D1759011

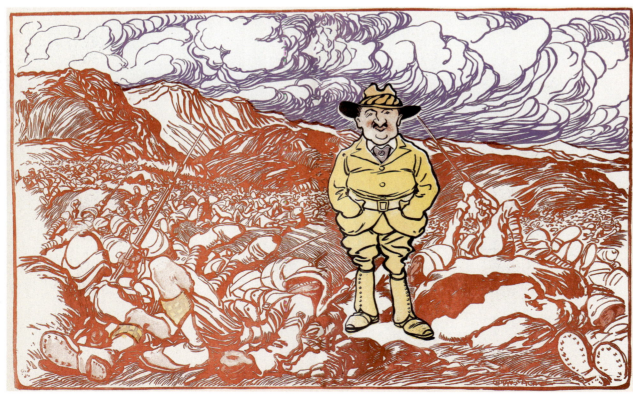

The History of
PRESS GRAPHICS
1819–1921

Réquisitoire
Conspiration sans but.

Alexander Roob

The History of
PRESS GRAPHICS
1819–1921

TASCHEN

The Classic Period of Press Graphics

Modern Press Graphics

Introduction

Alongside the beginnings of modern journalism, the use of illustration in the press developed gradually in the course of the 16th and 17th centuries, during the Wars of Religion and the Age of Enlightenment. It was a genuinely democratic art form, and also developed as a complement to the academic styles of high art. As such its place was not in the sacred temple of the Muses or the salons of the elite, but in the public space, the domain of the res publica. However, before the works of graphic artists could appear in news kiosks or on billboards the restrictions of taxation and censorship had first to be overcome, as well as obstacles to distribution, and these struggles would last several decades.

The period during which press graphics were at their most influential lasted for about a hundred years, from the satirical campaigns of William Hone in the late 1810s through until the First World War. After that date, illustration was used less and less often for images printed in newspapers as the result of improvements in photomechanical reproduction techniques. In terms of politics, the initial rise of the illustrated press was closely linked to the actions of English radicals agitating for parliamentary reform and the freedom of the press. The illustrated pamphlets they distributed in great numbers inspired Republicans in France to use caricatures in their attacks against the corrupt July Monarchy in 1830, and also, a little later, led to the creation of The Penny Magazine in England, the first mass-market illustrated review. The launch of this liberal-conservative cultural magazine was intended to break the hegemony of the radical reformers in popular journalism and their influence on the working class, but it also marked the first widespread, and indeed international appearance of press graphics when it was followed by the advent of the first major illustrated newspapers in the 1840s. For more than 50 years, this new form of historical art – which was quick to produce in response to events and was ideally suited for voicing criticism – remained the principal visual medium for printed news. It set the standard for modern times, and against it the revolutions in the arts of the 19th and early 20th centuries found their points of reference.

The same qualities that were strengths for press graphics, however, their topicality and diversity, have also proved to be obstacles when trying to present a general overview of the material. Moreover, within the hierarchical system used for classifying art history, which is traditionally based on the Platonic ideal of eternity, press graphics have tended to be consigned to the bottom drawer with various kinds of ephemera, the lowest category that is relevant for no more than a day, and left there to be forgotten. Cultural studies, meanwhile, have filed them according to theme and interpreted them from narrow regional or national perspectives, in spite of the international connections that were established early on between illustrated magazines and the developments that naturally followed. The fact that historians of photography and comic strips from an early date set out to distinguish individual areas within their field and treat them separately has also contributed to a distortion rather than a greater understanding of the context of press graphics. To make matters worse, the heyday of press graphics coincided with the most energetic phase of Eurocentric imperialism, an era that still has many unanswered questions, while the racial and social stereotypes that marked this period of uncertainty and discovery were to a large extent shaped by magazine illustrations. For a long time, the 19th century was understood as being determined by competing nationalisms and a dynamic drive for globalisation that was primarily characterised by colonialism, while 19th-century studies were seen as an anachronism. More recently though such misgivings have been replaced by an awareness that these very aspects are in fact increasingly relevant for our understanding of current political developments. Many of the war zones from which early journalists sent their images and reports are the hot spots of today's world politics, while the social conflicts described in a previous age have lost much of their historical remoteness. Even the key theme, in terms of emancipation for the press, of the fight against censorship seems more topical today than ever.

The illustrators for the press were known as special artists, or specials for short. Their particular duties included not only supplying on-site illustrations to accompany reports but also journalistic research, which at times might extend to full-scale investigations into details of geography or ethnography. Some of these early pictorial journalists became celebrated in their own right, and became adept at presenting themselves as bold adventurers. As such they became known for their contributions

←←**Charles Philipon (concept)
& Honoré Daumier (del.)**

Detail from:
Robert Macaire and the Coal, 1839
(see p. 128)

Syd B. Griffin (del.) & J. Ottmann (lith.)

The Evil Spirits of the Modern Daily Press, 1888
(see p. 383)

to illustrated magazines, but also through travel books, auto-biographies and public lectures. Many of them had trained as painters of historical subjects. However, unlike their academic colleagues they were much more exposed to the level of competition in the new media, and some of them developed their own specific style of improvisation in response to the pressure of continually having to depict current events. The mobile methods of documentation developed by these early pictorial journalists were in turn a source of fascination to Impressionist artists.

Generally speaking, the reporting activities of the *special artist* were distinct from those of the *home artist* or editorial draughtsman, although the two roles often overlapped and particularly so in the case of the most popular illustrators. The most noteworthy feature of press graphic art was not so much its openness to specialisation as its stylistic flexibility and broad range, which could include political or humorous cartoons, genre illustrations and excursions into science fiction and fantasy, alongside its basic documentary function. Histories of illustration that typically treat pictorial journalism and caricature as separate genres not only ignore the overlaps in the works of individual artists but also fail to acknowledge the close genealogical connections which can be traced back to such pioneers of social reportage as Pieter Bruegel, Jacques Callot and William Hogarth, whose caricature-styled works shaped the classic, formative phase of press graphics. The proliferation of grotesque imagery in these early graphic works had a significant influence on the period novels of Dickens and Balzac, as well as the development of social realism in art, which in France found great success with *caricatures*.

Documentary press illustration and caricature did not in fact begin to develop along separate lines until the late 1860s, when the introduction of new methods for reproducing graphic works also coincided with new generations being recruited to the staff of magazines, which together resulted in a paradigm shift for the design of illustrated magazines and a permanent change to their visual presentation. The uniform appearance of classic press graphics began to lose its hold and was replaced by a spectacular variety of individual styles. In documentary illustration, the fine lines of a new photographic realism were combined with expressive, individual techniques. The impact of the motifs and structural graphic elements of this expressive pictorial journalism can be demonstrated by their influence on Vincent van Gogh's paintings and drawings, and indeed a whole chapter is devoted later on to this artist who was also a keen collector of engravings and an advocate of contemporary illustrated graphic works.

Another innovation in modern press graphics was the use of illustrated articles on politics and other topics in the new medium of popular journalism, and from the 1880s the ghostly forerunners of Surrealism made an early appearance in the illustrations accompanying sensationalist reports. However, the break with reality that became evident in a variety of different ways in the hybrid imagery of illustrated magazines around the turn of the century was not an unknown phenomenon in the context of the press. A degree of fragmentation and lack of coherence had been associated with printed images in newspapers from the beginning, and the chance encounter of the most diverse news items or their unconnected juxtaposition in the columns on the page corresponded to a tendency in press illustration towards multiple images in pictorial formats that were arranged like patchwork. In England in the early 18th century there had already appeared a disjunctive form of graphic collage known as *medley prints* (ill. p. 30), which was closely linked to the rise of journalism.

When the use of caricatures in France became prominent once again at the end of the 19th century, this random method of structuring press graphics was given a systematic boost which had significant consequences. Incoherence was now the rallying cry of a group of artists, many of whom supplied works to illustrated magazines, who took up arms against the bastions of academic art through parody and experimental methods. In later decades the caricatural anti-art of this Incoherents art movement (ills. pp. 500–505) was taken up by Dada and Surrealist artists. At the turn of the century in the thriving art capital of Paris, there was scarcely any artist with innovative ideas who was not also working for illustrated magazines, and likewise almost every modern "ism" in the arts benefited from interchanges with press graphics. In terms of the history of illustration though, it can be said that there was no Big Bang in modernism after the First World War. Instead, and viewed within this complementary perspective, the artistic avant-gardes of the 20th century represented a sort of rearguard action of the age of press graphics.

PUCK.

THE EVIL SPIRITS OF THE MODERN DAILY PRESS.

Einleitung

Mit den Anfängen des neuzeitlichen Journalismus bildete sich in Europa während der Konfessionskriege des 16. und 17. Jahrhunderts und der Zeit der Aufklärung allmählich auch das Genre der Presseillustration heraus. Es handelte sich dabei um eine genuin demokratische Kunstform, die sich komplementär zur akademischen Hochkunst entwickelte. Ihr Ort war nicht der sakrale Musentempel oder der feudale Salon, sondern der öffentliche Raum, der die Domäne der *res publica* ist. Bevor sich allerdings die Werke der Pressezeichner an den Kiosken und Litfaßsäulen zeigen konnten, mussten in jahrzehntelangem Ringen Restriktionen durch Steuerauflagen und Zensurmaßnahmen beseitigt sowie Distributionshindernisse überwunden werden.

Die Epoche, in der die Pressegrafik bestimmend war, dauerte ungefähr ein Jahrhundert lang, von den satirischen Kampagnen William Hones am Ende der 1810er-Jahre bis zum Ersten Weltkrieg, als die Illustration durch die verfeinerten fotomechanischen Reproduktionsverfahren zunehmend aus dem Druckbild der Zeitungen verdrängt wurde. Politisch war der Aufstieg der illustrierten Presse eng mit den Agitationen der englischen Radikalen für Parlamentsreform und Pressefreiheit verbunden. Die Bildpamphlete, die sie massenweise in Umlauf brachten, inspirierten 1830 in Frankreich den republikanischen Karikaturkampf gegen die korrupte Julimonarchie und wenig später in England die Gründung der ersten Massenillustrierten *Penny Magazine*. Mit diesem liberal konservativen Kulturmagazin, das die Hegemonie der radikalen Reformer in der Populärpublizistik und Arbeiterbildung brechen sollte, begann der Aufstieg der Pressegrafik, die sich schließlich in den 1840er-Jahre mit den Gründungen der ersten großen Nachrichtenillustrierten international durchsetzte. Mehr als ein halbes Jahrhundert lang blieb diese neue Form einer beschleunigten und im Bereich des Cartooning auch kritischen Historienkunst das bildnerische Leitmedium, der Maßstab für *modernité*, an dem sich die Kunstrevolutionen des 19. und frühen 20. Jahrhunderts orientieren konnten.

Die Vorzüge der Pressegrafik – ihre Aktualität und Diversität – standen einer Überblicksdarstellung bislang eher im Weg. Im hierarchischen Ordnungssystem der Kunstgeschichte, das traditionellerweise am platonischen Ewigkeitsideal ausgerichtet ist, wies man ihr die unterste Schublade der Ephemera, der minderwertigen Eintagsobjekte, zu und vergaß sie dort.

Die Kulturwissenschaft hat sie thematisch filetiert und ungeachtet der frühen internationalen Vernetzung im Illustriertengewerbe und der daraus resultierenden Entwicklungszusammenhänge meist unter engen nationalen und regionalen Gesichtspunkten interpretiert. Auch dass die Fotografie- und Comichistoriker früh einzelne Bereiche herausgelöst und separiert behandelt haben, hat mehr zur Verzerrung als zum Verständnis der Zusammenhänge beigetragen. Erschwerend kommt hinzu, dass die Blütezeit der Pressegrafik mit der wenig verarbeiteten Phase des eurozentrischen Imperialismus zusammenfällt. Die rassistischen und sozialen Stereotypen, die diese prekäre Epoche bestimmt haben, wurden vor allem von der Illustriertengrafik geprägt. Lange Zeit stand die Auseinandersetzung mit dem 19. Jahrhundert als einem Zeitalter, das von Nationalismen und einer kolonial geprägten Globalisierungsdynamik bestimmt war, unter dem Verdacht des Anachronismus. Mittlerweile ist dieser Vorbehalt jedoch der Erkenntnis gewichen, dass diese Themen eine zunehmende Relevanz für das Verständnis der aktuellen politischen Entwicklungen haben. Viele der Kriegsschauplätze, von denen die frühen Bildjournalisten berichteten, sind die weltpolitischen Konfliktherde von heute, und auch die sozialen Konflikte, die sie schilderten, haben an historischer Ferne eingebüßt. Selbst das emanzipatorische Leitmotiv des Zensurkampfs scheint aktueller denn je.

Die grafischen Reporter wurden *special artists* oder kurz *specials* genannt. Zu ihren Sonderaufgaben zählte nicht nur die grafische Berichterstattung vor Ort, sondern auch die journalistische Recherche, die in manchen Fällen zu veritablen Forschungsarbeiten mit geo- und ethnografischen Schwerpunkten anwachsen konnte. Einige dieser frühen Bildjournalisten avancierten zu Medienstars, die es verstanden, sich abenteuerlich in Szene zu setzen. Sie waren nicht nur durch ihre Illustriertenbeiträge präsent, sondern auch mit Reisebüchern, Autobiografien und Vortragsveranstaltungen. Etliche hatten eine Ausbildung als Historienmaler durchlaufen. Allerdings waren sie viel unmittelbarer als ihre akademischen Kollegen dem Wettbewerb neuer Medien ausgesetzt, und einige entwickelten unter dem Druck der Aktualitäten eine spezifische Kunst der Improvisation. Die Künstler des Impressionismus waren von diesen ambulatorischen Aufzeichnungsweisen des frühen Bildjournalismus beeindruckt.

←←**Olaf Gulbransson**

Detail from:
The Blind Tsar, 1905
(see p. 560 t.)

Mstislav Dobuzhinsky

Detail from:
October Idyll, 1905
(see p. 560 b.l.)

In der Regel wurde die Reportertätigkeit des *special artist* von der Arbeit des *home artist* oder Redaktionszeichners unterschieden. Gerade bei den populärsten Illustratoren überlappten sich diese beiden Bereiche jedoch häufig. Die Besonderheit pressegrafischer Kunst lag weniger in ihren Spezialisierungen als vielmehr in der stilistischen Flexibilität und einem breiten Spektrum, das neben dem Bereich des Dokumentarischen auch das politische Cartooning, die grafische Humoreske sowie Genre-, Science-Fiction- und Fantasy-Illustration beinhalten konnte. Eine Illustrationshistorie, die es gewohnt ist, Bildjournalismus und Karikatur als separate Genre zu behandeln, ignoriert nicht nur diese Überschneidungen im Werk einzelner Künstler, sondern verkennt auch den engen genealogischen Zusammenhang, der auf Pioniere der Sozialreportage, wie Pieter Bruegel, Jacques Callot und William Hogarth, zurückgeht, die mit ihren karikaturesken Arbeiten die klassische, formative Phase der Pressegrafik geprägt haben. Die grotesken Typologien dieser frühen Illustriertengrafik hatten nicht nur einen bedeutenden Einfluss auf die epochalen Romane eines Honoré de Balzac und Charles Dickens, sondern auch auf die Entwicklung der sozialrealistischen Kunst, die in Frankreich unter der Flagge der *caricature* reüssierte.

Dokumentargrafik und Karikatur entwickelten sich erst in den späten 1860er-Jahren auseinander. Damals hatte die Einführung neuer Reproduktionsverfahren im Zusammenspiel mit einem Generationswechsel im Mitarbeiterstab der Zeitschriften einen gestalterischen Paradigmenwandel zur Folge, der das Antlitz der Illustrierten nachhaltig veränderte. Die Uniformität der klassischen Pressegrafik begann aufzubrechen und wurde durch eine spektakuläre Vielfalt von Individualstilen abgelöst. Im dokumentarischen Bereich traf ein filigraner fotografischer Realismus auf Tendenzen expressiver Handschriftlichkeit. Wie einflussreich nicht nur die Motive, sondern auch die grafischen Strukturen dieser pressegrafischen Ausdruckskunst waren, belegt das zeichnerische und malerische Werk von Vincent van Gogh. Der Perspektive dieses passionierten Sammlers und Anwalts der zeitgenössischen Illustriertengrafik ist hier ein eigenes Kapitel gewidmet.

Ein weiteres Novum in der modernen Pressegrafik stellte die Bildpublizistik der noch jungen Boulevardpresse dar. In ihren illustrierten Sensationsmeldungen kündigten sich seit den 1880er-Jahren bereits die Phantasmen des Surrealismus an. Der Wirklichkeitsbruch, der um die Jahrhundertwende in den hybriden Bildwelten der Illustrierten auf sehr vielfältige Weise offenbar wurde, war im Pressekontext allerdings kein fremdes Phänomen. Fragmentierung und Inkohärenz lagen dem Druckbild der Zeitungen von Anfang an zugrunde. Dem zufälligen Zusammentreffen unterschiedlichster Nachrichten und ihrem unverbundenen Nebeneinander im Spaltensatz entsprach in der Illustriertengrafik eine Tendenz zu pluralen, patchworkartigen Bildformaten. In England war bereits zu Anfang des 18. Jahrhunderts mit dem *medley print* eine disjunktive Form der grafischen Collage aufgetaucht (Abb. S. 30), die in engem Zusammenhang mit dem boomenden Journalismus stand.

Im Kontext der zweiten französischen Karikaturbewegung erfuhr dieses aleatorische Strukturmerkmal der Pressegrafik gegen Ende des 19. Jahrhunderts eine programmatische Aufladung, die ungemein folgenreich war. Inkohärenz wurde zum Kampfbegriff einer von Illustriertengrafikern dominierten Gruppierung, die auf experimentell-parodistische Weise gegen die Grundfesten der akademischen Künste anging. Die Dadaisten und Surrealisten schlossen Jahrzehnte später an diese karikatureske Antikunst der *Arts Incohérents* an (Abb. S. 500–505). Im Kunstzentrum Paris gab es zur Jahrhundertwende nur wenige innovative Künstler, die nicht für Magazine zeichneten, und kaum einen modernen Ismus, der nicht vom Austausch mit der Pressegrafik profitierte. Aus illustrationshistorischer Sicht war kein Urknall der Moderne nach den Weltkriegen auszumachen. Vielmehr stellen sich aus dieser komplementären Perspektive die künstlerischen Avantgarden des 20. Jahrhunderts als eine Art Nachhut des Zeitalters der Pressegrafik heraus.

Introduction

Avec les débuts du journalisme moderne, pendant les guerres de Religion des XVIe et XVIIe siècles et au siècle des Lumières, le genre de l'illustration de presse se développa peu à peu en Europe. Il s'agissait là d'une forme d'art profondément démocratique qui évolua en complément du grand art académique, non dans les temples de muses sacrés ou dans les salons raffinés, mais dans l'espace public, qui est le domaine de la *res publica*. Mais avant que puissent apparaître les travaux des dessinateurs de presse dans les kiosques ou sur les colonnes Morris, maintes restrictions dues aux lois fiscales et aux mesures de censure durent être abolies pendant de longues années, ainsi que des difficultés de distribution surmontées.

L'époque à laquelle le dessin de presse fut déterminant dura environ un siècle, des campagnes satiriques de William Hone à la fin des années 1810 jusqu'à la Première Guerre mondiale, lorsque l'illustration fut de plus en plus évincée des impressions des journaux par les procédés photographiques de reproduction mécaniques plus affinés. Sur le plan politique, la montée de la presse illustrée est étroitement liée aux agitations des radicaux anglais luttant pour une réforme du Parlement et pour la liberté de la presse. Les innombrables pamphlets illustrés qu'ils mirent en circulation inspirèrent en France, en 1830, le combat républicain par la caricature contre la monarchie de Juillet corrompue et, un peu plus tard, entraînèrent en Angleterre la fondation du premier magazine illustré de masse, le *Penny Magazine*. C'est avec ce magazine à visée éducative d'obédience libérale-conservatrice, qui devait briser l'hégémonie des réformistes radicaux dans les domaines du journalisme populaire et de la culture ouvrière, que commença l'ascension du dessin de presse, qui s'imposa finalement au niveau international dans les années 1840 avec la fondation des premières grandes revues illustrées d'information. Durant plus d'un demi-siècle, cette nouvelle forme de la peinture d'histoire – plus rapide dans son exécution et par ailleurs critique dans le secteur du dessin satirique – demeura le medium iconographique majeur, le critère de *modernité*, d'après lequel les révolutions artistiques du xixe et du début du xxe siècle purent s'orienter.

Jusqu'alors, les atouts du dessin de presse – actualité et diversité – étaient plutôt un obstacle à une représentation globale. Dans le système d'ordre hiérarchique de l'histoire de l'art traditionnellement orienté vers l'idéal platonique d'éternité, on lui concédait le tiroir du bas, celui de l'éphémère, des objets mineurs d'une seule journée, et on l'y oubliait. La science culturelle l'a fileté par thèmes et interprété sous des critères étriqués d'ordre national et régional, indépendamment de l'interconnexion internationale précoce et des évolutions en résultant. Le fait que les historiens de la photographie et de la bande dessinée aient très tôt étudié les secteurs un par un et les aient traités séparément a davantage contribué à la distorsion qu'à la compréhension du contexte. Pour aggraver les choses, l'âge d'or du dessin de presse coïncide avec la phase peu traitée de l'impérialisme eurocentrique. Les stéréotypes racistes et sociaux qui ont marqué cette époque précaire ont été surtout déterminés par la gravure d'illustration. Pendant longtemps, l'analyse du XIXe siècle comme période soumise aux nationalismes et à un dynamisme de globalisation à tendance coloniale était soupçonnée d'anachronisme. Entre-temps, ce jugement réservé a toutefois laissé place au constat que ces thèmes ont une importance grandissante pour la compréhension des évolutions politiques actuelles. Un grand nombre des territoires en guerre, d'où les reporters d'images d'autrefois faisaient leurs rapports, sont les foyers de conflit d'aujourd'hui à l'échelle politique mondiale, et les conflits sociaux qu'ils décrivaient ont perdu de leur distance historique. Même le leitmotiv émancipatoire de la lutte contre la censure semble plus actuel que jamais.

Les illustrateurs de presse étaient appelés *special artists* ou, en abrégé, *specials*. Leurs tâches « spéciales » ne consistaient pas seulement en des reportages illustrés *in situ*, mais comprenaient aussi la recherche journalistique, qui dans bien des cas pouvait s'étendre à de véritables travaux d'investigation dans les domaines géographique et ethnographique. Plusieurs de ces reporters d'images de la première heure devinrent des stars médiatiques qui savaient audacieusement se mettre en scène. Ils étaient omniprésents, non seulement par leurs articles pour les magazines, mais aussi par des guides de voyage, des autobiographies et des conférences. Un grand nombre avait suivi une formation de peintre d'histoire. Cependant, ils étaient beaucoup plus directement que leurs confrères académiques confrontés à la concurrence des nouveaux médias, et certains, sous la pression de l'actualité, développèrent un art spécifique

←← **Paul Iribe**

Detail from:
To M. Chauchard, a Rich Man, 1903
(see p. 557 t.)

Georges Scott

→ Detail from:
*An Accident on the Elevated Railroad
in New York*, 1905
(see p. 456 b.r.)

→→ **J.J. Grandville & Benjamin Roubaud**

Detail from:
Grand Funeral of a Fat Constitutional Member, 1834
(see p. 119)

de l'improvisation. Les artistes impressionnistes étaient fascinés par ces méthodes de documentation ambulatoires du journalisme d'images précoce.

Généralement, l'activité de reporter du *special artist* se distinguait du travail du *home artist* ou dessinateur de rédaction. Pourtant, chez les illustrateurs les plus populaires justement, ces deux secteurs se recoupaient fréquemment. La particularité des arts graphiques de presse résidait moins dans leurs spécialisations que dans la flexibilité stylistique et dans une vaste palette qui pouvait également inclure, en plus du secteur du documentaire, le dessin politique, humoristique, ainsi que l'illustration de genre, de science-fiction et de fantastique. Une histoire de l'illustration qui a pour habitude de traiter le journalisme illustré et la caricature comme des genres séparés passe sous silence non seulement ces recoupements dans l'œuvre des artistes, mais méconnaît aussi l'étroit rapport généalogique, qui remonte aux pionniers du reportage social, comme Pieter Bruegel, Jacques Callot et William Hogarth, qui avec leurs travaux de caricature ont marqué la phase classique et formatrice du dessin de presse. Les grotesques typologies de ce dessin d'illustration précoce n'eurent pas seulement une influence majeure sur les romans d'époque d'un Honoré de Balzac ou d'un Charles Dickens, mais aussi sur l'évolution de l'art social réaliste, qui fit florès en France sous l'étendard de la *caricature*.

Ce n'est qu'à la fin des années 1860 que le dessin documentaire et la caricature évoluèrent séparément. À cette époque, l'apparition de nouveaux procédés de reproduction coïncida avec un changement de générations dans le personnel des magazines illustrés et entraîna un renouvellement de modèle de création, qui transforma durablement le visage des illustrés. L'uniformité de l'illustration de presse classique commença à éclater et fut supplantée par une spectaculaire diversité de styles individuels. Dans le secteur du documentaire, un réalisme photographique tout en finesse de traits rejoignit les tendances d'une écriture expressive. Les dessins et les peintures de Vincent van Gogh témoignent de l'influence non seulement des motifs, mais aussi des structures graphiques de cet art d'expression journalistique. Un chapitre entier est consacré ici à la perspective de ce grand collectionneur de gravures et ardent défenseur du dessin d'illustration contemporain.

Le journalisme illustré de la presse à sensation encore jeune présenta une autre nouveauté dans le dessin de presse moderne. Dans ses nouvelles illustrées spectaculaires s'annoncèrent dès les années 1880 les fantasmes du surréalisme. La rupture avec la réalité, qui devint manifeste de manière très variée dans les univers imagés hybrides des illustrés, n'était toutefois pas un phénomène inconnu dans le contexte de la presse. Dès le début, la fragmentation et l'incohérence étaient sous-jacentes à l'image imprimée des journaux. Dans l'illustration de magazine, une tendance favorisant les formats d'images multiples distribués en patchwork correspondait à la convergence des nouvelles les plus diverses et à leur juxtaposition improvisée en colonnes. En Angleterre, dès le début du XVIIIe siècle était apparue avec le *medley print* une forme disjonctive de collage graphique (ill. p. 30) qui était en relation étroite avec le journalisme en pleine expansion.

Dans le contexte du second mouvement de caricature français, cette caractéristique structurelle aléatoire du dessin de presse connut vers la fin du XIXe siècle une charge programmatique qui eut d'immenses répercussions. L'incohérence devint la notion de combat d'un groupement dominé par des dessinateurs de magazines illustrés, qui s'attaquait aux fondations des arts académiques de façon expérimentale et parodique. Plusieurs décennies plus tard, les dadaïstes et les surréalistes se rallièrent à cet anti-art caricatural des *Arts incohérents* (ills. p. 500-505). Dans le centre artistique qu'était Paris, il y avait au tournant du siècle peu d'artistes innovateurs ne dessinant pas pour les magazines et pas un Isme moderne ne profitant pas de l'échange avec le dessin de presse. Du point de vue de l'historique de l'illustration, aucun big bang de modernisme ne fut observé après les guerres mondiales. Dans cette perspective complémentaire les avant-gardes du XXe siècle se sont plutôt avérées comme une espèce d'arrière-garde de l'ère du dessin de presse.

Early Illustrated News

Pictorial journalism in Europe first developed in early modern times with the advent of woodcuts and letterpress printing. The imaginatively illustrated news items from all parts of the known world that were thus produced were then distributed by pedlars in the form of printed single sheets. This method of transmitting news, which was essentially derived from hearsay, was not uncommonly accompanied by a recitation delivered by a performer known by the Italian name of *cantastoria* (story-singer). Research by the sinologist Victor Mair has in fact shown that this was a global phenomenon and was known in India from as early as the sixth century, although evidence for it in Europe can only be traced back as far as the 16th century (ill. p. 20). At that date the itinerant trade in illustrated prints was already dominated by a small number of publishing houses, which had an extensive network available for distributing their wares. One pioneer of this flourishing trade was the painter and etcher Hieronymus Cock in Antwerp, who for the most part published maps and reproductions of paintings. Among the famous artists to have worked for him was Pieter Bruegel the Elder, whose satirically ethnographic work had a fundamental influence on the typological tradition of press graphics. Frans Hogenberg, one of the best draughtsmen and engravers in Cock's workshop, went on to establish his own engraving business in Cologne in 1570. His published work included maps and topographical prints, but he was also especially successful, as a Protestant in exile, with his extensive series of news sheets recounting events during the Wars of Religion. Over 400 such illustrated reports from his workshop have survived (ill. p. 29 t.).

The artisans in Hogenberg's workshop had to take great care when preparing the illustrations for news items to ensure they were plausible, since they were examined and discussed by a critical and educated public. For their research though they were able to consult details within the workshop's own extensive archives. By the late 16th century there was already a wide range of printed material with pictorial documentation, including cosmographies and collections of city views from around the world, such as the *Orbis civitates terrarum* with engravings by Hogenberg himself, together with works on animals and plants and a substantial number of illustrated travel accounts. Amongst the *special artists* known by name at this early date and whose pioneering work contributed to Hogenberg's later success were Erhard Reuwich, Christoph Weiditz (ills. pp. 24–25), Hans Weiditz, Sebald Beham, Melchior Lorck and Jost Amman (ill. p. 20). Amman specialised in illustrations showing scenes from everyday life and the world of work, which then appeared in costume books and books of trades. A related class of social subjects showed local tradesmen with the street cries they used to advertise their products, and an early example of this in broadsheet form is known from Hogenberg's workshop. The first of these depictions had appeared in Paris in around 1500, and illustrations of street cries went on to become astonishingly popular for several hundred years before eventually being absorbed into investigative social reporting and urban ethnography in England in the early 19th century. Overall, however, many of Hogenberg's illustrated subjects cannot simply be explained as new versions of older ideas, while his publishing company must also have had some sort of basic network of corresponding graphic artists, along with engineers involved with siege warfare and fortifications who could send pictures drawn *in situ* from various battle zones.

Jost Amman & Theodor de Bry

A Pedlar with the Latest Newspaper, 1588
Der Kramer mit der newe Zeittung
Marchand ambulant avec le nouveau journal
Etching
Staatsbibliothek zu Berlin, Abteilung
Historische Drucke

Together with illustrated calendars, pedlars would also offer the latest illustrated news sheets. In the example shown here the Spanish Armada is being armed before setting sail for England, as seen in the background.

Zusammen mit illustrierten Kalendern bietet der fliegende Händler die neuesten Bildnachrichtenblätter an, auf denen bereits das Aufrüsten der spanischen Armada dargestellt ist, die im Hintergrund gegen England ausläuft.

En plus des calendriers illustrés, le marchand ambulant propose les feuilles volantes diffusant les nouvelles illustrées sur lesquelles est représenté l'armement de l'Armada espagnole qui, à l'arrière-plan, met les voiles en direction de l'Angleterre.

Daniel Chodowiecki

Moral Improvement, 1786
Verbesserung der Sitten | Amélioration des mœurs
Etching
Staatliche Museen zu Berlin, Kupferstichkabinett

This satirical image of the way in which early
popular and sensationalist journalism was published
associates the illustrated reports used by the two
story-singers in the foreground with the work of
the graphic artists themselves. The figure of the
pictorial journalist on the left of the picture, who is
occupied with sketching various accidents nearby,
is based on a self-portrait of Chodowiecki's role
model, William Hogarth.

Die satirische Ansicht von den Produktionsabläu-
fen der zeitgenössischen Sensationspublizistik
führt die Bildnachrichten der beiden Bänkelsänger
im Vordergrund auf die Arbeit grafischer Reporter
zurück. Der Bildjournalist, der am linken Bildrand
Unglücksfälle aller Art aufzeichnet, ist einer Selbst-
darstellung von Chodowieckis Vorbild William
Hogarth nachempfunden.

La représentation satirique des processus de production du journalisme à sensation contemporain
attribue les nouvelles illustrées des deux baladins,
au premier plan, au travail de dessinateurs chroniqueurs. L'artiste journaliste, qui au bord à gauche
croque des mésaventures de toutes sortes, est inspiré d'un autoportrait du modèle de Chodowiecki,
William Hogarth.

The close connection between press graphics, cartogra-
phy and illustrated city views, which constituted the output of
Hogenberg's workshop and which continued to do so when his
son Abraham took over (ill. p. 29 b.), can be seen most strikingly
in the work of Hogenberg's most famous employee, Wenceslaus
Hollar. An engraver and draughtsman originally from Bohemia,
he had acquired a special talent for producing copies during his
apprenticeship with the topographic engraver Matthäus Merian
and from his own studies of Dürer's graphic works. In 1637 he
moved to England, the home of the illustrated press, where he
introduced a style of restrained but highly detailed documentary illustration to the still fledgling graphic culture which then
existed. In hundreds of illustrated city and architectural views,
portraits and pictures of events, he left to posterity a kaleido-
scopic panorama of London during the English civil wars and
subsequent Restoration.

Hollar's groundbreaking style of realism in his illustrated journalism is exemplified by his depiction of the execution of the
Earl of Strafford in May 1641 (ill. pp. 26/27). This event marked
a decisive turning point in the struggle for power between
Parliament and the Monarchy, and was thus widely referred to
in print. Hollar, however, avoided the usual viewpoint taken from
an imaginary position high up and instead, based on his experience with using a *camera obscura,* modelled his perspective on
that of an observer at ground level which then gave the viewer
the impression of being an eye witness. The central event of the
execution was in this way somewhat sidelined, since the attention of viewers was also caught by other details, such as the
spectators' stand collapsing in the background on the right.

The events of the English Civil War, which began the year
after this execution of one of King Charles I's close advi-
sors, were also significant in the history of press graphics. In
1643, only a few decades after the first newspapers had been
launched in Strasbourg and Amsterdam, the first illustrated version appeared in London, the *Mercurius Civicus.* It was issued on
a weekly basis and featured crude woodcut portraits of notable

politicians and military figures. Although the *Mercurius* backed
the same anti-absolutist cause as Parliament, its appearance,
like that of every other publication at the time, was constantly
under threat of government censorship. In reaction to this the
Puritan poet John Milton published his pamphlet *Areopagitica* in
1644, the first modern defence of freedom in the press. Milton's
clear and incisive arguments set the standard for all subsequent
disputes about censorship and restrictions to liberty, such as the
protests when the infamous Stamp Act was introduced in Britain
in 1712 as an instrument of rule by taxation with the intention
of suppressing any publications that were critical of the government and ensuring that large sections of the population had no
political rights.

While only a small number of illustrated reports from the
time of the English Civil War have actually survived, in mainland Europe the Thirty Years' War (1618–1648), which was then
in full spate, proved to be a golden age for early pictorial journalism. The draughtsman, engraver and etcher Jacques Callot
(ills. p. 33) from the Duchy of Lorraine was an exceptional figure in the field of illustrated graphic work, not least because he
was unsatisfied with merely depicting the usual battle scenes
and chose instead to emphasise the disastrous effects of war on
local populations. From reports at the time it seems that many of
his images of beggars, vagrants and those wounded in war who
appeared in his series *Les Gueux* (1622–1623) were drawn from
life and directly in the presence of each subject. In doing so,
Callot initiated a revolutionary approach to socially realistic illustrated documentation, and the added depth conveyed an empa-
thy for these social outcasts. However, his multifaceted output
was not only of fundamental importance in the development of
illustrated social reporting since the series of grotesques he
also produced (which employed themes taken from the works
of Hieronymus Bosch and Pieter Bruegel, and also made use of
characters from the Italian *commedia dell'arte*) had an enormous
influence in turn on satirical press graphics. The art of Grandville,
for example, who was the first really big name amongst French

Verbesserung der Sitten

caricaturists and who was also from Lorraine, follows in a direct line from Callot's grotesque works.

By way of contrast, in England pictorial journalism developed at a rather slower rate, although the Glorious Revolution of 1688/89 did result in a strengthening of civil rights, which included the abolition of press censorship. When William III of Orange, steward of the Dutch Republic, achieved the "glorious" taking of the throne of England, the events were commemorated with an outburst of propaganda illustrated by the engraver, poet and painter Romeyn de Hooghe. As with Callot, De Hooghe's graphic works covered a wide range of styles, including Baroque illustrated news sheets as well as allegorical satires of social and political subjects. These satirical works led to charges of pornography and blasphemy against De Hooghe in the Netherlands, and to diplomatic incidents involving France and England. In 1701, however, he launched the first illustrated satirical weekly magazine, *Aesopus in Europa*, and it was De Hooghe's work that marked the establishment of political caricature as an artistic genre in its own right (see ill. p. 35).

The influence of Dutch graphic work did not become fully apparent in England, however, until a few decades later with the emergence of the highly original painter and engraver William Hogarth, who found fame with his series of illustrated studies that were issued in the style of broadsheets and showed what he called "modern moral subjects". These key scenes in the lives and actions of characters presented as types enabled Hogarth to shine a critical light on social conditions at the time. With his invention of dramatic scenes told in pictures he was also playing a part in the development of a sequential style of art which began to appear in press graphics during the 1840s with publication of the illustrated novels of Rodolphe Töpffer (see ill. p. 157). Hogarth's pictorial dramas were characterised by the raw realism of everyday life, as influenced by the rise of daily newspapers in towns and cities, and also featured regular journalistic references to current events. Acting as an artistic counterpart to the literary excursions of the satirical social reporter Ned Ward (ill. p. 39), who documented the lower walks of city life in his periodical *The London Spy*, Hogarth threaded his way through the different districts of London to record his visual impressions. If he ran out of paper while he was off on one of these trips he would apparently jot down observations in shorthand on his fingernails. A century before Baudelaire, this art from urban strolling was celebrated by Hogarth's friend, the poet John Gay, in his poem *Trivia* from 1716. Gay also provided Hogarth with the scenic model for his modern moral subjects (ill. pp. 36/37) by way of his own popular satire *The Beggar's Opera* (1728) and the social criticism it contained.

Hogarth's urban social realism was styled as a form of *comic history*, at the halfway point between the highest forms of historical art and the lowly genre of the grotesque. The antagonistic relationship between high art and popular art, which to this day continues to determine how the history of illustration is assessed, first takes on a certain virulence in Hogarth's work that can also be seen as instructive. His deep personal understanding of art was informed by the painting used in advertising, that is the most republican of all forms of art, in which he had worked himself at the start of his career and which was also the model for his representations of urban spaces shown as if they have been assembled in sections (ill. p. 38). The symbolic clutter that also characterises his pictorial scenes was similarly derived from a particular class of graphic works he had studied previously, that were known as *quodlibets* in the Netherlands and in England as *medley prints* (ill. p. 30). This genre of illusionistic pseudo-collage (ill. p. 39) anticipated the scrapbook aesthetic of the style of multiple press graphics in the 19th century.

Hogarth's ideal of a democratic art was developed in direct opposition to the academic absolutism of his fellow painters. In 1762, he organised an exhibition of advertising signs by unnamed artists as a counterpart for the ordinary person in the street to the exclusive exhibition held to mark the founding of the Society of Artists (ill. p. 44). The list of exhibits for this spectacular "Sign Painters' Exhibition" suggests that Hogarth in fact took found

Christoph Weiditz

*The Costume Book of His Journey to Spain
and the Netherlands, c. 1530–1540*
*Das Trachtenbuch von seinen Reisen nach Spanien
und den Niederlanden*
*Le recueil de costumes de ses voyages en Espagne
et aux Pays-Bas*
Watercolour on parchment
Nuremberg, Germanisches Nationalmuseum,
Hs 22474

This collection of 154 coloured drawings by the Strasbourg painter and illustrator Christoph Weiditz represents an early form of travel account. It mostly records Weiditz's impressions following a trip to Spain, with significant emphasis on illustrations showing aspects of slavery and punishment. In Madrid, he witnessed a number of performances by indigenous people from the Americas that had been organised at the Imperial court of Charles V by the conquistador Hernan Cortés. The sequential nature of the illustrations for these performances indicates the interest of this early *special artist* in sequences of movement. It is very likely that copies of this travel account with its details on social behaviour circulated in German humanist circles, although the title the series of drawings later acquired does not remotely cover the range of ethnographic contents.

Bei dem Konvolut von 154 kolorierten Zeichnungen des Straßburger Malers und Illustrators Christoph Weiditz handelt es sich um eine frühe Reisereportage. Sie gibt überwiegend Eindrücke einer Spanienreise wieder. Auffällig ist die Fokussierung auf Praktiken der Versklavung und der Bestrafung. In Madrid erlebte Weiditz Aufführungen amerikanischer Indigena, die der Konquistador Hernán Cortés am Kaiserhof Karls V. organisiert hatte. Die sequenzielle Art der Aufzeichnung unterstreicht das Interesse des frühen *special artist* an Bewegungsabläufen. Kopien dieses Reise- und Sozialreports zirkulierten aller Wahrscheinlichkeit nach in deutschen Humanistenkreisen. Der Titel eines Trachtenbuchs, den diese Zeichnungsfolge erst später erhielt, greift allerdings zu kurz, um ihrer ethnografischen Dimension auch nur annähernd gerecht zu werden.

Le recueil de 154 dessins coloriés du peintre et illustrateur strasbourgeois Christoph Weiditz constitue l'un des tout premiers récits de voyage. Il exprime surtout les impressions d'un voyage en Espagne. Il est frappant que les dessins aient pour thèmes centraux l'esclavage et le châtiment. À Madrid, Weiditz a assisté à des spectacles d'indigènes américains que le conquistador Hernán Cortés avait organisés à la cour impériale de Charles Quint. Le caractère séquentiel du dessin met en valeur l'intérêt que le *special artist* précoce porte aux séquences de mouvement. Selon toute vraisemblance, des copies de ce reportage de voyage sociologique circulaient dans les cercles humanistes allemands. Toutefois, le titre de «recueil de costumes» qu'il ne reçut qu'ultérieurement est quelque peu réducteur et ne cerne que très approximativement sa dimension ethnographique.

↑ *This is an Indian, who is lying on his back and throwing into the air with his heels a wooden staff that is as long and as heavy as a man, and on the ground beneath him is a piece of leather as big as a calf's hide.*

This is how he throws the staff up into the air using his feet.

And this is how he catches the staff with his feet in the same way.

Das ist ein Indianer, der liegt auf dem Rücken, und wirft ein Holz aus seinen Fersen heraus, das so lang und so schwer ist wie ein Mann, er hat auf der Erde unter ihm ein Leder, das so groß ist wie ein Kalbsfell.

So wirft er das Holz über sich hinweg mit den Füßen.

Genauso fängt er das Holz mit den Füßen auf, wie er's hinaufgeworfen hat.

Couché sur le dos un Indien lance avec ses talons un bout de bois aussi long et aussi lourd qu'un homme, il est allongé par terre sur un morceau de cuir aussi grand qu'un pelage de veau.

Ainsi il se sert de ses pieds pour jeter le bout de bois au-dessus de sa tête.

Puis il rattrape le bout de bois à l'aide de ses pieds, de la même manière qu'il l'a jeté.

→ *Self-portrait in Sailor's Costume*
Selbstporträt in nautischer Kleidung
Autoportrait en tenue de marin

signs and others he had commissioned and then overpainted or added to them, so as to present a kind of satirical metatext to the Society's exhibition of high art. He can thus be considered one of the pioneers in the early history of anti-art and artistic parodies which went on to become so important in Paris in the mid-19th century with the illustrations of a number of well-known graphic artists.

The only other work from this period that had a comparable influence on the development of press graphics was the monumental *Encyclopédie, ou Dictionnaire raisonné des sciences, des arts et des métiers* (ill. p. 48 t.), edited by Denis Diderot and Jean-Baptiste le Rond d'Alembert and published in Paris between 1751 and 1780 in 17 volumes of text and a further 11 volumes of plates. Artistic direction of the illustrations, which amounted to 2,885 copper engravings, was overseen by the mathematician and draughtsman Louis-Jacques Goussier. In preparation for illustrating the plates he spent 10 years travelling throughout France to visit various factories and workplaces and study the different manufacturing processes, manual as well as mechanical. Through his collected graphic work for the *Encyclopédie* Goussier set new standards for pictorial documentation, in terms of both the scope of research it represented and also the high level of precision.

In German-speaking areas, pictorial documentation was represented by the work of the illustrator and engraver Daniel Chodowiecki. As a chronicler of life at the Prussian royal court and the daily lives of the bourgeoisie, he was a compulsive draughtsman who worked quickly and, by his own admission, made his sketches in every kind of situation, whether "standing, walking or on horseback" (ill. p. 23). The artist Adolph Menzel, who became one of the most internationally influential illustrators of the 19th century, saw his work in pictorial journalism as being in direct succession to Chodowiecki's own.

By the end of the 18th century the print trade had become increasingly industrialised. In England, the mass audience for good-quality prints that Hogarth had attracted with his popular series of illustrations gave impetus to the new market, although widespread "Hogarthomania" only really set in after his death when the entrepreneurial print publisher John Boydell issued a complete collection of his graphic works, which went through several editions. Boydell was the Hieronymus Cock of his day, and by running his business with a clear division of labour and large print runs he introduced lasting changes in the art trade and the market for graphic works. In mainland Europe, similar figures such as the engraver Hieronymus Löschenkohl, who sold

Also ist der Stoffell vorydis
mit dem kolman golen
schmidt Jhen???
geworn.

Execution des Grafen Thomæ von Stafford Stattha

A. Doct. Usher Primat in Irland.   C.   Der Graf

B. Rahts Herren von Londen   D.   Seine anv

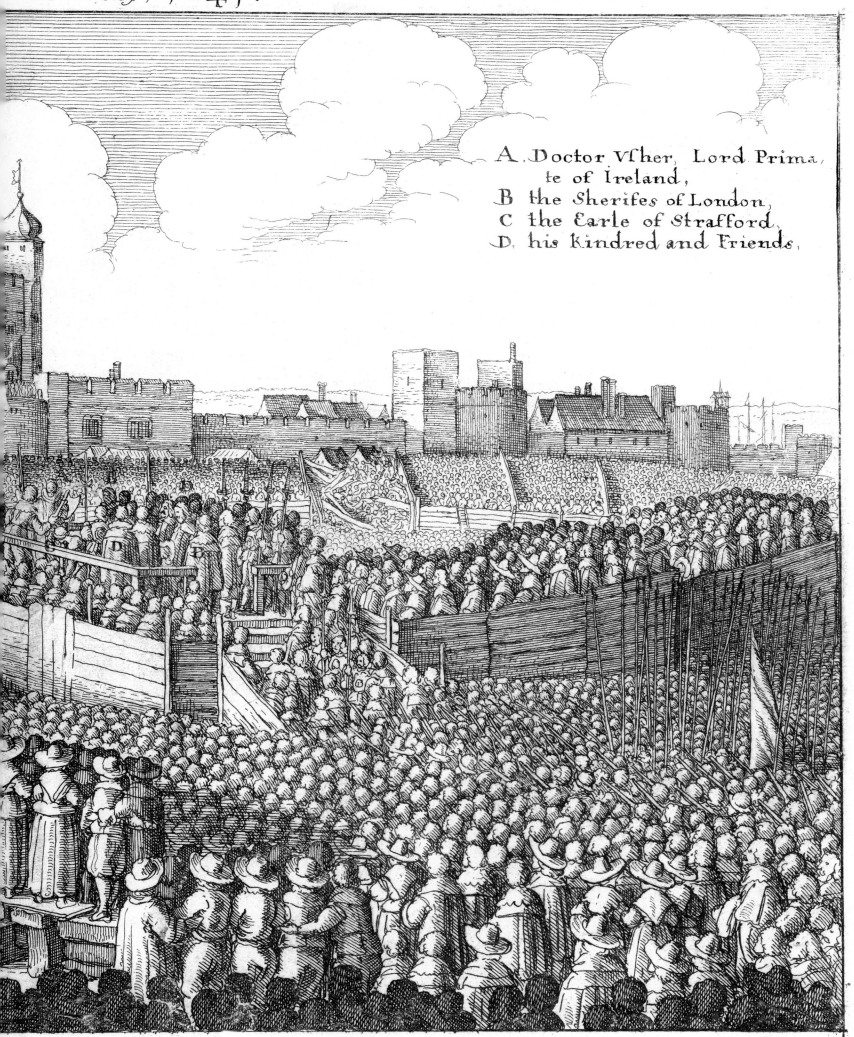

A. Doctor Vſher, Lord Prima,
  te of Ireland,
B the Sherifes of London,
C the Earle of Strafford,
D. his kindred and Friends,

es in Irland auf dē Tawers platz in Londen 12 Maj 1641.
n Stafford.
ꞷanten vnd freūnde.

←←Wenceslaus Hollar (del. & sc.)*

The True Maner of the Execution of Thomas Earle of Strafford, Lord Lieutenant of Ireland, upon Tower-hill, the 12th of May 1641, London, 1641
Execution des Grafen Thomae von Strafford, Statt-halter in Irland, auf dem Tower Hill, 12. Mai 1641
La véritable forme d'exécution du comte Thomas Strafford sur la Tower Hill, le 12 mai 1641
Copper engraving
(see also p. 32)

Studio of Frans Hogenberg

→ *The Execution of the Counts Egmont and Horn on 5 June 1568*, Cologne, 1568–1575
Hinrichtung der Grafen Egmont und Horn am 5. Juni 1568
Exécution des comtes d'Egmont et de Horne, le 5 juin 1568
Copper engraving

The sentencing by a special Spanish court of the two Dutch resistance leaders and their subsequent beheading in the market square in Brussels led to open revolt against foreign rule by the Spanish crown.

Mit der Verurteilung der beiden niederländischen Widerstandsführer durch ein spanisches Sonder-gericht und ihrer Enthauptung auf dem Marktplatz in Brüssel begann der offene Aufstand gegen den als Fremdherrschaft empfundenen spanischen Absolutismus.

La condamnation des deux chefs de résistance néerlandais par un tribunal d'exception espagnol et leur décapitation sur la Grand-Place de Bruxelles déclenchèrent la révolte ouverte contre l'absolutisme espagnol, ressenti comme une domination étrangère.

Studio of Abraham Hogenberg

↘ *The Election and Coronation of Ferdinand II as Emperor in Frankfurt am Main on 9 September 1619*, Cologne, 1619–1621
Kaiserwahl und Krönung Ferdinands II. in Frankfurt am Main am 9. September 1619
Élection et couronnement de l'empereur Ferdinand II à Francfort-sur-le-Main, le 9 septembre 1619
Copper engraving with etching

While sequences of scenes had been illustrated as separate sheets under Frans Hogenberg, in the workshop of his son and successor Abraham the events associated with the election of Ferdinand II were combined on a single sheet. The press graphics of the 19th century frequently made use of this Baroque scheme with its several pictorial panels.

Während die Werkstatt seines Vaters Frans Hogenberg szenische Abläufe noch als Folgen von Einzel-blättern realisiert hatte, wurden die Ereignisse um die Kaiserwahl in der Werkstatt seines Sohnes und Nachfolgers Abraham Hogenberg in einem einzigen Ensemble zusammengezogen. Die Pressegrafik des 19. Jahrhunderts griff das Schema der barocken Multipanel-Grafik vielfach auf.

Alors que l'atelier de son père Frans Hogenberg avait réalisé des séquences scéniques en séries de feuilles volantes, l'atelier de son fils et succes-seur Abraham Hogenberg a réuni les événements entourant l'élection de l'empereur sur une seule feuille. Le dessin de presse du XIXᵉ siècle s'est maintes fois inspiré de la peinture baroque sur panneaux multiples.

coloured illustrated news sheets in large numbers in Vienna, and the publishers François Buisson and Friedrich Justin Bertuch, who launched the first illustrated fashion magazines in Paris and Weimar respectively in the mid-1780s, properly prepared the way for the age of press graphics. Bertuch established a cultural empire of industry in Weimar which had an extensive network of connections and at times employed as many as 500 people. Back in London, the business founded by the Saxon publisher, draughtsman and inventor Rudolph Ackermann, who had settled in the city in 1795, operated along much the same lines. He also employed a number of outstanding English artists, and his business included a drawing school, a gallery from which graphic works could be taken out on loan, a library that was open to the public and a publishing house with its own printing works. The periodicals he published beginning in 1809, including the influential *Ackermann's Repository of Arts* and the first literary annual, *Forget-Me-Not*, later prompted the publisher Charles Knight to issue *The Penny Magazine*, the first popular illustrated weekly. Ackermann profited especially from the new hunger for pictures and the hobby painting that developed from the Picturesque Movement, which had begun in the mid-1780s in response to a series of illustrated travel guides by the amateur artist William Gilpin. Among Ackermann's most successful publications were two he produced with the satirical artist Thomas Rowlandson, namely the *Tour of Dr. Syntax* series, an early comic work that lampooned the craze for people going off in search of picturesque subjects, and *The Microcosm of London*, a portrait of the city in folio format consisting of over 100 hand-coloured pictures depicting animated scenes (ill. p. 49). Alongside his friend James Gillray, who was almost exactly the same age, and the much younger George Cruikshank, Rowlandson was one of the best-known caricature artists in England.

The first such caricatures in England had appeared during the explosive decade of the 1760s, when radicalism first properly took root in Britain, to be followed by a torrent of graphic works that were polemical as well as satirical in their response to

events in France after the Revolution. It has been estimated that during the 60-year reign of George III, that is up until 1820, some 12,000 caricatures were published in England, issued by specialist dealers as single-sheet prints in runs of between 500 and 1,500 copies. The undisputed champion of this wave of pictorial satire, from the 1780s onwards, was James Gillray, and the influence of his uncompromising designs reached as far afield as the graphic work being produced in France at the time. Gillray's technique relied heavily on the grotesque distortion of faces that had also characterised the Baroque drawing style of *caricare* (Italian "to load"), which had been used as one of the avant-garde teaching methods in Bologna in the late 16th century at the art academy run by Annibale, Agostino and Ludovico Carracci.

The influence of English social grotesques and political caricatures can also be seen in Goya's mysterious graphic works, which were identified by Baudelaire as a form of pictorial satire. Although only a small part of the published edition of his series *Los Caprichos* was in fact bought before the rest was withdrawn, individual sheets were circulated in artists' circles in France from 1824 at the latest (after Goya had moved to Bordeaux) and these designs left a strong mark, notably in Charles Philipon's magazine *La Caricature*.

In Japan meanwhile in the 1810s, the highly popular painter and woodblock artist Katsushika Hokusai issued the first of his 15 volumes of *Hokusai Manga*, a series of sketches in which he illustrated a huge range of subjects from nature, everyday life and the supernatural (ill. p. 53 b.). A few editions of this work had managed to appear in the West in the years prior to Japan being forced to open up to the rest of the world in the mid-19th century, yet despite that, Hokusai's considerable influence on press graphics with his subject matter and his whimsical compositions was not fully felt until about 20 years later.

---

*Editorial note on the abbreviations: del. (delineavit) = drawn by; sc. (sculpsit) = engraved by; lith. = lithographed by; photo. = photographed by

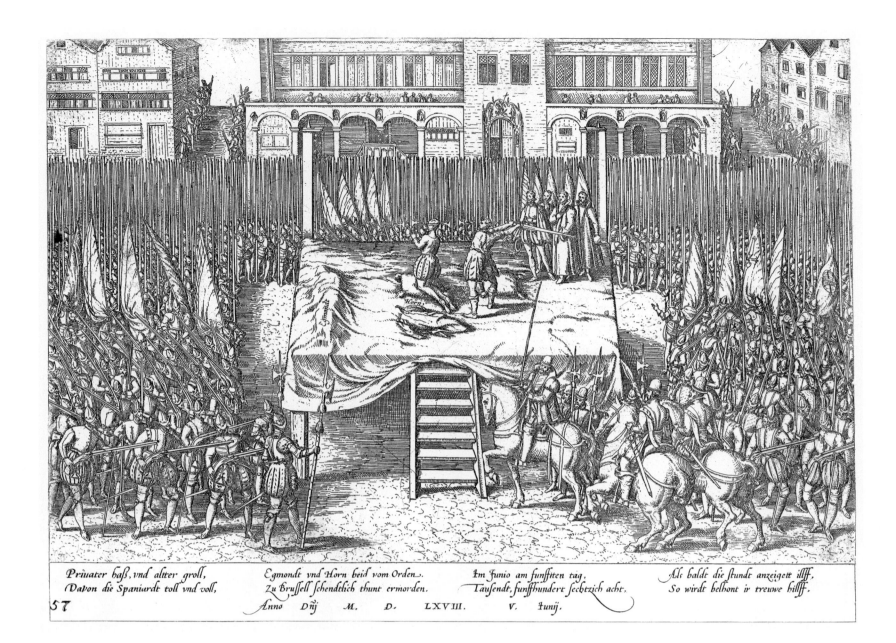

Prïuater haß, vnd alter groll,   Egmondt vnd Horn beid vom Orden.   Im Junio am funffiten tag.   Als baldt die stunde anzeigett ißff,
(Davon die Spaniardt toll vnd voll,   Zu Brußell schendtlich thunt ermorden.   Tausendt, funffhundert sechtzich acht.   So wirdt belhont ir treuwe hilßf.
57   Anno Dñj   M.   D.   LXVIII.   V.   Junij.

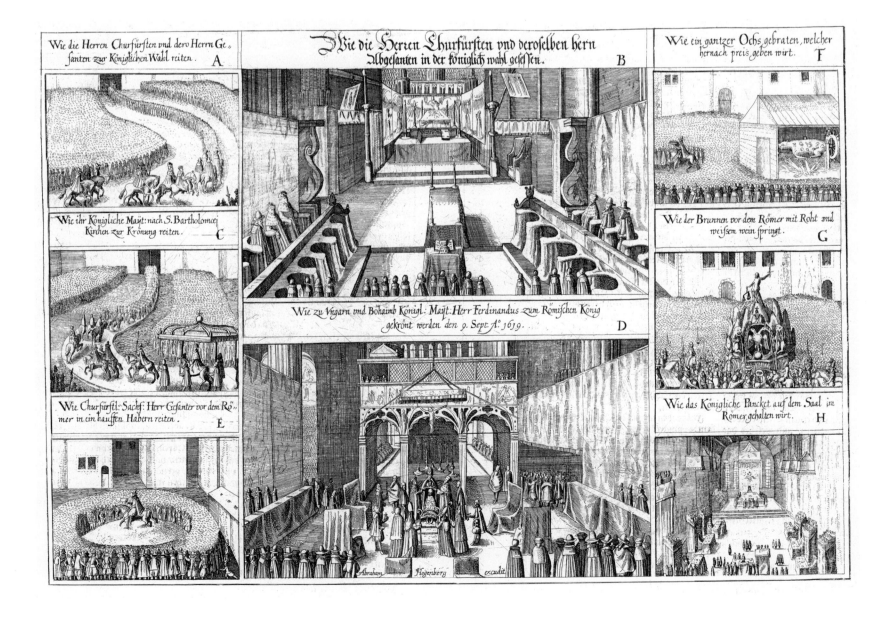

Wie die Herren Churfürsten vnd dero Herrn Ge=
santen zur Königlichen Wahl reiten.   A

Wie die Herren Churfürsten vnd deroselben hern
Abgesanten in der königlich wahl gesessen.   B

Wie ein gantzer Ochs gebraten, welcher
hernach preis geben wirt.   F

Wie ihr Königliche Maÿst: nach S. Bartholomej
Kirchen zur Krönung reiten.   C

Wie der Brunnen vor dem Römer mit Roht vnd
weisem wein springt.   G

Wie zu Vngarn vnd Böhaimb Königl: Maÿst: Herr Ferdinandus zum Römischen König
gekrönt werden den 9. Sept: A: 1619.   D

Wie Churfürstl: Sachs: Herr Gesanter vor dem Rö=
mer in ein hauffen Habern reiten.   E

Wie das Königliche Pancket auf dem Saal in
Römer gehalten wirt.   H

Abraham   Hogenberg   excudit

THE THREE FALSE BRETHREN.

A Deformed head in the Pillory.

What awkard ill-look'd Fellow's y.
He has an ugly frightfull Phys:
And sure as black his conscience is!
Cadaverous, black, blue, and green,
Nor fit in publick to be seen.
With dirt besmear'd, & goggle-ey'd
With a long Nose, & Mouth as wide;

With blobber Lips, & Lockram Jaws,
Warts Wrinkles, Wens, & other Flaws:
With nutty beard, & Neck that's scabby,
And in a dress that's very shabby,
Who this should be I do not know,
Unless a Whig? I guess he's so.
If I am right, pray take a Throw.

B R Sculp.

OLIVER CROMWELL

A Whig & Tory, a Wrestling.

Angry and Fierce are both, both very Bold,
Long did they struggle, yet maintain'd their hold.
Both did stand out against the Kick and Trip,
But the poor Whig is got upon the Hip:
And after all his pains of sweat and toil,
Is like to get a Fall, at least a Foil.
And now the Tory has him, 'tis well known,
And has with strength & Judgment Cast him down.

If we may trust to Metoposcopy,
To lines o'th' Face, and Language of y. Eye.
We find him thoughtfull, resolute, & Sly.
He knew when to cajole, and to dissemble.
And so to make his Foes m.st blust'ring tremble,
But yet, this bold & mighty daring Hector,
Is gone I fear to Hell, to be Protector.

Here's Daniel, the Pope, and the Devil well match'd,
By whose Crafty Inventions all mischief is hatch'd:
In deceiving poor Creatures their chief Talent lies,
Altho' to us Mortals they'd seem otherwise.
From crafty deceivers, Good Lord, set us free,
And keep us secure from the snares of these Three.

On the Calves head Feast.

Fanaticks base, a Calves head Feast still hold:
In Scorn of Charles, a pious King and bold.
For which (may Cuckoldome, be all their fates,
And Horns of Calves heads, still adorn their Pates.

THE Whigs Medly

By G.B. Ingraver.
M.DCC.XI.

Frühe Bildnachrichten

Der Bildjournalismus entwickelte sich im Europa der frühen Neuzeit mit dem aufkommenden Holzschnitt und Buchdruck. Reisende Händler verbreiteten fantasiereich ausgemalte Meldungen aus aller Welt in der Form von Einblattdrucken. Nicht selten war diese kolportierende Nachrichtenübermittlung mit einer rezitativen Aufführungspraxis verbunden, dem sogenannten Bänkelsang (ital. *cantastoria*). Dabei handelte es sich den Forschungen des Sinologen Victor H. Mair zufolge um ein globales Phänomen, das seinen Ausgang im Indien des 6. Jahrhunderts genommen hatte und erst ab dem 16. Jahrhundert in Europa nachweisbar ist (Abb. S. 20). Der mobile Grafikhandel wurde zu dieser Zeit bereits von einigen wenigen Verlagen dominiert, die über ein weitreichendes stationäres Distributionsnetz verfügten. Ein Pionier dieses aufblühenden Gewerbes war der Antwerpener Maler und Kupferstecher Hieronymus Cock, der vor allem kartografische Werke und Gemäldereproduktionen herausgab. Zu seinen bekanntesten Mitarbeitern zählte Pieter Bruegel d. Ä., der mit seinem satirisch-ethnografischen Werk einen elementaren Einfluss auf die typologische Tradition der Pressegrafik ausübte. Einer der besten Zeichner und Stecher der Cock-Factory, Frans Hogenberg, gründete 1570 in Köln ein eigenes Grafikunternehmen. Neben topografischen und kartografischen Werken waren es vor allem umfangreiche Folgen von Aktualitätenblättern über Ereignisse in den Konfessionskriegen, mit denen der protestantische Glaubensflüchtling als Verleger reüssierte. Über 400 Bildreportagen sind aus seiner Werkstatt bekannt (Abb. S. 29 o.).

Hogenbergs Mitarbeiter mussten bei der visuellen Umsetzung der Nachrichten sorgfältig vorgehen, da die Plausibilität von einem gebildeten Publikum kritisch geprüft und diskutiert wurde. Sie konnten bei den Recherchen auf ein umfangreiches verlagseigenes Archiv zurückgreifen. Im späten 16. Jahrhundert lag bereits eine breite Palette an gedruckten dokumentarischen Bildmaterialien vor: Kosmografien und Kompendien von internationalen Städteansichten, darunter die berühmte verlagseigene *Civitates orbis terrarum*, daneben Tier- und Pflanzenbücher sowie eine Vielzahl von grafischen Reiseberichten. Zu den namentlich bekannten *special artists* der Frühzeit, auf deren Pionierarbeit Hogenbergs Bildjournalismus aufbauen konnte, zählten Grafiker wie Erhard Reeuwijk, Christoph Weiditz (Abb. S. 24–25), Hans Weiditz, Sebald Beham, Melchior Lorck und Jost Amman (Abb. S. 20). Letzterer war auf Darstellungen der Arbeits- und Alltagswelt spezialisiert, die in sogenannten Stände- und Trachtenbüchern abgedruckt wurden. Ein verwandtes Genre der Sozialgrafik waren die sogenannten Kaufrufe (frz. *les cris*, engl. *street cries*). Ein frühes Exemplar dieser bilderbogenartigen Darstellungen lokaler Händlertypen fand sich in Hogenbergs eigenem Verlagsprogramm. Um 1500 in Paris begründet, durchlief die Kaufruf-Grafik im Lauf der Jahrhunderte eine erstaunliche internationale Karriere, bis sie schließlich in England zu Anfang des 19. Jahrhunderts in das Feld der investigativen Sozialreportage und urbanen Ethnografie mündete. Viele der Bildnachrichten Hogenbergs lassen sich allerdings nicht allein durch die Kompilation von Sekundärmaterialien erklären. Der

---

George Bickham (del. & sc.) *

The Three False Brethren: The Whig's Medly,
London, 1711
Die drei falschen Brüder: das Whig-Medly
Les trois faux frères : le medly des Whigs
Copper engraving
London, The British Museum

Assembled from parts of other publications and printed matter, this illustration presents a critical portrait of Daniel Defoe in the manner of a broken mirror. Defoe was the most controversial journalist of his time, and is seen as the inventor of the realistic novel and a modern form of reporting that emphasised the importance of eye-witness accounts.

Das aus publizistischen Fragmenten montierte Tableau gibt in der Art eines zerbrochenen Spiegels ein kritisches Porträt Daniel Defoes wieder. Der umstrittenste Journalist der Zeit gilt als Begründer

des realistischen Romans und einer modernen Form der Reportage, die auf die Authentizität von Augenzeugenberichten Wert legt.

Ce tableau, composé à partir de fragments de publications, présente à la manière d'un miroir brisé un portrait critique de Daniel Defoe. Le journaliste le plus controversé de son temps est considéré comme le père du roman réaliste et d'une forme moderne de reportage, qui met l'accent sur l'authenticité des témoignages vécus.

Anonymous

*The Earle of Strafford for Treasonable Practises
Beheaded on the Tower-hill (c. 1642)*, London, 1885
*Der Graf von Strafford wird wegen verräterischer
Akte auf dem Tower Hill enthauptet*
*Le comte Strafford est décapité sur la Tower Hill
pour acte de trahison*
Facsimile wood engraving after a woodcut
From: Mason Jackson, *The Pictorial Press*,
London, 1885

A year after the event, Strafford's execution was
made the subject of an eight-page illustrated newspaper. Wenceslaus Hollar's use of a subjective
perspective was discarded in favour of a pictorial
narrative that functioned more like a pictogram
to focus primarily on the execution.

Ein Jahr nach der Hinrichtung wurde der Fall
Strafford Gegenstand einer achtseitigen Bilderzei-
tung. Wenzel Hollars subjektive Perspektive wurde
dabei in eine piktogrammatische Bilderzählung
aufgelöst, die die Exekution ins Zentrum rückt.

Un an après l'exécution, l'affaire Strafford devint le
sujet d'un journal illustré de huit pages. La perspective subjective de Wenceslaus Hollar y fut transfor-
mée en un pictogramme qui place l'exécution au
centre de ce récit en images.

Verlag muss auch über ein rudimentäres grafisches Korres-
pondentennetz verfügt haben, zu dem auch Festungs- und
Belagerungsingenieure zählten, die in den Kriegsgebieten vor
Ort aufzeichneten.

Der enge Zusammenhang zwischen Bildreportage, Kartogra-
fie und Vedutengrafik, der das Hogenberg'sche Programm auch
unter der späteren Leitung seines Sohns Abraham (Abb. S. 29 u.)
bestimmte, zeigt sich auf besonders prägnante Weise im Werk
des prominentesten Mitarbeiters Wenzel Hollar. Der böhmische
Stecher und Zeichner hatte sich in seiner Lehrzeit bei dem Topo-
grafen Matthäus Merian sowie durch das Studium von Albrecht
Dürers Grafiken einen besonderen Ethos des Mimetischen an-
geeignet. Es war Hollar, der die Anschauung einer ebenso nüch-
ternen wie akribischen Form des Dokumentarismus in die noch
in den Kinderschuhen steckende grafische Kultur Englands im-
plementierte, nachdem er sich 1637 im Mutterland der illustrierten Presse niedergelassen hatte. In Hunderten von grafischen
Veduten, Architekturansichten, Porträts und Ereignisbildern
überlieferte er der Nachwelt ein kaleidoskopisches Panorama
Londons zur Zeit des beginnenden Bürgerkriegs und der anschließenden Restauration.

Hollars bahnbrechende bildjournalistische Sachlichkeit zeigte
sich auf exemplarische Weise in seiner grafischen Aufnahme der
Hinrichtung des Earl of Strafford im Mai 1641 (Abb. S. 26/27).
Das Ereignis markierte einen entscheidenden Wendepunkt im
Tauziehen um die Macht zwischen englischem Königtum und
Parlament und wurde daher vielfach kolportiert. Hollar vermied
die übliche Betrachtung aus einer imaginären Aufsicht, sondern
nahm einen an der Benutzung der Camera obscura geschul-
ten ebenerdigen Betrachterstandpunkt ein, der die Authentizität einer Augenzeugenschaft suggerierte. Das zentrale Ereignis
der Hinrichtung wurde dabei an den Rand gedrängt und musste
im Grad der Aufmerksamkeit sogar noch mit einer einstürzenden
Zuschauertribüne im Hintergrund konkurrieren.

Die Geschehnisse um den englischen Bürgerkrieg, der mit
der Hinrichtung dieses engen Vertrauten von König Karl I.

eingeläutet wurden, spielen pressehistorisch eine bedeutsame
Rolle. 1643 wurde, nur wenige Jahrzehnte nachdem in Straß-
burg und in Amsterdam die frühesten Zeitungen gegründet
worden waren, in London mit dem *Mercurius Civicus* das erste
illustrierte Periodikum aus der Taufe gehoben. Diese Kriegs-
illustrierte erschien in wöchentlichen Lieferungen und war mit
groben Holzschnittporträts führender Politiker und Militärs versehen. Obgleich das Blatt die antiabsolutistische Sache des
Parlaments vertrat, waren sein Erscheinen und das aller anderen
Publikationen ständig von einer parlamentarischen Vorzensur
bedroht. Der puritanische Dichter John Milton veröffentlichte
daraufhin mit seinem Pamphlet *Areopagitica* (1644) eine erste
neuzeitliche Verteidigung der Pressefreiheit. Mit der Scharfsinnig-
keit seiner Argumentation setzte Milton damit Maßstäbe für alle
weiteren Auseinandersetzungen um Zensur und andere Restriktionen, wie die Erhebung der berüchtigten Stempelsteuer.
Diese war in England 1712 als Herrschaftsinstrument eingeführt
worden, um regierungskritische Publikationen zu unterdrücken
und weite Teile der Bevölkerung in politischer Unmündigkeit
zu halten.

Während vom Bürgerkrieg in England nur wenige zeichnerische Zeugnisse überliefert sind, erwies sich der Dreißigjähri-
ge Krieg (1618–1648), der zur gleichen Zeit auf dem Kontinent
tobte, als eine Blütezeit des frühen Bildjournalismus. Herausragend war der lothringische Zeichner, Kupferstecher und Ra-
dierer Jacques Callot (Abb. S. 33). Callot gab sich nicht mit den
üblichen Schlachtenszenen zufrieden, sondern nahm vor allem
die verheerenden Folgen für die Bevölkerung in den Blick. Zeitgenössischen Berichten zufolge sind etliche seiner Darstellungen von Bettlern, Kriegsinvaliden und Vaganten aus der Serie
Les Gueux (1622–1623) direkt vor den Betroffenen entstanden.
Callot eröffnete dem grafischen Dokumentarismus damit eine
revolutionäre sozialrealistische Tiefendimension, die von Empathie mit den Außenseitern der Gesellschaft getragen war. Sein
facettenreiches Werk erwies sich allerdings nicht nur als grund-
legend für die Entwicklung der grafischen Sozialreportage. Die

Jacques Callot (del. & sc.)

The Sick Man
Der Kranke | Le Malade
Etching
From the series *Les Gueux*, Nancy, 1622–1623

Franca Trippa, Fritellino
Etching
From: *Balli di Sfessania*, Nancy, c. 1621–1622
New York, The Metropolitan Museum of Art

grotesken Bilderserien, in denen er auf Motive von Hieronymus Bosch und Pieter Bruegel zurückgriff und sich des Figurenrepertoires der italienischen Commedia dell'Arte bediente, hatten auch einen immensen Einfluss auf den satirischen Zweig der Pressegrafik. So stand beispielsweise die Kunst seines lothringischen Landsmanns Grandville, des ersten Stars der französischen Karikaturbewegung, ganz in der Nachfolge Callots.

In England entwickelte sich der Bildjournalismus hingegen nur schleppend. Dabei hatte die Glorious Revolution von 1688/89 dem Land eine Stärkung der bürgerlichen Rechte beschert, einschließlich der Aufhebung der Pressezensur. Die „glorreiche" Übernahme des britischen Throns durch den Statthalter der Niederlande, Wilhelm III. von Oranien, war von dem Kupferstecher, Dichter und Maler Romeyn de Hooghe auf vielfältige Weise bildpropagandistisch begleitet worden. De Hooghe deckte in der Nachfolge Callots ein weites grafisches Spektrum ab, das von barocken Bildnachrichtenblättern bis zu allegorischen Sozial- und Politsatiren reichte. Letztere führten in den Niederlanden zu Anklagen wegen Pornografie und Blasphemie und hatten diplomatische Zwischenfälle mit Frankreich und England zur Folge. 1701 brachte er mit seinem *Aesopus in Europa* ein erstes bildsatirisches Wochenmagazin in Umlauf. Mit de Hooghes Werk begann sich die politische Karikatur als komplexes und konsistentes künstlerisches Genre zu behaupten (Abb. S. 35).

In der englischen Kunst fand der Einfluss der niederländischen Grafik allerdings erst einige Jahrzehnte später im Werk des eigensinnigen Kupferstechers und Malers William Hogarth einen programmatischen Niederschlag. Hogarth wurde mit einer Reihe bilderbogenartiger Grafikfolgen bekannt, die er als *modern moral subjects* bezeichnete. Es handelte sich dabei um Schlüsselszenen aus dem Leben prototypischer Charaktere, deren Werdegänge ein kritisches Licht auf die sozialen Verhältnisse werfen sollten. Mit seiner Erfindung von Theaterstücken in Bildern schrieb sich Hogarth in die Genealogie einer sequenziellen Kunst ein, die pressegrafisch ab den 1840er-Jahren durch den Abdruck von Rodolphe Töpffers Bilderromanen

(siehe Abb. S. 157) eine Rolle zu spielen begann. Hogarth' Bildertheater zeichnete sich durch einen rohen Alltagsrealismus aus und war – beeinflusst vom Aufstieg der großstädtischen Tagespresse – vom journalistischen Paradigma der Tagesaktualität durchsetzt. In künstlerischer Entsprechung zu den literarischen Streifzügen des satirischen Gesellschaftsreporters Ned Ward (Abb. S. 39), der in seiner Gazette *The London Spy* von der Londoner Unterwelt berichtete, durchkreuzte Hogarth die Quartiere Londons, um visuelle Eindrücke für seine Bildgeschichten aufzuzeichnen. Es wird berichtet, dass er seine Beobachtungen in Ermangelung von Notizpapier stenogrammartig auf die Fingernägel skizzierte. Ein Jahrhundert vor Charles Baudelaire wurde diese Kunst des urbanen Flanierens von Hogarth' Freund, dem Dichter John Gay, in seinem Poem *Trivia* (1716) gefeiert. Gay war es auch, der Hogarth mit seiner sozialkritischen Erfolgsoperette *The Beggar's Opera* (1728) das inszenatorische Modell für die *modern moral subjects* geliefert hatte (Abb. S. 36/37).

Hogarth verortete seinen urbanen Sozialrealismus als *comic history* im Schnittbereich zwischen sublimer Historienkunst und niederer Groteske. Der Antagonismus zwischen Hoch- und Populärkunst, der die Rezeptionsgeschichte der Illustration bis heute bestimmt, wird in seinem Werk erstmals auf exemplarische Weise virulent. Sein künstlerisches Selbstverständnis gründete auf der Reklamemalerei, der republikanischen Kunst par excellence, die er zu Anfang seiner Karriere selbst betrieben hatte und die auch seine patchworkartig aufgelösten Darstellungen des Stadtraums bestimmte (Abb. S. 38). Die zeichenhafte Klitterung seiner Bildräume profitierte ebenso davon, dass er die Sammelsurium-Grafiken studierte, die in den Niederlanden als *quodlibets* und in England als *medley prints* (Abb. S. 30) bekannt waren. Dieses Genre illusionistischer Pseudocollagen (Abb. S. 39) antizipierte die Scrapbook-Ästhetik der pluralen Pressegrafik des 19. Jahrhunderts.

Hogarth' Ideal einer demokratischen Kunst verstand sich in erklärter Opposition zu dem absolutistisch geprägten Akademismus seiner Malerkollegen. 1762 kuratierte er als plebejisches

William Hogarth & Thomas Cook (sc.)

Bambridge on Trial for Murder by a Committee of the House of Commons (c. 1729), London, 1803
Bambridge wird von einem Ausschuss des Unterhauses des Mordes angeklagt
Bambridge est accusé de meurtre devant un comité de la Chambre des Communes
Copper engraving with etching

In around 1729, William Hogarth depicted the decisive phase in the investigation into allegations of torture that had been brought against the corrupt warden of the Fleet Prison, in the process making the first image of such an examination by a democratic supervisory authority. In the same way as his ardent admirer Charles Dickens, Hogarth had encountered the abuses of the prison system early on in life when his father had been imprisoned.

Um 1729 hielt William Hogarth die entscheidende Phase der Untersuchung von Foltervorwürfen gegen den korrupten Direktor des Fleet-Gefängnisses fest und setzte damit erstmals die Aufklärungsarbeit einer demokratischen Kontrollinstanz ins Bild. Wie sein Anhänger Charles Dickens war Hogarth durch die Inhaftierung seines Vaters früh mit den Missständen des Strafvollzugs konfrontiert worden.

Vers 1729, William Hogarth a dépeint la phase décisive de l'enquête touchant aux accusations de torture à l'encontre du directeur corrompu de la prison de la Fleet et a ainsi, pour la première fois, fixé sur image le travail d'investigation d'une instance démocratique de contrôle. Comme son disciple Charles Dickens, Hogarth avait été très tôt confronté aux abus du système pénitentiaire quand son père avait été emprisonné.

Romeyn de Hooghe (del. & sc.)

→ *Falling Monarchs*, 1689
Die fallenden Monarchen | *Les Monarques tombants*
Etching
London, The British Museum

The two monarchs in question are James II, the deposed Catholic king of England who went into exile and then in trying to regain the throne found his invasion was thwarted by the unicorn of England, together with his ally Louis XIV of France, the Sun King. Their plans to institute a widespread conflagration of absolute monarchical rule were stopped by the events of the Glorious Revolution, as seen in the background, not to mention the Dutch sailor in the foreground with his enema pump.

Bei den beiden Monarchen handelt es sich um Jakob II., den abgesetzten katholischen König von England, der ins Exil ging und bei seinem Versuch, den Thron zurückzuerobern, feststellte, dass seine Invasion durch das Einhorn von England vereitelt wurde, und seinen Verbündeten Ludwig XIV. von Frankreich, den Sonnenkönig. Ihre Pläne, einen Flächenbrand absolutistischer Herrschaft auszulösen, wurden durch die Ereignisse der Glorious Revolution gestoppt, wie im Hintergrund zu sehen ist, ganz zu schweigen von dem holländischen Matrosen im Vordergrund mit seiner Klistierpumpe.

Les deux monarques tombants sont Jacques II, le roi d'Angleterre catholique destitué qui s'était exilé et avait découvert lors de sa tentative de reconquérir le thrône que son invasion avait été contrecarrée par la licorne anglaise et son allié français Louis XIV, le Roi-Soleil. Ses projets visant à provoquer une flambée du pouvoir absolutiste sont réduits à néant par les événements de la Glorieuse Révolution d'Angleterre, figurée à l'arrière-plan, sans oublier le marin hollandais armé d'une pompe à lavement, visible au premier plan.

→→**William Hogarth & William Blake (sc.)**

A Scene from "The Beggar's Opera" VI (1731), London, 1790
Eine Szene aus „Die Bettleroper"
Une scène de « L'Opéra du gueux »
Copper engraving with etching

The original painting by William Hogarth on which this engraving was based had already established the close connections between theatrical drama and socially realistic pictorial journalism which were later to be of such importance for press graphics. In early 1788, the publisher and engraver John Boydell commissioned the artist William Blake, who had much experience as an engraver, to produce this detailed reproduction; the financial security of his fee enabled Blake to proceed with his groundbreaking experiments in the technique of relief etching.

Das Gemälde von William Hogarth, das dem Stich zugrunde liegt, begründete einen engen Zusammenhang zwischen Theatergenre und sozialrealistischer Bildpublizistik, der nachfolgend in der Pressegrafik eine wichtige Rolle spielte. Anfang 1788 beauftragte der Grafikunternehmer John Boydell den versierten Reproduktionsgrafiker William Blake mit diesem aufwendigen Nachstich und ermöglichte ihm damit, sich eine finanzielle Grundlage für bahnbrechende Experimente mit der Technik der Hochätzung zu schaffen.

Le tableau de William Hogarth servant de modèle à la gravure établit un lien étroit entre le genre théâtral et le journalisme illustré socio-réaliste, qui joua par la suite un rôle important dans le dessin de presse. Au début de 1788, l'éditeur et graveur John Boydell commanda à William Blake, artiste graveur chevronné, cette reproduction élaborée, lui offrant ainsi une base financière pour les expériences révolutionnaires réalisées grâce à la technique de la taille d'épargne.

VELUTI IN SPECULUM

UTILE DULCI

William Hogarth (del. & sc.)

The Times, London, 1762
Die Zeiten | Les Temps
Copper engraving with etching
Kunsthalle Bremen, Kupferstichkabinett

Gegenstück zu der exklusiven Gründungsausstellung der Society of Artists eine Ausstellung anonymer Werbeschilder (Abb. S. 44). Die Exponatenliste dieser spektakulären „Sign Painters' Exhibition" lässt vermuten, dass er eigene, gefundene und in Auftrag gegebene Schilder durch Übermalungen und Applikationen zu einem satirischen Metatext gegen die konkurrierende Hochkunstausstellung arrangierte. Hogarth reihte sich damit als einer der Pioniere in eine Frühgeschichte der Antikunst und Kunstparodie ein, die erst Mitte des 19. Jahrhunderts in Paris durch die Aktivitäten bekannter Pressezeichner an Bedeutung gewann.

Das einzige Werk dieser Zeit, das einen der Populärkunst von Hogarth vergleichbaren Einfluss auf die Entwicklung der Pressegrafik nahm, war die von Denis Diderot und Jean-Baptiste le Rond d'Alembert herausgegebene monumentale *Encyclopédie ou Dictionnaire raisonné des sciences, des arts et des métiers* (Abb. S. 48 o.), die in Paris zwischen 1751 und 1780 in 17 Text- und elf Bildbänden erschien. Die künstlerische Regie über den aus 2885 Kupferstichen bestehenden Abbildungsteil lag bei dem Mathematiker und Illustrator Louis-Jacques Goussier. Zehn Jahre lang hatte er die französischen Departements bereist, um in Fabriken und Manufakturen die manuellen und maschinellen Fertigungsabläufe für seine Darstellungen zu

studieren. Mit dem grafischen Corpus der *Encyclopédie* setzte Goussier neue Maßstäbe für die bildnerische Berichterstattung, sowohl was den Umfang der Recherche als auch die Präzision der Aufzeichnung betraf.

Im deutschsprachigen Raum verkörperte der Illustrator und Kupferstecher Daniel Chodowiecki den Topos des grafischen Reporters. Der Chronist des preußischen Königshofs und des bürgerlichen Alltags war ein besessener Schnellzeichner, der seine grafischen Notate nach eigenem Bekunden in allen Lebenslagen – „stehend, gehend, reitend" – anfertigte (Abb. S. 23). Adolph Menzel, der zu den international einflussreichsten Illustratoren des 19. Jahrhunderts zählte, verortete seine eigene Kunst in der bildjournalistischen Nachfolge Chodowieckis. Das ausgehende 18. Jahrhundert erlebte eine zunehmende Industrialisierung des Grafikhandels. In England hatte Hogarth das Eis gebrochen, indem er der anspruchsvolleren Druckgrafik mit seinen populären Bilderfolgen ein Massenpublikum erschlossen hatte. Die internationale „Hogarthomanie" setzte allerdings erst nach seinem Tod ein, als der Grafikunternehmer John Boydell eine voluminöse Gesamtausgabe seiner Werke herausbrachte, die mehrere Auflagen erlebte. Boydell war der Hieronymus Cock seiner Zeit. Mit seinem arbeitsteiligen Unternehmen und den

George Bickham (del. & sc.)

Sot's Paradise, London, 1706
Säufers Paradies | Paradis d'ivrogne
Copper engraving with etching
New York, The Metropolitan Museum
of Art

The subject of this pseudo-collage by George Bickham is the conflict between high art and popular art. The portrait of Philippe de Champaigne, the painter and one of the founders of the Académie Royale de Peinture et de Sculpture in Paris, is overlaid with pieces of satirical social commentary. In this way, the Catholic heaven of history painting collides with the drunkards' paradise of Ned Ward and Jacques Callot's defecating peasants.

George Bickhams Pseudocollage thematisiert den Konflikt zwischen Hoch- und Populärkunst. Das Porträt von Philippe de Champaigne, Maler und Mitbegründer der Académie Royale de Peinture et de Sculpture in Paris, wird von satirischen und sozialrealistischen Druckerzeugnissen überlagert. Der katholische Himmel der Historienkunst trifft hier auf das Säuferparadies Ned Wards und die scheißenden Bauern Jacques Callots.

Le pseudo-collage de George Bickham a pour thème le conflit entre le grand art et l'art populaire. Le portrait de Philippe de Champaigne, peintre et membre fondateur de l'Académie royale de peinture et de sculpture, est recouvert de matériel satirique et socio-réaliste. Le ciel catholique de la peinture d'histoire rencontre ici le paradis des ivrognes de Ned Ward et les paysans déféquant de Jacques Callot.

Francisco Goya & Anonymous engraver

The Disasters of War, c. 1807–1815/1865
Die Schrecken des Krieges
Les Désastres de la guerre
Wood engraving after etching with aquatint
From: *Le Monde illustré*, Paris, 11 November 1865

Francisco Goya began his series of dramatic scenes relating to the Spanish War of Independence as early as 1807, although they were not published until the 1860s, after he had died. Only one of the 82 engravings can definitely be said to be based on direct experience (top illustration), however, many of the allegorical representations are tinged with journalistic input and were derived from press reports or word of mouth.

Die Serie mit drastischen Szenen aus dem spanischen Befreiungskrieg hatte Francisco de Goya bereits 1807 begonnen. Allerdings konnte sie erst postum in den 1860er-Jahren veröffentlicht werden. Nur eine der 82 Radierungen (obere Abbildung)

geht verbürgterweise auf unmittelbar Erlebtes zurück. Viele der allegorischen Darstellungen sind jedoch journalistisch gefärbt und haben Pressemeldungen oder orale Überlieferungen als Hintergrund.

Francisco de Goya avait commencé la série des scènes dramatiques de la guerre d'indépendance d'Espagne dès 1807. Toutefois, elles ne purent être publiées que dans les années 1860. Seule une des 82 estampes (illustration du haut) est avérée témoignage d'un événement vécu. Un grand nombre de représentations allégoriques sont cependant teintées d'expérience journalistique et s'appuient sur des reportages de presse ou des récits rapportés par le bouche-à-oreille.

Massenauflagen veränderte er den Kunsthandel und den Grafikmarkt auf nachhaltige Weise. Auf dem Kontinent waren es Unternehmer wie der Kupferstecher Hieronymus Löschenkohl, der in Wien kolorierte Bildnachrichten im großen Stil vertrieb, oder die Verleger François Buisson und Friedrich Justin Bertuch, die in Paris und Weimar Mitte der 1780er-Jahre erste illustrierte Modemagazine herausbrachten, die den Boden für das Zeitalter der Pressegrafik bereiteten. Bertuch errichtete in Weimar ein weitverzweigtes kulturindustrielles Imperium, das zeitweilig bis zu 500 Personen beschäftigte. Ähnlich breit strukturiert war das Londoner Unternehmen des sächsischen Verlegers, Zeichners und Erfinders Rudolph Ackermann, der sich 1795 in der englischen Metropole etabliert hatte. Er beschäftigte eine Reihe der hervorragendsten englischen Künstler in seinem Unternehmen, das aus einer Zeichenschule, einer musealen Galerie mit Grafikausleihe, einer öffentlichen Bibliothek sowie einem Verlag mit Druckerei bestand. Die Periodika, die er seit 1809 herausbrachte, darunter das aufwendige *Ackermann's Repository of Arts* sowie der erste englischsprachige Almanach *Forget-me-not*, haben später den Verleger Charles Knight zur Herausgabe der ersten Populärillustrierten *Penny Magazine* stimuliert. Ackermann profitierte vor allem vom Bilderhunger und von der Hobbykunst der pittoresken Bewegung, die Mitte der 1780er-Jahre durch eine Reihe illustrierter Reiseführer des Laienkünstlers William Gilpin angestoßen worden war. Zu Ackermanns erfolgreichsten Publikationen zählten zwei Werke, die er mit dem satirischen Zeichner Thomas Rowlandson realisiert hatte: die frühe Comicserie *The Tour of Dr. Syntax*, in der die touristische Jagd nach pittoresken Motiven aufs Korn genommen wurde, sowie *The Microcosm of London*, ein aus über 100 handkolorierten Wimmelbildern bestehendes Porträt der Metropole London im Folioformat (Abb. S. 49). Rowlandson gehörte neben seinem nahezu gleichaltrigen Freund James Gillray und dem weitaus jüngeren George Cruikshank zu den bekanntesten Exponenten der englischen Karikaturbewegung.

Diese hatte in den explosiven 1760er-Jahren, der Gründungsphase des britischen Radikalismus, ihren Ausgang genommen und in der Auseinandersetzung mit den revolutionären Ereignissen in Frankreich eine Flut an grafischen Polemiken und Satiren hervorgebracht. Man schätzt, dass in der 60-jährigen

Regentschaft von Georg III. etwa 12 000 Karikaturen in England erschienen sind, die von spezialisierten Händlern als Einblattdrucke in Auflagen von 500 bis 1500 Exemplaren in Umlauf gebracht wurden. Der unbestrittene Champion dieser bildsatirischen Welle hieß seit den 1780er-Jahren James Gillray. Der Einfluss seiner drastischen Bildfindungen strahlte auch auf die französische Revolutionsgrafik aus. Gillray griff mit seiner Technik der physiognomischen Verzerrung auf den barocken Zeichenmodus des *caricare* (italienisch: überladen) zurück, der Ende des 16. Jahrhunderts zu den avantgardistischen Unterrichtsmethoden der Bologneser Kunstakademie der Brüder Annibale, Agostino und Ludovico Carracci zählte.

Der Einfluss britischer Sozialgroteske und Politkarikatur ist auch im mysteriösen grafischen Werk von Francisco de Goya auszumachen, das Baudelaire dem Bereich der Bildsatire zugeordnet hat. Obgleich von dessen Zyklus *Los Caprichos* nur ein geringer Teil der Auflage in Umlauf gekommen ist, zirkulierten einzelne Blätter spätestens seit Goyas Emigration nach Frankreich 1824 in den hiesigen Künstlerkreisen und haben dort ihre Spuren hinterlassen, nicht zuletzt in Charles Philipons Magazin *La Caricature*.

In den 1810er-Jahren schuf der populäre japanische Maler und Holzschneider Katsushika Hokusai seinen fünfzehnbändigen grafischen Lehrbuchkorpus *Hokusai Manga*, in dem er die Gesamtheit irdischer und überirdischer Phänomene dokumentierte (Abb. S. 53 u.). Einzelne Ausgaben zirkulierten im Westen bereits kurz nach der erzwungenen Öffnung Japans zur Mitte des 19. Jahrhunderts. Ihren deutlichen Niederschlag in der westlichen Pressegrafik fand der enorme Reichtum an Alltagsszenen, Naturstudien und surrealen Capriccis allerdings erst zwei Jahrzehnte später.

*Editorische Anmerkung zu den Abkürzungen: del. (delineavit) = gezeichnet; sc. (sculpsit) = gestochen; lith. = lithografiert; photo. = fotografiert

LE MONDE ILLUSTRÉ

Les portraits historiques de Goya sont nombreux, ils sont tous ou presque tous réunis au musée de Madrid ou conservés dans les résidences; et on peut juger de l'ampleur de l'exécution de ces belles toiles qui pourraient vieillir à cause du costume un peu ridicule déjà de nos jours, mais qui se sauveront et resteront éternellement jeunes, grâce à la fraicheur du coloris.

Le plus grand mérite de Goya comme portraitiste, celui que tous les artistes admirent le plus, 'est le sacrifice qu'il sait faire au profit de son modèle, de ces mille détails dont

LES DÉSASTRES DE LA GUERRE, *fac-simile* de l'eau-forte avec la légende : « J'ai vu cette scène ».

la lumière ne tient jamais compte, et qu'elle baigne dans une pénombre où ils ne s'accusent quepar des reflets. Il voit juste et peint ce qu'il voit et non ce qui est, et sa peinture arrive à ce degré d'impersonnalité qui fait qu'elle semble une fenêtre ouverte sur la nature et non une convention qui traduit; immense qualité qui se retrouve à un si haut degré dans le merveilleux *Esope* de Valasquez, dans *les Menines*, le *omédien* et l'étonnant *Ménippe*, don précieux qu'on a appelé de nos jours l'*Enveloppe* et qui est bien nommé : Problème résolu de la fusion de la ligne et de la lumière, des contours et de l'air ambiant à laquelle sont arrivés les grands Vénitiens et les Florentins de la renaissance.

Goya, peintre de quatre rois, Charles III, Charles IV, Ferdinand VII et le roi Joseph, a peint beaucoup de portraits historiques; mais il y a dans son œuvre des portraits peints en une séance qui se tiennent à côté de ses meilleurs.

L'aqua-fortiste a laissé un grand nombre de planches· les *Caprices* sont célèbres, elles contiennent au milieu de fantaisies et de rêves singuliers de mordantes attaques contre les hommes politiques d'alors la *Toromaquia* (33 planches), eau-forte et aquateinte, reproduit toutes les péripéties des combats de taureaux, Goya vivait beaucoup avec les toréros et excellait aux jeux du cirque. *Les désastres de la guerre* (80 planches) c'est là son chef-d'œuvre, on n'a jamais poussé plus loin la vie, le mouvement et la science du dessin. Une série de gravures à l'eau-forte, d'après les portraits de Velasquez d'une belle exécution, sévère et patiente, enfin quelques pièces détachées, entre autres

FRANCISCO DE GOYA Y LUCIENTES, peintre espagnol.

(D'après le portrait gravé par lui-même en tête des *Caprices*.)

la fameuse planche *le Garot*, le mode de supplice en usage en Espagne. Le nombre de dessins et de croquis est énorme, et tableaux de genre sont innombrables. C'est sur ces derniers qu'on l'a jugé en France, et tout Goya n'est pas là; on ne saurait se prononcer sur lui sans avoir vu les grandes œuvres.

Nous ne cessons pas de le répéter, nous ne voulons dans le *Monde illustré* prendre que la fleur des sujets, et ce recueil mondain moins futile qu'on pourrait le croire veut donner une notion juste sur tout élément nouveau d'actualité. Goya vient d'entrer au Louvre pour la première fois depuis la dispersion de la galerie espagnole; nous voulons qu'on sache qui il était, ce qu'il a produit, pourquoi il mérite l'honneur de figurer parmi les grands maitres. L'étude esthétique sérieuse nous l'écrivons en ce moment pour la plus solennelle et la plus enviée des revues, nous traçons ces lignes spéciales pour accompagner le portrait et les deux eaux-fortes que nous publions. Le portrait est de Goya lui-même, il figure en tête des *Caprices*, célèbre recueil d'eaux-fortes du maitre, les artistes apprécieront toute la valeur de ce croquis robuste qui donne bien l'idée de ce singulier genre, les eaux-fortes sont des *fac-simile* des planches très-rares des *Désastres de la guerre*, que nous avons dû réunir à grand peine pour avoir sous les yeux tous les éléments d'étude sur le peintre, elles représentent des scènes déchirantes de carnage et font allusion à l'invasion de l'empire. Sur l'une d'elles, en marge, Goya a écrit : « J'ai vu cette scène. » Quel motif d'intérêt pour l'astiste ! Sur la seconde, il a écrit de son crayon fiévreux : — « No se puede mirar. » « On ne saurait regarder. »

Nous ne suivons pas ici Goya dans sa longue existence; peintre de quatre rois, comblé d'honneurs et de gloire, il ne voulut pas donner à sa patrie le spectacle de sa décrépitude et finit sa carrière à Bordeaux en 1828, tenant encore d'une main tremblante la pointe et le pinceau et jusqu'au tombeau poursuivant de ses satires et de ses railleries les apostasies et les ridicules.

Goya est un maitre, la lumière se fait aujourd'hui sur cette organisation prodigieuse, nous avons suivi son œuvre du nord au midi de l'Espagne et espé-

LES DÉSASTRES DE LA GUERRE, *fac-simile* d'eau-forte de Goya.

LIEU.' GOVER.' GALL-STONE, inspired by ALECTO; ___ or ___ The Birth of MINERVA. "From his head, she sprung, a Goddess's Arm'd." Milton.

To the Opinions of The right hon.ble EDWARD, LORD THURLOW, the EARLS CAMDEN, BUTE, BATHURST, and COVENTRY, George Touchet BARON-AUDLEY, and PHILIP THICKNESSE Jun.r Esq.r to the LITERATI, the ROYAL-SOCIETY, the MILITARY, MEDICAL and OBSTETRIC Bodies, this attempt to Elucidate the properties of HONOR and COURAGE, INTELLIGENCE and PHILANTHROPY, is most respectfully submitted . by their humble servant , J.s Gillray.

Premières informations en images

Le journalisme illustré se développa en Europe au début des temps modernes avec l'émergence de la gravure sur bois et de l'imprimerie. Les marchands ambulants répandirent avec beaucoup d'imagination des nouvelles dessinées venant du monde entier sous forme d'imprimés individuels. Il n'était pas rare que cette diffusion de nouvelles colportées soit accompagnée d'une tradition récitative scénique appelée ritournelle (en italien *cantastoria*). Selon les recherches du sinologue Victor H. Mair, il s'agissait là d'un phénomène global, qui avait débuté en Inde à partir du VIe siècle et dont il est prouvé qu'il n'apparut en Europe qu'au XVIe siècle (ills. p. 20). À cette époque, le commerce ambulant de gravures était déjà dominé par quelques rares maisons d'édition qui disposaient sur place d'un vaste réseau de distribution. Le peintre et chalcographe anversois Hieronymus Cock, qui publiait avant tout des œuvres cartographiques et des reproductions de tableau, fut un pionnier de ce commerce émergent. Parmi ses plus célèbres collaborateurs se trouvait Pieter Bruegel l'Ancien, qui avec son œuvre satirico-ethnographique exerça une influence élémentaire sur la tradition typologique du dessin de presse. Frans Hogenberg, l'un des meilleurs dessinateurs et graveurs de l'usine Cock, fonda sa propre entreprise de gravure à Cologne en 1570. En plus des œuvres topographiques et cartographiques, ce sont surtout de volumineuses séries de feuilles d'actualité sur les événements survenus au cours des guerres de Religion qui consolidèrent la réussite comme éditeur de cet exilé protestant. Plus de 400 reportages issus de son atelier nous sont connus (ill. p. 29 h.).

Les collaborateurs d'Hogenberg devaient procéder soigneusement à la transposition visuelle des informations, car leur véracité était examinée sous un angle critique et discutée par un public cultivé. Pour leurs recherches, ils pouvaient recourir aux vastes archives de la maison d'édition. À la fin du XVIe siècle existe déjà un large éventail d'imprimés illustrés à visée documentaire : des cosmographies et des recueils de panoramas internationaux de villes, dont le fameux *Civitates orbis terrarum*, sans oublier les ouvrages sur le monde des animaux et des plantes ainsi qu'une multitude de récits de voyages illustrés. Parmi les *special artists* des tout débuts, sur le travail novateur desquels le journalisme illustré d'Hogenberg pouvait se fonder, il convient de citer des dessinateurs comme Erhard Reeuwijk, Christoph Weiditz (ills. p. 24–25), Hans Weiditz, Sebald Beham, Melchior Lorck et Jost Amman (ill. p. 20). Ce dernier s'était spécialisé dans les représentations de l'univers quotidien et du monde du travail, qui furent imprimées dans des ouvrages sur les métiers et les costumes. *Les cris* étaient un genre apparenté au dessin social. Un exemple précoce de ces représentations, semblables à des pages illustrées, de types de commerçants locaux et autres petits métiers se trouvait dans le propre programme éditorial d'Hogenberg. Créées à Paris vers 1500, les gravures des *cris de Paris* connurent au fil des siècles une étonnante carrière internationale avant de déboucher finalement en Angleterre au début du XIXe siècle sur le domaine du reportage social d'investigation et d'ethnographie urbaine. Un grand nombre des informations illustrées d'Hogenberg ne peuvent toutefois pas s'expliquer par la

---

James Gillray (del. & sc.) *

Lieutenant Governor Gall-stone, inspired by Alecto; or The Birth of Minerva, London, 15 February 1790
Vizegouverneur Gallenstein, inspiriert von Alekto; oder Die Geburt der Minerva
Le vice-gouverneur Calcul-Biliaire, inspiré par Alecto; ou La Naissance de Minerve
Hand-coloured etching with aquatint

The graphic invective heaped on the writer Philip Thicknesse in this work is one of the few illustrations by James Gillray not to have been based on current political events. It is also one of his most famous

designs, and its influence can be seen in mainland Europe from the following year in the works of such Neoclassical artists as Joseph Anton Koch and Jacques-Louis David.

Die grafische Invektive auf den Schriftsteller Philip Thicknesse ist eines der wenigen Werke James Gillrays, denen kein tagespolitisches Ereignis zugrunde liegt. Es handelt sich um eines seiner einflussreichsten Blätter, dessen Spuren sich ab 1791 auch auf dem Kontinent in Grafiken neoklassizistischer Künstler wie Joseph Anton Koch und Jacques-Louis David nachweisen lassen.

L'invective dirigée contre l'écrivain Philip Thicknesse est une des rares œuvres de James Gillray qui ne trouve aucun fondement dans un événement politique contemporain. Il s'agit de l'une de ses plus célèbres planches, dont l'influence aura des retombées sur le continent dès 1791 dans les dessins d'artistes néoclassiques comme Joseph Anton Koch et Jacques-Louis David.

THE COMBAT

Anonymous

The Combat, London, 1762
Der Kampf | *Le Combat*
Etching
London, The British Museum

In the guise of a modern Don Quixote, William Hogarth with his "Sign Painters' Exhibition" leads a phantom army of young sign painters into battle against the great and established artists of the Society of Artists. The long-standing and enduring conflict between elitist high art and a self-confident popular culture is seen here from the viewpoint of a caricaturist at the time.

William Hogarth führt mit seiner „Sign Painters' Exhibition" als moderner Don Quichotte eine Geister-armee junger Schildermaler in einen Kampf gegen die arrivierten Großkünstler der Society of Artists. Der sich anbahnende Dauerkonflikt zwischen elitä-rer Hochkunst und einer selbstbewussten Populär-kultur wird aus der Sicht eines zeitgenössischen Karikaturisten gezeigt.

Tel un Don Quichotte moderne, avec sa « Sign Painters' Exhibition » William Hogarth conduit une armée fantôme de jeunes peintres d'enseignes dans le combat mené contre les grands artistes parvenus de la Society of Artists. Le conflit à long terme qui s'installe entre le grand art élitiste et une culture populaire assumée est croqué par un cari-caturiste contemporain.

compilation de documents de seconde main. La maison d'édi-tion devait aussi disposer d'un réseau rudimentaire de correspon-dants illustrateurs dont des ingénieurs de forteresse et de places fortes qui dessinaient dans les territoires en guerre.

La relation étroite entre reportage imagé, cartographie et védutisme, qui détermina le programme d'Hogenberg, plus tard aussi sous la direction de son fils Abraham (ill. p. 29 b.), est pré-sente de façon particulièrement marquante dans l'œuvre de son collaborateur le plus célèbre, Wenceslaus Hollar. Pendant son apprentissage chez le topographe Matthäus Merian de même que par ses analyses des dessins de Dürer, le graveur et des-sinateur originaire de Bohême s'était approprié un ethos parti-culier du mimétisme. Ce fut Hollar qui mit en place la concep-tion d'une forme aussi sobre que minutieuse de documentarisme dans la culture du dessin en Angleterre alors à ses tout débuts, après s'être installé dans la patrie de la presse illustrée en 1637. Dans des centaines de vues illustrées, de dessins d'architec-ture, de portraits et de gravures d'événements, il a légué aux générations futures un panorama kaléidoscopique de Londres au temps de la première révolution anglaise à ses débuts et de la restauration qui s'ensuivit.

Le réalisme révolutionnaire d'Hollar en matière de journalisme illustré apparaît de manière exemplaire dans le cliché dessiné qu'il réalisa de l'exécution du comte de Strafford en mai 1641 (ill. p. 26/27). Cet événement marqua un tournant décisif dans la lutte pour le pouvoir opposant la royauté anglaise et le Parle-ment, et fut pour cette raison colporté de multiples façons. Au lieu de procéder selon l'approche habituelle d'une observation imaginaire, Hollar adopta de plain-pied le point de vue de l'ob-servateur qui, entraîné dans l'utilisation de la *camera obscura*, suggérait l'authenticité du témoignage vécu. L'événement cen-tral de l'exécution devint toutefois secondaire et dut même de surcroît, dans le niveau d'attention, rivaliser avec l'écroulement d'une tribune de spectateurs à l'arrière-plan.

Les péripéties de la guerre civile anglaise, qui commen-cèrent par l'exécution d'un homme de confiance proche du

roi Charles Iᵉʳ, jouent un rôle considérable dans l'histoire de la presse. En 1643, quelques décennies seulement après que les tout premiers journaux avaient été fondés à Strasbourg et à Amsterdam, le premier périodique illustré, *Mercurius Civicus*, vit le jour à Londres. Ce magazine était un hebdomadaire illustré de portraits grossiers, réalisés en gravure sur bois, de politiciens et de militaires de premier plan. Bien que cette gazette repré-sentât la cause anti-absolutiste du Parlement, sa parution – tout comme celle de toutes les autres publications – était constam-ment menacée d'une précensure parlementaire. Le poète puri-tain John Milton publia alors son pamphlet *Areopagitica* (1644), un premier plaidoyer moderne pour la liberté de la presse. Par la subtilité de son argumentation, Milton posa les jalons pour toutes les confrontations ultérieures touchant à la censure et aux autres restrictions, comme la levée du tristement célèbre droit de timbre. Celui-ci avait été instauré en Angleterre en 1712 comme instrument de domination afin de réprimer les publica-tions critiques à l'égard du gouvernement et pour maintenir de larges couches de la population sous tutelle politique.

Alors que seuls de rares témoignages illustrés nous sont parvenus de la guerre civile en Angleterre, la guerre de Trente Ans (1618-1648), qui à la même époque faisait rage sur le conti-nent, s'avéra l'âge d'or du journalisme visuel précoce, et le des-sinateur, graveur sur cuivre et maître de l'eau-forte Jacques Callot fut un artiste d'exception (ills. p. 33). Callot ne se contenta pas des scènes de batailles habituelles, mais mit l'accent sur les conséquences désastreuses pour la population. Selon des récits contemporains, un grand nombre de ses représentations de mendiants, d'invalides de guerre et de vagabonds de la série *Les Gueux* (1622-1623) ont été réalisées devant les person-nages concernés. Callot apporta ainsi au documentarisme gra-phique une dimension profonde et révolutionnaire de réalisme social, caractérisée par l'empathie qu'il portait aux marginaux de la société. Son œuvre aux multiples facettes ne fut toutefois pas seulement fondamentale pour l'évolution du reportage illustré social. Les séries de dessins grotesques – dans lesquels il se

James Gillray (del. & sc.)

The King of Brobdingnag and Gulliver,
London, 26 June 1803
Der König von Brobdingnag und Gulliver
Le Roi de Brobdingnag et Gulliver
Hand-coloured etching with aquatint

Taking his lead from Jonathan Swift's novel *Gulliver's Travels*, James Gillray here represents the relative sizes of his two characters in huge contrast, and moreover in reverse. The revolutionary French giant Napoleon has shrunk to the size of a small dwarf and is trembling as he stands in the hand of the enormous King George III of England, after the latter had once again declared war on France in response to Napoleon's plans to invade.

Wie in Jonathan Swifts Roman *Gullivers Reisen* stehen die Größenverhältnisse in starkem Kontrast. Der revolutionäre französische Riese Napoleon ist zu einem Winzling geschrumpft, der in der Hand des riesigen englischen Königs Georg III. zittern muss, nachdem dieser Frankreich als Reaktion auf Napoleons Invasionspläne erneut den Krieg erklärt hatte.

Comme dans le roman de Jonathan Swift *Voyages de Gulliver*, les proportions de taille sont en grand contraste. Le géant révolutionnaire Napoléon est réduit à la hauteur d'un nain qui tremble dans la main du gigantesque roi anglais George III, après que l'Angleterre a de nouveau déclaré la guerre et que les premières tentatives de Napoléon pour envahir l'île ont échoué.

→→ **Anonymous**

The Many Headed Monster of Sumatra, or Liberty's Efforts against Ministerial Oppression; a Vision,
10 June 1768
Das vielköpfige Ungeheuer von Sumatra oder Das Ringen der Freiheit gegen ministerielle Unterdrückung; eine Vision
Le monstre à plusieurs têtes de Sumatra ou La Lutte de la liberté contre l'oppression ministérielle ; une vision
Etching
London, The British Museum

The wave of caricatures in England really began in the 1760s in response to the Wilkes riots. Through a series of attacks on the government the journalist and member of parliament John Wilkes had succeeded in stirring up the political awareness of a large section of the public. The attributes used by his followers to represent him as a libertarian hero (the aggressive squint, Phrygian cap and staff) were taken from a satirical depiction of him by William Hogarth, who was opposed to his views.

Die englische Karikaturwelle begann in den 1760er-Jahren mit den Wilkes-Aufständen. Dem Journalisten und Parlamentarier John Wilkes war es mit seinen Attacken gegen die Regierung gelungen, die breiten Massen zu politisieren. Die Attribute, mit denen er von seinen Anhängern als Freiheitsheld in Szene gesetzt wurde – offensives Schielen, phrygische Mütze und Stab –, gehen auf ein Spottblatt seines Gegners William Hogarth zurück.

La vague anglaise de caricatures commença dans les années 1760 avec les révoltes de Wilkes. Par ses attaques à l'encontre du gouvernement, le journaliste et parlementaire John Wilkes avait réussi à politiser une grande partie du public. Les attributs avec lesquels ses partisans le représentaient comme héros de la liberté – strabisme agressif, bonnet phrygien et bâton – proviennent d'un pamphlet satirique de son adversaire William Hogarth.

The Shades of Night had long prevail'd,
When Sleep my weary Eyes assail'd:
Sunk in my Bed in soft repose,
This Strange Fantastic Vision rose.
   Methought convey'd by unknown Power
I just had gain'd some distant Shore,
Where Nature seem'd to scatter Joys,
Yet all was wild affright and Noise;
Scar'd at this seeming Contradiction
It thus was clear'd & prov'd No fiction.

A Monster by the...
Worse than St. Anton...
With many Heads, can...
A stranger Sight no...
A Laird, A Judge, A...
A Parson too, Right...
And pray for what c...
What but to Conquer...
Oft she assail'd and ...
And oft Inglorious ...

TRA, *or* LIBERTY'S EFFORTS *against*
...RESSION; A VISION.

Again she at the Land arrives,
And in a favourite Son revives,
Whose friends pursue with Joy each Plan,
To kill the Monster, if they can
The fight was fierce, each did his best
And the noise wak'd me from my rest,
When surely every one must Laugh
I found my self in England safe.

Publish'd according to Act of Parliamt. June 10th. 1768. Price 6d.

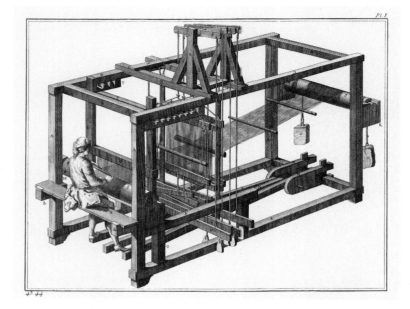

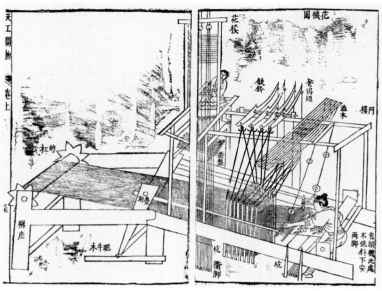

Anonymous

Loom for the Production of Marly Gauze, c. 1765
Webstuhl für die Herstellung von Marly-Gaze | *Métier à tisser de Marly*
Copper engraving
From: Denis Diderot & Jean-Baptiste le Rond d'Alembert (eds.), *Encyclopédie, ou Dictionnaire raisonné des sciences, des arts et des métiers*, Paris, c. 1765

↙ *Working at the Loom*, c. 1637
Arbeit am Webstuhl
Le travail sur métier à tisser
Woodblock print
From: Song Yingxing (ed.), *Tiangong Kaiwu or The Exploitation of the Works of Nature*, 1637

Since most of the illustrations that appeared in the *Encyclopédie* were unsigned then in the same way as the subjects being represented they should not be understood as works of art associated with individuals but as collective artefacts. It is none the less known, however, that the majority of the illustrations were done by Louis-Jacques Goussier, and the work of engraving on copper by Robert Bénard. In the long tradition of reference works from China, the illustrations in Song's encyclopaedia mark a huge leap forward in terms of the precise detail they incorporate, in the same way that Goussier's volumes of plates did in Europe with the *Encyclopédie*.

Die Bildwerke der *Encyclopédie* waren in der Regel nicht signiert. In Entsprechung zu den dargestellten Sujets sollten sie nicht als individualisierte Kunstwerke erscheinen, sondern als kollektive Artefakte. Bekannt ist jedoch, dass die meisten Entwürfe von Louis-Jacques Goussier stammen und von Robert Bénard in Kupfer übersetzt wurden. Die Abbildungen in Songs Enzyklopädie markieren in der langen Tradition chinesischer Nachschlagewerke einen ähnlichen Quantensprung hinsichtlich der Präzision der Beschreibung wie Goussiers Tafelbände für die *Encyclopédie* Diderots in Europa.

En général, les illustrations de l'*Encyclopédie* n'étaient pas signées. Correspondant aux sujets représentés elles ne devaient pas apparaître commes des œuvres d'art individualisées, mais comme des artefacts collectifs. Il est néanmoins reconnu que la plupart des ébauches sont de Louis-Jacques Goussier et ont été transposées sur cuivre par Robert Bénard. Dans la longue tradition d'ouvrages illustrés de référence en Chine, les illustrations de l'encyclopédie de Song marquent, quant à la précision de la description, un saut quantique analogue aux volumes de planches de Goussier pour l'*Encyclopédie* de Diderot en Europe.

référait aux motifs de Jérôme Bosch et de Pieter Bruegel et se servait du répertoire des personnages de la commedia dell'arte italienne – eurent une influence immense sur la branche satirique du dessin de presse. Ainsi son compatriote lorrain Grandville, la première star du mouvement de caricature français, fut-il par ses œuvres le digne successeur de Callot. En revanche, le journalisme illustré ne se développait qu'avec lenteur en Angleterre. Même si la Glorieuse Révolution de 1688-1689 avait procuré au pays un renforcement des droits civiques, avec notamment la suppression de la précensure. La prise «glorieuse» du trône d'Angleterre par le gouverneur des Pays-Bas, Guillaume III d'Orange, fut accompagnée d'une florissante propagande iconographique par le graveur sur cuivre, poète et peintre Romeyn de Hooghe. À l'instar de Callot, De Hooghe couvrait une vaste gamme d'œuvres graphiques, allant des feuilles baroques d'information illustrée aux complexes satires allégoriques, sociales comme politiques. Ces dernières lui valurent aux Pays-Bas des plaintes pour pornographie et blasphème et déclenchèrent des incidents diplomatiques avec la France et l'Angleterre. En 1701, il livra *Aesopus in Europa*, le premier hebdomadaire illustré satirique. Avec l'œuvre de De Hooghe, la caricature politique commença à s'affirmer comme un solide genre artistique (ill. p. 35).

L'influence du dessin néerlandais n'a cependant des répercussions programmatiques dans l'art anglais que plusieurs dizaines d'années plus tard, dans l'œuvre du très original peintre et graveur sur cuivre William Hogarth. Il dut sa notoriété à plusieurs séries de dessins réalisées dans le style d'images populaires et qu'il désigna sous le nom de *modern moral subjects*. Elles représentaient des scènes clés, tirées de la vie de personnages prototypes dont les parcours devaient faire découvrir les conditions sociales sous un jour critique. Avec son invention de pièces de théâtre en images, Hogarth s'inscrivit dans la généalogie d'un art séquentiel qui commença à jouer un rôle dans le dessin de presse à partir des années 1840 grâce aux romans illustrés de Rodolphe Töpffer (voir ill. p. 157). Le théâtre en images d'Hogarth se caractérisait par un réalisme brut de la vie quotidienne et – influencé par la montée en puissance de la presse quotidienne – était émaillé du paradigme journalistique de l'actualité au jour le jour. Pendant artistique des excursions littéraires du reporter social satirique Ned Ward (ill. p. 39), qui dans sa gazette *The London Spy* écrivait des articles sur les bas-fonds londoniens, Hogarth sillonna les quartiers de Londres dans le but de consigner ses impressions visuelles pour ses bandes dessinées. Selon les dires, il esquissait ses observations en signes sténographes sur les ongles de ses doigts s'il manquait de papier à dessin. Un siècle avant Charles Baudelaire, cet art de la flânerie urbaine fut déjà célébré par l'ami d'Hogarth, le poète John Gay, dans son poème *Trivia* (1716). C'est aussi Gay qui avec *The Beggar's Opera* (1728), sa très populaire opérette aux accents de critique sociale, avait procuré à Hogarth le modèle scénique des *modern moral subjects* (ill. p. 36/37).

Hogarth situait son réalisme social comme *comic history* à l'intersection entre la peinture d'histoire sublime et le grotesque trivial. L'antagonisme entre le grand art et l'art populaire qui domine jusqu'à nos jours l'historique de la réception de l'illustration devient pour la première fois virulent dans son œuvre de façon exemplaire. Sa conception profonde de l'art reposait sur la peinture de réclames, de l'art républicain par excellence, qu'il avait lui-même cultivé au début de sa carrière et qui caractérisait aussi ses représentations de l'espace urbain agencées en patchwork (ill. p. 38). L'assemblage significatif de ses champs d'images profitait également du fait qu'il étudiait les dessins

**Augustus Charles Pugin &
Thomas Rowlandson/J. Hill (sc.)**

Pass-room Bridewell, 1808–1810
Vorläufiger Verwahrraum in Bridewell
Cellule provisoire à Bridewell
Stencil-coloured aquatint
From: Rudolph Ackermann (ed.), *The Microcosm
of London,* London, 1808–1810

Ackermann's groundbreaking illustrated study of life
in a big city was first issued in a series of monthly
parts. It was produced through the outstanding col-
laborative efforts of Pugin, who supplied the architectural settings, Rowlandson, who added the
human figures, and the writer and illustrator William
Henry Pyne, who oversaw the research and wrote
much of the text.

Die wegweisende Großstadtreportage erschien
zuerst in monatlichen Lieferungen. Sie war das Produkt einer perfekten Teamarbeit. Pugin war für die
architektonischen Settings verantwortlich, Thomas
Rowlandson besorgte die Figurationen, und der
Autor und Illustrator William Henry Pyne war für die
Recherchen und Texte zuständig.

Le concept novateur de reportage dédié à une
grande ville parut d'abord sous forme de livraisons
mensuelles. Il était le produit d'un remarquable travail d'équipe. Pugin était responsable des décors
architecturaux, Thomas Rowlandson fournissait les
figurations, et l'auteur et illustrateur William Henry
Pyne était chargé des recherches et des textes.

hétéroclites, connus dans les Pays-Bas sous le nom de *quodlibets* et appelés *medley prints* (ill. p. 30) en Angleterre. Ce genre
de pseudo-collages oniriques (ill. p. 39) anticipa l'esthétique de
scrapbook propre au dessin de presse du XIXᵉ siècle.

L'idéal d'Hogarth d'un art démocratique se concevait en
opposition assumée à l'académisme empreint d'absolutisme de
ses collègues peintres. En 1762, il organisa une exposition d'enseignes commerciales anonymes en contrepartie plébéienne de
la première exposition exclusive de la Society of Artists (ill. p.
44). La liste des pièces d'exposition de cette spectaculaire « Sign
Painters' Exhibition » laisse supposer que par des surcharges et
des applications il transforma ces enseignes, les siennes comme
celles trouvées ou commanditées, en un métatexte satirique en
contraste avec l'exposition concurrente de grand art. Hogarth
s'inscrit ainsi comme pionnier dans l'histoire précoce de l'anti-art
et de la parodie artistique, qui ne prit de l'importance à Paris
qu'au milieu du XIXᵉ siècle à travers les activités de célèbres
illustrateurs de presse.

La seule œuvre de cette époque ayant eu une influence
comparable à celle de l'art populaire d'Hogarth sur l'évolution du dessin de presse fut la monumentale *Encyclopédie
ou Dictionnaire raisonné des sciences, des arts et des métiers*
(ill. p. 48 h.), parue à Paris entre 1751 et 1780 en 17 volumes
de textes et 11 volumes de planches et éditée par Denis Diderot
et Jean-Baptiste le Rond d'Alembert. C'est le mathématicien
et dessinateur Louis-Jacques Goussier qui assuma la direction
artistique du corpus d'illustrations, composé de 2 885 gravures
sur cuivre. Dix années durant, il avait sillonné les provinces françaises et étudié les processus de fabrication, manuels comme
mécaniques, dans les usines et manufactures pour réaliser
ses planches. Par ses travaux graphiques pour l'*Encyclopédie*,

Goussier établit de nouvelles normes du reportage illustré, qu'il
s'agisse de l'ampleur de ses recherches ou de la précision du
dessin.

Dans l'espace germanophone, c'était l'illustrateur et graveur
sur cuivre Daniel Chodowiecki qui incarnait le topos du reporter illustrateur. Ce chroniqueur de la cour royale prussienne et
de la vie quotidienne des bourgeois était un dessinateur pas-
sionné qui, selon ses propres affirmations, réalisait ses notices
dessinées dans toutes les situations de la vie – « debout, en
marche, à cheval (ill. p. 23) ». Adolph Menzel, qui comptait parmi
les illustrateurs du XIXᵉ siècle les plus influents à l'échelle internationale, situait son art dans la lignée du journalisme illustré de
Chodowiecki.

Le XVIIIᵉ siècle finissant vit une industrialisation croissante
du commerce d'estampes. Hogarth avait brisé la glace en Angleterre en conquérant un public de masse pour les estampes de
qualité grâce à ses séries de dessins populaires. L'« hogarthomanie » ne prit toutefois son essor qu'après sa mort, lorsque
John Boydell, un éditeur spécialisé dans les reproductions gravées, publia une volumineuse édition intégrale de ses œuvres,
qui connut plusieurs tirages. Boydell fut le Hieronymus Cock de
son temps. À l'aide de son entreprise où les tâches étaient clairement réparties et grâce à d'énormes tirages, il transforma le
commerce d'art et le marché de l'estampe de façon durable. Sur
le continent, ce furent des entrepreneurs comme le graveur sur
cuivre Hieronymus Löschenkohl, qui commercialisait des informations en images coloriées à Vienne, ou les éditeurs François Buisson et Friedrich Justin Bertuch, qui publièrent les premiers magazines de mode illustrés à Paris et à Weimar au milieu
des années 1780, qui posèrent les jalons de l'ère du dessin de
presse. Bertuch établit à Weimar un empire culturel à échelle

←← Anonymous

The Purifying Pot of the Jacobins, 1793
Der Läutertopf der Jakobiner
La Marmite épuratoire des Jacobins
Stencil-coloured aquatint
Reprinted in: Ernest Jaime (ed.), *Musée de
la caricature*, Paris, 1838

The giant figure of Maximilien Robespierre, a
Gulliver to the Lilliputian Jacobins before him,
is separating the good ones from the bad with a
skimming spoon. This graphic commentary on
the purges being made within the faction was
one of the few illustrations expressing criticism
of the regime to be published in France before
the end of the Terror.

Als riesiger Gulliver trennt hier Maximilien de
Robespierre mit einem Sieb die guten von den
schlechten Jakobinern. Der grafische Kommentar zu den innerparteilichen Säuberungsaktionen
war eines der wenigen regimekritischen Blätter,
die in Frankreich vor dem Ende des Terreur erschienen.

Représenté comme le géant Gulliver, Robespierre
sépare ici avec une passoire les bons des mauvais
Jacobins. Ce commentaire imagé des purges à l'intérieur du camp révolutionnaire fut l'une des rares
feuilles volantes critiques du régime à paraître en
France avant la fin de la Terreur.

Anonymous

→ *The Newspapers*, 1814
Die Zeitungen | *Les Journaux*
Stencil-coloured etching
From: *Le Nain jaune*, Paris, 15 December 1814
London, The British Museum

Following the end of Napoleon's dictatorship there
was a period of freedom for the press that lasted
four months, during which the symbolic figure of
the yellow dwarf (the "*nain jaune*") was able to shoot
his arrows of satire at the rival newspapers of both
the Royalists and the Jesuits. *Le Nain jaune* was the
forerunner of a great wave of caricature in France
that swept across the country 16 years later after the
Bourbon Restoration had been brought to a close.

Nach dem Ende der napoleonischen Diktatur gab
es eine viermonatige Phase der Pressefreiheit, in
der die Symbolfigur des gelben Zwergs *("nain jaune")*
ihre satirischen Pfeile auf die royalistischen und
jesuitischen Konkurrenzblätter abschießen konnte.
Der *Nain jaune* war der Vorbote einer großen Karikaturwelle, die 16 Jahre später, nach dem Ende der
Restauration, über Frankreich hereinbrechen sollte.

Après la fin de la dictature napoléonienne il y eut
pendant quatre mois une période de liberté de la
presse, au cours de laquelle la figure symbolique
du nain jaune pouvait lancer ses flèches satiriques
sur les publications concurrentes des royalistes et
des Jésuites. Le *Nain jaune* fut le précurseur d'une
grande vague de caricature qui, seize ans plus tard,
après la fin de la Restauration, devait déferler sur la
France.

Katsushika Hokusai

↘ *Manga Scenes*, 1817
Manga-Szenen | *Scènes de* La Manga
Woodblock print with ink and colour
From: *Denshin Kaishu: Hokusai Manga*,
vol. 6, 1817

The sixth volume of Hokusai's *Manga* depicted
different sequences of movements as used in
various techniques in martial arts.

Der sechste Band von Hokusais *Manga* konzentrierte sich auf Bewegungsabläufe von Kampf-
sporttechniken.

Le sixième volume de *La Manga* de Hokusai s'est
concentré sur les séquences de mouvement des
techniques appliquées aux arts martiaux.

industrielle qui disposait d'un vaste réseau et employait tempo-
rairement jusqu'à 500 personnes. L'entreprise londonienne de
l'éditeur, dessinateur et inventeur saxon Rudolph Ackermann,
qui s'était installé dans la métropole anglaise en 1795, présentait une structure de semblable envergure. Il sollicita plusieurs
des plus remarquables artistes anglais dans son entreprise qui
consistait en une école de dessin, une galerie de musée avec
prêt d'estampes, une bibliothèque publique ainsi qu'une maison
d'édition avec imprimerie. Les périodiques qu'il publiait depuis
1809, dont le dispendieux *Ackermann's Repository of Arts* ainsi
que le premier almanach en langue anglaise *Forget-me-not*, ont
par la suite encouragé l'éditeur Charles Knight à publier le premier magazine illustré populaire *Penny Magazine*. Ackermann
profita surtout de la soif d'images et de l'art des loisirs du mouvement pittoresque qu'une série de guides de voyage illustrés
de l'artiste amateur William Gilpin avait fait naître au milieu des
années 1780. Deux œuvres, réalisées en collaboration avec
le dessinateur satirique Thomas Rowlandson, faisaient partie
des publications d'Ackermann les plus populaires : *The Tour
of Dr. Syntax*, une des premières séries de bandes dessinées
dans laquelle la chasse touristique de motifs pittoresques était
prise pour cible, et *The Microcosm of London*, un portrait de
la métropole londonienne en format folio, composée de plus
de 100 images fourmillantes et coloriées à la main (ill. p. 49).
Avec son ami James Gillray, qui avait presque le même âge, et
George Cruikshank, nettement plus jeune, Rowlandson comptait
parmi les plus célèbres représentants du mouvement de caricature anglais.

Celui-ci avait débuté dans les explosives années 1760, pendant la phase fondatrice du radicalisme britannique, et entraîné
une multitude de dessins polémiques et de satires résultant de
l'analyse des événements révolutionnaires en France. On estime
que, pendant le règne de George I I qui dura soixante ans,
quelque 12 000 caricatures furent diffusées en Angleterre par
des négociants spécialisés en planches grand format et dans
des tirages allant de 500 à 1 500 exemplaires. Le champion

incontesté de ce raz-de-marée d'images satiriques depuis les
années 1780 s'appelait James Gillray. L'influence de ses rudes
créations picturales s'étendit aussi sur le dessin révolutionnaire
en France. Avec sa technique de distorsion physiognomonique,
Gillray se référait au style de dessin baroque de la surcharge
(en italien *caricare*) qui, à la fin du XVIe siècle, était une des
méthodes d'enseignement avant-gardistes à l'École de Bologne
des frères Annibale, Agostino et Ludovico Carracci.

L'influence du grotesque social et de la caricature politique
britanniques transparaît aussi dans les mystérieuses gravures
de Francisco de Goya que Baudelaire a associées au domaine de
la satire imagée. Bien que seule une infime partie du tirage de
son cycle *Los Caprichos* fût diffusée, au plus tard après l'émigration de Goya en France en 1824 des planches individuelles cir-
culèrent dans les cercles artistiques français et y ont laissé leur
empreinte, en particulier dans le magazine de Charles Philipon
La Caricature.

Dans les années 1810, le très populaire peintre et graveur
japonais Katsushika Hokusai réalisa sa collection d'estampes
réparties en quinze carnets, *Hokusai Manga*, dans laquelle
il livra une documentation intégrale d'épisodes de la vie et de
phénomènes surnaturels (ill. p. 53 b.). Plusieurs éditions isolées furent déjà diffusées en Occident peu avant l'ouverture forcée du Japon au milieu du XIXe siècle. Néanmoins, sa profonde
influence sur le graphisme de presse ne se reflétera que vingt
ans plus tard dans la profusion de scènes quotidiennes, d'études
de la nature et de *capricci* surréalistes.

Note éditoriale sur les abréviations : del. (delineavit) = dessiné ;
sc. (sculpsit) = gravé ; lith. = lithographié ; photo. = photographié

The Classic Period
of Press Graphics

1819–1868

The Industrial Turn

The explosive surge in illustrated graphic work at the start of the 19th century can only be explained in relation to the rapid industrialisation of paper production and printing, in particular the development of the first high-speed printing press in 1811. Three years later, the London *Times* adopted this new invention and became the first daily newspaper to be printed using a steam-operated press. However, this system of mechanised mass reproduction was only suitable for letterpress copy, typesetting and the relatively coarse illustrations of woodcut graphics. In order to meet the public's new-found hunger for images, which had been awakened by the detailed engraving work issued by William Hogarth, John Boydell and Rudolph Ackermann, a technique was needed that could combine the quality of fine lines found in prints made with copper engraving, and the advantages of relief printing, namely reproduction at speed. In 1790, the Newcastle engraver Thomas Bewick had published an encyclopaedic work on animals for young readers which achieved exactly that. The subtle quality of the illustrations in Bewick's *General History of Quadrupeds* with their distinct tonal gradations had been made in wood using engravers' printing tools, yet not in the soft wood with the grain (which can only be worked with knives or gouges on account of the fibrous texture of the wood) but instead the hard end sections where the wood is cut at right angles to the grain and which thus has a similarly consistent surface to metal. A wood engraving produced in this way is equivalent to a letterpress plate which can be perfectly integrated into the typographic set-up of the printed page and printed at the same time as one process.

While Bewick was of course not the inventor of wood engraving, which had been used in a more rudimentary form in textile printing in Armenia and in the printed illustrations of the Renaissance, he can be credited with reviving interest in it. There is certainly an element of paradox in this too, since there is otherwise no indication that a technique originally associated with Bewick's idyllic illustrations from nature would go on to become a medium for industrialised mass production. However, its educational potential was already evident in the inventiveness and versatility of Bewick's designs, such as *A Cheviot Ram* or the vignettes showing mist and rain or the artist's own fingerprint (ills. p. 58). The illustrations were very small, only about 8 x 6 cm (roughly corresponding to a section of hard box-wood), but even so they stand as some of the artistic masterpieces of their time alongside watercolours by Thomas Girtin, John Sell Cotman and J.M.W. Turner. The fascination Bewick's designs have continued to hold for the more than six generations of artists that followed him still applies even today, and especially if they are examined with a magnifying glass, that essential tool for wood engravers. Before such engravings became widely available with the first illustrated magazines in the 1840s, they had gone through a phase of incubation for 40 years during which they appeared in book illustrations and political pamphlets. Two opposing tendencies had emerged early on though amongst Bewick's students, many of whom had gone on to hold important positions in the print trade in London, namely interpretative wood engraving, also called tone engraving, and facsimile engraving. The first of these corresponds to the work done by Bewick, in which

Robert William Buss (del.) & William James Linton (sc.)

Figurative Initial, 1861
Figürliche Initiale | *Initiale figurative*
Wood engraving
From: John Jackson and W.A. Chatto,
A Treatise on Wood Engraving,
London, 1861

Seen here is the typical workplace of
a wood engraver working at night. The
glass globe filled with water focuses
the light from the lamp on the block,
which rests on a leather pad filled with
sand so that it can easily be moved
about and kept in position during the
engraving.

Typischer Arbeitsplatz eines nachts
arbeitenden Xylografen. Die mit Was-
ser gefüllte Schusterkugel fokussiert
das Lampenlicht. Der Druckstock
liegt auf einem mit Sand gefüllten
Lederkissen, sodass er sich während
der Gravurarbeit leicht drehen lässt.
Lieu de travail typique d'un xylographe
travaillant la nuit. La boule en verre
remplie d'eau concentre la lumière
de la lampe vers son ouvrage. Le bloc
d'impression se trouve sur un coussin
de cuir rempli de sable et peut être
ainsi aisément tourné lors du travail
de gravure.

←←**J.J. Grandville &
Eugène Forest (lith.)**

In Pursuit of Liberty, 1832
(see pp. 110/111)

the pictorial details were transposed relatively freely into tonal
values using white lines. Facsimile engraving, on the other hand,
proceeds from the black outline of a design and seeks to reproduce it as faithfully as possible. Those who were opposed to
facsimile engraving thus belittled it for being no more than sla-
vish copying and for its imitation of conventional printing techniques. Even so, it became established and quite successful in
London owing to the efforts of the illustrator William Harvey and
the engraver Allen Robert Branston. Charles Thompson, a student of Branston's, opened a wood-engraving workshop in Paris
in 1817 and thereby introduced the method to mainland Europe.
Other establishments later appeared in Munich and Leipzig in
the early 1840s.

In order to meet the demand for magazine illustrations, newspaper publishers were quick to set up their own wood-engraving
workshops and supplied them with the designs to be used from
in-house illustration departments (see ill. p. 61). The pressure of
printing deadlines also meant it was necessary to organise the
production of these large-format engravings by division of labour.
The individual pieces that together combined to make the printing blocks were divided amongst a corresponding number of
engravers and only assembled when all the work was done. In
the early 1850s a method of screwing together the pieces was
developed, which made the job of collective engraving a considerably easier process. For anyone looking closely, however, this
method of assembling the blocks could often be identified by
visible grid lines on the printed image. These tell-tale traces in
turn took on an important function in Adolph Menzel's illustrations

for Heinrich von Kleist's comedy *The Broken Jug*, whereby in
Menzel's media-conscious interpretation the segmented printing
block became a symbol for the loss of the meaningful creative
unity that was Kleist's theme in the text (ill. p. 63). In this way
Menzel made a parallel between the method of production, with
its division of labour and assembly of separate elements, and the
level of incoherence in press-graphic image collections that had
become evident by the 1870s. Another noticeable aspect that
resulted from the extended chains of transmission that were a
feature of this way of working was that since one or more editorial draughtsmen were generally involved as well as the engravers, most of the magazine images diverged markedly from the
original drawings. But overall, the classic period of press graphics
was characterised by standardisations of style that were the consequence of collective interpretations. As such, it made sense
entirely that to begin with illustrations were not signed by the
draughtsmen, but carried the mark of the engravers' workshop
that produced them. The second development in printing that
affected press graphics had nothing to do with styles of interpretation. In lithography, printing is done on a flat bed where the
image is drawn with some form of greasy substance on to a prepared stone plate before being chemically treated so that the ink
can be applied. It was developed in Munich in 1796 by the play-
wright and music publisher Alois Senefelder where it was used
for printing sheet music. The new technique became popular with
artists because in comparison with wood engraving, which had
then been in use for a few years, reproductions could be made
with greater fidelity and a wider range of graphic options were

Thomas Bewick (del. & sc.)

Mist and Rain, 1797
Nebel und Regen | *Brouillard et pluie*
Tail Piece | Schlussvignette |
Cul-de-lampe
Wood engraving
From: Thomas Bewick,
History of British Birds, vol. I,
Newcastle, 1797

The technique of wood engraving
is ideally suited for illustrating atmospheric scenes. In this example, the
evocative subject of the two lonely
horses reappears again later in Thomas
Bewick's celebrated last work *Waiting
for Death*, from 1828.

Die Technik des Holzstichs eignete
sich hervorragend zur Umsetzung
atmosphärischer Szenen. Das empathische Motiv der isolierten Pferde
verweist auf Thomas Bewicks berühm-
tes Abschlusswerk *Waiting for Death*
von 1828.

La technique de gravure sur bois était
particulièrement appropriée à la représentation de scènes d'atmosphère. Le
motif empathique des chevaux isolés
se réfère à *Waiting for Death,* célèbre
dernière œuvre de Thomas Bewick
réalisée en 1828.

↓ *Fingerprint,* 1797
Tail Piece | Schlussvignette |
Cul-de-lampe
Wood engraving
From: Thomas Bewick,
History of British Birds, vol. I,
Newcastle, 1797

Bewick's own fingerprint served as his
trademark, and he sometimes used it
as a form of signature for his works. Its
oval shape matches the format of his
engravings, which open up like a lens
in the paper to draw the viewer into the
depths of their miniature worlds.

Der Fingerabdruck war Thomas
Bewicks Markenzeichen, mit dem
er auch gern signierte. Das Oval des
Abdrucks entspricht dem Schema
seiner Holzstiche, die sich wie Iris-
blenden im Papiergrund öffnen, um
den Betrachter so in die Tiefe ihrer
Miniaturwelten zu ziehen.

L'empreinte digitale était la marque de
fabrique de Thomas Bewick, qu'il utili-
sait volontiers pour signer ses œuvres.
L'ovale de l'empreinte fait écho au
schéma de ses gravures sur bois qui
s'ouvrent comme des diaphragmes
d'iris au dos du papier, entraînant ainsi
l'observateur dans les profondeurs de
leurs univers en miniature.

available. Tonal effects could be achieved by the use of chalks
and washes, and fine lines could be reproduced with ink applied
with a brush or pen.

Lithography first became established as an artistic medium
in France, where it went on to make a particularly lasting impression, although this was not due to the efforts of major figures such as Eugène Delacroix or Honoré Daumier but rather
to the now largely forgotten military painter and printmaker
Nicolas Toussaint Charlet. He was a close friend of the painter Géricault's, and during the time of the Bourbon Restoration
he proceeded to issue huge quantities of subversive pamphlets
promoting Bonapartist propaganda (see ill. p. 69 b.). Charlet had
studied with the painter Antoine-Jean Gros, who had taken over
the teaching studio of Jacques-Louis David when he went into
exile. Under Gros, the studio held to its Republican tradition of
history painting but also became known for its training in lithographic techniques, which, still a new medium at this date,
Charlet undertook to learn. He became adept at using it com-
mercially to strong effect and was able to inspire several of
his fellow students to use it as well. In particular, he taught the
future publisher Charles Philipon the technique of using a lithographic crayon for drawing the image to be printed. Philipon
went on to establish lithography as a medium for press graphics
with the caricatures he issued in the course of his campaigns
against the Restoration and the July Monarchy.

While the cost of Philipon's revolutionary weekly magazine *La
Caricature* meant that only upper-class subscribers could afford
to buy it, the lithographic illustrations themselves were seen by
a larger number of people since they were also displayed in the
publisher's shop windows and could be bought as individual
prints. However, producing a magazine that combined two different methods of printing proved to be a problem. Where the use
of lithography made the illustrations a sort of foreign body inser-
ted into the rest of *La Caricature*, Philipon tried to integrate the
flat printing of images more successfully into the typographical layout of the next magazine he launched, *Le Charivari*. In the
long run though the effort involved in this twofold printing process was found to be too much, while the quality of the lithographic illustrations suffered noticeably when printed on newsprint.
As a result, the experimental combination of printing techniques
in *Le Charivari* did not lead to increased use of lithography in the
press, but instead showed the economic advantages of using
wood engraving.

Wood engraving was also much more suitable for use in illustrated magazines that exchanged images across an international
network, and for the worldwide distribution of illustrated news.
For large print runs, which were standard for newspapers, metal
copies known as clichés had to be made from the wood engravings. In 1838, the laborious casting process these required
began to be replaced by the much more accurate method of
electrolytic copper-plating, or electrotyping. A busy trade in
these electrotype plates soon developed between countries, so
that for instance engravings used in *The Penny Magazine* in
London, founded in 1832, were being used only a few weeks
later in publications in France, Germany, the Netherlands, Italy,
Greece, Sweden, Norway and the United States.

Adolph Menzel & Eduard Kretzschmar (sc.)

*A Scene from the Life of Frederick
the Great*, 1840
*Szene aus der Geschichte
Friedrichs des Großen*
*Scène tirée de l'histoire de
Frédéric le Grand*
Wood engraving
From: Franz Kugler, *Geschichte
Friedrichs des Großen*, Leipzig, 1840

The illustrations in an early
Impressionist style that Adolph
Menzel designed for Franz Kugler's
biography of Frederick II of Prussia
brought him fame around the world.
Of greater significance, however,
Eduard Kretzschmar's work set new
standards in facsimile engraving.

Mit seinen frühimpressionistischen
Grafiken für Franz Kuglers Biografie
von Friedrich II. stieg Adolph Menzel
zu einem der international einflussreichsten Illustratoren auf. Es waren
vor allem die Gravuren Eduard
Kretzschmars, die einen neuen Standard auf dem Gebiet des Faksimilestichs setzten.

Avec ses estampes de l'impressionnisme précoce réalisées pour la
biographie de Frédéric II par Franz
Kugler, Adolph Menzel devint l'un
des illustrateurs les plus influents à
l'échelle internationale. Ce sont surtout les œuvres d'Eduard Kretzschmar
qui établirent un nouveau standard
dans le domaine de la gravure en
fac-similé.

Adrien Dauzats & Héliodore Pisan (sc.)

↓ *The Iron Gates, leaving the last
narrow gorge*, 1839–1844
*Eisernes Tor, Ausgang aus der
letzten Felsenge*
Portes de Fer, sortie du dernier défilé
Wood engraving on pressed
India paper
From: Charles Nodier, *Journal
de l'expédition des Portes de Fer*,
Paris, 1844

The illustrations in Charles Nodier's
report of a colonial expedition to
Algeria are considered the high point
of early French wood engraving. The
finest engravers in France worked
on the designs, including Héliodore
Pisan whose later work with Gustave
Doré established his reputation as
a major influential figure in pictorial
wood engraving.

Die Illustrationen in Charles Nodiers
Bericht über die koloniale Expedition
nach Algerien gelten als Spitzenleis-
tungen des frühen französischen
Holzstichs. An der Umsetzung waren
die bedeutendsten französischen
Graveure beteiligt, darunter Héliodore
Pisan, der später durch seine Koope-
rationen mit Gustave Doré als stil-
bildender Vertreter des malerischen
Tonstichs bekannt wurde.

Les illustrations du rapport de l'expédition coloniale en Algérie de Charles
Nodier est considéré comme la référence absolue de la gravure française
précoce. Les graveurs français les
plus éminents ont participé à sa réalisation, dont Héliodore Pisan, qui à travers sa collaboration aux travaux de
Gustave Doré se forgea plus tard une
réputation de figure majeure de la
gravure picturale sur bois.

ILLUSTRATED NEWS:

A SKETCH OF THE RISE AND PROGRESS OF PICTORIAL JOURNALISM.

(*Continued from page* 158.)

Before sketching the production of a modern illustrated newspaper it may be as well to premise that the material used for wood engraving is Box-wood, which is preferred to all other kinds of wood on account of its close grain, hardness, and light colour. It admits of finer and sharper lines being cut upon it than any other wood, and great quantities are consumed in producing the engravings of an illustrated newspaper. According to Mr. J. R. Jackson, Curator of the Kew Museum, the box-tree is at the present time widely distributed through Europe and Asia, being found abundantly in Italy, Spain, Southern France, and on the coast of the Black Sea, as well as China, Japan, Northern India, and Persia. The box of English growth is so small as to be almost useless for commercial purposes. What is called Turkey box-wood is the best, and this is all obtained from the forests that grow on the Caucasus, and is chiefly shipped at Poti and Rostoff. The forests extend from thirty to a hundred and eighty miles inland, but many of them are in the hands of the Russian Government, and are closed to commerce. Within the last few years a supply of box-wood has been obtained from the forests in the neighbourhood of the Caspian Sea; but Turkey Box is becoming dearer every year and inferior in quality. After the wood is cut in the

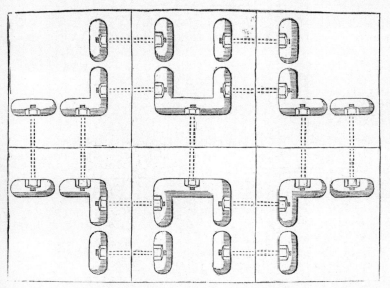

BACK OF A BLOCK, SHOWING THE WAY IN WHICH THE PARTS ARE FASTENED TOGETHER.

forest, it is brought down on horseback to the nearest river, put on board flat-bottom boats, and floated down to the port of shipment. It arrives in this country either at Liverpool or London, chiefly the former, and is usually in logs about four feet long and eight or ten inches across.

The wood intended for engraving purposes is first carefully selected and then cut up into transverse slices about an inch thick. After being cut the pieces are placed in racks something like plate racks, and thoroughly seasoned by slow degrees in gradually heated rooms. This seasoning process ought to last on an average four or five years. They are then cut into parallelograms of various sizes, the outer portion of the circular section near the bark being cut away, and all defective wood rejected. These parallelograms are then assorted as to size, and fitted together at the back by brass bolts and nuts. By this means blocks of any size can be made, and they possess the great advantage of being capable of being taken to pieces after a drawing is made, and distributed among as many engravers as there are pieces in the block. This invention of making bolted blocks was brought forward just about the time the *Illustrated London News* was started, when large blocks and quick engraving came to be in demand. In the days of the *Penny Magazine* blocks were made by simply glueing the pieces of wood together, or they were fastened by means of a long bolt passing through the entire block. The cut given above represents the back of a half-page block of the *Illustrated London News*, and shows the way in which the bolts and nuts are used for fastening the different parts of the block together.

For the production of a pictorial newspaper a large staff of draughtsmen and engravers is required, who must be ready at a moment's notice to take up any subject, and, if necessary, work day and night until it is done. The artist who supplies the sketch has acquired by long practice a rapid method of working, and can, by a few strokes of his pencil, indicate a passing scene by a kind of pictorial shorthand, which is afterwards translated and extended in the finished drawing. The sketch being completed on paper, the services of the draughtsman on wood come into requisition, for it is not often that the drawing on the block is made by the same person who supplies the sketch. Sometimes the sketch to be dealt with is the production of an amateur, or is so hastily or indifferently done that it has to be remodelled or rearranged before it can be drawn on the wood. Faulty or objectionable portions have to be left out or subdued, and perhaps a point in the sketch that is quite subordinate is brought forward and made to form a prominent part of the picture. All this has to be done without doing violence to the general truth of the representation, and with due consideration for the particular

A BLOCK BEFORE IT IS TAKEN TO PIECES.

conditions of the moment, such as the amount of finish and distribution of light and shade suitable for rapid engraving and printing.

Sometimes more than one draughtsman is employed on a drawing where the subject consists of figures and landscape, or figures and architecture. In such a case, if time presses, the two parts of the drawing are proceeded with simultaneously. The whole design is first traced on the block; the bolts at the back of the block are then loosened, the parts are separated, and the figure-draughtsman sets to work on his division of the block, while another draughtsman is busied with the landscape or architecture, as the case may be. Occasionally, when there is very great hurry, the block is separated piece by piece as fast as the parts of the drawing are finished—the engraver and draughtsman thus working on the same subject at the same time. Instances have occurred where the draughtsman has done his work in this way, and has never seen the whole of his drawing together. The double-page engraving of the marriage of the Prince of Wales in the *Illustrated London News*, March 21, 1863, was drawn on the wood by Sir John Gilbert at 198, Strand, and as fast as each part of the drawing was done it was separated from the rest and given to the engraver. Considering that the artist never saw his drawing entire, it is wonderful to find the engraving so harmonious and effective. Photographing on the wood is sometimes resorted to, and, in the hands of skilful and artistic engravers, with the happiest results.

The drawing on wood being completed, it passes into the hands of the engraver, and the first thing he does is to cut or set the lines across all the joins of the block before the different parts are distributed among the various engravers. This is done partly to ensure as far as possible some degree of harmony of colour and texture throughout the subject. When all the parts are separated and placed in the hands of different engravers each man has thus a sort of *key-note* to guide him in the execution of his portion, and it should be his business to

imitate and follow with care the colour and texture of the small pieces of engraving which he finds already done at the edge of his part of the block where it joins the rest of the design. The accompanying cuts represent a block entire and the same subject divided.

Though this system of subdividing the engraving effects a great saving of time, it must be admitted that it does not always result in the production of a first-rate work of art as a whole. For, supposing the subject to be a landscape with a good stretch of trees, the two or three engravers who have the trees to engrave have, perhaps, each a different method of rendering foliage; and when the whole is completed, and the different pieces are put together, the trees perhaps appear like a piece of patchwork, with a distinct edge to each man's work. To harmonise and dovetail (so to speak) these different pieces of work is the task of the superintending artist, who retouches the first proof of the engraving and endeavours to blend together the differences of colour and texture. This is often no easy task, for the press is generally waiting, and the time that is left for such work is often reduced to minutes when hours would scarcely suffice to accomplish all that might be done. Or the block to be engraved may be a marine subject with a stormy sea. In this case, like the landscape, two or three engravers may be employed upon the water, each of them having a different way of representing that element. Here it is even more difficult than in the landscape to blend the conflicting pieces of work, and requires an amount of "knocking about" that sometimes astonishes the original artist. All this is the necessary result of the hurry in which the greater part of newspaper engravings have to be produced. When the conditions are more favourable, better things are successfully attempted, and of this the illustrated newspapers of the day have given abundant proofs.

It is obvious that when a block is divided and the parts are distributed in various hands, if any accident should occur to one part the whole block is jeopardised. It is much to the credit of the fraternity of engravers that this rarely or ever happens. I only remember one instance of a failure of this kind within my own experience. An engraver of decidedly Bohemian character, after a hard night's work on the tenth part of a page block, thought fit to recruit himself with a cheering cup. In the exhilaration that followed, he lost the piece of work upon which he had been engaged, and thereby rendered useless the efforts of himself and his nine compatriots.

When the block is finished the parts are screwed together by means of the brass bolts and nuts at the back of the block. It is then electrotyped and delivered to the printer, who has

THE SAME SUBJECT DIVIDED.

Mason Jackson (del. & sc.)

← *A Sketch of the Rise and Progress of Pictorial Journalism*, 1879
Ein Abriss zu Aufkommen und Entwicklung des Bildjournalismus
Un description de l'essor et de l'évolution du journalisme illustré
Wood engravings
From: *The Illustrated London News*, 30 August 1879

Mason Jackson's article on engraving refers to the work being done by division of labour and also shows how the printing blocks were screwed together. Jackson had been trained in the tradition established by Thomas Bewick and went on to work for 30 years as art editor of *The Illustrated London News*. His brother John, a student of Bewick's, held the same position for *The Penny Magazine*.

Mason Jacksons Beitrag zeigt den arbeitsteiligen Gravurprozess mit der Aufteilung und Verschraubung der Druckstöcke. Jackson war in der Tradition von Thomas Bewick ausgebildet und 30 Jahre lang Art Editor der tonangebenden *Illustrated London News*. Sein Bruder John Jackson, ein Schüler Bewicks, unterhielt eine vergleichbare Stellung beim *Penny Magazine*.

L'article de Mason Jackson décrit le processus de gravure, et notamment la répartition du travail et le vissage des blocs d'impression. Jackson avait été formé dans la tradition de Thomas Bewick et fut, trente années durant, l'éditeur d'art de la revue phare l'*Illustrated London News*. Son frère John Jackson, un élève de Bewick, occupait une situation comparable au *Penny Magazine*.

Anonymous

The Engravers' Workshop for L'Illustration
Gravuratelier von L'Illustration
Atelier des graveurs de L'Illustration
Wood engravings
From: *L'Illustration*, Paris, 2 March 1844

Two views showing the wood-engraving workshop of the important French illustrated magazine *L'Illustration* by day and by night. In the middle of the room are the hand presses which the engravers used to make trial prints to check their work.

Einblicke in das xylografische Atelier der führenden französischen Illustrierten *L'Illustration* bei Tag und bei Nacht. In der Raummitte standen die Handpressen, auf denen die Graveure zur Kontrolle Probedrucke abziehen konnten.

Vues de jour et de nuit de l'atelier de xylographie du magazine illustré français *L'Illustration*. Au centre de la pièce se trouvent les presses manuelles sur lesquelles les graveurs tirent des épreuves d'essai pour vérifier leur travail.

8   L'ILLUSTRATION, JOURNAL UNIVERSEL.

(Atelier des Graveurs de *l'Illustration* pendant le jour.)

(Atelier des Graveurs de *l'Illustration*.)

Die industrielle Wende

Der explosionsartige Anstieg der Illustrationsgrafik zu Beginn des 19. Jahrhunderts ist nur vor dem Hintergrund der raschen Industrialisierung im Bereich der Papierfertigung und des Druckereiwesens zu erklären. Diese Entwicklung kulminierte 1811 in der Einrichtung der ersten Schnellpresse. Drei Jahre später übernahm die Londoner *Times* diese Erfindung und druckte als erste Tageszeitung im automatisierten Dampfbetrieb. Allerdings waren nur Hochdruckvorlagen, Letternsätze und die relativ groben Holzschnittgrafiken für eine solch dynamisierte Massenvervielfältigung geeignet. Um den Bildunger breiter Massen zu stillen, der durch die anspruchsvollen Tiefdruckproduktionen eines William Hogarth, John Boydell oder Rudolph Ackermann stimuliert worden war, bedurfte es einer Technik, die die filigranen Eigenschaften des Kupferstichs mit den Vorzügen des Hochdrucks – nämlich einer schnellen Reproduzierbarkeit – verbinden konnte. 1790 brachte ein Metallgraveur aus Newcastle, Thomas Bewick, ein Tierlexikon für Jugendliche auf den Markt, das genau eine solche Methode zur Anwendung brachte. Die subtilen Grafiken der *General History of Quadrupeds* mit ihren differenzierten tonalen Abstufungen waren mit den Stichwerkzeugen des Tiefdrucks in Holz realisiert worden, allerdings nicht in das weiche Längsholz, das sich wegen seiner faserigen Ausrichtung nur mit Messern und Hohleisen bearbeiten lässt, sondern in das harte Hirnholz, das quer zum Stamm geschnitten wird und ähnlich homogene Eigenschaften wie eine Metallplatte besitzt. Das Resultat eines solchen Holzstichs ist eine Hochdruckform, die sich perfekt in das typografische Druckbild integrieren und im gleichen Druckvorgang abziehen lässt.

Bewick kann nicht als Erfinder gelten, wohl aber hat er den Holzstich aufleben lassen, der bereits im armenischen Stoffdruck und im Bilderdruck der Renaissancezeit rudimentäre Verwendung gefunden hatte. Dass sich eine Technik, die durch Bewicks Grafiken mit idyllischen Naturbeobachtungen assoziiert war, zu einem industrialisierten Massenmedium entwickeln würde, war paradox und kaum abzusehen. Das schulbildende Potenzial ließ sich allerdings bereits im Erfindungsreichtum und Modulationsspektrum von *A Cheviot Ram* oder Werken, die Nebel und Regen oder den Fingerabdruck des Künstlers zeigen, ausmachen (Abb. S. 58). Obwohl diese Vignetten Bewicks alle nur etwa 8 x 6 cm messen, was in etwa der Größe einer hartholzigen Buchsbaumscheibe entspricht, sind sie zu den künstlerischen Ikonen der Zeit zu zählen, vergleichbar den Aquarellen Thomas Girtins, John Sell Cotmans und William Turners. Die Faszinationskraft, die sie in ungebrochener Folge auf mehr als sechs Generationen von Künstlern ausgeübt haben, lässt sich auch noch heute nachvollziehen, vor allem wenn man sich ihnen mit der Lupe, dem unentbehrlichen Werkzeug der Xylografen, nähert. Bevor der Holzstich in den 1840er-Jahren mit den ersten Illustrierten massentauglich wurde, hatte er bereits eine 40-jährige Inkubationszeit im Bereich der Buchillustration und des politischen Pamphlets hinter sich. Unter Bewicks Schülern, von denen etliche in London zentrale Positionen im Reproduktionsgewerbe eingenommen hatten, bildeten sich schon früh zwei antagonistische Richtungen heraus: die Schule des interpretativen Holzstichs, der auch als Tonstich bekannt war, und die des Faksimilestichs. Erstere konnte sich auf das

Adolph Menzel & Brendamour's Workshop (sc.)

The Flight of Adam, the village magistrate, 1877
Die Flucht des Dorfrichters Adam
La chute d'Adam, le magistrat éponyme du village
Wood engraving
From: Heinrich von Kleist, *Der zerbrochne Krug*,
Berlin, 1877

Caught up in the lattice-work that corresponds
to the individual pieces of the wood engraving are
traces of his fall left behind by Adam, the village
magistrate in Heinrich von Kleist's cabbalistic comedy, when fleeing from Eve's room.

Im verräterischen Gitter der Holzstichsegmente
haben sich Spuren vom Fall Adams verfangen, die
der gleichnamige Dorfrichter in Heinrich von Kleists
kabbalistischer Komödie auf seiner Flucht aus dem
Zimmer Evas hinterlassen hat.

Dans le perfide treillis des segments de gravure sur
bois se sont perdues les traces de la chute d'Adam
que le magistrat éponyme du village a laissées derrière lui en s'enfuyant de la chambre d'Ève dans la
comédie cabalistique de Heinrich von Kleist.

Beispiel Bewicks berufen. Wie in Bewicks Vignetten wurden hier malerische Vorlagen mittels Weißlinien relativ frei in Tonwerte übersetzt. Die Schule des Faksimilestichs hingegen ging vom schwarzen Lineament einer zeichnerischen Vorlage aus und war bestrebt, es möglichst originalgetreu nachzustechen. Von ihren Gegnern wurde sie daher mit dem Vorwurf belegt, sklavische Kopierarbeit zu leisten und herkömmliche Tiefdrucktechniken zu imitieren. Der Illustrator William Harvey und der Graveur Allen Robert Branston verhalfen dem Faksimilestich in London zum Erfolg. Ein Schüler Branstons, Charles Thompson, eröffnete 1817 in Paris ein xylografisches Atelier und etablierte damit den Holzstich auf dem Kontinent. Weitere xylografische Zentren folgten in den frühen 1840er-Jahren in München und in Leipzig.

Um dem Abbildungsbedarf der Illustrierten nachkommen zu können, gründeten die Zeitungsverlage schon bald eigene xylografische Ateliers, die von hauseigenen Zeichnungsabteilungen mit Vorlagen beliefert wurden (siehe Abb. S. 61). Aufgrund des Termindrucks im Nachrichtengewerbe lag es nahe, die Anfertigung großformatiger Holzstiche arbeitsteilig zu organisieren. Die einzelnen Segmente, aus denen die großflächigen Druckstöcke zusammengesetzt waren, wurden dabei auf eine entsprechende Anzahl von Graveuren aufgeteilt und erst im Stadium der Nachbearbeitung zusammengeleimt. Anfang der 1850er-Jahre setzte sich allmählich eine Methode der Verschraubung durch, die das kooperative Gravieren enorm erleichterte. Für den aufmerksamen Leser war diese Art der Zusammenfügung nicht selten anhand einer Gitterstruktur im Druckbild auszumachen. In Adolph Menzels Illustrationen zu Heinrich von Kleists Komödie

Der zerbrochne Krug spielt diese verräterische Struktur eine wichtige Rolle. Der segmentierte Druckstock wurde in Menzels medienreflexiver Interpretation zum Sinnbild für den Verlust einer sinnstiftenden schöpferischen Einheit, den Kleist in seinem Stück thematisiert (Abb. S. 63). Menzel unterstrich damit einen Zusammenhang zwischen den arbeitsteiligen, montageartigen Produktionsweisen und der Inkohärenz pressegrafischer Bildensembles, der in den 1870er-Jahren evident wurde. Die langen Übertragungsketten, in die neben den Xylografen in der Regel auch ein oder mehrere Redaktionszeichner involviert waren, hatte außerdem zur Folge, dass die Illustriertendrucke meist erheblich von den Ausgangszeichnungen abwichen. Die klassische Phase der Pressegrafik war stilistisch vor allem von den Standardisierungen geprägt, die aus solchen arbeitsteiligen Interpretationen resultierten. Dass es anfangs nicht die Illustratoren waren, die signierten, sondern die xylografischen Ateliers, war in dieser Hinsicht nur folgerichtig. Die zweite Drucktechnik, die pressegrafisch bedeutsam wurde, war nicht mit interpretativen Leistungen verbunden. Beim Flachdruckverfahren der Lithografie wird eine Zeichnung entweder direkt mit fetthaltigem Material oder per Umdruck auf eine präparierte Steinplatte aufgebracht, die dann durch chemische Behandlung druckfähig gemacht wird. Die Lithografie wurde 1796 von dem Münchener Komponisten Alois Senefelder für den Notendruck entwickelt. Von den Künstlern wurde die jüngere Technik favorisiert, da sie gegenüber dem Holzstich, dessen Einführung zu diesem Zeitpunkt bereits einige Jahre zurücklag, eine originalgetreuere Wiedergabe und eine größere Bandbreite an grafischen

Anonymous

↑↗ *The Paris Wine Market*, 1869
Der Pariser Weinmarkt | Le marché aux vins à Paris
Printing block, front and rear view

→ *The Paris Wine Market*, 1869
Der Pariser Weinmarkt | Le marché aux vins à Paris
Wood engraving
From: *The Illustrated London News*, 1 December 1869

Möglichkeiten erlaubte. Mit Kreiden und Lavuren ließen sich tonale Effekte erzielen, und mit fetthaltiger Tusche, die mit Pinsel oder Feder aufgetragen wurde, war die Wiedergabe feiner Linien möglich. Dass sich die Lithografie als Populärmedium zuerst in Frankreich durchsetzen und dort mit besonderer Nachhaltigkeit behaupten konnte, ist in erster Linie nicht etwa einem Eugène Delacroix oder Honoré Daumier zu verdanken, sondern dem weitgehend vergessenen Militär- und Genregrafiker Nicolas-Toussaint Charlet, einem engen Freund Théodore Géricaults, der das Land zu den Zeiten der bourbonischen Restauration mit seinen subversiven bonapartistischen Propagandablättern regelrecht zu fluten begann (siehe Abb. S. 69 u.). Charlet hatte bei Antoine-Jean Gros studiert. Das Lehrstudio, das dieser von dem geflohenen Jacques-Louis David übernommen hatte, blieb einer republikanischen Tradition der Historienmalerei verpflichtet und galt zudem als Zentrum lithografischer Ausbildung. Charlet konzentrierte sich noch während seiner Lehrzeit auf das neue Medium. Indem er es erfolgreich kommerziell zu nutzen wusste, motivierte er auch eine Vielzahl seiner Kommilitonen. Unter anderem unterrichtete er den späteren Verleger Charles Philipon in der lithografischen Kreide-Manier *(crayon)*. Philipon setzte dann die Lithografie im Zug seiner Karikaturkampagnen gegen die Restauration und die Julimonarchie als pressegrafisches Medium durch.

Obgleich der Kauf seines revolutionären Wochenmagazins *La Caricature* wegen des hohen Preises einem großbürgerlichen Abonnentenkreis vorbehalten blieb, erreichten die lithografischen Bildseiten über die Schaufensteraushänge des Verlags und den Einzelblattverkauf ein viel breiteres Publikum. Die Produktion einer aus zwei Druckverfahren kombinierten Zeitschrift erwies sich allerdings als problematisch. Während die Lithografie in *La Caricature* ein eingebundener Fremdkörper blieb, versuchte Philipon, den Flachdruck der Bilder in der nachfolgenden Tageszeitung *Le Charivari* mehr in das typografische Umfeld zu integrieren. Der Aufwand für den doppelten Druckvorgang war auf Dauer jedoch zu groß. Außerdem litt die Qualität der Lithografie merklich durch den Abdruck auf Zeitungspapier. Die Folge war, dass das drucktechnische Experiment des *Charivari* nicht zum verstärkten Einsatz von Lithografie im Pressewesen führte, sondern eher den Nachweis für die ökonomische Notwendigkeit der Xylografie lieferte.

Letztere hatte dazu noch den unschätzbaren Vorzug, dass sie einer internationalen Vernetzung der Illustrierten und der globale Verbreitung der Bildnachrichten entgegenkam. Für Massenauflagen, wie sie im Zeitungswesen die Regel waren, mussten nämlich von den Holzgravuren Metallkopien angefertigt werden, sogenannte Klischees (franz. *cliché*). Ab 1838 konnte das umständliche Abgussverfahren durch eine wesentlich präzisere Methode elektrolytischer Kupferablagerung ersetzt werden, die sogenannte Galvano- oder Elektrotypie. Von Anfang an wurde mit diesen Klischees ein reger internationaler Handel getrieben, sodass die Holzgravuren des 1832 gegründeten Londoner *Penny Magazine* bereits wenige Wochen später in verwandten französischen, deutschen, holländischen, italienischen, griechischen, schwedischen, norwegischen und amerikanischen Gazetten Verwendung finden konnten.

510   THE ILLUSTRATED LONDON NEWS   [DEC. 1, 1860.

1.—THE BRANDY QUARTER.   2.—RUES DE LANGUEDOC AND DE LA CÔTE D'OR.   3.—THE CELLARS.

THE PARIS WINE MARKET.—SEE SUPPLEMENT, PAGE 520.

Le tournant industriel

L'essor fulgurant du dessin d'illustration au début du XIXᵉ siècle ne peut s'expliquer que dans le contexte de l'industrialisation galopante dans le domaine de la fabrication du papier et de l'imprimerie, notamment avec l'inauguration de la presse à cylindre en 1811. Trois ans plus tard, le *Times* londonien était le premier quotidien imprimé sur une presse à vapeur. Toutefois, seuls les blocs d'impression en relief, les compositions de caractères et les dessins gravés sur bois, relativement grossiers, se prêtaient à une telle multiplication de masse. Pour étancher la soif de culture des masses que les gravures en taille-douce de William Hogarth, John Boydell ou Rudolph Ackermann avaient attisée, il fallait une technique qui puisse combiner les qualités de finesse des traits de la gravure sur cuivre aux avantages de l'impression en relief – c'est-à-dire une reproductibilité rapide. En 1790, Thomas Bewick, un graveur sur métal de Newcastle, lança sur le marché une encyclopédie sur les animaux à l'attention des jeunes lecteurs qui tirait parti de ces nouvelles techniques d'impression. Les subtiles illustrations de la *General History of Quadrupeds* avec leurs dégradés de tons bien distincts avaient été réalisées dans du bois au moyen des outils de gravure de taille-douce, non dans le tendre bois de fil – qui, à cause de sa consistance fibreuse, ne peut être travaillé qu'avec un couteau ou une gouge – mais dans le rigide bois de bout que l'on coupe perpendiculairement au sens des fibres et qui possède les mêmes qualités homogènes qu'une plaque de métal. Le résultat d'une gravure sur bois de ce type est une plaque typographique, qui peut être parfaitement intégrée dans l'image typographique imprimée ou imprimée à part au cours de la même étape

d'impression. Bewick ne peut en être considéré comme l'inventeur, mais c'est bien lui qui offre une deuxième naissance à la gravure sur bois, laquelle avait surtout été utilisée de façon rudimentaire dans l'impression textile en Arménie et dans l'impression d'images au temps de la Renaissance. Outre que ce soit paradoxal, rien ne laissait prévoir qu'une technique, associée aux illustrations idylliques de la nature de Bewick, se développe jusqu'à devenir un média de masse industrialisé. Un potentiel pédagogique se dégageait déjà d'œuvres inventives et polyvalentes comme *A Cheviot Ram* ou des œuvres représentant brouillard et pluie ou encore l'empreinte digitale de l'artiste (ills. p. 58). Bien que d'un format de 8 x 6 cm environ, soit la taille d'une rondelle de buis en bois dur, les vignettes de Bewick font partie des icônes artistiques de l'époque, comparables aux aquarelles de Thomas Girtin, John Sell Cotman et J. M. W. Turner. La formidable fascination qu'elles n'ont cessé d'exercer sur plus de six générations d'artistes se justifie aujourd'hui encore, surtout si on les examine à la loupe, cet outil indispensable aux xylographes. Avant que les gravures sur bois ne deviennent accessibles au grand public avec les premiers magazines illustrés dans les années 1840, elles avaient déjà connu une phase d'incubation de quarante ans dans le domaine de l'illustration livresque et du pamphlet politique. Parmi les élèves de Bewick, dont un grand nombre avaient occupé des positions centrales dans le secteur de la reproduction à Londres, se formèrent très tôt deux orientations antagonistes : l'école de la gravure d'interprétation, connue aussi sous le terme de bois de teinte, et celle du fac-similé. La première pouvait se référer à l'exemple de

Paul Gavarni & François Pierdon (sc.)

A Tale of Two Tattlers, 1857
Geschichte mit ein paar
passenden Worten
Histoire d'en dire deux
Wood engraving
From: *Le Monde illustré*, Paris,
22 August 1857

Whilst this illustration might seem to
be a chalk lithograph, it is actually a
wood engraving. Several years before
the paradigm shift occurred with the
introduction of using photography to
reproduce the image to be engraved,
the early Impressionist artist François
Pierdon transferred a number of pencil drawings by Paul Gavarni to the
linear medium of relief printing in a
deceptively similar manner.

Was aussieht wie eine Kreidelitho-
grafie, ist tatsächlich ein Holzstich.
Etliche Jahre vor dem mimetischen
Paradigmenwechsel, der durch die
Fotoxylografie eingeleitet wurde,
übersetzte der frühimpressionistische
Künstler François Pierdon einige
Crayon-Zeichnungen Paul Gavarnis
auf täuschend ähnliche Weise ins
lineare Hochdruckmedium.

Ce qui ressemble à une lithographie
à la craie est en réalité une gravure
sur bois. Bien des années avant le
changement de paradigme mimétique
qui fut introduit par la xylophotographie, l'artiste impressionniste précoce
François Pierdon transposa de façon
faussement similaire quelques dessins au crayon de Paul Gavarni sur ce
medium linéaire d'impression en relief.

Bewick. Comme dans les vignettes de Bewick, les modèles picturaux étaient transposés ici relativement librement en valeurs
tonales à l'aide de lignes blanches. L'école de gravure en fac-
similé, en revanche, partait du tracé noir d'un modèle illustré et
cherchait à le reproduire le plus fidèlement possible. Pour cette
raison, leurs concurrents les accusèrent de fournir un servile travail de copie et d'imiter les traditionnelles techniques de taille-
douce. L'illustrateur William Harvey et le graveur Allen Robert
Branston contribuèrent au succès de la gravure en fac-similé à
Londres. Un élève de Branston, Charles Thompson, ouvrit un
atelier de xylographie à Paris en 1817 et imposa ainsi la gravure
sur bois sur le continent. D'autres centres de xylographie virent
le jour à Munich et à Leipzig au début des années 1840.

Pour répondre au besoin d'illustrations des magazines illustrés, les éditeurs de journaux fondèrent de bonne heure leurs
propres ateliers de xylographie, qui recevaient des modèles du
service Illustration (voir ill. p. 61). À cause de la pression des
délais de bouclage, il devint nécessaire d'organiser la répartition
de travail pour la production de gravures grand format. Les segments isolés qui composaient les blocs d'impression de grande
surface furent répartis en un nombre correspondant de graveurs
et rassemblés seulement au moment de la finition. Une méthode
de fixation par vis, qui facilitait énormément le gravage coopéra-
tif, s'imposa peu à peu au début des années 1850. Le lecteur
attentif pouvait souvent déceler cette forme d'assemblage dans
la structure en treillis de l'image imprimée. Dans les illustrations
de la comédie de Heinrich von Kleist *La Cruche cassée* réalisées
par Adolph Menzel, cette structure mise à nu joue un rôle

important. Dans l'interprétation réflexive du medium de Menzel, le
bloc d'impression segmenté devint le symbole de la perte d'une
unité créatrice emplie de sens que Kleist thématise dans sa pièce
(ill. p. 63). Menzel faisait ainsi le parallèle entre les méthodes de
production avec répartition des tâches et assemblage des éléments et l'incohérence d'un ensemble pictural dans la presse
illustrée qui devint patent au cours des années 1870. Les longues chaînes de transmission, dans lesquelles en plus des xylographes un ou plusieurs illustrateurs de rédaction étaient en
général également impliqués, avaient pour conséquence que la
plupart des épreuves des magazines divergeaient considérablement des dessins d'origine. D'un point de vue stylistique, la phase
classique de l'illustration et du dessin de presse fut surtout marquée par les standardisations qui résultaient des interprétations
liées à la répartition du travail. À cet égard, il était donc parfaitement logique qu'au début les ateliers de xylographie apposèrent
leur signature sur les œuvres, et non les illustrateurs. La deuxième technique d'impression qui eut une place importante dans
l'illustration et le dessin de presse n'était pas associée à des performances d'interprétation. Dans le procédé d'impression à plat
de la lithographie, un dessin devient imprimable par traitement
chimique, soit directement avec du matériel de dessin gras soit
par transfert sur une plaque de pierre enduite. Elle fut développée en 1796 par le compositeur munichois Alois Senefelder pour
l'impression de notes de musique. Les artistes favorisaient cette
technique récente parce que, en comparaison de la xylographie
dont l'utilisation remontait alors déjà à plusieurs années, elle permettait une reproduction plus fidèle de l'original et une plus large

Anonymous

→ *Rue Saint-Maur-Popincourt*
The Barricade, 1848
Die Barrikade | *La barricade*
Wood engravings
From: *L'Illustration*, Paris, 1 July 1848

In this first printed report to use photography the quality of reproduction of the new medium was the main point of interest. The technique improved with the development of photoxylography in the 1860s.

Bei dieser ersten gedruckten Fotoreportage stand vor allem die Wiedergabe des neuen Mediums im Vordergrund; eine mimetische Haltung, die durch die Entwicklung der Fotoxylografie in den 1860er-Jahren weiter verstärkt wurde.

Pour ce premier reportage photographique, c'est surtout la reproductibilité de ce nouveau medium qui revêt le plus grand intérêt, lequel ira grandissant avec le développement de la photoxylographie pendant les années 1860.

M. Thibault

Rue Saint-Maur-Popincourt
Barricades before the Attack, 25 June 1848
Barrikaden vor dem Angriff
Barricades avant l'attaque
Daguerreotype
Paris, Musée d'Orsay

The photo shows the fighting on the barricades during the June Days uprising in Paris in 1848. Photography was in fact developed as a result of various chemical experiments undertaken to improve lithography, although for more than 50 years the new medium was reliant on manual transfers for it to be reproduced on a large scale, in particular wood engraving.

Ene Aufnahme vom Barrikadenkampf während der Aufstände im Juni 1848. Fotografie war ein Resultat chemiegrafischer Experimente, die zur Weiterentwicklung der Lithografie unternommen worden waren. Zur Massenvervielfältigung war das neue Medium noch mehr als ein halbes Jahrhundert lang auf manuelle Übersetzungen angewiesen, vor allem auf den Holzstich.

Un instantané des combats de barricades durant les journées insurrectionnelles de juin 1848 à Paris. La photographie était le résultat d'expériences chimico-graphiques entreprises pour améliorer la lithographie. Pendant plus d'un demi-siècle, ce nouveau medium fut dépendant de transpositions manuelles, en particulier de la gravure sur bois.

palette de possibilités graphiques. Les effets de teintes étaient obtenus au moyen de craies et de lavis, et de fines lignes étaient reproduites avec de l'encre de Chine appliquée au pinceau ou à la plume.

Le fait que la lithographie pût s'imposer comme medium populaire d'abord en France, et ce, de façon durable n'est pas le mérite d'Eugène Delacroix ou d'Honoré Daumier, mais du peintre et dessinateur spécialisé dans la scène de genre à sujet militaire Nicolas-Toussaint Charlet, largement tombé dans l'oubli. Il était un proche ami de Théodore Géricault qui commença à littéralement inonder le pays de ses feuilles volantes subversives de propagande bonapartiste pendant la Restauration des Bourbons (voir ill. p. 69 b.). Charlet avait étudié auprès d'Antoine-Jean Gros. L'atelier, que ce dernier avait repris de Jacques-Louis David en exil, resta attaché à une tradition républicaine de peinture historique et était de plus considéré comme un centre de formation lithographique. Pendant sa période d'apprentissage, Charlet se concentra sur le nouveau medium. Sachant l'utiliser avec succès à des fins commerciales, il motiva aussi un grand nombre de ses camarades étudiants. Il enseigna notamment au futur éditeur Charles Philipon la technique du crayon lithographique. Par la suite, dans le cadre de ses campagnes de caricatures contre la Restauration et la monarchie de Juillet, Philipon utilisa la lithographie comme medium du dessin de presse.

Bien qu'à cause de son prix élevé l'achat de son hebdomadaire révolutionnaire *La Caricature* restât le privilège d'un cercle d'abonnés de la haute bourgeoisie, les pages illustrées de lithographies touchèrent un bien plus vaste public grâce à leur affichage dans les vitrines de la maison d'édition et à leur vente en feuilles volantes. La fabrication d'un journal associant deux procédés d'impression s'avéra pourtant problématique. Alors que la lithographie restait un corps étranger inséré dans *La Caricature*, Philipon essaya d'intégrer davantage l'impression à plat des images dans le contexte typographique dans le journal qu'il fonda ensuite, *Le Charivari*. Mais à la longue, l'effort fourni pour ce double processus d'impression était trop important. En outre, la qualité de la lithographie souffrait considérablement de l'impression sur papier journal. Il en résulta donc que l'expérience de technique d'impression du *Charivari* n'entraîna pas une utilisation renforcée de la lithographie dans la presse, mais fournit plutôt la preuve de la nécessité économique de la xylographie.

Celle-ci offrait d'ailleurs l'avantage inestimable d'être adaptée à un réseau international de magazines illustrés et à la diffusion globale d'informations en images. Pour les gros tirages, qui étaient la règle dans le secteur journalistique, il fallait fabriquer à partir de gravures sur bois des copies en métal, appelées clichés. Dès 1838, le laborieux processus de moulage put être remplacé par une méthode nettement plus précise de cuivrage par électrolyse, également appelée galvanotypie ou électrotypie. Ces clichés furent très rapidement l'objet d'un commerce international intense, à tel point que les gravures sur bois du *Penny Magazine*, fondé à Londres en 1832, purent être utilisées quelques semaines plus tard dans des gazettes associées françaises, allemandes, néerlandaises, italiennes, grecques, suédoises, norvégiennes et américaines.

La barricade de la rue Saint-Maur-Popincourt le dimanche matin,
d'après une planche daguerréotypée par M. Thibault.

La barricade de la rue Saint-Maur-Popincourt le lundi après l'attaque,
d'après une planche daguerréotypée par M. Thibault.

**Nicolas-Toussaint Charlet
& François le Villain (lith.)**

It's the End of the World!, 1824
Es ist das Ende der Welt!
C'est la fin du monde !
Lithograph
From: Nicolas-Toussaint Charlet,
Croquis lithographiques, Paris, 1824

In this illustration Charlet is passing
comment on his own excessive production in self-mocking fashion. As
in a deluge, his pictorial albums rain
down on mankind and announce that
the end of the world is nigh. Even the
spirit of the burlesque, who tries in
vain to find a secure footing on a slab
of limestone, cannot escape the curse
of mass reproduction by lithography.

Auf selbstironische Weise kommentiert Nicolas-Toussaint Charlet hier
die eigene Überproduktion. Sintflut-
artig prasseln seine Alben auf die
Menschheit hernieder und kündigen
das nahe Weltende an. Auch dem
Genius der Burleske, die vergeblich
festen Halt auf einer Kalksteinplatte
sucht, gelingt es nicht, dem Fluch der
lithografischen Massenreproduktion
zu entrinnen.

Nicolas-Toussaint Charlet illustre
ici avec autodérision ses propres
excès de production. Tel un déluge,
ses albums s'abattent sur l'humanité
et annoncent la fin imminente du
monde. Même le génie du burlesque,
qui cherche en vain à prendre appui
sur une solide plaque de calcaire, ne
parvient pas à échapper à la malédiction de la reproduction lithographique
de masse.

C'est la fin du monde!

Realism and Caricature

While reproducing images by means of a *camera obscura* had been in common use for some time, and also through the first early experiments in photography, such visual documentation played only a marginal role in the initial phase of the illustrated popular press, where the taste for pictorial journalism was located elsewhere. As William Blanchard Jerrold, a journalist himself and an expert on the subject, noted at the time, the pictorial style "was distinctly the creation of our caricaturists" (Jerrold 1882, p. 93). By this he was referring to the tradition of social satire and its schematic representation of figures, and indeed early press graphics were full of the exaggerated physiognomies depicted by illustrators such as William Hogarth. It is also no coincidence that many of the terms associated with the ideological implications of classifying social and ethnic categories according to physical characteristics have been adopted from their use in the illustrations of press graphics: "types", "stereotypes" and "clichés", for instance were all words that were coined and introduced in this early period.

The approach of pictorial journalism from the outset was to be incisive and confrontational. This position was formulated in a spirit of resistance to the repressions being enforced throughout Europe at the time, and in the context of the social unrest that developed, first in England and then in France, with the Industrial Revolution. One such workers' protest in Manchester and its bloody suppression became the subject of a radical reformist pamphlet by William Hone and George Cruikshank, *The Political House that Jack Built*, which introduced the use of wood engraving in popular journalism in 1819, and in so doing established

the era of pictorial journalism (ills. pp. 76–79). Hone was already something of a folk hero, having successfully defended himself in a high-profile court case two years earlier against charges of blasphemy and distributing inflammatory writings. His acquittal also meant he had a certain immunity to further charges of a similar nature. Moreover, the consistency of his later pictorial campaigns against the corrupt regime of the English Prince Regent was grounded in the extensive research into the history of parody and pictorial satire he had undertaken in the course of his spectacular self-defence in court (see ill. p. 71).

The illegal, and unstamped publications issued by various radicals also helped to stimulate the growth of the illustrated press. When liberal and loyalist groups attempted to break the dominance of this faction in the media the consequence was the founding in 1832 of the first mass-circulation illustrated magazine, *The Penny Magazine*, which aimed to be both popular and informative. However, while the democratisation of knowledge in England had come about as part of a broad public debate, in France it still remained the privilege of a small elite. Earlier in the 19th century the Comte de Saint-Simon, whose progressive ideology had influenced a number of newspaper publishers, had applied the military term avant-garde (meaning the vanguard of an advancing force) to the cultural sphere.

To begin with, the caricature movement in France was entirely avant-garde. It developed out of the elite style of historical art in the time of Napoleon, with Eugène Delacroix being one of the earliest to work in this field, and under the leadership of the caricaturist and publisher Charles Philipon it grew

" We twa hae paidl't"—   BURNS.

William Hone (concept) & George Cruikshank (del.)

"We twa hae paidl't", c. 1827
„Wir beide sind gepaddelt"
«Nous avons galéré tous deux»
(a line from Robert Burns's poem
"Auld Lang Syne", based on an earlier
folk song)
Wood engraving
From: William Hone, *Facetiae and
Miscellanies*, London, 1827

During the three years they worked
together, the writer William Hone and
illustrator George Cruikshank produced a whole series of extremely successful pictorial satires. Behind the
apparent simplicity of their works lay a
sophisticated and calculated strategy
based on extensive research into the
possible combinations of illustrations
and text to achieve their parodic effect.

Im Verlauf ihrer dreijährigen Zusammenarbeit produzierten der Autor
William Hone und der Karikaturist
George Cruikshank eine Serie immens
erfolgreicher Bildsatiren. Hinter der
vordergründigen Simplizität ihrer Publizistik verbarg sich ein raffiniertes
strategisches Kalkül, dem eine intensive Recherche über die Möglichkeiten
parodistischer Bild- und Textkombina-
torik zugrunde lag.

Au cours de leur collaboration de
trois années, l'auteur William Hone
et le caricaturiste George Cruikshank
produisirent une série de satires en
images extrêmement populaire. Derrière une apparente simplicité se
cachait un calcul stratégique raffiné,
basé sur une recherche intensive
quant aux possibilités d'association
parodique d'illustrations et de textes.

into an industry run along military lines and directed against the
Restoration policies of the "Citizen King" Louis-Philippe. The war
on which Philipon duly embarked in *La Caricature*, the magazine he founded in 1830, was modelled on Hone's campaigns
against the Prince Regent. This became still more evident during Philipon's dramatic appearance in court in November 1831
when he too defended himself against charges of treason. As
with Hone though, the trial only backfired on the authorities,
and when Philipon was able to produce as evidence in court
a drawing showing the resemblance between the king's head
and a ripe pear, his campaign was given an enormous boost. As
students used the image in graffiti and it appeared on pictures
hung in shop windows, the pear became a symbol of the stupid-
ity and corruption of the political system as a whole, and spread
like wildfire.

In his campaigning, Philipon relied much more on the power
of a single image to convey his arguments than was the case
with the radicals in England. For him, press graphics were a
democratised continuation of history painting under conditions
of more rapid change. In this way he was building on the propagandist art used under Napoleon, which had propelled the history painting of mainland Europe into the present and connected
it to the more open possibilities of genre painting. As such, caricature was itself too restrictive a form to cater for the range of
interventionist styles of art that Philipon sought to present in
his magazines. To that end he also included early illustrations of
social realism by Nicolas Toussaint Charlet, Edmé Jean Pigal,
Charles-Joseph Traviès, Honoré Daumier and Philippe-Auguste

Jeanron, who in turn paved the way for artists such as Jean-
François Millet and Gustave Courbet.

After a range of rigid censorship measures were introduced
in 1835, *La Caricature*'s years of Republican struggle were
brought to a close and Philipon transferred his efforts to a harm-
less form of social satire in his magazine *Le Charivari*. His illustrators now often adapted popular figures from the boulevard
theatres or even created characters of their own that went on to
become successful on the stage. The trend for social types and
their classification culminated in a gigantic plan for a serialised
panorama of society, which had been conceived by Philipon's
former colleague Honoré de Balzac under the general heading of the *Comédie Humaine*. Its basic concept of the analogy
between social groups and animal species was a form of caricature and was modelled on the zoomorphic illustrations by
Grandville which also appeared in *La Caricature*. At the same
time in England, Charles Dickens, who was then working as
a journalist, and the illustrators Robert Seymour and George
Cruikshank were collaborating in the style of Hogarth's "modern
moral subjects" on serialised novels set in a very similar territory
between types of the grotesque and social realism. The works of
these two most popular writers of the 19th century, Balzac and
Dickens, were inspired by press graphics and in turn made their
own contributions to the development of pictorial journalism.

Realismus und Karikatur

Obgleich retinale Aufzeichungspraktiken durch die Praxis der Camera obscura seit Langem populär und bereits auch erste fotografische Experimente unternommen worden waren, spielte der visuelle Dokumentarismus in der initialen Phase der illustrierten Populärpresse nur eine marginale Rolle. Der Sinn für Bildjournalismus kam aus einer anderen Richtung. Nach Überzeugung von William Blanchard Jerrold, einem der besten Kenner der Materie, war er „eindeutig das Werk unserer Karikaturisten" (Jerrold 1882, S. 93). Gemeint war damit die sozialsatirische Tradition mit ihren schematisierten Charakterdarstellungen. Die frühe Pressegrafik war durchdrungen von dem physiognomischen Hype, den William Hogarth mit ausgelöst hatte. Es ist kein Zufall, dass die meisten Termini, die man mit den ideologischen Implikationen solcher an Körpermerkmalen orientierten sozialen und ethnischen Klassifizierungen verbindet, dem reproduktionsgrafischen Bereich der illustrierten Massenpresse entlehnt sind: Typen, Stereotypen und Klischees; sie wurden in dieser frühen Phase geprägt und einstudiert.

Die Codes des frühen Bildjournalismus waren scharf und konfrontativ. Sie formulierten sich im Widerstand gegen die Repressionen der europaweiten Restauration und im Spannungsfeld der sozialen Konflikte, die als Folge der industriellen Revolution zuerst in England und dann in Frankreich aufbrachen. Es war ein radikalreformatorisches Pamphlet über eine blutig niedergeschlagene Arbeiterdemonstration in Manchester – William Hones und George Cruikshanks *The Political House that Jack Built* –, das 1819 die Technik des Holzstichs im Bereich der Massenpublizistik etablierte und damit die bildjournalistische

Epoche begründete (Abb. S. 76–79). Hone genoss den Status eines Volkshelden, da er sich zwei Jahre zuvor in einem aufsehenerregenden Prozess erfolgreich gegen eine Anklage wegen Blasphemie und der Verbreitung aufrührerischer Schriften verteidigt hatte. Auch war er dadurch weitgehend immun gegenüber weiteren Anklagen ähnlicher Art. Die Konsistenz seiner nachfolgenden Bildkampagnen gegen das korrupte Regime des englischen Prinzregenten beruhte auf den ausgedehnten Recherchen zur Geschichte der Parodie und der Bildsatire, die er im Zusammenhang mit seiner spektakulären Selbstverteidigung unternommen hatte (siehe Abb. S. 71).

Die illegalen, ungestempelten Periodika der Radikalen trieben die Entwicklung der illustrierten Presse weiter voran. Der Versuch liberaler loyalistischer Kreise, die publizistische Hegemonie dieser Subkultur zu brechen, führte 1832 zur Gründung des ersten Bildermagazins in Massenauflagen, des populärwissenschaftlichen *Penny Magazine*. Während die Demokratisierung von Wissen sich in England im Rahmen einer breiten öffentlichen Auseinandersetzung durchgesetzt hatte, blieb sie in Frankreich das Projekt einer kleinen Elite. Graf Saint-Simon, dessen progressivistische Ideologie viele Zeitungsverleger motivierte, hatte den militärischen Begriff der Avantgarde *(Vorhut)* zu Beginn des Jahrhunderts auf den kulturellen Bereich übertragen.

Durch und durch avantgardistisch war die französische Karikaturbewegung in ihren Anfängen ausgerichtet. Sie entstand im elitären Zirkel napoleonischer Historienkunst mit Eugène Delacroix als einem ihrer frühesten Vertreter und entwickelte sich unter der Führung des Karikaturisten und Verlegers Charles

George Cruikshank (del. & sc.)

Bank Restriction Note, 1819
Bankrestriktionsnote
Billet bancaire de restriction
Etching
From: William Hone, *Facetiae and Miscellanies*, London, 1827

This satirical bank-note, distributed by William Hone in large numbers, is a masterful example of interventionist graphics. Its effect even reached as far as the fiscal policy of the time, which oversaw the issuing of small amounts of money in cheaply printed notes that were easy to counterfeit and which thus, by way of a harsh judicial system, were responsible for numerous death sentences.

Die satirische Banknote, die William Hone massenweise in Umlauf brachte, war ein Glanzstück interventionistischer Grafik. Sie verfehlte nicht ihre Wirkung gegen eine Fiskalpolitik, die niedrige Geldbeträge in billig gedruckten und leicht zu imitierenden Scheinen ausgab und die damit im Zusammenhang mit einer rigiden Rechtssprechung für eine Flut von Todesurteilen verantwortlich war.

Le billet de banque satirique, que William Hone fit diffuser à grande échelle, fut un exemple éclatant de dessin interventionniste. Il ne manqua pas d'influencer une politique fiscale qui imprimait à moindres frais des billets faciles à contrefaire et qui, en accointance avec une juridiction inflexible, entraîna ainsi une vague de condamnations à mort.

Philipon zu einer militärisch operierenden Unternehmung, die gegen die restaurative Politik des sogenannten Bürgerkönigs Louis-Philippe gerichtet war. Der Krieg, den Philipon in seinem 1830 gegründeten Magazin *La Caricature* gegen Louis-Philippe führte, war der Kampagne Hones gegen den englischen Prinzregenten nachgebildet. Dies wurde auch in Philipons spektakulärem Gerichtsauftritt deutlich, mit der er sich im November 1831 gegen eine Anklage wegen Majestätsbeleidigung verteidigte. Wie im Fall Hones ging auch hier für die Obrigkeit der Schuss nach hinten los. Der zeichnerische Nachweis einer Analogie zwischen dem Kopf des Königs und einer reifen Birne, den er vor Gericht erbringen konnte, beschied seiner Kampagne einen enormen Auftrieb. Über studentische Graffitiaktionen und Schaufensteraushänge verbreitete sich die Birne als Symbol für die Dummheit und Korruption des ganzen politischen Systems wie ein Lauffeuer.

Philipon setzte in seinen Kampagnen viel stärker auf die argumentative Kraft des Einzelbilds, als dies bei den englischen Radikalen der Fall war. Pressegrafik war für ihn eine demokratisierte Fortsetzung der Historienkunst unter beschleunigten Voraussetzungen. Er knüpfte damit an die napoleonische Propagandakunst an, die die kontinentale Historienmalerei in die Gegenwart katapultiert und an die offenen Möglichkeiten des Genrebilds angeschlossen hatte. Karikatur war dementsprechend auch ein viel zu enges begriffliches Korsett, um die Vielfalt interventionistischer Kunst zu fassen, die Philipon in seinen Magazinen versammelte. Dazu zählten auch eine Reihe früher sozialrealistischer Grafiken von Nicolas-Toussaint Charlet,

Edmé-Jean Pigal, Charles-Joseph Traviès, Honoré Daumier und Philippe-Auguste Jeanron, die Künstlern wie Jean-François Millet und Gustave Courbet den Weg gewiesen haben.

Nachdem die republikanische Kampfphase von *La Caricature* 1835 durch ein Bündel rigider Zensurmaßnahmen beendet worden war, wich Philipon in seinem Journal *Le Charivari* auf eine unverfängliche Form der Sozialsatire aus. Nicht selten adaptierten seine Zeichner hier populäre Gestalten des Boulevardtheaters oder kreierten Charaktere, die wiederum auf den Bühnen erfolgreich waren. Die Tendenz zur sozialen Typisierung und Klassifizierung kulminierte in dem gigantomanen Plan zu einem serialisierten Gesellschaftspanorama, den Philipons ehemaliger Mitarbeiter Honoré de Balzac unter dem Oberbegriff einer *Comédie humaine* gefasst hatte. Die zugrunde liegende Vorstellung einer Analogie zwischen sozialen Gruppen und Tiergattungen war karikaturesk und an das Vorbild der zoomorphen Illustrationen des *La-Caricature*-Zeichners Grandville angelehnt. Zeitgleich arbeitete Balzacs englischer Kollege, der Journalist Charles Dickens, in enger Kollaboration mit den Illustratoren Robert Seymour und George Cruikshank und in Anlehnung an Hogarth' *modern moral subjects* an Feuilletonromanen, die in einem ganz ähnlichen Schnittbereich zwischen grotesker Typologie und sozialem Realismus angesiedelt waren. Die Werke der beiden populärsten Schriftsteller des 19. Jahrhunderts, Balzac und Dickens, waren pressegrafisch inspiriert und waren in der Folge wiederum prägend für die Entwicklung des Bildjournalismus.

Réalisme et caricature

Bien que les procédés rétiniens de reproduction fussent depuis longtemps populaires grâce à l'utilisation de la *camera obscura* et que les premières expériences photographiques eussent aussi déjà été effectuées, le documentarisme visuel ne joua qu'un rôle marginal au cours de la phase initiale de la presse populaire illustrée. L'engouement pour le journalisme illustré est venu d'une autre direction. Selon la conviction de William Blanchard Jerrold, l'un des experts en la matière, il est « sans conteste l'œuvre de nos caricaturistes » (Jerrold 1882, p. 93). Il entendait par là la tradition de satire sociale et ses représentations schématiques de caractères. À ses débuts, le dessin de presse était imprégné du courant de médiatisation physiognomonique que William Hogarth, entre autres, avait déclenché. Ce n'est pas par hasard que la majorité des termes que l'on associe aux implications idéologiques de telles classifications sociales et ethniques en fonction des caractéristiques physiques sont empruntés au secteur du dessin de presse de masse illustrée : types, stéréotypes et clichés ; ils furent façonnés et inculqués pendant cette phase précoce. Les codes du journalisme illustré naissant étaient rigoureux et orientés vers la confrontation. Ils s'articulèrent comme résistance contre les répressions de la Restauration instaurée à l'échelle européenne et dans le contexte tendu des conflits sociaux qui, suite à la révolution industrielle, éclatèrent d'abord en Angleterre, puis en France. C'est un pamphlet réformateur et radical sur une manifestation d'ouvriers réprimée dans le sang à Manchester – *The Political House that Jack Built* conçu par William Hone et George Cruikshank – qui instaura en 1819 la technique de la gravure

sur bois dans le domaine des médias de masse et inaugura ainsi l'ère du journalisme illustré (ills. p. 76–79). Hone jouissait du statut de héros populaire, parce que, deux ans auparavant, il s'était défendu contre une plainte pour blasphémie et propagation d'écrits séditieux dans un procès retentissant. C'est pourquoi aussi il était largement immunisé contre toute autre accusation du même ordre. La consistance des futures campagnes illustrées qu'il mena contre le régime corrompu du Prince Régent anglais reposait sur les recherches poussées qu'il avait entreprises dans le contexte de son spectaculaire plaidoyer sur l'histoire de la parodie et de la satire en images (voir ill. p. 71).

Les périodiques illégaux et non timbrés des radicaux contribuèrent à promouvoir davantage encore l'essor de la presse illustrée. La tentative des cercles libéraux et loyalistes de briser l'hégémonie médiatique de cette subculture entraîna en 1832 la création du premier magazine illustré à haut tirage, le *Penny Magazine* à vocation à la fois populaire et scientifique. Tandis que la démocratisation du savoir s'était établie en Angleterre dans le cadre d'une large discussion publique, elle restait en France le projet d'une élite restreinte. Le comte de Saint-Simon, dont l'idéologie progressiste avait motivé un grand nombre d'éditeurs de presse, avait au début du siècle appliqué le concept militaire d'avant-garde (première ligne de l'armée) à la sphère culturelle.

À ses débuts, le mouvement de caricature français était complètement orienté vers l'avant-garde. Il vit le jour dans le club élitiste de l'art de l'épopée napoléonienne, dont l'un des tout premiers représentants fut Eugène Delacroix, et devint sous la direction du caricaturiste et éditeur Charles Philipon une

J.J. Grandville

Le Charivari, 1833
Title vignette | Titelvignette |
Vignette de titre
Wood engraving
From: *Le Charivari*, Paris,
24 November 1833

The band of noise-makers are, from left to right: Eugène Forest (lithographer, with violin), Bernard-Romain Julien (lithographer, cymbals), Michel Altaroche (writer, lyre), Gabriel Aubert (publisher, cymbals), Charles Philipon (editor-in-chief and publisher, drum), Honoré Daumier (illustrator, tambourine), Auguste Desperret (lithographer, guitar), Charles-Joseph Traviès (illustrator, bassoon), Grandville (illustrator, transverse flute).

Die versammelten Radaubrüder von links nach rechts: Eugène Forest (Lithograf, mit Geige), Bernard-Romain Julien (Lithograf, Becken), Michel Altaroche (Autor, Leier), Gabriel Aubert (Verleger, Becken), Charles Philipon (Chefredakteur und Verleger, Trommel), Honoré Daumier (Zeichner, Tambourin), Auguste Desperret (Lithograf, Gitarre), Charles-Joseph Traviès (Zeichner, Fagott), Grandville (Zeichner, Querflöte).

Les chahuteurs réunis de gauche à droite : Eugène Forest (lithographe, avec violon), Bernard-Romain Julien (lithographe, cymbales), Michel Altaroche (auteur, lyre), Gabriel Aubert (éditeur, cymbales), Charles Philipon (rédacteur en chef et éditeur, tambour), Honoré Daumier (dessinateur, tambourin), Auguste Desperret (lithographe, guitare), Charles-Joseph Traviès (illustrateur, basson), Grandville (illustrateur, flûte traversière).

entreprise opérant dans un style militaire et luttant contre la politique de restauration de Louis-Philippe, également appelé le roi bourgeois. La guerre que Philipon mena contre Louis-Philippe dans *La Caricature*, son magazine créé en 1830, était calquée sur le modèle de la campagne dirigée par Hone contre le Prince Régent anglais. Ceci devint particulièrement évident quand au cours d'une spectaculaire apparition au tribunal Philipon se défendit contre une plainte pour lèse-majesté en novembre 1831. Comme dans le cas d'Hone, l'effet escompté par les autorités tourna ici aussi en fiasco. La preuve, dessin en main, d'une analogie entre la tête du roi et une poire mûre qu'il put avancer en salle d'audience donna à sa campagne un gigantesque élan. À l'aide d'actions de graffittis d'étudiants et d'affiches en vitrines, l'image de la poire se propagea comme une traînée de poudre et devint le symbole de la bêtise et de la corruption de tout un système politique.

Dans ses campagnes, Philipon misait beaucoup plus sur la force d'argumentation d'une seule image que ne le faisaient les radicaux anglais. Pour lui, le dessin de presse était une prolongation démocratisée de la peinture d'histoire dans des conditions accélérées. Il se référait ainsi à l'art de propagande napoléonien qui avait catapulté la peinture d'histoire continentale dans le présent et avait fait siennes les possibilités étendues de l'image de genre. La caricature était aussi par conséquent un corset beaucoup trop étroit de conception pour saisir l'éclectisme de l'art interventionniste que Philipon présentait dans ses magazines. En faisaient également partie une série de dessins socio-réalistes de la première heure, signés Nicolas-Toussaint Charlet, Edmé-Jean Pigal, Charles-Joseph Traviès, Honoré Daumier et Philippe-Auguste Jeanron, qui avaient ouvert la voie à des artistes comme Jean-François Millet et Gustave Courbet.

Après que la phase de combat républicain de *La Caricature* fut stoppée 1835 par un lot de rigides mesures de censure, Philipon se décida pour une forme inattaquable de la satire sociale dans son journal *Le Charivari*. Ses dessinateurs y adaptaient fréquemment des figures populaires du théâtre de boulevard ou créaient des personnages qui, eux, remportaient de vifs succès sur la scène. La tendance à une spécification sociale et à une classification culmina dans le projet mégalomane d'un panorama de société présenté sous forme de série, que l'ancien collaborateur de Philipon, Honoré de Balzac, avait conçu sous le terme générique de *Comédie humaine*. L'idée originelle d'une analogie entre les groupes sociaux et les races animales était caricaturale et s'inspirait du modèle des illustrations zoomorphes de Grandville, dessinateur pour *La Caricature*. Simultanément, le collègue anglais de Balzac Charles Dickens travaillait, en étroite collaboration avec les illustrateurs Robert Seymour et George Cruikshank et, en référence aux *modern moral subjects* d'Hogarth, à des romans-feuilletons qui s'inscrivaient dans un segment tout à fait analogue entre typologie grotesque et réalisme social. Les œuvres des deux écrivains les plus populaires du XIXe siècle, Balzac et Dickens, étaient sous l'inspiration du dessin de presse, et par conséquent eux aussi déterminants pour l'essor du journalisme illustré.

THE POLITICAL
HOUSE
THAT
JACK BUILT.

" A straw—thrown up to show which way the wind blows."

WITH THIRTEEN CUTS.

The Pen and the Sword.

Tenth Edition.

LONDON:
PRINTED BY AND FOR WILLIAM HONE, LUDGATE HILL.

1819.

ONE SHILLING.

William Hone (concept) & George Cruikshank (del.)

The Political House that Jack Built, London, 1819
Das politische Haus, das Jack gebaut hat
La Maison politique que Jack a construite
Wood engraving

No other work of illustrated propaganda in the 19th century had such a far-reaching and significant effect as this 10-page pamphlet, whose print run reached 100,000 copies soon after it was first published, alongside numerous forgeries and imitations that were also in circulation. The event that provoked its stinging attack on the government at the time was the killing of several of those who had gathered for a peaceful rally at St. Peter's Field near Manchester to demand parliamentary reform and the repeal of the Corn Laws. The bloodbath unleashed by the local militia became known as the Peterloo Massacre, in reference to the Battle of Waterloo.

Kein bildpropagandistisches Werk des 19. Jahrhunderts hatte eine so weitreichende und durchschlagende Wirkung wie dieses zehnseitige Pamphlet, das bereits kurz nach Erscheinen in einer Auflagenhöhe von ca. 100 000 Exemplaren sowie in unzähligen Imitationen und Travestien kursierte. Auslöser

für die bissige Abrechnung mit der amtierenden Regierung war ein Massaker an den Teilnehmern einer friedlichen Massenkundgebung, die sich auf dem St. Peter's Field bei Manchester eingefunden hatten, um für eine Wahlrechtsreform und die Aufhebung von Getreidezöllen zu demonstrieren. Das von örtlichen Militärs angerichtete Blutbad ging in Anspielung auf das Gemetzel von Waterloo als Peterloo-Massaker in die Annalen ein.

Aucune œuvre de propagande du XIXᵉ siècle n'eut un impact aussi étendu et aussi radical que ce pamphlet de dix pages qui, juste après sa publication, circula avec un tirage de quelque 100 000 exemplaires et d'innombrables imitations et contrefaçons. L'événement déclencheur de cet âpre règlement de compte avec le gouvernement en place fut le massacre des participants à une grande manifestation pacifique, qui s'étaient rendus au St. Peter's Field près de Manchester pour réclamer une réforme du droit de vote et l'abolition des droits sur les céréales. Le bain de sang perpétré par les militaires locaux passa dans les annales sous le nom de massacre de Peterloo, allusion à la bataille de Waterloo.

← Title-page | Titelseite | Page de titre

The Duke of Wellington, following his victory in the Battle of Waterloo, had been newly appointed to the Tory government of the day. He is shown throwing his sword into the political balance for the weighty argument it represents, in support of a series of repressive laws and the curtailing of the freedom of opinion.

Der Duke of Wellington, Sieger von Waterloo, war erst kürzlich in die amtierende Tory-Regierung einberufen worden. Als schwerwiegendes Argument wirft er sein Schwert in die politische Waagschale, um ein Bündel repressiver Gesetze zu flankieren und die Meinungsfreiheit auszustechen.

Le duc de Wellington, vainqueur de Waterloo, n'avait été nommé que récemment dans le gouvernement Tory alors en exercice. Il jette son épée comme un argument de poids dans la balance politique afin de soutenir une série de lois répressives et de torpiller la liberté d'opinion.

This Is the House that Jack Built
Das ist das Haus, das Jack gebaut hat
La Maison, que Jack a construite

The constitutional structure built for himself by Everyman Jack was designed originally with freedom and equality placed at the summit. These civil rights had been guaranteed by two of the items in Jack's treasure chest, *Magna Carta* and the *Bill of Rights*.

Das konstitutionelle Gebäude, das sich Jack, der Jedermann, erbaut hat, war ursprünglich auf Freiheit und Gleichheit an der Spitze ausgerichtet. Garantiert waren diese Bürgerrechte durch die Schätze der *Magna Carta* und der *Bill of Rights*.

L'édifice constitutionnel que Jack, Monsieur-tout-le-monde, s'est construit était initialement axé – à son sommet – sur la liberté et l'égalité. Ces droits civiques étaient garantis par les trésors de la *Magna Carta* et du *Bill of Rights*.

The Thing | Das Ding | La Chose

The Thing that will see off the vermin and the government's draconian repression is the printing press.

Das Ding, das dem Pack und den drakonischen Repressionsmaßnahmen der Regierung trotzen wird, ist die Druckerpresse.

La Chose qui bravera la vermine et les mesures de répression draconniennes du gouvernement est la presse d'impression.

The Vermin | Das Pack | La Vermine

Jack's treasure, freedom, is looted by a nasty-looking group of government officials and their henchmen, together with the Manchester magistrate who read the Riot Act during the demonstration.

Jacks Schatz der Freiheit wird von einer sinistren Reihe von Regierungsrepräsentanten und deren Büttel geplündert, darunter auch der Amtsrichter von Manchester.

Le trésor de Jack, la liberté, est saccagé par une sinistre rangée de représentants gouvernementaux et leurs huissiers, dont le juge de première instance de Manchester fait partie.

" A distant age asks where the fabric stood."

THIS IS THE HOUSE THAT JACK BUILT.

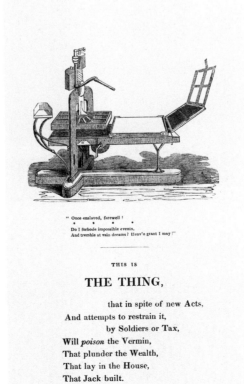

" Once enslaved, farewell !
* * *
Do I forbode impossible events,
And tremble at vain dreams ? Heav'n grant I may !"

THIS IS

THE THING,

that in spite of new Acts,
And attempts to restrain it,
by Soldiers or Tax,
Will *poison* the Vermin,
That plunder the Wealth,
That lay in the House,
That Jack built.

————" A race obscene,
Spawn'd in the muddy beds of Nile, came forth,
Polluting Egypt: gardens, fields, and plains,
Were cover'd with the pest;
The croaking nuisance lurk'd in every nook;
Nor palaces, nor even chambers, 'scap'd;
And the land stank — so num'rous was the fry."

THESE ARE

THE VERMIN

That plunder the Wealth,
That lay in the House,
That Jack built.

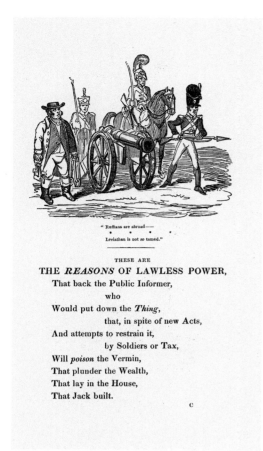

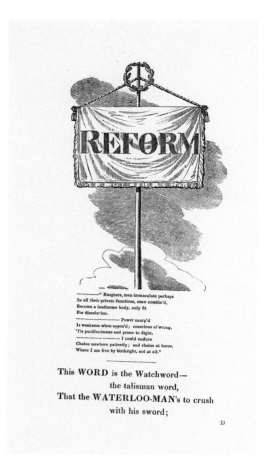

William Hone (concept) & George Cruikshank (del.)

The Reasons of Lawless Power
Die Gründe gesetzloser Macht
Les Raisons d'un pouvoir anarchique

Just as Percy Bysshe Shelley wrote in his contemporaneous poem about the Peterloo Massacre, *The Masque of Anarchy*, Hone accused the Tories in government of a form of lawlessness that could only be sustained by the arguments of state oppression.

Wie Percy Bysshe Shelley in seinem zeitgleichen Poem zum Peterloo-Massaker *The Masque of Anarchy* klagt Hone die amtierende Tory-Regierung einer Form von Gesetzlosigkeit an, die sich allein auf die Argumente staatlicher Gewalt stützen kann.

Comme Percy Bysshe Shelley dans son poème contemporain *The Masque of Anarchy*, Hone accuse le gouvernement Tory en place d'une forme d'anarchie qui ne peut s'appuyer que sur les arguments du pouvoir étatique.

The Dandy of Sixty
Der Dandy von sechzig
Le Dandy de soixante ans

The Prince Regent and future King George IV was much given to lavish pomp and ceremony during his despotic rule, and since he also ran the affairs of state on behalf of his mentally ill father he was a prime target for ridicule. Hone's campaign was the inspiration for Charles Philipon's pictorial satires attacking the "Citizen King" Louis-Philippe, and also Thomas Nast's later campaign against the Tammany Hall organisation in New York.

Der zu exzessivem Pomp und Despotismus neigende Prinzregent und spätere König Georg IV., der in Vertretung seines geistig umnachteten Vaters die Regierungsgeschäfte leitete, war eine bevorzugte Zielscheibe des Spotts. Hones Kampagne inspirierte Charles Philipons Karikaturkrieg gegen Bürgerkönig Louis-Philippe und später auch Thomas Nasts Feldzug gegen die New Yorker Tammany Hall.

Le Prince Régent et futur roi George IV avait un penchant pour la pompe excessive et le despotisme. Il dirigeait les affaires de l'État à la place de son père mentalement détraqué et fut fréquemment la cible de railleries. La campagne d'Hone inspira la guerre caricaturale de Charles Philipon contre le « roi bourgeois » Louis-Philippe ainsi que, plus tard, la campagne de Thomas Nast contre le Tammany Hall à New York.

The Word | Das Wort | Le Mot

"Reform" was the watchword for the Peterloo demonstrators, that was later to be suppressed with brute force by Wellington, the Waterloo Man. More than any other published source, this pamphlet by Hone and Cruikshank made the Peterloo Massacre a landmark in the annals of the radical reform movement and the international labour movement.

„Reform" hieß die magische Parole der Demonstranten von Peterloo, die der Waterloo-Man Wellington künftig mit roher Gewalt unterdrücken sollte. Es war nicht zuletzt der Publizistik von Hone und Cruikshank zu verdanken, dass Peterloo-Massaker zu einem Markstein in den Annalen der radikalen Reformbewegung und der internationalen Arbeiterbewegung wurde.

« Reform », tel était le mot d'ordre magique des manifestants de Peterloo que Wellington, l'homme de Waterloo, devait à l'avenir opprimer avec une implacable brutalité. Ce furent surtout les publications d'Hone et de Cruikshank qui firent du massacre de Peterloo une pierre angulaire dans les annales du mouvement réformiste et du mouvement ouvrier international.

→ *The People | Das Volk | Le Peuple*

The contrast between the caricatural representation of the pompous monarch in *The Dandy of Sixty* and the realistic depiction of the hardship and oppression endured by the common people had its influence 10 years later in the Republican journalism published by Charles Philipon. In place of the Peterloo Massacre, for his Regent Louis-Philippe it was the silk workers' uprisings in Lyon and the massacre in the Rue Transnonain in Paris (ills. pp. 107 t., 119 b.).

Der Kontrast zwischen der karikaturesken Repräsentanz des aufgeblasenen Monarchen im Bild *Der Dandy von sechzig* und einer realistischen Darstellung von Not und Unterdrückung auf Seiten des Volks bestimmte eine Dekade später die republikanische Publizistik von Charles Philipon. Das Peterloo seines Regenten Louis-Philippe waren die Weberaufstände in Lyon und das Massaker in der Rue Transnonain in Paris (Abb. S. 107 o., S. 119 u.).

Dix ans plus tard, le contraste entre la représentation caricaturale du monarque bouffi d'orgueil de l'image *Le Dandy de soixante ans* et une représentation réaliste de la misère et de l'oppression endurées par le peuple caractérise les publications républicaines de Charles Philipon. Les révoltes des canuts de Lyon et le massacre de la rue Transnonain à Paris furent le Peterloo de son souverain Louis-Philippe (ills. p. 107 h., 119 b.).

"Portentous, unexampled, unexplain'd!
——————————— What man seeing this,
And having human feelings, does not blush,
And hang his head, to think himself a man?
——————————— I cannot rest
A silent witness of the headlong rage,
Or heedless folly, by which thousands die——
Bleed gold for Ministers to sport away."

THESE ARE

THE PEOPLE

all tatter'd and torn,

Who curse the day

wherein they were born,

On account of Taxation

too great to be borne,

And pray for relief,

from night to morn :

Who, in vain, Petition

in every form,

Anonymous

The Palace of John Bull, Contrasted with the Poor "House that Jack Built", London, 1820
Der Palast von John Bull gegenüber dem ärmlichen „Haus, das Jack gebaut hat"
Le Palais de John Bull, en contraste avec la pauvre «Maison que Jack a construite»
Hand-coloured copper engravings

Amongst the numerous imitations and plagiarisms of William Hone's pamphlet on the Peterloo Massacre, *The Palace of John Bull* stands out as being a cut above the rest. The contrast between a thriving loyalist England and the failed attempts of the radicals to replace it is emphasised by the use of the detailed engraving work, which was also intended to make it more eye-catching than the cheap letter-press printing of the original.

Unter den unzähligen Nachahmungen und Gegenentwürfen zu William Hones Pamphlet über das Peterloo-Massaker sticht *The Palace of John Bull* hervor. Der Kontrast zwischen einem blühenden loyalistischen England und einer gescheiterten Version der Radikalen wird durch die Verwendung des aufwendigen Tiefdrucks unterstrichen, der sich medial vom billigen Hochdruck des Originals abheben soll.

The Palace of John Bull se démarque de la masse ces innombrables imitations et plagiats du pamphlet sur le massacre de Peterloo réalisé par William Hone. Le contraste entre une Angleterre ardemment loyaliste et une version ratée des Radicaux est souligné par le choix d'une gravure en creux élaborée, notamment pour se distinguer de la gravure en relief bon marché de l'original.

THE
PALACE OF JOHN BULL,
Contrasted
WITH
THE POOR "HOUSE THAT JACK BUILT."

" Answer a Fool according to his Folly."—KING SOLOMON.
" England, with all thy Faults I love thee still."—COWPER.

WITH EIGHT COPPER-PLATES:

Radical Balance—The Palace—Radical Reform—England's Pyramid—
Radical's Pyramid—Radical's Triumph—Ruffian Assemblies
—Vessel of State, and Radical Lugger.

THE RADICAL BALANCE

First see the fair SCALES of JUSTICE suspended:
Shall a FEATHER outweigh what BRITONS defended?
The Sceptre and Crown,– and bless'd inspired Word:
Our Laws of renown,– and Justices' Sword.

London,
PUBLISHED BY G. GREENLAND, 3, FINSBURY-PLACE;
AND SOLD BY ALL BOOKSELLERS.
PRINTED BY C. HAZARD, 50, BEECH-STREET.
1820.

THE RADICALS' FINAL TRIUMPH.

The Radical topsy-turvey Pyramid breaking

By the cumberous load, the walls are all crush'd.   *Heav'n thundering above–Hell yawning beneath,*
And Jack and his rabble, to silence are hushed.   *With a curse on their folly they sink deep in death.*

" Touch'd with the torch the train,
'Tis fir'd
Spire, vaults, the shrine, the spoil, the slain,
The *Radical* victors, the *Luddite* band,
All that of living or dead remain
Hurl'd on high with the shiver'd fane
In one wild roar expir'd!"   LORD BYRON.

15

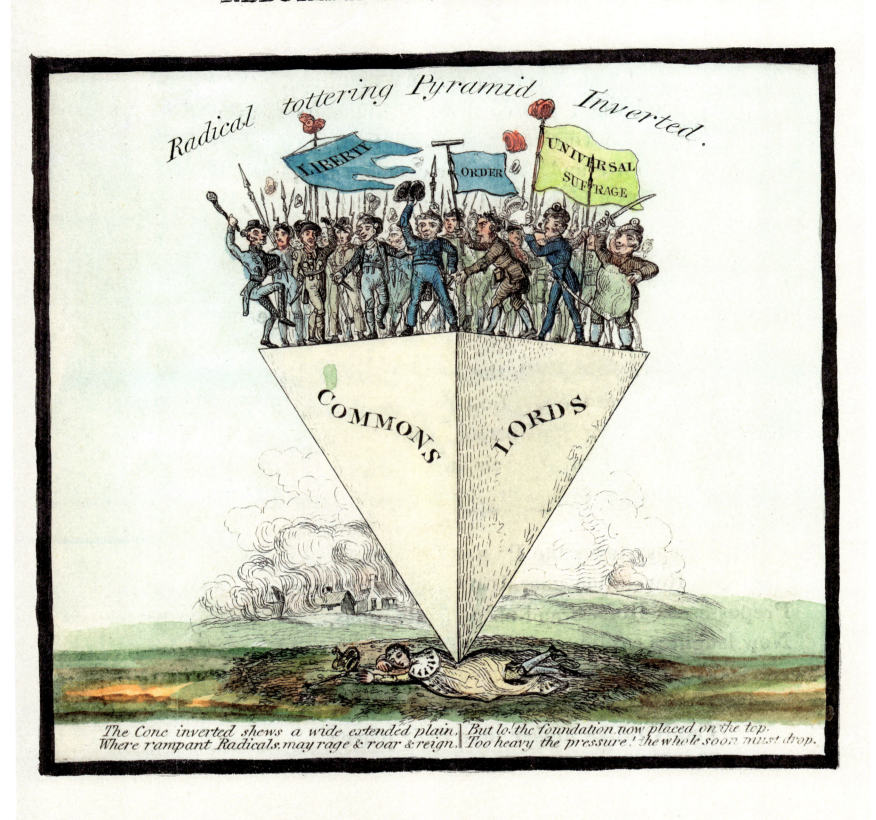

The Cone inverted shews a wide extended plain, | But lo! the foundation now placed on the top.
Where rampant Radicals, may rage & roar & reign. | Too heavy the pressure! the whole soon must drop.

" He started up with more of fear
Than if an armed foe were near.
God of my fathers! what is here?"

LORD BYRON.

14

BRIDGE-STREET GANG.

" The Freeborn Englishman."

William Hone (concept) & George Cruikshank (del.)

The Freeborn Englishman, 1821
Der frei geborene Engländer | L'Anglais né libre
A page from the newspaper parody | Eine Seite aus der
Zeitungsparodie | Un page de la parodie de journal
A Slap at Slop and the Bridge-street Gang
Wood engraving
From: William Hone, *Facetiae and Miscellanies,*
London, 1827

William Hone and George Cruikshank's caricature
of "The Freeborn Englishman", who stands gagged and
shackled by the oppressive laws of the Six Acts, can
be traced back to an illustration from the group associated with the early English radical and proto-communist
Thomas Spence, who was sent to prison on several
occasions. The portrait of Arthur Thistlewood, a follower
of Spence's, was used for the French version of this
image (bottom).

William Hones und George Cruikshanks Karikatur des
„frei geborenen Engländers", der mundtot unter den
Knebelgesetzen der *Six Acts* vegetiert, geht auf einen
Cartoon aus dem Umkreis des mehrfach inhaftierten
englischen Frühkommunisten Thomas Spence zurück.
In die französische Version (unten) ist das Porträt des
Spenceaners Arthur Thistlewood eingearbeitet.

La parodie faite par William Hone et George Cruikshank
de «L'Anglais né libre», bâillonné et végétant sous les
lois oppressives des *Six Acts*, est une référence à un
dessin humoristique issu du cercle entourant Thomas
Spence, communiste anglais de la première heure, qui
fut plusieurs fois incarcéré. C'est le portrait d'Arthur
Thistlewood, disciple de Spence, qui transparaît dans
la version française (en bas).

Voici l'Anglais.

L'ANGLAIS NÉ LIBRE.

Anonymous

*Here is the Freeborn Englishman
(Arthur Thistlewood), c.* 1821
Hier der frei geborene Engländer
Voici l'Anglais, né libre
Etching with aquatint

William Hone (concept) & George Cruikshank (del.)

A Slap at Slop and the Bridge-street Gang, London, 1821
Wood engravings
London, The British Library

This newspaper parody was designed to mock the loyalist line of John Stoddart, the editor of *The Times*, who is identified with the incompetent Dr. Slop from Lawrence Sterne's *Tristram Shandy*. However, in using wood engravings for its illustrations it was not following in the tradition of an existing format but instead anticipating later satirical illustrated magazines such as *Figaro in London* or *Punch*.

Die Zeitungsparodie zielte auf den loyalistischen Kurs des Verlegers der *Times*, John Stoddart, der mit dem nichtsnutzigen Dr. Slop aus Lawrence Sternes *Tristram Shandy* identifiziert wird. Mit ihren holzgravierten Abbildungen bezog sie sich allerdings nicht auf ein existierendes Format, sondern antizipierte vielmehr zukünftige satirische Illustrierte wie *Figaro in London* oder *Punch*.

La parodie de journal visait la position loyaliste de John Stoddart, l'éditeur du *Times*, ici assimilé au vaurien Dr. Slop du *Tristram Shandy* de Lawrence Sterne. Toutefois, avec ses illustrations gravées sur bois elle ne se réfère pas à un format déjà existant, mais anticipait plutôt des magazines satiriques futurs comme *Figaro in London* ou *Punch*.

Le Supplice

Géricault (Lh.)
le N°140. du Catalogue de Mr Clément

Théodore Géricault

The Gallows, London, c. 1820
Der Galgen | *Le Supplice*
Chalk with wash
Musée des Beaux-Arts de Rouen

The reformer Thomas Spence was one of the most influential figures in the English radical movement. While Théodore Géricault was in London early in 1820 he was able to sketch the execution of a group of Spence's followers, including Arthur Thistlewood, who had plotted to murder the cabinet in retaliation for the Peterloo Massacre. The execution even led to riots in Paris.

Der Landreformer Thomas Spence war einer der einflussreichsten Vertreter des britischen Radikalismus. Als Théodore Géricault Anfang 1820 in London zeichnete, konnte er die Exekution einer Gruppe von Spenceanern dokumentieren, darunter Arthur Thistlewood, die in Vergeltung für das Peterloo-Massaker einen Anschlag auf das englische Kabinett geplant hatten. Die Hinrichtung löste auch in Paris Unruhen aus.

Le réformateur politique Thomas Spence fut l'une des figures les plus influentes du radicalisme britannique. Lorsque Théodore Géricault dessinait à Londres au début de 1820, il put documenter l'exécution d'un groupe d'adeptes de Spence, dont faisait partie Arthur Thistlewood qui avait fomenté une attaque du Cabinet anglais en représailles au massacre de Peterloo. À Paris aussi cette exécution provoqua des troubles.

Théodore Géricault & Charles Joseph Hullmandel (lith.)

↓ *Pity the Sorrows of a Poor
Old Man*, 1821
*Habt Erbarmen mit den Sorgen
eines armen alten Mannes*
*Ayez pitié des chagrins d'un pauvre
vieillard*
Lithograph
From: Théodore Géricault, *Various
Subjects Drawn from Life and on
Stone*, London, 1821
Paris, École Nationale Supérieure
des Beaux-Arts

→ *The Piper*, 1821
Der Dudelsackspieler
Le Joueur de cornemuse
Lithograph
From: Théodore Géricault, *Various
Subjects Drawn from Life and on
Stone*, London, 1821
Paris, École Nationale Supérieure
des Beaux-Arts

In 1820, Théodore Gericault travelled
to London with his friend, the well-
known illustrator and lithographer
Nicolas Toussaint Charlet, to assess
whether he might be able to find work
there in the print trade. The resulting
project was a series of 12 lithographs
about the great city, which sold well
in London as well as Paris.

1820 hielt sich Théodore Géricault in
London auf, um in Begleitung seines
Freundes, des populären lithografischen Zeichners Nicolas-Toussaint
Charlet, die Möglichkeiten zu sondie-
ren, sich auf dem dortigen Druckgra-
fikmarkt zu etablieren. Das Resultat
war ein aus zwölf Blättern bestehen-
der Großstadtzyklus, der sowohl in
London als auch in Paris erfolgreich
vermarktet werden konnte.

En 1820, Théodore Géricault séjour-
na à Londres en compagnie de son
ami, l'illustrateur lithographe populaire
Nicolas-Toussaint Charlet, afin de
sonder la possibilité de s'établir sur
le marché local de l'illustration imprimée. Il en résulta une série de douze
lithographies sur la grande ville, qui
obtint un vif succès à Londres comme
à Paris.

Following the Coalition Wars against
France, the populations of England's
cities swelled with an army of destitute
soldiers and uprooted commoners.
Géricault's gloomy series of lithographs reveals his close study of
representations of the poor in English
illustrations of the time, which also
had a considerable influence on the
social realism of his friend Nicolas-
Toussaint Charlet.

Die englischen Metropolen waren
nach den Koalitionskriegen gegen
Frankreich von einem Heer mittel-
loser Soldaten und vertriebener Bau-
ern bevölkert. Théodore Géricaults
düsterer Zyklus verrät eine intensive
Auseinandersetzung mit der zeitge-
nössischen englischen Pauperismus-
Grafik, die auch einen beträchtlichen
Einfluss auf das sozialrealistische
Werk seines Freundes Nicolas-
Toussaint Charlet hatte.

Suite aux guerres de coalition dirigées
contre la France napoléonnienne, les
métropoles anglaises étaient peuplées
d'une armée de soldats démunis et de
paysans déracinés. La série particulièrement sombre de Théodore Géricault
témoigne d'une analyse approfondie
de la représentation des pauvres par
le dessin anglais contemporain, lequel
eut par ailleurs une influence considérable sur l'œuvre socio-réaliste de son
ami Nicolas-Toussaint Charlet.

John Thomas Smith (del. & sc.)

Blind Beggar, c. 1816
Blinder Bettler | *Mendiant aveugle*
Etching
From: John Thomas Smith,
*Vagabondiana; or, Anecdotes of
Mendicant Wanderers through
the Streets of London*, London, 1817

The engraver and antiquary John
Thomas Smith was the first artist to
make an extensive study of the social
misery in the lives of those who inha-
bit big cities. He first made sketches,
with his pupil John Constable, of the
hovels in which the poor lived on the
outskirts of London, and then turned
his attention to the beggars and pedlars in the centre of the city.

Der Graveur und Altertumsforscher
John Thomas Smith war der erste
Künstler, der sich intensiv mit der
großstädtischen Sozialmisere auseinandersetzte. Nachdem er zuerst
mit seinem Schüler John Constable
die Hütten der Armen am Stadtrand
Londons gezeichnet hatte, dokumentierte er die Situation der Bettler und
Hausierer im Stadtzentrum.

Le graveur et antiquaire John Thomas
Smith fut le premier artiste à avoir
étudié en profondeur la misère sociale
des grandes villes. Après avoir dessiné les taudis des pauvres à la péri-
phérie de Londres avec son élève
John Constable, il documenta la situation des mendiants et des colporteurs
au centre de la cité.

A Jewish Mendicant, c. 1816
Ein jüdischer Bettler | *Un mendiant juif*
Etching
From: John Thomas Smith,
*Vagabondiana; or, Anecdotes of
Mendicant Wanderers through the
Streets of London*, London, 1817

Smith's research was undertaken
with the extreme objectivity of an
archaeologist of the present, and his
pioneering work had a revolutionary
effect on the development of investigative journalism and urban ethnography. His *Vagabondiana* was widely
distributed, and featured 31 illustrations with commentaries depicting the
different struggles for survival on the
streets of London.

Smith verfolgte in seinen Untersu-
chungen einen sehr sachlichen,
gegenwartsarchäologischen Ansatz,
der sich bahnbrechend auf die Entwicklung des investigativen Journalismus und der urbanen Ethnografie
ausgewirkt hat. Sein weitverbreitetes
Werk *Vagabondiana* enthielt 31 kommentierte Grafiken, die vom Überle-
benskampf auf den Straßen Londons
berichteten.

Tel un archéologue du présent, Smith
poursuivit dans ses recherches une
approche extrêmement objective qui
influença de façon révolutionnaire
l'évolution du journalisme et de l'ethnographie urbaine. Sa publication largement répandue *Vagabondiana* comprenait 31 illustrations commentées,
qui décrivaient la lutte pour la survie
dans les rues de Londres.

William Henry Pyne

→ *Dustmen*, c. 1803
Müllmänner | *Éboueurs*
Stencil-coloured lithograph
From: William Henry Pyne,
The Costume of Great Britain,
London, 1804

The art critic and illustrator William
Henry Pyne had a comparable influence on the social realism of Théodore
Géricault and Nicolas-Toussaint
Charlet as had his fellow artist John
Thomas Smith. Taking the form of
a costume book, his comprehensive
account of working conditions in his
day covered everyone from dustmen
to members of parliament.

Der Kunstkritiker und Zeichner William
Henry Pyne hat auf das sozialrealistische Werk von Théodore Géricault
und Nicolas-Toussaint Charlet in vergleichbarer Weise eingewirkt wie
sein Freund John Thomas Smith. Im
Gewand eines Kostümbuchs hatte
er eine umfassende Darstellung zeitgenössischer Arbeitsverhältnisse
geliefert, die vom Müllmann bis zum
Parlamentarier reichte.

Le critique d'art et illustrateur William
Henry Pyne influença l'œuvre socio-
réaliste de Théodore Géricault et de
Nicolas-Toussaint Charlet de manière
analogue à son ami John Thomas
Smith. Sous la forme d'un recueil de
costumes, il dressa un portrait
exhaustif des conditions de travail
contemporaines allant de l'éboueur
au parlementaire.

Théodore Géricault & Godefroy Engelmann (lith.)

Dustmen, Paris, 1823
Die Müllmänner | Les Boueux
Lithograph
New York, Brooklyn Museum

Théodore Géricault's dark social realism was part of a culture of Republican resistance to the Bourbon Restoration, which had begun to take form in the schools of history painting under Napoleon. The studio where Baron Gros taught painting, and where Géricault's friend Nicolas Toussaint Charlet became so influential, was kept under observation by the authorities on the grounds of the security of the state.

Théodore Géricaults düsterer Sozialrealismus war Teil einer Kultur des republikanischen Widerstands gegen die bourbonische Restauration, die sich in den Schulen der napoleonischen Historienmalerei zu formieren begann. Das Lehrstudio des Barons Gros, in dem sein Freund Nicolas-Toussaint Charlet eine dominierende Rolle spielte, stand unter Beobachtung des Staatsschutzes.

Le sombre réalisme social de Théodore Géricault faisait partie d'une culture de la résistance républicaine à la Restauration des Bourbons, qui commença à prendre forme dans les écoles de la peinture d'histoire napoléonienne. L'atelier de formation du baron Gros, au sein duquel son ami Nicolas-Toussaint Charlet joua un rôle dominant, fut mis sous observation par les organes de protection de l'État.

Nicolas-Toussaint Charlet & Charles Motte (lith.)

Become a Bricklayer, if that's what You Do Best!, c. 1821
Werden Sie doch lieber Maurer, wenn das Ihr Talent ist!
Soyez plutôt maçon, si c'est votre talent!
Lithograph

The workman's remark is addressed to the two noblemen in the background seen passing beside a historical arched opening while laden with their ministerial portfolios. This direct attack on the politics of the Restoration was the work of the same printer who had produced the confrontational caricatures of Charlet's young admirer Eugène Delacroix (ills. p. 90 t. and b.).

Der Spruch des Arbeiters ist auf die beiden Adligen im Hintergrund gemünzt, die mit ihren ministerialen Portefeuilles auf ein antiquiertes Portal zustreben. Der Frontalangriff auf die Politik der Restauration wurde vom gleichen Drucker verantwortet, der sich auch der oppositionellen Karikaturen von Charlets jungem Bewunderer Eugène Delacroix annahm (Abb. S. 90 o. und u.).

La phrase lancée par l'ouvrier s'adresse aux deux aristocrates à l'arrière-plan qui, munis de leurs serviettes de ministres, se dirigent vers un portail de style classique. L'attaque frontale à l'égard de la politique menée sous la Restauration est due au même imprimeur que celui qui assuma les caricatures engagées du jeune admirateur de Charlet, Eugène Delacroix (ills. p. 90 h. et b.).

Nicolas-Toussaint Charlet (del. & lith.)

↓ *Form before Colour*, 1823
Die Form vor der Farbe
La Forme avant la Couleur
Lithograph
From: Nicolas-Toussaint Charlet,
Croquis lithographiques, Paris, 1823

Notwithstanding the Neoclassical
motto proclaimed by the drunken
sign-painter's apprentice, Nicolas-
Toussaint Charlet's illustration work
was based entirely on tonal values.
This example has something in
common with the tradition of artistic
parody made famous by William
Hogarth, who had also championed
sign painting as an art of the people
in opposition to academic high art.

Entgegen dem klassizistischen Leit-
spruch aus dem Mund des angetrun-
kenen Schildermalergehilfens setzte
Nicolas-Toussaint Charlets Zeichen-
kunst ganz auf Tonwerte. Das Blatt
bewegt sich in der kunstparodistischen Tradition eines William Hogarth,
der die Schildermalerei als plebeji-
sche Gegenkunst zum Akademismus
in Stellung gebracht hatte.

À l'inverse de la devise néo-classique
clamée par l'apprenti peintre d'enseignes éméché, l'art de Nicolas-
Toussaint Charlet illustrateur s'ap-
puyait sur des valeurs tonales. Cette
planche s'inscrit dans la tradition
de parodie artistique d'un William
Hogarth, qui avait placé la peinture
d'enseignes comme une forme
d'art plébéienne par opposition à
l'académisme.

→ *What a Beautiful Arm! It's like an
Arm from Antiquity!*, 1823
*Der schöne Arm! Das ist wie
die Antike!*
Le beau bras! C'est comme l'antique!
Lithograph

Almost like a prosthesis, the arm of
the gnarled old cobbler is here being
held aloft. Charlet's proletarian
genre art rubbed shoulders with the
unworldly Classical ideal of history
painting, as promoted by his tutor
Antoine-Jean Gros (who was himself
following in the footsteps of Jacques-
Louis David), and who together paved
the way for the realism of Gustave
Courbet.

Wie eine Prothese hält die verwachse-
ne Gestalt des alten Flickschusters
den eigenen Arm in der Hand. Nicolas-Toussaint Charlets proletarische
Genrekunst rieb sich am weltfernen
klassischen Ideal einer Historienmalerei, die von seinem Lehrer Antoine-
Jean Gros in der Nachfolge Jacques-
Louis Davids propagiert wurde, und
bereitete damit dem Realimus Gustave
Courbets den Boden.

Telle une prothèse, la silhouette défor-
mée du vieux cordonnier tient dans sa
main son propre bras. Le genre artistique prolétarien de Nicolas-Toussaint
Charlet se frottait à l'idéal classique
et éloigné de la réalité d'une peinture
d'histoire, que propageait son professeur Antoine-Jean Gros à l'instar de
Jacques-Louis David, et ouvrait ainsi la
voie au réalisme de Gustave Courbet.

Le beau bras! C'est comme l'antique!

La Forme avant la Couleur!

Litho. de C. Motte, R. des marais.

Les Ecrevisses à Longchamps.

Miroir (Journal).

Lithog: de C. Motte

Le Déménagement.

N.º 1. Maison à louer.
   2. Pain-de-Sucre.
   3. Une Mazure.
   4. La Chaise.
   5. d'Outre-zèle.

6. Cadet-Roussel.
7. un Viellard.
8. une Lourde-Oye.
9. un Anonyme.

Miroir (Journal).

Eugène Delacroix & Charles Motte (lith.)

← *The Crayfish at Longchamps*, 1822
Die Flusskrebse bei Longchamps
Les Écrevisses à Longchamps
Lithograph
From: *Le Miroir*, Paris, 4 April 1822
Kupferstichkabinett, Staatliche
Museen zu Berlin

In the same way as Théodore
Géricault, Eugène Delacroix used his
art for journalistic ends, and it is little
surprise therefore that he became
successful as a political caricaturist.
In this example the subject is a fundamental ideological conflict, in which
the liberal faction is seen to be moving along with the current of the times
while the powerful ultra-royalists,
walking backwards with the crayfish,
are heading off in their own direction.

Eugène Delacroix verfolgte wie
Théodore Géricault ein journalisti-
sches Ideal von Kunst. Es verwundert
daher kaum, dass er als politischer
Karikaturist reüssierte. Hier visualisiert er einen fundamentalen ideologischen Konflikt. Während die liberalen
Kräfte dem Strom der Zeit folgen, hat
sich die mächtige Fraktion der Ultra-
royalisten mit ihrer krebsartigen Rück-
schrittlichkeit ins Abseits verirrt.

Tout comme Théodore Géricault,
Eugène Delacroix poursuivait un idéal
artistique journalistique. Il n'est donc
guère étonnant qu'il réussit comme
caricaturiste politique. Il illustra ici un
conflit idéologique fondamental. Tandis que les forces libérales suivent
le courant de l'époque, la puissante
fraction des ultra-royalistes a pris la
tangente à la manière d'écrevisses
marchant à reculons.

↙ *The Censors Moving House*, 1822
Der Umzug der Zensur
Le Déménagement de la Censure
Lithograph
From: *Le Miroir*, Paris,
11 February 1822
Kupferstichkabinett, Staatliche
Museen zu Berlin

A phase of liberalisation swept in
during the more balanced reign of
Louis XVIII, and this caricature
expresses the hope that censorship
would at last be abolished. However,
shortly after it was published prospects for the future grew dark once
again when Louis's reactionary brother Charles X became king.

Unter der ausgleichenden Herrschaft
von Ludwig XVIII. gab es eine Phase
der Liberalisierung. Die Karikatur gibt
der Hoffnung Ausdruck, dass die Zensur damit endgültig aufgehoben wird.
Kurze Zeit nach der Veröffentlichung
verfinsterten sich die Aussichten
allerdings wieder unter dem Regime
seines reaktionären Bruders Karl X.

Sous le règne équilibré de Louis XVIII
survint une phase de libéralisation.
Cette caricature exprime l'espoir que
la censure sera définitivement suppri-
mée. Cependant, peu après sa publication, la perspective s'assombrit à
nouveau sous la férule de Charles X,
son frère réactionnaire.

Le baume d'acier?

Louis-Léopold Boilly & François-Séraphin Delpech (lith.)

The Dentist's Forceps, 1823
Der Trost des Stahls | *Le Baume d'acier*
Lithograph
From: Louis-Léopold Boilly, *Recueil
de grimaces*, Paris, 1823

The well-regarded Neoclassical genre
painter Louis-Léopold Boilly laid
the foundations for the popularity of
portrait caricature in France with his
series of 97 illustrations of people
depicted with various different grimaces, which were published at irregular
intervals between 1823 and 1828.

Der beliebte klassizistische Genre-
maler Louis-Léopold Boilly legte mit
einer aus 97 Blättern bestehenden
Serie von Grimassendarstellungen,
die er in loser Folge zwischen 1823
und 1828 publizierte, die Grundlage
für die Popularität der Porträtkarikatur
in Frankreich.

Louis-Léopold Boilly, peintre de genre
néo-classique très apprécié, posa les
fondements de la popularité de la
caricature de portrait avec une série
composée de 97 planches figurant
des représentations de grimaces, qu'il
publia à intervalles irréguliers entre
1823 et 1828.

Époux parisiens.   N.°3.

Une Visite au Protecteur.

Charles Philipon & Joseph Langlumé (lith.)

Visiting the Guardian, 1825
Ein Besuch beim Wohltäter
Une Visite au protecteur
Lithograph
From: Charles Philipon, *Époux
parisiens*, no. 3, Paris, 1825

Before Charles Philipon became the
driving force of the caricature movement in France with the founding of
the Aubert publishing house in 1829,
he himself had worked as a freelance
illustrator. This print shows him as a
shrewd observer of the etiquette of
relationships amongst the bourgeoisie,
and the studies he made in this series
appeared at the same time as the literary sketches on similar themes written by his friend Honoré de Balzac.

Bevor Charles Philipon 1829 mit der
Gründung des Verlagshauses Aubert
zum Motor der französischen Karikaturbewegung wurde, betätigte er sich
einige Jahre als freier Illustrator. Das
Blatt zeigt ihn als pointierten Beob-
achter bürgerlicher Beziehungsmuster.
Diese Studien entstanden zeitgleich
mit thematisch verwandten literarischen Skizzen seines Freundes
Honoré de Balzac.

Avant que Charles Philipon ne
devienne le moteur du mouvement
caricaturiste français en fondant la
maison d'édition Aubert en 1829, il
travailla plusieurs années comme illustrateur indépendant. Cette planche
le représente comme un observateur
sagace des modèles de relations bourgeois. Ces études virent le jour en
même temps que les esquisses littéraires de son ami Honoré de Balzac,
qui traitaient de thèmes analogues.

William Heath (del. & sc.)

French Expedition against Algiers – New Publications: Musick, 1830
Französische Expedition gegen Algier – Neuerscheinungen: Musick
Expédition française contre Alger – Nouvelles publications : Musique
Etching
From: Thomas McLean (ed.), *The Looking Glass*, vol. 1, no. 5,
London, May 1830

While he was staying in Glasgow for work, the London illustrator William Heath launched the very first magazine of caricatures, *The Glasgow Looking Glass*, at the early date of 1825. When he returned he then engraved the first issues of the London edition of this satirical magazine, the fifth issue of which featured a comment on the French invasion of Algeria.

Bereits 1825 hatte der Londoner Illustrator William Heath bei einem Arbeitsaufenthalt in Glasgow mit dem *The Glasgow Looking Glass* das allererste Karikaturmagazin begründet. Nach seiner Rückkehr radierte er dann die ersten Nummern der Londoner Ausgabe. Der satirische Weltspiegel Nr. 5 enthält einen Kommentar zur französischen Invasion Algeriens.

Dès 1825, lors d'un séjour de travail à Glasgow, l'illustrateur londonien William Heath avait fondé le tout premier magazine de caricatures, *The Glasgow Looking Glass*. Après son retour, il grava alors les premiers numéros de l'édition londonienne. La revue mondiale satirique no 5 contient un commentaire sur l'invasion française en Algérie.

Robert Seymour (del. & lith.)

John Bull and the Bread Riots of 1830
John Bull und die Brotunruhen von 1830
John Bull et les émeutes du pain de 1830
Lithograph
From: Thomas McLean (ed.), *The Looking Glass*, vol. 1, no. 12,
London, December 1830

Despite the fact that he died when he was still only young, Robert Seymour was considered the most important English caricaturist apart from George Cruikshank and was much copied by his fellow artists in France. The expressive image of his times he created here presents a depressing view of living conditions in England in the person of a down-at-heel John Bull: a number of reforms are waiting to be dealt with and social tensions are boiling over.

Der früh verstorbene Robert Seymour galt als bedeutendster englischer Karikaturist neben George Cruikshank, er wurde viel kopiert, auch von seinen französischen Kollegen. Das ausdrucksstarke Zeitbild, das er von den englischen Verhältnissen in der Gestalt eines abgewrackten John Bull entwirft, ist deprimierend: Der Reformstau ist enorm, und die sozialen Spannungen sind am Siedepunkt.

Robert Seymour, qui mourut jeune, était considéré comme le caricaturiste le plus important aux côtés de George Cruikshank. Il fut maintes fois copié, y compris par ses homologues français. Le tableau expressif qu'il dresse des conditions de vie en Angleterre en la personne d'un miteux John Bull est déprimant : le besoin de réformes est immense, et les tensions sociales au bord de l'explosion.

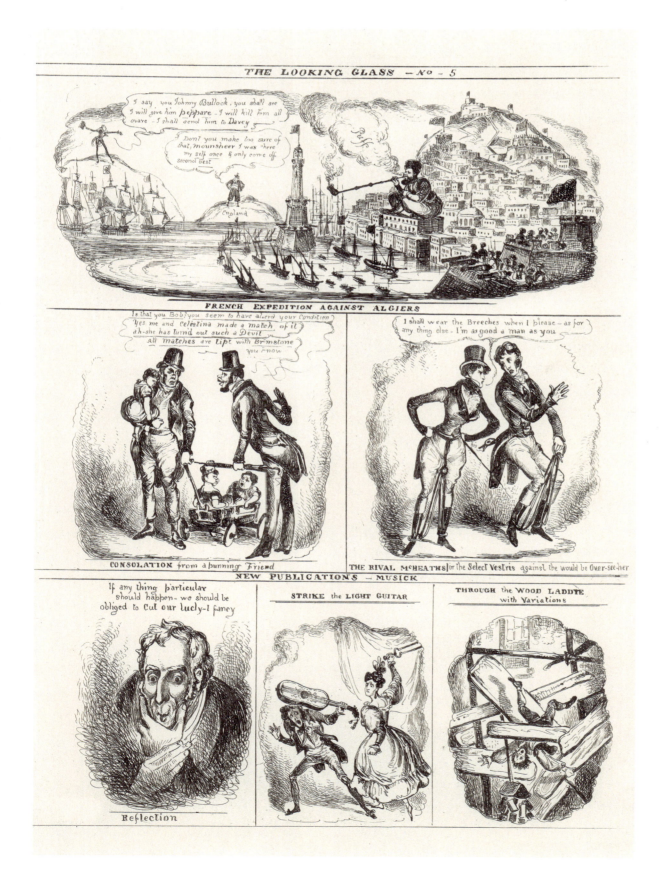

Anonymous & Joseph Langlumé (lith.)

Run along You Stupid Fellow, I'm Thirty-three Million Times Stronger than You Are,
Paris, 21 August 1830
Wirst du so dumm sein, ich bin dreiund-dreißig Millionen mal stärker als du
Vas-t'en donc imbécille, je suis trente trois millions de fois fort que toi
Hand-coloured lithograph

The hollow threats of King Charles X against the forces of the July Revolution seem ridiculous in relation to the real balance of power. In the tradition of Honoré Daumier's adaptations of scale, the motif of a gigantic embodiment of the sovereignty of the people became a recurrent theme in socialist illustrations.

Die Drohgebärden von König Karl X. gegenüber den Juliaufständischen wirken lächerlich in Anbetracht der wahren Machtverhältnisse. Über die Adaptionen

von Honoré Daumier wurde dieses Motiv einer gigantischen Verkörperung der Volkssouveränität zu einem zentralen Topos sozialistischer Grafik.

Les gestes menaçants du roi Charles X à l'égard des révolutionnaires de Juillet paraissent ridicules en comparaison des réels rapports de force. À travers les adaptations d'Honoré Daumier, ce motif d'une incarnation massive de la souveraineté du peuple devint un thème central de l'imagerie socialiste.

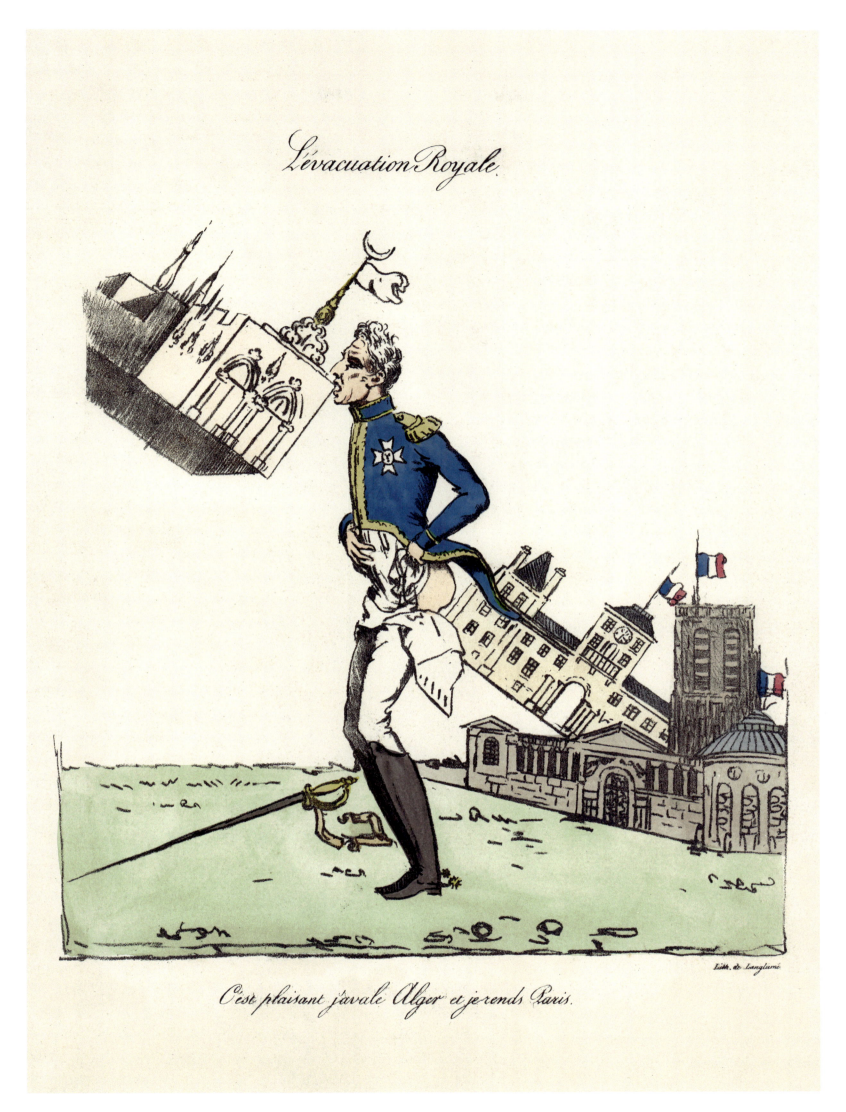

L'évacuation Royale

C'est plaisant j'avale Alger et je rends Paris.

Lith. de Langlumé

Anonymous & Joseph Langlumé (lith.)

The Royal Evacuation. Here's a Pretty Pass, I'll Eat up Algiers and Excrete Paris, Paris, 1830
Königliche Entleerung. Ein Spass, Algier zu verschlingen und Paris abzugeben
L'évacuation royale. C'est plaisant j'avale Alger et je rends Paris
Stencil-coloured lithograph

Shortly after Charles X, the last of the Bourbon rulers, had annexed Algiers at the end of June 1830, he lost the Palais-Royal in the July Revolution. Faecal jokes are some of the oldest and most effective techniques used in political caricature.

Kurz nachdem sich der letzte Bourbonenherrscher Karl X. Ende Juni 1830 Algier einverleibt hatte, kam ihm auch schon im Verlauf der Julirevolution sein Palais-Royal abhanden. Fäkale Verspottung gehört zu den ältesten und wirksamsten Techniken der politischen Karikatur.

Peu après que Charles X, le dernier Bourbon, eut annexé Alger à la fin du mois de juin 1830, il perdit son Palais-Royal au cours de la révolution de Juillet. Le sarcasme de nature fécale était l'une des techniques les plus anciennes et les plus effectives de la caricature politique.

PI. XLIV.   T. 3

Habit de Casimir, Boutons pareils — Cravatte de Satin,
Chemise de Batiste plissée à larges plis.

L'Administration de la Mode est Rue du Helder, Nᵒ 25.

Paul Gavarni & Vittore Pedretti (sc.)

A Kerseymere Suit with Self-covered Buttons, with Satin Cravat and Wide-pleated Cambric Shirt, 1830
Wolljackett aus Kasimir mit überzogenen Knöpfen – Satinkrawatte mit plissiertem Batisthemd
Habit de Casimir, Boutons pareils – Cravatte de satin, Chemise de Batiste plissée à larges plis
Stencil-coloured steel engraving
From: *La Mode,* Paris, 1830
Paris, Bibliothèque nationale de France

Paris's reputation as the fashion capital of the world can be traced back to the large number of fashion magazines that were first published at the start of the July Monarchy, in the new spirit of economic liberalism. With his outstanding work for one of the main such magazines, *La Mode,* Paul Gavarni established himself as the most important illustrator of genre scenes since Nicolas Toussaint Charlet.

Der Ruf von Paris als Hauptstadt der Mode geht auf die Gründung einer Vielzahl von Modejournalen zu Beginn der wirtschaftsliberalen Julimonarchie zurück. Mit seinen herausragenden Arbeiten für das führende Magazin *La Mode* begründete Paul Gavarni seine steile Karriere als wichtigster französischer Genregrafiker nach Nicolas-Toussaint Charlet.

La renommée de Paris comme capitale de la mode est due à la création d'un grand nombre de journaux de mode au début de la monarchie de Juillet, empreinte de libéralisme économique. Grâce à ses excellents travaux pour la grande revue *La Mode,* Paul Gavarni s'imposa au cours de sa fulgurante carrière comme le plus important dessinateur de scènes de genre après Nicolas-Toussaint Charlet.

La Mode.

Gravé d'après Gavarni par Trueb.

Toilette Composée.

Paul Gavarni & Trueb (sc.)

Morning Dress, 1830
Vormittagskombination
Toilette composée
Stencil-coloured steel engraving
From: *La Mode*, Paris, 1830

J.J. Grandville, Michel Delaporte & Joseph Langlumé (lith.)

The Bacchanalia of 1831
Die Bacchanalien von 1831
Les Bacchanales de 1831
Plates 32 & 33
Stencil-coloured lithographs
From: *La Caricature*, Paris, 17 February 1831

The idea of a series of illustrations showing groups of people in different costumes seems originally to have been Charles Philipon's. His first experience of political activism occurred during the carnival in his home town of Lyon, when he was arrested for staging a mock funeral. The accompanying text for these plates was written by Honoré de Balzac, although he left the magazine in the same month they appeared. In the parade of figures from *La Caricature*, fantastic characters such as the symbolic jester mingle with significant individuals associated with the July Monarchy. These include the "Citizen King" Louis-Philippe, who is glancing furtively at the costume of his predecessor, who ruled as an absolute monarch; in fact, Louis-Philippe's increasingly repressive policies meant he soon followed in the same footsteps.

Die Konzeption des kostümierten Bilderreigens geht wohl auf Charles Philipon zurück. Der hatte erste Erfahrungen mit politischem Aktionismus während des Karnevals in seiner Heimatstadt Lyon gesammelt. Wegen einer inszenierten Bestattung war er damals inhaftiert worden. Der Begleittext der Abbildung stammt von Honoré de Balzac, der das Blatt allerdings im gleichen Monat noch verließ. Fantastische Gestalten wie die närrische Symbolfigur von *La Caricature* wechseln sich ab mit führenden Repräsentanten der Julimonarchie, darunter auch Bürgerkönig Louis-Philippe. Verstohlen schaut er auf das Kostüm seines absolutistischen Vorgängers, und tatsächlich sollte er schon bald mit seiner zunehmenden Repressionspolitik in dessen Fußstapfen treten.

Le concept de séries d'images en costumes remonte sans doute à Charles Philipon. Il avait fait ses premières armes avec l'activisme politique pendant le carnaval dans sa ville natale de Lyon. Il fut emprisonné à l'époque pour avoir mis en scène un enterrement. Le texte qui l'accompagne est signé Honoré de Balzac, qui toutefois quitta le journal au cours du même mois. Des figures fantastiques, tel le personnage symbolique du bouffon dans *La Caricature* alternent avec des représentants importants de la monarchie de Juillet, dont Louis-Philippe le «roi bourgeois». Il regarde furtivement le costume de son prédécesseur absolutiste, dont il suivra bientôt les traces avec sa politique de plus en plus répressive.

J.J. Grandville, Michel Delaporte & Joseph Langlumé (lith.)

The Third Restoration, 1830
Die dritte Restauration | *3ᵉ Restauration*
Lithograph
From: *La Caricature, prospectus*, pl. 1,
Paris, October 1830

This illustration from the brochure announcing
Charles Philipon's new magazine depicts the fear
that Charles X might return from exile and the
country be returned to rule by absolute monarchy.
Grandville's fantastical composition, with its cryptic
symbolism, set the tone for *La Caricature* before it
was superseded in about 1834 by Honoré Daumier's
classic style of exaggerated physiognomies.

Die Grafik der Ankündigungsnummer von Charles
Philipons neuem Magazin visualierte die Furcht vor
einer Rückkehr des geflohenen Karl X. und einem
erneuten Rückfall in den Absolutismus. Die fantastische Kunst Grandvilles war mit ihrer abgründigen
Emblematik tonangebend in *La Caricature*, bis sie
gegen 1834 vom klassisch-physiognomischen Stil
Honoré Daumiers verdrängt wurde.

L'illustration du prospectus annonçant le nouveau
magazine de Charles Philipon décrit la peur d'un
retour de Charles X, alors en exil, et du retour à
l'absolutisme. Avec son symbolisme énigmatique,
la composition fantastique de Grandville donne le
ton dans *La Caricature* avant d'être supplanté vers
1834 par le style classique et physiognomonique
d'Honoré Daumier.

La Caricature (Journal.) N.º 51.

Auguste Raffet (del. & lith.)

The King's Prosecutor, 1831
Königliche Staatsanwaltschaft
Parquet Royal
Stencil-coloured lithograph
From: *La Caricature*, Paris,
28 April 1831

A trio of ultra-royalist lawmakers is in
the process of cutting the thread of
the Republican life of the nation, for
which a large number of people had
died a martyr's death between 1815
and 1822 in resistance to the Restoration. In the same way as Nicolas
Toussaint Charlet and Charles Philipon,
Auguste Raffet had learned his craft
in Baron Gros's studio, and followed in
the tradition of using history painting
to represent the themes of the day.

Ein Trio ultraroyalistischer Juristen ist
gerade dabei, den republikanischen
Lebensfaden der Nation zu zerschnei-
den, für den sich im Widerstand gegen
die Restauration 1815 und 1822
eine Reihe Märtyrer geopfert hatten.
Auguste Raffet war wie Nicolas-
Toussaint Charlet und Charles Philipon
im Lehrstudio von Baron Gros ausgebildet worden und verfolgte die
gleiche Idee einer tagesaktuellen
Historienkunst.

Un trio de juristes ultra-royalistes
coupe le cordon de la vie républicaine
de la nation, pour laquelle un grand
nombre de martyrs s'étaient sacrifiés
en résistant contre la Restauration
entre 1815 et 1822. Auguste Raffet,
tout comme Nicolas-Toussaint Charlet
et Charles Philipon, avait fait son
apprentissage dans l'atelier de formation du baron Gros et poursuivait la
même idée d'une peinture d'histoire
brûlante d'actualité.

Charles Philipon, Michel Delaporte & Joseph Langlumé (lith.)

↓ *The People's Weapons/Weapons of the Juste Milieu*, 1831
Waffen des Volkes/Waffen des Juste milieu
Armes du Peuple/Armes du juste milieu
Stencil-coloured lithograph
From: *La Caricature*, Paris, 26 May 1831

To mark the occasion when the royal coat of arms was changed, Charles Philipon felt compelled to suggest two designs of his own. Alongside one for the people, with its attributes of manual work and Republican rebellion, he proposed a crest for the ruling liberal-conservative "Juste Milieu" (centre right), consisting of the insignia of petit-bourgeois narrow-mindedness and Imperial arrogance.

Anlässlich der Änderung des königlichen Wappens fühlte sich Charles Philipon berufen, zwei eigene Entwürfe anzubieten. Einem Schild des Volkes, das mit Symbolen eines rebellischen Republikanismus und der Arbeit gespickt ist, stellt er ein Wappen des regierenden liberalkonservativen „Juste milieu" (rechte Mitte) entgegen, das aus Insignien spießiger Borniertheit und imperialer Attitüden besteht.

À l'occasion de la modification du blason royal, Charles Philipon se sentit exhorté à proposer deux esquisses de sa façon. À un écusson du peuple, doté de symboles d'un républicanisme rebelle et du travail, il oppose un écusson du «juste milieu» libéral conservateur alors au pouvoir, composé des insignes du sectarisme petit-bourgeois et de l'arrogance impérialiste.

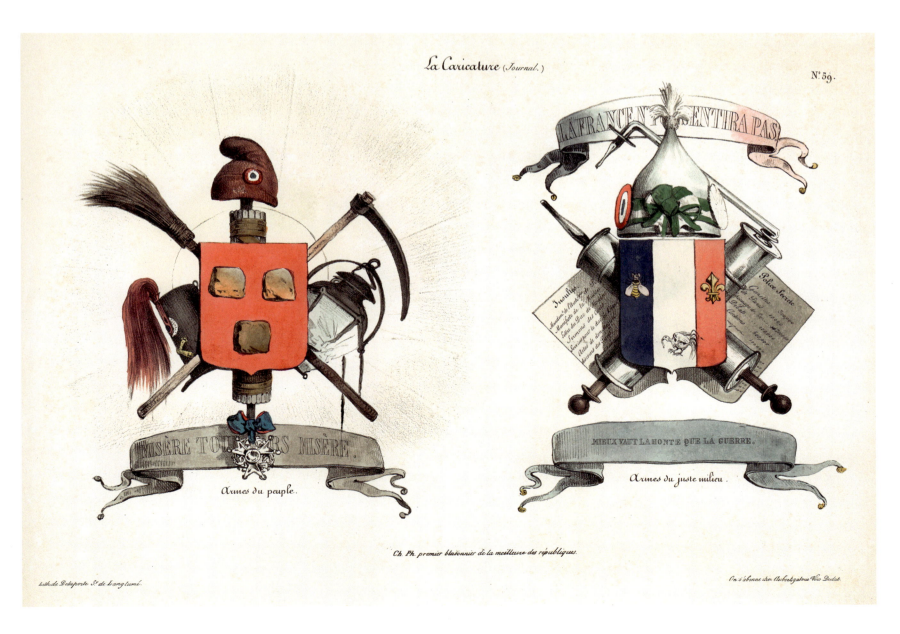

La Caricature (Journal.) Nᵒ 68.

Philippe-Auguste Jeanron & Michel Delaporte (lith.)

He Is Dying of Starvation from Having Lived too long in Hope, 1831
Er stirbt an Erschöpfung, weil er zu lang von der Hoffnung gelebt hat
Il meurt d'inanition pour avoir vécu trop longtemps d'espérances
Lithograph
From: *La Caricature*, Paris, 23 June 1831

The vital force of the fighter in the July Revolution dwindles before the heap of broken promises as they spill out on to the street from the black horn of plenty and the Chamber of Deputies in the distance. Philippe-Auguste Jeanron was a pioneer of early socialist realism, and when he later became director of the Louvre he was instrumental in promoting realism in art.

Der Lebensmut des Julirevolutionärs sackt in sich zusammen angesichts der Flut von gebrochenen Versprechungen, die das schwarze Füllhorn aus der fernen Abgeordnetenkammer auf die Straße ergießt. Philippe-Auguste Jeanron war ein Pionier des frühsozialistischen Realismus. Als späterer Direktor des Louvre war er auch maßgeblich an der Durchsetzung des Realismus in der Kunst beteiligt.

L'énergie vitale du révolutionnaire de Juillet s'effondre devant le torrent de promesses brisées, issues de la lointaine assemblée de députés et que la corne d'abondance noire déverse sur la rue. Philippe-Auguste Jeanron fut un pionnier du réalisme socialiste précoce. Devenu par la suite directeur du Louvre, il a largement contribué à imposer le réalisme dans l'art.

Charles Philipon & Michel Delaporte (lith.)

Dupinade, 1831
Lithograph
From: *La Caricature*, Paris,
30 June 1831

Where Nicolas Toussaint Charlet had counselled ministers of the Restoration to become bricklayers (see ill. p. 88), his pupil Charles Philipon here demonstrates that the same technique can be put to good use in politics, if the bricklayer's name is Louis-Philippe and the mortar used is "Dupinade" (from the verb *duper,* to deceive). This illustration resulted in the famous "Pear Trial" being brought against Philipon, and a separate prison sentence as well (see ill. p. 106).

Nicolas-Toussaint Charlet hatte den Vertretern der Restauration das Maurerhandwerk empfohlen (siehe Abb. S. 88). Sein Schüler Charles Philipon demonstriert hier, dass sich mit dieser Technik politisch gut arbeiten lässt, wenn der Maurer Louis-Philippe und der Mörtel *Dupinade* (nach *duper*: täuschen) heißt. Das Blatt bescherte seinem Autor den berühmten Birnen-Prozess und eine Haftstrafe obendrein (siehe Abb. S. 106).

Nicolas-Toussaint Charlet avait conseillé aux représentants de la Restauration le métier de maçon (voir ill. p. 88). Son élève Charles Philipon démontre ici que cette technique peut bien être utilisée en politique, quand le maçon s'appelle Louis-Philippe, et le mortier *Dupinade* (nom dérivé de *duper*). Cette planche valut à son auteur le fameux « procès de la poire » et une peine de prison en sus (voir ill. p. 106).

La Carica

Lith. de Delaporte.

Peuple affranchi, d
Croise les bras, après

Peuple!... repose to

18,000,000 de liste civile, budjet d'un milliard, impots augmentés, lois de pr
coups de bourse, marchés onéreux, paix honteuse, commerce anéanti, couleu
traitres de l'ex-nation et peuple misérable.

(Coté positif.)

(Journal.)

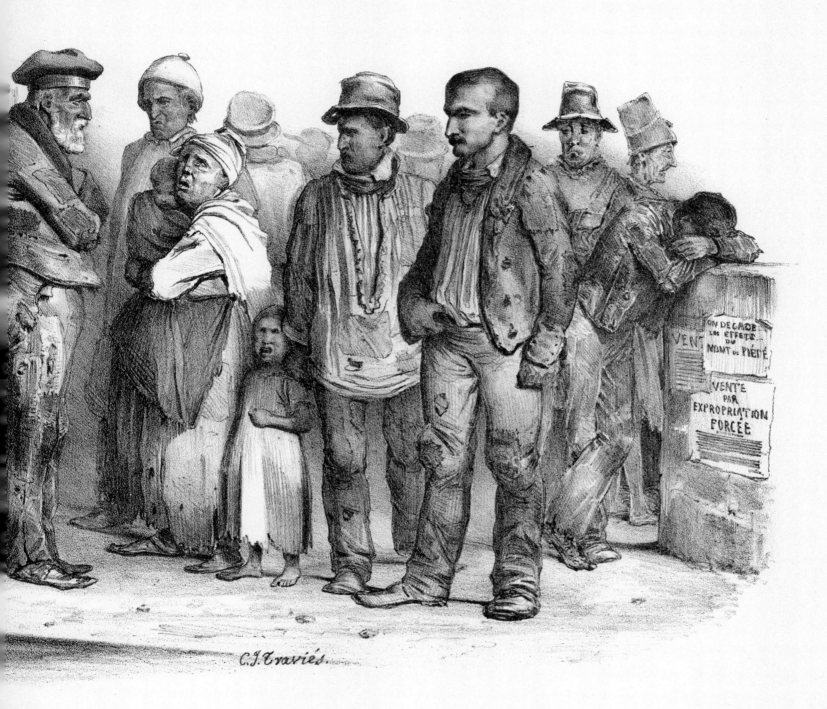

C.J.Traviés.

bonheur commence,
vre immense !

. . . .

(Côté poétique)

e , arrestations et visites illégales, arrestations sans motif, prisons encombrées,
tionales proscrites, patriotes assassinés, assomeurs publics payés, trésor gaspillé, sinécuristes,

On s'abonne chez Aubert, Galerie véro dodat.

←←Charles-Joseph Traviès & Michel Delaporte (lith.)

Liberated People, whose Good Fortune Begins…, 1831
Befreite Menschen, deren Glück beginnt…
Peuple affranchi, dont le bonheur commence…
Lithograph
From: *La Caricature*, Paris,
27 October 1831

The text underneath the illustration lists the grievances of the people and the government's abuses of power in summary fashion and in the style of a black book of misdeeds. The unwavering realism, which shows how large parts of the population have fallen into poverty, leaves nothing to the imagination in terms of its clarity. This issue of the magazine was confiscated after it was published.

Die Inschrift listet die herrschenden Missstände und die Vergehen der Regierung summarisch in der Art eines Schwarzbuchs auf. Auch der schonungslose Realismus, der die Verelendung breiter Bevölkerungs-schichten zeigt, lässt an Deutlichkeit nichts zu wünschen übrig. Die Ausgabe wurde nach dem Erscheinen beschlagnahmt.

L'inscription dresse la liste sommaire des abus perpétrés et des transgressions du gouvernement sous la forme d'un livre noir. L'implacable réalisme qui dénonce la pauvreté grandissante de larges couches de la population ne laisse rien à désirer en matière de clarté. Cette édition fut confisquée après sa publication.

Charles-Joseph Traviès

↓*A Grievous Burden*, 1832
Üble Last | Mauvaise charge
Lithograph
From: *La Caricature*, Paris,
19 July 1832

Charles Philipon succeeded in turning his trial into a media event, and not only that but he also managed to prove with a drawing that Louis-Philippe's head was indeed the same shape as a pear. Charles-Joseph Traviès here combines this symbolism of the pear with the inverted social pyramid, a recurrent theme in revolutionary graphic work, whereby the fourth estate has to carry the whole burden.

Charles Philipon hatte den Prozess gegen ihn in ein Happening verwandelt, in dessen Verlauf ihm der zeichnerische Nachweis für eine Ähnlichkeit des Kopfes von Louis-Philippe mit der Gestalt einer Birne gelang. Charles-Joseph Traviès kombinierte die Birnensymbolik mit dem aus der Revolutionsgrafik geläufigen Motiv der verkehrten Sozial-pyramide, in welcher der vierte Stand alle Last zu tragen hat.

Charles Philipon avait fait du procès intenté contre lui un événement, au cours duquel il réussit à prouver une similitude entre la tête de Louis-Philippe et la forme d'une poire. Charles-Joseph Traviès combina le symbolisme de la poire avec un motif récurrent du graphisme révolutionnaire, la pyramide sociale inversée, dans laquelle le quart-état doit porter toute la charge.

Charles-Joseph Traviès & Michel Delaporte (lith.)

Perfect Order Prevails in Lyon too, 1832
Die perfekteste Ordnung herrscht auch in Lyon
L'ordre le plus parfait règne aussi dans Lyon
Lithograph
From: *La Caricature*, Paris, 5 January 1832

In the previous November, a revolt by silk workers in Lyon had been crushed by a massive army of soldiers. Charles-Joseph Traviès here shows the city while it was under occupation, and the contrast between the somewhat grotesque style used to depict the officer of the national guard and the realism of the rest of the scene highlights the rift between the bourgeoisie and the socialist labour force.

Ein Weberaufstand in Lyon war im vorangegangenen November mit einem gewaltigen Militäraufgebot niedergeschlagen worden. Charles-Joseph Traviès zeigt die Stadt im Zustand der Okkupation. Der Unterschied zwischen dem grotesken Modus, in dem der Nationalgardist gehalten ist, und dem Realismus der Umgebung indiziert einen Bruch zwischen der Bourgeoisie und der sozialistisch organisierten Arbeiterschaft.

Au cours du mois de novembre précédent, une révolte des canuts à Lyon avait été écrasée par une intervention massive de l'armée. Charles-Joseph Traviès montre la ville en état d'occupation. La différence de traitement graphique entre le soldat de la Garde nationale, figuré de manière grotesque, et son entourage immédiat, illustré avec réalisme, met en exergue le fossé entre la bourgeoisie et une classe ouvrière organisée selon des principes socialistes.

Charles Philipon (concept)
& Charles-Joseph Traviès (del.)

Aubert Publishers, 1831
Verlagshaus Aubert | *Aubert Éditeur*
Lithograph
From: *La Caricature*, Paris, 22 December 1831

The worker facing out from *La Caricature*'s windows is gesturing that the government has a "most peculiar head". He is referring not only to the pear-shaped caricatures seen behind him but also to the similar-shaped helmets worn by the national guard. The suggested despotism of a police state resulted in another ban for the magazine.

Der Arbeiter vor dem Schaufenster von *La Caricature* weist darauf hin, dass die Regierung hier einen „ziemlich seltsamen Kopf" aufweise. Er spielt damit nicht nur auf die Birnenförmigkeit der ausgestellten Karikaturen an, sondern auch auf die analoge Form des Helms, die der Nationalgardist trägt. Die Suggestion des polizeistaatlichen Despotismus bescherte dem Journal ein erneutes Verbot.

L'ouvrier posté devant la vitrine de *La Caricature* signale que le gouvernement présente une « tête plutôt bizarre ». Il ne fait pas seulement allusion ici aux caricatures en forme de poires mais aussi à la forme similaire du casque que porte le soldat de la Garde nationale. Cette insinuation d'un despotisme policier valut au journal une nouvelle interdiction.

Je séparerai l'ivraie du bon grain (Jésus ch.)

J.J. Grandville & Eugène Forest (lith.)

*I Shall Separate the Wheat
from the Chaff*, 1831
Ich werde die Spreu vom Weizen trennen
Je séparerai l'ivraie du bon grain
Lithograph
From: *La Caricature*, Paris, 6 October 1831

Marianne, the personification of the French Republic,
is shaking her basket to separate out the worthless
upper echelons from the Juste Milieu. Grandville's
illustration, which frequently reappeared in various
similar forms in socialist graphic works during the
20th century, was itself clearly derived from the
Revolutionary engraving of 1793, *The Purifying Pot
of the Jacobins* (ill. pp. 50/51).

Marianne, die Personifikation der französischen
Republik, sieht die Oberen des „Juste milieu" als
wertlos aus. Grandvilles Darstellung, die in der sozialistischen Grafik des 20. Jahrhunderts vielfach vari-
iert wurde, ist offensichtlich an ein Motiv aus der
Revolutionsgrafik von 1793 angelehnt, *Der Läutertopf der Jakobiner* (Abb. S. 50/51).

Marianne, personnification de la République française, sépare les classes supérieures du «juste
milieu» comme étant sans valeur. La représentation
de Grandville, qui fut l'objet de nombreuses varia-
tions dans l'imagerie socialiste du XXᵉ siècle, est
manifestement inspirée de la gravure révolutionnaire de 1793, *La Marmite épuratoire des Jacobins*
(ill. p. 50/51).

J.J. Grandville & Eugène Forest (lith.)

The Resurrection of Censorship, 1832
Wiederauferstehung der Zensur
Résurrection de la Censure
Lithograph
From: *La Caricature*, Paris,
5 January 1832

In a diabolical imitation of the resurrection
of Christ, the French Minister of the Interior
rises from the tomb of the July Revolution
in the form of a censor. Grandville here
makes use of certain pictorial elements
from Eugène Delacroix's caricature *The
Censors Moving House*, while inverting

the content (ill. p. 90 b.). The figure of
Anastasia, whose name derives from the
Greek word for resurrection, later appeared
similarly armed with a giant pair of scissors
as the symbol of censorship.

In diabolischer Nachahmung Christi steigt
der Innenminister als Zensor aus dem Grab
der Julirevolution empor. Grandville greift
hier auf das Bildvokabular von Eugène
Delacroix' Karikatur *Der Umzug der Zensur* zurück und verkehrt es inhaltlich (Abb.
S. 90 u.). Die Figur der Anastasia, deren
Name sich von dem griechischen Wort
für Auferstehung ableitet, erschien später

ebenfalls mit einer riesigen Schere als
Symbol der Zensur bewaffnet.

En une imitation diabolique du Christ, le
ministre de l'Intérieur, représenté en censeur, s'élève du tombeau de la révolution
de Juillet. Grandville se réfère ici au voca-
bulaire pictural du *Déménagement de la
Censure*, caricature d'Eugène Delacroix,
et en inverse le contenu (ill. p. 90 b.). Le
personnage d'Anastasia, dont le nom est
dérivé du mot grec signifiant résurrection,
apparut plus tard également armée de
ciseaux géants, symboles de la censure.

Auguste Bouquet & the Becquet Brothers (lith.)

← *Father Saw*, 1832
Vater-Säge | *Père-Scie*
Stencil-coloured lithograph
From: *La Caricature*, Paris, 14 June 1832

The use of a sawfish head to represent the magistrate Jean-Charles Persil is based on a play on words on his last name (which in French sounds like *Père-Scie*) and also the fact that he had a prominent nose. The delinquent lying apparently untroubled on blocks made up of bundled-up copies of *La Caricature* may be recognised as a young Honoré Daumier, who had recently been sentenced to six months in prison for contempt of the government and insulting the king.

Dem Motiv des Sägefischs liegt ein Wortspiel mit dem Namen des Generalstaatsanwalts Jean-Charles Persil und dessen prägnanter Nase zugrunde. In dem Delinquenten, der entspannt auf einem Richtblock aus *Caricature*-Exemplaren liegt, hat man den jungen Honoré Daumier ausgemacht, der erst kurz zuvor wegen Majestätsbeleidigung zu einer sechsmonatigen Haftstrafe verurteilt worden war.

Le motif du poisson-scie repose sur un jeu de mots en allusion au nom du Procureur de la République, Jean-Charles Persil, et à son nez proéminent. Dans le délinquant qui, détendu, est allongé sur billot fait d'exemplaires de *La Caricature* on a pu reconnaître le jeune Honoré Daumier ; peu auparavant, celui-ci avait été condamné à une peine de prison de six mois pour lèse-majesté.

J.J. Grandville & Eugène Forest (lith.)

In Pursuit of Liberty, 1832
Die Jagd auf die Freiheit
La Chasse à la liberté
Stencil-coloured lithograph
From: *La Caricature*, Paris,
1 November 1832

It is the start of the hunting season, and Louis-Philippe's cabinet and court, led by the willing figure of Justice, have sounded the horn for a general attack on civil liberties, which have foolishly allowed themselves to be caught in the nets of criminal law. Following the June Rebellion by republicans and a crisis in the government in October, the persecution of opposition forces had steadily increased.

Eröffnung der Jagdsaison: Das Kabinett und der Hofstaat von Louis-Philippe und allen voran eine willfährige Justiz blasen zum Generalangriff auf die bürgerlichen Freiheitsrechte, die sich kopflos in die Netze des Strafrechts treiben lassen. Nach dem republikanischen Juniaufstand und einer Regierungskrise im Oktober hatte die Verfolgung oppositioneller Kräfte zugenommen.

Ouverture de la saison de la chasse : le Cabinet et la cour de Louis-Philippe précédés d'une Justice arbitraire sonnent la charge pour une attaque générale des droits civiques de liberté, qui se laissent stupidement prendre dans les filets du droit pénal. Après la révolte des journées de Juin suivie d'une crise gouvernementale en octobre, la persécution des forces d'opposition s'était amplifiée.

PI. 214

LA LIBERTÉ.

Charles-Joseph Traviès & the Becquet Brothers (lith.)

→ *It Was a Magnificent Celebration and the Merriment Was Enjoyed by Everyone*, 1832
Das Fest war wunderschön und die Heiterkeit allgemein
La fête a été magnifique et l'allégresse universelle
Lithograph
From: *La Caricature*, Paris,
30 August 1832

The juxtaposition in this illustration of the splendid ballroom with the dank dungeons for political prisoners showed the Juste Milieu in an entirely different light from the way they were depicted in the court bulletins that appeared in the loyalist press. With his rather sculptural style of drawing, that alternated fluidly between realism and symbolism, Charles-Joseph Traviès prepared the way for Honoré Daumier, who at this stage was still uncertain about how to proceed.

Der grafische Schwenk vom prunkvollen Festsaal hinunter ins trostlose Verlies für politische Häftlinge zeigt das „Juste milieu" in einem ganz anderen Licht als die Hofberichterstattungen der loyalistischen Presse. Mit seinem plastischen Zeichenstil, der virtuos zwischen Realismus und Emblematik changiert, hat Charles-Joseph Traviès dem damals noch unentschiedenen Honoré Daumier den Weg gewiesen.

La composition graphique de ce dessin, qui juxtapose la fastueuse salle de banquet au sinistre cachot pour prisonniers politiques, présente le «juste milieu» sous un tout autre jour que les rapports obséquieux de la presse loyaliste. Par son choix esthétique, alternant entre réalisme et symbolisme, Charles-Joseph Traviès a tracé la voie d'Honoré Daumier, alors encore indécis.

La Caricature (Journal) N°117.   Pl.243.

LA RÉPUBLIQUE A PÂLI......

Imp. Lith. de Becquet, rue childebert, N°9   On s'abonne chez Aubert, galerie véro-dodat

Philippe-Auguste Jeanron

The Republic Has Faded Away…, 1833
Die Republik ist verblichen… | *La République a pâli…*
Lithograph
From: *La Caricature*, Paris, 31 January 1833

The Citizen King's sarcastic comment on the failed June Rebellion of the republicans proved to be a gift for *La Caricature* in the context of the bloody suppression that had left some 800 people dead. Here in the mortuary, the grotesque unreality of the Juste Milieu is confronted with a reality that prefigures Honoré Daumier's *Rue Transnonain, 15 April 1834* (ill. p. 119 b.).

Der sarkastische Kommentar des Bürgerkönigs zum gescheiterten Juniaufstand der Republikaner lieferte *La Caricature* angesichts der blutigen Niederschlagung mit rund 800 Toten eine wahre Steilvorlage. Im Leichenschauhaus wird die groteske Unwirklichkeit des „Juste milieu" mit einer Realität konfrontiert, die bereits auf Honoré Daumiers *Rue Transnonain, 15. April 1834* vorausweist (Abb. S. 119 u.).

Le commentaire sarcastique du «roi bourgeois» sur la révolution manquée de Juin fut du pain béni pour *La Caricature*, au regard de la sanglante répression qui fit quelque 800 morts. À la morgue, la grotesque irréalité du «juste milieu» est confrontée à une réalité qu'Honoré Daumier avait déjà préfigurée dans *Rue Transnonain, le 15 avril 1834* (ill. p. 119 b.).

La Caricature (Journal)
N°95

Pl. 195.

La fête à été magnifique
et l'allégresse universelle.
(Moniteur)

Robert Seymour

FIGARO IN LONDON.

Satire should, like a polish'd razor keen,
Wound with a touch that's scarcely felt or seen.—LADY MONTAGUE.

'Political Pasquinades and Political Caricatures are parts (though humble ones,) of Political history. They supply information as to the personal habits, and often as to the motives and objects of public men, which cannot be found elsewhere.''—CROKER's NEW WHIG GUIDE.

No. 16.]   SATURDAY, MARCH 24, 1832.   [Price One Penny.

THE POLITICAL GAME OF HIGH-COCKOLORUM.   AN IRISH POLITICAL KANGAROO.

THE STATE BEGGAR'S OPERA.

Our readers are doubtless aware that there is a certain game played by little boys, and called *High-cockolorum*, in which there are two sides, one of which jumps on to the backs of the other party, and sits there till its weight breaks down its supporters.—Much after this fashion have those *high cocks o'law*, the English and Irish Chancellors, been playing a game with John Bull, who, poor fellow, is ready to sink beneath his ponderous burden.

The woolsack is indeed a very comfortable seat. Eldon and Lyndhurst have each made the most of it in their time, and the party with whom they act has at length thought proper to bring to task its present occupants.—"*Set a thief to catch a*

thief," is a most admirable maxim, and surely on this principle the delinquencies of Lord Plunkett could not have a more appropriate expositor than Mr. Gentleman Dawson. He certainly was never more entertaining in his life, than when he expressed himself horrified at the jobbing practised by the Irish Chancellors; and nothing more humorous could be conceived, considering its source, than the eulogium which he passed on public honesty. Lord Plunkett, it seems, is one of those tender parents, who no sooner gets into a good thing himself, than he manages to find room for the whole of his family. He excuses himself by saying, that it is but natural he should have a desire to provide for his own children, and indeed we

Figaro in London, 1832
Title-page | Titelseite | Page de titre
Wood engraving
From: *Figaro in London*, London, 24 March 1832

With its use of wood engraving for illustrations, the satirical magazine *Figaro in London*, edited by Gilbert Abbott à Beckett, opened up new possibilities for pictorial journalism. Seymour's designs were modest in comparison with the rich quality of the lithographs in *La Caricature*, but they could be printed in far greater numbers because of the cheaper productions costs.

Durch den Einsatz der Xylografie eröffnete das von Gilbert Abbott à Beckett herausgegebene Satireblatt *Figaro in London* dem illustrierten Journalismus neue Perspektiven. Seymours Grafiken nahmen sich zwar bescheiden aus im Vergleich zu den opulenten Lithografien von *La Caricature*, durch die niedrigeren Produktionskosten konnten jedoch weitaus höhere Auflagen gedruckt werden.

En optant pour la xylographie, le magazine satirique *Figaro in London*, publié par Gilbert Abbott à Beckett, ouvrit de nouvelles perspectives au journalisme illustré. Les gravures de Seymour sont modestes, comparées aux opulentes lithographies de *La Caricature*, mais elles purent être imprimées en beaucoup plus grand nombre grâce aux frais modiques de fabrication.

Charles Philipon

Louis-Philippe, King of the French, 1834
Louis-Philippe, König der Franzosen
Louis-Philippe, Roi des Français
Letterpress with metal type
From: *Le Charivari*, 27 February 1834

While he was still in prison, in December 1832 Charles Philipon published the first issue of *Le Charivari*, with its groundbreaking format as an illustrated daily magazine. In the same way as Gilbert Abbott à Beckett's *Figaro in London*, the aim with Philipon's format was to achieve a better integration of image and text. This was expressed most incisively in the typograms such as this one that were a reaction to the precensor's ban on illustrations.

Noch aus der Haft heraus hatte Charles Philipon im Dezember 1832 mit *Le Charivari* das bahnbrechende Format eines illustrierten Tagesjournals gegründet. Wie in Gilbert Abbott à Becketts *Figaro in London* wollte man mit diesem Format eine bessere Integration von Bild und Text erzielen. In pointiertester Form kommt sie in den Typogrammen zum Ausdruck, mit denen der Verleger auf Bildverbote der Vorzensur reagierte.

Charles Philipon avait fondé avec *Le Charivari* le format novateur d'un quotidien illustré en décembre 1832, alors qu'il était encore en prison. Comme dans le *Figaro in London* de Gilbert Abbott à Beckett, le but recherché avec ce format était d'obtenir une meilleure intégration de l'image et du texte. Elle trouve son expression la plus achevée dans les calligrammes et typogrammes avec lesquels l'éditeur réagissait aux interdictions d'images imposées par la précensure.

27 février 1834.   Troisième année.   N° 58. — Jeudi.

Le Charivari,

JOURNAL PUBLIANT CHAQUE JOUR UN NOUVEAU DESSIN.

Nous donnons ci-dessous, conformément à la volonté de nos juges, le dispositif et l'arrêt du jugement en dernier ressort qui a frappé le *Charivari*. Le jugement de nos derniers juges est absolument pareil à celui de nos seconds juges, lequel était lui-même la reproduction de celui de nos premiers juges. Tant il est vrai que les beaux esprits se rencontrent. Comme ce jugement, tout spirituel qu'il soit, risquerait d'offrir peu d'agrément à nos lecteurs, nous avons tâché de compenser du moins par la forme, ce qu'il pourrait y avoir d'un peu absurde au fond.

Louis-Philippe, roi des Français, à tous présens et à venir salut. La cour d'assises du département de Seine-et-Oise, séant à Versailles, a rendu l'arrêt suivant. — La cour, etc. — Considérant que l'opposition est régulière, — Reçoit Cruchet opposant à l'arrêt par défaut du 20 mars dernier. — Faisant droit sur son opposition, et statuant par arrêt nouveau. — Considérant que la question de compte rendu ne pourrait être examinée par la cour sans remettre en question la compétence irrévocable ment fix ée par l'arrêt de la cour d'asises de Sein e-et-Oise du dix août dernier et celui de la cour de cassation le 19 octobre suivant. — Considérant d'ail leurs, que les articles incriminés relatant les interrogatoir es des prévenus et et les dépositions des témoins entendus dans les audiences de la cour d'assises de la Seine, des onze et douze mars dernier, renfermant ainsi, un véritable compte-rendu de ces audiences. — Considérant que de la comparaison des deux articles incriminés avec le procès-verbal dressé par les membres de la cour d'assises de la Seine le dix-neuf mars dernier, il résulte que le compte qu'ils contiennent, des audiences de ladite cour des onze et douze mars dernier, dans le procès, concernant Bergeron et Benoist est infidèle, qu'en effet les interrogatoires des accusés, les dépositions des témoins, les paroles pro non cées par le président et par le procureur-général y sont pour la plupart tronquée et dénatu rés, qu e même on y prête au président, au procureur-général et à plusieurs des témoins des paroles qui n'ont pas réellement été proférées. — Considérant que ces infidélités ont pour motif de jeter le ridi cul e soit sur l'accusation, soit sur le président, et que d'ailleurs les deux articles dont il s'agit sont remplies de réflexions et de qualifications offensantes pour le président et le procureur-général ; d'où il suit que le compte-rendu l'a été de mauvaise foi, et qu'il est injurieux pour le président et le procureur-général. — Considérant que Cruchet a de son aveu signé lesdits articles comme gérant responsable. — Déclare Cruchet coupable d'avoir, dans le journal le *Charivari*, dont il est gérant, imprimé, vendu et distribué, rendu de mauvaise foi un compte non seulement infidèle des audiences de la cour d'assises de la Seine des 11 et 12 mars dernier, mais encore injurieux pour le président et le procureur-géné ral, ce qui constitue le délit prévu par les articles 7, 16, de la loi du 25 mars 1822 ; 26 de la loi du 26 mai 1819 ; 11 de la loi du 9 juin 1819, et 14 de la loi du 18 juillet 1828, lus à l'audience par le président. — Faisant application de ces dispositions de lois. — Condamne Isidore Mathias Cruchet, en un mois d'emprisonnement et en 5,000 fr. d'amende. — Interdit pendant un an aux éditeurs du journal dit le *Charivari* de rendre compte des débats judiciaires. — Condamne ledit Cruchet aux frais du procès. — Ordonne en exécution dudit article 26 de la loi du 26 mai 1819 la destruction desdits numéros du journal le *Charivari* qui pourraient être ultérieurement saisis. — Ordonne que dans le mois, à partir de ce jour, le gérant du journal le *Charivari*, sera tenu d'insérer dans l'une des feuilles dudit journal qui paraîtront, un extrait contenant les motifs et le dispositif du présent arrêt. — Ordonne que le présent arrêt sera exécuté à la diligence du procureur du roi, conformément à la loi. — Fait et jugé à Versailles en audience publique au Palais-de-Justice le lundi 9 décembre 1833 en présence de M. Salerai, procureur du roi, par MM. Antoine Aimé Marie Lefebvre, conseiller à la cour royale de Paris, président de la cour d'assises, Louis Claude Mirofle, vice-président du tribunal de première instance de l'arrondissement de Versailles, et Arnould Teissier, juge au même tribunal composant la cour d'assises du département de Seine-et-Oise, qui ont signé avec Jean Marie Fontaine, commis greffier assistant. — En foi de quoi la minute du présent arrêt a été signée par le président et le commis greffier ainsi signé Lefebvre Mirofle, Tessier et Fontaine.

THE PENNY MAGAZINE

OF THE

Society for the Diffusion of Useful Knowledge.

36.]   PUBLISHED EVERY SATURDAY.   [OCTOBER 27, 1832.

THE BOA CONSTRICTOR.

[The Boa Constrictor about to strike a Rabbit.]

ONE of the most interesting objects in the fine collection of animals at the Surrey Zoological Gardens, is the Boa Constrictor. Curled up in a large box, through the upper grating of which it may be conveniently examined, this enormous reptile lies for weeks in a quiet and almost torpid state. The capacity which this class of animals possess of requiring food only at very long intervals, accounts for the inactive condition in which they principally live; but when the feeling of hunger becomes strong they rouse themselves from their long repose, and the voracity of their appetite is then as remarkable as their previous indifference. In a state of confinement the boa takes food at intervals of a month or six weeks; but he then swallows an entire rabbit or fowl, which is put in his cage. The artist who made the drawing for the above wood-cut, saw the boa at the Surrey Zoological Gardens precisely in the attitude which he has represented. The time having arrived when he was expected to require food, a live rabbit was put into his box. The poor little quadruped remained uninjured for several days, till he became familiar with his terrible enemy. On a sudden, while the artist was observing the ill-sorted pair, the reptile suddenly rose up, and, opening his fearful jaws, made a stroke at the rabbit, who was climbing up the end of the box; but, as if his appetite was not sufficiently eager, he suddenly drew back, when within an inch of his prey, and sunk into his wonted lethargy. The rabbit, unconscious of the danger which was passed for a short season, began to play about the scaly folds of his companion; but the keeper said that his respite would be brief, and that he would be swallowed the next day without any qualms.

All the tribe of serpents are sustained by animal food. The smaller species devour insects, lizards, frogs, and snails; but the larger species, and especially the boa, not unfrequently attack very large quadrupeds. In seizing upon so small a victim as a rabbit, the boa constrictor would swallow it without much difficulty; because the peculiar construction of the mouth and throat of this species enables them to expand, so as to receive within

Anonymous

Page spread
Doppelseite | Double page
Wood engravings
From: *Le Magasin pittoresque*,
Paris, 13 April 1833

A French equivalent to *The Penny Magazine*, the *Magasin pittoresque* was founded by Édouard Charton in January 1833, while four months later the German *Pfennig Magazin* was launched in Leipzig by the publisher Johann Jakob Weber. Both publications were independent, but for the first few years they relied on wood engravings from England owing to a lack of trained wood engravers where they were produced.

Im Januar 1833 kam das von Édouard Charton herausgegebene französische Pedant zum *Penny Magazine* heraus, und bereits vier Monate später hatte in Leipzig das von Johann Jakob Weber edierte deutsche *Pfennig Magazin* Premiere. Beide Blätter waren zwar unabhängig, blieben in den ersten Jahren allerdings von den englischen Holzstichexporten abhängig, da es vor Ort an ausgebildeten Xylografen mangelte.

Cette réplique française du *Penny Magazine* fut publiée en janvier 1833 par Édouard Charton, et quatre mois plus tard le *Pfennig Magazin*, édité par Johann Jakob Weber, sortait déjà son premier numéro à Leipzig. Ces deux journaux étaient indépendants, mais furent cependant tributaires des exportations de gravures sur bois anglaises, car sur place les xylographes de profession faisaient défaut.

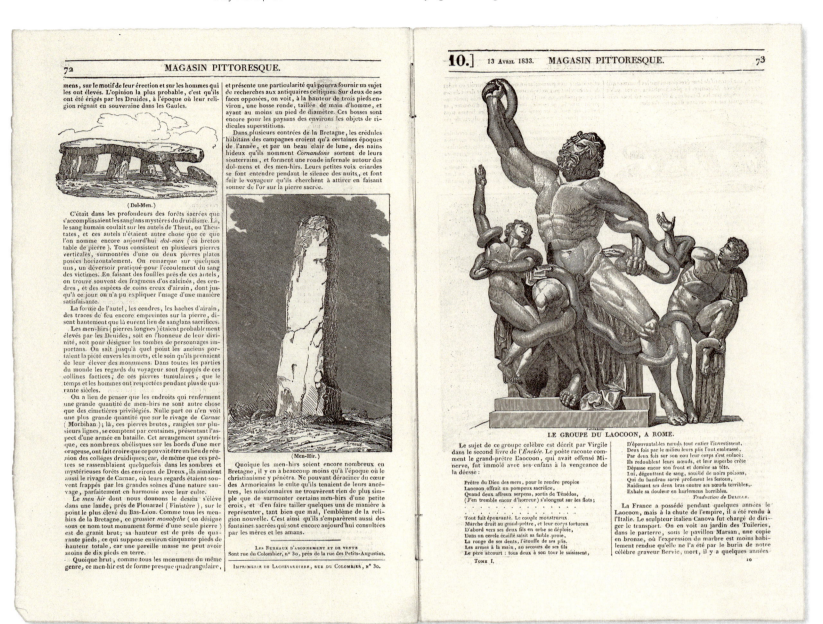

Anonymous

← *The Penny Magazine*, 1832
Title-page | Titelseite | Page de titre
Wood engraving
From: *The Penny Magazine*, London,
27 October 1832

The illustrations for *The Penny Magazine*, published by Charles Knight for the liberal-conservative Society for the Diffusion of Useful Knowledge, were also produced as wood engravings. The Society was opposed to leaving the education of the working class to forces campaigning for radical reform, and by making its content mostly popular science the magazine was able to avoid the extra costs associated with stamp duty.

In Holz graviert waren auch die Illustrationen des von Charles Knight herausgegebenen *Penny Magazine* der liberal konservativen Society for the Diffusion of Useful Knowledge. Diese wollte die Bildung der Industriearbeiterschaft nicht länger den radikalen Reformkräften überlassen. Mit den populärwissenschaftlichen Inhalten umging sie die preistreibende Stempelsteuer.

Les illustrations du *Penny Magazine*, le journal de la Society for the Diffusion of Useful Knowledge publié par Charles Knight, furent également gravées dans du bois. La Société ne voulait pas laisser plus longtemps l'éducation de la classe laborieuse de l'industrie aux mains des forces radicales militant pour la réforme. Avec un contenu centré sur la culture populaire, elle évita le fort coûteux droit de timbre.

La Caricature (Journal) N°162.   Pl.33g

POIRES POUR LA SOIF...

MARTE

Chez Aubert Galerie vero Bedat.   L. de Becquet rue Furstenberg 6.

À quelle sauce la voulez-vous ?

Auguste Bouquet & the Becquet Brothers (lith.)

Which Sauce Do You Want with That?, 1833
In welcher Soße wollt ihr sie?
À quelle sauce la voulez-vous ?
Lithograph
From: *La Caricature*, Paris, 13 December 1833

Dressed as a chef in the style of a character from
La Caricature, Charles Philipon is leading his Pear
Campaign (French *poire* being slang for "fool").
As a symbol protesting against the rule of Louis-
Philippe and more generally the politics of repres-
sion, images of pears appeared throughout France
at this time and were even used in graffiti on the
pyramids in Egypt.

Als Küchenchef im *Caricature*-Kostüm befehligt
Charles Philipon die Birnen-Kampagne (franz. *poire*,
umgangssprachlich Dummkopf). Das Symbol gegen
die Herrschaft von Louis-Philippe und die Repressionspolitik im Allgemeinen war nicht nur in Frankreich allgegenwärtig. Selbst an den ägyptischen
Pyramiden wurden damals Birnen-Graffitis bezeugt.

Vêtu comme un chef de cuisine dans le costume de
La Caricature, Charles Philipon dirige la campagne
des poires («poire» étant synonyme d'«idiot»). Ce
symbole contre le règne de Louis-Philippe en particulier et contre la politique de répression en général
n'était pas omniprésent qu'en France. À l'époque,
des grafittis en forme de poires apparurent même
sur les pyramides d'Égypte.

Anonymous

⊾ *Pont Lafayette, Lyon*
*The Toll Booth on the City Side as It Appears
Today*, 1834
*Aktueller Zustand des Zollhäuschens,
von der Stadt aus gesehen*
*Situation actuelle du Pavillon de péage,
du côté de la ville*
Wood engraving
From: *Le Charivari*, Paris, 15 May 1834

The illustrated reports of the workers' revolt in Lyon,
which appeared in 1834 in the first illustrated daily
magazine, *Le Charivari*, followed only a few days
after the events they described and can thus be
seen as an early form of live reporting. By employing
picture correspondents who worked on location,
Charles Philipon anticipated the graphic journalism
of the daily news that began in New York in 1873.

Die Bildberichte über den Arbeiteraufstand in Lyon,
die 1834 in der ersten Tagesillustrierten *Le Charivari*
erschienen, können mit einer minimalen zeitlichen
Verzögerung von nur wenigen Tagen als frühe Form
der Livereportage gelten. Durch den Einsatz von
Bildkorrespondenten vor Ort antizipierte Charles
Philipon den grafischen Tagesjournalismus, der
1873 in New York begann.

Les articles illustrés de la révolte des canuts à Lyon,
parus en 1834 dans le premier quotidien illustré *Le
Charivari*, n'avaient que quelques jours de décalage
sur les événements et peuvent être considérés
comme la forme initiale du reportage en direct. En
employant des correspondants dessinateurs sur les
lieux, Charles Philipon anticipa le dessin de presse
quotidien qui fit ses débuts à New York en 1873.

Grand enterrement du gros Constitutionnel décédé en son hôtel rue Montmartre N°121, enface de l'apothicaire et du Marchand de Brioches.

J.J. Grandville & Benjamin Roubaud

↑ *Grand Funeral of a Fat Constitutional Member*, 1834
Großes Begräbnis eines fetten Constitutionnel
Grand Enterrement du gros Constitutionnel
Stencil-coloured lithograph
From: *La Caricature*, Paris,
16 January 1834

When the pro-government newspaper *Le Constitutionnel* suffered a massive loss of subscribers a wave of malicious glee spread through the opposition press. The grotesque funeral procession here led by *Le Charivari*'s drummer also harks back to Charles Philipon's visit to Lyon (see ill. pp. 98/99), while the raucous noise of charivari has long been a traditional way of expressing in public an opposition to corruption or unpopular figures.

Schadenfreude über den massiven Abonnentenverlust des regierungstreuen Journals *Le Constitutionnel* herrschte bei der oppositionellen Presse. Der groteske Leichenzug, der vom Trommler des *Charivari* angeführt wird, spielt auf Charles Philipons Lyoneser Happening an (siehe Abb. S. 98/99). Charivari-Lärm war eine traditionelle Praxis, um Korruption anzuprangern.

La presse d'opposition se réjouit de la perte massive d'abonnés au journal *Le Constitutionnel*, fidèle au gouvernement. Le cortège funèbre, conduit par le tambour du *Charivari*, est une allusion au passage de Charles Philipon à Lyon (voir ill. p. 98/99). Le bruit de charivari était une pratique de la rue pour dénoncer la corruption.

Honoré Daumier & Delaunois (lith.)

Rue Transnonain, 15 April 1834
Lithograph
From: Charles Philipon (ed.),
L'Association mensuelle, Paris,
October 1834
Dresden, Staatliche Kunstsammlungen

The disturbance that spread from Lyon to Paris was ruthlessly put down using military techniques from the guerrilla war in Algeria. A few months later, the massacre of innocent civilians in an apartment building on the Rue Transnonain offered Charles Philipon the opportunity of launching a scathing attack on the hated regime of Louis-Philippe, which he did by way of a special edition. "This is not a caricature, nor is it any kind of exaggeration, rather it is a bloody page in the modern history of our country […]. Daumier has risen to great heights with this illustration, in which he has created an image that, although it is only done in black and on just a sheet of paper, will be no less acknowledged for its merits and will prove as long-lasting as any other form of image" (Charles Philipon, *La Caricature*, 2 October 1834).

Die Unruhen, die von Lyon auf Paris übergegriffen hatten, wurden rigoros mit militärischen Mitteln aus dem algerischen Guerillakrieg beantwortet. Das Massaker an unbeteiligten Zivilisten in einem Mietshaus in der Rue Transnonain bot Charles Philipon einige Monate später im Rahmen einer Sonderedition die Gelegenheit, das verhasste Regime von Louis-Philippe empfindlich zu treffen. „Das ist keine Karikatur, das ist keine Übertreibung, das ist eine blutige Seite unserer modernen Geschichte […]. Daumier hat sich mit dieser Zeichnung auf eine große Höhe geschwungen, er hat ein Gemälde geschaffen, das, obgleich es nur in Schwarz und auf ein Papier gemalt ist, nicht weniger geschätzt und von Dauer sein wird" (Charles Philipon, *La Caricature*, 2. Oktober 1834).

Les troubles qui de Lyon avaient atteint Paris furent réprimés sans pitié avec les moyens militaires utilisés dans la guérilla en Algérie. Le massacre de civils innocents perpétré dans un bâtiment locatif de la rue Transnonain fournit quelques mois plus tard à Charles Philipon l'occasion de lancer dans une édition spéciale une flèche cinglante au gouvernement tant haï de Louis-Philippe. «Ce n'est point une caricature ; ce n'est point une charge ; c'est une page sanglante de notre histoire moderne […]. Daumier, dans ce dessin, s'est élevé à une grande hauteur, il a créé un tableau qui, quoique peint en noir et sur une feuille de papier, n'en sera ni moins estimé ni moins durable» (Charles Philipon, *La Caricature*, 2 octobre 1834).

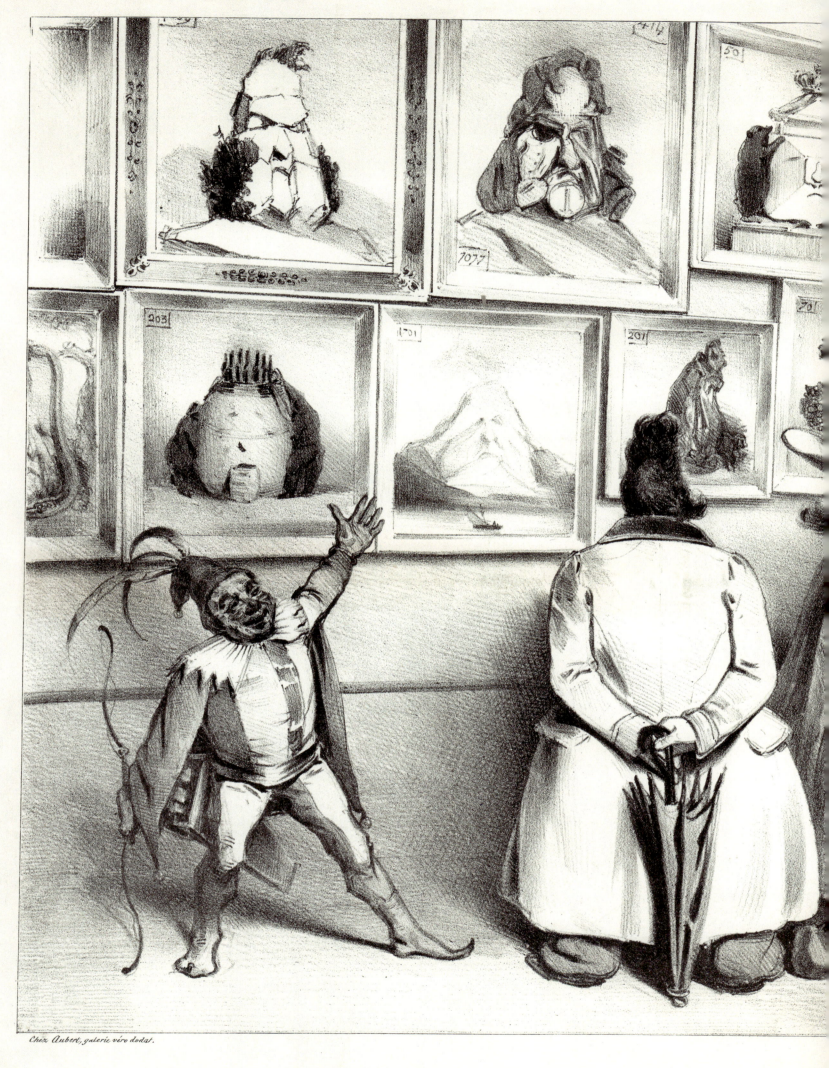

Pl. 366, 367.

L. de Benard.

honneur d'exposer journellement.

ye qu'en s'abonnant et il faudrait vraiment ne pas avoir 13 f dans sa poche

Roi et de son Auguste famille.

! baound! baound!!

←←Charles-Joseph Traviès & the Becquet Brothers (lith.)

Gentlemen, We Have the Honour of Presenting to You Here and Every Day…, 1834
Meine Herrschaften, hier das, was wir die Ehre haben, jeden Tag auszustellen…
Voici Messieurs, ce que nous avons l'honneur d'exposer journellement…
Lithograph
From: *La Caricature*, Paris, 3 June 1834

This illustration is less concerned with the way the Pear Campaign had become known ubiquitously throughout France, and is more a central argument in Charles Philipon's defence. As a result of their delusional paranoia, the assembled spectators, who consist only of the king and crown prince, can see nothing in the simple images but allusions to themselves.

Hier geht es weniger um die Ubiquität der Birnenkampage, sondern um ein zentrales Argument in Charles Philipons Verteidigung. Offenbar aufgrund eines paranoiden Defekts vermag das Publikum, das einzig aus dem Monarchen und dem Kronprinzen besteht, in den harmlosen Bildern nur Anspielungen auf sich selbst zu erkennen.

Ici, il s'agit moins de l'ubiquité de la campagne des poires que d'un argument central pour la défense de Charles Philipon. Conséquence manifeste de troubles paranoïdes, le public, composé seulement du monarque et du dauphin, ne peut distinguer dans les innocentes images que des allusions à lui-même.

Anonymous & Junca (lith.)

Sauzet's Infernal Machine, 1835
Höllenmaschine des Sauzet
Machine infernale de Sauzet
Lithograph
From: *La Caricature*, Paris, 20 August 1835

In response to a bloody attempt at assassinating the king using a volley gun with several barrels (later known as the "infernal machine"), the deputy Paul Jean Pierre Sauzet announced a series of stringent censorship measures which are here being fired against the opposition press. The jester for *La Caricature* is lying injured on the ground, but the drummer for *Le Charivari* stands thumbing his nose at the infernal machine of the law.

Als Reaktion auf einen blutigen Attentatsversuch auf den König, der mit einem mehrläufigen Schussapparat verübt worden war, verkündete der Abgeordnete Sauzet eine Reihe von rigiden Zensurmaßnahmen, die hier auf die oppositionelle Presse abgefeuert werden. Der *Caricature*-Narr liegt getroffen am Boden, doch der *Charivari*-Trommler zieht der juristischen Höllenmaschine eine lange Nase.

En réaction à une tentative sanglante d'assassinat du roi perpétrée avec la machine infernale, une arme à feu faite de plusieurs canons de fusil, Sauzet, membre du Parlement, annonça une série de mesures de censure restrictives destinées ici à viser la presse d'opposition. Le bouffon de la *Caricature* gît blessé à terre, mais le tambour du *Charivari* fait un pied de nez à la machine infernale de la justice.

Honoré Daumier & Delaunois (lith.)

The Modern Galileo: And Yet It Does Move, 1834
Moderner Galilei. Und sie bewegt sich doch
Moderne Galilée. Et pourtant elle marche
Lithograph
From: *La Caricature*, Paris,
6 November 1834

The rioting in Lyon and Paris in April led to 2,000 people being arrested and convicted. Persil, the Minister of Justice, appears here as a stern-faced inquisitor, but cannot break the prisoner's certainty that republicanism will prevail in the end. This modern Galileo has the combined features of two early socialist activists, Louis-Auguste Blanqui and Armand Barbès.

Die Aprilaufstände in Lyon und Paris zogen 2000 Verhaftungen und Anklagen nach sich. Generalstaatsanwalt Persil tritt als grimmiger Inquisitor in Erscheinung, doch er kann die Gewissheit des Gefangenen nicht brechen, dass sich der Republikanismus am Ende durchsetzen wird. Der moderne Galilei trägt Züge der beiden frühsozialistischen Aktivisten Louis-Auguste Blanqui und Armand Barbès.

Les révoltes de Lyon et de Paris en avril entraînèrent 2 000 arrestations et condamnations. Le procureur général Persil apparaît comme un sinistre inquisiteur, mais il ne peut pas briser la certitude du prisonnier que le républicanisme finira par s'imposer. Le Galilée moderne porte les traits de deux activistes socialistes de la première heure, Louis-Auguste Blanqui et Armand Barbès.

Honoré Daumier & Junca (lith.)

It really Was Worth Dying for!, 1835
Es hat sich wahrlich gelohnt, dafür zu sterben!
C'était vraiment bien la peine de nous faire tuer!
Lithograph
From: *La Caricature*, Paris,
27 August 1835

The fallen freedom fighters of the July Revolution look out from their graves and discover the sobering fact that the repressive conditions have not changed at all. Honoré Daumier was responsible for designing this final illustration for *La Caricature*, which was obliged to cease publication because of the pressures of inflexible pre-censorship.

Die gefallenen Freiheitskämpfer der Julirevolution schauen aus ihren Gräbern hervor und müssen ernüchtert feststellen, dass sich an den repressiven Verhältnissen nichts geändert hat. Die Ausführung dieses finalen Blatts von *La Caricature*, die unter dem Druck einer rigiden Vorzensur ihr Erscheinen einstellen musste, war dem aufstrebenden Honoré Daumier zugefallen.

Les combattants de la liberté de la révolution de Juillet tombés surgissent de leurs tombes et constatent, désabusés, que rien n'a changé quant aux dispositions répressives. Honoré Daumier fut chargé de l'exécution de cette dernière page de *La Caricature*, qui dut stopper la publication sous la pression d'une précensure intransigeante.

C'était vraiment bien la peine de nous faire tuer!

Charles-Joseph Traviès

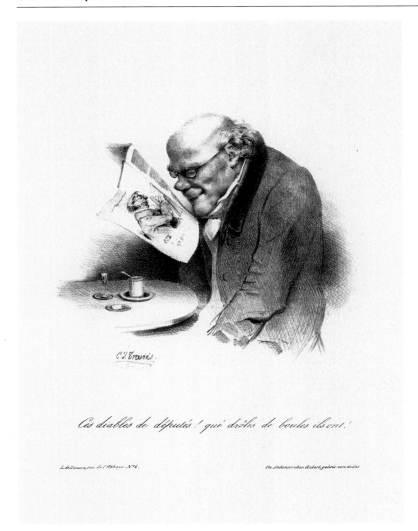

These Damned Members of Parliament, What Funny Heads They Have!, 1833
Diese Teufel von Parlamentarier, was für komische Köpfe die haben!
Ces diables de députés! Qué drôles de boules is ont!
Lithograph
From: Le Charivari, Paris, 13 March 1833

That Scoundrel Figaro! The Rogue Has Such Wit and Talent!!, 1833
Der Spitzbube vom Figaro! Geist hat er und Talent, dieser Schelm!!
Cré coquin de Figaro! A-t-il de l'esprit et du talent, ce farceur-là!!
Lithograph
From: Le Charivari, Paris, 31 March 1833

The Bureaucrat: Shameless, Idle and Lazy, 1833
Der Bürokrat: Unverschämt, träge und faul
Le Bureaucrate: Insolent, musard et paresseux
Lithograph
From: Le Charivari, Paris, 13 April 1833

→ The Man of Private Means: Trifler, Simpleton, Bored and Boring, 1833
Der Privatier: Tagedieb, Fliegenschnapper, gelangweilt und langweilig
Le Rentier: Musard, gobe-mouche, ennuyeux et ennuyé
Lithograph
From: Le Charivari, Paris, 2 May 1833

In contrast to the caricatures of manners by his fellow artists Honoré Daumier and Paul Gavarni, Charles-Joseph Traviès presented a bitter picture of the dreadful conditions in society with his series of physiognomic portraits. Baudelaire called him the "Prince of Bad Luck" while at the same time acclaiming his powers of observation and stating that "there is a serious and tender side to his talent that makes him peculiarly engaging."

Im Gegensatz zu den versöhnlichen Sittenkarikaturen seiner Kollegen Honoré Daumier und Paul Gavarni zeichnete Charles-Joseph Traviès in seinen physiognomischen Serien ein bitteres und abgründiges Bild der gesellschaftlichen Verhältnisse. Charles Baudelaire attestierte diesem „Fürst des Missgeschicks" eine „vorzügliche Beobachtungsgabe" und einen „Ernst und eine Zärtlichkeit, die ihm eine sonderbare Anziehungskraft verleihen".

À l'inverse des scènes de mœurs indulgentes réalisées par ses collègues Honoré Daumier et Paul Gavarni, Charles-Joseph Traviès dressa un tableau amer des dramatiques conditions sociales dans ses séries physiognomoniques. Charles Baudelaire confirme que ce «prince du guignon» dont le «talent a quelque chose de sérieux et de tendre qui le rend singulièrement attachant» était «très observateur».

Types et Portraits de Fantaisie.

Le rentier.

Musard, gobe-mouche, ennuyeux et ennuyé.

Frédéric Bouchot & Delaunois (lith.)

Théâtre des Variétés
Father Goriot, 1835
Vater Goriot | Le Père Goriot
Lithograph
From: *Le Charivari*, Paris, 6 April 1835

Shortly after Honoré de Balzac's key work of literary realism had been published, *Le Père Goriot* also became successful on the stage. Through the gradual decline of the simple-headed Goriot, Balzac analysed the changes in attitudes in the transition from a late-feudal society to a capitalist market economy. In *Le Charivari*, the dramatic reality of the stage and the critical social comment merge into one.

Kurz nach der Veröffentlichung von Honoré de Balzacs *Le Père Goriot* feierte dieses Schlüsselwerk des literarischen Realismus auch auf den Bühnen Erfolge. Am Beispiel des Niedergangs des naiven Goriot analysierte Balzac den Mentalitätswandel im Übergang vom Spätfeudalismus zur kapitalistischen Marktwirtschaft. In *Le Charivari* gingen Bühnenwirklichkeit und sozialkritisches Cartooning ineinander über.

Peu après sa parution, *Le Père Goriot* d'Honoré de Balzac, roman clé du réalisme littéraire, remportait aussi un grand succès sur les scènes des théâtre. À travers l'exemple du naïf Goriot, Balzac fit une analyse du changement des mentalités lors du passage du féodalisme tardif à l'économie de marché capitaliste. Dans *Le Charivari*, la réalité de la comédie et le dessin socio-critique ne firent qu'un.

Jules Bourdet & Junca (lith.)

← *Visiting-Cards*, 1836
Visitenkarten | *Les Cartes de visites*
Lithograph
From: *Le Charivari*, Paris, 15 January 1836

As the dense thickets of advertising encroach on people's private lives, the new market economy is shown to be governed by appearances and commercial promotion. The popular stage character Robert Macaire, an unscrupulous swindler (see ill. p. 128), has left his mark here already, while in his criticism of the increasing commercialisation of everyday life Jules Bourdet does not spare his own publisher Aubert, which trades in illustrations.

Dass die neue Marktwirtschaft von Schein und Marketing regiert wurde, suggeriert der Wald aus Werbemitteln, der bis in die Privatsphäre vordringt. Ebenso hat die populäre Bühnenfigur des Straßenräubers und Betrügers Robert Macaire (siehe Abb. S. 128) hier bereits seine Marke hinterlassen. Jules Bourdet spart auch den Grafikhandel des eigenen Verlagshauses Aubert nicht von der Kritik an der allgemeinen Kommerzialisierung der Lebensverhältnisse aus.

Que la jungle des réclames vienne s'immiscer jusque dans la sphère privée dénonce une nouvelle économie de marché dominée par les apparences et les stratégies commerciales. Le personnage de théâtre populaire du bandit et escroc Robert Macaire a déjà laissé sa trace ici (voir ill. p. 128). Dans sa dénonciation de la marchandisation générale qui affecte la vie courante, Jules Bourdet n'épargne pas sa propre maison d'édition Aubert qui fait commerce de dessins.

Béotisme parisien
Lithographs
From: Jules Bourdet, *Béotisme parisien*, Paris, 1837

Béotisme parisien, no. 19
The Great Artist, 1836
Der große Künstler | *Le Grand Artiste*

In his series *Béotisme parisien* (The Philistines of Paris), which first appeared in *Le Charivari* and was later issued as a separate collection, Jules Bourdet confronted the cultural ignorance of the new wealthy elite. The childish drawings which this mother, seized by the cult of genius, takes as a sign of her son's artistic talent became established as a style of illustration from the late 1840s.

In der Reihe *Béotisme parisien* (Pariser Tölpelei), die zuerst in *Le Charivari* und später als Album erschien, rechnete Bourdet mit der kulturellen Ignoranz des neuen Geldadels ab. Das kindische Gekritzel, das eine vom Geniekult ergriffene Mutter als Zeichen der künstlerischen Begabung ihres Sohns zu erkennen glaubt, begann sich ab Ende der 1840er-Jahre als Illustrationsstil durchzusetzen.

Dans la série *Béotisme parisien*, qui parut d'abord dans *Le Charivari* puis sous forme d'album, Bourdet règle ses comptes avec l'ignorance culturelle de la nouvelle aristocratie financière. Le gribouillage infantile dans lequel une mère entichée du culte du génie croit voir le signe du talent artistique de son fils commença à s'imposer comme style d'illustration dès la fin des années 1840.

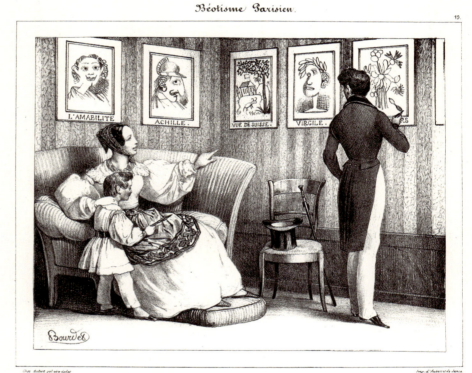

Regardez, Monsieur, les ouvrages de mon Auguste, son maître en est très content, il n'y a pas retouché du tout. — Ces dessins sont délicieux, il y a là Madame, un avenir de grand artiste.

Béotisme parisien, no. 24
Postermania, 1836
Der Plakatwahn | *L'Affichomanie*

Bourdet was another of Baron Gros's students who went on to work with Charles Philipon. He was influenced by Nicolas-Toussaint Charlet's work and paid special attention to the background in his illustrations, for which he developed a system of reference. Following William Hogarth he was one of the first artists to deal with the commercialisation of urban space, and for that reason he is known as a pioneer in the history of pictorial design.

Jules Bourdet war ein weiterer Schüler des Baron Gros in der Riege Charles Philipons. Unter dem Einfluss Nicolas-Toussaint Charlets hatte er den Bildhintergründen besondere Aufmerksamkeit gewidmet und für sie eine Verweisstruktur entwickelt. Nach William Hogarth war er der erste Künstler, der die Kommerzialisierung des Stadtraums thematisierte und der sich damit als ein weiterer Wegbereiter in die Historie der Bildmontage einschrieb.

Jules Bourdet fut un autre élève du baron Gros dans l'équipe de Charles Philipon. Sous l'influence de Nicolas-Toussaint Charlet il avait développé une attention particulière pour la structure référentielle des arrière-plans d'images. Après William Hogarth, il fut le premier artiste qui thématisa la commercialisation de l'espace urbain et gagna ainsi sa place de pionnier dans l'histoire du montage pictural.

L'affichomanie.
Cette affaire ne peut manquer d'être bonne, voyez mon affiche, 25 pieds carrés, on réserve des jours pour les avisés, c'est une opération colossale — Le public s'étonne, se passionne et devient action.

Charles Philipon (concept) & Honoré Daumier (del.)

Robert Macaire and the Coal, 1839
Robert Macaire und die Kohle
Robert Macaire et la houille
Lithograph
From: Charles Philipon & Honoré Daumier,
Les Cent et un Robert-Macaire, Paris, 1839

The fictional character of Robert Macaire was the embodiment of speculation, investment and dubious public relations. A symbolic figure, he also set the tone for the obituary of the July Monarchy as later written by Karl Marx in 1850 in which it was summed up as "nothing but a joint stock company for the exploitation of France's national wealth […]. Louis-Philippe was the director of this company, and Robert Macaire sat upon the throne."

Die fiktive Figur des Robert Macaire wurde zum Inbegriff für Spekulation, Investition und zweifelhafte Public Relations. Als Symbolfigur bestimmte er auch den Nekrolog auf die Julimonarchie, den Karl Marx 1850 verfasst hatte: Diese „war nichts als eine Aktienkompanie zur Exploitation des französischen Nationalreichtums […]. Louis-Philippe war der Direktor dieser Kompanie – Robert Macaire auf dem Throne."

Robert Macaire, personnage fictif, devint l'incarnation de la spéculation, des investissements et des relations publiques douteuses. Cette figure symbolique détermina aussi la nécrologie de la monarchie de Juillet que Karl Marx avait rédigée en 1850 : cette dernière « n'était qu'une société par actions pour l'exploitation de la richesse nationale française […]. Louis-Philippe était le directeur de cette compagnie : Robert Macaire sur le throne ».

To all Those with Capital to Lose, 1838
An alle Personen, die Kapital zu verlieren haben
À toutes les personnes qui ont des capitaux à perdre
Stencil-coloured lithograph
From: Charles Philipon & Honoré Daumier,
Caricaturiana (Les Robert-Macaire), no. 20,
Paris, 1838

Charles Philipon achieved his greatest coup against the July Monarchy while the censorship laws were still in force. In the *Caricaturiana* series, which appeared in *Le Charivari* from 1836 to 1842, he adapted the stage character of the crooked Robert Macaire and combined him with the new market liberalism under Louis-Philippe and its unbridled greed for profit.

Der größte Coup gegen die Julimonarchie gelang Charles Philipon unter der Knute der Zensurgesetze. In der Serie *Caricaturiana*, die in *Le Charivari* von 1836 bis 1842 lief, adaptierte er die Bühnenfigur

des Betrügers Robert Macaire und führte sie mit der ungehemmten Profitgier des neuen Marktliberalismus unter Louis-Philippe zusammen.

Charles Philipon réussit le plus grand coup contre la monarchie de Juillet sous le joug des lois de censure. Dans la série *Caricaturiana* qui parut dans *Le Charivari* de 1836 à 1842, il reprit le personnage imaginaire d'escroc Robert Macaire et l'associa à la soif de profit effrénée du nouveau libéralisme de marché sous Louis-Philippe.

Auguste Raffet

The March on Constantine, October 1837, 1838
Vormarsch auf Constantine, Oktober 1837
Marche sur Constantine, Octobre 1837
Hand-coloured lithograph
From: Auguste Raffet, *Prise de Constantine*,
Paris, 1838

Auguste Raffet played a major role in the development of pictorial journalism. He was a student of Nicolas Toussaint Charlet's and working with the realism of Napoleonic historical art he depicted scenes in the form of cinematic sequences which, like this reconstruction of the capture of the Algerian city of Constantine, were based on meticulous research and detailed studies.

Auguste Raffet spielt in der Entwicklung des grafischen Journalismus eine überragende Rolle. Der Schüler Nicolas-Toussaint Charlets überführte den Realismus bonapartistischer Historienkunst in filmische Folgen, die wie diese Rekonstruktion der Einnahme der algerischen Metropole Constantine auf akribischen Recherchen und Detailstudien beruhten.

Auguste Raffet joua un rôle majeur dans l'évolution du journalisme illustré. Élève de Nicolas-Toussaint Charlet, il prit le parti de transposer l'épopée napoléonienne en épisodes cinématographiques, lesquels, à l'image de cette reconstitution de la prise de la ville algérienne de Constantine, reposaient sur des recherches acribiques et des études de détail.

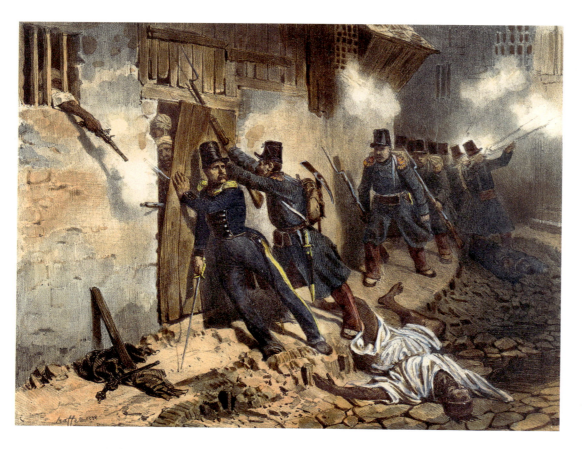

The Brilliant Captain Th. Le Blanc: Mortally Wounded in the Streets of Constantine, 1838
Der geniale Hauptmann Th. Le Blanc. Tödlich verwundet in den Straßen von Constantine
Le Capitaine de Génie Th. Le Blanc. Blessé à mort dans les rues de Constantine
Hand-coloured lithograph
From: Auguste Raffet, *Prise de Constantine*,
Paris, 1838

The scenes of fighting in the streets, showing sniper attacks, exploding booby traps and armed raids, that Raffet illustrated in a series of 18 designs would later find their modern counterparts in the guerrilla warfare of the 20th and 21st centuries.

Die urbanen Kampfszenen wie Heckenschützenattacken, Sprengstofffallen und Razzien, die Auguste Raffet in der 18-teiligen Folge schildert, sollten sich als charakteristisch für die Guerillakriege des 20. und 21. Jahrhunderts herausstellen.

Les scènes de combats de rue, avec attaques de tireurs d'élite, pièges explosifs et razzias, qu'Auguste Raffet a retracées dans une série de 18 épisodes, allaient se révéler caractéristiques des guérillas des XXᵉ et XXIᵉ siècles.

George Cruikshank (del. & sc.)

Air-um Scare-um Travelling, 1843
Leichtsinnige Luftreisen
Téméraires Voyages dans les airs
Etching
From: George Cruikshank, *The Comic Almanack for 1843*, London, 1844

In the popular series of *Comic Almanacks* that were published for 19 years beginning in 1835, George Cruikshank was able to present the full breadth of his styles from political caricatures to social satire and fantastic illustrations. This parody of the craze for ballon-powered flight, inspired by the artist William Heath's satirical responses to technology, was in turn an influence on later science-fiction illustration.

In seiner populären *Comic-Almanack*-Reihe, die ab 1835 für 19 Jahre erschien, konnte George Cruikshank sein breites Spektrum vom politischen Cartooning über die Gesellschaftssatire bis zur Fantasy-Illustration ausspielen. Die Parodie auf den Ballonflug-Hype, die an Techniksatiren von William Heath angelehnt ist, hat das Genre der Science-Fiction-Illustration beeinflusst.

Dans sa série populaire *Comic Almanack*, qui parut pendant dix-neuf ans à partir de 1835, George Cruikshank déploya un large éventail de croquis politiques depuis la satire sociale jusqu'à l'illustration fantastique. La parodie d'un lancement de ballon, inspirée des dessins satiriques sur la technologie de William Heath, influença le genre de l'illustration d'anticipation.

Superior
fast going
BALLOON
To
PARIS
Every
quarter
of an
hour —
Fares 6.d

Excursion
To
MONT BLANC
(To eat ice creams)
Returning the same
day — Parties wishing
to watch the Ava=
=lanches, may be
accomodated with
private Balloons
by the day or hour

The Balloon
Packet
for
Pekin & Canton
Every day —
NB Balloons from
Pekin (via) Bombay
every day, calling
three days a week
at Teneriffe

On Sunday
next
A Charity
Sermon
will be preached
in aid of the
Tumbleing
Fund

South
America
Every Day's

George Cruikshank

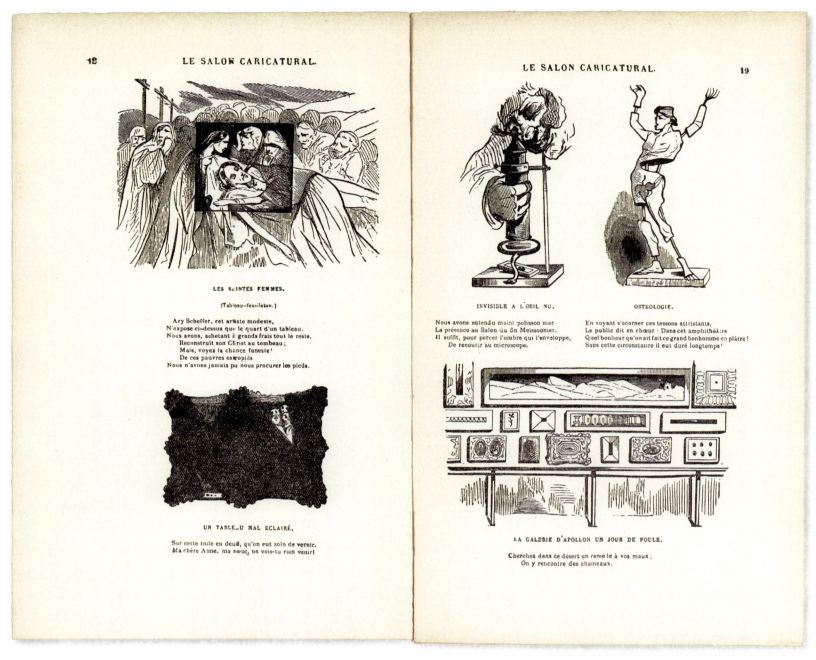

Charles Baudelaire & Raymond Pelez (attr.)*

An Exhibition of Caricatures, 1846
Der Karikatursalon
Le Salon caricatural
Wood engravings
From: Anonymous, *Le Salon caricatural. Critique en vers et contre tous: illustrée de soixante caricatures dessinées sur bois*, Paris, 1846

* attributed / zugeschrieben / attribué

While Honoré Daumier produced a number of caricatures of works that were intended to be typical of artists he had invented, the parodies in this collection were based on real artists and whole exhibitions. The first such *Salon* appeared in 1843, with illustrations by Bertall and Raymond Pelez, and the edition for 1846 featured ambiguous commentaries by Charles Baudelaire to the parodied works of artists such as Ary Scheffer and Ernest Meissonier.

Während Honoré Daumier ideal-typische Werke erfundener Künstler karikierte, zielten die nachfolgenden Parodien auf reale Künstler und ganze Ausstellungszusammenhänge. Die ersten *Salons caricaturaux* der Zeichner Raymond Pelez und Bertall waren 1843 erschienen. Charles Baudelaire verfasste 1846 die doppelbödigen Kommentare zu parodierten Gemälden von Künstlern wie Ary Scheffer und Ernest Meissonier.

Alors qu'Honoré Daumier réalisait des caricatures d'œuvres imaginaires incarnant les canons artistiques, les parodies suivantes visaient des artistes bien réels et des contextes entiers d'expositions. Les premiers *Salons caricaturaux* des illustrateurs Raymond Pelez et Bertall avaient paru en 1843. En 1846, Charles Baudelaire rédigea des commentaires ambigus sur les tableaux parodiés d'artistes comme Ary Scheffer et d'Ernest Meissonier.

Honoré Daumier

Salon de 1841
The Ascension of Jesus Christ, 1841
Christi Himmelfahrt
Ascension de Jésus-Christ
After the Original Painting by
Nach dem Originalgemälde von
D'après le tableau original de
M. Brrdhkmann
Hand-coloured lithograph
From: *Le Charivari*, Paris, 1 April 1841

The Paris Salon, the official exhibition of the Académie des Beaux-Arts, had long been a favourite subject for satirical illustrations with social content. The caricature shown here takes aim at the neo-religious paintings of the Nazarene school, focusing for the first time on individual works in the exhibition. Honoré Daumier's illustration established a genre of critical parodies of artistic works, which went on to greater popularity with the different editions of the *Salon caricatural*.

Der Salon de Paris, die offizielle Ausstellung der Académie des Beaux-Arts, war bislang ein beliebtes Thema für satirische Gesellschaftsstudien gewesen. Mit dieser Verspottung der neosakralen Malerei nazarenischer Schule konzentrierte sich die Karikatur erstmals auf die Exponate. Honoré Daumier begründete damit ein Genre grafischer Kunstkritik, die mit den Ausgaben des *Salon caricatural* zu größerer Popularität gelangte.

Le Salon de Paris, exposition officielle de l'Académie des Beaux-Arts, avait été jusqu'alors un motif de prédilection pour les caricatures du milieu artistique. Par cette raillerie de la peinture néo-sacrale selon l'école nazaréenne, la caricature prend cette fois pour cible les œuvres exposées. Honoré Daumier inaugura ainsi un genre de parodies critiques d'œuvres artistiques, qui jouit d'une grande popularité grâce à diverses éditions du *Salon caricatural*.

Imp. d'Aubert & Cie

Chez Bauger R du Croissant 16

ASCENSION DE JESUS-CHRIST

D'après le Tableau original de M. Brrdhkmann

George Cruikshank (del. & sc.)

Oliver Asking for More, 1837
Oliver bittet um einen Nachschlag
*Oliver demande une ration
supplémentaire*
Etching
From: *Bentley's Miscellany*, London,
1 February 1837

After the death of Robert Seymour, George Cruikshank was the second illustrator to work with Charles Dickens, a young journalist at the time, on developing the plots for his realistic social satires. The basic structure of *Oliver Twist*, the workhouse novel that was published as a serial in the literary magazine *Bentley's Miscellany*, was derived from a number of illustrations by William Hogarth.

George Cruikshank war, nachdem Robert Seymour verstorben war, der zweite Illustrator, mit dem der junge Journalist Charles Dickens die Plots seiner sozialrealistischen Satiren entwickelte. Das Grundgerüst der Armenhausnovelle *Oliver Twist*, die als Fortsetzungsgeschichte in dem Literaturmagazin *Bentley's Miscellany* erschien, basierte auf einer Grafikfolge von William Hogarth.

Après la mort de Robert Seymour, George Cruikshank fut le deuxième illustrateur avec lequel le jeune journaliste Charles Dickens développa les intrigues de ses satires socio-réalistes. La structure de base du roman des bas-fonds *Oliver Twist*, qui parut en feuilleton dans le magazine littéraire *Bentley's Miscellany*, reposait sur une série d'illustrations réalisées par William Hogarth.

John Leech & Ebenezer Landells (sc.)

Sir Robert Macaire
Endeavouring to Do an Exchequer Bill, 1841
Beim Versuch, einen staatlichen Wechsel einzulösen
Essayant d'endosser une lettre de change
Wood engraving
From: *Punch, or The London Charivari*,
6 November 1841

The English counterpart to Charles Philipon's *Charivari* was *Punch*, and enjoyed a similar success. Its founders included Henry Mayhew, who had already been involved with *Figaro in London*, together with Douglas Jerrold, Mark Lemon and the wood engraver Ebenezer Landells, a student of Thomas Bewick's. One of the magazine's chief targets was the conservative Prime minister Robert Peel, whose fiscal policies were compared with the devious schemes of Robert Macaire.

Die britische Replik auf Charles Philipons *Charivari* hieß *Punch* und war ähnlich erfolgreich. Zu den Gründern zählten Henry Mayhew, der bereits im *Figaro in London* involviert war, sowie Douglas Jerrold, Mark Lemon und der Holzstecher Ebenezer Landells, ein Schüler Thomas Bewicks. Eine bevorzugte Zielscheibe war der konservative Premier Robert Peel, dessen Fiskalpolitik mit den Machenschaften Macaires verglichen wird.

La réponse britannique au *Charivari* de Charles Philipon fut intitulée *Punch* et jouit d'un succès analogue. Parmi ses fondateurs comptèrent Henry Mayhew, qui avait déjà été impliqué dans *Figaro in London*, ainsi que Douglas Jerrold, Mark Lemon et le xylographe Ebenezer Landells, un élève de Thomas Bewick. Le Premier ministre conservateur Robert Peel, dont la politique fiscale est comparée aux machinations de Robert Macaire, était une cible privilégiée.

SIR ROBERT MACAIRE
ENDEAVOURING TO DO AN EXCHEQUER BILL.

"Henry" Asking for More, 1844
„Henry" bittet um einen Nachschlag
«Henry» demande une ration supplémentaire
Wood engraving
From: *Punch, or The London Charivari*,
30 March 1844

Henry Brougham, the founder of the Society for the Diffusion of Useful Knowledge, is pictured here in the guise of the orphaned Oliver Twist asking for a further helping of food at mealtime in the workhouse. Although he was a reformist Whig politician, Brougham was said to have ambitions to obtain a ministerial office in the conservative government of Robert Peel.

Henry Brougham, der Begründer der Society for the Diffusion of Useful Knowledge, ist hier als Waisenkind Oliver Twist porträtiert, das bei der Essensausgabe im Armenhaus auf einen Nachschlag drängt. Dem liberalen Reformpolitiker wurden Ambitionen auf ein Ministeramt in der konservativen Regierung unter Robert Peel nachgesagt.

Henry Brougham, le fondateur de la Society for the Diffusion of Useful Knowledge, est représenté ici comme l'orphelin Oliver Twist qui réclame une deuxième portion pendant la distribution de repas dans l'asile des pauvres. Le bruit courait que le politicien réformiste libéral ambitionnait un poste de ministre dans le gouvernement conservateur dirigé par Robert Peel.

"HENRY" ASKING FOR MORE.

Vide "OLIVER TWIST."

Kenny Meadows; John Orrin Smith & William James Linton (sc.)

The Chimney-sweep, 1840
Der Kaminkehrer | *Le Ramoneur*

The English Peasant, 1840
Der englische Bauer | *Le Paysan anglais*

The Bricklayer's Labourer, 1840
Der Maurergehilfe | *L'Aide-maçon*

The Capitalist, 1840
Der Kapitalist | *Le Capitaliste*

Wood engravings
From: Douglas Jerrold (ed.), *Heads of the People; or, Portraits of the English*, London, 1840/41

The two-volume collection in which these English character sketches are found was compiled by the satirist Douglas Jerrold in conjunction with the illustrator Kenny Meadows and a number of their journalist colleagues. The portraits mark the beginning of a wave of depictions of social types that influenced classic press graphics around the world.

Die zweibändige Sammlung englischer Charakterskizzen, die der Satiriker Douglas Jerrold in Zusammenarbeit mit dem Karikaturisten Kenny Meadows und einer Reihe befreundeter Journalisten realisierte, stand am Beginn einer Welle sozialer Typologien, die die klassische Pressegrafik international geprägt haben.

La collection en deux volumes d'esquisses de stéréotypes sociaux anglais, que le satiriste Douglas Jerrold produisit en collaboration avec le caricaturiste Kenny Meadows et un groupe d'amis journalistes, fut le début d'une vague de typologies sociales qui influenceront le dessin de presse classique.

THE CHIMNEY-SWEEP.

I reverence these young Africans of our own growth—who from their little pulpits (the tops of chimnies) in the nipping air of a December morning preach a lesson of patience to mankind.

ESSAYS OF ELIA.

THE ENGLISH PEASANT.

Poor and content, is rich and rich enough.

SHAKSPERE.

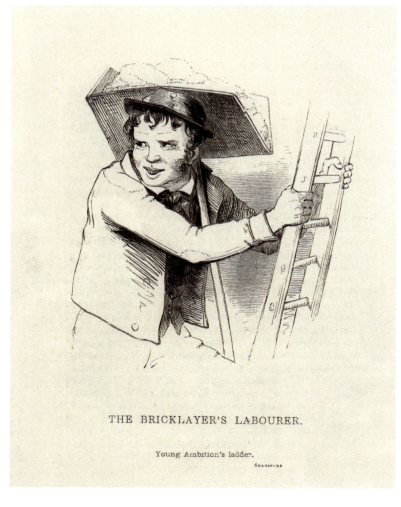

THE BRICKLAYER'S LABOURER.

Young Ambition's ladder.

SHAKSPERE.

THE CAPITALIST.

Nothing comes amiss, so money comes with all.

SHAKSPERE.

164   LA PORTIÈRE.

crainte des mauvaises charges des polissons du quartier.

Le chat est peu sédentaire, il va et vient, n'est jamais en place; assez bien vu dans quelques parties de la mai-

son, fort mal dans d'autres; il fournit rarement une longue carrière.

Chaque année, les cages reçoivent de nouveaux locataires: cette odeur de pipe et de *ratatouille*, qui constamment règne dans la loge, est en grande partie une des causes principales de l'émigration de leurs habitants.

Les petits cochons d'Inde pullulent d'une manière effrayante; ils se trouveraient assez bien de la loge, ils s'y plairaient bien davantage encore si tous n'étaient condamnés à être servis sur la table de leurs honorés maître et maîtresse. Jamais je n'en mangeai, mais je tiens de ma portière, qui en consomme fréquemment, que c'est un mets très-délicat et très-recherché.

Chez les garçons, la portière remplit souvent les fonctions de femme de ménage; c'est même une des belles cordes de son arc, quand elle a le talent de la bien faire jouer: un garçon n'y regarde jamais de près, et, si son heureuse étoile veut que le cher homme prenne ses déjeuners chez lui, elle trouve facilement moyen de sustenter, haut la main, elle et tous les siens, à ses frais et dépens.

Plus encore que la femme de ménage, la portière, qui va et vient à toute heure de jour et de nuit, à l'abri de tout contrôle, a beau jeu pour faire, comme on dit, ses orges; aussi la gaillarde fait-elle danser à *belle baise-*

Henry Monnier & Purret (sc.)

The Door-keeper, c. 1839
Die Portiersfrau | *La Portière*
Wood engraving
From: Léon Curmer (ed.),
Les Français peints par eux-mêmes,
Paris, 1840–1842

In France, the counterpart to Douglas Jerrold's miscellaneous collection of social types took the form of a truly monumental social panorama. This five-volume set, an "Encyclopaedia of 19th-century Morals and Manners", was in part conceived by Balzac, who was also one of its authors and at the time was engaged in the publication of his *Comédie humaine*. Curmer's collection featured the work of several well-known press illustrators, such as Nicolas Toussaint Charlet, Paul Gavarni and Honoré Daumier.

Die französische Erwiderung auf Douglas Jerrolds lose Typensammlung hatte die monumentale Dimension eines Sozialpanoramas. Die fünfbändige „Enzyklopädie der Sitten des 19. Jahrhunderts" war von Honoré de Balzac geprägt, der auch einer der Autoren war. Parallel begann er mit der Herausgabe seiner *Comédie humaine*. Beteiligt waren renommierte Pressegrafiker wie Nicolas-Toussaint Charlet, Paul Gavarni und Honoré Daumier.

La réponse française à la collection désordonnée de stéréotypes sociaux créée par Douglas Jerrold possédait les dimensions monumentales d'un panorama social. L'ouvrage sous-titré *Encyclopédie morale du XIXe siècle* fut largement influencé par Honoré de Balzac, qui en était aussi l'un des auteurs. Ce dernier entreprit simultanément la publication de sa *Comédie humaine*. De célèbres illustrateurs de presse comme Nicolas-Toussaint Charlet, Paul Gavarni et Honoré Daumier y apportèrent leur contribution.

Kenny Meadows & Ebenezer Landells (sc.)

The "Milk" of Poor-law "Kindness", 1843
Die „Milch" der „Güte" des Armengesetzes
Le « Lait » de la « bonté » de la Loi sur les indigents
Wood engraving
From: *Punch, or The London Charivari*,
28 January 1843

The idea behind this allegorical illustration of the inhuman consequences of the Poor Law that had recently been introduced, which separated mothers from their children and condemned men to the brutal working conditions found in prisons, may again be traced back to Douglas Jerrold. He and even more so his colleague Henry Mayhew were responsible for the confrontational tone *Punch* adopted in its early years in relation to the unacceptable violence of social reforms.

Die Idee zu dieser Allegorie über die inhumanen Konsequenzen des neuen Armengesetzes, das die Mütter von ihren Kindern trennte und die Männer unter gefängnisartigen Bedingungen verrohen ließ, stammte von Douglas Jerrold. Ihm vor allem und seinem Kollegen Henry Mayhew war der konfrontative sozialreformatorische Kurs geschuldet, den der *Punch* in den ersten Jahren einschlug.

L'idée de cette allégorie sur les conséquences inhumaines des nouvelles Poor Law (lois pour les indigents), qui séparaient les mères de leurs enfants et brutalisaient les hommes dans des conditions pénitenciaires, vint de Douglas Jerrold. Lui et surtout son collègue Henry Mayhew avaient pour mission de dénoncer la violence des réformes sociales, une ligne éditoriale qui caractérisa le *Punch* pendant ses premières années.

PUNCH'S PENCILLINGS.—Nº. LXII.

THE "MILK" OF POOR-LAW "KINDNESS."

SUBSTANCE AN

CARTOON, N°. I.

SHADOW.

CAPITAL AND LABOUR

←← **John Leech**

Cartoon No. I
Substance and Shadow, 1843
Substanz und Schatten
Substance et ombre
Wood engraving
From: *Punch, or The London Charivari*,
12 August 1843

The generic term "cartoon" can be traced back to its use here in titling John Leech's sarcastic caricature. His use of the word refers to illustrations on card for a competition of historical designs, but as the chief illustrator for *Punch* what he shows is the feudal mentality embedded in an exhibition of such designs in the Houses of Parliament, in contrast to the widespread misery that was the life of those on the streets of London outside.

Der Genrebegriff Cartoon leitet sich von John Leechs sarkastischer Kunstkarikatur ab. Er bezieht sich auf die Entwurfskartons für einen Historienwandbild-Wettbewerb. Der Chefzeichner des *Punch* zeigt hier den feudalen Habitus einer aktuellen Ausstellung mit diesen Entwurfskartons im Parlamentsgebäude im Kontrast zur epidemischen Not auf den Straßen Londons.

Le terme générique «cartoon» est dérivé de la caricature artistique et sarcastique de John Leech. Il est une référence aux esquisses sur carton destinées à un concours de fresques historiques. Le dessinateur en chef de *Punch* présente ici l'habitus féodal d'une exposition de ces dessins sur carton dans la Chambre du Parlement, lequel contraste avec l'immense misère régnant dans les rues de Londres.

CARTOON, No. V.

SHALLABALA

R.J. Hamerton (Shallabala)

Cartoon No. V
Capital and Labour, 1843
Kapital und Arbeit | *Capital et travail*
Wood engraving
From: *Punch, or The London Charivari*,
29 July 1843

The critical commentary in this historical cartoon is directed at the catastrophic failings revealed by a report on child labour in England in mines and factories. Hamerton compares the appalling working conditions in Manchester at a time of unregulated capitalism with slavery and the condition of slaves (see also ill. p. 142).

Das kritische Historienbild Nr. V kommentiert die katastrophalen Missstände, die ein Untersuchungsbericht über Kinderarbeit in englischen Bergwerken und Manufakturen offenbart hatte. Der Cartoonist vergleicht die schockierenden Arbeitsverhältnisse im unregulierten Manchester-Kapitalismus mit dem Zustand der Sklaverei (siehe auch Abb. S. 142).

L'image historique et critique n° V dénonce les désastreuses conditions de travail qu'un rapport d'enquête avait révélées sur l'emploi des enfants dans les mines et manufactures anglaises. Le dessinateur compare les scandaleuses conditions de travail du capitalisme incontrôlé de Manchester avec l'état d'esclavage (voir aussi ill. p. 142).

CHILDREN'S EMPLOYMENT COMMISSION. 49

because it is graphic, not only because it is true, but to show that the wretched condition of these children was just the same 15 years ago and upwards (we know not how long), previous to the establishment of the recent Commission.

The next species of employment to which children are put in the mines, as soon as they are strong enough, is that of dragging the loaded corves from the workings to the foot of the shaft. In some districts this is done by fixing a girdle round the naked waist, to which a chain from the corve is hooked and passed between the legs, and the boys or girls crawl on their hands and knees, drawing the corve full of coal after them. This is called "drawing by girdle and chain." In other districts the same kind of work is done by pushing with the head and hands from behind. This is called "putting," or "hurrying." Sometimes both the above methods are combined, as in the following illustration.

The printed evidence of the children, taken from various districts, will show the severe pain which this mode of labour inflicts. They attest that the girdle and chain frequently rub the skin off them, make blisters "as large as shillings and half-crowns," and otherwise injure the boys and girls. They get no rest all day, unless for a few moments at a time, and in general "only when something is the matter with the engine." The *human* engine, it will be perceived, is treated without any such consideration, though there is continually something the matter with it. The galling modes of work are various :—

Katharine Logan, 16 years old, coal-putter :—"Began to work at coal-carrying more than five years since ; works *in harness* now ; draws backwards, with face to the tubs ; the ropes and chains go under pit-clothes ; it is o'er sair work, especially when we crawl." (Franks, Report and Evidence, App. Pt. II., p. 389.)

Rosa Lucas, aged 18, Lamberhead Green :—" Do you find it very hard work ?—Yes, it is very hard work for a woman. I have been so tired many a time that I could scarcely wash myself. I could scarcely ever wash myself at night, I was
VOL. I.

so tired ; and I felt very dull and stiff when I set off in the morning." (Kennedy, Evidence, No. 92: App. Pt. II., p. 231, l. 53.)—James Crabtree, aged 15, Mr. Dearden's, near Todmorden :—" Is it hard work for the lads in winter ?—My brother falls asleep before his supper, and the little lass that helps him is often very tired." (Ibid. No. 71: p. 229, l. 11.) —Peter Gaskell, Mr. Lancaster's, near Worsley :—" Has four sisters, and they have all worked in the pits ; one of them works in the pits now ; she sometimes complains of the severity of her work. Three years ago, when they had very hard work, I used to hear her complain of the boils on her back, *and her legs were all eaten with the water* ; she had to go through water to her work ; she used to go about four or five o'clock in the morning, and stay till three or four in the afternoon, just as she was wanted ; I have known her to be that tired at night that she would go to sleep before she had anything to eat." (Ibid. No. 29: p. 217. l. 36.)

North Lancashire Coal and Iron Mines.—Mr. Austin, after giving a deplorable picture of the labour of young children in the thin-seam mines, illustrates its effect by the words of the parents of some young workers. "I wish," one of them states, "you could see them come in ; they come as tired as dogs, and throw themselves on the ground like dogs (here pointing to the hearthstone before the fire) ; we cannot get them to bed." (Austin, Report, § 11: App. Pt. II., p. 803.)

But whence, it will be asked, do all these poor boys and girls bring their heavy loads of coal ? From the remote darkness of a low, narrow den, in the bowels of the mine, at a distance from the shaft, perhaps, of upwards of 1000 yards, perhaps of 200, perhaps 2000, and through a passage of not more than from 18 to 20 inches in height. At the end of this there is the gloomy den called a "facing," a "heading," a "working," or a "man's room ;" and in that "room" lies the man at his work.

It has been seen, that a foolish lord has been angry at the sketches given by the Commission, and declared them to be exaggerations, and so forth. The following extract will show that many more startling sketches might have been made. There are abundant instances ; they were not illustrated ; but are not the words pictures ?

In this district (the West Riding of Yorkshire) girls are almost universally employed as trappers and hurriers in com-
E

Anonymous

Richard Henry Horne
Children's Employment Commission, 1843
Kommission zur Kinderarbeit
Commission sur le travail des enfants
Wood engraving
From: Douglas Jerrold (ed.), *The Illuminated Magazine*, vol. 1, London, May to October 1843

The report on which *Cartoon No. V* was based (pp. 140/141) was written by the critic and poet Horne, who later went on to work for Charles Dickens. Extracts from it were printed in *The Illuminated Magazine*, which was edited by Douglas Jerrold (who also wrote for *Punch*) and featured articles on such taboo subjects as suicide rates and conditions for inmates in mental asylums.

Der Bericht, auf den sich *Cartoon No. V* (siehe S. 140/141) bezog, wurde von dem Dichter Horne, einem späteren Mitarbeiter von Charles Dickens, abgefasst. Er wurde auszugsweise im *Illuminated Magazine* abgedruckt, einem von dem *Punch*-Redakteur Douglas Jerrold herausgegebenen Periodikum, das sich mit Tabuthemen wie Suizidalität und den Zuständen in psychiatrischen Kliniken auseinandersetzte.

Le rapport auquel se réfère *Cartoon No. V* (voir p. 140/141) fut rédigé par le poète Horne, futur assistant de Charles Dickens. Des extraits furent imprimés dans l'*Illuminated Magazine*, un périodique édité par le rédacteur de *Punch* Douglas Jerrold, qui abordait des sujets tabous comme le taux de suicides et les conditions d'internement dans les asiles psychiatriques.

William James Linton (del. & sc.)

The Deluge, 1839
Die Sintflut | *Le Déluge*
Wood engraving
From: *The National: A Library for the People*,
London, 22 June 1839

The expressive power of the cover illustrations for
The National was unparalleled for the graphic reproduction of the time. The designs are marked by an
early expressionistic style that was later championed
by William James Linton, one of the leading propo-
nents of wood engraving, and which notably influenced the artistic development of Van Gogh.

Die Ausdruckskraft der Titelillustrationen des
National war beispiellos im reproduktionsgrafischen
Kontext der Zeit. Hier kündigte sich bereits eine
frühexpressionistische Anschauung an, die William
James Linton später als tonangebender Xylografie-
Theoretiker propagieren sollte und die nicht zuletzt
auch Einfluss auf die künstlerische Entwicklung
van Goghs hatte.

La force expressive des illustrations de titre du
National était unique dans le contexte des reproductions illustrées de l'époque. Une approche de
l'expressionnisme précoce est ici manifeste, que
William James Linton comme théoricien de la
xylographie devait propager ultérieurement et
qui influença notamment l'évolution artistique
de Van Gogh.

THE DELUGE.

Fall of the Niagara, 1839
Fall des Niagara | *Chute du Niagara*
Wood engraving
From: *The National: A Library for the People*,
London, 23 February 1839

The National magazine was the work of the writer
and wood engraver William James Linton, and was
intended to be the journal of the new workers' movement in England and a republican counterpart to the
loyalist educational agenda of *The Penny Magazine*.
By way of alternative contents Linton featured a
selection of important texts relating to freedom and
emancipation together with some of his own politically propagandist poetry.

The National war ein Autorenmagazin des Xylografen und Dichters William James Linton, das sich als
Programmzeitung der neuen englischen Arbeiterbewegung sowie als republikanische Antwort auf das
loyalistische Bildungsprogramm des *Penny Magazine*
verstand. Als alternativen Kanon bot Linton ein Kom-
pendium klassischer emanzipatorischer Schriften
und eigene Agitprop-Lyrik an.

The National était une gazette du xylographe et
poète William James Linton, qui se voulait journal
programmatique du nouveau mouvement ouvrier
anglais et réponse républicaine au *Penny Magazine*.
Comme canon alternatif, Linton proposait un compendium d'écrits classiques émancipatoires et sa
propre poésie «agitprop».

FALL OF THE NIAGARA.

Richard Doyle

Thomas Hood
The Song of the Shirt, 1843
Das Lied vom Hemd
La Chanson de la chemise
Wood engraving
From: *Punch, or The London Charivari*,
December 1843

Thomas Hood's poem about the abject poverty of an underpaid worker in Victorian England seems out of place in the humorous Christmas edition of *Punch*, as seen in the comical vignettes by Richard Doyle. The enormous response to the poem, which was published anonymously, can be ascribed in part to this contrast.

Thomas Hoods Gedicht über die bittere Not einer viktorianischen Billiglohnarbeiterin wirkte in der humoresken Weihnachtsausgabe des *Punch* mit den verspielten Umrahmungen von Richard Doyles Vignetten ziemlich deplatziert. Die kolossale Resonanz, die das anonym erschienene Gedicht erfuhr, ist auch auf diesen Kontrast zurückzuführen.

Le poème de Thomas Hood sur l'affreuse misère d'une ouvrière sous-payée de l'ère victorienne, encadré des vignettes amusantes de Doyle, parut déplacé dans l'édition humoristique de Noël de *Punch*. La résonance colossale du poème qui fut publié anonymement peut être aussi attribuée à ce contraste.

260   PUNCH'S TRIUMPHAL PROCESSION!

THE SONG OF THE SHIRT.

WITH fingers weary and worn,
    With eyelids heavy and red,
A Woman sat, in unwomanly rags,
    Plying her needle and thread—
        Stitch! stitch! stitch!
In poverty, hunger, and dirt,
    And still with a voice of dolorous pitch
She sang the "Song of the Shirt!"

"Work! work! work!
While the cock is crowing aloof!
    And work—work—work,
Till the stars shine through the roof!
It 's O! to be a slave
    Along with the barbarous Turk,
Where woman has never a soul to save,
    If this is Christian work!

"Work—work—work
Till the brain begins to swim;
    Work—work—work
Till the eyes are heavy and dim!
Seam, and gusset, and band,
    Band, and gusset, and seam,
        Till over the buttons I fall asleep,
    And sew them on in a dream!

"O! Men, with Sisters dear!
    O! Men! with Mothers and Wives!
It is not linen you 're wearing out,
    But human creatures' lives!
        Stitch—stitch—stitch,
In poverty, hunger, and dirt,
Sewing at once, with a double thread,
    A Shroud as well as a Shirt.

"But why do I talk of Death?
    That Phantom of grisly bone,
I hardly fear his terrible shape,
    It seems so like my own—
    It seems so like my own,
Because of the fasts I keep,
Oh! God! that bread should be so dear,
    And flesh and blood so cheap!

"Work—work—work!
    My labour never flags;
And what are its wages?   A bed of straw,
    A crust of bread—and rags.

That shatter'd roof—and this naked floor—
    A table—a broken chair—
And a wall so blank, my shadow I thank
    For sometimes falling there!

"Work—work—work!
From weary chime to chime,
    Work—work—work—
As prisoners work for crime!
    Band, and gusset, and seam,
    Seam, and gusset, and band,
Till the heart is sick, and the brain benumb'd,
    As well as the weary hand.

"Work—work—work,
In the dull December light,
    And work—work—work,
When the weather is warm and bright—
While underneath the eaves
    The brooding swallows cling
As if to show me their sunny backs
    And twit me with the spring.

"Oh! but to breathe the breath
Of the cowslip and primrose sweet—
    With the sky above my head,
And the grass beneath my feet,
    For only one short hour
    To feel as I used to feel,
Before I knew the woes of want
    And the walk that costs a meal!

"Oh but for one short hour!
    A respite however brief!
No blessed leisure for Love or Hope,
    But only time for Grief!
A little weeping would ease my heart,
    But in their briny bed
My tears must stop, for every drop
    Hinders needle and thread!"

With fingers weary and worn,
    With eyelids heavy and red,
A Woman sate in unwomanly rags,
    Plying her needle and thread—
        Stitch! stitch! stitch!
In poverty, hunger, and dirt,
And still with a voice of dolorous pitch,
    Would that its tone could reach the Rich!
She sang this "Song of the Shirt!"

Thomas Sibson & William James Linton (sc.)

Bob Thin, 1845
Bob Spule | Bob effilé
Wood engraving
From: W.J. Linton, *Bob Thin, Part I: The Life
and Adventure of Bob Thin*, London, 1845

The success of Thomas Hood's poem *The Song of
the Shirt* prompted William James Linton to embark
on a project with one of the most complex illustration schemes that had yet been seen. The four parts
of this new poem, about a weaver called Bob Thin
(sounds like "bobbin") who escaped from the poorhouse and found a safe haven in a rural community,
were illustrated by Linton and three artist colleagues
of his within a carefully integrated overall plan. It was
published in Douglas Jerrold's *Illuminated Magazine*
and a number of special editions.

Der Erfolg von Thomas Hoods *The Song of the Shirt*
motivierte William James Linton zu einem der kom-
plexesten Illustrationsprojekte. Die vier Teile seines
Gedichts über einen Weber namens Bob Thin (klingt
wie „bobbin" – „Garnspule"), der aus dem Armenhaus
flieht und Erfüllung in einer Landkommune findet,
wurde von Linton und drei befreundeten Künstlern
auf ganz unterschiedliche Weise grafisch orchestriert.
Das Werk wurde in Douglas Jerrolds *Illuminated
Magazine* und in Sonderdrucken publiziert.

Le succès de *The Song of the Shirt* de Thomas
Hood incita William James Linton à réaliser l'un
des projets d'illustration les plus complexes. Les
quatre parties de son poème sur un tisserand nommé Bob Thin (sonne comme „bobbin" – «bobine»)
qui fuit l'hospice des pauvres et trouve son salut
dans une commune rurale furent coordonnées, gra-
phiquement parlant, par Linton et trois amis artistes
de manières différentes. L'œuvre fut publiée dans
l'*Illuminated Magazine* de Douglas Jerrold et dans
des éditions spéciales.

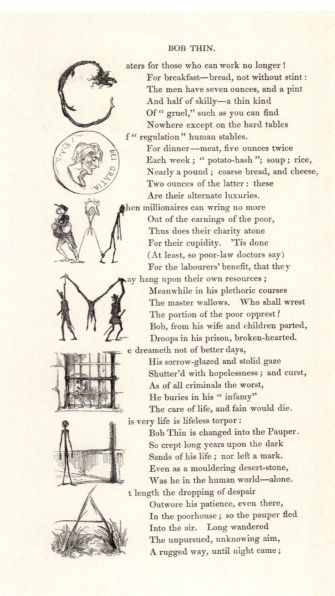

William James Linton (del. & sc.)

Song of the Stream, 1845
Lied vom Bach | Chanson du ruisseau
Wood engraving
From: W.J. Linton, *Bob Thin, Part II:
The Poorhouse Fugitive*, London, 1845

To show his support for the Chartist Land Plan,
William James Linton published this poetic work
which was inspired by William Blake's close integration of text and image in his own works. It first
appeared in *The Illuminated Magazine*, where Linton
had taken over from Douglas Jerrold as editor, and
again in various special editions.

Zur Unterstützung des Landbesiedlungsplans der
Chartisten publizierte William James Linton das
von William Blakes vielschichtigen Bild- und Text-
bezügen inspirierte Werk zuerst im *Illuminated Magazine*, dessen Herausgeberschaft er von Douglas
Jerrold übernommen hatte, sowie in verschiedenen
Sonderdrucken.

Afin de soutenir le plan agraire des chartistes, William
James Linton publia d'abord l'œuvre inspirée des
références multiples tant sur le plan du texte que de
l'image de William Blake dans l'*Illuminated Magazine*,
où il avait succédé à Douglas Jerrold comme éditeur,
ainsi que dans diverses éditions spéciales.

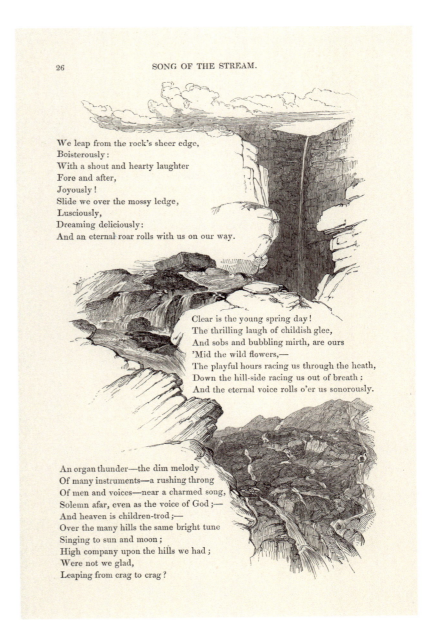

The Rise of Illustrated Journalism

In May 1842, the first mass-circulation illustrated news magazine was published with the launch of the weekly *Illustrated London News*. The publisher Herbert Ingram, a former printer and newsagent, had noticed that newspapers such as the *Observer* and the *Weekly Chronicle* sold better when they featured pictures of notable events. However, with costs being high because of the stamp duty on newspapers it was only when the weekly satirical magazine *Punch* became successful that he felt encouraged to risk the huge financial investment required to produce a popular news magazine. To begin with, Ingram hired several illustrators who had worked on *Punch* to help with the workload. A year later, two important news magazines were launched in quick succession in mainland Europe, firstly in Paris with *L'Illustration* and then in Leipzig with the *Illustrirte Zeitung*, both of which took their lead from the popular educational journal *The Penny Magazine*.

At a time when widespread repression and a precarious economic situation were so bad that the decade became known, in Britain, as the Hungry Forties, the liberal ethos of social reform associated with the founding of these first illustrated magazines was potentially highly explosive. Indeed, it would be difficult to overestimate the influence of the rise of illustrated news magazines on the dynamics of the revolutions that took place across Europe in 1848. Conversely though, when these uprisings were suppressed, the press landscape was itself changed with lasting effect. Political illustrations, which had just had a brief but dramatic run of popularity, now all but disappeared, and only a few,

rather lightweight satirical magazines were able to survive the reactionary ice age that set in. In France, where a conservative Republic had been formed with a nephew of Napoleon's as president, the reactionary picture stories of Rodolphe Töpffer and his successor Cham were particularly successful. These early comic strips were also welcomed by the German press where they were combined with a style that emphasised line and contour after the Nazarene school of artists, with the aim of invoking an Old German national identity. Although England mostly escaped revolution and conflict, the conservative change of course was nevertheless clearly reflected in the English illustrated press. The best indicator of this was the groundbreaking magazine *Punch* which, after the departure of its co-editor and founder, the social reformer and satirist Henry Mayhew, increasingly became a vehicle for loyalist propaganda and loudly barked its patriotism during the British Empire's colonial wars.

A new era of imperialism began in December 1851 when Louis Napoléon organised a bloody coup which replaced the Second Republic with a new Bonapartist Empire. The photographic realism that was now required as state art also increasingly determined the appearance of illustrated magazines. Social satire and grotesquely exaggerated physiognomies, which had played an important subliminal role in the oppositional realism of illustrators such as Gustave Courbet, were now seen as anachronistic and troublesome. As such, caricature and documentary press graphics began to move apart during the 1850s, a shift that manifested itself most clearly in the genre change

A. Door to the cart-house.   B. Door by which the officers entered.   C. Stable window.   D. Loft-door.

Anonymous

Stable Where the Cato Street
Conspirators Met, 1820
Stall, in dem sich die Verschwörer
von der Cato Street trafen
Étable où se rencontraient les
conspirateurs de la Rue Cato
Wood engraving
From: The Observer, London,
5 March 1820

Even before the days of illustrated
news items, a few popular newspapers occasionally included pictures
with their reports. This example from
The Observer shows the base that
was used by a group of supporters of
the early proto-communist Thomas
Spence while they plotted their attack
on the Prime Minister and his cabinet.

Hin und wieder gab es in einigen
populären Zeitungen bereits vor der
Ära der Illustrierten bebilderte Nachrichten. Das Beispiel aus dem Observer zeigt den Ort, an dem eine Gruppe
von Anhängern des Frühkommunisten
Thomas Spence einen Anschlag auf
das britische Kabinett geplant hatte.

Bien avant l'époque des magazines
illustrés, quelques journaux populaires publiaient déjà de temps à
autre des nouvelles avec des images.
Cet exemple de l'Observer montre
l'endroit où un groupe de supporters
de Thomas Spence, communiste de
la première heure, avait fomenté une
attaque contre le Cabinet britannique.

and artistic conflicts of the exceptionally talented young artist
Gustave Doré.

The Crimean War (1853–1856), in which Britain and France
joined forces against the expansion of the Russian Empire, was
the first major conflict for countries in Europe since the Battle of
Waterloo. The media spectacle it represented brought enormous
challenges for the editors of illustrated news magazines, and
since at this time there was still no proper network of professional picture correspondents it was often necessary to rely on
sketches made by the troops themselves. The most prominent
special artists working in Crimea were Henri Durand-Brager, who
was there on behalf of L'Illustration in France, and Constantin
Guys, representing The Illustrated London News. Both of these
pioneers of illustrated war reporting also had military training in
common, which was of considerable help when communicating
in the field. In terms of their professional qualities, however, they
were almost polar opposites since Durand-Brager, who was also
a brilliant writer, brought a meticulously naturalistic style of documentation to his precise illustrations, whereas Guys preferred a
freer and more general drawing style. He was later identified by
the Impressionist avant-garde as a key figure in pictorial journalism because of his rapid, roving method of working.

While written reports could be transmitted at this time by
telegraph, sending drawings in could often take several weeks.
As a result, the illustrations that appeared in the press were not
synchronised with the events actually being reported. Even so,
illustrators did not have to worry about competition from war

photographers, for although their sketches were often signifi-
cantly distorted by the work of editorial draughtsmen and engravers, they still had the decisive advantage over photography in
that because they did not require long exposure times they could
reproduce the action as it happened.

The media war set against a backdrop of eye-catching scenes
in the east gave the illustrated magazines a huge boost in circulation and helped to consolidate the new business of pictorial
reporting. Among the many periodicals launched elsewhere in
the world in the wake of the Crimean War mention should be
made of two in the United States, Frank Leslie's Illustrated Newspaper (1855) and Harper's Weekly (1857), whose high-quality
illustrated reporting soon rivalled that in European magazines.
During the American Civil War (1861–1865) these magazines
established a veritable cult of the picture reporter. The illustrator, referred to as "our artist", acted as a direct agent for readers
to ensure they felt as though they were personally involved in
the events on the battlefields. The young special artist Thomas
Nast was one who was partly responsible for this situation,
since he knew how to promote himself more successfully than
anyone else.

Der Aufstieg des Bildjournalismus

Im Mai 1842 erschien mit der Startausgabe der wöchentlichen *The Illustrated London News* die erste Nachrichtenillustrierte in Großauflage. Der Herausgeber Herbert Ingram, ein erfahrener Drucker und Zeitungshändler, hatte die Beobachtung gemacht, dass sich Zeitungen wie der *Observer* oder der *Weekly Chronicle* immer dann besonders gut verkauften, wenn sie anlässlich besonderer Ereignisse Bilder enthielten. Erst das Beispiel des erfolgreichen satirischen Wochenmagazins *Punch* hatte ihn jedoch ermutigt, den enormen finanziellen Einsatz zu riskieren, der notwendig war, um ein populäres Nachrichtenmagazin gegen die Teuerung durch die Stempelsteuer durchzusetzen. In der Anfangszeit griff Ingram auch auf die Mitarbeit etlicher Grafiker des Magazins *Punch* zurück. Die beiden kontinentalen Gründungen großer Nachrichtenillustrierten, die ein Jahr später in schneller Folge zuerst in Paris (*L'Illustration*) und dann in Leipzig (*Illustrirte Zeitung*) folgen sollten, bauten hingegen auf den redaktionellen Strukturen des populärwissenschaftlichen *Penny Magazine* auf.

Der liberale sozialreformatorische Ethos, der mit diesen ersten Illustriertengründungen verbunden war, hatte angesichts der repressiven Umstände und der prekären ökonomischen Situation einer Zeit, die als „Hungry Forties" bekannt wurden, eine ganz besondere Brisanz. Auf die Dynamik der europaweiten 1848er-Revolutionen hatte der Aufstieg des illustrierten Nachrichtenwesens einen kaum zu überschätzenden Einfluss. Die Niederschlagungen dieser Aufstände veränderte die Presselandschaft auf nachhaltige Weise. Die politische Karikatur, die

gerade eine kurze und heftige Blütezeit erlebt hatte, verschwand weitgehend von der Bildfläche. Nur wenige handzahme Satiremagazine waren in der Lage, die einsetzende Eiszeit der Reaktion zu überleben. In Frankreich, wo sich eine konservative Republik unter der Präsidentschaft eines Neffen von Napoleon Bonaparte herausgebildet hatte, machten die reaktionären Bildergeschichten Rodolphe Töpffers und seines Nachfolgers Cham Furore. Diese frühen Comics fielen auch in der deutschen Presse auf fruchtbaren Boden und verbanden sich dort mit einem nazarenischen Konturstil, der eine altdeutsche Nationalidentität beschwören sollte. Obgleich England von revolutionären Konflikten weitgehend verschont geblieben war, schlug sich auch dort der konservative Kurswechsel in in der Bildpresse deutlich nieder. Bester Indikator war das tonangebende Magazin *Punch*, das sich nach dem Weggang seines Begründers und Mitherausgebers, des sozialreformerischen Satirikers Henry Mayhew, immer mehr zu einem loyalistischen Propagandablatt entwickelte, das die Kolonialkriege des britischen Weltreichs mit chauvinistischem Gebell begleitete.

Eine neue Ära des Imperialismus kündigte sich im Dezember 1851 an, als Louis Napoléon die Zweite Republik nach einem blutigen Putsch in ein weiteres bonapartistisches Kaiserreich überführte. Der fotografische Realismus, der als Staatskunst propagiert wurde, bestimmte zunehmend auch das Erscheinungsbild der Illustrierten. Sozialsatire und physiognomische Groteske, die im oppositionellen Realismus eines Gustave Courbet eine wichtige unterschwellige Rolle spielten, wurden

Anonymous

Somerset House Stamp Office, 1842
Unloading the Illustrated London News
Abladen der Illustrated London News
Déchargement des Illustrated London News
Wood engraving
From: *The Illustrated London News*,
24 September 1842

Until stamp duty in England was abolished
in 1855, newspapers had to be transported
to the central tax office at Somerset House
before it was permitted for them to be
distributed.

Bis zur Aufhebung der Stempelsteuer – in
England 1855 – mussten die Zeitungen vor
ihrer Auslieferung ins zentrale Steuerbüro
transportiert werden.

Jusqu'à la suppression du droit de timbre –
en 1855 en Angleterre – les journaux
devaient être transportés au bureau central
des impôts avant d'être livrés.

als anachronistisch und heikel empfunden. Karikatur und dokumentarische Pressegrafik begannen sich in den 1850er-Jahren
langsam auseinanderzuentwickeln; ein Phänomen, das sich in
den Genrewechsel und den künstlerischen Konflikten des jugendlichen Ausnahmetalents Gustave Doré auf exemplarische
Weise zeigte.

Der Krimkrieg (1853–1856), in dem England und Frankreich
gemeinsam gegen das expandierende russische Zarenreich vor-
gingen, war der erste Großkrieg seit der Schlacht von Waterloo.
Das Medienspektakel stellte die Redaktionen der Illustrierten
vor enorme Herausforderungen. Da es noch kein geeignetes
Netzwerk professioneller Bildkorrespondenten gab, musste man
häufig auf Vorlagen von Truppenangehörigen zurückgreifen.
Die führenden *special artists* auf der Krim waren Henri Durand-
Brager, der für die französische *L'Illustration* arbeitete, und
Constantin Guys, der die britische *Illustrated London News* vertrat. Gemeinsam war beiden Pionieren des grafischen Kriegs-
journalismus, dass sie über eine militärische Ausbildung verfügten, was ihnen die Kommunikation vor Ort erheblich erleichterte.
Darüber hinaus verkörperten sie jedoch zwei geradezu entgegengesetzte Qualitäten ihrer Profession. Durand-Brager, der
auch ein brillanter Autor war, antizipierte in der Präzision seiner
Beschreibungen eine akribische, naturalistische Form der Reportage. Guys hingegen bevorzugte einen freien, synoptischen
Zeichenstil. Die impressionistische Avantgarde erkor ihn später
aufgrund seiner beschleunigten, ambulanten Aufzeichnungswei-
se zur bildjournalistischen Leitfigur.

Während Textbeiträge bereits telegrafisch übermittelt werden konnten, dauerte der Transport der Zeichnungen oft mehrere Wochen. Dementsprechend asynchron verhielten sich
die Bildnachrichten zur Nachrichtenlage. Die Konkurrenz der
Kriegsfotografen brauchten die Zeichner allerdings noch nicht
zu fürchten. Obgleich ihre Skizzen durch die Interpretationen
der Redaktionszeichner und Xylografen oft erheblich verfälscht
wurden, hatten diese gegenüber der Fotografie, die mit langen
Belichtungszeiten operieren musste, den entscheidenden Vorteil, dass sie Handlung wiedergeben konnten.

Der Medienkrieg vor der pittoresken orientalischen Kulisse
beschied den Illustrierten phänomenale Auflagensteigerungen
und trug mit dazu bei, das junge Gewerbe zu konsolidieren.
Zu den vielen internationalen Neugründungen im Kielwasser
des Krimkriegs zählten auch die beiden führenden nordamerikanischen Illustrierten *Frank Leslie's Illustrated Newspaper*
(1855) und *Harper's Weekly* (1857), deren hochwertige grafische Berichterstattung schon bald mit den europäischen Magazinen konkurrieren konnte. Während des Sezessionskriegs
(1861–1865) zelebrierten sie einen regelrechten Kult um den
Bildreporter. Als *our artist* wurde der Zeichner zum Agenten
der Leserschaft stilisiert, der für eine persönliche Teilhabe an
den Geschehnissen auf den Schlachtfeldern zu sorgen hatte.
Mit verantwortlich für diesen Hype war der jugendliche *special*
Thomas Nast, der sich bei seinen Einsätzen wirkungsvoll wie
kein anderer in Szene zu setzen wusste.

L'Essor des nouvelles illustrées

En mai 1842, avec le premier numéro de l'hebdomadaire *The Illustrated London News* parut le premier magazine d'informations illustré à grand tirage. L'éditeur Herbert Ingram, un imprimeur et marchand de journaux expérimenté, avait observé que des journaux comme l'*Observer* ou le *Weekly Chronicle* se vendaient extraordinairement bien quand ils contenaient des images relatives à des événements particuliers. Mais c'est seulement l'exemple du succès du magazine hebdomadaire satirique *Punch* qui l'avait encouragé à risquer l'énorme investissement financier nécessaire au lancement d'un magazine d'informations populaire contre la hausse du prix due au droit de timbre. Dans les premiers temps, Ingram eut recours également à la collaboration de nombreux dessinateurs du magazine *Punch*. La création de deux grands magazines illustrés sur le continent, qui devait survenir un an plus tard à peu d'intervalle, d'abord à Paris (*L'Illustration*), puis à Leipzig (*Illustrirte Zeitung*), s'inspirait, elle, des structures rédactionnelles du journal d'esprit populaire et scientifique, *Penny Magazine*.

Face aux conditions répressives et à la situation économique précaire d'une époque connue sous le nom de « Hungry Forties », l'éthique libérale aspirant à des réformes sociales qui soustendait ces premières créations de magazines renfermait un potentiel explosif. La montée en puissance du secteur des informations illustrées eut une influence certaine sur la dynamique des révolutions de 1848 à travers l'Europe entière. L'écrasement de ces révoltes transforma le paysage médiatique de façon durable. La caricature politique, qui venait de connaître une courte et vigoureuse apogée, disparut quasiment de la scène. Seuls de rares magazines complaisants furent capables de survivre à l'ère de glace imposée en réaction. En France, où une république conservatrice s'était formée sous la présidence d'un neveu de Napoléon Bonaparte, les histoires illustrées réactionnaires de Rodolphe Töpffer et de son successeur Cham faisaient un tabac. Ces toutes premières bandes dessinées trouvèrent aussi dans la presse allemande un sol fertile et adoptèrent un style aux contours nazaréens qui devait raviver une identité nationale allemande conservatrice. Bien que l'Angleterre restât dans l'ensemble préservée des conflits révolutionnaires, là encore le changement de cap conservateur de la presse illustrée eut des répercussions certaines. Le meilleur indicateur en fut le magazine *Punch* qui donnait le ton et qui, après le départ de son fondateur et coéditeur Henry Mayhew, un satiriste favorable à des réformes sociales, se transforma à vue d'œil en un journal de propagande loyaliste qui accompagnait les guerres coloniales de l'Empire britannique d'aboiements chauvinistes.

En décembre 1851, une nouvelle ère d'impérialisme s'annonça lorsqu'après un putsch sanglant Louis-Napoléon remania la Deuxième République en un nouvel empire bonapartiste. Le réalisme photographique que Napoléon propageait comme art officiel définit de plus en plus aussi l'apparence des magazines. La satire sociale et le grotesque physiognomonique qui jouaient un rôle latent mais important dans le réalisme contestataire d'un Gustave Courbet étaient ressentis comme anachroniques et scabreux. Pendant les années 1850, caricature et

Gustave Courbet

Long Live the Republic, 1848
Es lebe die Republik
Vive la République
Wood engraving
From: *Le Salut public*, Paris, 1848

The title vignette for the second issue of Charles Baudelaire's revolutionary newspaper *Le Salut public* is the only example of press graphic work by Gustave Courbet that did not suffer at the hands of the censor. The adaptation of Eugène Delacroix's famous painting *La Liberté guidant le peuple* (*Liberty Leading the People*, 1830) suggests that the freedom envisioned by Delacroix had yet to be won.

Bei der Titelvignette für die zweite Ausgabe von Charles Baudelaires Revolutionszeitung *Le Salut public* handelt es sich um die einzige Pressegrafik Gustave Courbets, die nicht einer Zensur zum Opfer gefallen war. Die Adaption von Eugène Delacroix' populärem Gemälde *La liberté guidant le peuple* (*Die Freiheit führt das Volk*, 1830) suggerierte, dass die Freiheit, die Delacroix vor Augen gehabt hatte, erst noch erkämpft werden musste.

La vignette de titre de la seconde édition du journal révolutionnaire de Charles Baudelaire *Le Salut public* est le seul dessin de presse de Gustave Courbet qui n'ait pas été victime de la censure. L'adaptation du tableau populaire d'Eugène Delacroix *La Liberté guidant le peuple* (1830) suggérait que la liberté telle que Delacroix la voyait devait encore être conquise.

dessin de presse documentaire commencèrent peu à peu à se dissocier, phénomène qui se manifesta de façon exemplaire dans les conflits artistiques et le passage à un autre genre du jeune et exceptionnellement talentueux Gustave Doré.

La guerre de Crimée (1853-1856), au cours de laquelle l'Angleterre et la France luttèrent ensemble contre l'Empire tsariste russe en pleine expansion, fut le premier conflit majeur depuis la bataille de Waterloo. Le spectacle médiatique posait d'énormes défis aux rédactions des magazines illustrés. Comme il n'existait pas encore de réseau approprié de photojournalistes professionnels, il fallait bien souvent avoir recours aux croquis de militaires. Les *special artists* de premier plan en Crimée étaient Henri Durand-Brager, qui travaillait pour le journal français *L'Illustration*, et Constantin Guys, qui représentait le magazine britannique *Illustrated London News*. Le point commun de ces deux pionniers du reportage de guerre illustré était qu'ils avaient reçu une formation militaire, ce qui facilitait considérablement la communication sur place. De plus, ils incarnaient deux qualités pratiquement opposées dans leur profession. Durand-Brager, brillant auteur au demeurant, anticipa dans la précision de ses descriptions une forme acribique et naturaliste de reportage. Guys, au contraire, préférait un style pictural libre et synoptique. L'avant-garde impressionniste l'adopta plus tard comme figure emblématique en raison de son style d'écriture rapide et changeant.

Alors que les rapports écrits pouvaient déjà être transmis par télégraphe, le transport de dessins durait souvent des semaines.

En conséquence, les informations par images n'étaient pas adaptées à la situation réelle. Toutefois, les dessinateurs ne devaient pas encore craindre la concurrence des photographes de guerre. Si les croquis étaient souvent falsifiés à travers les interprétations des dessinateurs de rédaction et des xylographes, ils présentaient par rapport à la photographie, qui devait opérer sur de longs temps d'exposition, l'avantage décisif de pouvoir reproduire l'action.

La guerre des médias se déroulant devant des coulisses orientales pittoresques fournit aux illustrés de fabuleuses augmentations de tirage et contribua à consolider le jeune secteur. Parmi les nombreuses nouvelles créations internationales dans le sillage de la guerre de Crimée, il convient de citer aussi les deux magazines américains de premier plan *Frank Leslie's Illustrated Newspaper* (1855) et *Harper's Weekly* (1857), dont la couverture illustrée accrocheuse haut de gamme put rapidement faire concurrence aux magazines européens. Pendant la guerre de Sécession (1861-1865) ils entretinrent un véritable culte du reporter illustrateur. Le dessinateur, désigné sous le nom de *our artist* fut promu au grade d'agent des lecteurs et devait participer en personne aux événements sur les champs de bataille. C'est le jeune *special* Thomas Nast qui déclencha cet engouement et qui, lors de ses interventions, savait comme aucun autre se mettre en valeur.

THE ILLUSTRATED LONDON NEWS

No. 1.] FOR THE WEEK ENDING SATURDAY, MAY 14, 1842. [SIXPENCE

OUR ADDRESS.

In presenting the first number of the ILLUSTRATED LONDON NEWS to the British Public, we would fain make a graceful entrée into the wide and grand arena, which will henceforth contain so many actors for our benefit and so many spectators of our career. In plain language, we do not produce this illustrated newspaper without some vanity, much ambition, and a fond belief that we shall be pardoned the presumption of the first quality by realizing the aspirations of the last. For the past ten years we have watched with admiration and enthusiasm the progress of illustrative art, and the vast revolution which it has wrought in the world of publication through all the length and breadth of this mighty empire. To the wonderful march of periodical literature it has given an impetus and a rapidity almost coequal with the gigantic power of steam. It has converted blocks into wisdom, and given wings and spirit to ponderous and senseless wood. It has in its turn adorned, gilded, reflected, and interpreted, nearly every form of thought. It has given to fancy a new dwelling-place, to imagination a more permanent throne. It has set up fresh land-marks of poetry, given sterner pungency to satire, and mapped out the geography of mind with clearer boundaries and more distinct and familiar intelligence than it ever bore alone. Art—as now fostered, and redundant in the peculiar and facile department of wood engraving—has, in fact, become the bride of literature ; genius has taken her as its handmaid, and popularity has crowned her with laurels that only seem to grow the greener the longer they are worn.

And there is now no staying the advance of this art into all the departments of our social system. It began in a few isolated volumes—stretched itself next over fields of natural history and science—penetrated the arcanæ of our own general literature—and made companionship with our household books. At one plunge it was in the depth of the stream of poetry—working with its every current—partaking of the glow, and adding to the sparkles of the glorious waters—and so refreshing the very soul of genius, that even Shakspeare came to us clothed with a new beauty, while other kindred poets of our language seemed as it were to have put on festive garments to crown the marriage of their muses to the arts. Then it walked abroad among the people, went into the poorer cottages, and visited the humblest homes in cheap guises, and, perhaps, in roughish forms ; but still with the illustrative and the instructive principle strongly worked upon, and admirably developed for the general improvement of the human race. Lastly, it took the merry aspect of fun, frolic, satire, and *badinage* ; and the school of *Charivari* began to blend itself with the graver pabulum of Penny Cyclopædias and Saturday Magazines.

And now, when we find the art accepted in all its elements, and welcomed by every branch of reading into which it has diverged ; now, when we see the spirit of the times everywhere associating with it, and heralding or recording its success ; we do hold it as of somewhat triumphant omen that WE are, by the publication of this very newspaper, launching the giant vessel of illustration into a channel the broadest and the widest that it has ever dared to stem. We bound at once over the billows of a new ocean—we sail into the very heart and focus of public life—we take the world of newspapers by storm, and flaunt a banner on which the words "ILLUSTRATED NEWS" become symbols of a fresher purpose, and a more enlarged design, than was ever measured in that hemisphere till now.

The public will have henceforth under their glance, and within their grasp, the very form and presence of events as they transpire, in all their substantial reality, and with evidence visible as well as circumstantial. And whatever the broad and palpable delineations of wood engraving can be taught to achieve, will now be brought to bear upon every subject which attracts the attention of mankind, with a spirit in unison with the character of such subject, whether it be serious or satirical, trivial or of purpose grave.

And, reader, let us open something of the detail of this great intention to your view. Begin, *par exemple*, with the highest region of newspaper literature—the Political. Why, what a field ! If we are strong in the creed that we adopt—if we are honest, as we pledge ourselves to be, in the purpose that we maintain—how may we lend muscle, bone, and sinew to the tone taken and the cause espoused, by bringing to bear upon our opinions, a whole battery of vigorous illustration. What "H. B." does amid the vacillations of parties, without any prominent opinions of his own, *we* can do

with double regularity and consistency, and therefore with more valuable effect. Moreover, regard the homely illustration which nearly every public measure will afford :—your Poor-laws—your Corn-laws—your Factory bills—your Income taxes ! Look at the field of public portraiture presented in your Houses of Legislature alone, and interesting to every constituency in the land. Open your police-offices, your courts of law, your criminal tribunals—all the pith and marrow of the administration of justice—you can have it broadly before you, with points of force, of ridicule, of character, or of crime ; and if the pen be ever led into fallacious argument, the pencil must at least be oracular with the spirit of truth.

In the world of diplomacy, in the architecture of foreign policy, we can give you every trick of the great Babel that other empires are seeking to level or to raise. Is there peace ? then shall its arts, implements, and manufactures be spread upon our page. The literature—the customs—the dress—nay, the institutions and localities of other lands, shall be brought home to you with spirit, with fidelity, and, we hope, with discretion and taste. Is there war ? then shall its seat and actions be laid naked before the eye. No estafette—no telegraph—no steam-winged vessel—no overland mail, shall bring intelligence to our shores that shall not be sifted with industry, and illustrated with skill in the columns of this journal ; and whether the cowardice of China or the treachery of Afffghanistan be the theme of your abhorrence or resentment, you shall at least have as much historical detail of both as, while it gratifies general curiosity, shall minister to the natural anxieties at home of those who have friends and relations amid the scenes delineated and the events described.

Take another fruitful branch of illustration, the pleasures of the people !—their theatres, their concerts, their galas, their races, and their fairs ! Again, the pleasures of the aristocracy—their court festivals, their *bals masqués*, their levees, their drawing rooms—the complexion of their grandeur, and the circumstance of all their pomp !

In literature, a truly beautiful arena will be entered upon ; for we shall not only, in most instances, have the opportunity of illustrating our own reviews, but of borrowing selections from the illustrations of the numerous works which the press is daily pouring forth, so elaborately embellished with woodcuts in the highest style of art.

In the field of fine arts——but let the future speak, and let us clip promise in the wing. We have perhaps said enough, without

condescending to the littleness of too much detail, to mark the general outline of our design ; and we trust to the kindness and intelligence of our readers to imagine for us a great deal more than we have been able to crowd into the compass of an introductory leader. Moreover, we would strongly premise an expression of gratitude for all suggestions that may hereafter reach us, and assure our volunteers of these, that wherever there seems a possibility of acting upon them creditably, that course shall be taken with promptitude, vigour, and effect.

Here we make our bow, determined to pursue our great experiment with boldness ; to associate its principle with a purity of tone that may secure and hold fast for our journal the fearless patronage of families ; to seek in all things to uphold the great cause of public morality, to keep continually before the eye of the world a living and moving panorama of all its actions and influences ; and to withhold from society no point that its literature can furnish or its art adorn, so long as the genius of that literature, and the spirit of that art, can be brought within the reach and compass of the Editors of the ILLUSTRATED LONDON NEWS !

DESTRUCTION OF THE CITY OF HAMBURGH BY FIRE.

By the arrival of the General Steam Navigation Company's boat Caledonia, off the Tower, on Tuesday evening, news has been brought of an immense conflagration which took place on Thursday morning, the 5th instant, at one o'clock, in that city. The district in which the fire broke out consists entirely of wood tenements, chiefly of five and six stories high, and covering an area of ground of about thirty to forty acres. The whole of the buildings on this large space have been totally consumed to the number of more than 1000. The fire was by some thought to have originated in the street known by the name of the Stein Twite, in the warehouse of a Jew, named Cohen, a cigar manufacturer, and who, upon good grounds, has been taken up on suspicion as the incendiary. The wind at the time blew a stout north-west, which caused the flames rapidly to spread ; and proceeding in the direction of Rodings-market, and from thence to Deich-street, entirely consuming the whole of the following streets, among which is the Hoppen-market, and St. Nicholas Church, a fine stone fabric, and the handsomest in Hamburgh. Grutz Twite, Cressnon (back end), Grosser Burstah, Muhlen Brucke, Alte Borse, Bohnen Strasse, Monkedam Twite, Altewalle Strasse, Grosse and Rlaire, Johannes Strasse, Nassewall (partially), Alter and Neuer Jungferstiey Berg, New Berg Strasse, St. Petrie Trichie, Kunigs Strasse, Greenhoff a Grasskiller (partially), Rathaus, Borsenhalle, Zuichhaus, Spinnhaus, and Detenwinshaus, Schmidt Wassenkunst (Nue Bose), Zuchstrausse Strasse, Kunst, Caulstrausse, Kobdam, Dullhaus, Sperort, and Steinstrausses.

View of the Conflagration of Hamburgh, from the Alster.

Anonymous

← *View of the Conflagration of Hamburgh*, 1842
Ansicht der Hamburger Feuersbrunst
Vue du grand incendie de Hambourg
Wood engraving
From: *The Illustrated London News*,
14 May 1842

The first illustrated newspaper to be published on a regular basis started out with a circulation of 26,000 copies. However, the documentary integrity promised by the two editors in their opening announcement was more a promise for the future. This illustration on the cover showing a fire in Hamburg, for example, was a product of the artist's imagination and had simply been engraved from a view of the city.

Die erste regelmäßig erscheinende Nachrichtenillustrierte ging mit 26 000 Exemplaren an den Start. Die dokumentarische Wahrheitstreue, die die beiden Herausgeber in ihrem Grußwort ankündigten, war allerdings eher ein in die Zukunft gerichtetes Versprechen. Die Abbildung des Brands von Hamburg auf dem Cover war beispielsweise ein reines Fantasieprodukt, das nach einer Vedutenvorlage gestochen war.

Le premier journal illustré à parution régulière fit ses débuts avec un tirage de 26 000 exemplaires. La véracité documentaire que les deux éditeurs promettaient dans leur préambule était toutefois plutôt une promesse pour l'avenir. Par exemple, l'illustration en une figurant l'incendie de Hambourg était un pur produit de l'imagination et fut gravée d'après une vue de la ville.

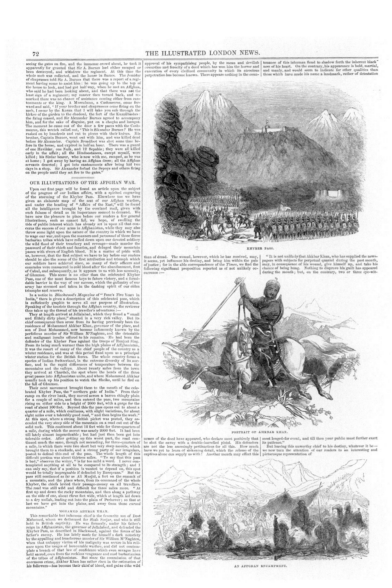

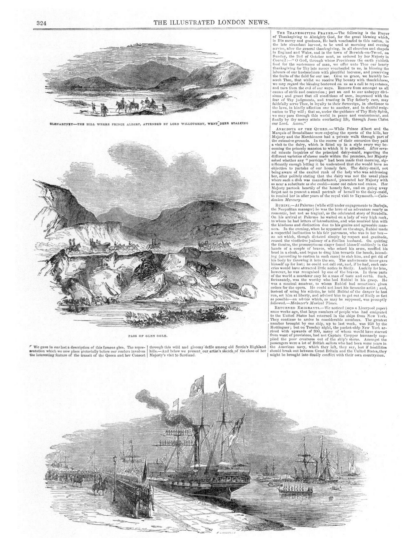

Anonymous

Illustrations of the Afghan War, 1842
Illustrationen des Afghanischen Kriegs
Illustrations de la guerre en Afghanistan
Wood engravings
From: *The Illustrated London News*,
11 June 1842

The *Illustrated London News* was also reliant on pictorial material from secondary sources for its initial reports on the wars in Afghanistan and Algeria. The illustrations were prepared by the wood engraver Henry Vizetelly, and together with Ebenezer Landells, a student of Thomas Bewick's and co-founder of *Punch*, he determined the artistic style for the newspaper.

Auch bei ihren ersten Kriegsreportagen aus Afghanistan und Algerien war die *Illustrated London News* auf grafisches Sekundärmaterial angewiesen. Verantwortlich für den Abbildungsteil war der Holzstecher Henry Vizetelly, der zusammen mit Ebenezer Landells, dem Thomas-Bewick-Schüler und Mitbegründer des *Punch*, die künstlerische Linie der Illustrierten bestimmte.

L'*Illustrated London News* aussi était tributaire de matériel iconographique de seconde main pour ses premiers reportages de guerre en Afghanistan et en Algérie. Le xylographe Henry Vizetelly était responsable de la partie illustrations et détermina la ligne artistique des magazines ilustrés en coopération avec Ebenezer Landells, élève de Thomas Bewick et cofondateur de *Punch*.

Ebenezer Landells & G.F. Sargent

The Royal Visit to Scotland, 1842
Königlicher Besuch in Schottland
Visite royale en Écosse
Wood engravings
From: *The Illustrated London News*,
1 October 1842

Ebenezer Landells was not only the main wood engraver for *The Illustrated London News* but also its first picture correspondent. His illustrated reports on the royal couple's visit to Scotland were a major feature of the newspaper's coverage for several weeks.

Ebenezer Landells fungierte für die *Illustrated London News* nicht nur als leitender Xylograf, sondern auch als erster künstlerischer Korrespondent. Seine grafische Dokumentationsreihe vom Besuch des englischen Königspaars in Schottland dominierte die Berichterstattung der Illustrierten über mehrere Wochen.

Ebenezer Landells n'était pas seulement le chef xylographe du *Illustrated London News*, mais aussi son premier correspondant artistique. Son reportage illustré sur la visite du couple royal en Écosse domine la couverture médiatique de l'événement par les magazines pendant plusieurs semaines.

THE ILLUSTRATED LONDON NEWS.

LORD MAYOR'S DAY.

The usual civic procession on Wednesday was honoured with a more numerous assemblage of spectators than on any occasion for many years past. The 9th of November, it will be recollected, was the anniversary of the birth of the Prince of Wales; and while the bells of the City steeples rang merry peals, as well in commemoration of that auspicious event as in celebration of the important civic day, those of the metropolitan churches "beyond the walls" responded in many a cheerful round in honour of the first event. The morning, too, was unusually fine, and altogether a Lord Mayor's Show has seldom within the memory of the oldest citizen presented a gayer appearance than that of Wednesday. It is to be deeply regretted, however, that the festive procession did not pass over without a very serious accident to one of the "men in armour," who, it will be seen, fell from his horse near Blackfriars-bridge, and broke his thigh.

At an early hour in the morning the Lord Mayor elect gave a public breakfast to the various civic functionaries, in the Council Chamber, at Guildhall. The procession was formed at a quarter past eleven, and differed in no particular calling for the slightest remark from those of preceding years. The boys of the Marine Society led the way, and were followed by the Goldsmiths' Company, with their various handsome banners, &c.; next came the Company of Tallow Melters, of which the chief magistrate is a liveryman. The various city officers, and the Sheriffs, with the late Lord Mayor and the Court of Aldermen, followed, the procession being closed by the Right Honourable the Lord Mayor elect, in his state carriage, and attended by his chaplain, the sword bearer, water bailiff, &c. The band of the 1st Life Guards with a company of that regiment, and a detachment of the Royal Horse Guards (Blue), were in attendance as usual.

The procession, contrary to the usual custom, proceeded through Cornhill and Gracechurch-street, to the Southwark side of London-bridge, and embarked at the

THE INAUGURATION.

PROCESSION BY WATER FROM LONDON BRIDGE.

southwest stairs, closely adjoining the range of warehouses belonging to his lordship, and known as the Kent and Sussex Wharf. Here the "silent highway" was witness to another departure from established rule, for some of the barges, in the place, as has been the custom "any time these hundred years past," of being propelled in the true and stately style of civic dignity, viz., by powerful sweeps in the hands of the renowned Thames watermen, were made fast to steamers, and "tugged" up to Westminster. The assistance of the steamers was not unattended with misfortune or vexation. The procession, on nearing Waterloo-bridge, ran foul of a revenue boat, which was capsized, and three of the crew were rescued with considerable difficulty. Immediately after this the state barge ran aground, and, as the tide was unusually low, a quarter of an hour elapsed before she could be got off and brought alongside all that remains of the ancient Cotton Garden, where temporary stairs were erected for the purpose of disembarking. The appearance of the gilded barges on the water, when com-

pletely under weigh, was really very grand and imposing, particularly the state barge and the barge of the Goldsmiths' Company, which shone like immense masses of floating gold. One steamer, which had been chartered for the sole use of the perambulating advertisers of the ILLUSTRATED LONDON NEWS, attracted universal notice by an imposing "salute" of broadsides, with which the civic dignitaries appeared to be highly pleased.

The procession arrived at Westminster shortly before three o'clock. The administration of the oaths and the customary ceremonies having been gone through, before the Barons of the Exchequer, his lordship, attended by the late Lord Mayor, the Sheriffs, Mr. Alderman Gibbs, and Mr. Alderman T. Wood, proceeded to the several courts of law and equity, where the Recorder, in his lordship's name, invited the Judges to the banquet at Guildhall. The number of persons at Westminster, and indeed throughout the line, was unusually great. The Court of Exchequer, as usual, was the chief point of attraction, and was crowded with elegantly-dressed ladies.

ENTERING WESTMINSTER HALL.

THE   RETURN   OF   THE

WESTMINSTER   TO   GUILDHALL.

His lordship re-embarked shortly after three o'clock, and on arriving at Blackfriars-bridge the procession was reformed—the Stationers' Company taking the first rank. While the procession was being arranged in order on the bridge, the very serious accident above alluded to took place. The man wearing a suit of brass scale armour, who has been accustomed to the same duty on several previous occasions, was observed to have some difficulty in managing his horse, and, before assistance could be rendered, the animal slipped down on its haunches, and rolled over on to its rider, fracturing his thigh in a most dreadful manner. The City Marshal, who was close to the spot, assisted by several police constables, immediately raised the unfortunate sufferer, who appeared to be in the most excruciating agony, and a stretcher having been procured, he was conveyed to St. Bartholomew's Hospital, where the armour was removed and the limb set.

The procession was joined at the corner of Farringdon-street by the Lady Mayoress, and the carriages of several of the nobility, and proceeded in the usual manner to Guildhall.

THE BANQUET.

The Guildhall was more crowded than usual. The hospitality of the Lord Mayor seemed to outrun the accommodation afforded by the hall, great as that is ; and at several tables parties were somewhat inconveniently crowded.

Sir R. Peel on his arrival was loudly and cordially greeted.

Any one who has ever attended at these festivals need not be told that few of the speeches are heard with any distinctness, and that the few who do succeed in rendering their sentences audible at some distance from the head table purposely abstain from any allusion to party topics. The character of the speeches on Wednesday did not differ from that hitherto observed—the grand staple of their composition was the veriest common-place. We shall not weary our readers by reporting what must be little else than a reprint of the addresses delivered in former years ; but shall give those points in the leading speeches which we think worthy of being noticed.

Amongst the guests were the following :—The Foreign Ministers, the Duke of Buccleuch, the Marquis of Downshire, Earl of Haddington, Earl of Arundel, Lord W. Lennox, Lord J. Russell, Lord Stanley, Viscount Lowther, Lord D. Stuart, Lord Fitzgerald and Vesci, Lord Denman and the Judges, Right Hon. Sir R. Peel, Mr. Goulburn, Sir E. Knatchbull, Hon. H. T. L. Corry, Hon. C. P. Villiers, Hon. W. Baring, Sir G. Clerk, Sir T. Fremantle, Sir H. Meux, Sir J. Easthope, Sir F. Booth, Sir C. Hunter, Sir P. Laurie, Mr. Hume, Sir J. Hensler, Captain Hensler, the Sergeants, Sir T. Wilde, Mr. J. Jervis, several of the Under Secretaries of State, Mr. Walter, the Aldermen, Recorder, &c.

The Lord Mayor, in giving the first toast, " The Queen," dwelt on the talent and energy exhibited by the present Sovereign since she ascended the throne—qualities which were outshone only by her exalted virtues. (Cheers.) Then followed the toasts of " Prince Albert," " The Queen Dowager," " The Prince of Wales." In reference to the last, his lordship observed, that that day being the anniversary of the birth of the Prince of Wales would long be memorable in the annals of the country. (Loud cheering followed this allusion.)

His lordship next gave " The Army and Navy." Colonel T. Wood returned thanks, and acknowledged, on the part of the two services, the joint compliment which had been paid them. He need not say that they were ready, whenever their country called on them, to do justice to any cause in which they might be engaged, and to emulate the great deeds of those who had gone before them.

The Lord Mayor next gave " The late Lord Mayor," who was loudly cheered, and returned thanks in a few words.

The Lord Mayor then proposed " The health of her Majesty's Ministers." (Cheers.) Though he differed from them in politics, he believed they had the interests of the country at heart ; and he unhesitatingly stated his belief that there was no man to whom her Majesty could with more safety entrust the administration of affairs than to Sir Robert Peel. (Cheers.)

Sir R. Peel, on rising to return thanks, was loudly cheered. He said, " My Lord Mayor and gentlemen—It is my duty, on behalf of the Ministers of the Crown, and in behalf of those members of the

CIVIC   PROCESSION   FROM

THE BANQUET AT GUILDHALL.

←←**John Gilbert**

Lord Mayor's Day, 1842
Festliche Amtseinführung Lord Mayors
Investiture solennelle de Lord Mayor
Wood engravings
From: *The Illustrated London News*,
12 November 1842

All the illustrations on this spread, in their various different styles, are by the history painter John Gilbert, who went on to become picture correspondent for court events in Victorian England. He was extremely prolific, and because of his ability to work consistently within the required parameters of journalism he may be seen as the first *special artist* of the age of illustrated newspapers and magazines.

Sämtliche Abbildungen dieser variationsreichen Doppelseite stammen von dem Historienmaler John Gilbert, der zum bildnerischen Hofberichterstatter der viktorianischen Ära avancierte. Gilbert war immens produktiv. In der Konsequenz, in der er sich auf die Parameter des Journalismus einließ, kann er als erster *special artist* des Illustriertenzeitalters gelten.

Toutes les illustrations de cette double page débordante de variété sont l'ouvrage du peintre d'histoire John Gilbert qui devint le correspondant de cour pictural de l'ère victorienne. Gilbert fut extrêmement prolifique. Vu qu'il accepta les paramètres du journalisme, il peut être considéré comme le premier *special artist* de l'époque des magazines illustrés.

L'ILLUSTRATION, JOURNAL UNIVERSEL. 504

Algérie.

OMBRES CHINOISES. — GARAGOUSSE (KARA-GEUZ).

(Les ombres chinoises à Alger.)

(Scènes de la pièce intitulée *Garagousse*.)

Anonymous

Algeria: Shadow-puppet Show –
Garagousse (Karagöz), 1846
Algerien: Schattenspiel – Karagöz
Algérie : Ombres chinoises –
Kara-Geuz
Wood engravings
From: *L'Illustration*, Paris,
10 January 1846

The French occupation of Algeria also featured as a subject in the traditional Turkish variety of shadow theatre, which was popular in Algiers as well. The protagonist of this ancestral form of motion pictures was Karagöz, who in the accompanying text is compared with Harlequin and such symbolic figures of the early caricature movement as Mayeux and Robert Macaire (see ill. p. 128). The heyday of shadow theatre in general occurred in Montmartre around the end of the 19th century.

Die französische Okkupation Algeriens war auch Thema des traditionellen türkischen Schattentheaters, das in Algier populär war. Karagöz, der Protagonist dieser Vorform des Kinos, wird im Begleittext mit Harlekin und Symbolfiguren der Karikaturbewegung, wie Mayeux und Robert Macaire, verglichen (siehe Abb. S. 128). Einen Höhepunkt erlebte das Schattenspiel zur Jahrhundertwende auf dem Montmartre.

L'occupation française de l'Algérie était aussi un thème cher au théâtre traditionnel d'ombres turc, alors très populaire à Alger. Dans un texte d'accompagnement, Kara-Geuz, le protagoniste de cet ancêtre du cinéma, est comparé à Arlequin et à des figures symboliques du mouvement caricatural comme Mayeux et Robert Macaire (voir ill. p. 128). Le spectacle d'ombres connut son heure de gloire à Montmartre au tournant du siècle.

Cham, after Rodolphe Töpffer

The Story of Mr. Cryptogam, 1845
Geschichte des Monsieur Cryptogame
Histoire de M. Cryptogame
Wood engavings
From: *L'Illustration*, Paris,
1 March 1845

While pirated editions of of Rodolphe Töpffer's picture stories had been available in France since 1839, they only became widely known with this publication of *M. Cryptogame*. The work for the wood engraving was done by the illustrator Cham, and with its anti-Muslim sentiment this early comic strip showed its support for France's aggressive colonial policy.

Obgleich in Frankreich bereits seit 1839 Raubdrucke in Umlauf waren, wurden Rodolphe Töpffers Bildergeschichten erst mit dieser Veröffentlichung von *Monsieur Cryptogame* populär. Die Aufbereitungen für den Holzstich besorgte der Grafiker Cham. Mit seinen antimuslimischen Ressentiments flankierte dieser frühe Comic die agressive französische Kolonialpolitik.

Bien que des contrefaçons eussent circulé en France dès 1839, les histoires en images de Rodolphe Töpffer n'obtinrent de succès qu'avec cette publication de *Monsieur Cryptogame*. C'est le dessinateur Cham qui fournit la matière pour la gravure sur bois. Avec ses préjugés contre les musulmans, cette bande dessinée précoce étaye la politique coloniale agressive de la France.

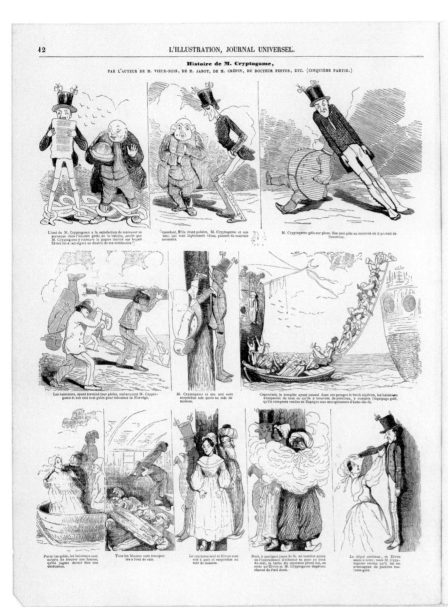

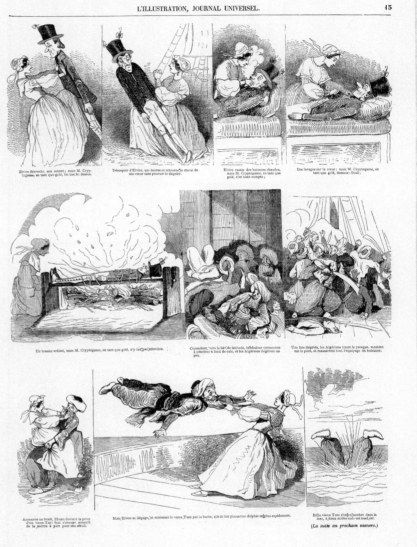

→→**Cham**

A Few Episodes from the Epic of the Railways, 1845
Einige Episoden aus dem Epos der Eisenbahn
Quelques épisodes de l'épopée des chemins de fer
Wood engravings
From: *L'Illustration*, Paris,
13 December 1845

Beginning in December 1843, Cham, who was one of Nicolas-Toussaint Charlet's last students, provided the satirical magazine *Le Charivari* and the weekly *L'Illustration* with regular pictorial news reports and illustrated stories inspired by the work of George Cruikshank and Rodolphe Töpffer.

Von Dezember 1843 an überzog der Zeichner Cham, ein später Schüler Nicolas-Toussaint Charlets, das Publikum des Satiremagazins *Le Charivari* und der Wochenillustrierten *L'Illustration* mit regelmäßigen Bildergeschichten und piktoralen Wochenschauen, die von George Cruikshank und Rodolphe Töpffer inspiriert waren.

À partir de décembre 1843, le dessinateur Cham, un élève tardif de Nicolas-Toussaint Charlet, submergea régulièrement les lecteurs du magazine satirique *Le Charivari* et de l'hebdomadaire *L'Illustration* d'histoires illustrées et d'actualités en images qui étaient inspirées de George Cruikshank et de Rodolphe Töpffer.

228   L'ILLUSTRATION, JOURNAL UNIVERSEL.

Quelques épisodes de l'épopée des chemins de fer, par Cham.

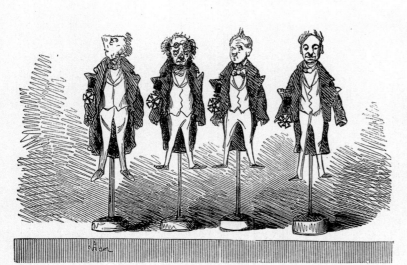

(Un conseil d'administration.)

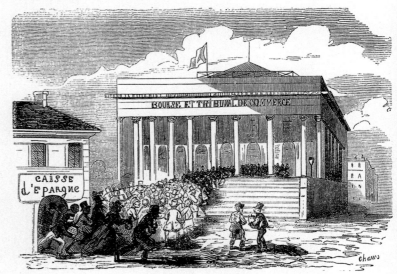

(Les actionnaires.)

(Une ligne de chemin de fer d'après le plan des ingénieurs.)

(Aspect réel de la même ligne.)

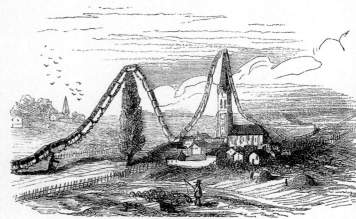

(Nouveau chemin de fer à train articulé.)

(Nouveau projet de chemin de fer atmosphérique. — Compagnie des Zéphyrs.)

(Compagnie des voyageurs.)

(La hausse et la baisse.)

(Un actionnaire venant de toucher son dividende.)

(Un actionnaire se créant des ressources.)

L'ILLUSTRATION, JOURNAL UNIVERSEL. 229

(Une minute d'avance et 50 mètres de barrières avant d'arriver au bureau.)

(Employé civil des chemins de fer.)

(Entente cordiale des ouvriers français et anglais.)

(Entêtement fatal.)

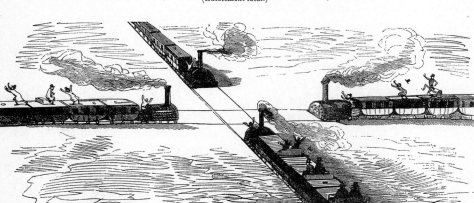

(La patte d'oie.)

(Cas non prévu par les polices d'assurance contre la grêle.)

HISTOIRE NATURELLE

(Amélioration de la race humaine par les chemins de fer.)

(Le dernier des chevaux, au jardin des Plantes en 1900.)

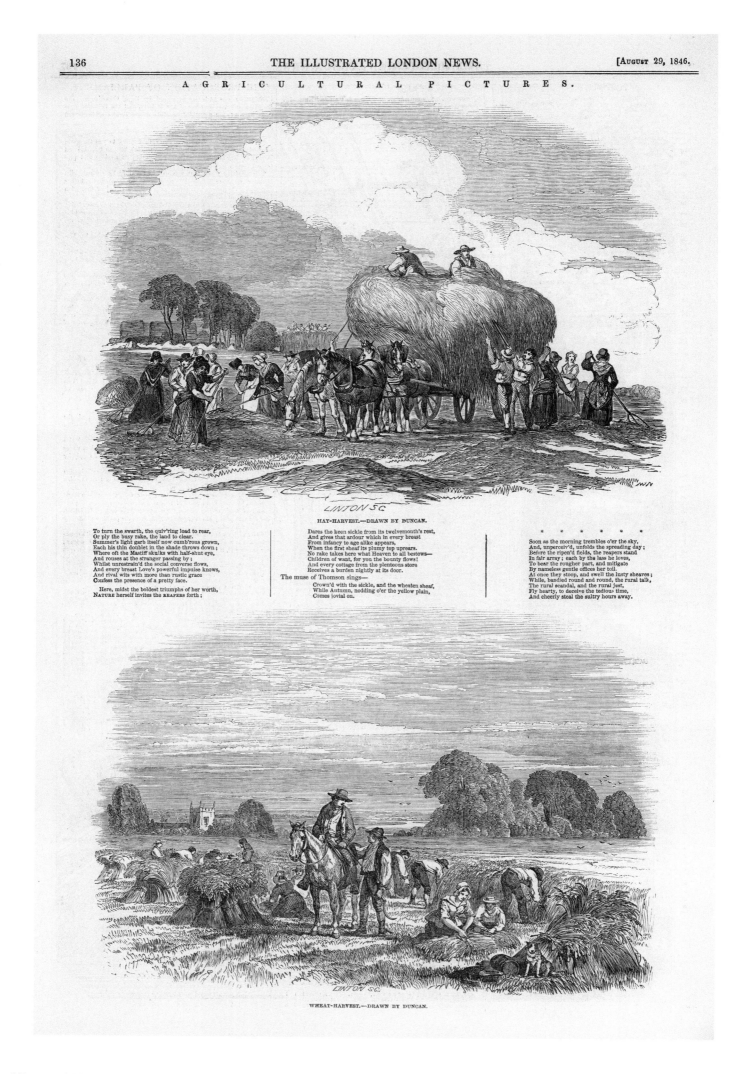

Edward Duncan & William James Linton (sc.)

Agricultural Pictures, 1846
Bilder der Landarbeit
Images du travail agricole
Wood engravings
From: *The Illustrated London News*,
29 August 1846

As a freelance wood engraver Linton was kept busier than most in his work for *The Illustrated London News*. He was a propagandist for the republican cause, and in his series of *Agricultural Pictures* he discarded the typical romanticised feudal image in favour of a remarkably sober view of rural life, and as the accompanying text stated these were "scenes from real life, not artistic compositions".

William James Linton war einer der meistbeschäftigten freien Xylografen der *Illustrated London News*. Mit der von ihm konzipierten Serie der *Agricultural Pictures* setzte der republikanische Propagandist der gängigen Feudalromantik eine bemerkenswert nüchterne Ansicht vom Landleben entgegen. „Szenen aus dem wirklichen Leben – keine malerischen Kompositionen", wie es im Begleittext heißt.

William James Linton était l'un des xylographes indépendants les plus occupés du *Illustrated London News*. En réalisant la série des *Agricultural Pictures*, le propagandiste républicain opposa au style roman féodal courant une vision remarquablement sobre de la vie rurale. « Scènes de la vie réelle – et non composition picturale », comme l'indique le texte qui l'accompagne.

116   THE ILLUSTRATED LONDON NEWS.   [Feb. 20, 1847.

SKETCHES IN THE WEST OF IRELAND.—BY MR. JAMES MAHONY.

BOY AND GIRL AT CAHERA.   THE VILLAGE OF MIENIES.

WE resume from our Journal of last week our Artist's Sketches of Scenes and Incidents from the distressed district of Skibbereen, and its neighbourhood; premising that our main object in the publication of this Series of Illustrations is to direct public sympathy to the suffering poor of these localities, a result that must, inevitably, follow the right appreciation of their extent and severity.

We left our Artist, last week, on the road to Dromdaleague, to inquire into the horrible circumstances of Leahey's death.

The first Sketch is taken on the road, at Cahera, of a famished boy and girl turning up the ground to seek for a potato to appease their hunger. "Not far from the spot where I made this sketch," says Mr. M., "and less than fifty perches from the high road, is another of the many sepulchres above ground, where six dead bodies had lain for twelve days, without the least chance of interment, owing to their being so far from the town. After leaving this fearful spot, we soon reached Dromdaleague, where I called upon the Rev. J. Creedon, and inquired of him as to the fate of Leahey. 'Not only do I know the statement to be true,' replied the reverend gentleman, 'but also prepared the man for death, and am ready to accompany you to the spot.' We, accordingly, started; and, within half an hour's drive, reached the village of Meinies, where the house of Leahey is situated, and of which I send you a sketch. Whilst making this, I learned from Mr. Creedon, and one of the villagers, that not only was the account of Leahey's house in the Diary true, but the case

was even more disgusting than there stated; and, horrifying as it was, the man's mother, who found the dogs about him, after having first lain him across the few remaining sparks of fire upon the floor, went out to beg as much as would purchase a coffin to bury him in."

"Having heard much of the wants of Dunmanway, I proceeded thither, and am delighted to say that this large and thriving town (of which I send you a sketch, taken from the bridge on the Cork road) seems to be the barrier to the dreadful want further west. Not, at the same time, but that much want does exist here, though nothing beyond what may be expected upon land where nature is not bountiful. The worst feature presenting itself, at this moment, all through the West, is the entire abandonment of agricultural occupation; and, during my entire excursion from Clonakilty round to Dunmanway, not more than ten or a dozen fields seemed to have been prepared for the spring; and the answer of all those to whom I addressed myself on the subject was, that if they put down, they did not know who would reap; and that, in case the crops were sown, the poor famished wretches would be there to eat them up long before they had time to grow.

"Again, all sympathy between the living and the dead seems completely out of the question; and the revolting practice will, doubtless, go on until it works its own remedy. I certainly saw from 150 to 180 funerals of victims to the want of food, the whole number attended by not more than 50 persons; and so hardened are the men regularly employed in the removal of the dead from the workhouse, that I saw one

MULLINS'S HUT, AT SCULL.

ENTRANCE TO DUNMANWAY, FROM THE BRIDGE ON THE CORK ROAD.

James Mahony & Frederick James Smyth (sc.)

Sketches in the West of Ireland, 1847
Skizzen vom Westen Irlands
Esquisses dans l'ouest de l'Irlande
Wood engravings
From: The Illustrated London News,
20 February 1847

The newspaper's picture editors used a combination of picturesque Romantic-styled scenery shot through with horrific details to convey the humanitarian catastrophe that was the very real result of the moral bankruptcy of England's free-trade liberalism.

Die Bildredaktion bemühte Schemata der pittoresken Schauerromantik, um eine humanitäre Katastrophe zu visualisieren, die nichts weniger als den moralischen Bankrott des englischen Freihandelsliberalismus bedeutete.

La rédaction fit le choix de présenter des motifs du romantisme pittoresque pimenté d'un frisson d'horreur afin d'illustrer une catastrophe humanitaire qui n'était rien de moins que la banqueroute morale du libéralisme anglais de libre-échange.

Anonymous

↓ *Epsom Downs One Derby Day*
Epsom Downs Eintages-Derby
Derby d'une journée à Epsom Downs, 1848
Wood engraving
From: *The Illustrated London News*,
27 May 1848

Horse races were a favourite subject for sports reports in England. The heyday of this popular genre occurred before the advent of illustrated magazines, when etchings with aquatint were produced by artists such as Samuel Howitt, Henry Alken and James Pollard, while in mainland Europe Théodore Géricault and his tutor Carle Vernet both also worked in this tradition of pictorial reporting.

Pferderennen waren das beliebteste Sujet des englischen Sportdrucks. Das populäre Genre hatte seine Blütezeit noch vor Beginn der Illustriertenära im Medium der Aquatinta-Radierung mit Exponenten wie Samuel Howitt, Henry Alken und James Pollard. Auf dem Kontinent arbeiteten Théodore Géricault und sein Lehrer Carle Vernet in dieser Tradition grafischer Reportage.

Les courses hippiques étaient le sujet favori des journalistes sportifs anglais. Ce genre très populaire connut son âge d'or bien avant le début de l'ère des magazines travaillant avec la gravure à l'aquatinte, représentée par des artistes tels que Samuel Howitt, Henry Alken et James Pollard. Sur le continent, Théodore Géricault et son professeur Carle Vernet travaillèrent dans cette tradition de reportage illustré.

Gustave Doré & Dumont (sc.)

→ *View of the Champs-Élysées on a Sunday*, 1849
Sonntäglicher Anblick der Champs-Élysées
Aspect des Champs-Élysées le dimanche
Wood engraving
From: *Journal pour rire*, Paris,
6 October 1849

In France, Richard Doyle's experiments with working in outline were taken up by Gustave Doré, the latest star in the world of illustrated caricatures. Charles Philipon had signed him up in February 1848 to his new humorous magazine *Journal pour rire*, when Doré was only 16, giving him the freedom to try out any styles he wanted.

Richard Doyles Experimente mit der Umrisslinie wurden in Frankreich von Gustave Doré, dem neuesten Stern am Karikaturenhimmel, aufgegriffen. Charles Philipon hatte den erst 16-Jährigen im Februar 1848 für sein neues Humormagazin *Journal pour rire* unter Vertrag genommen und bot ihm dort den Freiraum, sich in allen möglichen Stilen auszuprobieren.

En France, les expériences de Richard Doyle avec les contours furent reprises par Gustave Doré, l'étoile montante dans le firmament des caricatures. En février 1848, Charles Philipon avait mis sous contrat le jeune garçon de 16 ans pour son nouveau magazine humoristique *Journal pour rire* et lui laissa la liberté d'expérimenter toutes sortes de styles.

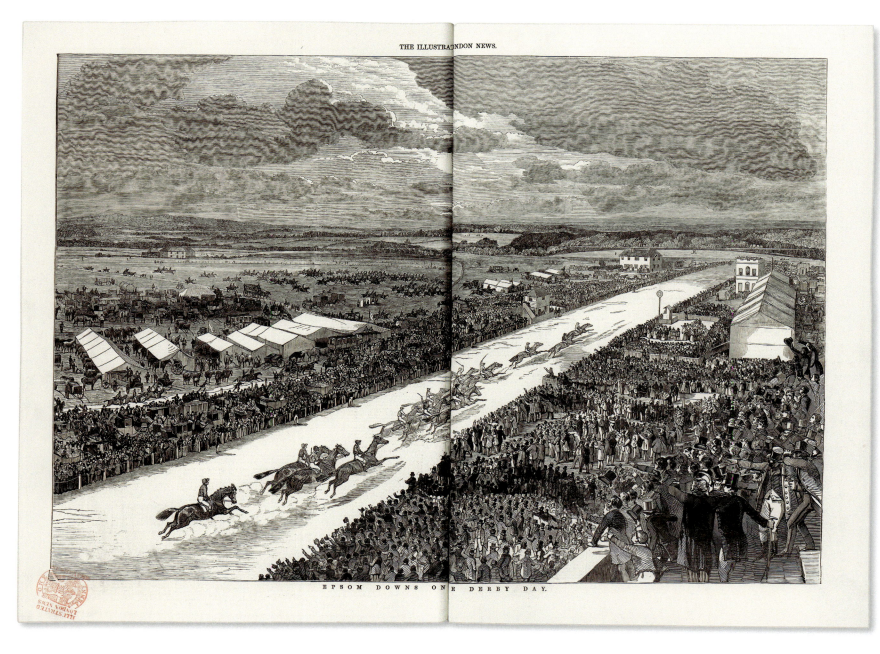

EPSOM DOWNS ONE DERBY DAY.

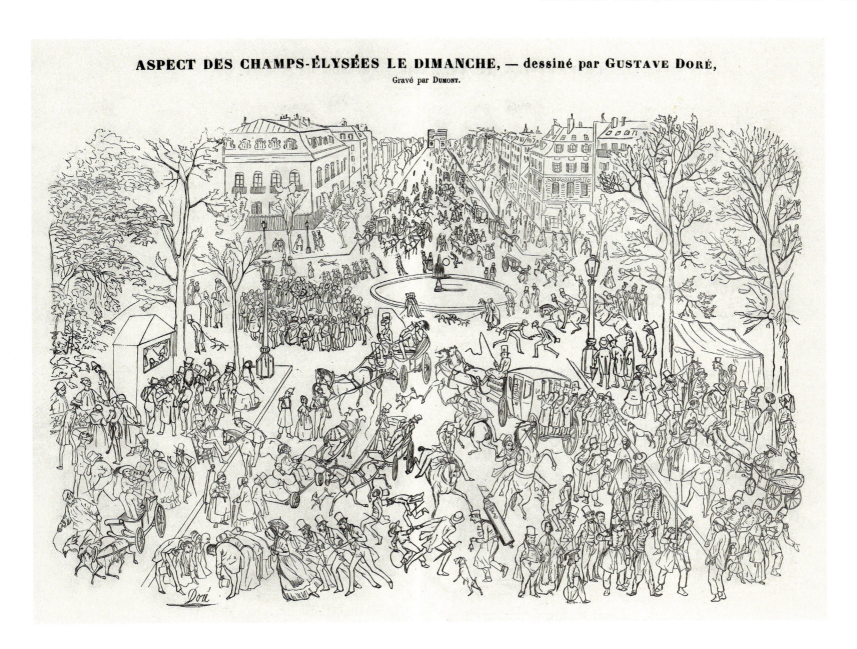

ASPECT DES CHAMPS-ÉLYSÉES LE DIMANCHE, — dessiné par GUSTAVE DORÉ,
Gravé par DUMONT.

Richard Doyle

Manners and Custom's of ye Englyshe in 1849, no. 7:
Ye National Sporte!!! of Steeple Chasynge
Sitten und Gebräuche der Engländer 1849, Nr. 7:
Der Volkssport!!! Steeplechase-Rennen
Mœurs et coutumes des Anglais en 1849, no. 7:
Le sport populaire!!! Course d'obstacles
Wood engraving
From: *Punch, or The London Charivari*, vol. XVI,
London, January–June 1849

Until he left the magazine in 1850 the young
Richard Doyle was one of the two main illustrators
for *Punch*, along with John Leech. With his series
on the manners and customs of the English he
introduced a childlike style into his illustrations (see
also ill. p. 375), while the emphasis on outlines, not
unlike the simplified forms in graffiti, can be seen
as a forerunner of the clear-line style later adopted
in cartoon strips.

Bis zu seinem Ausscheiden 1850 war der junge
Richard Doyle zusammen mit John Leech Chefzeichner des *Punch*. Mit seiner Serie über die Gebräuche der Engländer führte er die Manier der
kindlichen Pseudokritzelei in die Illustrationsgrafik
ein (siehe auch Abb. S. 375). In der graffittiartigen
Betonung der Umrisslinie kann sie als Vorläufer
des Ligne-claire-Stils des Comicstrips gelten.

Jusqu'à son départ en 1850, le jeune Richard Doyle
était dessinateur en chef du *Punch* avec John Leech.
Avec sa série sur les coutumes des Anglais, il introduisit le style du pseudo-griffonnage enfantin dans
les illustrations (voir aussi ill. p. 375). Avec ses lignes
de contour accentuées comme dans un graffiti, elle
peut être considérée comme le précurseur du style
de ligne claire des bandes dessinées.

MANNERS·AND·CVSTOM'S·OF·Ye·ENGLYSHE·IN·1849.   No. 7.

Ye NATIONAL SPORTE !!! OF STEEPLE·CHASYNGE.

Mr. Pips his Diary.

Monday, April 23, 1849. Down the Road to a Steeple Chase, which I had never seen before, and did much long to behold; for of all Things I do love Diversion and Merriment; and both MR. STRAPPES and SIR WILLIAM SPURKINS did tell me there would be rare Sport. Got a Place in the Grand Stand, cost me half a Guinea, which was loth to part with, but thought I should have brave Entertainment for so much Money. Did find myself here in fine Company, Dukes, and Earls, and Lords and Ladies too, which did please me; but among them some Snobs, in Stable-cut Clothes, with spotted Neckcloths and Fox-headed Breast-pins; though some of these were Lords too, who seemed to have been at Pains to look like Ostlers. To see the Crowd on Horseback and in Carriages, and those on Foot pushing and scrambling, and trampling each other to get a Sight of the Course, as if there had been going to be a Coronation, or a Man hanged! The Course, marked out with Flaes, and having Hurdles, Posts, Fences, Rails, Hedges, Drains, Ditches, and Brooks in the Way; and this Sportsmen do call the Country, and say such a Country is a Teaser, and so I should think. By-and-by the Jockies in their Saddles, but their word is Pig-skins, looking, in their gay Colours, like Tulips on Horseback, which was a pretty sight. Then a Bell rung to clear the Course, and the Horses with their Riders drawn up ready to start, and presently a Flag flourished for a Signal; and so they off. Good lack, to see them galloping helter-skelter, like mad, through Rivers, and over Hedges and Ditches, and the whole Thing done in ten Minutes! Some did jump the Fences and Hedges, which they

about me did term Raspers, clean over; but others not so lucky, and stuck in Brambles or on Stakes, or between double Rows of Posts, with a Quickset in the Middle, whereof the cant name is Bullfinchers. Others upset in Ditches; and one or two of them not able to get up again, and carried away upon some of the Hurdles; and when the Race was over, three Horses found lying with their Backs broken, and so shot. SIR WILLIAM did inform me that it was a tidy Field, which I could not agree, with the Raspers and Palisades upon it, and the Horses spiked, or sprawling with their Riders on the Ground with broken Backs and Limbs. Nor did I understand the Fun of this Part of the Thing; wherefore I suppose I must be dull; for it do seem to be the chief Delight that People take in it. For, as if the Gates and Rails belonging to the Ground were not dangerous enough, they do set up others called made Fences, being stubborn Posts and Stakes twisted with Briars and Brambles, which do seem to be meant for nothing but to be tumbled over, and in that Case to do as much Mischief, as may be, to Man and Beast. The Horses mostly ridden by Jockeys for Hire; but some by their Owners, who, methinks, do set a sufficient Value upon their own Existence when they venture their Necks in riding a Steeple Chase; but I do blame them for risking the Life of a useful Horse.

Printed by William Bradbury, of No. 13, Upper Woburn Place, in the Parish of St. Pancras; and Frederick Mullet Evans, of 7, Church Row, Stoke Newington, both in the County of Middlesex, Printers, at their Office in Lombard Street, in the Precinct of Whitefriars, in the City of London, and Published by them at No. 85, Fleet Street, in the Parish of St. Bride, in the City of London.—SATURDAY, APRIL 28th, 1849.

Paul Gavarni, after Constantin Guys

Defenders of the Barricade, 1848
Verteidiger der Barrikade | *Défenseurs de la barricade*
Wood engraving
From: *The Illustrated London News*,
11 March 1848

The events in Paris of the French Revolution of February 1848 resulted in huge increases in circulation for illustrated newspapers and magazines. The eccentric Constantin Guys was dispatched from London to send back reports, and with his military experience, enthusiasm and ability to draw quickly he seemed ideally suited for the job of a picture correspondent.

Die Ereignisse der Pariser Februarrevolution hatten immense Auflagensteigerungen im Illustriertengewerbe zur Folge. Aus London schickte man den exzentrischen Constantin Guys. Der enthusiastische Schnellzeichner schien mit seinen militärischen Erfahrungen für den Job des Bildreporters bestens geeignet.

Les événements de la révolution de Février à Paris entraînèrent d'énormes augmentations de tirage dans le secteur des magazines illustrés. L'excentrique Constantin Guys y fut envoyé de Londres. De par ses expériences militaires, ce créateur zélé de croquis rapides semblait convenir de façon idéale pour le job de reporter d'images.

In the Throne-room, 1848
Im Thronsaal | *Dans la salle du trône*
Wood engraving
From: *The Illustrated London News*,
4 March 1848

The French illustrator Paul Gavarni, who happened to be in London at the time on the invitation of his fellow artist Constantin Guys, was hired by *The Illustrated London News* to work up Guys's sketches for publication. Gavarni added a dramatic quality to the simple outline work of the self-taught Guys, and also drew the finished versions of the illustrations on to the wooden blocks for the engravers.

Die *Illustrated London News* engagierten den französischen Illustrator Paul Gavarni, der sich gerade auf Vermittlung seines Freunds Constantin Guys in London aufhielt, um dessen Skizzen aus Paris bildredaktionell aufzuarbeiten. Gavarni theatralisierte die grafischen Stenogramme des Autodidakten Guys und zeichnete die ausgearbeiteten Versionen für die Xylografen auf die Holzblöcke auf.

L'*Illustrated London News* engagea l'illustrateur français Paul Gavarni, qui séjournait justement à Londres grâce aux bons offices de son ami Constantin Guys, afin qu'il retouche les esquisses parisiennes de ce dernier en vue de la publication. Gavarni dramatisa les sténogrammes graphiques de l'autodidacte Guys et dessina les versions finales pour les xylographes sur des blocs de bois.

SOUVENIRS DES JOURNÉES DE JUIN, 1848.

ENLÈVEMENT D'UNE BARRICADE, RUE PERDUE (Quartier du Panthéon)

Édouard de Beaumont & Eugène Cicéri (lith.)

Remembering the June Days of 1848
Erinnerungen an die Junitage 1848
Souvenirs des journées de Juin 1848
Lithographs
From: *Le Charivari*, Paris, July–September 1848

Rue Perdue
Storming a Barricade, 1848
Abtragung einer Barrikade
Enlèvement d'une barricade

At the end of June 1848, workers in Paris rose up in protest at plans to close the system of national workshops that were intended to guarantee employment. The uprising sharply divided the radicalised workers from the liberal bourgeoisie and precipitated a violent crisis. Charles Philipon's *Charivari* was the only publication that featured detailed illustrated reports of the three days of bloody slaughter.

Ende Juni war es in Paris zu einem proletarischen Aufstand gegen die Aufhebung des staatlichen Arbeitsbeschaffungsprogramms gekommen. Er führte zu einer folgenreichen Spaltung zwischen radikalisierter Arbeiterschaft und liberalem Bürgertum. Charles Philipons *Le Charivari* war die einzige Illustrierte, die eine detaillierte grafische Dokumentation des dreitägigen Juni-Massakers brachte.

Fin juin, les ouvriers de Paris s'insurgèrent contre la fermeture des ateliers nationaux. Cette insurrection entraîna une scission lourde de conséquences entre les travailleurs radicalisés et la bourgeoisie libérale. *Le Charivari* de Charles Philipon fut le seul magazine illustré à avoir publié une documentation illustrée détaillée des trois sanglantes journées de Juin.

SOUVENIRS DES JOURNÉES DE JUIN, 1848.

RUE S' ANTOINE.

Rue St. Antoine, 1848

Where Charles Philipon's press had been on the side of the protesters during the uprising in Lyon (see ills. pp. 107 t., 118 b.), the coverage for the June uprising in Paris took the viewpoint of the national guard. This time the rebellious workers were depicted as a bloodthirsty mob, and the shift in perspective influenced reports in the liberal press of social unrest later on in the 19th century.

Während die Charles-Philipon-Presse bei den Bürgerkriegen in Lyon (siehe Abb. S. 107 o., 118 u.) noch auf der Seite der Aufständischen gestanden hatte, repräsentierte ihre Juni-Dokumentation die Perspektive der Nationalgarde. Die rebellierenden Arbeiter traten als blutrünstiger Mob in Erscheinung. Diese veränderte Sichtweise bestimmte die weitere Berichterstattung der liberalen Presse über die sozialen Kriege des 19. Jahrhunderts.

Alors que pendant les révoltes de Lyon la presse de Charles Philipon (voir ills. p. 107 h., 118 b.) était encore du côté des insurgés, sa documentation de juin représentait la perspective de la Garde nationale. Les ouvriers révoltés y apparaissaient comme une meute assoiffée de sang. Ce changement de point de vue détermina le cours des reportages ultérieurs de la presse libérale sur les troubles sociaux du XIXᵉ siècle.

Félix Nadar

The Public and Private Life of Mossieu Réac, 1849
Das öffentliche und private Leben des Mossieu Réac
La vie publique et privée de Mossieu Réac
Wood engravings
From: Nadar (ed.), *La Revue comique à l'usage
des gens sérieux*, Paris, 7 April 1849

Chapter V
News by Telegram
Telegrafische Nachrichten
Nouvelles télégraphiques

Chapter III
*Fortune Smiles on His Attempts at Industry
and Philanthropy*
*Das Glück lächelt über seine ökonomischen
und philantrophischen Bemühungen*
*La fortune sourit à ses efforts industriels et
philantrophiques*

Chapter VI
*Mossieu Réac Realises He Was a Republican
Two Days Earlier*
*Mossieu Réac merkt, dass er ein Republikaner
von vorgestern ist*
*Mossieu Réac s'aperçoit qu'il est républicain
de l'avant-veille*

The caricaturist Nadar's cartoon series about
Mossieu Réac took up the format of the comical
story told in pictures that had been developed by
Rodolphe Töpffer and Cham and given a counter-
revolutionary bias. A left-wing republican, Nadar
used it against the reactionary Louis Napoléon,
the nephew of Napoleon I, in his bid to become
president.

Mit seiner Cartoonserie *Mossieu Réac* griff der
linksrepublikanische Karikaturist Nadar das Format der lustigen Bildergeschichte auf, das durch
Rodolphe Töpffer und Cham konterrevolutionär
konnotiert war, und setzte es gegen die reaktionäre
Präsidentschaftskanditatur von Louis Napoléon,
dem Neffen Napoleons I., ein.

Avec sa série de dessins *Mossieu Réac*, le caricaturiste Nadar, républicain de gauche, reprend le
format de l'histoire comique en images, qui grâce
à Rodolphe Töpffer et à Cham présentait des connotations contre-révolutionnaires, et l'utilisa contre
la candidature réactionnaire à la présidence de
Louis-Napoléon, le neveu de Napoléon Iᵉʳ.

LA VIE PUBLIQUE ET P[...]
CHAP. V. — *Nou[...]*

Mossieu Réac, préfet, monte sur le
télégraphe pour avoir des nouvelles de Paris. Tout est tranquille et mossieu Réac aussi.

Diable!... Cela se gâte!...
L'opposition veut faire des banquets
réformistes ..

LA VIE PUBLIQUE ET P[...]
CHAP. III. *La fortune sourit à ses [...]*

Il faut dire que mossieu Réac, outre *la banque* de
son agent de change et les manœuvres remarquables de ses innombrables courtiers, n'a pas
négligé de faire hommage de quelques actions
à mademoiselle Loulou Mouillefarine (dite *la
Ci gale turbulente*), jolie danseuse, qui a l'o-
reille du ministre,— si j'ose m'exprimer ainsi '

...non plus qu'au célèb[...]
de Marseille, qui a [...]
qu'assez dans es [...]

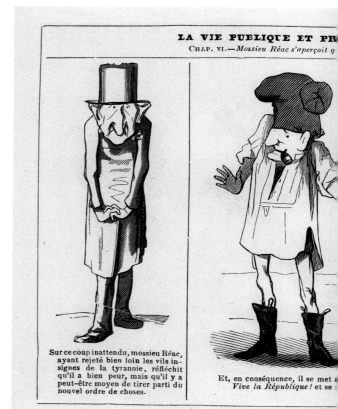

LA VIE PUBLIQUE ET PR[...]
CHAP. VI.—*Mossieu Réac s'aperçoit q[...]*

Sur ce coup inattendu, mossieu Réac,
ayant rejeté bien loin les vils insignes de la tyrannie, réfléchit
qu'il a bien peur, mais qu'il y a
peut-être moyen de tirer parti du
nouvel ordre de choses.

Et, en conséquence, il se met a [...]
Vive la République! et se [...]

gand Odilon Barrot
, à sa tête.

Mais le gouvernement défendant les banquets, le grand Odilon Barrot a peur et recule. — Mossieu Réac est rassuré.

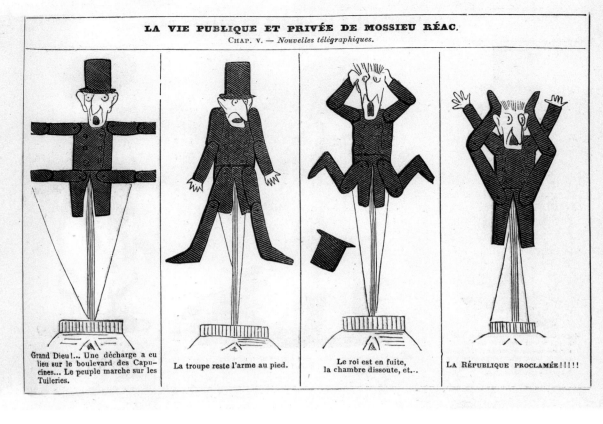

Grand Dieu!.. Une décharge a eu lieu sur le boulevard des Capucines... Le peuple marche sur les Tuileries.

La troupe reste l'arme au pied.

Le roi est en fuite, la chambre dissoute, et...

LA RÉPUBLIQUE PROCLAMÉE !!!!!

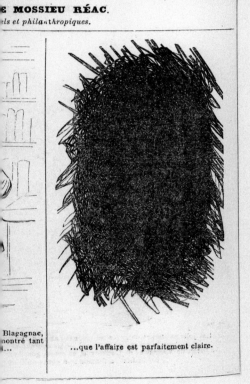

Blagagnac,
ontré tant
...

...que l'affaire est parfaitement claire.

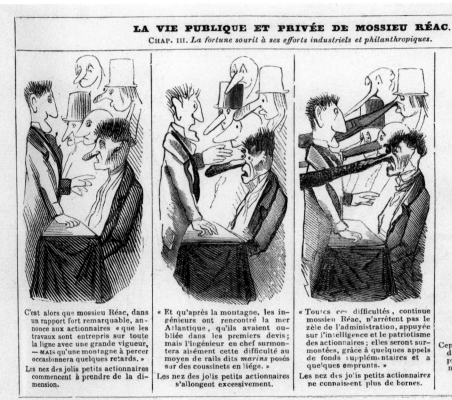
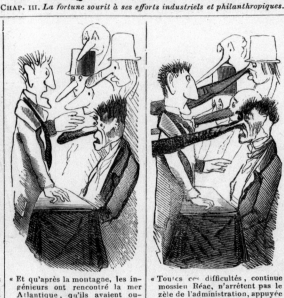
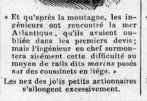

C'est alors que mossieu Réac, dans un rapport fort remarquable, annonce aux actionnaires « que les travaux sont entrepris sur toute la ligne avec une grande vigueur, — MAIS qu'une montagne à percer occasionnera quelques retards. »
Les nez des jolis petits actionnaires commencent à prendre de la dimension.

« Et qu'après la montagne, les ingénieurs ont rencontré la mer Atlantique, qu'ils avaient oubliée dans les premiers devis; mais l'ingénieur en chef surmontera aisément cette difficulté au moyen de rails dits *marins* posés sur des coussinets en liége. »
Les nez des jolis petits actionnaires s'allongent excessivement.

« Toutes ces difficultés, continue mossieu Réac, n'arrêtent pas le zèle de l'administration, appuyée sur l'intelligence et le patriotisme des actionnaires; elles seront surmontées, grâce à quelques appels de fonds supplémentaires et à quelques emprunts. »
Les nez des jolis petits actionnaires ne connaissent plus de bornes.

Report des nez des jolis petits actionnaires.

Cependant les actions baissent dans la même proportion. — La prime disparaît et les versements ne se font plus.

ates ses forces :
sans culotte.

Cependant, s'apercevant que ce costume négatif est mal interprété, il se contente d'arborer une cocarde de taille et du rouge le plus vif.

Et la quitte bientôt pour en prendre une autre de la même dimension mais tricolore.

Et comme les Polonais étaient fort bien portés, il eut l'idée ingénieuse de prendre leur costume national, afin de se rendre intéressant.

Arrivé à Paris, mossieu Réac va au club le plus ardent et débite cette théorie neuve, qu'il faut faire renaître la *confiance, mère du crédit,*

et le crédit, *fils de la confiance.*
(*La suite à la prochaine livraison.*)

Andreas Achenbach & Arnz & Co. (lith.)

*Pegasus Leaves Prussia for Fear of Being
Eaten*, 1848
*Pegasus verlässt die preußischen Staaten,
weil er Gefahr läuft, aufgefressen zu werden*
*Pégase quitte les États prussiens, parce qu'il
court le risque d'être mangé*
Lithograph
From: *Düsseldorfer Monatshefte*, 1848
Düsseldorf, Universitäts- und Landesbibliothek

The *Düsseldorfer Monatshefte* was the press outlet
for a generation of Rhineland artists who supported
the March Revolution of 1848 in Germany with
their critical style of history illustration. Andreas
Achenbach's picture associates the increase in the
number of slaughterhouses where horses were
being killed because of famine in the population with
the hostile climate to cultural expression under
absolute Prussian rule.

Die *Düsseldorfer Monatshefte* waren das publizistische Organ einer rheinischen Künstlergeneration,
die die deutsche Märzrevolution mit einer kritischen

Genre- und Historienkunst unterstützte. Andreas
Achenbachs Grafik verknüpft die vermehrte Einrichtung von Pferdeschlachtereien gegen die Hungersnot mit dem kulturfeindlichen Klima unter dem preußischen Absolutismus.

Les *Düsseldorfer Monatshefte* étaient l'organe journalistique d'une génération d'artistes rhénans qui sou-
tenaient la révolution de Mars allemande sous une
forme de peinture d'histoire. Le dessin d'Andreas
Achenbach associe la multiplication des abattoirs
pour chevaux afin de combattre la famine au climat
anti-culturel sous l'absolutisme prussien.

Theodor Hosemann & Arnz & Co. (sc.)

The Barricade at Louisenplatz, 1849
Barrikade am Louisenplatz
Barricade sur la Louisenplatz
Wood engraving
From: *Düsseldorfer Monatshefte*, 1849
Düsseldorf, Universitäts- und Landesbibliothek

In the same way as *La Caricature* on which it had
been modelled, the *Monatshefte* initially consisted
of political caricatures, pictorial news reports and
illustrated parodies of manners and customs.
Theodor Hosemann, whose work documented the
revolutionary events in Berlin, went on to become
Heinrich Zille's tutor and was thus an important
precursor of Berlin's social realism movement.

Wie das Vorbild *La Caricature* bestanden die *Monats-
hefte* anfangs aus einer Kombination von politischem
Cartooning, grafischem Report und Sittenkarikatur.
Theodor Hosemann, der die Revolutionsereignisse
in Berlin dokumentierte, wurde später als Lehrer von
Heinrich Zille zu einem wichtigen Wegbereiter des
Berliner Sozialrealismus.

Comme leur modèle *La Caricature*, les *Monatshefte*
consistaient au début en une combinaison de dessins politiques, de reportages illustrés et de scènes
de mœurs. Theodor Hosemann, qui documenta les
événements révolutionnaires à Berlin, devint par la
suite le professeur d'Heinrich Zille et ainsi un important précurseur du réalisme social berlinois.

lith. Inst. von Arnz & Co in Düsseldorf

„ Wat heulst'n kleener Hampelmann?

„ — Jck habe Jhr'n Kleenen 'ne Krone jeschnitzt, nu will er se nich! — "

(April 49.)

Ferdinand Schröder & Arnz & Co. (lith.)

"What Are You Crying for, Little Jumping Jack?", 1849
„Wat heulst 'n kleener Hampelmann?"
«Pourquoi chiales-tu, p'tit pantin?»
Tinted lithograph
From: *Düsseldorfer Monatshefte*,
April 1849
Düsseldorf, Universitäts- und Landesbibliothek

The president of the German parliament stands in tears before the female personification of Prussia, complaining that her son, who is playing with the bear of Russian autocracy, has rejected the imperial crown. The headless statue of Germania shows that the revolutionaries' hopes for national unity and democratic rule have been completely destroyed.

Heulend steht der Präsident des deutschen Parlaments vor Frau Preußen und beschwert sich, dass ihr Sohn, der gerade mit dem russischen Autokratiebären spielt, die Kaiserkrone abgelehnt habe. Wie die kopflose Statue der Germania zeigt, haben sich damit wohl die Hoffnungen der Revolutionäre auf eine nationale Einigung unter demokratischen Vorzeichen zerschlagen.

Le président du Parlement allemand se tient en larmes devant madame la Prusse et lui reproche que son fils, en train de jouer avec l'ours de l'autocratie russe, ait refusé la couronne d'empereur. Comme en témoigne la statue sans tête de Germania, les espoirs des révolutionnaires d'une unité nationale sous prémisses démocratiques sont ainsi anéantis.

Alfred Rethel & August Gaber (sc.)

Another Dance of Death, Fifth Sheet, 1849
Auch ein Todtentanz, Fünftes Blatt
Encore une danse macabre, cinquième planche
Wood engraving
From: Alfred Rethel, *Auch ein Todtentanz*,
Leipzig, 1849

The liberal satire from the period before the March Revolution faded away to a large extent after the autocratic coup d'état towards the end of 1848, yet Alfred Rethel's reactionary adaptation of Hans Holbein's *Dance of Death* broke all records for sales of an illustrated publication. This major work of counter-revolutionary propaganda went through numerous editions and had a huge influence on press graphics.

Während die liberale Satire des Vormärz nach den autokratischen Staatsstreichen weitgehend zum Erliegen kam, brach Alfred Rethels reaktionäre Adaption von Hans Holbeins altdeutschem *Totentanz* alle bildpublizistischen Rekorde. Das Hauptwerk konterrevolutionärer Propaganda erlebte unzählige Neuauflagen und war auch pressegrafisch enorm einflussreich.

Alors qu'après les coups d'État autocrates la satire libérale du Vormärz sombrait dans l'immobilisme, l'adaptation réactionnaire qu'Alfred Rethel fit de la *Danse macabre* d'Hans Holbein battit tous les records de publications illustrées. L'œuvre principale de la propagande contre-révolutionnaire connut d'innombrables rééditions et exerça une énorme influence sur le dessin de presse.

Theodor Kaufmann & Carl Weber (sc.)

Blessed with Powder and Lead, 1849
Begnadet zu Pulver und Blei
Béni par la poudre et le plomb
Wood engraving
From: Anonymous, *Trost für 1849*, Düsseldorf, 1849
Düsseldorf, Universitäts- und Landesbibliothek

The history painter Theodor Kaufmann, a left-wing follower of Hegel who had fought on the barricades, provided an antidote to Alfred Rethel's sarcastic depictions of Death in the form of a skeleton with scenes such as this of republican martyrs. His response had to be published anonymously, and after fleeing his homeland Kaufmann went to New York, where he taught Thomas Nast, the most politically influential artist in all press graphics.

Der linkshegelianische Historienmaler und Barrikadenkämpfer Theodor Kaufmann entgegnete Alfred Rethels sarkastischen Knochenmann-Darstellungen mit republikanischen Märtyerszenen. Seine Replik auf den *Todtentanz*-Zyklus musste er anonym veröffentlichen. Nach seiner Flucht wurde Kaufmann in New York Lehrer von Thomas Nast, dem politisch einflussreichsten Künstler des Pressegrafikzeitalters.

Theodor Kaufmann, peintre d'histoire de l'aile gauche hégélienne et combattant des barricades, opposa aux représentations sarcastiques de la Mort par Alfred Rethel des scènes de martyrs républicains. Il dut publier sa réplique au cycle de la *Danse macabre* de façon anonyme. Après avoir fui son pays, Kaufmann devint à New York le professeur de Thomas Nast, l'artiste politiquement parlant le plus influent de l'époque du dessin de presse.

Kaspar Braun (del. & sc.)

The Emigrants, 1849
Die Auswanderer | *Les Émigrants*
Wood engraving
From: *Fliegende Blätter*, no. 205,
Munich, 1849

The wave of emigration that followed the revolutions in Europe became the subject of a series of cartoons that appeared between 1849 and 1861 in the *Fliegende Blätter*, the oldest and most influential German satirical magazine. The writer Kaspar Braun was its founder and co-editor, and being also a wood engraver he established the practice in Germany.

Die Emigrationswelle aus dem post-revolutionären Europa wurde in einer Cartoonserie thematisiert, die 1849–1861 in den *Fliegenden Blätter* erschien, dem ältesten und einfluss-reichsten deutschen Satiremagazin. Der Autor Kaspar Braun war auch Begründer und Mitherausgeber der Illustrierten. Als Xylograf hat er den Holzstich in Deutschland etabliert.

La vague d'émigration qui suivit les révolutions en Europe fut thématisée dans une série de desssins qui parut de 1849 à 1861 dans les *Fliegende Blätter*, le plus ancien et le plus influent magazine satirique allemand. Kaspar Braun en était le fondateur et le co-éditeur. C'est ce xylographe qui a établi la gravure sur bois en Allemagne.

Disgrazia D'un Uccellatore

Antonio Masutti

↑ *A Bird-catcher's Disgrace*, 1849
Ein Vogelfänger im Unglück
Disgrâce d'un oiseleur
Lithograph
From: *Il Don Pirlone*, Rome,
16 January 1849

Lured by the parrot of Pope Pius IX, who had promised half-hearted reforms in the Papal States, the winged ideal of Italian unification and independence is in danger of being caught up in the demonic nets of reaction in Rome. Antonio Masutti was the main illustrator for the most important satirical magazine in the Roman Republic, even as the state was threatened by intervention from monarchist forces.

Angelockt vom Ruf des Papageien Papst Pius IX., der halbherzige Reformen im Kirchenstaat versprochen hatte, droht sich das beflügelte italienische Einigungs- und Unabhängigkeitsideal in Rom in den teuflischen Netzen der Reaktion zu verfangen. Antonio Masutti war Chefzeichner des wichtigsten Satiremagazins der von monarchistischen Interventionen bedrohten römischen Republik.

Attiré par le perroquet de Pie IX, qui avait promis de tièdes réformes dans les États pontificaux, l'idéal ailé d'unification et d'indépendance italienne menace à Rome de se laisser attraper dans les filets diaboliques de la réaction. Antonio Masutti était chef illustrateur du magazine satirique le plus important de la République romaine, menacée d'interventions monarchistes.

Henry Ritter

The Terrible Tale of Alfred the Butcher, 1849
Die schreckliche Geschichte vom Schlächter Alfred
L'horrible histoire du boucher Alfred
Stencil-coloured wood engraving
From: Henry Ritter, *Der politische Struwwelpeter*, Düsseldorf, 1849
Düsseldorf, Universitäts- und Landesbibliothek

In this parody of the collection of cautionary tales for children *Der Struwwelpeter* (Shockheaded Peter), Henry Ritter, who was also a co-editor of the *Düsseldorfer Monatshefte*, dealt with the various reasons for the failure of the revolutions in Europe in 1848. The killings committed by Alfred the Butcher allude to the uprisings in Vienna and Berlin that were suppressed by the generals Windisch-Grätz and Wrangel respectively.

In seiner Parodie des autoritären Kinderbuchs *Der Struwwelpeter* setzte sich der Mitherausgeber der *Düsseldorfer Monatshefte* Henry Ritter mit den vielfältigen Gründen für das Scheitern der 1848er-Revolutionen auseinander. Die Metzeleien des Schlächters Alfred spielen auf die Niederschlagungen der Aufstände in Wien und Berlin durch die Generäle Windisch-Graetz und Wrangel an.

Dans sa parodie de *Der Struwwelpeter*, un livre pour enfants autoritaire, le coéditeur des *Düsseldorfer Monatshefte* Henry Ritter analyse les diverses raisons qui ont conduit à l'échec des révolutions de 1848. Les tueries du boucher Alfred font allusion à l'écrasement des insurrections de Vienne et de Berlin par les généraux Windisch-Graetz et Wrangel.

VI. Die schreckliche Geschichte vom Schlächter Alfred. Erstes Bild.

Schlächter war des Alfred's Vater,
Schwein' und Ochsen schlachten that er
In 'nem Dorf in Oesterreich;
Wüßt' ich nur den Namen gleich!
In dem Hause war viel Blut,
Wie's bei Schlächtern hergehn thut.
So ward Alfred gar nicht bange
Vor dem Blut, und stundenlange
Konnte er dem Schlachten zu-
sehen mit der größten Ruh!
Dadurch kam es, daß sein Herz
Niemals kannt' des Mitleids Schmerz.
Rohe Kraft und Grausamkeit
Weg' ihm mehr als Menschlichkeit.

Nicht gar ferne wohnt' ein Mann,
Der manchmal zum Alfred kam.
(Man nannte ihn im Land umher
Nur den bitter=bösen Bär.)
Dieser Nachbar, Nikolas
Hatte seinen größten Spaß

Sah er Alfred bis zum Knie
Waten in dem Blut, und wie
Ein kanibalisch Ungethüm,
Armen Schaaf' die Haut abziehn.
Spornt ihn an mit Wort und Rath
Einst wie's sonst der Teufel that,
Schenkt ihm auch für sein Talent
Was man Ehrenzeichen nennt.

Der Vater war ein schwacher Mann,
Und Niklas kömmt's nicht d'rauf an
Ob's hundert Thaler oder zwei,
Ob's gar ein größ'rer Vorschuß sei,
Der ihm den Alten ganz und gar
In seine Hand gibt Haut und Haar.
Den Alten fängt mit seinen Ränken,
Den Alfred er mit den Geschenken.
So faßte Posto er im Haus
Und gibt für stammverwandt sich aus;
Und scheinbar gänzlich ungefährlich,
Ist Nachbar Niklas unentbehrlich.

Kaspar Braun (del. & sc.)

The Goose Song, 1849
Das Lied von der Gans
La Chanson de l'oie
Wood engraving
From: *Münchener Bilderbogen*, no. 7,
Munich, 1849

Illustrated stories presented in sequence and in the large format of a broadsheet had been appearing in Philipon's *Journal pour rire* since December 1847 (ill. p. 178). Braun followed suit six months later with his own series in the same format, and by 1898 some 1,200 episodes of the *Münchener Bilderbogen* had appeared, including a large number by Wilhelm Busch from 1858 onwards.

Seit Dezember 1847 druckte Charles Philipon in seinem *Journal pour rire* grafische Bildergeschichten im raumgreifenden Broadsheet-Format ab (Abb. S. 178). Ein halbes Jahr später folgte ihm Kaspar Braun mit einer Serie von Einblattdrucken in gleicher Größe nach. Bis 1898 waren vom *Münchener Bilderbogen* rund 1200 Folgen erschienen, darunter ab 1858 auch etliche Sequenzen von Wilhelm Busch.

Dès décembre 1847, Charles Philipon fit imprimer dans son *Journal pour rire* des histoires dessinées séquencées en vignettes en un généreux grand format (ill. p. 178). Six mois plus tard, Kaspar Braun l'imitait avec une série de planches imprimées de même format. Jusqu'en 1898, quelque 1 200 épisodes du *Münchener Bilderbogen* étaient parus, dont à partir de 1858 de nombreuses séquences signées Wilhelm Busch.

Das Lied von der Gans.

7

Was trägt die Gans auf ihrem Schnabel? —
Einen Ritter mit sammt dem Sabel
Trägt die Gans auf ihrem Schnabel.

Was trägt die Gans auf ihrem Kopf? —
Den dicken Koch mit sammt dem Topf
Trägt die Gans auf ihrem Kopf.

Was trägt die Gans auf ihrem Rücken? —
Ein altes Weib mit sammt den Krücken
Trägt die Gans auf ihrem Rücken.

Was trägt die Gans auf ihrem Bauch? —
Ein altes Weinfaß mit sammt dem Schlauch
Trägt die Gans auf ihrem Bauch.

Was trägt die Gans auf ihren Zehen? —
Eine Jungfrau, die thut ihr Hemdlein nähen,
Trägt die Gans auf ihren Zehen.

Was trägt die Gans auf ihrem Schwanze? —
Eine Jungfrau mit sammt dem Hochzeitskranze
Trägt die Gans auf ihrem Schwanze.

Was trägt die Gans auf ihren Füßen? — Die Braut, den Bräutigam zu begrüßen, Trägt die Gans auf ihren Füßen.

Münchener Bilderbogen.
10. Auflage.   **Nro. 7.**
Kgl. Hof- und Universitäts-Buchdruckerei von Dr. C. Wolf & Sohn in München.   Herausgegeben und verlegt von K. Braun und F. Schneider in München.

Max Haider

Two Stories: The Big Fish, and The Bad Billy-goat and the Swing, 1856
Zwei Geschichten: Vom großen Fisch und vom bösen Ziegenbock mit der Schaukel
Deux histoires : du grand poisson et du méchant bouc avec la balançoire
Stencil-coloured wood engraving
From: *Münchener Bilderbogen*, no. 187, Munich, 1856

The animal painter Max Haider, who specialised in hunting scenes, was one of the pioneers of proto-cinematic movement sequences. The technique was soon taken up by Wilhelm Busch, who developed this episodic illustrated storytelling into a popular form. In the 1880s the genre was given fresh impetus by the introduction of chronophotography.

Der auf Jagdmotive spezialisierte Tiermaler Max Haider zählte zu den Pionieren protofilmischer Bewegungsfolgen. Ihm folgte kurze Zeit später Wilhelm Busch, der das Format der episodischen Bilderzählung popularisierte. In den 1880er-Jahren erhielt die sequenzielle Grafik durch die Chronofotografie einen neuen pressegrafischen Auftrieb.

Max Haider, peintre d'animaux et spécialiste des motifs de chasse, comptait parmi les pionniers de séquences animées proto-cinématographiques. Peu de temps après, il fut suivi de Wilhelm Busch, qui popularisa la narration illustrée en épisodes. Dans les années 1880, le dessin séquentiel reçut une nouvelle impulsion dans le dessin de presse grâce à la chronophotographie.

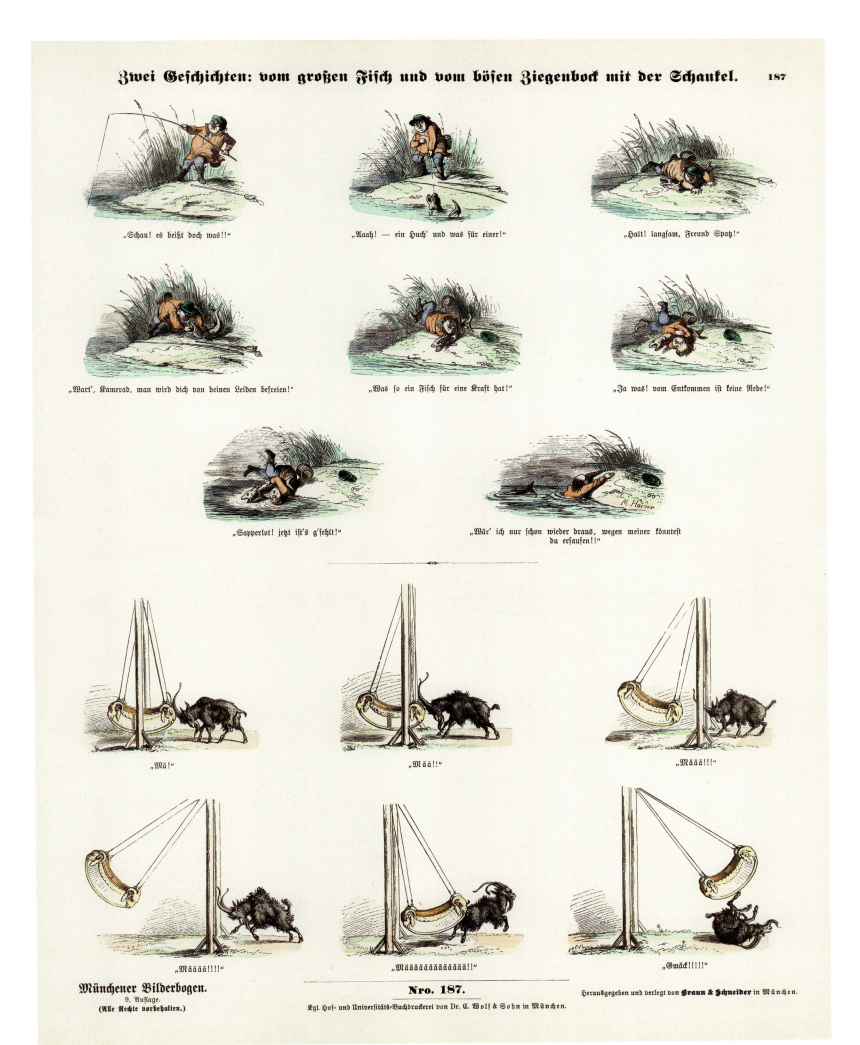

Anonymous

*Newcastle-upon-Tyne and Gateshead during
the Recent Conflagration*, 1854
*Newcastle-upon-Tyne und Gateshead während
der jüngsten Feuersbrunst*
*Newcastle-upon-Tyne et Gateshead pendant
le dernier grand incendie*
Wood engraving
From: *The Illustrated London News*,
14 October 1854

Following the introduction of printing blocks made
as separate pieces that could be screwed together,
which meant there could be a division of labour for
the wood engravers, illustrations that depicted large
fires tended to be produced in bigger formats. The
subject was ideally suited to allowing the artistic
qualities of the engraving work to develop freely and
with a variety of different results.

Verheerende Großbrände wurden seit der Einführung verschraubter Blockverbindungen, die ein
arbeitsteiliges Gravieren ermöglichten, bevorzugt im
Großformat abgebildet. Das Sujet war prädestiniert,
um die malerischen Effekte des Tonstichs relativ frei
und variantenreich zur Entfaltung zu bringen.

Suite à l'introduction de blocs d'impression vissés,
qui permettaient aux xylographes de se partager le
travail, les grands incendies étaient représentés de
préférence en grand format. Le sujet était prédes-
tiné pour permettre aux effets picturaux de la gravure sur bois de s'épanouir assez librement et dans
une grande diversité.

Félix Nadar & Dumont (sc.)

Review of the Second Quarter of 1851
Zweite Vierteljahresrundschau 1851
Revue du deuxième trimestre de 1851
Wood engraving
From: *Journal pour rire*, Paris, 28 July 1851

After the new censorship laws imposed during the
presidency of Louis Napoléon had forced Nadar
to shut down his *Revue comique* (ills. pp. 166/167),
he moved on to engage in a furious competition of
graphic work with Gustave Doré and Bertall in
the *Journal pour rire*. In his quarterly pictorial review

here he commented amongst other things on the
increasingly hard-line approach being adopted by
the police state, which a few months later resulted
in a coup d'état.

Nachdem Nadar sein eigenes Magazin *Revue
comique* (Abb. S. 166/167) aufgrund neuer Zensurgesetze unter der Präsidentschaft von Louis
Napoléon hatte einstellen müssen, lieferte er sich im
Journal pour rire mit Gustave Doré und Bertall einen
furiosen grafischen Wettstreit. In seiner vierteljähr-
lichen piktoralen Rundschau kommentierte er auch
die zunehmenden polizeistaatlichen Maßnahmen,

die wenige Monate später in einen Staatsstreich
münden sollten.

Après avoir dû interrompre la parution de son propre
magazine *Revue comique* (ill. p. 166/167) à cause
de nouvelles lois de censure sous la présidence de
Louis-Napoléon, Nadar se livra à une furieuse com-
pétition par dessins interposés avec Gustave Doré
et Bertall dans le *Journal pour rire*. Dans sa revue
de presse picturale et trimestrielle, il commentait également les mesures policières de plus en plus dictato-
riales, qui devaient aboutir à un coup d'État quelques
mois plus tard.

Un numéro tous les vendredis.　　　　Prix du numéro : 45 centimes.　　　　25 Juillet 1851

Numéro 182.

On s'abonne
CHEZ
AUBERT et Cⁱᵉ.
PLACE DE LA BOURSE.
PRIX :
3 mois : 4 fr. 25
6 mois : 8 50
12 mois : 16 »

LE JOURNAL POUR RIRE

Journal d'images, journal comique, critique, satirique et moqueur,

DIRIGÉ PAR

Ch. PHILIPON, fondateur de la Maison Aubert et Cⁱᵉ, du *Charivari*, de la *Caricature politique*, du *Musée Philipon*, des *Modes Parisiennes*, etc.

Étranger,
SELON LES DROITS DE POSTE
On s'abonne
AUBERT et Cⁱᵉ.
PLACE DE LA BOURSE.
PRIX :
3 mois : 4 fr. 25
6 mois : 8 50
12 mois : 16 »

Toute demande d'abonnement non accompagnée d'un bon sur la Poste ou d'un bon à vue sur *Paris* est considérée comme nulle et non avenue. Les messageries nationales et les messageries générales font les abonnements sans frais pour le souscripteur. — On souscrit aussi chez tous les libraires de France, — chez les correspondants de l'Agence d'abonnement, rue du Ponceau. — A Lyon, au magasin de papiers peints, rue Centrale, 27. — A Londres, chez Delizy et Cⁱᵉ, 13, Regent-street. — A Saint-Pétersbourg, chez Isakoff. — A Leipzig, chez Michelsen et chez C. Tweetmeyer.

REVUE DU DEUXIÈME TRIMESTRE DE 1851, — par NADAR,
Gravé par DUMONT.

L'homme à sonnette...

— Ce malade n'a rien. Mais comme il se trouve entre deux autres en traitement, nous le soumettrons au même régime jusqu'à ce que ses voisins soient guéris.

Beautés (modéré-e) de l'histoire de France (honnê-te). Un monsieur *honnête* vient proposer à un enragé *modéré* de trahir ses devoirs et d'être parjure à sa conscience.

Le modéré, pas *honnête*, a soin d'aposter quelques amis et un sténographe pour recueillir cette vilaine proposition. N. B. *Les deux tableaux vont très-bien comme pendants et ne valent pas cher.*

— A quelle sauce voulez-vous être revisés, légitimiquement, orléaniquement ou napoléoniquement ! — Mais nous ne voulons pas être revisés ! — Vous sortez de la question.

Au congrès agricole, M. Dupin a cru devoir donner encore une représentation de son éternelle pièce.

Dans sa monomanie d'arrérages, l'ex-roi *Jérôme* va demander aux Westphaliens son arriéré de traitement de roi.

— Pourriez-vous me donner des nouvelles de toutes ces sociétés californiennes, qui firent tant de bruit et de promesses il y a quelques mois !....

« Les banquets, c'est ma tribune à moi ! »

Le résultat de la discussion sur les sucres, qui ne satisfait personne et mécontente tout le monde.

La proposition de M. *Chapot* contre le droit de pétition est flambée !!

Le Belge au Français. — Eh bien ! vous qui nous traitez toujours si dédaigneusement, en voilà un procès !

Expédition de Kabylie. — Nous continuons à civiliser le pays.

— Mais je ne vois ai rien fait, général ! — Misérable ! je crois bien que tu ne m'as rien fait ! Juge un peu si tu m'avais fait quelque chose !

La vraie prolongation. — Allongement d'un nez connu devant la nomination de la commission pour l'examen des pétitions révisionnistes.

Report du même nez.

— M. *Veuillot* devrait pourtant bien savoir qu'il est défendu de déposer de ces choses-là ici.

Une fable de La Fontaine.

L'exposition de Londres. — Quel beau soleil !

Quel mouvement d'affaires !

MM. Thiers et Dupin à Londres — ou le plus curieux produit de notre exposition française.

Envoi français. Machine à voter de la force de 750 représentants.

Loi qui dote Lyon d'une préfecture de police.

Le spectre rouge. — Une dernière charge de ce farceur de Romieu.

LE HANNETON ROUGE
COCO ROMIEU
PRORROGATION
EMPIRE

L'homme qui est pour la force !

Fermeture des Italiens, et départ de la troupe de M. Lumley.

M. de Riancey et la garde nationale. — Mais, mon bon et tendre ami, si je monte à votre place vos deux heures de faction, c'est pour que vous ne perdiez pas votre temps, si précieux à l'ouvrier.

(Suite). — Eh bien ! monsieur de Riancey, voilà que la conscription me prend sept ans de ce temps si précieux à l'ouvrier. C'est le cas de prendre ma place. Ça ne me regarde pas ! tâchez d'acheter comme moi un remplaçant.

Ah ! dame ! M. de Riancey ne veut pas que tout le monde puisse être garde national !

Continuation du système Riancey. Dans vingt ans, le garde national sera un objet de curiosité et d'antiquité

VOYAGE SUR LES BORDS DU RHIN (Suite), — par GUSTAVE DORÉ,

Gravé par PONTENIER et SOTAIN.

On y trouve encore quelques caveaux où l'on peut se promener et trouver des trésors.

En effet je viens d'en trouver un !... Je viens de voir l'or briller.

Déception ! Je mets la main sur une calotte Keeloise à bords fourrés et à passementeries dorées.

Le lendemain je prends un guide pour visiter les ruines qui dominent le village.

Je sors en jurant que je ne visiterai plus de caveaux de ma vie.

En grimpant à un tronc de lierre, j'arrive au haut d'une tour. Deux poètes étaient assis sur le mur absorbés dans leurs méditations.

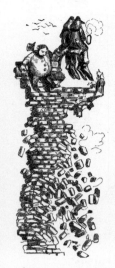

À peine étais-je arrivé au sommet qu'une partie du mur s'écroule en emportant mon guide !... Les flegmatiques poètes ne sourcillent pas.

L'horizon retentit de mes cris... Les poètes ne semblent pas entendre..

Survient la pluie... Nous subissons le sort des gargouilles d'église. Les deux poètes se donnent si peu de mouvement, que l'herbe des ruines prend racine sur eux.

Et toujours ils méditaient... Désespoir cruel, la faim me dévorait, j'attendais impatiemment un coup de vent qui voulût tout anéantir.....

Dieu est grand ! ! m'écriai-je en voyant poindre mon salut au milieu du ciel... « Mosieu Poitevin criai-je... » Les deux poètes étaient muets... ils méditaient toujours.

Sauvé !... Môsieu Poitevin m'a entendu et est venu à moi. Malgré nos instances, les deux poètes n'ont pas voulu quitter leurs méditations sur les ruines et la chute des empires. Tant mieux pour le cheval.

Nous n'avons pas de chance à la descente.. Nous tombons sur une cheminée surmortée d'un nid de cigogne.

Ce qui nous vaut une rosée cruelle des indigènes, qui ont pour les cigognes un culte particulier.

Nous nous relevons moulus. Môsieu Poitevin m'avertit que je lui dois 4,000 fr... Comprends pas...

Je paye enfin ; mais je n'ai plus même assez pour continuer mon voyage en bateau.

Je visite l'antique Stolzenfels, résidence seigneuriale du prince de Prusse. Il y a là un portier qui raconte à qui vent l'entendre et payer la légende suivante : *Légende naïve des bords du Rhin.*

Or la belle Euryane vit de sa tour le beau Solérol.

Aussi le beau Solérol fut pris d'une si grande passion que son cheval s'emporta.

Cette passion ne cessait d'accroître.

Par un hasard fort étonnant, son cheval galopant sans cesse le mena à la rencontre de l'armée sainte....

Donc il se joignit noblement à l'armée sainte, et pourfendit les *inchrétiens.*

Fier de ses exploits, Solérol retourna à Stolzenfels demander la main d'Euryane. Mais le père, qui était un dur seigneur, détourna la tête.

Puis il jeta sa fille dans un noir cachot, parce qu'elle avait aimé un chrétien.

Le beau Solérol désespéré gagna la plaine.

Et comme il était sensible, il résolut de mourir de chagrin.

Qu'allais-tu faire, langoureux chevalier, lui dit la fée Grillette, qui sortit d'un bluet ; moi je vais te rendre heureux...

Et aussitôt le beau Solérol changé en hanneton gagna avec les ailes de l'Amour la prison de la belle Euryane.

Et la belle Euryane que l'amour éclairait vit bien aux manières de ce hanneton que ce n'était pas un hanneton ordinaire.

Mais Tarabin, son petit frère, qui était un enfant terrible, prit un jour ce hanneton et joua...

Ce jeune chevalier conçut alors l'idée très-répandue aujourd'hui d'armer en tournoi deux hannetons, et de leur planter la tarière dans du liège.

Ce amusa beaucoup môsieur son père, qui était très-guerrier. Si bien que le seigneur se mit à dire : « Sans doute, si je savais un chevalier preux comme ce hanneton, je lui donnerais la main d'Euryane.

Et à ces mots le hanneton redevint le beau Solérol !...

La noce se fit en grande pompe ! chacun disait en voyant cela : Bossana ! preux chevalier, qui naquit à 25 ans du corps d'un hanneton. Respectons toujours les hannetons !

Une charte de ces temps rap° porte que cette princesse pleure fonda une abbaye, où elle se retira, trois jours après son mariage, du consentement de son époux.

Gustave Doré; Pontenier & Sotain (sc.)

Journey along the Banks of the Rhine, 1851
Reise an die Ufer des Rheins
Voyage sur les bords du Rhin
Wood engraving
From: *Journal pour rire*, Paris, 6 June 1851

The large format of the *Journal pour rire*, and its use of rapid storytelling in pictures, enabled the publisher of *Le Charivari* to reach a much broader and especially younger public. In comparison with the firework bursts of new graphic ideas set off by the young Gustave Doré, the earlier style of caricatures by Honoré Daumier and Paul Gavarni now looked antiquated and bland.

Mit dem großformatigen *Journal pour rire*, das auf rasante grafische Narration setzte, war es dem Verleger des *Charivari* gelungen, ein viel breiteres und vor allem jüngeres Publikum zu erreichen. Gemessen an dem Feuerwerk grafischer Einfälle, das der junge Gustave Doré entzündete, nahmen sich die tonangebenden Genrekarikaturen eines Honoré Daumier und Paul Gavarni antiquiert und blass aus.

Avec le *Journal pour rire* grand format, qui misait sur une narration graphique au pas de charge, l'éditeur du *Charivari* avait réussi à atteindre un beaucoup plus large et surtout plus jeune public. Comparé au feu d'artifice des trouvailles graphiques que le jeune Gustave Doré allumait, les scènes de genre prédominantes d'un Honoré Daumier ou d'un Paul Gavarni paraissaient dépassées et fades.

→ **Bertall; Dumont, Pothey & Riault (sc.)**

Comic Review of the Exhibition of Painting, Sculpture, Architecture etc., etc., etc., 1849
Humoristische Rückschau auf den Salon für Malerei, Skulptur, Architektur usw., usw., usw.
Revue comique du Salon de peinture, de sculpture, d'architecture, etc., etc., etc.
Wood engraving
From: *Journal pour rire*, Paris, 28 July 1849

After Gustave Doré had tried his hand with some unsubtle caricatures of the Salon the previous year, Charles Philipon decided to leave the field to the more experienced Bertall. The contest between Neoclassicism and Romanticism became Bertall's main theme, by way of the political conservatism he associated with Ingres and the anarchism he attributed to Eugène Delacroix.

Nachdem Gustave Doré sich im Jahr zuvor wenig pointiert in der Salonkarikatur versucht hatte, überließ Charles Philipon das Feld wieder dem erfahreneren Bertall. Der nahm als zentrales Thema das Duell zwischen Neoklassizismus und Romantik aufs Korn, zwischen Jean-August-Dominique Ingres, dem er den politischen Konservatismus zuordnet, und Eugène Delacroix, den er mit Anarchismus assoziierte.

Après que Gustave Doré eut tenté de caricaturer platement le Salon un an plus tôt, Charles Philipon laissa à nouveau le champ libre à Bertall qui était plus expérimenté. Il choisit comme thème central de ses charges le duel entre le néoclacissisme et le romantisme, entre Jean-Auguste-Dominique Ingres, affilié au conservatisme politique, et Eugène Delacroix, qu'il associait à l'anarchisme.

→→ **Bertall**

Humorous Review of the Exhibition of 1850
Unterhaltsame Rückschau auf den Salon von 1850
Revue pour rire du Salon de 1850
Wood engraving
From: *Journal pour rire*, Paris, 7 March 1851

Bertall clearly had no difficulty in identifying the salient characteristics of some of the paintings by Gustave Courbet that had caused a stir at the exhibition, in particular the huge work *Un Enterrement à Ornans* (*A Burial at Ornans*; middle of the page). As critics at the time noted, the outrageous exaggerations Courbet used in his paintings were essentially the same as those used in caricatures.

Bertall fiel es offensichtlich nicht schwer, die Charakteristika einiger der Gemälde herauszuarbeiten, mit denen Gustave Courbet im Salon Aufsehen erregt hatte, allen voran das riesige *Un enterrement à Ornans* (*Ein Begräbnis in Ornans*: in der Mitte der Seite). Wie die zeitgenössische Kritik bemerkte, waren die skandalträchtigen Zuspitzungen in Courbets Malereien der Karikatur wesensverwandt.

Manifestement, il ne fut pas difficile à Bertall d'isoler les caractéristiques de quelques-uns des tableaux, avec lesquels Gustave Courbet avait fait sensation au Salon, en particulier l'immense *Enterrement à Ornans* (au centre de la page). Comme la critique contemporaine en fit la remarque, les exagérations scandaleuses des peintures de Courbet présentaient des ressemblances certaines avec la caricature.

→→→ **Anonymous**

View Inside the Palace of the Exhibition in London, 1851
Innenansicht des Londoner Ausstellungspalastes
Vue intérieure du Palais de l'Exposition de Londres
Wood engraving
From: *L'Illustration*, Paris, 15 March 1851

For the first World's Fair, a new type of modular building was constructed in London in Hyde Park to house under one roof the collected exhibits of the 94 countries taking part. The structure became known as the Crystal Palace, a name that was coined by Douglas Jerrold in *Punch*.

Für die erste Weltausstellung wurde im Londoner Hyde Park ein Gebäude in neuartiger Modulbauweise errichtet, das die Exponate der 94 beteiligten Länder unter einem Dach versammelte. Der Name Crystal Palace, unter dem die Konstruktion bekannt wurde, war von Douglas Jerrold in der Zeitschrift *Punch* geprägt worden.

Pour la première Exposition universelle un bâtiment de construction modulaire, qui abritait les pièces d'exposition des 94 pays participants sous un même toit, fut érigé au Hyde Park de Londres. Le nom Crystal Palace, sous lequel la construction devint célèbre, avait été inventé par Douglas Jerrold dans le magazine *Punch*.

An de grâce 1849. — Avec la permission de M. le Maire et d'autres Autorités constituées.

REVUE COMIQUE

DU

SALON DE PEINTURE, DE SCULPTURE, D'ARCHITECTURE, ETC., ETC., ETC.,

Chargée de nombreux dessins par BERTALL, gravés par DUMONT, POTHEY et RIAULT;

AVEC DISSERTATIONS VARIÉES SUR LES COULEURS POLITIQUES ET CONSIDÉRATIONS VAGUES SUR LE DANGER DE S'EXPOSER.

Douleur des populations en apprenant que
Thomas Couture n'a rien mis au salon.

Vu l'état de siège, un des plus farouches gardiens
est spécialement chargé de surveiller les meutes,
afin qu'il ne soit pas laissé le moindre prétexte
à l'insurrection.

Le citoyen Thoré déclare que les tableaux sont
fort mal éclairés aux Tuileries, cet antique
foyer des ténèbres monarchiques.

Théophile Gautier examine avec un dédain qu'il ne
cherche pas à déguiser certains tableaux où les
paysagistes ont sacrifié au préjugé en peignant
des arbres.

Mais il n'approuve nullement que la réaction vexe les
gardiens en rendant leur figure glabre de barbe et
dépourvue de moustaches et de favoris, ces moississures
du fromage humain.

La Feste d'Elliant.

Mourir pour la patrie, mourir pour la patrie,
C'est le sort le plus beau…

Ce tableau est une diatribe violente contre l'administration des pompes funèbres, qui
a si mal fait son service pendant la durée de l'épidémie. Il y a du courage à oser
manifester des pensées aussi audacieuses sous le régime de l'état de siège.

Ma foi, tant pis! nous autres qui avons le courage de notre opinion, nous
avouons nos regrets pour la monarchie; non pas certes parce qu'elle nous
donnait un roi, nous prisons peu ce genre de fonctionnaires, mais bien à
cause de certaines institutions parmi lesquelles, en première ligne, se trouve le
jury. Où est il donc, bon Dieu, ce ravissant jury qui fonctionnait si bien sous
la monarchie? ce jury qui a abat-jour comme le *Constitutionnel*, à perruque comme
M. Molé, brèche-dent comme M. Pasquier, à lunettes comme M. Thiers; ce
jury qui portait si bien, si allégrement, toutes les accusations, toutes les iniqui-
tés, toutes les injures? — Bon jury monarchique, quelles ravissantes tartines
n'a-t-il pas fourni à ce littérateur qui est peintre, à ce peintre qui est littérateur, à cette littérature, à cette peinture que l'on nomme Théophile Gautier
et Thoré, ce critique….. blond qui a tant de barbe et si peu de chapeaux, à
comme il le tripotait de main de maître, ce pauvre jury, comme il lui flanquait
à la figure son indignation de son mépris; en cette belle et bonne prose socialiste qu'adorait alors le *Constitutionnel*, et qu'il subventionnait de son or, à
5 sous la ligne. Thoré n'a point eu de veine plus superbe, si ce n'est ces
magnifiques tirades que lui inspirèrent les chênes de Fontainebleau immolés
par une liste civile impure. Les chênes et le jury ont fait la fortune politique de
Thoré, le jury a posé Théophile Gautier. Chose étrange, ces deux hommes
éminents que le jury trouvait toujours au premier rang revêtus de la cuirasse
d'or de la science et de l'arme flamboyante et acérée du style, furent profondément divisés sur la question des chênes. C'était au moment où Thoré pleurait
en larmes de sang sur le sort de ces malheureux arbres de Fontainebleau si
méchamment mis à mort par la liste civile, que Gautier lançait son aphorisme audacieux, *l'arbre est un préjugé*, aphorisme de première qualité, père
putatif de celui que lança plus tard le glorieux citoyen P.-J. Proudhon. Il ne
nous appartient pas de décider la question entre ces deux maîtres de l'art, ni
de découvrir comment Thoré, cet apôtre de la liberté, prenait si chaudement
parti pour les chênes; constatons seulement que c'est au jury et à la liste civile,
deux institutions monarchiques s'il en fut, que nous devons la manifestation
de ces intelligences énormes!

Certes le jury qui produit de tels hommes est un jury bien regrettable, et
nous le pleurons d'autant plus que, si maintenant le salon n'est pas très-riche
et très-foisonnant en chefs-d'œuvre, si les artistes persistent, comme par le
passé, à rouler peu le carrosse, ce n'est plus le jury qui en est la seule cause.
Où donc est-elle? Nous n'en savons rien; M. Thiers y est-il pour quelque chose,
ou bien M. Proudhon, ou l'empereur Nicolas, ou le docteur Fattet; nous ne
devons rien décider à cet égard. Contentons-nous d'exposer avec exactitude les
tableaux que notre dessinateur a copiés au salon, et offrons les au public qui
jugera par lui-même. Peut-être parfois le crayon peu académique de l'artiste,
aura-t-il échoué dans son intention de rendre la finesse, ou l'élégance, ou la
vigueur du modèle, nous en demandons humblement pardon à qui de droit.

Bergers chaldéens observant les astres et la planète de M. Leverrier. Les
bergers chald ens naissan mathématiciens, prennent naturellement des
poses mathématiques.

Le mauvais Riche (épisode).

La pensée de l'auteur, M. Biennoury, est juste et humanitaire; il trouve
que le riche est trop bien nourri, et que le pauvre ne l'est pas assez.
Pour rendre encore plus odieux le mauvais riche, déjà si bien nourri,
il a eu l'heureuse idée de le représenter au moment où il va manger
son ange gardien à la coque, ce qui est le comble de la gourmandise et
de la scélératesse. C'est une bonne peinture socialiste faite avec des
procédés réactionnaires.

Le tableau
de M. de Tournemine,
44e édition,
fac-similé garanti.

Ce petit endroit était réservé au
tableau de M. Jules Laure,
n° 1246 : Milton aveugle. —
M. Laure n'est point aveugle,
il s'en faut, mais il est un peu
sourd, ce qui nous fait craindre qu'il n'entende pas très-
bien la plaisanterie. Bornons-
nous à constater qu'il entend à
merveille la composition et la
couleur.

RÉPUBLIQUE DES ARTS.

Duel à outrance entre M. Ingres, le Thiers de la ligne, et M. Delacroix, le Proudhon de la couleur.

Il n'y a point de quartier à espérer; si M. Ingres triomphe, la couleur sera proscrite sur toute la ligne, et l'insurgé que l'on trouverait muni de la moindre vessie sera livré aux
derniers supplices. Si Delacroix est vainqueur, on interdira la ligne avec tant de rigueur que les gens surpris à pêcher à la ligne sous le Pont-Neuf seront immédiatement passés par
les armes. Quelques personnes ont bien osé parler de fusion entre la ligne et la couleur; mais ce projet a paru si ridicule et si extravagant, que nous n'en parlons ici que pour
mémoire.

Terrains d'automne.
Tableau en terre cuite au four par M. Rousseau.

Vache égarée dévorée par les carpes que la famine fait sortir de l'eau.

Ce tableau, œuvre probable d'un socialiste, nous paraît être un appel à la violence. Nous désignons
le tableau et l'auteur à l'œil vigilant de M. Carlier.

Les joueurs de Lansquenet.

Ce tableau est remarquable en ce sens qu'il présente l'étude consciencieuse de la frisure et du tire-bouchon,
appliquée à la peinture. Celui qui perd est plus défrisé que les autres. Heureuse intention.

Junon jalouse.

M. Galimard a compris avec beaucoup d'intelligence que la ligne
droite est préférable à la ligne tire-bouchonnée pour les sujets
grecs. La figure a du ressort. M. Galimard entre avec résolution
dans la voie de M. Bard.

Portrait de M. Ferdinand Flocon.

Au moment où il est représenté, était-il encore représentant?
O peintre, pourquoi nous laisser dans cette douloureuse anxiété?
Du reste, Ferdinand est triste comme s'il venait d'être fait au
même.

REVUE POUR RIRE DU SALON DE 1850. (Suite.)

Les mansardes du grand Salon ayant été uniquement réservées aux sujets affreux et criminels, ces mansardes ont naturellement pris le nom de *Mansardes du crime.* — Nous faisons suivre ici quelques-uns des sujets qui illustrent ces mansardes.

MANSARDE DU CRIME.
Épisode de la bataille de Colique au veau.

Ce tableau qui se trouve justement placé entre le Banquet des Girondins et le tableau de Duveau, fut, dit-on, commandé par le czar pour dégoûter les moujiks des banquets et du veau, cette source de bouleversements et de coliques dans l'ordre social.

MANSARDE DU CRIME.
337. Boxe parlementaire.

Le retour du marché, par Courbet, maître peintre.

Rien n'égale l'enthousiasme produit sur le public par les tableaux de Courbet. — Voilà de la *vérité vraie*, sans chic ni ficelles. — On ne sent point là le poncif de l'école, et les absurdes traditions de l'antique. Tout y est naïf, heureux et gai. Courbet avait dix-huit mois quand il a peint ce tableau.

MANSARDE DU CRIME.
Scène d'intérieur.

MANSARDE DU CRIME.
Saint Sébastien percé de flèches.

Modèle de pelote destiné aux personnes pieuses.

778. Le Giaour par Eugène Delacroix.

684. Quelques points de Couture.

Ce magnifique dessin représente quelques mèches de cheveux appartenant à Béranger. Le génie sait donner de l'importance et du prix aux moindres choses.

259.

André Vesale, étudiant pas doux, s'occupe à décrocher le cadavre d'une charmante jeune fille qu'on a eu l'indélicatesse de pendre.   BLAGBON.

1499. Daniel dans une fausse position.

La couleur est assez fausse. Quant aux lions ils ont une figure humaine de nature à tranquilliser le spectateur.

Buste de l'ambassadeur du Népaul.

Il paraît d'après cette sculpture que les gens du Népaul ont l'habitude de se coiffer d'un panier. Nous n'avons rien à dire à ça. — Tous les goûts sont dans la nature.

Portrait de famille.

Ce portrait représente quatre enfants jolis comme des petits cœurs. Cette peinture fait l'éloge du cœur de l'artiste qui est une demoiselle.

10. EFFET DE PERREQUES.
Lecture du testament de Louis XIV. — Peinture Alaux et à l'huile.

Ce tableau renferme une allusion fine au corps académique. En récompense l'auteur a été nommé membre de l'Académie. — C'est justice.

L'enterrement d'Ornans, par Courbet, maître peintre.

Cette toile est celle que l'on remarque le plus au Salon, et à juste titre. Un enterrement est généralement chose assez triste. M. Courbet qui n'accepte point les traditions vermoulues, et ne marche pas dans les sentiers battus, a combiné son enterrement de telle sorte qu'on est pris d'une gaieté folle en le regardant. — C'est là un trait de génie.

1851. Tableau des misères réservées aux hommes politiques.

— Est-il vrai, Monsieur le baron, que vous serez bientôt représentant ?
— On le dit !
— Eh bien alors payez-moi tout de suite ma petite note, ou je vous fais fourrer à Clichy, et vivement.

— Bravo! Voilà Meissonnier qui se lance dans les grandes toiles! son tableau me rappelle la Smala d'Horace Vernet.
— Le fait est qu'on pourrait se tailler là-dedans cinq ou six tableaux délicieux.

Devant l'intérieur grec de Gérôme.

— Cette peinture est fort belle, c'est vrai, mais le sujet est peut-être un peu... chose.
— Moi je ne trouve pas; l'auteur a eu l'heureuse idée de faire les femmes en fer-blanc, ce qui sauve toutes les convenances.

Un tableau inédit de M. Courbet.

" Les relations étendues qu'entretient le *Journal pour rire*, nous ont mis à même de donner à nos abonnés une idée de cette magnifique toile, chef-d'œuvre de Courbet. — C'est M. Masson, le premier bras de France, qui en est l'heureux possesseur; il promène ce tableau par toutes les villes et bourgades, et fait, dit-on, par ce moyen, des recettes admirables. — C'est pour cela probablement que ce chef-d'œuvre n'a pu figurer cette année au Salon de peinture.

NOTA. — On nous apprend que le président a fait de nombreuses commandes à M. Courbet. Nous comprenons à merveille cette tactique. Un homme m me M. Courbet, s'il se lançait dans la caricature politique, serait évidemment des plus redoutables.

Ugolin déjeunant avec sa famille.

Manger ses enfants ce doit être bien dur pour un père, surtout quand les enfants sont aussi maigres. Heureusement le peintre qui est boulanger s'est arrangé pour rendre la tâche plus facile au malheureux père. — Il a fait de chacun d'eux fils d'Ugolin autant de croûtes.

NOTA. — Nous regrettons vivement que le président de la chambre n'ait pas songé à Boulanger pour faire son portrait. — Boulanger devait naturellement faire Dupin. Nous sommes certain que l'honorable fonctionnaire se reprochera vivement un pareil oubli des convenances.

Les Mannequins.

LEHMANN. — Quinze études consciencieuses d'après des pièces mécaniques allemandes.

Ce tableau peint à merveille la désolation des océanides au pied du roc de Prométhée. Il est rare que ceux qui les regardent n'éprouvent pas la désolation qu'elles expriment; le peintre lui-même, lorsqu'il examine son tableau, doit être désolé.... de l'avoir fait; car il a fait beaucoup mieux. — Aucune ordonnance de police ne peut nous empêcher de dire ici que les portraits de Lehmann et ceux de Chaplin sont les plus beaux portraits du salon.

Les Casseurs de pierre.

M. Courbet ayant observé que les peintres ses confrères avaient eu jusqu'alors la coutume de mettre les jambes dans les culottes qu'ils avaient à peindre, a cru devoir s'affranchir de cette routine. — Un pareil trait de génie est au-dessus de tout éloge.

QUARTIER FRANÇAIS.

VUE INTÉRIEURE DU PA

OSITION DE LONDRES.   QUARTIER FRANÇAIS.

SPECIMENS FROM MR. PUNCH'S INDUSTRIAL EXHIBITION OF 1850.

(TO BE IMPROVED IN 1851).

John Leech

↑ *Specimens from Mr. Punch's Industrial Exhibition of 1850*
Beispiele aus Mr Punchs Industrieausstellung von 1850
Spécimens de l'exposition industrielle de 1850 de M. Punch
Wood engraving
From: *Punch, or The London Charivari*, London, 13 April 1850

During the preparations for the Great Exhibition, the *Punch* co-founder Henry Mayhew published a series of investigative articles on London's poor in the *Morning Chronicle* (see ills. p. 185). In this illustration Mr. Punch is proposing to Prince Albert, who organised the event, that these unknown ethnic groups from the slums of London should also be exhibited, or else action should be taken to change their social conditions.

Während der Vorbereitungen zur Weltausstellung erschien von Henry Mayhew, dem Mitbegründer des *Punch*, im *Morning Chronicle* eine investigative Artikelserie über die Armen Londons (siehe Abb. S. 185). Mr Punch schlägt hier Prinz Albert, dem Initiator der Ausstellung, vor, der Welt entweder diese unbekannten Ethnien aus den Londoner Slums zu präsentieren oder die Verhältnisse zu ändern.

Pendant les préparatifs pour l'Exposition universelle, Henry Mayhew, le cofondateur de *Punch*, publia dans le *Morning Chronicle* une série d'articles très approfondis sur les pauvres de Londres (voir ills. p. 185). Mr Punch propose ici au prince Albert, l'initiateur de l'Exposition, soit de présenter au monde ces peuplades inconnues des bas-fonds de Londres, soit de changer les conditions sociales.

Henry George Hine, after Richard Beard (photo.), & E. Whimper (sc.)

The London Costermonger, 1851
Der Londoner Straßenhändler
Le Marchand de quatre-saisons londonien
Wood engraving

The Coster-girl, 1851
Die Straßenhändlerin
La Marchande de quatre-saisons
Wood engraving

Long-song Seller, 1851
Liedblattverkäufer
Vendeur de partitions de chansons
Wood engraving

Archibald Henning, after Richard Beard (photo.), & William Measom (sc.)

The Mud-lark, 1851
Der Schmutzfink | *Le Gamin de la rue*
Wood engraving

All illustrations from | Alle Abbildungen aus | Toutes les images:
Henry Mayhew, *London Labour and the London Poor*, vol. I, London, 1851

Following on from the work of John Thomas Smith, the book edition of Henry Mayhew's spectacular series of articles, *London Labour and the London Poor*, is a significant milestone in the development of investigative social journalism. The work's examination of costermongers, who sold fruit and vegetables from a barrow in the street, is acknowledged as a pioneering achievement in the research of a particular sub-culture. For the illustrations Mayhew used artists from *Punch*, who in most cases worked from daguerreotypes taken by Richard Beard.

Die Buchfassung von Henry Mayhews spektakulärer Artikelserie *London Labour and the London Poor* stellt nach den Arbeiten von John Thomas Smith einen weiteren Meilenstein in der Entwicklung des investigativen Sozialjournalismus dar. Die Untersuchung über die *costermongers*, die mobilen Obst- und Gemüsehändler Londons, gilt als Pionierleistung der Subkulturforschung. Für die Illustrationen griff Mayhew auf Grafiker des *Punch* zurück, die größtenteils nach Daguerreotypien von Richard Beard arbeiteten.

Après les travaux de John Thomas Smith, la version livresque de la spectaculaire série d'articles d'Henry Mayhews *London Labour and the London Poor* constitue une nouvelle pierre angulaire dans l'évolution du journalisme social d'investigation. L'analyse des *costermongers*, les marchands ambulants de fruits et légumes de Londres, est considérée comme une performance révolutionnaire de la recherche des subcultures. Pour les illustrations, Mayhew fait appel aux dessinateurs du *Punch*, qui travaillaient la plupart du temps d'après des daguerréotypes de Richard Beard.

London Labour and the London Poor.

THE LONDON COSTERMONGER.

"Here Pertaters! Kearots and Turnups! fine Brockello-o-o!"

[*From a Photograph.*]

THE COSTER-GIRL.

"Apples! An 'aypenny a lot, Apples!"

[*From a Photograph.*]

LONG-SONG SELLER.

"Two under fifty for a fardy'!"

[*From a Photograph.*]

THE MUD-LARK.

[*From a Photograph.*]

Honoré Daumier

↓ *The Northern Bear, the Most Unpleasant of All Known Bears*, 1854
Der Bär des Nordens, der unangenehmste aller bekannten Bären
L'Ours du nord, le plus désagréable de tous les ours connus
Lithograph
From: *Le Charivari*, Paris,
17 April 1854

With this menacing image of a warlike bear and its enslaved subjects, *Le Charivari* showed its sympathy for the combustible anti-Russian sentiment of the day. The cartoon was published soon after Louis Napoléon's Second Empire sided with Britain following the outbreak of war in the Crimea.

Mit der sinistren Darstellung eines kriegerischen Bären, der seine Untertanen versklavt, stimmte der *Charivari* in die hochkochenden antirussischen Ressentiments der Zeit ein. Der Cartoon erschien kurz nach dem Ausbruch des Krimkriegs, an dem das zweite französische Kaiserreich unter Louis Napoléon zusammen mit Großbritannien beteiligt war.

Avec la sinistre représentation d'un ours belliqueux qui réduit ses sujets en esclavage, le *Charivari* s'inscrit dans l'atmosphère anti-russe hautement explosive de l'époque. Ce dessin parut peu de temps après le déclenchement de la guerre de Crimée, quand le Second Empire sous Louis-Napoléon entra en guerre aux côtés de la Grande-Bretagne.

Gustave Doré & Soutain (sc.)

The History of Holy Russia,
Paris, 1854
Geschichte des heiligen Russland
Histoire de la Sainte Russie
Stencil-coloured wood engraving
From: Gustave Doré, *L'Histoire dramatique, pittoresque et caricaturale de la Sainte Russie*, Paris, 1854
Paris, Bibliothèque nationale de France

When the Crimean War broke out, Gustave Doré exploited all the available resources in the early forerunners of graphic novels to produce his enormous, nonsensical digression on the barbarity of Russian history, and in support of his propagandist intentions he pushed the medium to the limits of its possibilities. The work also marks Doré's shift from designing humorous caricatures to Napoleonic illustration and historical art.

Zu Beginn des Krimkriegs zog Gustave Doré in seinem riesigen Nonsens-Exkurs über die Barbarei der russischen Historie alle Register des frühen Autorencomic und führte das Medium mit propagandistischen Intentionen an die Grenzen seiner Möglichkeiten. Das Werk markiert Dorés Wende vom komischen Karikaturfach zur bonapartistischen Illustrations- und Historienkunst.

Au début de la guerre de Crimée, Gustave Doré exploita tous les registres d'une forme précoce de la bande dessinée d'auteur dans son immense digression sur la barbarie de l'histoire russe et, avec des intentions propagandistes, amena le medium aux limites de ses possibilités. Cette œuvre marque le passage de Doré du domaine de la caricature comique à l'illustration et à la peinture d'histoire napoléonienne.

ACTUALITÉS.   36

L'Ours du nord, le plus désagréable de tous les ours connus.

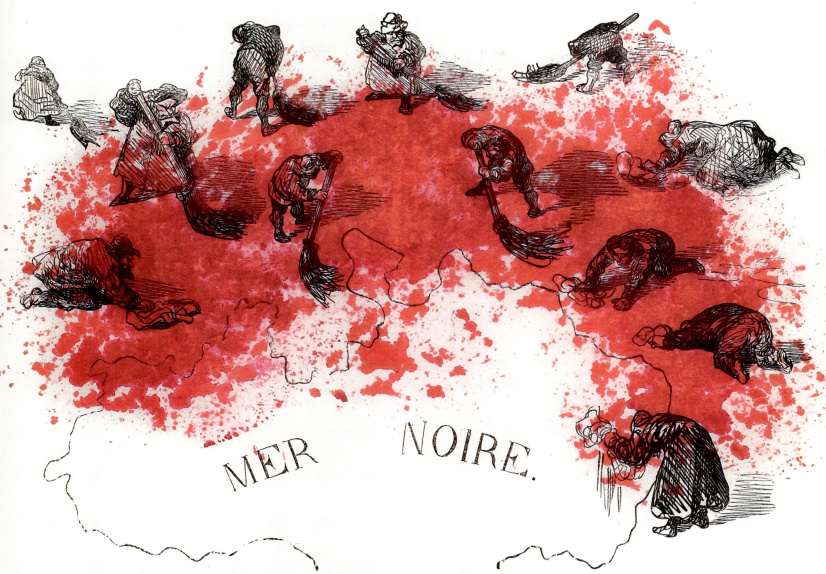

Les puissants et honorables successeurs d'Ivan mettent toute leur gloire à récurer le sol de la Russie.

Mais la discorde s'étant glissée parmi les récureurs, ils tâchent d'en finir au plus vite par un vigoureux coup de torchon.

Mais cela va bien plus loin qu'on n'avait pu le supposer ; les partis se reforment et se livrent des guerres affreuses. Tous les jours il en surgit de nouveaux et de plus terribles. De là des exterminations, des désastres, des débordements de tout genre, et, pour l'historien, une confusion plus grande que jamais. C'est de ce chaos formidable que surgit, après de longues et cruelles années, la nouvelle race des Romanoff, qui commence l'ère glorieuse et pacifique de la Russie.

Et maintenant, chapeau bas devant le colossal réformateur de la sainte Russie.

220   GLEASON'S PICTORIAL DRAWING-ROOM COMPANION.

OMAR PASHA.

The picture we give herewith represents the commander of the Sultan's troops, mounted. The history of this man is one of considerable interest, especially as he is now so prominently before the world. His proper name is Lattas. His family are immigrants in Croatia; consequently, by birth, Omar Pasha is an Austrian subject. His father held a military post in the Austrian service. He had an uncle, who was a Greek priest, of more than ordinary merit. A son of that priest is also an officer in the Austrian army. Omar Pasha himself is said to have been born in the year 1811—another account gives 1801—at Plaski, in the district of Ogulin, in Austrian Croatia. Frequenting the military normal high school in that city, he acquired the knowledge and mental discipline whence have flowed his power and distinction. Among acquirements of a much higher kind, he formed a beautiful hand, which proved of no small service in the commencement of his career. Afterwards he became a pupil in the mathematical school at Thurm, near Carlstadt. On completing his studies in that institution, he was incorporated in the Ogulin regiment in the capacity of cadet. Then he accepted a civil office, in which his calligraphy was his chief recommendation. Major Cajetan Kreczig, his employer, is said to have taken special pains to improve and guide the young man, who, however, seems to have neglected his duties, and in consequence found it convenient to relinquish his post. Hastening into Bosnia, he entered the service of a Turkish merchant. There his higher qualifications became known, and received recognition. Having renounced Christianity, and given his allegiance to the prophet of Mecca, Omar Pasha was made domestic tutor by his employer, whose children he accompanied to Constantinople. Considerable and important service has gained for Omar Pasha the full confidence of the Sultan, and the present crisis of the Turkish nation will afford ample scope for his military knowledge and skill. When active operations are chronicled, we look for much good generalship from him, and wish him abundant success against Russia. At the present moment the waters of the Danube may be reddened with blood.

EQUESTRIAN PORTRAIT OF OMAR PASHA, COMMANDER OF THE TURKISH FORCES.

SCHUMLA, TURKEY.

Any locality near the seat of European warfare at the present time is interesting. The view which we present below represents the plains and town of Schumla, and is taken from the inside of the Fort of Fidieh-Tabiassi, situated a mile and a half from the town. The visitors have arrived, with two orderlies (artillerymen) as their escort, a *valet-de-place* and interpreter, and the aide-de-camp. In the foreground are piles of shot; and upon the walls are the travellers, sketching and viewing the distant country—Schumla lying between the two mountains on the right. The town is nearly encircled by a chain of hills. They are in no part of very great height, but rise almost perpendicularly above the town, and contain some charming glens. At first sight one would imagine that, when thus overlooked, Schumla must be all but untenable as a military post, for any line of defence which embraced the hills would require an enormous army to man it, vastly larger, in fact, than the importance of the place, in any point of view, would warrant. In reality, however, they form the great source of its strength, and have rendered it famous by the various checks which the Russians have sustained before it. They are covered throughout the whole extent by thick brushwood, the remains of old forests, the height in most places of a man's shoulders, and so stiff and close that it is almost impossible for one to make his way through it, even along the path, without a guide. In the same manner it forms an excellent barrier against any attack on every side but the east, as it would be impossible for troops to deploy in the thickets; and, if the two narrow roads were well defended, it would be equally impossible even for scattered detachments to penetrate, without being separated and cut off by any foe who knew the ground. These natural advantages have rendered Schumla the great stumbling-block of the Russians in all their wars with the Turks; and as long as it remained unto them, an advance upon Constantinople was attended with no small danger. The approaches on the side next Varna are defended by several batteries as well as by the enceinte which surrounds the whole place, making it a place whose defences make it quite impregnable.

FORT OF FIDIEH-TABIASSI—VIEW OF THE TOWN AND PLAIN OF SCHUMLA.

Anonymous & Constantin Guys

Omar Pasha, 1854
*Fort of Fidieh-Tabiassi, Schumla
View of the Town and the Plain
Ansicht der Stadt und Ebene
Vue de la ville et de la plaine*
Wood engravings
From: *Gleason's Pictorial Drawing-room Companion*, Boston,
8 April 1854

Pictures of what was also known as the Eastern War were later published as well, after an interval of several weeks, in the first American illustrated periodical, which had been founded in 1851. Constantin Guys supplied the image of the Turkish headquarters, and as Charles Baudelaire noted, his drawings were a unique archive with an unmatched wealth of detail and lively spirit.

Bilder vom sogenannten Orientkrieg wurden mit mehrwöchiger Verspätung auch in der 1851 gegründeten ersten amerikanischen Nachrichtenillustrierten abgedruckt. Die Aufnahme vom türkischen Hauptquartier stammte von Constantin Guys. Seine Zeichnungen stellten nach Charles Baudelaire ein einzigartiges Archiv dar, das an Detailfülle und Lebendigkeit nicht zu überbieten sei.

Les images du conflit portant le nom de guerre de Crimée furent également imprimées avec plusieurs semaines de retard dans le premier magazine illustré américain fondé en 1851. La reproduction du quartier général turc est signée Constantin Guys. Selon Charles Baudelaire, ses dessins représentaient des archives uniques dont l'abondance de détails et la vitalité ne pouvaient pas être surpassées.

Constantin Guys

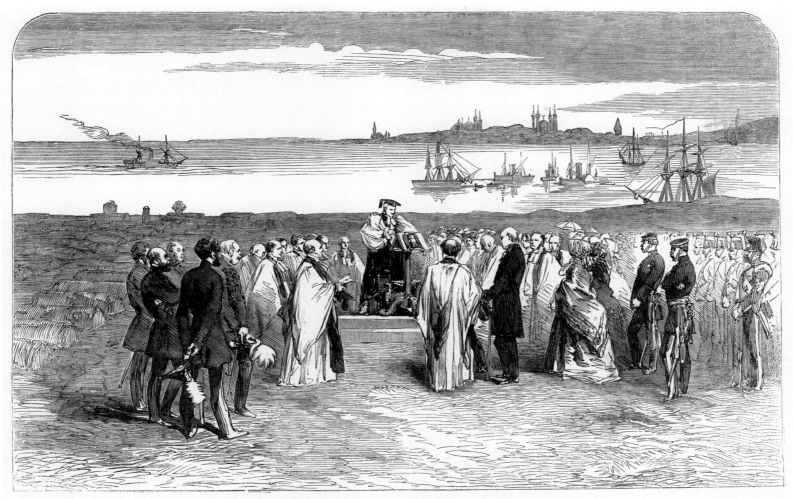

CONSECRATION OF THE BURIAL-GROUND AT SCUTARI, BY THE BISHOP OF GIBRALTAR.—(SEE NEXT PAGE.)

↑ *Consecration of the Burial-ground at Scutari, by the Bishop of Gibraltar, 1855*
Einsegnung des Friedhofs in Scutari durch den Bischof von Gibraltar
Consécration du cimetière de Scutari par l'évêque de Gibraltar
Wood engraving
From: *The Illustrated London News,*
9 June 1855

This illustration showing the English cemetery at Istanbul particularly impressed Baudelaire: "The pictures-que quality of the scene, which resides in the contrast between its Eastern setting and the Western clothing and poses of those involved, is achieved in a striking manner that suggests a view seen in a dream." (1863)

Die Szene auf dem englischen Fried-hof in Istanbul hatte Baudelaire be-sonders beeindruckt. „Der malerische Charakter des Schauspiels, der auf dem Kontrast zwischen der orienta-lischen Umgebung und den abend-ländischen Haltungen und Uniformen der Teilnehmer beruht, ist auf eine packende, suggestive, zum Träumen verführende Weise wiedergegeben" (1863).

Cette scène d'un cimetière anglais à Istanbul avait particulièrement impressionné Baudelaire. «Le carac-tère du spectacle, qui consiste dans le contraste de la nature orientale envi-ronnante et les attitudes et uniformes occidentaux des assistants, est rendu d'une manière saisissante, suggestive, grosse de rêveries» (1863).

↓ *Our Artist on the Battle-field of Inkerman, 1855*
Unser Künstler auf dem Schlachtfeld von Inkerman
Notre Artiste sur le champ de bataille d'Inkerman
Wood engraving
From: *The Illustrated London News,*
3 February 1855

Upon seeing this cavalry officer, "who, with his head slightly raised seems to be breathing in the terrible poetry of the battlefield, while his horse sniffs at the ground as it picks its way between the scattered corpses", Baudelaire perceived a new type of artist who captured a fleeting reality by way of his roaming eye.

In dem Reiter, „der erhobenen Haup-tes aussieht, als atme er die schreck-liche Poesie des Schlachtfeldes ein, während sein Pferd, am Boden schnuppernd, sich einen Weg sucht zwischen den übereinandergehäuften Leichen", nahm Baudelaire einen neuen Künstlertypus wahr, der eine vergängliche Wirklichkeit als wandeln-des Auge rezipiert.

Dans ce cavalier «qui, la tête relevée, a l'air de humer la terrible poésie d'un champ de bataille, pendant que son cheval, flairant la terre, cherche son chemin entre les cadavres amoncelés», Baudelaire perçut un nouveau type d'artiste qui capte une réalité passagère comme un œil en mouvement.

OUR ARTIST ON THE BATTLE-FIELD OF INKERMAN.

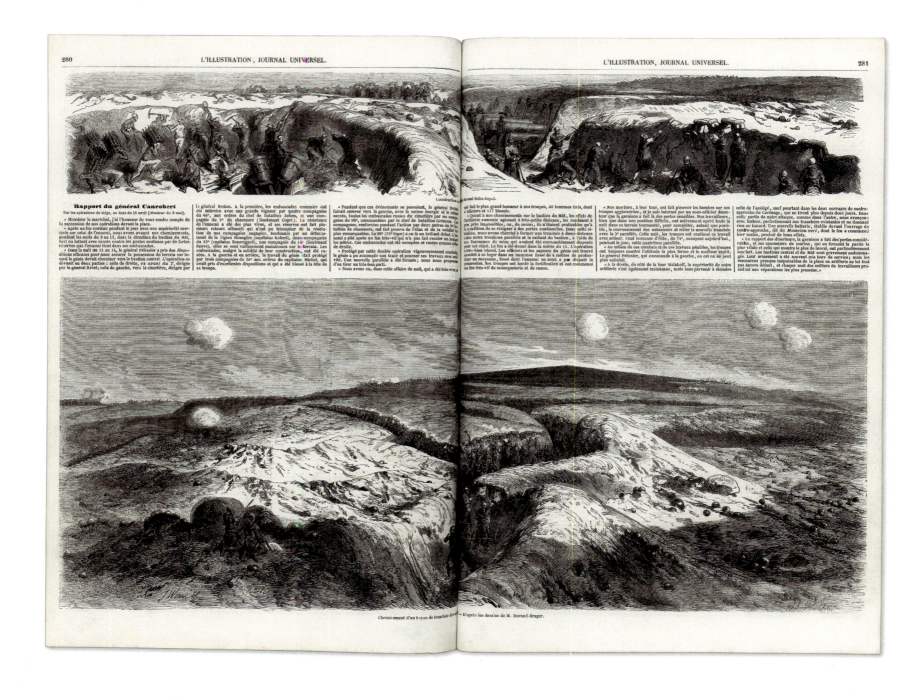

Henri Durand-Brager & Jules Worms (sc.)

Report by General Canrobert, 1855
Bericht des Generals Canrobert
Rapport du général Canrobert
Wood engraving
From: *L'Illustration*, Paris, 5 May 1855

Henri Durand-Brager was the main picture correspondent on the French side, and like Constantin Guys he had had military training in the past. Where Guys was concerned with process, however, Durand-Brager, a painter of seascapes and an experienced officer who had first worked for the press during the French campaign in Morocco, was more attentive to topographical accuracy in his illustrations.

Henri Durand-Brager war der führende Bildreporter der französischen Seite. Wie Constantin Guys verfügte er über eine militärische Ausbildung. Im Unterschied zu dessen prozesualer Anschauung ging es dem versierten Marinemaler und Offizier, der erste journalistische Erfahrungen während des Marokkofeldzugs gesammelt hatte, um die Präzision der topografischen Wiedergaben.

Henri Durand-Brager fut le peintre reporter le plus important du côté français. Comme Constantin Guys, il avait reçu une formation militaire. À la différence de la vision procédurale de ce dernier, ce peintre de marine et officier expérimenté, qui avait accumulé une première expérience de journaliste pendant la campagne du Maroc, recherchait la précision de la reproduction topographique.

THE SIEGE OF SEBASTOPOL, GENERAL VIEW.—SKETCHED FROM THE HEIGHTS.—(SEE NEXT PAGE.)

Constantin Guys

The Siege of Sebastopol. General View, Sketched from the Heights, 1854
Die Belagerung von Sewastopol. Gesamtüberblick von der Anhöhe aus skizziert
Le Siège de Sébastopol, vue générale dessinée depuis les hauteurs
Wood engraving
From: *The Illustrated London News*, 9 December 1854

The subjective viewpoint with its limited perspective in this scene combines the movement of the troops in the foreground with a detailed view of the general topography. Synoptic illustrations such as this revealed Constantin Guys to be an "advocate of a self-reflexive and relative, rather than a naively *absolute* form of authenticity in reportage" (Keller 2001).

Die subjektive und limitierte Betrachterperspektive auf die vorbeiziehenden Truppen im Vordergrund sind mit einer konstruierten topografischen Übersicht kombiniert. Constantin Guys erwies sich mit solchen synoptischen Aufnahmen als „Verfechter einer selbstreflexiven und *relativen* statt einer naiven *absoluten* Form von Authentizität in der Reportage" (Keller 2001).

La perspective subjective et limitée de l'observateur voyant les troupes défiler à l'arrière-plan est combinée à une vue d'ensemble topographique échafaudée. Par de telles images synoptiques, Constantin Guys se révéla comme «le défenseur d'une forme auto-réflexive et *relative* plutôt que naïvement *absolue* de l'authenticité dans le reportage» (Keller 2001).

William Simpson & E. Walker (lith.)

← *Commissariat Difficulties. The Road from Balaklava to Sebastopol, at Kadikoi, during Wet Weather*, 1854
Schwierigkeiten für die Intendantur. Die Straße von Balaklawa nach Sewastopol nahe Kadiköy bei feuchter Witterung
Difficultés pour l'intendance. La route menant de Balaklava à Sébastopol près de Kadiköy, par temps humide
Tinted lithograph
From: William Simpson, *The Seat of War in the East: First Series,* London, 9 February 1855

When winter came, the British army found itself ravaged by hunger and frostbite, and once the reports of this situation reached London, courtesy of the new independent correspondents, the cabinet was forced to resign. William Simpson was one of the few picture correspondents who remained in the field over the winter, and since he was dependent on protection from the army his reports of the terrible conditions were somewhat diluted.

Im Winter wurde die britische Armee durch Hunger und Erfrierung aufgerieben. Dass das Kabinett in London deshalb zurücktreten musste, war eine Folge der neuen unabhängigen Textberichterstattung. Zu den wenigen Zeichnern, die im Winter vor Ort verblieben waren, gehörte William Simpson. Da er auf die Protektion der Militärs angewiesen war, gab er die Missstände auf moderate Weise wieder.

Pendant l'hiver, l'armée britannique fut ravagée par la faim et le froid. La démission pour cette raison du Cabinet à Londres fut une conséquence de récents comptes rendus indépendants. William Simpson comptait parmi les rares dessinateurs restés sur place durant l'hiver. Comme il dépendait de la protection de l'armée, il décrivit de façon modérée les horribles conditions.

William Simpson & Edmond Morin (lith.)

↙ *Embarkation of the Sick at Balaklava*, 1854
Einschiffung der Kranken in Balaklawa
Embarcation des malades à Balaklava
Tinted lithograph
From: William Simpson, *The Seat of War in the East: First Series,* London, 24 April 1855

William Simpson's depiction of the procession of the sick and wounded is one of the most famous images of the Crimean War. Despite such unheroic representations he was still able to count on the army's support, unlike his colleague William Russell, who provided written reports for *The Times* but met with considerable difficulties because of the critical tone he used.

William Simpsons Prozession der Kranken und Verwundeten zählt zu den bekanntesten Bildern des Krimkriegs. Trotz solcher unheroischen Darstellungen konnte der Künstler auf die Unterstützung der Militärs rechnen, ganz im Gegensatz zu seinem Freund William Russell, dem Textkorrespondenten der *Times*, der wegen seiner kritischen Beiträge auf erhebliche Schwierigkeiten stieß.

La procession des malades et des blessés de William Simpson est l'une des images les plus connues de la guerre de Crimée. Malgré de telles représentations non héroïques, l'artiste pouvait compter sur le soutien de l'armée, à l'inverse de son ami William Russell, le correspondant de presse du *Times*, qui essuya de notables revers à cause de ses rapports critiques.

William Simpson & Jonathan Needham (lith.)

The Valley of the Shadow of Death, 1855
Das Tal des Todesschattens
La Vallée de l'ombre de la mort
Tinted lithograph
From: William Simpson, *The Seat of War in the East: First Series,* London, 11 June 1855

Simpson's watercolours were printed and sold in large editions in London and had a lasting effect in the way they depicted the Crimean War as a picturesque spectacle. As a trained lithographer Simpson was at first inspired by the designs of Carle Vernet and Auguste Raffet, which centred on the action of events, but in time he developed a more restrained and naturalistic way of working (see also ills. pp. 390, 391 b.).

William Simpsons Aquarelle wurden in London in riesigen Auflagen druckgrafisch verbreitet. Sie bestimmten den Eindruck vom Krimkrieg als pittoreskes Spektakel auf nachhaltige Weise. Der gelernte Lithograf orientierte sich zuerst an der Action-Grafik Carle Vernets und Auguste Raffets, entwickelte dann aber einen zunehmend verhaltenen und veristischen Stil (siehe auch Abb. S. 390, 391 u.).

Les aquarelles de William Simpson furent imprimées à grand tirage et distribuées à Londres. Elles procurèrent l'impression durable que la guerre de Crimée était un spectacle pittoresque. Le lithographe en formation s'inspira des illustrations centrées sur l'action de Carle Vernet et d'Auguste Raffet avant d'élaborer par la suite un style de plus en plus réservé et véristique. (voir aussi ills. p. 390, 391 b.).

Henri Durand-Brager & Lemercier (lith.)

View of Kamiesch, Paris, 1855
Ansicht von Kamiesch | *Vue de Kamiesch*
Lithograph
Published by E. Gambart & Co. (London) and Bisson Frères (Paris)

The photography that was used during the Crimean War was restricted to still subjects because of the long exposure times required. However, the resulting static, atmospheric images were purposely employed to discredit more critical forms of reporting. Henri Durand-Brager was the first *special artist* to experiment with the new medium.

Die Fotografie, die im Krimkrieg zum Einsatz kam, war durch ihre langen Belichtungszeiten zu unbewegten Motiven gezwungen. Sie wurde dementsprechend auch gezielt eingesetzt, um kritische Berichterstattungen durch statuarische Stimmungsbilder zu diskreditieren. Henri Durand-Brager war der erste *special artist*, der mit dem neuen Medium experimentierte.

La photographie, qui fut utilisée pendant la guerre de Crimée, était réduite à des motifs immobiles à cause des longs temps d'exposition. Ces images d'atmosphère statiques furent délibérément exploitées afin de discréditer les reportages critiques. Henri Durand-Brager fut le premier *special artist* à expérimenter ce nouveau medium.

Gustave Doré

↓ *The Siege of Sebastopol – Retreat of the Russians*, 1855
Die Belagerung von Sewastopol – Rückzug der Russen
Le Siège de Sébastopol – La retraite des Russes
Wood engraving
From: *The Illustrated London News*,
3 November 1855

At the same time as he was working on his vast project for an illustrated canon of world literature Gustave Doré spent two years working in pictorial journalism converting the sketches of picture correspondents in the field into a monumental series of moving images in a late-Romantic style. William Simpson's scene of Balaklava (ill. p. 192 b.), for example, was intensified into an apocalyptic vision of the Russian retreat from Sebastopol.

Parallel zu seinem Megaprojekt eines illustrierten Kanons der Weltliteratur arbeitete Gustave Doré zwei Jahre lang im bildjournalistischen Gewerbe und übersetzte Motive der Korrespondenten vor Ort in spätromantisches Monumentalkino. William Simpsons Balaklawa-Szene (Abb. S. 192 u.) steigerte er in eine endzeitliche Vision vom russischen Rückzug aus Sewastopol.

Parallèlement à son immense projet d'un canon illustré de la littérature mondiale, Gustave Doré travailla pendant deux ans dans le secteur du journalisme illustré et transmua les motifs des correspondants se trouvant sur place en un cinéma monumental du romantisme tardif. Il intensifia la scène de Balaklava de William Simpson (ill. p. 192 b.) en une vision apocalyptique de la retraite russe de Sébastopol.

THE SIEGE OF SEBASTOPOL.—RETREAT OF THE RUSSIANS FROM THE SOUTH TO THE NORTH SIDE.—DRAWN BY GUSTAVE DORE.—(SEE NEXT PAGE.)

Charles A. Barry (sc.), after Mazury & Silsbee (photo.)

The Chippewa Indians, 1856
Die Chippewa-Indianer | *Les Indiens Chippewa*
Wood engraving
From: *Ballou's Pictorial*, Boston, 19 January 1856

As is shown by this group portrait of six Chippewa
Indians on the cover of the magazine that followed on
from *Gleason's Pictorial*, relatively free transfers of
photographic originals were normal practice only a few
years before photographs could be exposed directly
on to printing blocks, and thus establish a new standard of accuracy for reproductions.

Wie das Gruppenporträt von Vertretern der Chippewa-
Indianern auf dem Cover des Nachfolgemagazin von
Gleason's Pictorial demonstriert, waren, nur wenige
Jahre bevor die direkte Aufbelichtung von Fotografien
auf die Druckstöcke einen neuen mimetischen Standard
etablierte, relativ freie Übertragungen fotografischer
Vorlagen üblich.

Comme en témoigne le portrait de groupe de représentants des Indiens Chippewa sur la couverture du magazine
qui succéda au *Gleason's Pictorial*, le transfert relativement
libre de photographies originales était monnaie courante,
quelques années seulement avant que l'exposition directe
de photographies sur les blocs d'impression établisse un
nouveau standard mimétique.

Winslow Homer

March Winds and *April Showers*, 1859
Märzwinde und *Aprilschauer*
Vents de mars et *giboulées d'avril*
Wood engravings
From: *Harper's Weekly*, New York, 2 April 1859

In the same way as many other important American artists,
Winslow Homer began his career as an illustrator for the
press. In 1859, he and Alfred Waud moved from *Ballou's
Pictorial* in Boston to the newly founded illustrated magazine *Harper's Weekly* in New York, where he went on to
work freelance for more than 20 years.

Wie viele führende amerikanische Künstler hatte Winslow
Homer seine Karriere als Pressegrafiker begonnen. 1859
war er zusammen mit Alfred Waud vom Bostoner *Ballou's
Pictorial* zu der erst kürzlich gegründeten New Yorker Illustrierten *Harper's Weekly* gewechselt, für die er mehr als
20 Jahr lang als freier Mitarbeiter tätig sein sollte.

Comme de nombreux artistes américains de premier plan,
Winslow Homer avait commencé sa carrière comme illustrateur de presse. En 1859, il était passé avec Alfred Waud
du *Ballou's Pictorial* de Boston au magazine illustré new-
yorkais *Harper's Weekly* récemment fondé, pour lequel il
allait travailler en free-lance pendant plus de vingt ans.

Constantin Guys

Sketches in Alexandria, 1855
Skizzen von Alexandria | *Esquisses à Alexandrie*
Wood engravings
From: *The Illustrated London News*, 18 August 1855

These two street scenes are among the few press illustrations in which traces of the compressed style with several focal points used by Constantin Guys have survived into the finished wood engravings. Nadar, who along with Manet and Émile Zola was one of the first collectors of this proto-Impressionist style of art, believed that snapshots were not invented with photography, but by Guys.

Die beiden Straßenszenen gehören zu den wenigen Illustriertenabbildungen, bei denen sich Reste von Constantin Guys, polyfokaler Schnellschrift in den xylografischen Übertragungen erhalten haben. Nadar, der neben Édouard Manet und Émile Zola zu den ersten Sammlern dieser protoimpressionistischen Kunst zählte, war der Ansicht, dass der Schnappschuss nicht durch die Fotografie, sondern durch Guys entdeckt worden sei.

Ces deux scènes de rue comptent parmi les rares images de journaux illustrés dans lesquelles sont conservées des traces de l'expression comprimée et multifocale dans les processus de tranfert de xylographie, utilisée par Constantin Guys. Nadar, qui avec Édouard Manet et Émile Zola fut l'un des premiers collectionneurs de cet art proto-impressionniste, pensait que l'instantané n'avait pas été une découverte de la photographie, mais de Guys.

Sketches in Madrid, 1856
Skizzen von Madrid | *Esquisses à Madrid*
Wood engravings
From: *The Illustrated London News*,
26 July 1856

In Baudelaire's view, Constantin Guys was especially attracted to subjects in which "all *the magnificence of life* in the capital cities of the civilised world is revealed […] the splendour of military life, elegant life and the gallant life" (1863). Guys typically insisted on being an anonymous *special artist*, but for these sophisticated snapshots of Madrid he allowed himself to be named.

Constantin Guys Neigung galt, laut Charles Baudelaire, vor allem jenen Sujets, in denen sich „die Pracht des Lebens" in den Hauptstädten der zivilisierten Welt […] entfaltet, der Glanz des militärischen, des eleganten, des galanten Lebens" (1863). Normalerweise beharrte Guys auf der Anonymität des *special artist*. Im Zusammenhang mit dieser mondänen Momentaufnahmen aus Madrid ließ er sich jedoch zur Preisgabe seiner Identität überreden.

Selon Baudelaire, Constantin Guys se sentait surtout attiré par les sujets dans lesquels « *la pompe de la vie* […] s'offre dans les capitales du monde civilisé, la pompe de la vie militaire, de la vie élégante, de la vie galante» (1863). Normalement, Guys insistait sur l'anonymité du *special artist*. Pourtant, en rapport avec ces clichés mondains de Madrid il accepta de révéler son identité.

Constantin Guys

Courtesans and Officers, undated
Kurtisanen und Offiziere | *Lorettes et officiers*
Ink with wash

↓ *Cavalry*, c. 1865
Kavallerie | *Cavalerie*
Ink with watercolour

When it was remarked that Guys's pictorial journalism always placed great importance on details of clothing, Baudelaire felt it necessary to justify his art with the newly coined notion of *modernity*: "For him, it is a matter of taking from fashion that part of it which has a temporary element of poetry [...]. Modernity is transitory, ephemeral and contingent, one half of art the other half of which is eternal and unchanging" (*The Painter of Modern Life*, 1863).

Die Beobachtung, dass Guys Bildjournalismus stets ein Augenmerk auf die Spezifik der Bekleidung legte, bewog Charles Baudelaire dazu, seine Kunst mit dem Neologismus der *modernité* zu belegen: „Für ihn geht es darum, der Mode das abzugewinnen, was sie im Vorübergehenden an Poetischem enthält [...]. Die *Modernität* ist das Vergängliche, das Flüchtige, das Zufällige, die eine Hälfte der Kunst, deren andere Hälfte das Ewige und Unwandelbare ist" (*Le peintre de la Vie moderne*, 1863).

L'observation, que Guys attachait une grande importance aux détails vestimentaires dans ses reportages illustrés, incita Charles Baudelaire à employer le néologisme de *modernité* pour définir son art : «Pour lui, il s'agit de dégager de la mode ce qu'elle peut contenir de poétique dans l'historique [...]. La *modernité*, c'est le transitoire, le fugitif, le contingent, la moitié de l'art, dont l'autre moitié est l'éternel et l'immuable (*Le peintre de la Vie moderne*, 1863).»

THE BRITISH LION'S VENGEANCE ON THE BENGAL TIGER.

. An uncontrollable desire for revenge was aroused throughout England on account of the horrible atrocities committed by the native Indian soldiers after the Mutiny.

John Tenniel & Joseph Swain (sc.)

*The British Lion's Vengeance
on the Bengal Tiger*, 1857
*Die Rache des britischen Löwen
am Bengal-Tiger*
*La Vengeance du Lion britannique
sur le Tigre du Bengale*
Wood engraving
From: *Punch, or The London Charivari*,
London, 22 August 1857

From 1850, after John Tenniel was made chief illustrator for *Punch*, the magazine's nationalistic tendency became more pronounced. His allegorical cartoons reflect his earlier experience as a history painter influenced by the German Nazarenes. With this depiction of a wrathful lion Tenniel supplied the British longing for revenge after the Cawnpore Massacre with a symbolic figure, which became enormously popular and was also featured on army banners.

Mit John Tenniels Engagement als Chefzeichner des *Punch* verstärkte sich seit 1850 die chauvinistische Tendenz des Satiremagazins. In den allegorischen Cartoons schlug sich seine Erfahrung als nazarenischer Historienmaler nieder. Den britischen Vergeltungsgelüsten nach dem Kanpur-Massaker verlieh Tenniel in der Darstellung des wütenden Löwen eine symbolische Gestalt, die immens populär wurde und sich auch auf den Bannern der Armee wiederfand.

À partir de 1850, après que John Tenniel fut engagé comme chef dessinateur au *Punch*, la tendance chauviniste du magazine satirique alla en augmentant. Ses dessins allégoriques reflètent son expérience en tant que peintre d'histoire nazaréen. Dans la représentation du lion furieux, Tenniel conféra à la soif de vengeance britannique après le massacre de Cawnpore une figure symbolique, qui obtint une immense popularité et se retrouva aussi sur les étendards de l'armée.

Anonymous

Top: *Underground Works at the Junction of Hampstead Road, Euston Road and Tottenham Court Road*
Bottom: *New Railway Carriage Built for the Use of the Prince and Princess of Wales on the Great Eastern Railway*
Oben: *U-Bahn-Bau an der Kreuzung von Hampstead Road, Euston Road und Tottenham Court Road*
Unten: *Neuer Eisenbahnwaggon, gebaut zur Benutzung durch den Prinzen und die Prinzessin von Wales auf der Great Eastern Railway*

En haut: *Travaux souterrains au croisement de l'Hampstead-Road, de l'Euston-Road et de la Tottenham-Court-Road*
En bas: *Nouveau wagon de chemin de fer, construit pour l'usage du prince et de la princesse de Galles sur le Great Eastern Railway*

Wood engravings
From: *The Illustrated London News*, 28 May 1864

THE ILLUSTRATIONS.

Fig. 1. *Walking Dress.* Dark lilac poplin robe, trimmed with black passementerie ornaments. The corsage is cut in the style known as the corsage Impératrice, without seam. Lilac crape bonnet, covered with black tulle, and ornamented with lilac marquérites beneath the front edge.

Fig. 2. *Carriage Dress.* Slate-coloured moire antique robe, trimmed with violet ribbon, fastened at intervals by bows of the dress material; the sleeves are similarly ornamented. Rice chip bonnet, edged in front with a trimming of black lace, and provided on one side, behind, with a violet bow and green leaf; a small bouquet of green leaves is also placed upon the violet silk bavolet.

Fig. 3. *Dress for a Watering-place.* — Robe of grey moire, which it is needless to describe, as the principal feature of this figure is the Maintenon mantle, composed of cashmere, lined with taffety. The hood is flat, trimmed with lace, and, forming a pelerine, falls over the shoulders when worn out of doors with a bonnet. With the hood raised over the head, as shown in our Illustration, this mantle will be very convenient for evening rambles in the country, or at the sea-side.

UNDERGROUND WORKS IN THE EUSTON-ROAD.

OUR Engraving represents a section of the underground works at the junction of Tottenham-court-road and Hampstead-road with Euston-road. The view is taken from beneath the north-west corner of Tottenham-court-road looking towards the east along the line of Euston-road. It will serve to show what extensive subterranean works are being constructed in different parts of London, yet which make no show on the surface, and the very existence of which is probably unknown to a very large portion of the inhabitants residing in the neighbourhood or daily walking over the site. We have chosen this particular locality because it is a point where the lines of a number of different works intersect each other. There is, first, immediately under the surface of the road, a double set of mains and pipes for supplying the district with water and gas. Beneath these passes, transversely, the

iron tube belonging to the Pneumatic Dispatch Company, through which parcels are constantly being conveyed backwards and forwards, and occasionally the mailbags also, between the General Post Office and this district. Under this tube, is the tunnel of the Metropolitan (or, as it is more generally called, the Underground) Railway, through which trains are constantly passing and repassing. The Pneumatic Dispatch Company's tube cuts through the crown of this tunnel. On each side of it run large sewers which form part of the London Main-Drainage works. Beneath all these structures we have shown a longitudinal section of the proposed Hampstead, Midland, North-Western, and Charing-cross Railway—a line which is not yet made, but which has been recommended by a Committee of the House of Commons, and is likely, sooner or later, to be constructed, passing the junction of Euston-road and Tottenham-court-road in the manner here displayed.

SALOON CARRIAGE FOR THE PRINCE OF WALES ON THE GREAT EASTERN RAILWAY.

A REPRESENTATION of the new and elegant saloon carriage, built expressly for the use of the Prince and Princess of Wales, in their journeys to Sandringham and back by the Great Eastern Railway, is engraved in our pages this week. Their Royal Highnesses, with the infant Prince, attended by their ordinary suite, travelled by this conveyance from the Bishopsgate terminus to the Wolferton station on the occasion of their last visit to Norfolk, when the Prince expressed himself much pleased with the arrangements made by the railway company, and especially with this beautiful carriage. It has been constructed in the workshops of the company at Stratford, by Mr. G. Attock, superintendent of the carriage department, from the designs of Mr. R. Sinclair, the chief engineer. Its total length is 26 ft., width 8 ft., and height 7 ft. 3 in. The interior is divided into three compartments—ante-room, saloon, and retiring room. The length of the saloon is 12 ft. 6 in., with doors leading to ante and retiring rooms. The fittings and decorations, by Mr. Thomas Fox, of 93, Bishopsgate Within, are very rich.

UNDERGROUND WORKS AT THE JUNCTION OF HAMPSTEAD-ROAD, EUSTON-ROAD, AND TOTTENHAM-COURT-ROAD.

NEW RAILWAY CARRIAGE BUILT FOR THE USE OF THE PRINCE AND PRINCESS OF WALES ON THE GREAT EASTERN RAILWAY.

Thomas Nast & Andrew Varick Stout Anthony (sc.)

When the recently founded *New York Illustrated News* commissioned its youngest employee, Thomas Nast, to cover the first boxing world championship match in England in early 1860, the occasion marked the start of the most successful career in press graphics. Nast had just left the major American weekly *Frank Leslie's Illustrated Newspaper* for the New York journal, and the 20-year-old *special artist* duly made a name for himself on both sides of the Atlantic with his reports on the spectacular sporting event, in which he also made sure to give himself a prominent mention.

Als die neu gegründete *New York Illustrated News* Anfang 1860 ihren jüngsten Mitarbeiter Thomas Nast damit beauftragte, über den weltweit ersten Boxweltmeisterschaftskampf in England zu berichten, war dies der Auftakt zur triumphalsten Karriere des Pressegrafikzeitalters. Nast war erst kürzlich von der führenden amerikanischen Illustrierten *Frank Leslie's Illustrated Newspaper* zur *New York Illustrated News* gewechselt. Mit seinen Berichten über das spektakuläre Sportereignis, in denen er sich selbst prominent in Szene setzte, machte sich der erst 20-jährige *special artist* auf beiden Seiten des Atlantiks einen Namen.

Lorsque le *New York Illustrated News* récemment fondé sollicita, début 1860, son plus jeune collaborateur Thomas Nast pour qu'il couvre le tout premier match de championnat du monde de boxe en Angleterre, démarra la carrière la plus triomphale de l'époque du dessin de presse. Nast venait de quitter le grand journal illustré *Frank Leslie's Illustrated Newspaper* pour entrer au *New York Illustrated News*. Grâce à ses reportages sur cet événement sportif spectaculaire, dans lesquels il se plaça lui-même sur le devant de la scène, le *special artist* de tout juste vingt ans se fit un nom des deux côtés de l'Atlantique.

THE RECEPTION OF OUR SPECIAL ARTIST, THOMAS NAST, ESQ., BY JOHN C. HEENAN, THE BENICIA BOY, AT THE HOUSE OF THE LATTER IN HARNHAM, WILTSHIRE

The Reception of Our Special Artist, Thomas Nast, Esq., by John C. Heenan, 1859
Der Empfang unseres Special Artist *Thomas Nast, Esq., durch John C. Heenan*
La Réception de notre special artist, *Thomas Nast, Esq., par John C. Heenan*
Wood engraving
From: *New York Illustrated News*, 1860

THE CHAMPIONSHIP FIGHT BETWEEN HEENAN AND SAYERS, ON APRIL 17, 1860
Jack Macdonald Billy Mulligan   Joseph Cusick   The "Benicia Boy"   Thomas Sayers   Morrissey   Jemmy Welsh Harry Brunton
From a sketch by our artist, Thomas Nast, Esq. Engraved by A. V. S. Anthony, Esq., on board the "Vanderbilt," on her return passage.

The Championship Fight between Heenan and Sayers on April 17, 1860
Der Meisterschaftskampf zwischen Heenan und Sayers
Le Combat de championnat entre Heenan et Sayers
Wood engraving
From: *New York Illustrated News*, 1860

Thomas Nast

*The Vote for Annexation
at Naples – Polling Booth
at Monte Calvario*, 1860
*Die Abstimmung über den
Anschluss in Neapel –
Wahllokal in Monte Calvario
Le Vote sur l'annexion
à Naples – Bureau de vote
à Monte Calvario*
Wood engraving
From: *The Illustrated
London News*,
10 November 1860

THE VOTE FOR ANNEXATION AT NAPLES.—POLLING BOOTH AT MONTE CALVARIO.—FROM A SKETCH BY T. NAST.—SEE PAGE 447.

*The Triumphal Entry of
Garibaldi into Naples*, 1860
*Der triumphale Einzug
Garibaldis in Neapel
L'Entrée triomphale
de Garibaldi dans Naples*
Wood engraving
From: *The Illustrated
London News*,
22 September 1860

THE TRIUMPHAL ENTRY OF GARIBALDI INTO NAPLES

Shortly after the great sporting event, Thomas Nast went to cover the most dazzling political spectacle of the time on behalf of American and also English journals. Together with more than 1,000 supporters of the revolution from all round the world, he joined the military expedition to Sicily led by the freedom fighter Garibaldi when they embarked from Genoa. Nast identified with Garibaldi's campaign for national unity, and produced heroic portraits of the republican idol and advocate of abolitionism. As such he put himself in prime position to become a propagandist for the Unionists during the American Civil War when it began in 1861.

Kurz nach dem größten Sportevent verfolgte Thomas Nast im Auftrag englischer und amerikanischer Illustrierten das glänzendste Politspektakel der Zeit. Zusammen mit über 1000 revolutionären Enthusiasten aus aller Welt schloss er sich in Genua der sizilianischen Intervention des italienischen Freiheitskämpfers Giuseppe Garibaldi an. Nast identifizierte sich mit der Einigungsbewegung Garibaldis und brachte heroische Darstellungen des republikanischen Idols und Verfechters des Abolitionismus in Umlauf. Er qualifizierte sich damit für eine herausragende Position als Propagandist der Union im amerikanischen Bürgerkrieg, der 1861 ausbrechen sollte.

Peu après sa couverture du grand événement sportif, Thomas Nast suivit un événement politique particulièrement grandiose pour le compte de magazines illustrés anglais et américains. Avec plus de 1 000 supporters révolutionnaires venus du monde entier, il rejoignit l'intervention sicilienne du combattant pour la liberté Giuseppe Garibaldi à Gênes. Nast s'identifiait au mouvement d'unité nationale de Garibaldi et fit circuler des représentations héroïques de l'idole républicaine et défenseur de l'abolitionisme. Par là même, il se distingua pour une position exceptionnelle comme propagandiste de l'Union pendant la guerre de Sécession, qui devait éclater en 1861.

CATASTROPHE DU BALLON LE *Géant.* — La nacelle rasant le sol à Nieubourg (Hanovre). — D'après les renseignements fournis par M. Nadar.

CATASTROPHE DU BALLON LE *Géant.* — Le Ballon vient de s'abattre à la lisière de la forêt de Nieubourg ; les aéronautes cherchent à dégager M*me* N..... prise sous la nacelle. — (D'après les renseignements fournis par M. Nadar.)

Henri de Montaut

The Le Géant *Balloon Disaster*, 1863
Katastrophe des Ballons Le Géant
Catastrophe du ballon Le Géant
Wood engravings
From: *Le Monde illustré*, Paris,
7 November 1863

Nadar's enthusiasm for aerial photo-graphy suffered a substantial setback when his huge balloon *Le Géant* crash-landed in a field near Hanover. The event was reconstructed after Nadar's description in these drawings by Henri de Montaut, who later illus-trated a number of fantastic novels by Jules Verne, a friend of Nadar's whose stories were inspired by his daring adventures.

Nadars Enthusiasmus für die Luftbild-fotografie erlebte einen Einbruch, als sein Riesenballon *Le Géant* auf einem Acker bei Hannover niederging. Henri de Montaut, der das Ereignis nach Angaben Nadars zeichnerisch rekons-truierte, illustrierte später einige der fantastischen Romane von Nadars Freund Jules Verne, die von Nadars Abenteurertum inspiriert waren.

L'enthousiasme de Nadar pour la pho-tographie aérienne s'émoussa quand son énorme ballon *Le Géant* s'écrasa sur un champ près de Hanovre. Henri de Montaut, qui reconstitua l'événe-ment par un dessin, illustra plus tard quelques-uns des romans fantas-tiques de Jules Verne, l'ami de Nadar, qui étaient inspirés des aventures intrépides de Nadar.

Félix Nadar

→ *Birth of the* Petit Journal pour rire, 1856
Geburt des Petit Journal pour rire
Naissance du Petit Journal pour rire
Stencil-coloured wood engraving
From: *Petit Journal pour rire*, no. 1,
Paris, 1856

The photographic studio that Nadar had set up and been operating since 1855 did not prevent him from contin-uing with his work as an illustrator for the press. Indeed the following year he helped his friend Charles Philipon establish a smaller version of the *Journal pour rire*, for which he later worked as co-editor and chief illus-trator. The small figure being lifted up by Nadar in the picture has been given a clown's costume and pencil, the same attributes that character-ised the symbolic mascot for *La Caricature* (see ill. pp. 18/19).

Das Fotoatelier, das Nadar seit 1855 betrieb, hinderte ihn nicht da-ran, seine pressegrafische Arbeit fortzuführen. Bereits im Jahr darauf half er als künftiger Mitherausgeber und Chefcartoonist, seinen Freund Charles Philipon von einem verklei-nerten Ableger des *Journal pour rire* zu entbinden. Der Sprössling, den Nadar hochhebt, war mit den gleichen Attributen, dem Narrenkostüm und Zeichenstift, versehen wie die Sym-bolfigur von *La Caricature* (siehe Abb. S. 18/19).

L'atelier photographique que Nadar dirigeait depuis 1855 ne l'empêchait pas de continuer à poursuivre son travail de dessinateur de presse. Un an plus tard déjà, en tant que futur coéditeur et chef dessinateur, il aida son ami Charles Philipon à fonder une plus petite version du *Journal pour rire*. Le rejeton que Nadar soulève dans ses bras était doté des mêmes attri-buts, costume de clown et crayon, que la figure symbolique de *La Caricature* (voir ill. p. 18/19).

Numéro 1.   Prix : 10 cent.

PETIT JOURNAL POUR RIRE.

AUX BUREAUX DU
JOURNAL AMUSANT, DU MUSÉE FRANÇAIS-ANGLAIS ET DES MODES PARISIENNES,
20, rue Bergère, 20.

Directeur, Ch. Philipon.   Rédacteur en chef, Nadar.

NAISSANCE DU PETIT JOURNAL POUR RIRE,
par Nadar (d'après Devéria).

Le PETIT JOURNAL POUR RIRE, qui vient de naître, est présenté aux populations attendries par une personne chargée de l'*élever*.
L'Abonné, l'homme à sac, qui se trouve sur le premier plan, et les physionomies de l'assistance semblent témoigner que l'enfant a
la figure heureuse. — Son père, dit présentement JOURNAL AMUSANT, qui vient de donner à son jeune fils son nom POUR
RIRE par avancement d'hoirie, semble aussi satisfait de son accouchement que peu disposé à s'habiller pour aller déjeuner au
dîner de l'Exposition. S'apprêterait-il à nous donner un jumeau, grand Dieu!...

N° 154. — 1858.   Prix du numéro : 45 centimes.   11 Décembre.

Rue Bergère, 20.   JOURNAL POUR RIRE,   *Rue Bergère*, 20

JOURNAL AMUSANT

JOURNAL ILLUSTRÉ,

Journal d'images, journal comique, critique, satirique, etc.

PRIX :
3 mois..... 5 fr.
6 mois..... 10 ·
12 mois..... 17 ·

PRIX :
3 mois..... 5 fr.
6 mois..... 10 ·
12 mois..... 17 ·

LES CONTEMPORAINS DE NADAR.

DESSIN PAR NADAR ET RIOU.   BIOGRAPHIE PAR NADAR.

COURBET.

Félix Nadar & Édouard Riou

Courbet, 1858
Nadar's Contemporaries
Nadars Zeitgenossen
Les Contemporains de Nadar
Wood engraving
From: *Journal amusant*, Paris,
11 December 1858

With this symbolic portrait of Gustave Courbet, Nadar was making a point about the antiquated two-dimensional style of his painting, which later also impressed Cézanne and the Cubists. Nadar's series of *Contemporaries* in Charles Philipon's new illustrated magazine, the *Journal amusant*, served as a model for the portraits of famous people by the future star of caricatures, André Gill, who began his career in this magazine in 1859 (see ill. p. 317).

In dem symbolischen Porträt Gustave Courbets thematisierte Nadar die archaische Flächigkeit von dessen Malerei, die später auch Paul Cézanne und die Kubisten beeindruckte. Nadars Reihe *Les contemporains* in Charles Philipons neuem Karikaturmagazin *Journal amusant* war Vorbild der Prominentenporträts des kommenden Karikaturstars André Gill, der seine Karriere 1859 im gleichen Magazin begann (siehe Abb. S. 317).

Dans le portrait symbolique de Gustave Courbet, Nadar thématisa la planéité archaïque de sa peinture, qui impressionna aussi plus tard Paul Cézanne et les cubistes. La série de Nadar *Les Contemporains*, dans le nouveau journal satirique de Charles Philipon *Journal amusant*, servit de modèle aux portraits de célébrités de la star montante de la caricature André Gill, qui entama sa carrière en 1859 dans le même journal (voir ill. p. 317).

N° 289. — 1861.　　　　Prix du numéro : 45 centimes.　　　　13 Juillet.

JOURNAL POUR RIRE,

JOURNAL AMUSANT

JOURNAL ILLUSTRÉ.

Journal d'images, journal comique, critique, satirique, etc.,

DIRIGÉ PAR

CH. PHILIPON, fondateur de la maison Aubert et Cie, du *Charivari*, de la *Caricature politique*,
du *Musée Philipon*, des *Modes Parisiennes*, etc.

ON S'ABONNE
CHEZ LE SUCCESSEUR
d'AUBERT et Cie,
RUE BERGÈRE, 20.

PRIX :
3 mois . . . . . 5 fr.
6 mois . . . . . 10 »
12 mois . . . . . 17 »

ÉTRANGER :
selon les droits de poste.

Toute demande non accompagnée d'un bon sur la Poste ou d'un bon à vue sur *Paris* est considérée comme nulle et non avenue. Les messageries impériales et les messageries Kellermann font les abonnements sans frais pour le souscripteur. On souscrit aussi chez tous les libraires de France. — A Lyon, au magasin de papiers peints, rue Centrale, 27. — Delizy, Davies et Cie, 1, Finch Lane.

Cornhill, London. — A Saint-Pétersbourg, chez Dufour, libraire de la Cour impériale. — A Leipzig, chez Goetze et Micriesch et chez Durr et Cie. — Prusse, Allemagne et Russie, on s'abonne chez MM. les directeurs des postes de Cologne et de Sarrebruck. — Bruxelles, Office de Publicité, rue Montagne de la Cour, 19.

ON S'ABONNE
CHEZ LE SUCCESSEUR
d'AUBERT et Cie,
RUE BERGÈRE, 20.

Les lettres non affranchies sont refusées.

L'administration ne tire aucune traite et ne fait aucun crédit.

DESSINS PAR
NADAR et DARJOU.

NADAR JURY
AU SALON DE 1861.

TEXTE PAR
NADAR.

LE DANTE ET VIRGILE DANS L'ENFER DES GLACES.
Michel-Ange Doré coupe ses damnés en morceaux, mais les morceaux en sont bons. — Tableau de glace, — peinture pleine de chaleur.

SATAN MÉDITE LA RUINE DE L'HOMME.
Ce que voyant, et pour parer à des inconvénients graves, M. DURANDEL s'empresse de passer Satan au bleu.

Pour être prisonnier, on n'en est pas moins père, — et soumis aux ordonnances de M. le préfet concernant l'échenillage.

Félix Nadar & Alfred Darjou

Nadar Jury
At the Exhibition of 1861
Im Salon von 1861
Au Salon de 1861
Wood engravings
From: *Journal amusant*, Paris,
13 July 1861

From 1857, Nadar worked with the history painter and picture correspondent Alfred Darjou to continue his popular series of caricatures from the annual exhibitions in Paris, *Nadar Jury*, in the *Journal amusant*. The series had first appeared in illustrated albums beginning in 1852.

In Kooperation mit dem Historienmaler und Bildreporter Alfred Darjou führte Nadar seit 1857 im *Journal amusant* seine erfolgreiche *Saloncaricatural*-Serie *Nadar Jury* fort, die er bereits 1852 im Albumformat begonnen hatte.

À partir de 1857, en coopération avec le peintre d'histoire et reporter illustrateur Alfred Darjou, Nadar poursuivit dans le *Journal amusant* sa série très populaire de *Salon caricatural Nadar Jury* qu'il avait commencé à publier en format d'album dès 1852.

John Everett Millais & Joseph Swain (sc.)

Sister Anne's Probation, 1862
Schwester Annes Bewährung
Probation de sœur Anne
Wood engraving
From: *Once a Week*, London, 12 April 1862

When the literary magazine *Once a Week* was founded in 1859 by Bradbury and Evans, the publishers of *Punch*, it ushered in a period of artistic press illustrations in England that went on to find international appeal. The style was defined by the work submitted by the Pre-Raphaelite artist John Everett Millais, whose original sketches were masterfully worked up by Joseph Swain.

Die Gründung der literarischen Zeitschrift *Once a Week* durch die Verleger der Zeitschrift *Punch*, Bradbury and Evans, leitete in England 1859 eine Periode der künstlerischen Illustrationsgrafik ein, die international ausstrahlte. Stilprägend waren die Beiträge des präraffaelitischen Malers John Everett Millais, dessen skizzenhafte Vorlagen von Joseph Swain auf kongeniale Weise wiedergegeben wurden.

La création de la revue littéraire *Once a Week* par les éditeurs du *Punch*, Bradbury et Evans, inaugura en Angleterre en 1859 une période de dessins d'illustration artistiques au rayonnement international. Le style en fut déterminé par les travaux du peintre préraphaélite John Everett Millais, dont les modèles en formes d'esquisses furent reproduits de façon congéniale par Joseph Swain.

Frederick Walker & the Brothers Dalziel (sc.)

Love in Death (A Woman in the Snow), 1862
Liebe im Tod (Eine Frau im Schnee)
L'Amour dans la mort (Une Femme dans la neige)
Wood engraving
From: *Good Words*, Edinburgh, 3 March 1862

The wood engraver Frederick Walker was one of the most important pioneers of expressive press illustrations during the 1870s. The socio-realist school favoured by *The Graphic* (see ills. p. 258) was essentially based on his style of poetic realism, and John Everett Millais considered the young illustrator and painter the greatest artist of the century.

Der Holzstecher Frederick Walker gehörte zu den wichtigsten Wegbereitern der expressiven Illustrationsgrafik der 1870er-Jahre. Die sozialrealistische Schule des *Graphic* (siehe Abb. S. 258) gründete wesentlich auf dem Vorbild seines poetischen Realismus. John Everett Millais hielt den jungen Illustrator und Maler für den größten Künstler des Jahrhunderts.

Le xylographe Frederick Walker comptait parmi les plus importants pionniers du dessin d'illustration expressif des années 1870. L'école socio-réaliste du *Graphic* (voir ills. p. 258) était largement basée sur le modèle de son réalisme poétique. John Everett Millais considérait le jeune peintre et illustrateur comme le plus grand artiste du siècle.

Arthur Boyd Houghton & the Brothers Dalziel (sc.)

The Vision of Sheik Hamil, 1866
Scheich Hamils Vision | *La Vision du cheikh Hamil*
Wood engraving
From: *The Argosy*, London, 1866

Arthur Boyd Houghton's work was inspired by that of the Pre-Raphaelites and he is regarded as one of the most influential figures in the artistic renaissance in illustration of the 1860s, together with Frederick Walker and John Everett Millais. His work is unsurpassed in terms of its graphic precision and inventiveness, while this portrait of a Sufi sheikh in a trance is in fact a self-portrait.

Der präraffaelitisch inspirierte Arthur Boyd Houghton zählte neben John Everett Millais und Frederick Walker zu den einflussreichsten Vertretern der künstlerischen Illustrationsrenaissance in den 1860er-Jahre. An grafischer Prägnanz und Erfindungsreichtum blieb sein Werk unübertroffen. Bei dem Bildnis eines Sufi-Scheichs in Trance handelt es sich um ein Selbstporträt.

Arthur Boyd Houghton était inspiré par les préraphaélites et comptait, dans les années 1860, parmi les représentants les plus influents de la renaissance artistique dans l'illustration aux côtés de John Everett Millais et de Frederick Walker. Son œuvre resta inégalé en densité graphique et en inventivité. Cette représentation d'un cheikh soufi en transe est en réalité un autoportrait.

James McNeill Whistler (del.)

The Relief Fund in Lancashire, 1862
Die Unterstützungskasse in Lancashire
Le Fonds de secours au Lancashire
Wood engraving
From: *Once a Week*, London, 26 July 1862

One of only a few contributions to *Once a Week* by the Impressionist painter and printmaker James McNeill Whistler, this eye-catching allegory shows the plight of English weavers. A crisis had developed following the shortage of cotton that resulted from the American Civil War, while the female figure here is apparently Joanna Hiffernan, who had posed for Whistler's series of paintings *Symphony in White*.

Unter den wenigen Beiträgen des impressionistischen Malers und Grafikers James McNeill Whistler für *Once a Week* sticht diese Allegorie über die Not der englischen Weber hervor, die durch die Baumwollverknappung im Zug des amerikanischen Bürgerkriegs verursacht worden war. Bei der Frauengestalt handelte es sich offenbar um Joanna Hiffernan, die für Whistlers Gemäldeserie *Symphony in White* Modell gestanden hatte.

Parmi les rares apports du peintre impressionniste et dessinateur James McNeill Whistler à *Once a Week,* cette allégorie sur la misère des tisserands anglais sort du lot. Celle-ci avait été causée par la pénurie de coton consécutive à la guerre de Sécession. La figure féminine est manifestement Joanna Hiffernan qui avait posé pour la série de tableaux de Whistler *Symphony in White.*

George du Maurier (del.)

George du Maurier studied painting with James McNeill Whistler in Paris, and before joining *Punch* in 1865 he provided illustrations in a Pre-Raphaelite style for *Once a Week*. In the *Punch* series *A Legend of Camelot* he poked fun at the Pre-Raphaelites' cult of the Middle Ages and their tendency to elegiac pathos.

George du Maurier hatte zusammen mit James McNeill Whistler in Paris Malerei studiert. Bevor er 1865 fester Mitarbeiter des *Punch* wurde, zeichnete er für *Once a Week* Grafiken im Stil der Präraffaeliten. In der *Punch*-Serie *A Legend of Camelot* nahm er dann den Mittelalterkult und den elegischen Pathos dieser Künstlerbewegung auf die Schippe.

George du Maurier avait étudié la peinture à Paris avec James McNeill Whistler. Avant de devenir un collaborateur permanent du *Punch* en 1865, il fit des dessins dans le style des préraphaélites pour *Once a Week*. Dans la série de *Punch*, *A Legend of Camelot*, il ironisait sur le culte du Moyen Âge et le pathos élégiaque de ce mouvement artistique.

→ *A Legend of Camelot, Part IV:*
"Two Royal Heads of Hair He Saw!", 1866
„*Zwei königliche Köpfe mit Haar sah er!*"
«*Deux têtes royales tout en cheveux il vit !*»
Wood engraving
From: *Punch, or The London Charivari*,
London, 24 March 1866

This somewhat surreal night vision was the most famous illustration in George du Maurier's *Camelot* series. It combines a number of anti-Semitic symbols and references, and as the most popular illustrated magazine of its time *Punch* exerted considerable influence in shaping racist stereotypes.

Die surreale Nachtvision war das bekannteste Blatt von George du Mauriers *Camelot*-Reihe. Es vereint eine Vielzahl antisemitischer Symbole und Anspielungen. Als meistverbreitetstes Karikaturmagazin der Zeit war der *Punch* maßgeblich an der Prägung rassistischer Stereotypen beteiligt.

Cette vision nocturne surréelle fut la planche la plus célèbre de la série *Camelot* de George du Maurier. Elle réunit une multitude de symboles et allusions antisémites. Étant le magazine de caricatures le plus répandu de son temps, le *Punch* contribua largement à l'établissement de stéréotypes racistes.

A Legend of Camelot, Part I:
"Behold the Wild Growth from Her Nape!", 1866
„*Seht den Wildwuchs in ihrem Nacken!*"
«*Voyez les cheveux sauvages déferlant de sa nuque !*»
Wood engraving
From: *Punch, or The London Charivari*,
London, 3 March 1866

A Legend of Camelot, Part II:
"Jew-laden on Her Way She Went!", 1866
„*Judenbeladen ging sie ihres Weges!*"
«*Chargée d'un Juif, elle alla son chemin !*»
Wood engraving
From: *Punch, or The London Charivari*,
London, 10 March 1866

Anonymous

*Sketches Made or Picked up by Our Eccentric
Artist at the Seat of War*, 1861
*Von unserem exzentrischen Künstler am Kriegs-
schauplatz angefertigte oder aufgegriffene Skizzen
Esquisses réalisées ou glanées par notre artiste
excentrique sur le lieu des combats*
Wood engraving
From: *Harper's Weekly*, New York, 15 June 1861

This cartoon sends up the *special artists* and the way
they sought to promote themselves, even though
their reports created such an impression in the press.
Right from the start of the American Civil War a real
cult had developed for the picture correspondents
and their taste for bravado and adventure.

Der Cartoon bezieht sich auf die medienwirksamen
Selbstinszenierungen der *special artists*. Bereits
in der Anfangsphase des amerikanischen Bürgerkriegs hatte sich ein regelrechter Kult um den
Bildreporter und sein sagenhaftes Abenteurertum entwickelt.

Ce dessin se réfère aux auto-mises en scène très
médiatiques des *special artists*. Dès les débuts de
la guerre de Sécession, un véritable culte s'était
développé autour du reporter d'images et de son
légendaire goût pour l'aventure.

John Tenniel & Joseph Swain (sc.)

Divorce à Vinculo, 1861
Scheidung vom Bunde | Divorce à Vinculo
Wood engraving
From: *Punch, or The London Charivari*,
London, 19 January 1861

The personification of South Carolina, the first
southern state to secede from the Union, here raises
a fist in anger at the figure of the liberal North who
is protecting a young slave from getting a beating.
Contrary to what the cartoon suggests, *Punch*, like
much of the imperialist media in Europe, was in
favour of the southern states breaking away.

Wütend erhebt die Personifikation von South Carolina, dem ersten Südstaat, der aus der amerikanischen Union ausgetreten war, ihre Faust gegen den
liberalen Norden, der gerade einem jungen Sklaven
Schutz vor ihren Misshandlungen bieten will. Anders
als der Cartoon vermuten lässt, trat der *Punch* wie
ein Großteil der imperialen europäischen Medien für
eine Sezession der Südstaaten ein.

La personnification de la Caroline du Sud, premier
État du Sud à quitter l'Union américaine, lève le
poing dans un geste de colère contre le Nord libéral qui veut offrir sa protection à un jeune esclave
qu'elle veut maltraiter. À l'inverse de ce que le dessin
laisse supposer, *Punch* – comme une grande partie
des médias européens impérialistes – était favorable
à une sécession des États du Sud.

Alfred Waud & Winslow Homer

Our Army before Yorktown, Virginia,
1862
Unsere Armee vor Yorktown in Virginia
Notre Armée devant Yorktown en
Virginie
Wood engraving
From: *Harper's Weekly*, New York,
3 May 1862

Winslow Homer and Alfred Waud, whose work features together in this illustration in several panels, already knew each other from the time they both worked in Boston for *Ballou's Pictorial*. Homer specialised in scenes showing military camps, which he sometimes developed into paintings, while Waud moved around with the troops in the field. Born in London, Waud trained as a stage painter before going to work as an illustrator for *Harper's Weekly* where he had been under contract since late 1861. He became the epitome of the *special artist*, and like Constantin Guys he developed a keen sense of the dynamics of troop movements while covering more battles in the Civil War than any other artist.

Winslow Homer und Alfred Waud, deren Arbeiten in dieser Multipanelgrafik kombiniert sind, kannten sich bereits von einem gemeinsamen Engagement beim Bostoner Magazin *Ballou's Pictorial*. Homer war auf Lagerszenen spezialisert, die er mitunter auch als Malereien umsetzte, während Waud mit den Truppen unterwegs war. Der britische Bühnenmaler, der seit Ende 1861 bei *Harper's Weekly* als Illustrator unter Vertrag stand, wurde zum Inbegriff des *special artists*. Wie Constantin Guys entwickelte er ein besonders Gespür für die Dynamik von Truppenbewegungen. Keiner hat mehr Bürgerkriegsschlachten festgehalten als er.

Winslow Homer et Alfred Waud, dont les travaux sont assemblés en vignettes sur cette double page, se connaissaient déjà depuis leur collaboration commune avec le magazine bostonien *Ballou's Pictorial*. Homer s'était spécialisé dans les scènes de camp qu'il transposait quelquefois aussi en peintures, tandis que Waud se déplaçait sur le terrain avec les troupes. Le peintre de décor de théâtre britannique, qui depuis la fin de 1861 était sous contrat comme illustrateur chez *Harper's Weekly*, devint l'incarnation du *special*. Comme Constantin Guys, il acquit un sens aigu de la dynamique des mouvements de troupes. Aucun autre artiste que lui n'a couvert plus de batailles de la guerre de Sécession.

OUR ARMY BEFORE YORKTOWN, VIRGINIA.—From Sketches by Mr. A. R. Waud and Mr. W. Homer.—[See Page 283.]

NEWS FROM THE WAR.—[DRAWN

CRVALRY

From Richmond

WOUNDED

HERALD

WEEKLY

HARPER'S

STAR

The Newspaper Train

SPECIAL ARTIST, MR. WINSLOW HOMER.]

Winslow Homer

←← News from the War, 1862
Nachrichten aus dem Krieg
Nouvelles de la guerre
Wood engraving
From: *Harper's Weekly*, New York,
14 June 1862

*↓ The Surgeon at Work at the Rear
during an Engagement*, 1862
*Der Wundarzt im Nachhuteinsatz
während des Gefechts*
*Le Chirurgien au travail à l'arrière-
garde pendant le combat*
Wood engraving
From: *Harper's Weekly*, New York,
12 July 1862

Winslow Homer's special field was
allegorical illustrations intended as
propaganda, which included a certain
amount of ideological content. This
large illustration deals with the subject
of news during wartime, and indicates
that the public should be prepared
when totals were announced for the
growing number of casualties. The
special artist labelled thus at the bottom left may well be Homer's fellow
artist Alfred Waud.

Winslow Homers Spezialität war die
allegorische Propagandagrafik, in
der ideelle Inhalte verhandelt wurden.
Mit dieser grafischen Reflexion über
das Kriegsnachrichtenwesen sollte
das Publikum auf wachsende Verlust-
zahlen eingeschworen werden. Bei
dem *special artist* links unten handelt
es sich wohl um Homers Freund
Alfred Waud.

La spécialité de Winslow Homer
était le dessin de propagande allégorique au contenu idéologique. Par
cette réflexion illustrée sur la nature
des informations de guerre, le public
devait être préparé aux chiffres gran-
dissants des pertes. Le *special artist*
en bas à gauche n'est autre que l'ami
d'Homer, Alfred Waud.

Since it was decided that the public
should not be exposed to the full horrors of war, the work of surgeons in
the field was only hinted at obliquely
in illustrations. From early depictions
of the Civil War such as this one
Winslow Homer went on to develop
the voluminous two-dimensional style
with which he later found success
as a painter (see ills. pp. 218/219,
293 b.).

Der Horror des Kriegs durfte dem
Publikum nicht explizit zugemutet werden. Die Arbeit der Chirurgen wurde
daher nur andeutungsweise gezeigt.
Winslow Homer entwickelte bereits in
diesen frühen Bürgerkriegsgrafiken
den voluminösen Flächenstil, mit dem
er dann als Maler reüssierte (siehe
Abb. S. 218/219, 293 u.).

Le public ne devait pas être confronté
de manière explicite avec les horreurs
de la guerre. Le travail du chirurgien
n'est donc que suggéré. Winslow
Homer développa dès ces premières
illustrations de la guerre de Sécession
le volumineux style bi-dimensionnel
avec lequel il réussit plus tard comme
peintre (voir ills. p. 218/219, 293 b.).

436

HARPER'S WEEKLY.

[July 12, 1862.

THE SURGEON AT WORK AT THE REAR DURING AN ENGAGEMENT.—[See Page 439.]

728 HARPER'S WEEKLY. 729

THE WAR FOR THE UNION—SURPRISE OF REBEL GUERRILLAS BY A SQUADRON OF UNITED STATES CAVALRY.

Thomas Nast

The War for the Union – Surprise of Rebel Guerrillas by a Squadron of United States Cavalry, 1862
Der Kampf für die Union – Aufständische Rebellen werden von einer Kavallerieschwadron der Vereinigten Staaten überrascht
La Guerre pour l'Union – Guérilleros rebelles surpris par un escadron de cavalerie des États-Unis
Wood engraving
From: *Harper's Weekly*, New York, 15 November 1862

Thomas Nast's scenes of the Civil War were action-packed fantasies designed to stir up the emotions, often with only a vague resemblance to reports from the front. The *special artists* had a particular dislike of *home artists* such as Nast or Gustave Doré since the latter used their designs without crediting the original artists and thus received the lion's share of the public's acclaim.

Thomas Nasts Bürgerkriegsszenen waren actionreiche Fantasien, die Emotionen schüren sollten und oft nur vage Bezüge zu den Frontberichten hatten. Bei den *specials* waren *home artists* wie Nast oder Gustave Doré verhasst, da sie ohne Urhebernennung auf deren Vorlagen zurückgriffen und dabei den Löwenanteil der Popularität genossen.

Les scènes de la guerre de Sécession illustrées par Thomas Nast regorgeaient d'actions qui devaient attiser les émotions et n'avaient souvent qu'une lointaine similitude avec les rapports du front. Les *specials* avaient les *home artists* comme Nast ou Gustave Doré en horreur, parce qu'ils avaient recours à leurs dessins sans aucune référence d'auteur et récoltaient ainsi la part du lion de la popularité.

→→ *The Emancipation of the Negroes – The Past and the Future*, 1863
Die Emanzipation der Schwarzen – Vergangenheit und Zukunft
L'Émancipation des Noirs – Passé et avenir
Wood engraving
From: *Harper's Weekly*, New York, 24 January 1863

With time, Nast increasingly turned away from his pseudo-documentary style and instead worked like Winslow Homer on illustrations of allegorical propaganda (see ill. pp. 212/213). In this he was also following the lesson of his tutor Theodor Kaufmann, who advocated an emancipatory symbolism for art (see ill. p. 170 b.). Nast was so successful with his pictorial reporting that Abraham Lincoln called him the "best recruiting sergeant" in all the northern states.

Thomas Nast kehrte sich zunehmend vom Pseudo-Dokumentarismus ab und sprang Winslow Homer auf dem Gebiet der allegorischen Propagandagrafik bei (siehe Abb. S. 212/213). Er folgte hier seinem Lehrer Theodor Kaufmann, der für eine Kunst der emanzipatorischen Emblematik plädierte (siehe Abb. S. 170 u.). Nast war mit seinen grafischen Kampagnen so erfolgreich, dass Abraham Lincoln ihn als besten Rekrutierungsoffizier *(best recruiting sergeant)* der Nordstaaten bezeichnete.

Thomas Nast se détourna de plus en plus du pseudo-documentarisme et rejoignit Winslow Homer dans le domaine du dessin de propagande allégorique (voir ill. p. 212/213). Il suivait là son professeur Theodor Kaufmann, qui plaidait pour un art emblématique et émancipatoire (voir ill. p. 170 b.). Nast obtint un tel succès avec ses reportages illustrés qu'Abraham Lincoln le qualifia de meilleur officier de recrutement *(best recruiting sergeant)* des États du Nord.

→→→ Winslow Homer

Our Watering-places – The Empty Sleeve at Newport, 1865
Unsere Seebäder – Der leere Ärmelkanal in Newport
Nos Stations balnéaires – La manche vide à Newport
Wood engraving
From: *Harper's Weekly*, New York, 26 August 1865

Winslow Homer often found ways to make subtle comments on the aftermath of the Civil War. Charles Parsons, who had been art director at *Harper's Weekly* since 1863 and in that role later became one of the most important promoters of young American artists, recognised the exceptional quality of Homer's illustration work and allowed him plenty of freedom for his designs.

Winslow Homer hat sich vielfach und auf subtile Weise mit den Nachwirkungen des amerikanischen Bürgerkriegs befasst. Charles Parsons, der seit 1863 Artdirector von *Harper's Weekly* war und in dieser Funktion einer der wichtigsten Förderer der jungen amerikanischen Künstlerszene werden sollte, erkannte die überragende Qualität von Homers Grafiken und gab ihnen einen breiten Raum.

Winslow Homer a souvent analysé de façon subtile les conséquences de la guerre de Sécession. Charles Parsons, qui était depuis 1863 le directeur artistique du *Harper's Weekly* et devait devenir à ce titre l'un des plus importants mécènes de la jeune scène artistique américaine, reconnut l'exceptionnelle qualité des œuvres d'Homer et lui laissa une grande latitude.

56

HARP

THE EMANCIPATION OF THE NEGROES, JANUARY, 1863—THE P

O THE FUTURE.—Drawn by Mr. Thomas Nast.—[See preceding Page.]

OUR WATERING-PLACES—THE EMPTY

E AT NEWPORT.—[SEE PAGE 534.]

Santiago Hernández

→ *The Eighth Wonder*, 1863
Das achte Wunder
La Huitième Merveille
Lithograph
From: *El palo de Ciego*, No. 11,
Mexico City, c. May 1863

As guerrilla warfare became more widespread in Mexico, the aerial correspondents of the liberal press spy danger looming in the distance. Being occupied in this way, however, they fail to notice the troop movements of the French right below them, who are well camouflaged and moving once again on Puebla and the capital. This is an early work by Santiago Hernández, who shortly afterwards took the place of Constantino Escalante when he died while still young.

Im Verlauf des offenen Guerillakriegs sehen die Luftfahrer der liberalen mexikanischen Presse Gefahr in der Ferne aufziehen. Dabei entgehen ihnen die nahen französischen Truppenbewegungen, die – gut getarnt – erneut auf Puebla und die Hauptstadt zuhalten. Es handelt sich um eine frühe Arbeit von Santiago Hernández, der schon bald die Nachfolge des früh verstorbenen Constantino Escalante antreten sollte.

Au cours de la guérilla ouverte, les aéronautes de la presse libérale mexicaine voient le danger monter dans le lointain. Ce faisant, ils ne remarquent pas les mouvements des troupes françaises proches qui, bien camouflées, se dirigent à nouveau vers Puebla et la capitale. Il s'agit ici d'une œuvre précoce de Santiago Hernández, qui devait bientôt succéder à Constantino Escalante, mort jeune.

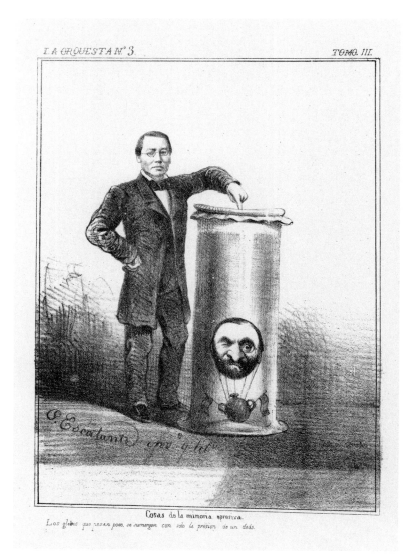

Constantino Escalante

What Transpires with the Oppressive Minority, 1862
Angelegenheiten der Minderheit, die Druck ausübt
Affaires de la minorité oppressive
Lithograph
From: *La Orquesta*, Mexico City,
7 May 1862

On the pretext of collecting foreign debts from the liberal Mexican government, French troops advanced as far as the strategically important city of Puebla. General Zaragoza, who was able to repel the invasion after a famous battle, here needs only the slightest pressure from one finger to stop the pot of debts, suspended from the head of the French ambassador, from leaving the ground.

Unter dem Vorwand, Auslandsschulden des liberal regierten mexikanischen Staats einzutreiben, waren französische Truppen bis zur strategisch bedeutsamen Stadt Puebla vorgedrungen. General Zaragoza, der die Invasion dort in einer legendären Schlacht stoppen konnte, macht hier mit leichtem Fingerdruck den Auftrieb des Schuldentopfs zunichte, der am Kopf des französischen Botschafters hängt.

Sous le prétexte de percevoir les dettes du gouvernement libéral du Mexique dues à l'étranger, des troupes françaises étaient parvenues jusqu'à la ville de Puebla, point stratégique important. Le général Zaragoza, qui put y repousser l'invasion au cours d'une bataille légendaire, réduit à néant d'une légère pression du doigt la progression du récipient contenant les dettes, fixé à la tête de l'ambassadeur français.

Sir, Spare a Penny, Please, 1862
Der Herr, ein Almosen, wenn es genehm ist
Monsieur, la charité, s'il vous plaît
Lithograph
From: *La Orquesta*, Mexico City,
9 June 1862

Faced with the superior power of the invading forces, the progress of republicanism in Mexico was temporarily halted. Constantino Escalante, the pioneer of Latin American political art, here takes as his subject the bankrupt constitution of the conservative junta which, in the guise of the future Emperor Maximilian (shown in an imaginary portrait) and his propaganda officer Juan Almonte, is begging for alms at the court of Napoleon III.

Angesichts der invasorischen Übermacht war der mexikanische Republikanismus vorerst ins Hintertreffen geraten. Constantino Escalante, der Pionier lateinamerikanischer Politkunst, thematisiert die bankrotte Konstitution der konservativen Junta, die in Gestalt des zukünftigen Kaisers Maximilian (ein Fantasieporträt) und seines Propagandisten Almonte am Hof Napoleons III. um Almosen bettelt.

Face à la supériorité de l'envahisseur, le républicanisme mexicain fut d'abord pris de court. Constantino Escalante, le pionnier de l'art politique sud-américain, prit pour motif la constitution en déroute de la Junte conservatrice qui, sous les traits du futur empereur Maximilien (un portrait imaginaire) et de son propagandiste Almonte, fait l'aumône à la cour de Napoléon III.

LA OCTAVA MARAVILLA.

Los Franceses, temerosos de los glovos guerrilleros, se dizfrazan.

EXPÉDITION DU MEXIQUE. — Butron, chef de pillards, exécuté dans l'enceinte de la citadelle à Mexico. (Croquis de M. Brunet, lieutenant d'artillerie.)

M. Brunet

Butron, the Leader of the Looters, Is Executed inside the Citadel in Mexico City, 1863
Butron, Anführer von Plünderern, wird auf dem Gelände der Zitadelle in Mexiko-Stadt hingerichtet
Butron, chef des pillards, exécuté dans l'enceinte de la citadelle à Mexico
Wood enrgaving
From: *Le Monde illustré*, Paris, 5 October 1863

The execution scene shown here took place following the capture of Mexico City by the invading French troops. The artist Édouard Manet, who was an outstanding analyst of press graphics and also profited from them himself, adapted this subject fours years later when the puppet Emperor Maximilian I, who had been installed by Napoleon III, was executed by Mexican republicans in a court martial.

Die hier gezeigte Exekutionsszene fand statt, nach-dem französische Interventionstruppen Mexiko-Stadt erobert hatten. Édouard Manet, der ein brillanter Analytiker und Profiteur der Pressegrafik war, hat das Motiv vier Jahre später adaptiert, als der von Napoleon III. installierte Marionettenkaiser Maximilian I. von einem Standgericht mexikanischer Republikaner hingerichtet wurde.

La scène d'exécution représentée ici eut lieu après la prise de Mexico par les troupes d'intervention françaises. Édouard Manet, un brillant analyste qui sut tirer profit de ce dessin de presse, adapta le motif quatre ans plus tard, quand l'empereur d'opé-rette Maximilien Ier, installé au pouvoir par Napoléon III, fut exécuté par une cour martiale formée de républicains mexicains.

Édouard Manet

The Execution of Emperor Maximilian, 1867
Die Erschießung des Kaisers Maximilian
L'Exécution de l'empereur Maximilien
Lithograph
Cleveland, Museum of Art

Émile Zola's observation that in Manet's painting Maximilian I is being shot by French troops can be verified from the press illustration he used as his model. Furthermore, the fact that the accused is there identified as "leader of the looters" underlines the anti-imperialist message of Manet's painting.

Émile Zolas Bemerkung, dass Maxi-milian I. auf Édouard Manets Gemälde von französischen Truppen erschos-sen werde, lässt sich anhand der pressegrafischen Vorlage verifizieren. Und mehr noch: Dass der Delinquent dort als ein „Anführer von Plünde-rern" *(chef des pillards)* bezeichnet wird, spitzt die antiimperialistische Botschaft von Manets Gemälde noch weiter zu.

La remarque d'Émile Zola notant que Maximilien Ier est fusillé par des troupes françaises dans le tableau d'Édouard Manet peut être vérifiée à partir des illustrations de presse qui lui servent de modèle. Par ailleurs, que le délinquant soit qualifié là-bas de *chef des pillards* souligne encore davantage le message anti-impéria-liste du tableau de Manet.

Henri Durand-Brager

A Visit to the Main Factories in Wales, 1865
Ein Besuch bei der Großindustrie von Wales | Une Visite aux grandes usines du pays de Galles
Wood engraving
From: *Le Tour du Monde*, Paris, no. 12, 1865

With its high-quality illustrated reports of journeys abroad, Édouard Charton's magazine *Le Tour du Monde* was intended to serve the interests of colonial exoticism. An article on forms of slavery that existed within Europe, as shown here with illustrations by Henri Durand-Brager and written by the mining engineer Louis Simonin based on the mining region of South Wales, was a notable exception.

Das von Édouard Charton begründete Magazin *Le Tour du Monde* bediente mit seinen hochwertig illustrierten Expeditionsberichten vor allem kolonialen Exotismus. Ein Bericht über innereuropäische Formen der Sklaverei, wie ihn Henri Durand-Brager zusammen mit dem Autor und Bergbauingenieur Louis Simonin anhand der Bergbauregion von Südwales ablieferte, blieb eine Ausnahme.

Avec ses reportages illustrés haut de gamme, le magazine *Le Tour du Monde* fondé par Édouard Charton traitait surtout de l'exotisme colonial. Un article sur les formes d'esclavage à l'intérieur de l'Europe, élaboré par Henri Durand-Brager avec l'auteur et ingénieur des Mines Louis Simonin et consacré à la région minière du sud du pays de Galles, resta une exception.

↑ *The Factories of the Taff Valley*, 1865
Die Fabriken im Taff Valley
Les Usines de la vallée du Taff

↓ *Women Collecting Grit in Cyfarthfa*, 1865
Die Aschensammlerinnen in Cyfarthfa
Les Chercheuses d'escarbilles, à Cyfarthfa

340   LE TOUR DU MONDE.

un nombre proportionné de trains de laminoirs et de marteaux-pilons pour achever le traitement métallurgique du fer.

La consistance de Cyfarthfa est moins importante que celle de Dowlais. L'usine n'a que sept hauts fourneaux, quatre-vingt-quatre fours à puddler, et n'occupe guère que six à sept mille ouvriers; mais c'est encore un assez beau lot.

De toutes ces vastes usines, le métal entré à l'état de minerai, sort à l'état de fonte moulée, mais surtout à l'état de fer marchand, en barres ou en verges, rond ou carré, en feuilles, lanières, rubans, enfin à l'état de rails. Jamais les usines ne chôment ni de jour ni de nuit. Les hauts fourneaux, géants des foyers métallurgiques,

hauts de quinze mètres, peuvent produire jusqu'à quarante mille kilogrammes de fonte par vingt-quatre heures. Dans d'autres districts d'Angleterre, à Ulverston par exemple, dans le North-Lancashire, au bord du canal d'Irlande, on a même construit des hauts fourneaux qui produisent jusqu'à quatre-vingt-dix mille kilogrammes de fonte par jour. C'est plutôt par l'augmentation de la quantité de vent soufflée par les machines dans ces immenses cuves et permettant aux *charges* de descendre d'autant plus vite qu'elles reçoivent plus d'air pour activer la combustion, que par l'augmentation des hauts fourneaux que l'on est arrivé aux étonnants résultats atteints à Ulverston. Cependant les dimensions

Les chercheuses d'escarbilles, à Cyfarthfa. — Dessin de Durand-Brager.

du creuset, partie inférieure du haut fourneau où s'élabore la fonte, ont dû être aussi augmentées en même temps que le nombre des tuyères amenant le *vent* dans l'appareil.

L'usine de Cyfarthfa appartient à M. Crawshay. Elle a été bâtie en 1765, et jusqu'en 1782 a fourni le gouvernement anglais de canons en fonte de fer. La famille Crawshay possède depuis longtemps ces usines. Le chef de cette illustre maison, Richard Crawshay, vint fort pauvre du Yorkshire à Londres, où il servit comme domestique. De là il passa dans le pays de Galles, et de simple ouvrier devint le plus grand maître de forges du pays. C'est ainsi qu'on arrive par le travail assidu et constant, et de tels exemples ne sont pas rares en Angleterre, où les Savery, les Newcomen, les Cowley, les

Watt, les Robert Stephenson, tous si glorieusement connus dans l'industrie, ont commencé par la plus obscure des conditions.

Aux forges de Merthyr Tydvil se rattache un fait historique, où le nom de Richard Crawshay se trouve mêlé, et que l'on ne peut passer sous silence. C'est à l'usine de Penydarren que fut construite, en 1803, par Trevithick, la première locomotive qui ait jamais fonctionné. Trevithick paria mille guinées (vingt-six mille francs), avec Richard Crawshay, que sa voiture à vapeur porterait une charge de fer de son usine à Navigation House, sur le *tram-way* ou chemin à ornières creuses en fonte qui descendait les charbons le long de la vallée du Taff. Ce chemin avait été construit depuis nombre d'années pour le transport économique de la houille; il était des-

→→**Joseph Keppler**

Puck's Holiday Plum-pudding, 1882
Pucks festtäglicher Plumpudding
Le Plumpudding festif de Puck
Tinted lithograph
From: *Puck*, New York,
27 December 1882

The angelic Puck cuts into the pudding of politics with a knife that means no harm to anyone. Joseph Keppler's moderate line with cartoons was diametrically opposed to Thomas Nast's attacking style, which aimed to hit his targets "right between the eyes". In an era of political gamesmanship Keppler's mild approach was preferred as Nast's sharp pencil fell from favour (see ill. p. 355 b.).

Mit einem Messer, das nichts Böses will, sticht der nette Puck in den Pudding der Politik. Joseph Kepplers moderierendes Verständnis von Cartooning stand in diametralem Gegensatz zu Thomas Nasts Zugriff, der die Gegner „direkt zwischen die Augen" zu treffen suchte. In einer Ära des politischen Lavierens war Kepplers weicher Modus en vogue, während Nasts spitzer Stift ins Abseits geriet (siehe Abb. S. 355 u.).

Le gentil Puck poignarde le pudding de la politique avec un couteau inoffensif. Le parti-pris modéré de Joseph Keppler est diamétralement opposé à l'attaque de Thomas Nast qui cherchait à toucher l'adversaire «directement entre les yeux». Dans une ère de tergiversation politique, le mode tiède de Keppler était en vogue, alors que le crayon acéré de Nast était discrédité (voir ill. p. 355 b.).

Henri Durand-Brager & Laplante (sc.)

A Visit to the Poor Districts of London:
A Dormitory in a "Common Lodging House", 1865
Ein Ausflug in die Armenviertel Londons:
Ein Schlafsaal im „common lodging house"
Une Excursion dans les quartiers pauvres de
Londres : Un dortoir de «common lodging house»
Wood engraving
From: *Le Tour du Monde*, Paris, no. 11, 1865

**Émile Bayard, after Henri Durand-Brager,
& J. Gauchard (sc.)**

↘*A Visit to the Poor Districts of London:*
The Poor Abandoned Creatures, 1865
Ein Ausflug in die Armenviertel Londons:
Die armen Findelmädchen
Une Excursion dans les quartiers pauvres
de Londres : Les pauvrettes abandonnées
Wood engraving
From: *Le Tour du Monde*, Paris, no. 11, 1865

A little later on, Henri Durand-Brager and Louis Simonin continued their journey into the underworld of industrialisation, this time in the slums of London. The investigative nature and content of Simonin's reporting was an inspiration to Émile Zola, while Durand-Brager's illustrations were soon adapted for Gustave Doré's popular survey of poverty, *London: A Pilgrimage* (ill. p. 287).

Ihre Expedition in die Unterwelt der Industrialisierung setzten Henri Durand-Brager und Louis Simonin kurze Zeit später in den Slums von London fort. Der investigative Gehalt von Simonins Reportagen hat Émile Zola inspiriert, und die Zeichnungen Durand-Bragers wurden wenig später in Gustave Dorés populärem Pauperismus-Report *London: A Pilgrimage* adaptiert (Abb. S. 287).

Peu de temps après, Henri Durand-Brager et Louis Simonin poursuivirent leur expédition dans l'univers sombre de l'industrialisation, cette fois dans les quartiers miséreux de Londres. La densité investigatrice des reportages de Simonin ont inspiré Émile Zola, et les dessins de Durand-Brager furent peu après adaptés dans l'enquête populaire de Gustave Doré sur la pauvreté, *London: A Pilgrimage* (ill. p. 287).

Anonymous

→ *Cross-section beneath a Street in London, at the Top of Hampstead Road*, 1865
Schnitt durch den Untergrund einer Londoner Straße auf Höhe der Hampstead Road
Coupe sous une rue de Londres, à la hauteur de Hampstead Road
Wood engraving
From: *Le Monde illustré*, Paris, 28 January 1865

60   LE MONDE ILLUSTRÉ

1. Conduite d'eau. — 2. Tubes pneumatiques pour le transport des dépêches. — 3. Chemin de fer métropolitain. — 4. Projet d'un chemin de jonction entre Hampstead et Charing-Cross.

Coupe sous une rue de Londres, à la hauteur de Hampstead-Road.

Modern
Press Graphics

1869–1921

The Chemigraphical Turn

In the 1870s, the uniform appearance that illustrated magazines had shared up until now began to fall away. As the American draughtsman, art director and historian of graphic art Joseph Pennell noted, this was "probably the most important [...] upheaval" (Pennell 1895, p. 39) in the history of illustrative art, and was the consequence of two complementary developments in letterpress printing technology, namely photoxylography and relief etching.

The first attempts at exposing photographs directly on to coated sections of wood had been made in the mid-1850s. The best-known example of such a photographic technique, Thomas Bolton's engraving *Deliver Us from Evil* (1861), shows how much these early experiments still relied on the technique of using strong outlines that was part of the classic style of reproduction illustrations (ill. p. 229). Special engraving machines were often used, but in August 1877 a group of American wood engravers upset this traditional approach with a spectacular series of engravings made from gouaches by James E. Kelly. The most radical of these engravers, Frederick Juengling, emphasised that "We do not busy ourselves with presenting a 'tasteful' arrangement of lines" (Anthony 1880, p. 447), yet such provocations angered the likes of William James Linton, the foremost American exponent of artistic wood-engraving. However, his accusation that these young American photographers, who as the New School of Wood Engraving soon found great success in museums and at world's fairs, were operating with no expression just like machines went right to the heart of the argument. With a studied indifference that much later would characterise some of those involved with Pop Art, the engravers of the New

School distanced themselves from the traditional objectivity of illustration in favour of simply scanning the surface of images, as if they were human scanners.

As photoxylography became less associated with the artistic need to produce a creative reproduction of an image and moved instead towards a structural format that would later manifest itself in grid networks and Pointillism, the developing technique of relief etching concentrated on the complementary importance above all of the line and of free expression. In this case the illustrations were transferred to metal plates using acid-resistant colours, before the plates were placed in acid baths where the etching was done in layers (ill. p. 239 b.). This technique of relief etching was invented in the late 1780s by the printer and poet William Blake who, at the same time as Thomas Bewick was rediscovering wood engraving, was looking for ways to combine text and image on the printed page for his illuminated poetry. It was more than 70 years before Blake's chemical experiments were adopted for use in press graphics.

The poet and wood engraver William James Linton was one of many people who explored the possibilities offered by relief etching, and in 1863 he produced the first edition of Blake's illustrations using the technique of cerography (ill. pp. 242/243). From a technical point of view this process was of only marginal importance, but the consequences for art were rather more far-reaching. With his discovery of line etching Linton hoped that the laborious work of reproduction could be consigned to the past and that engraving could now develop into an expressive art form. In his trial work Linton was assisted by his pupil Walter Crane and colleague William Luson Thomas; a few years later

Thomas Bolton (sc.), after John Flaxman

Deliver Us from Evil, 1861
Erlöse uns vom Bösen | Délivre-nous du mal
Wood engraving
From: John Jackson & W.A. Chatto, *A Treatise on Wood Engraving*, London, 1861

The popularity of photoxylography in England increased substantially when this image was published in the second edition of John Jackson and W.A. Chatto's masterful history of wood engraving.

Mit der Veröffentlichung dieser Abbildung in der zweiten Auflage von John Jacksons und W. A. Chattos einflussreicher Geschichte des Holzstichs wurde die Fotoxylografie in England bekannt.

La xylophotographie fut popularisée en Angleterre grâce à la publication de cette illustration dans la seconde édition de l'histoire magistrale de la gravure sur bois de John Jackson et W.A. Chatto.

Thomas was involved in making Linton's ideal a reality when an expressive art of printmaking was seen in published form in *The Graphic* (1869), which later had a profound influence on Vincent van Gogh.

Ultimately, however, the success of line etching was not down to Linton's wax-coating technique but rather a zinc-etching process that had been patented in 1850 by the French printer Firmin Gillot. For many draughtsmen working with the old methods, the shift to chemical engraving spelled the end of their career. Even so, when Thomas Nast's illustrations stopped being produced as wood engravings in 1877 and were replaced with ink drawings, it became clear that much of the visual power of his illustrations was the result of them being reproduced as wood engravings. For many younger illustrators though, the new possibilities for reproducing images led to an increase in works that were drawn by hand. The trend was shaped in part by the sketch-like illustrations of the pictorial journalist Melton Prior, and the delicate graphic style of the illustrator Daniel Vierge, whose work has been likened to Tachism. These were followed in the 1890s by a whole generation of illustrators, including Walter Crane, Adolphe Willette, Caran d'Ache, Phil May, Henri de Toulouse-Lautrec, Félix Vallotton, Winsor McCay, Thomas Theodor Heine and Aubrey Beardsley, whose new art was perfectly suited to what could be achieved with line etching.

With this method of relief etching it was not only possible to reproduce linear drawings but also complete illustrations, by transposing them to the metal plates with special transfer papers that were developed early on and had different coatings adapted to the various drawing techniques. Chalk drawings,

for instance, could be imitated by using a grained paper, while Honoré Daumier's successors made extensive use of the opportunity to reproduce the effect of lithographic crayons in relief etching. Daumier himself preferred to continue drawing on stone, yet in order for them to appear in the press his lithographic prints now had to be transferred and etched on to metal plates. Such involved processes became unnecessary by the late 1870s when, in a manner similar to photoxylography, it was discovered how to expose photographs of illustrations directly on to metal plates. This technique of photomechanical engraving also enabled the size of the reproduction to be varied, which in turn greatly increased the design possibilities for page layouts. However, the fact that the dimensions were no longer the same as those of the originals meant there was a noticeable loss of coherence and visual conciseness.

By the turn of the century, reproduction graphic work had reached a point where the actual method used was often hard to distinguish, so that what might seem to be an elaborate wood engraving, for instance, could easily be an image on a scrape board printed with relief etching (ill. p. 239 t.). To begin with, and while work still had to be finished by hand, the fact that chemigraphers signed each piece in the same way as engravers meant there were few distinguishing details. In 1880, a scrape board with a stamped grid pattern became available that enabled grey tones to be imitated, which soon led to the invention of halftone printing. This process made it possible to reproduce photographs by breaking them down into black and white units with a grid installed in the reproduction camera. However, for the first few decades when this technique was in use, the quality of the

Timothy Cole (sc.), after James E. Kelly

The Gillie Boy, 1877 (right: detail)
Der Jagdbursche | *Le Jeune Chasseur*
Wood engraving
From: *A Portfolio of Proof Impressions
Selected from Scribner's Monthly and
St. Nicholas*, New York, 1880

Timothy Cole's interpretation of James
Kelly's original gouache painting *The
Gillie Boy* was the first illustration that
appeared in a spectacular series of
reproductions compiled by Alexander
Wilson Drake, the daring art director
at *Scribner's Monthly*. In this example
it was no longer the content of a work
that was the main point of interest,
but its texture.

Timothy Coles Interpretation von
James Kellys Gouachemalerei *The
Gillie Boy* war die erste Abbildung
einer aufsehenerregenden Reihe von
Reproduktionen, die der experimentierfreudige Artdirector von *Scribner's
Monthly*, Alexander Wilson Drake, zu
verantworten hatte. Hier stand nicht
länger der Inhalt eines Werks im Vordergrund, sondern seine Textur.

L'interprétation de Timothy Cole de
la peinture à la gouache de James
Kelly *The Gillie Boy* fut la première
illustration d'une spectaculaire série
de reproductions due à Alexander
Wilson Drake, le très aventureux
directeur artistique de *Scribner's
Monthly*. Ici, le contenu d'une œuvre
n'était plus de première importance,
mais sa texture.

halftone engravings was so poor that they were no match for
photoxylography, while they were also reliant on finishing work
from the engravers since most of the halftone plates had to be
retouched with burins. Furthermore, the monotony of the grid
pattern in the printed image created a strange effect. To con-
form to what the public was used to seeing in terms of the
diversity of detail in wood engravings, the photographic plates
were covered in part or in whole by wood-engraving screens.
An effect similar to that of these so-called xylotype engravings
was obtained by using a grid with an irregular mesh for halftone photographs.

What reproduction graphics was striving for at this time,
through various methods, was to achieve a balance between
the diffuse style of the photographic image and the razor sharpness of engravings. Photographs that were out of focus were
retouched at length with brushes or airbrushes, and the subjects were often entirely overpainted or altered to appear in a
more photorealistic manner. The retouching departments, which
gradually replaced the wood-engraving workshops for bigger
newspapers, were mostly run by painters with academic training. The range of printed images seen in newspapers and magazines was never more varied or more exciting than in the 1890s,
when line etchings, photographic reproductions, retouched and
photographic copies of painted images, wood engravings, pseu-
do-wood engravings and all kinds of hybrid techniques existed

side by side (ills. pp. 246–249). It was not until the digital age
that a comparable range of options was again available for
manipulating images.

Photomechanical relief etching was the key development
that enabled the modern illustrated mass press to become properly established. In 1889, William Luson Thomas revolutionised
this sector of the media when he launched *The Daily Graphic* in
London. By the turn of the century, Thomas's newspaper was
using an international network of 2,000 picture correspondents,
who from 1908 were able to wire in their illustrations by telegraph. Of similar significance was the publication in Paris in
1884 of the first illustrated Sunday edition of *Le Petit Journal*
by the newspaper publisher and inventor Hippolyte Marinoni.
Its attractive four-colour printing was produced by a six-cylinder
rotary press Marinoni had designed, which was capable of printing and folding 10,000 newspapers an hour. *The Daily Graphic*
was also printed on Marinoni presses, and involved shaping the
copper tops of the picture plates into semicircles and then casting them in lead. The improved machines used 14 years later by
Joseph Pulitzer to print the illustrated Sunday edition of his *New
York World* had four times the capacity, and could also print the
delicate halftone plates using the rotary cylinders.

Richard Caton Woodville Jr.

Illustration for the Novel | Illustration zu dem Roman | Illustration pour le roman They Were Married, 1882
Calotype of gouache painting
From: Franz von Lipperheide (ed.), *Mustersammlung von Holzschnitten*, Berlin, 1885–1888

This juxtaposition of illustration works reproduced by photoxylography and photomechanical means is part of a sample portfolio that was published at great expense by the Berlin publisher Franz von Lipperheide. It was designed to enable German illustrators, whose work he felt to be largely behind the times, to become more familiar with the standard of wood engraving being produced elsewhere around the world.

Die Gegenüberstellung von Fotoxylografie und fotomechanisch reproduzierter Malereivorlage gehört zu einer Mustermappe, die der Berliner Verleger Franz von Lipperheide aufwendig produziert hatte, um die seiner Ansicht nach rückständigen deutschen Illustratoren mit den internationalen Standards auf dem Gebiet des Tonstichs vertraut zu machen.

La juxtaposition de la xylophotographie et de la reproduction photomécanique de modèles peints fait partie d'un portfolio de spécimens que l'éditeur berlinois Franz von Lipperheide avait produit à grands frais pour familiariser les illustrateurs allemands, qu'il jugeait rétrogrades, avec les standards internationaux dans le secteur de la xylogravure.

Richard Caton Woodville Jr.

Illustration for the Novel | Illustration zu dem Roman | Illustration pour le roman They Were Married, 1882
Wood engraving
From: Franz von Lipperheide (ed.), *Mustersammlung von Holzschnitten*, Berlin, 1885–1888

Die chemiegrafische Wende

In den 1870er-Jahren brach das uniforme Erscheinungsbild der Illustrierten auf. Nach Ansicht des amerikanischen Zeichners, Artdirectors und Grafikhistorikers Joseph Pennell war der „wohl wichtigste […] Umbruch" in der Geschichte der Illustrationskunst die Folge zweier komplementärer Innovationen im Bereich der Hochdrucktechnik, der Fotoxylografie und der Hochätzung (Pennell 1895, S. 39).

Erste Versuche, Fotos direkt auf beschichtete Holzstöcke aufzubelichten, waren bereits Mitte der 1850er-Jahre unternommen worden. Das bekannteste Beispiel einer solchen Fotografik, Thomas Boltons Stich *Deliver Us from Evil* (1861), zeigt, wie sehr diese frühen Experimente noch dem umrissbetonten linearen Paradigma klassischer Reproduktionsgrafik verpflichtet waren (Abb. S. 229). Oft kamen dabei sogenannte Tonschneidemaschinen zum Einsatz. Mit einer spektakulären Serie von Stichen nach Gouachen von James E. Kelly warf im August 1877 eine Gruppe amerikanischer Xylografen diese Konvention über den Haufen. „Wir beschäftigen uns nicht damit, eine geschmackvolle Zusammenstellung von Linie zu präsentieren", betonte ihr radikalster Vertreter Frederick Juengling (Anthony 1880, S. 447). Die Provokationen erregten den Zorn von William James Linton, dem führenden Vertreter der künstlerischen Xylografie. Sein Vorwurf, dass die jungen amerikanischen Fotografiker, die schon bald als New School of Wood Engraving museal und auf Weltausstellungen reüssierten, ausdruckslos wie Maschinen operierten, traf jedoch den Nagel auf den Kopf. Mit einer betonten Indifferenz, die an die Programmatik der Pop-Art erinnerte, entfernten sich die Protagonisten der New School aus der tradierten grafischen Gegenständlichkeit, um sich stattdessen wie

menschliche Scanner auf eine reine Abtastung von Bildoberflächen zu konzentrieren.

Während sich die Fotoxylografie vom auktorialen Anspruch einer kreativen Übersetzungsleistung entfernte und auf Strukturen zubewegte, die das Netzraster und den Pointillismus vorwegnahmen, feierte die parallele Technik der Hochätzung das komplementäre Primat der Linie und des freien Ausdrucks. Die Grafiken wurden hierbei mit säureresistenten Farben auf Metallplatten übertragen. Die Gravurarbeit übernahmen dann die Säurebäder, in denen die Druckplatten schichtenweise heruntergeätzt wurden (Abb. S. 239 u.). Erfunden wurde diese Technik der Hoch- oder Reliefätzung Ende der 1780er-Jahre von dem Drucker und Dichter William Blake. Für seine illuminierten Dichtungen hatte dieser zeitgleich mit Thomas Bewick, dem Wiederentdecker des Holzstichs, nach Möglichkeiten gesucht, wie sich Schrift und Bild in einer Druckform sinnvoll vereinen ließen. Es dauerte mehr als 70 Jahre, bis Blakes chemiegrafische Versuche pressegrafisch bedeutend wurden.

Zu den vielen Experimentatoren auf dem Gebiet der Hochätzung zählte auch der Dichter und Xylograf William James Linton, der 1863 mit seiner Methode der Kerografie die erste Buchausgabe mit Grafiken Blakes realisierte (Abb. S. 242/243). In technischer Hinsicht war die Bedeutung dieses Verfahrens eher marginal. Umso weitreichender waren allerdings die künstlerischen Folgen. Linton erhoffte sich nämlich mit dem Durchbruch der Linienätzung ein Ende der sklavischen Reproduktionsarbeit und eine Entwicklung der Xylografie zur Ausdruckskunst. Involviert in diese Experimente war neben Lintons Schüler Walter Crane auch sein Assistent William Luson Thomas. Dieser verhalf

Frederick Juengling (sc.), after Frank Duveneck

The Professor, 1880
Der Professor | Le Professeur
Wood engraving
From: William James Linton, *The History of
Wood-engraving in America*, Boston, 1882

Frederick Juengling's engraving, based on an
Impressionist portrait by Frank Duveneck, was exhibited in Paris at the Salon for 1881 where it helped
to gain recognition for the New School of Wood Engraving. In the same year, the well-known print curator Sylvester Rosa Koehler featured the work of the
new American graphic artists in a groundbreaking
exhibition at the Museum of Fine Arts in Boston.

Frederick Juenglings Stich nach einem impressio-
nistischen Porträt von Frank Duveneck wurde 1881
im Pariser Salon gezeigt und verhalf der New School
of Wood Engraving zu internationalem Ansehen.
Im gleichen Jahr präsentierte der bekannte Kurator
Sylvester Rosa Koehler die junge amerikanische
Fotografik in einer bahnbrechenden Ausstellung im
Bostoner Museum of Fine Arts.

La gravure de Frederick Juengling d'après un portrait impressionniste de Frank Duveneck fut exposée au Salon de Paris en 1881 et contribua à la
renommée internationale de la New School of Wood
Engraving. La même année, le célèbre conservateur de musée Sylvester Rosa Koehler présenta
les nouvelles photographies américaines dans une
exposition révolutionnaire au Museum of Fine Arts
de Boston.

wenige Jahre später Lintons Ideal einer expressiven Holzstich-
kunst durch die Gründung der auflagenstarken Illustrierten *The
Graphic* (1869) zum entscheidenden Durchbruch. Vincent van
Goghs Kunst war entscheidend von den Anschauungen des
Graphic geprägt.

Die Linienhochätzung setzte sich schließlich nicht mithilfe
Lintons Technik der Wachsbeschichtung durch, sondern durch
ein Verfahren der Zinkätzung, das der französische Drucker
Firmin Gillot bereits 1850 patentieren ließ. Für viele Zeichner
der alten Schule war diese chemiegrafische Wende mit einem
Niedergang ihrer Karriere verbunden. Als Thomas Nasts Cartoons ab 1877 nicht mehr in der Form von Holzstichen, sondern als Federzeichnungen erschienen, wurde offenbar, dass
die visuelle Kraft seiner Cartoons zu einem nicht geringen Teil
den xylografischen Interpretationen geschuldet war. Bei vielen
jüngeren Zeichnern provozierten die neuen Möglichkeiten der
Faksimilierung eine Emphase der Handschriftlichkeit. Stilbildend
waren hier die skizzenartigen Grafiken des Bildreporters Melton
Prior und die nervösen Grafismen des Illustrators Daniel Vierge,
der ein *tachiste* genannt wurde. In den 1890er-Jahren folgte
der Aufstieg einer Generation von Grafikern wie Walter Crane,
Adolphe Willette, Caran d'Ache, Phil May, Henri de Toulouse-
Lautrec, Félix Vallotton, Winsor McCay, Thomas Theodor Heine
und Aubrey Beardsley, deren neue Kunst auf die Möglichkeiten
der Linienätzung zugeschnitten war.

Die Technik der Hochätzung erlaubte jedoch nicht nur Reproduktionen linearer Zeichnungen. Für die Übertragung der
Grafiken auf die Metallplatten wurden bereits früh spezielle Um-
druckpapiere entwickelt, deren Beschichtungen den jeweiligen

Zeichentechniken angepasst waren. Mit gekörnten Papieren
ließen sich beispielsweise Kreidezeichnungen imitieren. Diese
Möglichkeit, den Effekt der lithografischen Crayon-Manier im
Hochdruck zu imitieren, nutzten Honoré Daumiers Nachfolger
ausgiebig. Er selbst hingegen bevorzugte es, weiterhin auf Stein
zu zeichnen. Für die Illustrierten mussten die lithografischen
Abzüge dann auf die Metallplatten umgedruckt und hochgeätzt
werden. Derart aufwendige Verfahren wurden Ende der 1870er-
Jahre obsolet, als es analog zur Fotoxylografie möglich wurde,
Aufnahmen von Grafiken direkt auf die Metallplatten aufzubelichten. Dass die Reproduktionsgrößen durch diese Technik der
fotomechanischen Hochätzung variabel wurden, erweiterte die
gestalterischen Möglichkeiten des Layouts zwar erheblich, die
Abkopplung von den Maßen der Originalgrafik brachte allerdings
auch einen deutlichen Verlust von Kohärenz und visueller Prägnanz mit sich.

Die Jahrhundertwende war eine Hochphase reproduktions-
grafischer Camouflage. Was wie ein aufwendiger Holzstich aus-
sah, konnte leicht der Abdruck eines gekratzten Schabekartons
sein, der als Reliefätzung reproduziert war (Abb. S. 239 o.). Da
die Chemiegrafen anfangs, als die manuelle Nachbearbeitung
noch eine wesentliche Rolle spielte, in der Art der Graveure signierten, gab es kaum Unterscheidungsmerkmale. Um Imitationen
von Grauwerten zu ermöglichen, kam 1880 ein Schabekarton
mit tiefengeprägtem Netzraster in den Handel, eine Entwicklung,
die kurze Zeit später in die Erfindung der Autotypie oder Halb-
tonhochätzung *(Halftone)* mündete. Dieses chemiegrafische
Verfahren ermöglichte es, Fotos abzudrucken, indem sie durch
ein in der Reproduktionskamera vorgeschaltetes Raster in

Timothy Cole (sc.), after George Romney

Lady Derby, 1902 (right: detail)
Boxwood printing block
with white pigment

The printing blocks produced by Timothy Cole and other artists of the New School themselves became prized collectors' items, and were often included in exhibitions alongside the prints on Japanese paper that had been made from them. In order for these blocks to give a clearer idea of how the printed image would appear, some areas were rubbed over with a white pigment.

Die Druckstöcke von Timothy Cole und anderen Exponenten der New School waren begehrte Sammlerobjekte, die zusammen mit den Abzügen auf Japanpapier in Ausstellungen präsentiert wurden. Um eine bessere Vorstellung vom Druckbild zu vermitteln, wurden einzelne Partien mit Weißpigment eingerieben.

Les blocs d'impression de Timothy Cole et d'autres exposants de la New School étaient des objets de collection convoités, qui furent présentés dans des expositions avec les copies sur papier Japon. Pour transmettre une meilleure idée de l'image imprimée, certaines parties étaient frottées séparément avec du pigment blanc.

schwarz-weiße Einheiten zerlegt wurden. Die Qualität der Autotypien war in den ersten Jahrzehnten allerdings so mangelhaft, dass sie weder die Fotoxylografie ersetzen noch ohne die manuelle Unterstützung von Graveuren auskommen konnten. Die meisten Halbtonklischees mussten mit Gravurstichlen nachgearbeitet werden. Hinzu kam, dass die Monotonie des Netzrasters im Druckbild befremdlich erschien. Um den Sehgewohnheiten eines an die Vielfalt xylografischer Strukturen gewohnten Publikums zu entsprechen, überzog man Fotoklischees teilweise oder gänzlich mit Holzstichstrukturen. Ein ähnlicher Effekt wie bei diesen sogenannten Xylotypogravuren wurde durch die Verwendung unregelmäßiger Strukturraster bei den Halbtonaufnahmen erzielt.

Das reproduktionsgrafische Abenteuer der Jahrhundertwende bestand darin, den diffusen Modus des Lichtbilds auf vielfältigste Weise mit der gestochenen Schärfe der Grafik auszutarieren. Verschwommene Fotos wurden aufwendigen Retuschen mit Pinsel und Airbrushgerät unterzogen. Oft wurden die Vorlagen dabei komplett übermalt oder in fotorealistischer Manier neu interpretiert. Die Retuscheabteilungen, die bei den großen Illustrierten allmählich die xylografischen Ateliers ersetzten, wurden meist von akademisch ausgebildeten Malern geleitet. Zu keiner Zeit war das Druckbild der Zeitungen vielfältiger und aufregender als in den 1890er-Jahren, als Strichhochätzungen, Fotoreproduktionen, Retusche- und Fotomalereien, Holzstiche, Pseudoxylografien und allerlei Hybride (Abb. S. 246–249)

koexistierten. Erst das digitale Zeitalter hat wieder eine vergleichbare Palette bildmanipulativer Möglichkeiten eröffnet.

Die fotomechanische Hochdruckätzung war die Voraussetzung für die Entwicklung der modernen illustrierten Massenpresse. 1889 revolutionierte William Luson Thomas mit der Gründung des Londoner *Daily Graphic* das Bildnachrichtenwesen auf nachhaltige Weise. Das Journal verfügte um die Jahrhundertwende über ein internationales Netz von etwa 2000 Zeichenkorrespondenten, die ihre Grafiken seit 1908 auch telegrafisch übermitteln konnten. Von vergleichbarer Bedeutung war 1884 die Herausgabe der ersten illustrierten Sonntagsausgabe des Pariser *Le Petit Journal* durch den Verleger und Erfinder Hippolyte Marinoni. Marinoni hatte für den attraktiven Vierfarbdruck eine spezielle Sechs-Zylinder-Rotationsdruckmaschine konstruiert, die in der Lage war, 10 000 Zeitungen pro Stunde zu drucken und zu falten. Auch der *Daily Graphic* wurde auf einer Marinoni gedruckt. Die Kupferhäute der Bildklischees mussten dafür in eine halbrunde Form gebracht und mit Blei hintergossen werden. Die etwas reicher ausgestattete Maschine, die Joseph Pulitzer 14 Jahre später für den Druck der illustrierten Sonntagsausgabe seiner *New York World* zum Einsatz brachte, konnte bereits die vierfache Menge bewältigen und war auch in der Lage, die besonders heiklen Autotypieklischees vom Rollenzylinder zu drucken.

Edward Duncan, after John Constable, & William James Linton (sc.)

The Cornfield (detail), 1860
Das Kornfeld | Le Champ de blé
Wood engraving
From: William James Linton, *Thirty Pictures by Deceased British Artists: Engraved Expressly for the Art-union of London*, London, 1860

William James Linton's rather old-school interpretation of Constable's painting was the result of a three-stage process. First, the painter and illustrator Edward Duncan sketched out the image and transferred it to a wooden block. The areas of shadow were then probably treated with a wash, and only then was the template for printing engraved using Linton's very free style and with white lines.

William James Lintons Old-School-Interpretation nach Constable war das Produkt einer dreifachen Übersetzung. Zuerst hatte der Maler und Illustrator Edward Duncan eine Skizze des Gemäldes angefertigt und auf den Holzstock übertragen. Die Schattenpartien waren vermutlich laviert. Danach erst wurde die Vorlage in Lintons betont freier Weißlinienmanier gestochen.

L'interprétation « old school » de William James Linton d'après Constable fut le résultat d'un processus en trois étapes. D'abord, le peintre et illustrateur Edward Duncan avait fait une esquisse du tableau et l'avait transposé sur le bloc de bois. Les parties d'ombre furent probablement traitées au lavis. Ensuite seulement, le modèle fut gravé en lignes blanches selon la méthode libre de Linton.

Timothy Cole (sc.), after John Constable

The Cornfield (detail), 1902
Das Kornfeld | Le Champ de blé
Wood engraving
From: Timothy Cole, *Old English Masters*, New York, 1902

The pointillist version of the same painting as done in the style of the New School was produced from an exposed photograph, whose tonal values were carefully interpreted by Timothy Cole in relation to the original work. Beginning in 1883, he spent 27 years travelling and visiting different museums in Europe on behalf of *Century Magazine*, in order to create his series of engraved masterpieces directly from the paintings themselves.

Die pointillistische New-School-Übersetzung des gleichen Gemäldes ist nach einer aufbelichteten Aufnahme entstanden, deren Tonwerte von Timothy Cole in aufwendiger Weise vor dem Original interpretiert wurden. Von 1883 an war er im Auftrag des *Century Magazine* 27 Jahre in europäischen Museen unterwegs, um seine Serie gestochener Meisterwerke vor Ort zu produzieren.

La transposition pointilliste New School du même tableau est réalisée d'après un cliché exposé dont la tonalité fut interprétée de l'original dans un processus élaboré par Timothy Cole. À partir de 1883 et pendant vingt-sept ans, il fit la tournée des musées européens pour le compte du *Century Magazine* afin de produire sa série de chefs-d'œuvre gravés.

Le tournant chimigraphique

C'est pendant les années 1870 que l'apparence uniforme des magazines émergea. Selon l'avis du dessinateur, directeur artistique et historien de la lithographie et de l'illustration Joseph Pennell, ce «bouleversement capital» dans l'histoire de l'art illustratif était la conséquence de deux innovations complémentaires dans le domaine de la technique d'impression en relief : la xylophotographie et la gravure (Pennell 1895, p. 39).

De premiers essais consistant à projeter directement des photographies sur des planches de bois enduites avaient déjà été entrepris au milieu des années 1850. L'exemple le plus connu de tels photogrammes, la gravure de Thomas Bolton *Deliver Us from Evil* (1861), montre à quel point ces toutes premières expériences étaient encore redevables du paradigme linéaire aux contours marqués du dessin classique de reproduction (ill. p. 229). Pour ce faire, des machines de découpe de bois étaient souvent utilisées. En août 1877, un groupe de xylographes américains bouleversa cette tradition avec une spectaculaire série de gravures inspirées des gouaches de James E. Kelly. «Nous ne nous préoccupons pas de présenter un arrangement harmonieux de lignes», soulignait son représentant le plus radical Frederick Juengling (Anthony 1880, p. 447). Ces provocations exacerbèrent la colère de William James Linton, le principal représentant de la xylographie artistique. Son reproche stipulant que les jeunes photographistes américains, qui bientôt obtinrent de grands succès dans les musées et dans les expositions universelles en tant que New School of Wood Engraving, opéraient sans expression comme des machines était toutefois parfaitement juste. Les protagonistes de la New School s'éloignèrent du figuratisme graphique traditionnel avec une indifférence délibérée, qui rappelait le programmatisme du Pop Art, et se concentrèrent uniquement comme des scanners humains sur le balayage des surfaces picturales.

Alors que la xylophotographie abandonnait l'exigence auctorielle d'une performance de transposition créatrice et se tournait vers des structures qui anticipaient le réseau en grille et le pointillisme, la technique parallèle de la gravure en relief célébrait la primauté complémentaire de la ligne et de la libre expression. Les dessins étaient dans ce cas transposés par des couleurs résistant à l'acide sur des plaques de métal. Ensuite, les bains acides dans lesquels les plaques d'impression étaient gravées par couches se chargeaient du travail de gravure (ill. p. 239 b.). Cette technique de gravure en relief fut inventée par l'imprimeur et poète William Blake à la fin des années 1780. Pour ses poésies enluminées, ce dernier avait à la même époque que Thomas Bewick, qui avait renouvelé la gravure sur bois, cherché à réunir judicieusement l'écriture et l'image dans une forme d'impression. Il faudra attendre plus de soixante-dix ans avant que les essais chimigraphiques de Blake acquièrent de l'importance pour le dessin de presse.

Le poète et xylographe William James Linton réalisa en 1863 la première édition des illustrations de Blake à l'aide de la

méthode de cérographie et comptait parmi ceux qui, nombreux, tentèrent des expériences dans le domaine de la gravure en relief (ill. p. 242/243). D'un point de vue technique, l'importance de ce procédé était plutôt marginale. Les conséquences artistiques n'en eurent qu'une plus grande portée. Linton espérait en effet qu'avec la découverte de la gravure des lignes le pénible travail de reproduction appartiendrait au passé et que la xylographie deviendrait un art expressif. Crane, élève de Linton Walter, prit part à ces expériences ainsi que son assistant William Luson Thomas. Quelques années plus tard, ce dernier contribua à la percée décisive de l'idéal de Linton d'un art expressif de la gravure en fondant le magazine illustré à grand tirage *The Graphic* (1869). L'art de Vincent van Gogh fut influencé de manière déterminante par *The Graphic*.

La gravure en relief des lignes ne s'imposa finalement pas à l'aide de la technique de revêtement de cire de Linton, mais par un procédé de gravure sur zinc que l'imprimeur français Firmin Gillot fit breveter dès 1850. Pour beaucoup de dessinateurs de l'ancienne école, ce tournant chimigraphique entraîna le déclin de leur carrière. Quand les croquis de Thomas Nast ne parurent plus sous la forme de gravures sur bois en 1877, mais comme dessins à la plume, il devint évident que la puissance visuelle de ses croquis était due en grande partie aux interprétations xylographiques. Pour beaucoup d'illustrateurs plus jeunes, les nouvelles possibilités de reproduction provoquèrent une emphase

de travaux exécutés à la main. Les dessins, semblables à des esquisses, du reporter dessinateur Melton Prior influencèrent la tendance ainsi que les dessins nerveux de l'illustrateur Daniel Vierge, décrit comme un *tachiste*. Les années 1890 virent l'ascension d'une génération d'artistes tels que Walter Crane, Adolphe Willette, Caran d'Ache, Phil May, Henri de Toulouse-Lautrec, Félix Vallotton, Winsor McCay, Thomas Theodor Heine et Aubrey Beardsley, dont le nouvel art s'accordait parfaitement au potentiel qu'offrait la gravure des lignes.

Néanmoins, la gravure en relief ne permettait pas seulement la reproduction de dessins linéaires. Des papiers de transfert, dont les revêtements étaient adaptés à chaque technique de dessin, furent développés pour la transposition des dessins sur les plaques de métal. Par exemple, le papier granulé permettait l'imitation de dessins à la craie. Les successeurs d'Honoré Daumier tirèrent largement profit de la possibilité d'imitation de l'effet de manière de crayon dans la gravure en relief. Lui-même, en revanche, préférait continuer à dessiner sur la pierre. Pour la presse, les tirages lithographiques devaient être ensuite transférés sur les plaques de métal et gravés en relief. De tels procédés laborieux devinrent obsolètes à la fin des années 1870, lorsqu'il devint possible comme pour la xylophotographie d'exposer les photographies de dessins directement sur les plaques de métal. Le fait que cette technique de gravure en relief photomécanique rendît la taille des reproductions variable

←←**Henry Wolf (del. & sc.)**

Henry Mills Alden, 1916
Wood engraving with pencil and ink; proof on book paper (left)
Wood engraving, proof on Japanese paper (right)

In the proof image the development of the tonal cross-hatching can be examined, as used in this case to represent the skin texture of Henry Mills Alden, the literary editor at *Harper's Monthly*.

Anhand des Korrekturabzugs lässt sich der Aufbau einer tonalen Kreuzschraffur studieren, mit der hier Hautstruktur von Henry Mills Alden, dem Literaturredakteur von *Harper's Monthly*, wiedergegeben wird.

L'épreuve permet d'étudier la structure d'une hachure croisée tonale, avec laquelle est reproduite ici la texture de peau d'Henry Mills Alden, le rédacteur littéraire du *Harper's Monthly*.

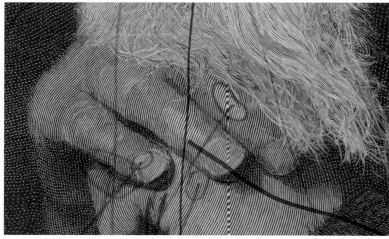

Henry Mills Alden (detail), 1916
Wood engraving with pencil and ink; proof on book paper

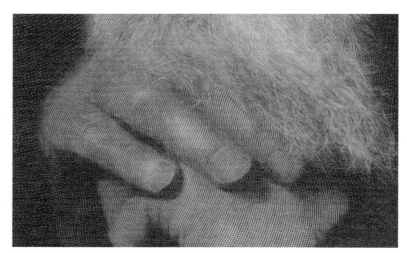

Henry Mills Alden (detail), 1916
Wood engraving, proof on Japanese paper

élargissait considérablement les possibilités de conception de la mise en page, mais la déconnexion des mesures du dessin d'origine entraînait une perte importante de cohérence et de dynamisme visuel.

Le tournant du siècle fut une haute phase de camouflage dans le domaine du dessin de reproduction. Ce qui ressemblait à une gravure sur bois élaborée pouvait facilement être la réimpression d'un carton gratté reproduit comme gravure en relief (ill. p. 239 h.). Au début, lorsque le travail de finition manuel jouait encore un rôle important, comme les chimigraphes apposaient leur signature à la manière des graveurs, il n'y avait guère de signes distinctifs. En 1880, pour permettre les imitations de teintes grises, un carton à gratter avec une trame quadrillée estampée fut commercialisé, une évolution qui aboutit peu de temps après à l'invention de la similigravure ou gravure en demi-teinte (halftone). Ce procédé chimigraphique permettait d'imprimer des photographies en les décomposant en unités noir-et-blanc avec une grille en amont dans la chambre photographique. Dans les premières décennies, la qualité des gravures en demi-teinte était cependant si mauvaise qu'elles ne pouvaient ni remplacer la xylographie ni se passer de l'appui manuel des graveurs. La plupart des clichés en demi-teinte devaient être retouchés avec des burins de gravure. De plus, la monotonie de la trame quadrillée dans l'image imprimée produisait un étrange effet. Pour répondre aux habitudes visuelles d'un public accoutumé à la diversité des structures xylographiques, les clichés photographiques furent recouverts en partie ou en totalité de structures de gravures sur bois. Un effet analogue aux gravures dites en xylotype fut obtenu par l'utilisation de grilles à la trame irrégulière pour les photographies en demi-teinte.

L'aventure du dessin de reproduction au tournant du siècle consista à trouver à travers les moyens les plus variés un équilibre entre le mode diffus de la photographie et la netteté tranchante des œuvres graphiques. Des photographies floues furent soumises à d'intensives retouches à l'aide du pinceau et de

l'aérographe. Les modèles étaient souvent entièrement surpeints ou réinterprétés de manière photoréaliste. Les départements de retouche, qui supplantèrent progressivement les ateliers de xylographie auprès des grands magazines illustrés, étaient le plus souvent dirigés par des peintres de formation académique. À aucun moment l'image imprimée des journaux ne fut plus diversifiée ni plus passionnante que dans les années 1890, lorsque gravures en relief au trait, reproductions de photographies, peintures retouchées et peintures-photos, gravures sur bois, pseudo-xylographies et autres hybrides (ills. p. 246–249) coexistèrent. Seule l'ère numérique offrit à nouveau une palette comparable de possibilités de manipulation d'images.

La gravure en relief photomécanique fut la condition qui permit à la presse illustrée moderne de masse d'évoluer. En 1889, William Luson Thomas révolutionna durablement le secteur de la presse illustrée en fondant le *Daily Graphic* à Londres. Au tournant du siècle, le journal disposait d'un réseau international de quelque 2 000 correspondants illustrateurs qui, à partir de 1908, pouvaient aussi transmettre leurs dessins par télégraphe. En 1884, la publication de la première édition dominicale du *Petit Journal* à Paris par l'éditeur et inventeur Hippolyte Marinoni fut d'une égale importance. Afin d'obtenir l'attractive impression en quadrichomie, Marinoni avait construit une presse rotative à six cylindres qui pouvait imprimer et plier 10 000 journaux par heure. Le *Daily Graphic* fut lui aussi imprimé sur une Marinoni. Pour ce faire, les feuilles de cuivre devaient être formées en demi-cercle et coulées dans du plomb. La machine un peu mieux équipée que Joseph Pulitzer utilisa quatorze ans plus tard pour imprimer l'édition illustrée du dimanche de son *New York World* disposait déjà d'une quadruple capacité et pouvait aussi imprimer, avec le cylindre rotatif, les clichés en similigravure particulièrement délicats.

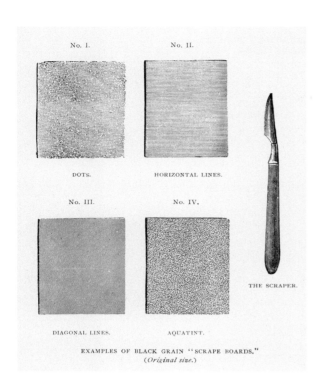

EXAMPLES OF BLACK GRAIN "SCRAPE BOARDS."
(*Original size.*)

Alfred Horsley Hinton

Examples of Black Grain "Scrape Boards", 1894
Beispiele für schwarz beschichtete
Schabekartons
Exemples de cartons grattés à grain noir
Relief etching
From: Alfred Horsley Hinton,
A Handbook of Illustration, New York, 1894

In addition to the black-coated scrape boards
that are still in use today, press illustrators working around the turn of the century could also
make use of special variants that included grid
markings. These could be removed with the
tip or edge of the scraper after the design had
been applied, and then these areas would be
touched up with a brush or quill pen.

Neben den noch heute gebräuchlichen Schabekartons mit schwarzen Beschichtungen
verwendeten die Pressegrafiker um die Jahrhundertwende auch spezielle Varianten mit
eingeprägten Strukturrastern, die dann, nachdem die Zeichnungen mit Pinsel oder Feder
aufgetuscht waren, in malerischer Weise mit
einem Schabemesser aufgehellt wurden.

En plus des cartons de grattage aux revêtements noirs encore en usage aujourd'hui,
les illustrateurs de presse utilisaient aussi au
tournant du siècle des variantes spéciales
avec des grilles structurales imprégnées qui
ensuite étaient éclaircies de manière artistique à l'aide d'un couteau racleur après que
les dessins ont été appliqués avec un pinceau
ou une plume d'oie.

Anonymous

Etchers' Workshop, c. 1905
Ätzerei | Atelier de graveur
Relief etching
From: Arthur W. Unger, *Die Herstellung von Büchern,*
Illustrationen, Akzidenzen usw., Halle, 1910

Chemical engravers etching zinc plates for printing
Chemiegrafen beim Ätzen von Zinkklischees
Graveurs chimiques travaillant sur des plaques
d'impression de zinc

AN EXPERIMENTAL DRAWING BY MR. THACKERAY.

William Makepeace Thackeray & William James Linton

Specimens of a New Process of Engraving for Surface-printing, 1861
Muster für ein neues Ätzverfahren im Hochdruck
Spécimens d'un nouveau procédé de gravure pour impression en surface
Relief etching

As an illustrator as well as being a novelist, William Makepeace Thackeray provided a design for the brochure William James Linton put together to advertise his relief-etching process. Linton's assistant William Luson Thomas was one of the first people to use cerography, a technique he employed in 1861 for various illustrations to Hans Christian Andersen's fairy tales.

Für den Werbeprospekt von William James Lintons Hochätzverfahren hatte auch der Schriftsteller und Cartoonist William Makepeace Thackeray eine Vorlage beigesteuert. Zu den ersten Praktikern der Kerografie zählte Lintons Assistent William Luson Thomas, der 1861 Illustrationen zu Hans Christian Andersens Märchen in dieser Technik realisierte.

L'écrivain et dessinateur humorisitique William Makepeace Thackeray avait aussi fourni un modèle pour la brochure publicitaire vantant le procédé de gravure en relief de William James Linton. William Luson Thomas, l'assistant de Linton qui réalisa en 1861 des illustrations pour les contes de Hans Christian Andersen à l'aide de cette technique, fit partie des premiers à pratiquer la cérographie.

PABLO DE SÉGOVIE. — CHAPITRE X.   105

J'éclatai de rire en voyant en quoi il faifait confifter l'art militaire, et je compris que c'était quelque coquin, car il n'eft point d'habitude plus déteftée parmi les foldats de cœur et de mérite, fi elle ne l'eft parmi tous.

Nous arrivâmes aux gorges du port; l'ermite récitait fes prières fur un chapelet qui valait fon pefant de bois et qui reffemblait à un jeu de boules; le foldat, de fon

Daniel Vierge & Charles Gillot (sc.)

Relief etching
From: Francisco de Quevedo y Santibáñez Villega, *Histoire de Don Pablo de Ségovie*, Paris, 1882

With his pen and ink drawings for this picaresque novel the enterprising Daniel Vierge established himself as the "father of modern illustration". The photomechanical method of relief etching invented by Charles Gillot here announced its success as an artistic technique for reproducing line illustrations with the spontaneous pen drawings of Vierge, who had been known up until this point for working in an early tachiste style.

Mit seinen Federzeichnungen zu dem Schelmenroman *Histoire de Pablo de Ségovie* avancierte der experimentierfreudige Daniel Vierge zum „Vater der modernen Illustration". Die von Charles Gillot entwickelte fotomechanische Linienhochätzung feierte mit den impulsiven Federzeichnungen des als *tachiste* (Kleckser) bekannten Vierge ihren Durchbruch als künstlerische Reproduktionstechnik.

Avec ses dessins à la plume pour le roman picaresque *Histoire de Pablo de Ségovie*, le fort entreprenant Daniel Vierge devint le «père de l'illustration moderne». Le procédé linéaire photomécanique de gravure en relief inventé par Charles Gillot célébra sa réussite comme technique de reproduction artistique avec les fulminants dessins à la plume de Vierge, connu jusqu'alors comme tachiste.

Walter Crane

The Capitalist Vampire, 1885
Der kapitalistische Vampir
Le Vampire capitaliste
Relief etching
From: *Justice*, London,
22 August 1885

Walter Crane had been involved
with the socialist cause since 1884
together with other figures in the Arts
and Crafts movement such as William
Morris and Emery Walker. A compilation of his politically engaged illustrations, which he had produced for the
periodicals of the Social Democratic
Federation and the Socialist League
for distribution around the world,
was published in 1896 with the title
Cartoons for the Cause.

Seit 1884 war Walter Crane gemeinsam mit weiteren Exponenten
der Arts-and-Crafts-Bewegung wie
William Morris und Emery Walker in
der sozialistischen Bewegung engagiert. Eine Kompilation seiner international verbreiteten Agitprop-Grafiken,
die er für Periodika der Social Democratic Federation und der Socialist
League gezeichnet hatte, erschien
1896 unter dem Titel *Cartoons for
the Cause*.

Depuis 1884, Walter Crane s'était
engagé pour la cause socialiste avec
d'autres exposants du mouvement
Arts and Crafts comme William Morris
et Emery Walker. Une compilation
de ses dessins «agitprop», qu'il avait
réalisés pour des périodiques de la
Social Democratic Federation et de la
Socialist League et qui furent distribués
à échelle internationale, parut en 1896
sous le titre *Cartoons for the Cause*.

→→ **William Blake & William James Linton (sc.)**

America, a Prophecy (1793), 1863
Amerika, eine Prophezeiung
Amérique, une prophétie
Relief etching
From: Alexander Gilchrist, *Life of
William Blake, "Pictor Ignotus"*,
London, 1863

William Blake's art first became more
widely known by way of the cero-
graphic versions William James Linton
made of some of his designs. The
two Pre-Raphaelite brothers Dante
Gabriel and William Rossetti had
recommended Linton for the task of
adapting Blake's illustrations for this
first biography of the "Pictor Ignotus"
(anonymous painter).

Die Kunst William Blakes wurde
erst durch die kerografischen Interpretationen William James Lintons
bekannt. Das präraffaelitische Brü-
derpaar Dante Gabriel und William
Rossetti hatte den umstrittenen
Holzstecher und Dichter für die Illustrierung dieser ersten Biografie des
„Pictor Ignotus" empfohlen.

Ce sont les interprétations céro-
graphiques de William James Linton
qui rendirent l'art de William Blake
célèbre. Les deux frères préraphaélites Dante Gabriel et William Rossetti
avaient recommandé le xylographe
et poète controversé pour l'illustration de cette première biographie
du «Pictor Ignotus».

Milnes's superb copy. Turning over the leaves, it is sometimes like an increase of daylight on the retina, so fair

and open is the effect of particular pages. The skies of sapphire, or gold, rayed with hues of sunset, against which stand out leaf or blossom, or pendant branch, gay with bright plumaged birds; the strips of emerald sward below, gemmed with flower and lizard and enamelled snake, refresh the eye continually.

Some of the illustrations are of a more sombre kind. There is one in which a little corpse, white as snow, lies gleaming on the floor of a green overarching cave, which close inspection proves to be a field of wheat, whose slender interlacing stalks, bowed by the full ear and by a gentle breeze,

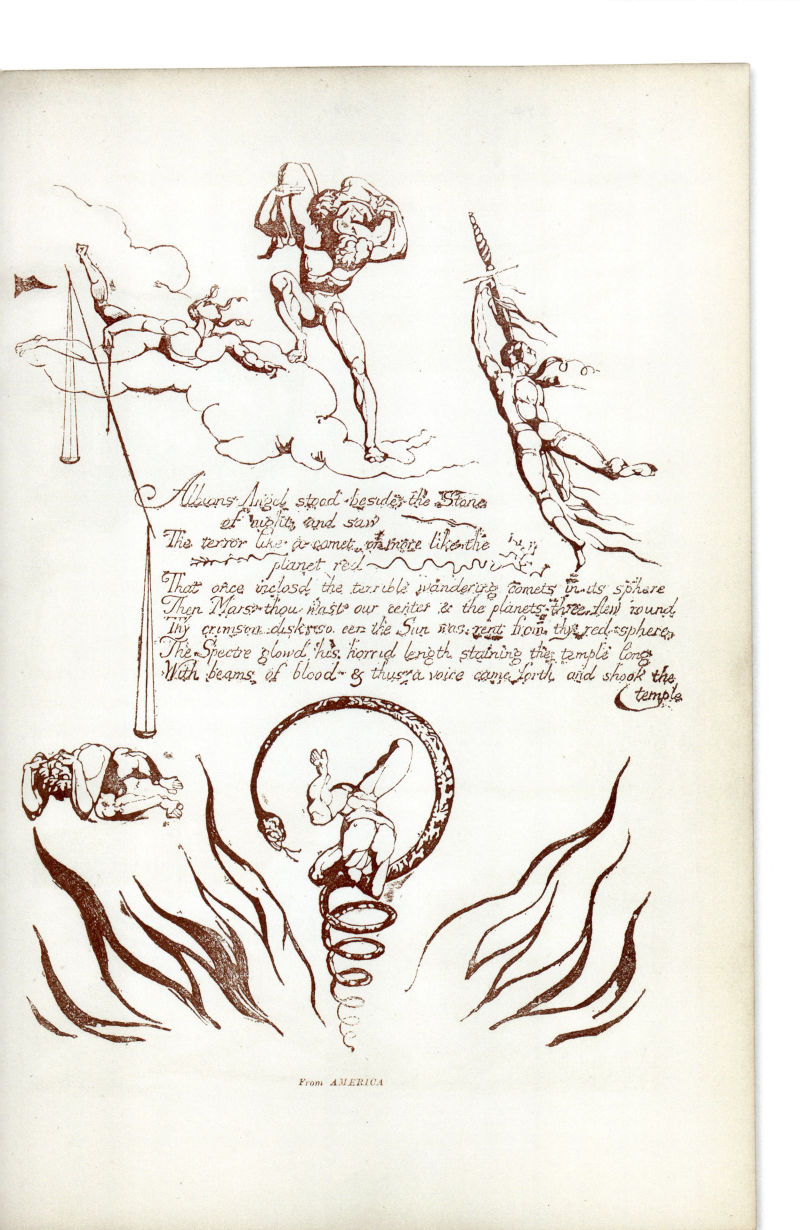

Albions Angel stood beside the Stone
      of night, and saw
The terror like a comet, or more like the
      planet red
That once inclosd the terrible wandering comets in its sphere
Then Mars, thou wast our center & the planets three flew round
Thy crimson disks; so eer the Sun was rent from thy red sphere
The Spectre glowd his horrid length staining the temple long
With beams of blood & thus a voice came forth and shook the
                                                              temple

From AMERICA

PRESENTED GRATIS WITH THE CHRISTMAS NUMBER OF "THE GRAPHIC"

THE
DAILY-GRAPHIC

A PRELIMINARY NUMBER OF THE NEW PAPER   PRICE ONE PENNY

*Ladies and Gentlemen,   "The Graphic"
has now been in existence for twenty years.
Its career has been remarkably successful. This success
is greatly due to the fact that it has been fortunate enough to
number on its staff Artists whose names and works are fam-
-iliar as household words; such as Luke Fildes, Herkomer, Woods,
Elizabeth Thompson, Caldecott and many others; while its
popularity has been greatly enhanced by the
contributions of such distinguished men as
Sir Frederick Leighton, Sir J. E. Millais and
Alma Tadema. Then, as regards literature
"The Graphic" has been honoured with the assistance of Charles Reade, Anthony Trollope, Victor
Hugo, Walter Besant and William Black, who have
worked in harmony with artists of high merit*

*The paper has undergone constant develop-
-ment, enlargement and improvement. In 1869
it consisted of 24 pages produced at an annual
cost of £54,000; now the pages
number 36, and the expenditure amounts to £74,000, an increase of
£20,000 per annum. This cordial appreciation and sympathy of an indulgent
public has been of so encouraging a nature that we have now to announce
our intention of embarking in an entirely new enterprise
We propose to publish a daily newspaper entirely distinct from "the Graphic"
with an independent literary, Artistic, and engraving staff of its own.*

SIR JOHN MILLAIS, BART., R.A.

THE FIRST NUMBER OF THE "DAILY GRAPHIC" WILL BE PUBLISHED ON JANUARY 4, 1890

C. Green, R.I.   Sydney P. Hall   H. Woods, A.R.A.   Luke Fildes, R.A.   J. Nash, R.I.

H. Herkomer, A.R.A.   E. J. Gregory, A.R.A.   The late F. Holl, R.A.   W. Small
G. Durand

SOME "GRAPHIC" ARTISTS

Anonymous

Relief etching
From: *The Daily Graphic*
(preliminary number),
London, December
1889

Joseph Pennell

→ *In the Streets of Berdychiv:
An Interrupted Sketch*, 1891
*In den Straßen von Berdytschiw:
Eine unterbrochene Skizze*
*Dans les rues de Berditchev:
une esquisse interrompue*
Relief etching
From: *The Illustrated London News*,
28 November 1891

While Joseph Pennell was drawing this view of the market square in Berdychiv, a city in Ukraine, he was arrested by the militia on suspicion that he was a spy. Pennell was an illustrator and historian of illustrations who had been inspired by the work of Melton Prior, Daniel Vierge and Whistler, and when his "interrupted sketch" was printed it meant nothing less for him than the liberation of press graphics from the need to be fully finished.

Während er die Marktplatzansicht im ukrainischen Berdytschiw zeichnete, wurde Joseph Pennell von Milizen unter Spionageverdacht festgenommen. Für den Zeichner und Illustrationshistoriker, der von den Grafiken Melton Priors, Daniel Vierges und James McNeill Whistlers inspiriert war, bedeutete der Abdruck dieser „unterbrochenen Skizze" nichts weniger als die Befreiung der Pressegrafik vom Zwang zur Vollendung.

Alors qu'il dessinait la vue sur la place du marché à Berditchev en Ukraine, Joseph Pennell, soupçonné d'espionnage, fut arrêté par la milice. Pour le dessinateur et historien de l'illustration qui était inspiré par les dessins de Melton Prior, de Daniel Vierge et de James McNeill Whistler, l'impression de cette « esquisse interrompue » ne signifiait rien de moins que la libération des dessins de presse du diktat de l'achèvement.

Charles Dana Gibson

People Who Will Have Their Own Way, 1899
Menschen, die ihren Willen bekommen
Des gens qui obtiennent ce qu'ils veulent
Relief etching
From: *Life*, New York, 1899

The success of *Life*, which was founded in 1883, was due in large part to Charles Dana Gibson's illustrations for the magazine. His elegant satires of high society, influenced by the work of *Punch* illustrators such as Charles Keene and George du Maurier, revolved around the figure of the self-confident new woman who, in Gibson's portrayal of her with an hourglass waist and hair pinned up, shaped the ideal of female beauty at the time.

Der Erfolg des 1883 gegründeten Magazins *Life* beruhte vor allem auf den Grafiken von Charles Dana Gibson. Im Zentrum seiner eleganten von *Punch*-Cartoonisten wie Charles Keene und George du Maurier beeinflussten Upper-Class-Satiren stand die selbstbewusste neue Frau, die in Gibsons Ausprägung mit Wespentaille und hochgesteckter Frisur das Schönheitsideal der Zeit prägte.

Le succès du magazine *Life* fondé en 1883 reposait surtout sur les dessins de Charles Dana Gibson. An centre de ses élégantes satires de la haute société, influencées par des illustrateurs de *Punch* comme Charles Keene et George du Maurier, trônait la femme nouvelle et sûre d'elle, qui dans la représentation ce Gibson avec sa taille de guêpe et ses cheveux relevés détermina l'idéal ce beauté de l'époque.

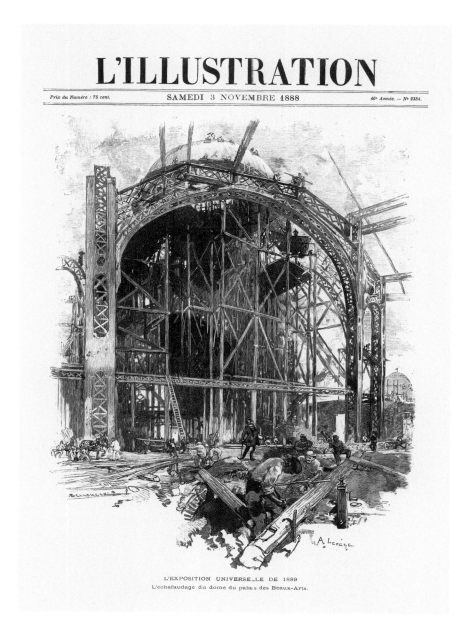

Albert Bellenger & Auguste Lepère (sc.)

The World's Fair of 1889
Die Weltausstellung von 1889
L'Exposition universelle de 1889
Wood engraving
From: *L'Illustration*, Paris, 3 November 1888

In November 1888, construction work for the World's Fair in Paris was in full swing. This impressionistic design was one of the last illustrations for the press produced by the experienced wood engraver Auguste Lepère. He subsequently made a name for himself as a pioneer of modern artist prints created by his experiments with various wood-engraving techniques, which in mainland Europe remained a largely undeveloped craft.

Im November 1888 waren die Bauarbeiten für die Pariser Weltausstellung in vollem Gang. Der impressionistische Tonstich zählte zu den letzten Pressegrafiken des versierten Holzstechers Auguste Lepère. Danach machte er sich durch seine Experimente mit der in Europa verdrängten Technik des Holzschnitts einen Namen als Wegbereiter der modernen Künstlerdruckgrafik.

En novembre 1888, les travaux pour l'Exposition universelle de Paris battaient leur plein. La gravure de teinte impressionniste était l'un des derniers dessins de presse du graveur sur bois expérimenté Auguste Lepère. Ensuite, grâce à son savoir-faire technique en matière de gravure sur bois, laquelle fut mise au ban en Europe, il se fit un nom comme précurseur des estampes artistiques.

Julien Antoine Peulot (sc.)

At the Fair – The Lift Tracks to the First Floor of the Eiffel Tower, 1889
In der Ausstellung – Aufzugbahn in der ersten Etage des Eiffelturms
À l'Exposition – Le chemin des ascenseurs du premier étage de la tour Eiffel
Wood engraving
From: *Le Monde illustré*, Paris, 18 May 1889

→→Anonymous

An Appalling Hotel Fire, 1899
Ein schrecklicher Hotelbrand
Un terrible incendie d'hôtel
Relief etching
From: *Leslie's Weekly*, New York, 30 March 1899

The various panels of this composite illustration use different degrees of retouching, from reproductions of only slightly reworked photographs to whole areas of painting in grisaille.

Das Multipanel-Ensemble vereint verschiedene Grade der Retusche, von der schwach überarbeiteten Fotoreproduktion bis hin zu vollflächigen Grisaillemalereien.

La double page composée de vignettes associe les différentes phases de retouche, de la reproduction de photographie légèrement retravaillée aux pleines surfaces en technique de grisaille.

REGISTERED AT THE GENERAL POST-OFFICE FOR TRANSMISSION ABROAD.

No. 2634.—VOL. XCV.   SATURDAY, OCTOBER 12, 1889.   TWO WHOLE SHEETS } SIXPENCE. By Post, 6½D.

THE FORTH BRIDGE: QUEENSFERRY NORTH CANTILEVER, BOTTOM MEMBER: AND GARVIE MAIN PIER (APRIL, 1889).

Anonymous

↑ *The Forth Bridge*, 1889
Die Brücke über den Forth | Le Pont du Forth
Relief etching
From: *The Illustrated London News*,
12 October 1889

In order to be able to compete with the depth of focus that could be reproduced with photoxylography, the photographic originals used to produce halftone engravings were generally retouched before the rasterised image was made. The zinc plate for this cover image for *The Illustrated London*
News would then have been trimmed and cropped using engraving tools while the large blank spaces were probably cut away with a fretsaw.

Um neben der tiefenscharfen Konkurrenz der Fotoxylografien bestehen zu können, wurden die fotografischen Vorlagen der Autotypien vor den Rasteraufnahmen meist retuschiert. Das Zinkklischee für die Titelabbildung der *Illustrated London News* wurde dann mit xylografischen Werkzeugen nachgeschnitten und freigestellt. Die Leerräume sind vermutlich mit einer Laubsäge ausgeschnitten worden.

Afin de pouvoir rivaliser avec la profondeur de champ des xylophotographies, les modèles photographiques des similigravures étaient la plupart du temps retouchés avant la prise des images rasterisées. Le cliché zinc pour la couverutre de titre des *Illustrated London News* fut ensuite découpé avec des outils xylographiques et détaché de son arrière-plan. Les espaces vides ont probablement été découpés à l'aide d'une scie à chantourner.

VIEW OF RUINS FROM FORTY-SEVENTH STREET AND FIFTH AVENUE—THE AMBULANCES' GRIM WORK.

JUST BEFORE THE COLLAPSE OF THE FORTY-SIXTH STREET WALL.

OUTBURST OF FLA

AN APPALLI

MANY PERSONS MEET FRIGHTFUL DEATH IN THE CONFLAGRATION WHICH DEVOURED THE WINDSOR, ONE OF THE BEST-KNOWN AND LUXURIOUS HOTELS
AND ANIMATED WITE THE GREAT CROWDS THAT HAD GATHERED IN THE VICINITY OF THE HOTEL TO WATCH THE ST. PATRICK'S-DAY PARADE
LOOKING UPON FIFTH AVENUE WAS FILLED WITH SMILING FACES, WHEN THE CRY OF FIRE AROSE. FIFTEEN MINUTES LATE
THE WINDSOR WAS THE FAVORITE NEW YORK STOPPING-PLACE OF PRESI

RUINS, FROM FIFTH AVENUE WITHIN AN HOUR FROM THE TIME THE FIRST JET OF FLAME SHOT FROM AN UPPER WINDOW.

THE WINDSOR HOTEL, A HOTEL OF WORLD-WIDE FAME.

SHOWING HOTEL AFTER THE OUTWARD COLLAPSE OF THE CENTRE SECTION.

CROWDS IN FORTY-SIXTH STREET WATCHING THE ENGULFING FLAMES.

IMMENSE VOLUME OF FLAME AND SMOKE POURING FROM THE UPPER FLOORS.

E ROOF FELL IN.

OTEL FIRE.

WORLD. THE FLAMES BROKE OUT AT QUARTER PAST THREE ON THE AFTERNOON OF MARCH 17TH, WHEN FIFTH AVENUE WAS BRIGHT WITH SUNSHINE
IRST COMPANY OF IRISH VOLUNTEERS HAD JUST PASSED, WITH BANDS PLAYING AND FLAGS FLYING, AND EVERY WINDOW OF THE WINDSOR
ME WINDOWS SHOWED FRENZIED HUMAN BEINGS LEAPING TO DEATH OR SINKING BACK INTO THE LURID GLARE OF FLAME.
NLEY AND OF PERSONS OF GREAT WEALTH, MANY OF WHOM PERISHED.

Van Gogh's "Bible for Artists"

Vincent van Gogh was a knowledgeable collector of socially realistic press graphics and was also one of the most original users of the form within his own art. His collection included around 1,500 pages from illustrated magazines from around the world, which he classified according to artist and subject and annotated at length. There were several political caricatures, but his main interest was in graphic work with a social theme and in particular the work of English illustrators of the 1870s for which he had developed a great liking while apprenticed to the London office of the art dealers Goupil & Cie. The new illustrated newspaper *The Graphic* had introduced him to the expressive designs of artists such as Hubert von Herkomer, Luke Fildes and William Small, whose subjects seemed to be taken directly from everyday life. These no-nonsense illustrations with their "types […] from the people for the people" (Van Gogh 1882; see Jansen, no. 291) appeared in stark contrast to the expensive print editions he had seen at Goupil's, with their lavish photomechanical reproductions of anaemic Salon art.

The Graphic was founded in 1869 by the wood engraver William Luson Thomas, a friend of Dickens's, with the aim of bringing greater variety into press illustrations. As reproducing graphics by hand became less and less important across the industry, Thomas continued to endorse the individual style of different illustrators alongside a transfer to wood-engraved copies that showed the work to best effect. He was inspired by the artistic illustrations in such literary periodicals as *Once a Week* (1859; ills. pp. 206 t., 207 b.) and *Good Words* (1860; ill. p. 206 b.) but clearly most of all by the ideas of his teacher William James Linton, who was seen as something of a champion of wood engraving and also a leading exponent of the art.

The combination of artistic illustration in *The Graphic* and the newspaper's commitment to social reform in the spirit of Dickens proved irresistibly attractive to Van Gogh. "It would have been the greatest honour, an ideal even, to have worked for *The Graphic* when it first began," he wrote to his brother Theo in December 1882 (see Jansen, no. 293). By this date he had already begun his own research on social issues in The Hague on the model of pictorial journalists in England. When he was invited to present this press graphics work at the local artists' association the response was dismissive because of the arrogant attitude of his fellow artists and their reservations concerning such "illustrative art". The reaction had a significant influence on his decision about where he would choose to work as an artist in future, and in June 1883 he told his brother that he was going to apply for a permanent job in England with the illustrated press. He increasingly saw his vocation as propagating a democratically expressive form of art, in the manner of the early illustrators for *The Graphic*. The famous illustration *The Empty Chair* by *The Graphic*'s Luke Fildes, which shows Dickens's chair beside his desk the day after he died, became

Vincent van Gogh

Gauguin's Chair, 1888
Gauguins Stuhl | *La Chaise de Gauguin*
Oil on canvas
Amsterdam, Van Gogh Museum

Luke Fildes

The Room in which Charles Dickens Wrote (The Empty Chair), 1870
Das Zimmer, in dem Charles Dickens schrieb (Der leere Stuhl)
La chambre dans laquelle Charles Dickens écrivait (La Chaise vide)
Wood engraving
From: *Harper's Weekly*, New York, 7 January 1871

"Empty chairs – there are many of them, later there will be even more, and in the end there will be nothing but empty chairs in place of Herkomer, Luke Fildes, Frank Holl, William Small etc."

„Empty chairs – es gibt viele, mehr werden hinzukommen, und früher oder später wird es an der Stelle von Herkomer, Luke Fildes, Frank Holl, William Small etc. nur empty chairs geben".

«Empty chairs – il y en a beaucoup, il en viendra beaucoup plus, et tôt ou tard à la place de Herkomer, Luke Fildes, Frank Holl, William Small etc. il n'y aura que des empty chairs.»

—Vincent van Gogh to his brother Theo, 11 December 1882

This illustration first appeared in the Christmas 1870 issue of *The Graphic*, with the title *The Empty Chair*.

Die Abbildung erschien erstmals in der Weihnachtsnummer 1870 des *Graphic* unter dem Titel *The Empty Chair*.

Cette illustration parut pour la première fois dans le numéro de Noël 1870 du *Graphic* sous le titre *The Empty Chair*.

a symbol for the affinity Van Gogh felt with the newspaper's agenda (ills. p. 251).

The purpose of his collection of press graphics, which ran to 18 volumes, now also appeared in a transfigured light, and he proposed that it was "a kind of Bible for artists [...] which they should keep in their studios at all times" (Jansen, no. 331). To begin with, Van Gogh mostly made use of the subject matter, but later on, as the social themes became less significant, he concentrated more on the different styles of wood engravings in the press illustrations. Over the course of many sleepless nights the now experienced specialist in graphic works pored over the engravings at length while examining the dynamic whirls and ecstatic groups of lines. The illustrations produced from the white-line engravings of such respected masters of wood engraving as Joseph Swain left a strong mark on his late paintings and reed-pen drawings (ills. p. 256).

Among the most important items in Van Gogh's "Bible for artists" were two major works of socially critical pictorial journalism, namely Arthur Boyd Houghton's burlesque travel account, *Graphic America* (1869–1870), and Gustave Doré's hellish vision of city life, *London: A Pilgrimage* (1867–1872). These were both ambitious and multi-layered meta-reports, which took the established forms of press graphics and re-examined and recodified them. They marked a culmination of press graphic work, and also a turning point since they coincided with two events that

were of fundamental importance in the industry's history: the Franco-Prussian War of 1870/71 and the subsequent founding of the Paris Commune. The bloody suppression of this short-lived attempt at creating a purely democratic republic resulted in an ideological readjustment for the press on a global level. In the emphatically Imperialist era that followed, pictorial journalism developed in an increasingly nationalistic climate.

While many of Van Gogh's favourite illustrators were involved in the Commune's struggles, either as reporters or as activists, this crucial event is not mentioned at all in his notes. In fact, like most of his fellow artists, his reaction was to turn away from the horrific situation in 1871. Even so, his collection, influenced by the writings of Émile Zola and Jules Michelet, reflected an increasing focus on analysing social and political content in the press, which gradually replaced his interest in the social romanticism of the Victorian age. In particular he studied the subtle milieu designs by the illustrator Paul Renouard, and compiled a large amount of material on various topics that would enable him to make a historical survey of social injustices.

Van Goghs Künstlerbibel

Vincent van Gogh war nicht nur einer der besten Kenner sozialrealistischer Pressegrafik, sondern auch einer ihrer eigenwilligsten künstlerischen Interpreten. Seine Sammlung umfasste etwa 1500 Blätter aus internationalen Illustrierten, die er mit großem Enthusiasmus nach Künstlern und Themen ordnete und kommentierte. Darunter befanden sich auch Konvolute politischer Karikatur. Der Schwerpunkt lag allerdings auf der Sozialgrafik, insbesondere englischer Illustratoren der 1870er-Jahre, für die er während seiner Ausbildung in der Londoner Filiale der Kunsthandlung Goupil & Cie eine Passion entwickelt hatte. In den Auslagen der neuen Illustrierten *The Graphic* war er der ausdrucksstarken Bildwelt von Zeichnern wie Hubert von Herkomer, Luke Fildes oder William Small begegnet, deren Motive direkt aus dem Alltagsleben gegriffen schienen. Diese kernigen Drucke mit „Typen … aus dem Volk für das Volk" (van Gogh 1882; siehe Jansen, Nr. 291) standen in diametralem Gegensatz zu Goupils hochpreisigen Editionen, die anämische Salonkunst in fotomechanischer Hochglanzreproduktion zeigten.

The Graphic war 1869 von dem Xylografen William Luson Thomas, einem Freund von Charles Dickens, mit dem Vorsatz begründet worden, mehr Vielfalt in der Presseillustration zuzulassen. Vor dem Hintergrund des drohenden Bedeutungsverlusts manueller Reproduktionsgrafik setzte er verstärkt auf die individuelle Handschrift der Zeichner und eine kongeniale xylografische Übersetzung. Inspiriert war er dabei von der künstlerischen Illustrationsgrafik in literarischen Periodika wie *Once a Week* (1859, Abb. S. 206 o., 207 u.) und *Good Words* (1860, Abb. S. 206 u.), doch offensichtlich vor allem von den Anschauungen seines Lehrers William James Linton, der als Propagandist und führender Vertreter des expressiven Holzstichs galt.

Auf van Gogh übte dieser künstlerische Impuls des *Graphic* im Zusammenhang mit einer an Dickens orientierten sozialreformatorischen Ausrichtung eine unwiderstehliche Anziehung aus. „Es wäre mir die größte Ehre gewesen, ein Ideal, ganz am Anfang für den *Graphic* gearbeitet zu haben", schrieb er im Dezember 1882 an seinen Bruder Theo (Jansen, Nr. 293). Zu dieser Zeit hatte er in Den Haag mit eigenen Sozialstudien nach dem Vorbild der englischen Bildreporter begonnen. Dass eine Einladung zur Präsentation seiner pressegrafischen Forschungstätigkeit im örtlichen Künstlerverein am Dünkel der Kollegenschaft und deren Vorbehalten gegenüber dem „Illustrativen" gescheitert war, trug nicht unwesentlich zur eigenen künstlerischen Standortbestimmung bei. Im Juni 1883 erwähnte er gegenüber seinem Bruder konkrete Pläne, sich bei englischen Illustrierten um eine ständige Anstellung zu bewerben. Seine Berufung sah er verstärkt darin, eine demokratische Ausdruckskunst in der Nachfolge der frühen *Graphic*-Illustratoren zu propagieren. Zum Sinnbild dieser Wahlverwandtschaft wurde ihm die berühmte Grafik *The Empty Chair* des *Graphic*-Zeichners Luke Fildes, die

William James Linton (del. & sc.)

Wood engraving
From: William Cullen Bryant, *The Flood of Years*,
New York, 1877

"The purpose of wood engraving is expression."
„Die Bestimmung des Holzstichs ist Ausdruck."
« L'objectif de la gravure sur bois est l'expression. »
—W.J. Linton, "Art in Engraving on Wood",
Atlantic Monthly, June 1879

Charles Dickens' leeren Schreibtischstuhl am Morgen nach dem Tod des Dichters zeigt (Abb. S. 251).

In einem verklärten Licht erschien ihm auch die Funktion seiner aus 18 Bänden bestehenden Sammlung. Er empfahl sie als „eine Art Bibel für den Künstler", die man „ein für alle Mal im Atelier haben" (Jansen, Nr. 331) solle. Anfänglich profitierte er vor allem von den Motiven. Später, als die Sozialthemen in den Hintergrund rückten, konzentrierte er sich zunehmend auf die xylografischen Strukturen der Illustriertenblätter. In vielen schlaflosen Nächten nahm der ausgebildete Grafikspezialist die Stiche unter die Lupe und inspizierte die dynamischen Wirbel und ekstatischen Linienbündel. Die Nachbilder von Weißlinienstichen eines verehrten Meisters ausdrucksstarker Xylografie wie Joseph Swain haben die Strukturen seiner späten Malereien und Rohrfederzeichnungen nachhaltig geprägt (Abb. S. 256).

Zu den Kernstücken von van Goghs Künstlerbibel zählten zwei Hauptwerke des sozialkritischen Bildjournalismus, Arthur Boyd Houghtons burlesker Reisebericht *Graphic America* (1869–1870) und Gustave Dorés abgründige Großstadtvision *London: A Pilgrimage* (1867–1872). Es handelte sich in beiden Fällen um vielschichtige Metareportagen, in denen etablierte pressegrafische Muster reflektiert und neu codiert wurden. Sie markierten einen Kulminations- und Wendepunkt, der mit einem Doppelereignis korrelierte, das pressehistorisch von weitreichender Bedeutung war: dem Deutsch-Französischen Krieg

von 1870/71 und der anschließenden Gründung der Pariser Kommune. Die blutige Niederschlagung dieses kurzzeitigen Versuchs, eine basisdemokratische Republik zu realisieren, hatte eine ideologische Neujustierung der internationalen Presselandschaft zur Folge. Bildjournalismus fand in der nachfolgenden hochimperialistischen Ära unter zunehmend chauvinistischen Vorzeichen statt.

Obgleich viele seiner favorisierten Illustratoren als Reporter oder Aktivisten in den Kampf um die Pariser Kommune involviert waren, blieb dieses einschneidende Ereignis in van Goghs Kommentaren ausgeblendet. Wie die meisten seiner Künstlerkollegen reagierte er in eskapistischer Weise auf das Inferno von 1871. Allerdings schlug sich in seiner Sammlung unter dem Einfluss der Schriften Émile Zolas und Jules Michelets ein zunehmend analytisches Interesse an sozialpolitischen Inhalten nieder, das seine Begeisterung für viktorianische Sozialromantik abzulösen begann. Er beschäftigte sich intensiv mit den subtilen Milieustudien des Zeichners Paul Renouard und legte umfangreiche Konvolute zu Themenfeldern an, die es ihm erlaubten, soziale Missstände im historischen Kontext zu studieren.

La bible pour artistes de Van Gogh

Vincent van Gogh n'était pas seulement l'un des plus fins connaisseurs du dessin de presse empreint de réalisme social, mais également l'un de ses interprètes les plus originaux dans le domaine artistique. Sa collection comprenait quelque 1 500 estampes provenant de revues illustrées internationales, qu'il classait par auteur et par thème et qu'il analysait avec ferveur. Parmi elles se trouvait toute une série de caricatures politiques. Toutefois, son intérêt se portait sur les œuvres graphiques à message social, en particulier sur celles des illustrateurs anglais des années 1870 pour lesquels il avait nourri une véritable passion pendant son apprentissage dans la filiale londonienne du magasin d'art Goupil & Cie. À travers les œuvres présentées dans la nouvelle revue *The Graphic*, il avait découvert l'univers illustré très expressif de dessinateurs comme Hubert von Herkomer, Luke Fildes ou encore William Small dont les motifs semblaient directement tirés de la vie quotidienne. Ces estampes intenses présentaient «des types [...] issus du peuple pour le peuple» (Van Gogh 1882; voir Jansen, n° 291) en contraste diamétral avec les éditions haut de gamme qui montraient l'art anémique de salon dans de somptueuses reproductions photomécaniques.

The Graphic avait été créé en 1869 par le xylographe William Luson Thomas, un ami de Charles Dickens, dans le but d'apporter une plus grande diversité dans l'illustration de presse. Dans le contexte d'une perte de vitesse grandissante du dessin manuel de reproduction, il accorda davantage d'importance au style individuel des dessinateurs et à une transposition xylographique congéniale. Le dessin d'illustration artistique de périodiques littéraires comme *Once a Week* (1859, ills. p. 206 h., 207 b.) et *Good Words* (1860, ill. p. 206 b.) et surtout, selon toute évidence, les idées de son professeur William James Linton, qui était considéré comme propagandiste et figure emblématique de la gravure sur bois expressive, furent ses sources d'inspiration.

Cette impulsion artistique du *Graphic* combinée à un engagement pour les réformes sociales dans l'esprit de Charles Dickens exercèrent sur Van Gogh une attirance irrésistible. «Cela aurait été pour moi le plus grand honneur, un idéal, d'avoir travaillé tout au début pour le *Graphic*», écrivit-il à son frère Theo en décembre 1882 (cfr. Jansen, n° 293). À cette époque, il avait personnellement entamé à La Haye des études sociales d'après le modèle des reporters d'images anglais. Le fait qu'une invitation à la présentation de ses recherches dans le domaine du dessin de presse dans un cercle d'artistes local se heurta à l'arrogance de ses collègues et à leur méfiance face à l'«illustratif» détermina en grande mesure le choix de son propre lieu de création artistique. En juin 1883, il annonça à son frère le projet concret de postuler à un emploi permanent auprès de magazines illustrés anglais. Il considérait que sa vocation profonde était de propager un art d'expression démocratique dans la lignée des premiers illustrateurs du *Graphic*. Le fameux croquis *The Empty Chair* du

Vincent van Gogh

The Potato Eaters, Nuenen,
April–May 1885
Die Kartoffelesser
Les Mangeurs de pommes de terre
Oil on canvas
Amsterdam, Van Gogh Museum
(Vincent van Gogh Foundation)

dessinateur de *Graphic* Luke Fildes, qui représente la chaise du bureau de Charles Dickens le lendemain de sa mort, devint pour lui le symbole de cette affinité élective (ills. p. 251).

La fonction de sa collection composée de 18 volumes lui apparaissait dans une lumière transfigurée. Il la recommanda comme «une sorte de Bible pour artiste», que l'on «devait avoir une fois pour toutes dans son atelier» (cfr. Jansen, n° 331). Au début, il profita surtout des motifs. Par la suite, lorsque les thèmes sociaux passèrent à l'arrière-plan, il se concentra de plus en plus sur les structures xylographiques des journaux illustrés. Pendant de nombreuses nuits d'insomnie, ce professionnel de l'estampe examina avec acribie les gravures et scruta les boucles dynamiques et les séries de lignes extatiques. Les illustrations copiées de gravures en lignes blanches d'un maître respecté comme Joseph Swain ont imprégné de manière durable ses futurs peintures et dessins à la plume de roseau (ills. p. 256).

Deux œuvres principales du journalisme illustré à tendance de critique sociale comptent parmi les éléments centraux de la bible artistique de Van Gogh : le récit burlesque de voyage d'Arthur Boyd Houghton *Graphic America* (1869–1870) et la vision intense d'une métropole, réalisée par Gustave Doré, *London: A Pilgrimage* (1867–1872). Il s'agit dans les deux cas de reportages complexes de grande envergure dans lesquels les motifs des dessins de presse furent reflétés et recodifiés. Ils marquèrent un point culminant et un tournant qui coïncida avec un double événement d'importance capitale pour l'histoire de la presse : la guerre franco-allemande de 1870/71 et l'instauration de la Commune de Paris qui s'ensuivit. La sanglante répression de cette tentative éphémère de réaliser une république à base démocratique eut pour conséquence un réajustement idéologique du paysage journalistique international. Au cours de l'ère suivante hautement impérialiste, le journalisme illustré se développa dans un climat de nationalisme.

Bien qu'un grand nombre de ses illustrateurs favoris fussent mêlés comme reporters ou activistes à la lutte pour la Commune de Paris, cet événement décisif n'est mentionné nulle part dans les commentaires de Van Gogh. Comme pour la plupart de ses collègues artistes, sa réaction fut de fuir l'enfer de 1871. Cependant, sous l'influence des œuvres d'Émile Zola et de Jules Michelet transparaît dans sa collection un intérêt croissant pour les messages de politique sociale qui succéda peu à peu à son enthousiasme pour le romantisme social de l'ère victorienne. Il analysa en profondeur les subtiles études de milieu du dessinateur Paul Renouard et établit de volumineux dossiers sur les champs thématiques qui lui permettaient d'étudier les injustices sociales dans le contexte historique.

Arthur Boyd Houghton & Joseph Swain (sc.)

Graphic America
Buffalo Hunting – Camping Out, 1871
Büffeljagd – Im Freien lagern
Chasse au buffle – camper en plein air
Wood engraving
From: *The Graphic,* London, 5 August 1871

"Coasting" at Omaha, 1871
Rutschpartie in Omaha | Glissade en Omaha
Wood engraving
From: *The Graphic*, London, 19 January 1871

The Religious Dance, 1870
Der religiöse Tanz | La Danse religieuse
Wood engraving
From: *The Graphic*, London, 14 August 1870

BUFFALO HUNTING—CAMPING OUT

"COASTING" AT OMAHA

Structural comparisons are shown here for certain details from Van Gogh's pen drawings and Arthur Boyd Houghton's wood engravings from the series *Graphic America.* Van Gogh wrote in relation to the latter that "When I can't sleep at night, which happens often, I return to the wood engravings and look through them again with renewed enjoyment."

Strukturvergleiche mit Details aus van Goghs Rohrfederzeichnungen und Arthur Boyd Houghtons Holzstichen aus *Graphic America,* über die

van Gogh schrieb: „Wenn ich nachts nicht schlafen kann, was oft passiert, stöber ich immer mit erneutem Vergnügen in den Holzstichen herum."

Comparaisons structurelles avec détails des dessins à la plume de roseau de Van Gogh et des gravures sur bois d'Arthur Boyd Houghton extraites de *Graphic America* à propos desquelles Van Gogh écrivait : «Quand je ne peux pas dormir la nuit, ce qui arrive souvent, je contemple les gravures sur bois avec un plaisir sans cesse renouvelé.»

Vincent van Gogh

Sunflowers, 1887
Sonnenblumen | *Tournesols*
Oil on canvas
Kunstmuseum Bern

Enclosed Wheat Field with Sun and Clouds, 1889
Eingezäuntes Weizenfeld mit Sonne und Wolken
Champ de blé avec soleil et nuages
Black chalk and reed pen
Otterlo, Kröller-Müller Museum

Wheat Field with Rising Sun, November/December 1889
Weizenfeld mit aufgehender Sonne | *Champ de blé au lever du soleil*
Black chalk and reed pen
Staatliche Graphische Sammlung München

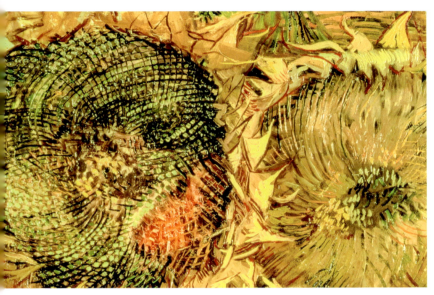

Hubert von Herkomer

Luke Fildes

↑ *Low Lodging House, St. Giles's*
(A Study from Life), 1872
Absteige, St. Giles's (Eine Studie nach dem Leben)
Bouge, St. Giles's (Une étude d'après la vie)
Wood engraving
From: *The Graphic*, London, 18 August 1872

In a letter to his friend the artist Anthon van Rappard
dated 26 February 1883, Van Gogh wrote that he
could "scarcely imagine anything more beautiful"
than this illustration. The scene showing a lodging
house for the poor in London was a source of inspiration for Van Gogh's Dutch colleagues, while in its
intimacy and dignified way of treating its delicate
subject matter it also served as a model for his own
important work, *The Potato Eaters* (1885; ill. p. 255).

Er könne sich „kaum etwas Schöneres vorstellen"
als diese Grafik, schrieb van Gogh an seinen Künst-
lerfreund Anthon van Rappard (Brief, 26. Februar
1883). Die Szene aus einer Londoner Pension für
Mittellose hatte nicht nur seinen niederländischen
Kollegen inspiriert. Die Intimität und Nobilität, mit
der das prekäre Sujet behandelt wird, war auch vorbildhaft für van Goghs Schlüsselwerk *Die Kartoffelesser* (1885; Abb. S. 255).

Van Gogh écrivit à son ami artiste Anthon van
Rappard qu'il ne pouvait «guère imaginer quelque
chose de plus beau» que cette illustration (Lettre,
26 février 1883). Cette scène d'une pension londonienne pour indigents n'a pas inspiré que son
collègue néerlandais. L'intimité et la noblesse, avec
lesquelles ce précaire sujet est traité, a aussi servi
de modèle à l'œuvre majeure de Van Gogh *Les
Mangeurs de pommes de terre* (1885; ill. p. 255).

Houseless and Hungry, 1869
Obdachlos und hungrig | *Sans abri et affamés*
Wood engraving
From: *The Graphic Portfolio*, London, 1877

This picture of a group of homeless people waiting to be let in to a night shelter appeared in
the first issue of *The Graphic* towards the end of
1869 and became a major work for the new style
of social realism, as exemplified by artists such
as Luke Fildes and especially his fellow student
Hubert von Herkomer. Van Gogh had a copy of it
in the special edition *Graphic Portfolio*, in which
the illustrations had been printed directly from the
original woodblocks.

Die Darstellung einer Gruppe Obdachloser, die
auf Einlass ins Nachtasyl wartet, war Ende 1869
in der Startnummer des *Graphic* erschienen und
wurde zum Schlüsselwerk eines neuen Sozialrealismus, für den neben Luke Fildes vor allem dessen Studienkollege Hubert von Herkomer stand.
Van Gogh verfügte über ein solches Exemplar aus
der Sonderedition *Graphic Portfolio*, das direkt
vom Holzstock gedruckt worden war.

La représentation d'un groupe de sans-abri,
qui attendent d'être admis dans un asile de nuit,
était parue fin 1869 dans le premier numéro
du *Graphic* et devint l'œuvre clé d'un nouveau
réalisme social. Son défenseur le plus assidu,
avec Luke Fildes, était surtout son compagnon
d'études Hubert von Herkomer. Van Gogh disposait d'une copie de l'édition spéciale *Graphic
Portfolio*, qui avait été directement imprimée à
partir du bloc de bois.

Hubert von Herkomer & Joseph Swain (sc.)

↑ *Blind Basket-makers*, 1870
Blinde Korbmacher | *Vanniers aveugles*
Wood engraving
From: *The Illustrated London News*,
30 September 1870

Van Gogh felt an affinity for Hubert von Herkomer since he had also "had to struggle with a kind of awkwardness" (letter to Theo, 3 February 1883). All the main stylistic features that inspired Van Gogh are apparent even in the earliest of Herkomer's socially realistic illustrations for the press, namely figures drawn in a strong manner with expressive use of lines, a claustrophobic depiction of space that pulled viewers in and a careful use of light.

Van Gogh fühlte sich Hubert von Herkomer nahe, da auch dieser „mit einer Art Ungeschicklichkeit zu kämpfen" (Brief an Theo, 3. Februar 1883) gehabt habe. Bereits in Herkomers frühester sozialrealistischer Pressegrafik sind alle wesentlichen Stilmerkmale ausgeprägt, die van Gogh inspiriert haben: markige Figurenzeichnung, expressives Lineament, klaustrophober Raumsog und eine pointierte Lichtregie.

Van Gogh se sentait proche d'Hubert von Herkomer parce que ce dernier aussi «avait eu à lutter avec une sorte de maladresse» (lettre à Théo, 3 février 1883). Déjà dans les dessins de presse précoces d'Herkomer imprégnés de réalisme social apparaissent toutes les caractéristiques de style qui ont inspiré Van Gogh : dessin vigoureux des figures, trait expressif, magnétisme spatial claustrophobe et une utilisation minutieuse de la lumière.

Hubert von Herkomer

Studies for Blind Basket-makers, 1870
Studien für Blinde Korbmacher
Études pour Vanniers aveugles
Pencil on paper

Before drawing his designs directly on to the wooden blocks, Herkomer prepared his illustrations by making detailed individual studies. Van Gogh adopted one of Herkomer's maxims that he had read in his writings: "Draw in a plain but forceful manner so that the engraver remains what he is supposed to be, the translator of the draughtsman's work, and does not in any way take over" (letter to Theo, 1 November 1882).

Hubert von Herkomer hatte, bevor er das Motiv direkt auf den Holzblock zeichnete, detaillierte Einzelstudien betrieben. Ein Motto aus seinen Lehrschriften hatte van Gogh sich zu eigen gemacht: „Zeichne sachlich und kraftvoll, damit der Stecher bleibt, was er soll, der Übersetzer der Arbeit des Zeichners, und er nicht die Oberhand gewinnt" (Brief an Theo, 1. November 1882).

Avant de dessiner le motif directement sur le bloc de bois, Hubert von Herkomer avait réalisé des études individuelles détaillées. Van Gogh avait fait sienne une devise de ses écrits didactiques : «Dessine avec sobriété et force pour que le graveur reste ce qu'il est, le traducteur du travail du dessinateur, et qu'il ne prenne pas le dessus» (lettre à Théo, Iᵉʳ novembre 1882).

Vincent van Gogh

At Eternity's Gate, 1882
An der Schwelle zur Ewigkeit | *Au seuil de l'éternité*
Transfer lithograph
Amsterdam, Van Gogh Museum

One of Van Gogh's models for his extensive series of drawings based on *Heads of the People* was this old pensioner in a home for veterans. In order to get closer to his ideal of an inexpensive form of popular illustration Van Gogh experimented with autographic ink and transfer paper. The result could then be reproduced as a relief engraving or, as in this case, a transfer lithograph.

Ein Pensionär aus einem Veteranenheim diente van Gogh als Modell für eine umfangreiche Serie von Zeichnungen nach dem Vorbild der *Heads of the People*. Um seinem Ideal preiswerter Populärgrafik näher zu kommen, experimentierte er mit autografischer Tusche und Umdruckpapier. Das Resultat konnte dann als Hochätzung oder wie in diesem Fall als Transferlithografie vervielfältigt werden.

Un retraité d'un home pour vétérans sert de modèle à Van Gogh pour une vaste série de dessins inspirés des *Heads of the People*. Pour se rapprocher de son idéal d'une illustration populaire peu coûteuse, il expérimenta à l'aide d'encre autographique et de papier transfert. Le résultat pouvait ensuite être reproduit sous forme de gravure en relief ou, comme c'est le cas ici, en lithographie sur papier transfert.

Hubert von Herkomer & C. Roberts (sc.)

Heads of the People II: The Agricultural Labourer – Sunday, 1875
Köpfe des Volkes II: Der Landarbeiter – Sonntag
Têtes du peuple II : Le Laboureur – Dimanche
Wood engraving
From: *The Graphic*, London, 9 October 1875

In June 1875 *The Graphic* began a second series of *Heads of the People* following on from the genre-defining study of types by Kenny Meadows (1840/41, ills. p. 136). By June 1883 nine portraits of English characters by different artists had appeared, on a sporadic basis, with personal attributes that were intended to reveal their social status. Van Gogh was deeply impressed by the powerful realism in some of these illustrations.

Im Juni 1875 startete der *Graphic* ein Sequel von Kenny Meadows' genreprägender Typologie *Heads of the People* (1840/41, Abb. S. 136). In loser Folge erschienen bis Juni 1883 von verschiedenen Autoren neun Porträts englischer Charaktere, deren Attribute den sozialen Stand verraten sollten. Van Gogh war vom kernigen Realismus einiger dieser Blätter nachhaltig beeindruckt.

En juin 1875, le *Graphic* lança une suite à la typologie marquante en son genre de Kenny Meadows *Heads of the People* (1840/41, ills. p. 136). À partir de juin 1883, neuf portraits de caractères anglais réalisés par différents auteurs parurent sporadiquement, et leurs attributs devaient révéler leur statut social. Van Gogh fut profondément impressionné par le puissant réalisme de certaines planches.

360   THE GRAPHIC   [*Oct.* 9, 1875

HEADS OF THE PEOPLE DRAWN FROM LIFE, II.
"THE AGRICULTURAL LABOURER—SUNDAY"

Hubert von Herkomer & Heinrich Sigismund Uhlrich (sc.)

Heads of the People VIII: The Coastguardsman, 1879
Köpfe des Volkes VIII: Der Küstenwachmann
Têtes du peuple VIII: Le garde-côte
Wood engraving
From: *The Graphic*, London, 20 September 1879

When *The Graphic* announced a forthcoming series for 1883 of academic portraits produced by chromolithography, Van Gogh viewed it as a real break with culture: "*The Graphic* now wants to do *Types of Beauty* (large heads of different women), according to its prospectus, doubtless to stand in for the *Heads of the People* […] And *The Graphic* is saying they'll be chromos!!! Give us Swain's workshop any time […] I can't do TYPES OF BEAUTY, but I'll do what I can for HEADS OF THE PEOPLE. […] I want to work in the same way as those who did when *The Graphic* started […], you know, taking some fellow, or a woman or child, from the street and drawing them in my studio. But no, what they'll say is 'Can you do some chromos for us, made under electric light?'" (letter to Theo, 11 December 1882).

Als der *Graphic* für 1883 eine Reihe mit akademischen Porträts in Chromolithografien ankündigte, nahm van Gogh das als regelrechten Kulturbruch wahr: „Der *Graphic* will jetzt *Types of Beauty* bringen (große Köpfe von Frauen), heißt es im Propekt, zweifellos um die *Heads of the People* zu ersetzen. […] Der *Graphic* sagt, sie wollten Chromos bringen!!!! Gebt uns die Werkstatt von Swain zurück. […] Ich kann keine TYPES OF BEAUTY machen – aber ich werd mein Bestes geben, um HEADS OF THE PEOPLE zu realisieren. […] Ich will so vorgehen wie die, die den *Graphic* gestartet haben […], nämlich einen Kerl oder eine Frau oder ein Kind von der Straße holen und es in meinem Atelier machen. Aber nein, sie würden verlangen: ‚Kannst du uns nicht Chromos bei Kunstlicht liefern?'" (Brief an Theo, 11. Dezember 1882).

Lorsqu'en 1883 le *Graphic* annonça une série de portraits académiques en chromolithographie, Van Gogh le ressentit comme une véritable rupture culturelle : « Le *Graphic* veut maintenant faire des *Types of Beauty* (grandes têtes de femmes), dit le prospectus, sans doute pour remplacer les *Heads of the People*. […] Le *Graphic* dit qu'ils veulent faire des chromos !!! Rendez-nous le studio de Swain. […] Je ne peux pas faire de TYPES OF BEAUTY – mais je ferai de mon mieux pour réaliser des HEADS OF THE PEOPLE. […] Je veux faire comme ceux qui ont commencé le *Graphic* […], c'est-à-dire aller chercher un type ou une femme ou un enfant de la rue et le faire dans mon atelier. Mais non, ils demanderaient : « Peux-tu nous faire des chromos à la lumière électrique ? » (Lettre à Théo, 11 décembre 1882).

HEADS OF THE PEOPLE—"THE COASTGUARDSMAN"
DRAWN BY HUBERT HERKOMER

Vincent van Gogh

The Postmaster Joseph Roulin, Arles, August 1888
Der Postmeister Joseph Roulin
Joseph Roulin, le postier
Reed pen and goose-feather quill pen
Los Angeles, Getty Museum Collection

A Zouave, Arles, July/August 1888
Ein Zuave | Un Zouave
Pencil, reed pen and goose-feather quill pen
New York, The Solomon R. Guggenheim Museum

Van Gogh's late *Heads of the People* were done with a Japanese reed pen, which gave results that were closer to the rough yet expressive style of wood engravings of years past than the chalks he had originally used for his drawings.

Seine späten *Heads of the People* realisierte van Gogh mit der japanischen Rohrfeder, die den schroffen und expressiven Strukturen der Old-School-Xylografie näherkam als die Kreiden, die er anfänglich für seine Zeichnungen verwendet hatte.

Van Gogh réalisa ses *Heads of the People* tardives en utilisant la plume de roseau japonaise qui donnait des résultats plus proches des structures rudes et expressives de la xylographie « old school » que les craies dont il s'était d'abord servi pour ses dessins.

←← **Arthur Boyd Houghton & Joseph Swain (sc.)**

Graphic America:
Barber's Saloon in New York, 1870
Barbiersalon in New York
Salon de barbier à New York
Wood engraving
From: *The Graphic*, London, 16 April 1870

Arthur Boyd Houghton's reports from North America appeared in *The Graphic* for almost three years. Van Gogh was fascinated by their illustrations, as was the established critic Harry Quilter who considered the Anglo-Indian Houghton an original genius and *Graphic America* the best illustrated travel reports ever to have been published in the press.

Arthur Boyd Houghtons Nordamerika-Reportage ist im *Graphic* über einen Zeitraum von fast drei Jahren erschienen. Van Gogh war von den Zeichnungen fasziniert, ebenso der namhafte Kritiker Harry Quilter, der den angloindischen Künstler für ein Originalgenie hielt und *Graphic America* für den besten illustrierten Reisebericht, der je in der Presse erschienen war.

Le reportage d'Arthur Boyd Houghton sur l'Amérique du Nord parut dans le *Graphic* sur une période de presque trois ans. Van Gogh était fasciné par les dessins, tout autant que le fameux critique Harry Quilter qui considérait l'artiste anglo-indien comme un génie original et *Graphic America* comme le meilleur récit de voyage illustré jamais paru dans la presse.

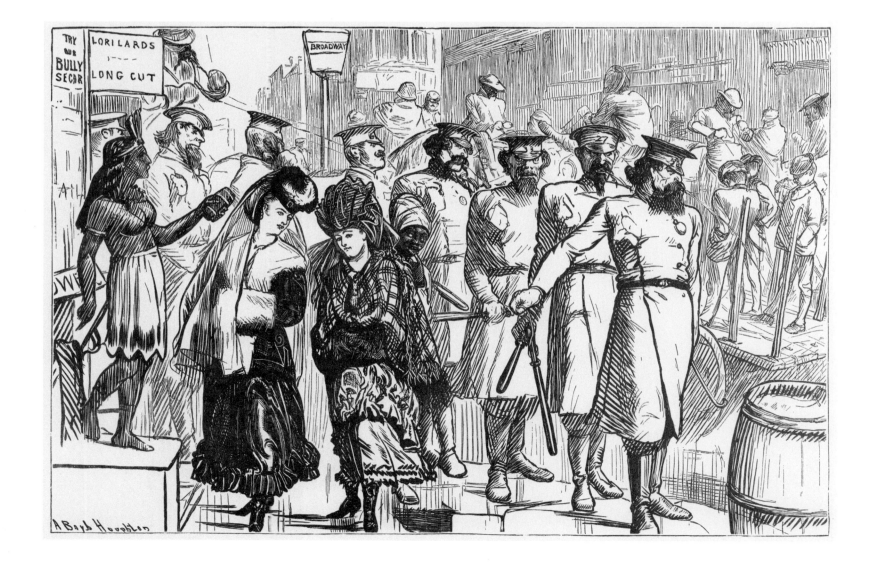

Arthur Boyd Houghton

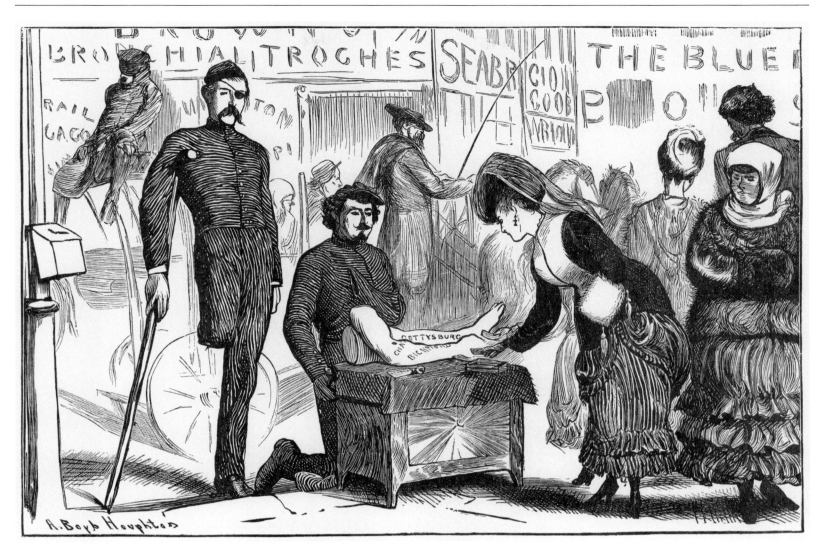

Graphic America:
Boston Pets, 1870
Bostoner Schätzchen | Chouchous de Boston
Wood engraving
From: *The Graphic*, London, 30 April 1870

The urban scenes in *Graphic America* convey a grim impression of life in the bigger cities in the period after the Civil War, when corruption and speculation were rife. Arthur Boyd Houghton's grotesque style of social realism was derived from the flourishes found in Pre-Raphaelite illustrations.

Die urbanen Szenen in *Graphic America* vermitteln einen sinistren Eindruck von der Vitalität der amerikanischen Metropolen während der von Korruption und Spekulantentum dominierten Aufbruchsphase nach dem Bürgerkrieg. Arthur Boyd Houghtons grotesker Sozialrealismus leitete sich von der arabesken präraffaelitischen Illustrationskunst ab.

Les scènes urbaines de *Graphic America* donne une sinistre impression de la vitalité des métropoles américaines pendant la période de reconstruction qui suivit la guerre de Sécession et fut dominée par la corruption et la spéculat on. Le grotesque réalisme social d'Arthur Boyd Houghton était dérivé des fioritures propres aux illustrations des préraphaélites.

Arthur Boyd Houghton

← *Graphic America:*
New York Police, 1870
New Yorker Polizei | Police de New York
Wood engraving
From: *The Graphic*, London, 16 April 1870

→ *Graphic America:*
Rag Collectors in Chicago, 1870
Lumpensammler in Chicago | Chiffonniers à Chicago
Wood engraving
From: *The Graphic*, London, 9 April 1870

Arthur Boyd Houghton & William Luson Thomas (sc.)

Graphic America:
In the Rag Trade, 1870
Im Lumpenhandel
Au commerce de chiffons
Wood engraving
From: *The Graphic*, London, 7 May 1870

Under its celebrated art director Charles Parsons, *Harper's Weekly* published a few examples from Arthur Boyd Houghton's socially critical reports. While certain parts were edited or redrawn to remove some of the more overt references, the scenes showing the run-down Five Points district of New York City still provoked a storm of outrage.

Unter seinem legendären Artdirector Charles Parsons entschied sich *Harper's Weekly*, Arthur Boyd Houghtons sozial-kritischen Report auszugsweise abzudru-cken. Doch obgleich einzelne Passagen entschärft worden waren, riefen vor allem die Szenen aus dem berüchtigten New Yorker Slumquartier Five Points einen Sturm der Entrüstung hervor.

À l'initiative de son directeur artistique légendaire Charles Parsons, *Harper's Weekly* décida d'imprimer des extraits du reportage de critique sociale réalisé par Arthur Boyd Houghton. Mais même si certains passages parurent dans une ver-sion édulcorée, les scènes dépeignant notamment Five Points, le quartier popu-laire mal famé de New York, suscitèrent une vague d'indignation.

Arthur Boyd Houghton

Graphic America:
The Rag-picker, 1870
Die Lumpensammlerin | La Chiffonnière
Wood engraving
From: *Harper's Weekly*, New York,
7 May 1870

In the watered-down American version the disrespectful portrayal of the police-man was changed and the street cleared of rubbish.

In der entschärften amerikanischen Fassung wurde die despektierliche Dar-stellung des Polizisten verändert und die Straße vom Müll befreit.

Dans la version américaine édulcorée, la représentation irrespectueuse du poli-cier fut modifiée, et la rue débarrassée de ses ordures.

→ **Arthur Boyd Houghton**

Graphic America:
Among the Aborigines, 1870
Unter den Ureinwohnern | Parmi les autochtones

→→ **Arthur Boyd Houghton**
& Joseph Swain (sc.)

Graphic America:
A Pawnee Camp in Midwinter/Pawnees
Gambling, 1870
Ein Pawnee-Lager mitten im Winter/Pawnees
beim Glücksspiel
Un Camp pawnee en plein hiver/Pawnees
en train de jouer
Wood engravings
From: *The Graphic*, London, 23 July 1870

While visiting a Pawnee reservation in Nebraska, Houghton witnessed the living conditions of the indigenous population which, far from presenting any kind of romantic image, were instead dominated by gambling and alcoholism. In his empathetic report Houghton, who was born in India, toyed with racist clichés while at the same time mocking his own participation as an intruder and voyeur.

In Nebraska wurde Houghton in einem Reservat der Pawnees Zeuge der wenig romantischen, von Spiel- und Alkoholsucht bestimmten Lebensumstände der indigenen Bevölkerung. In seinem empathischen Report spielt der angloindische Künstler mit rassistischen Klischees und nimmt dabei auch die eigene Rolle als Eindringling und Voyeur aufs Korn.

Dans une réserve de Pawnees du Nebraska, Houghton fut témoin des conditions de vie peu romantiques et dominées par l'addiction au jeu et l'alcoolisme de la population autochtone. Dans son reportage empathique, l'artiste anglo-indien joue avec les clichés racistes et raille aussi par la même occasion son propre rôle d'intrus et de voyeur.

Arthur Boyd Houghton & Joseph Swain (sc.)

Graphic America:
Shaker Evans at Home, 1871
Shaker Evans zu Hause
Shaker Evans à la maison
Wood engraving
From: *The Graphic*, London,
26 August 1871

On his journey west Houghton visited the Shaker sect in Ohio and drew their evening ceremony. Van Gogh saw "something in the style of Goya" in the somnambulistic atmosphere of these illustrations, "but then all of a sudden there is something else like an undercurrent that in its extraordinary severity recalls [Charles] Meryon" (letter to Theo, 26/27 January 1883).

Auf seiner Reise in den Westen besuchte Houghton in Ohio die Sekte der Shaker und zeichnete deren Abendzeremoniell. Van Gogh nahm in der somnambulen Atmosphäre dieser Grafiken „etwas Goya-artiges" wahr, „aber dann taucht auf einmal in der unteren Schicht etwas auf, das wegen der außerordentlichen Strenge an [Charles] Meryon erinnert" (Brief an Theo, 26./27. Januar 1883).

Au cours de son voyage à l'Ouest, Houghton rendit visite à la secte des shakers dans l'Ohio et dessina leur cérémonie vespérale. Van Gogh perçut l'atmosphère somnambulique de ces esquisses comme « goyaesque, mais tout à coup apparaît quelque chose qui rappelle [Charles] Meryon en raison de son extraordinaire austérité » (lettre à Théo, 26/27 janvier 1883).

GRAPHIC AMERICA

AMONG THE ABORIGINES

WHAT would be the future of the American Indian has always been somewhat a mystery, and how he should be treated somewhat of a puzzle, to the white invaders and conquerors of his ancient hunting grounds. Would he gradually be absorbed in the white race—gradually, in succession of generations, changing the hue of his skin, the manner of his life, the object of his worship; becoming a citizen and a voter running for Congress, and preaching from Methodist pulpits? Or would he cleave to his old nature and habits, reject the proffered prizes of another civilisation, and like Achilles, sit for ever sulking in his tent. If so, how to deal with him? should he be permitted still to occupy, without subduing and cultivating, the heart of the continent, and devote its most fruitful plains and valleys to hunting wild deer and buffaloes, and, while warring upon his savage neighbours, bloodily repelling the advance of white settlements? Or should he be driven back—back to the innermost depths of the far western wilds, to the farthest corners of obscure mountain ranges and remotest forests by the bayonet and the cannon, and the fatal force of civilised discipline? The question remains to be answered. The Indian will not mix with the white man. He looks with a sort of contempt even upon him whom he with apparent reverence calls "The Great Father"—none other than the President of the White House. He recedes farther and farther from the white settlements, year by year. Now and then he sweeps down upon an infant colony with hellish clamour, and massacres helpless emigrants, and bears thence in trophy the scalps of babes, and the long hair of women. His preference for the old savagery is indomitable, and he will never be brought to live in cities, to drudge, and by the sweat of his brow to earn his daily bread. The race is dying out; and it is an inevitable death. The Indians are fewer every year, their domain is each year narrowing; their resistance to civilisation is each year feebler. One cannot see the visibly approaching extinction of so noble a race, in many respects, without an emotion of pity and sadness. How stout was the strength and how splendid the valour of the Indian warrior a short century ago. Who of our readers has not read the glowing pages of Fenimore Cooper, and wept over the fatal courage of the "Last of the Mohicans," and been thrilled by the exciting scenes, adventures, and escapes which abound in his pages, presenting us with a vivid picture of the early contact of the white race with the red? Where, within the life of men now living, the tribes were wont to worship the Old Man in the Clouds, and to dance the wild, weird scalp dance by glimmering bonfires—there are now cities and commonwealths; cities, note you, where Henry Ward Beecher delivers lectures, where ladies in late Paris fashions and the Grecian bend, promenade these summer evenings, and go to the opera; where you may find thousands of copies of the stories of beloved Dickens; where there are woman suffrage conventions, and mercantile halls, and gas lights, and water, hot and cold, in the bath-rooms. But the Indian, whilst savage and morose for ever, has not in vain felt the contact with the whites. He has not absolutely shunned communication with his conquerors. Possibly for all the good that contact has done him, it were better it had never taken place. Chippewa and Sioux, Hiawatha and Minne-ha-ha, seem to have a marvellous faculty for catching up and clinging to the vices, while utterly passing by and ignoring the virtues of his enlightened unwelcome neighbour. With a superstitiously reverent nature, he has become a curser and swearer, outcursing and outswearing the most inveterate Far Western scallawag whom you may find gambling on Mississippi steamboats, or guzzling abominable whisky at a pioneer military station. The thoroughly inoculated Indian is profane with a gusto and enthusiasm such as takes aback ears most familiar with the ingenious oaths of an alley bar-room. He swears on the slightest occasion, when he is pleased as when he is wroth; whether he be calm or excited; whether in company with delightful companion scallawags, or whether squatted before his hut, smoking the calumet with his squaw, and toying bearishly with his ugliest and favourite papoose. He swears as if it were a keen luxury newly discovered, a fresh language learned, with as much relish as a fashionable young lady, from a fashionable boarding school, experiments her French in the presence of an admiring family on landing at Calais; 'Son of the Forest conceiving it a rare triumph to outswear his rival Painted Eagle, and crowing over poor discomfited Painted Eagle threat.

Then, too, the modern Hiawatha drinks. Indeed, "fire water," was not wanting to the primitive Indian described by Cooper. In the days of the American Revolution we hear of Indians selling themselves, to serve as spies and guerillas, for "fire water." It was an excitement which seemed to suit their strong, fiery, impulsive natures. A taste once had of brandy, whisky, and gin, and they were no longer content with the fresh pure springs which bubbled up in the depths of the forest; they no longer endured the bark cup of water with a spicing of honey pressed into it out of the comb; nor the beverages which they were wont to concoct out of innocent roots, herbs, and flowers. Almost the first we hear of the communion of Indians with the whites, is of the exchange of mocassins and painted bags for whisky. We may well believe that the New England Indians, the tribes of "Massachusetts," did not derive any such temptation of the Evil One from the Puritans; as little is it to be imagined that Pennsylvanian chieftains quaffed strong drinks in their conferences with good William Penn, the Quaker; though, possibly, that liberal-minded founder of commercial commonwealths may not unlikely have brought out some nutty sherry or fine old crusted port, after the conclusion of an especially satisfactory treaty with Delaware sachems or Alleghany chiefs. Penn, though a Quaker, was no Puritan; but a courtier of the sleek order, and not grumpish in the matter of beverages. More probably the Indians derived their first experiences of "fire-water" either from the pleasure-loving Cavalier colony of Virginia or the Catholic one of Maryland; or, as possibly, from the French and English settlers in Canada. However they came by it, they were soon drawn to it as a moth to the candle-light; and now, whatever Indian by any odd chance gets involved in a city or village of the whites is almost certain to be the champion drunkard of the place. Government, in past times, has not disdained to ply them with whisky, and has been able to obtain from them, in return, substantial concessions in the matter of treaties—a disgraceful practice which in these latter more enlightened times has happily been abandoned, but abandoned too late to save the poor savage race from the evils of intoxication and moral ruin. Meaner men—the scallawags of the borders—still take advantage of this peculiar weakness of the Indian: he is robbed by thieves, bamboozled by marauders, violated at his hearth-stone, cheated by cheats; because he can never resist the ugly bottleful of spitfire poison which they thrust in his face. As for the sexes, there is but little difference in this matter of loving "fire-water." The Indian squaw is but a shade less masculine than her Hiawatha; Minne-ha-ha is no delicately coppery beauty. The poem is an imagination, beautiful but misleading, especially as far as it regards the heroine:—

> Minne-ha-ha, laughing water,
> Loveliest of Dacotah women,

is found by the modern traveller, who ventures into the tents of the "ancient arrow-maker," to have, indeed, "her moods of shade and sunshine"—mostly the former—"eyes that smile and frown alternate,"—the alternate frown preponderating :—

> Feet as rapid as the river,
> Tresses flowing like the water—

UTE SQUAWS

the feet very large, and the tresses like horsehair. But the modern traveller must look long before he finds the "musical laughter;" or before any later Minne-ha-ha inspires him, or would seem capable of inspiring even Hiawatha, with "dreams of beauty." The belles of the forest are more faithfully, if unpoetically, depicted by our artist, who gives us a view of two tender young mothers bearing their babes up across a mountain pass. Were it not for their dress you would never imagine their sex. Their faces are wooden in their hardness and fixed expression; and the men, any more than the women, do not have beards. That femininity is not feminine among the aborigines is easily accounted for when we think of the hard climate to which they are subjected, the fearful drudgery which they are called upon to undergo, and the enthralled condition in which their lives are passed. We have seen somewhere an account of an Indian courtship, which was as amusing as it was contrary to our own sentimental Saxon "ideas of what a courtship should be." The gambollings of the lovers were elephantine, and the mutual attentions as rough and as little shy as one might well imagine. Not that the passion of love is not strong in the aboriginal breast. The Indian has a lion-like, chivalrous, and often touching affection for his squaw, which causes him to guard her with extreme jealousy, often impels him to murder, and which is never dimmed by age, by ugliness, or even by drunkenness. The women not only drink as sedulously as their lords, but they gamble even more sedulously. In two pictures the artist gives us a view of gambling parties in the camps and prairies. In that depicting "Pawnees gambling," the reader has a vivid portraiture of a company of squaws, young and old, engaged in playing at chequers, in which he has faithfully reproduced, not only a scene frequently to be encountered in the outskirts of the Western settlements, but the minutest details of the Indian physiognomy and dress; and has given us in the faces, postures, and adornments, an excellent hint of the female Indian character. They are not, however, specimens of that primitive and uncorrupted Indian race which we have so admired in the glowing pictures of the "Deerhunter" and the "Last of the Mohicans," but the commonplace reality of these modern days: coarse passions and vulgarity evident in their expression; grovelling dispositions in attitude and gesture, grossly fond of sensual excitement, yet retaining all the old barbarian rudeness, courage, and strength; and suffering the association of whites because these have introduced them to the luxuries of crime. The games of cards played by the Indians are those mostly in vogue among the Western card-players, among which figure prominently cribbage, "seven-up," "high, low, jack," whist, and euchre. Whether the fashionable game of bezique has penetrated to the aborigines or not we are unable to report; but they are shrewd players, and can cheat as deftly as did the men with whom Little Nell's grandfather played in the churchyard. The picture of the "Pawnee

CARDS ON THE PRAIRIE

Camp in Midwinter" explains itself; some of the Indians are bringing in sticks for their fires and hay for their horses, while one is shown at the side dressing skins.

THE Foreign Office has issued a notice recommending all those who mean to try Continental travelling to look to their passports, and see that they are duly *viséd* for the countries they intend to visit.

A PAWNEE CAMP IN MIDWINTER

PAWNEES GAMBLING

Arthur Boyd Houghton & Joseph Swain (sc.)

Graphic America:
Crossing a Cañon, 1871
Durchquerung eines Canyons
Traversée d'un canyon
Wood engraving
From: *The Graphic*, London,
29 July 1871

Arthur Boyd Houghton called himself a "one-eyed artist" because of an accident he had suffered when he was a child, but this did not prevent him during his trek to the west coast of the United States from joining a buffalo-hunting expedition with the world-famous Buffalo Bill. The two-dimensional spatial quality of this somewhat spectral scene, with its different points of focus, reveals his interest in Japanese prints.

Arthur Boyd Houghton nannte sich „one-eyed artist", weil er als Kind einen Unfall gehabt hatte. Das hielt ihn aber auf seinem Weg zur Westküste nicht davon ab, sich einem Büffeljägertreck unter der Leitung des legendären Buffalo Bill anzuschließen. Die flächige, polyfokale Raumauffassung der gespenstischen Szene verrät seine Auseinandersetzung mit japanischer Druckgrafik.

Arthur Boyd Houghton se décrivait lui-même comme « artiste borgne » à cause d'un accident survenu dans son enfance. Ce qui toutefois ne l'empêcha pas de se joindre à un groupe de chasseurs de buffles mené par le légendaire Buffalo Bill sur la route le menant vers la côte ouest. La conception spatiale, plate et polyfocale, de la scène fantomatique révèle son analyse des estampes japonaises.

Graphic America:
Buffalo Hunting – Camping out, 1871
Büffeljagd – Im Freien lagern
Chasse au buffle – camper en plein air
Wood engraving
From: *The Graphic*, London,
5 August 1871

As an illustrator, Arthur Boyd Houghton provided his engravers with an exact template by drawing his designs directly on to the wooden blocks with pencil, pen, wash and opaque white. Many of the expressive illustrations for *Graphic America* were produced in Joseph Swain's workshop, and Van Gogh preferred the engravings made there to even those made by such old masters as Rembrandt and Jacob van Ruisdael.

Arthur Boyd Houghton gehörte zu den Illustratoren, die ihren Graveuren präzise Vorlagen lieferten, indem sie mit Bleistift, Feder, Lavur und Deckweiß direkt auf die Blöcke zeichneten. Viele der expressiven Stiche von *Graphic America* wurden von der Werkstatt Joseph Swain ausgeführt, deren Xylografien van Gogh sogar den Stichen von Altmeistern wie Rembrandt oder Jacob van Ruisdael vorzog.

Arthur Boyd Houghton était l'un des illustrateurs qui fournissaient à leurs graveurs des modèles précis en les dessinant directement sur les blocs avec mine de plomb, plume, lavis et blanc opaque. Nombre des gravures expressives de *Graphic America* furent élaborées par l'atelier de Joseph Swain, dont Van Gogh préférait même les xylographies aux gravures de grands maîtres comme Rembrandt ou Jacob van Ruisdael.

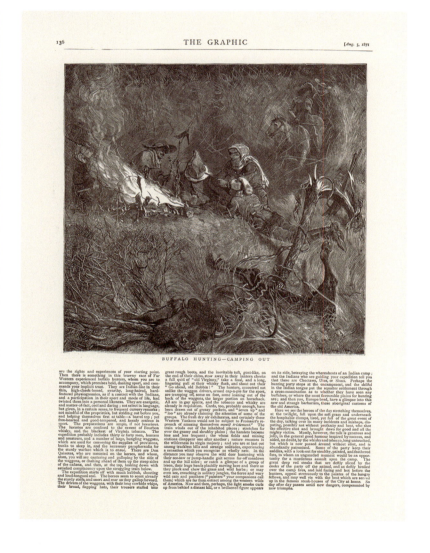

Ernest Griset

→ *A Dogs' Dinner Party in Paris*
(from a Sketch by Balloon Post),
1870
Eine Dinnerparty für Hunde in
Paris (nach einer per Ballonpost
zugestellten Skizze)
Un Dîner pour chiens à Paris
(d'après un croquis expédié par
ballon courrier)
Wood engraving
From: *The Graphic*, London,
10 December 1870

When the Franco-Prussian War began in July 1870 *The Graphic* saw its opportunity to assert itself as a serious rival to the main newspaper of the day, *The Illustrated London News*. This illustration of a pack of starving dogs reflects the dire situation in the French capital after months of being besieged by the German forces.

Der Krieg, der im Juli 1870 zwischen Frankreich und Preußen ausgebrochen war, bot dem *Graphic* die Gelegenheit, sich gegenüber der marktführenden *Illustrated London News* als ernst zu nehmender Konkurrent zu behaupten. Die Abbildung der verhungernden Hunde gibt die Misere in der von Truppen des deutschen Bundes eingekesselten französischen Hauptstadt wieder.

La guerre qui avait éclaté en juillet 1870 entre la France et la Prusse fournit au *Graphic* l'occasion de s'affirmer comme concurrent à prendre au sérieux face aux *Illustrated London News* qui dominaient le marché. La représentation des chiens affamés reflète la misère de la capitale française encerclée par les troupes allemandes.

A DOGS' DINNER PARTY IN PARIS
(FROM A SKETCH BY BALLOON POST)

THE PARIS MOB—A

ARRICADE IN PARIS

THE ILLUSTRATED LONDON NEWS

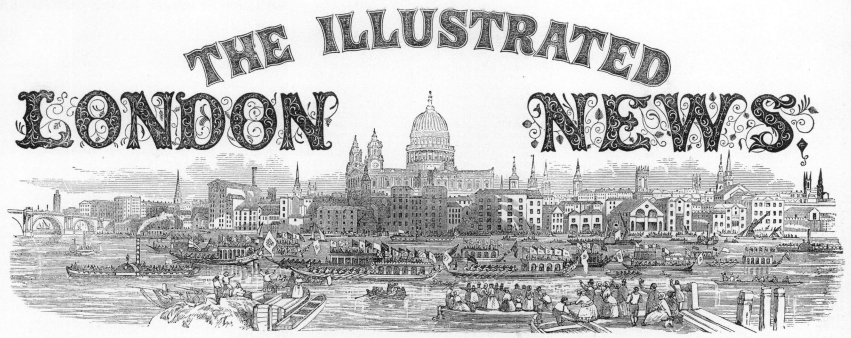

REGISTERED AT THE GENERAL POST-OFFICE FOR TRANSMISSION ABROAD.

No. 1648.— VOL. LVIII.   SATURDAY, APRIL 29, 1871.   PRICE FIVEPENCE
BY POST, 5½D.

THE CIVIL WAR IN FRANCE: A SHELL AT SURESNES.—FROM A SKETCH TAKEN IMMEDIATELY AFTER THE EXPLOSION.
SEE PAGE 423.

←←Arthur Boyd Houghton & Horace Harral (sc.)

Daniel Vierge & Auguste Lançon

The Paris Mob –
A Barricade in Paris, 1871
Der Pariser Pöbel –
Eine Barrikade in Paris
La Foule de Paris –
Une barricade à Paris
Wood engraving
From: *The Graphic*, London,
8 April 1871

After the French had surrendered,
disputes boiled up between the
bourgeois executive government and
the National Guard, and when an
attempt was made to disarm these
reserve forces a revolt broke out,
which Arthur Boyd Houghton was
on hand to record. The fighting on
the barricades, a subject Eugène
Delacroix had earlier depicted as a
heroic stand, was transformed by
Houghton into a delirious scene that
looked more like a black mass.

Nach der französischen Kapitulation
war es zu Konflikten zwischen der
bürgerlichen Exekutivregierung und
der Nationalgarde gekommen. Bei
dem Versuch, sie zu entwaffnen,
brach eine Revolte aus, die von Arthur
Boyd Houghton festgehalten wurde.
Das Motiv des Barrikadenkampfs,
das durch Eugène Delacroix heroisch
konnotiert war, verkehrte er in ein
schwarzmagisches Delirium.

Après la capitulation française, des
conflits étaient survenus entre le
gouvernement bourgeois exécutif et
la Garde nationale. Pendant une tentative de désarmement, une révolte
éclata, qu'Arthur Boyd Houghton fixa
sur image. Le motif du combat de barricades, auquel Eugène Delacroix a
conféré des accents héroïques, tourne
chez lui au délire de magie noire.

The Civil War, 1871
Der Bürgerkrieg | La Guerre civile
Wood engraving
From: *Le Monde illustré*, Paris,
22 April 1871

The fighting between the rebel forces
and the troops of the Versailles government is shown here as seen from
Montmartre, where the revolt had
begun following the attempt to disarm
the National Guard. The Spanish-born
Daniel Vierge, whose work Van Gogh
admired, began his phenomenal career
as an illustrator for the press with his
reports on the civil war in France.

Die Gefechte zwischen den Revolutionären und den Versailler Regierungstruppen vom Montmartre aus gesehen,
wo die Ereignisse durch den Ent-
waffnungsversuch der Nationalgarde
ihren Ausgang genommen hatten.
Der von van Gogh bewunderte spanische Zeichner Daniel Vierge startete
mit seinen Kriegsberichten in Frankreich eine phänomenale Karriere als
Pressegrafiker.

Les combats opposant les révolutionnaires et les troupes du gouvernement
de Versailles sont observés depuis
Montmartre où avaient éclaté les événements dus à la tentative de désarmement de la Garde nationale. Le
dessinateur espagnol Daniel Vierge,
que Van Gogh admirait, amorça une
carrière phénoménale de dessinateur
de presse grâce à ses reportages de
guerre en France.

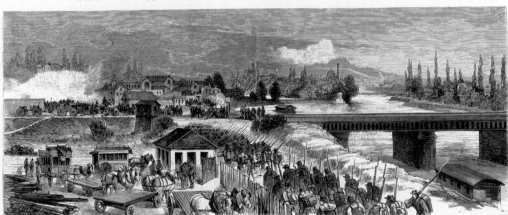

Matthew White Ridley, after William Simpson

← *The Civil War in France: A Shell at*
Suresnes – From a Sketch Taken
Immediately after the Explosion, 1871
Der Bürgerkrieg in Frankreich: Eine
Granate in Suresnes – Nach einer
unmittelbar nach der Explosion
angefertigten Skizze
La Guerre civile en France: une
grenade à Suresnes – D'après un
croquis réalisé juste après l'explosion
Wood engraving
From: *The Illustrated London News*,
29 April 1871

Amongst the large number of *special*
artists associated with the *Illustrated*
London News was the veteran William
Simpson, who witnessed at first hand
the bombardment by the forces of
the Paris commune of a farmhouse
in Suresnes where members of the
Versailles government were shelter-
ing. His sketch was completed by
Matthew White Ridley, who later
worked mostly for *The Graphic*.

Unter dem Großaufgebot von *special*
artists der *Illustrated London News* befand sich auch der erfahrene William
Simpson. In einem Bauernhaus in
Suresnes erlebte er die Bombardierung der nach Versailles geflohenen
Regierung durch die Pariser Aufständischen hautnah mit. Seine Skizze
wurde von Matthew White Ridley
umgesetzt, der später hauptsächlich
für den *Graphic* arbeitete.

Dans la vaste équipe de *specials* des
Illustrated London News se trouvait
aussi William Simpson, rompu à l'exercice. Dans une ferme à Suresnes il
vécut de très près le bombardement
du gouvernement alors en fuite à
Versailles par les communards parisiens. Son esquisse a été transposée
par Matthew White Ridley qui, plus
tard, travailla surtout pour le *Graphic*.

Anonymous

Fall of the Column in the Place Vendôme, Paris, 1871
Sturz der Säule auf der Place Vendôme
Démolition de la colonne de la place Vendôme
Wood engraving
From: *The Illustrated London News*, 27 May 1871

The toppling and dismantling of Napoleon's Victory Column, which was clad in bronze panels made from captured cannons, followed Gustave Courbet's proposal on behalf of the Commune's committee. It was intended as a pacifist act and a signal to the nternational community, and its anti-imperialist message had tremendous symbolic force in the press all around the world.

Der Sturz der aus Kanonen gegossenen bonapartistischen Triumphsäule geschah auf Betreiben des Mitglieds des Kommunerats Gustave Courbet und sollte als pazifistisches Signal an die Weltgemeinschaft verstanden werden. Der antiimperialistische Akt war von ungeheurer Symbolkraft und manifestierte sich in der internationalen Presse auf entsprechende Weise.

La démolition de la colonne de la Victoire érigée par Napoléon et coulée dans le bronze de canons eut lieu sous l'impulsion de Gustave Courbet, membre du Conseil de la Commune dans le but d'envoyer un signal pacifique à la communauté internationale. Cet acte anti-impérialiste était d'un formidable pouvoir symbolique et eut sa place en conséquence dans la presse internationale.

Godefroy Durand

← *Following the "Gentle Craft" – At the Pont de Neuilly*, Paris, 1871
Den Angelsport pflegen
Pêcher à la ligne
Wood engraving
From: *The Graphic*, London, 20 May 1871

After the government troops were able to summon reinforcements with the permission of the occupying German forces, they took up positions to surround Paris. The idyllic scene in the foreground here, unaffected by the events of the war taking place elsewhere, prefigures the artists of the Impressionist movement whose strict sense of escapism must be understood in the context of the breakdown of the previous bourgeois order.

Nachdem die Regierungstruppen mit Einwilligung der deutschen Besatzer aufgestockt werden konnten, begannen sie, Paris einzukesseln. Die Idyllik, die sich vom martialischen Geschehen unbeeindruckt gibt, weist bereits auf die impressionistische Bewegung voraus. Deren strikter Eskapismus lässt sich nur vor dem Hintergrund des vorangegangenen Zusammenbruchs der bürgerlichen Ordnung erklären.

Après que les troupes gouvernementales avaient pu être renforcées avec l'accord des occupants allemands, elles commencèrent à encercler Paris. La scène idyllique, qui se veut insensible aux événements guerriers, préfigure déjà le mouvement impressionniste. Son imperturbable fuite de la réalité ne peut s'expliquer que dans le contexte de l'effondrement antérieur de l'ordre bourgeois.

Horace Castelli

A Church Women's Club in the Batignolles in Paris under the Commune, 1871
Ein Frauenclub in der Kirche des Batignolles zu Paris während der Herrschaft der Kommune
Un Club féminin à l'église des Batignolles à Paris pendant la Commune
Wood engraving
From: *Über Land und Meer*, no. 44, Stuttgart, 1871

While Arthur Boyd Houghton reacted to the subject of political power being given to women by stereotypically depicting them as witches, Horace Castelli in his work for the French and German illustrated press used the similarly dismissive cliché of the blue-stocking, who shakes the institution of the family to its foundations by rejecting the role of motherhood.

Während Arthur Boyd Houghton dem Phänomen politischer Frauenpower mit dem Stereotyp der Hexe begegnete, bediente Horace Castelli französische und deutsche Illustrierte mit dem Klischee des intellektuellen Blaustrumpfs, der die familiären Grundfeste durch eine Negation der Mutterschaft ins Wanken bringt.

Alors qu'Arthur Boyd Houghton opposait au phénomène du pouvoir politique des femmes le stéréotype de la sorcière, Horace Castelli présentait aux magazines français et allemands le cliché du bas-bleu, qui ébranle les fondations de la famille par une négation de la maternité.

Ein Frauenclub in der Kirche des Batignolles zu Paris während der Herrschaft der Kommune. Originalzeichnung von Horace Castelli. (S. 14.)

Arthur Boyd Houghton & Horace Harral (sc.)

Paris under the Commune – Women's Club at the Boule Noire, Boulevard Rochechouart, 1871
Paris unter der Kommune – Frauenclub im Boule Noire
Paris pendant la Commune – Club féminin à la Boule Noire
Wood engraving
From: *The Graphic*, London, 3 June 1871

During the Commune, women gathered together at night to discuss their own new ideals of emancipation, before asserting these rights to the Commune's committee. Arthur Boyd Houghton, who attended one such meeting in Montmartre, responded in the spirit of the conservative fears of his Victorian readership with this animated scene done in the style of Goya.

Die Frauen der Kommune formulierten in nächtlichen Debattierklubs zukunftsweisende emanzipatorische Ziele, die sie auch gegenüber dem Kommunerat durchzusetzen wussten. Arthur Boyd Houghton, der bei solch einer Veranstaltung auf dem Montmartre zugegen war, entsprach mit seiner goyanesken Schilderung den wertkonservativen Ängsten seiner viktorianischen Leserschaft.

Les femmes de la Commune formulaient des ambitions révolutionnaires d'émancipation, qu'elles savaient aussi imposer face au Conseil de la Commune, dans des clubs de débats nocturnes. Avec sa description goyaesque, Arthur Boyd Houghton, présent à l'une de ces sessions à Montmartre, répondait aux frayeurs conservatrices de ses lecteurs victoriens.

Anonymous

*The End of the Commune –
Execution of a Pétroleuse*, 1871
*Das Ende der Kommune –
Hinrichtung einer Pétroleuse*
*La Fin de la Commune –
Exécution d'une pétroleuse*
Wood engraving
From: *Harper's Weekly*,
New York, 8 July 1871

When Versailles government troops entered Paris at the end of May and the Commune's prospects looked hopeless, rebel soldiers set fire to several important buildings. The rumour that spread, that these arson attacks were the work of "depraved" working-class women and prostitutes who were known as *pétroleuses*, was in fact part of the nobility's campaign to demonise the rebel forces.

Als die Versailler Truppen Ende Mai in Paris eindrangen und die Lage aussichtslos wurde, setzten Soldaten der Kommune eine Reihe repräsentativer Bauten in Brand. Das Gerücht, dass diese Brandstiftungen auf das Konto „verkommener" Arbeiterfrauen und Prostituierten gingen, den sogenannten *Pétroleuses*, war Teil der großbürgerlichen Dämonisierungskampagne.

Quand les troupes versaillaises pénétrèrent dans Paris fin mai et que la situation devenait désespérée, des soldats de la Commune mirent le feu à une série d'édifices parisiens. Le bruit selon lequel ces incendies étaient le crime de femmes ouvrières et prostituées «dépravées», qu'on appelait pétroleuses, était un élément de la campagne de diabolisation menée par la grande bourgeoisie.

SUMMARY EXECUTIONS IN PARIS—SHOOTING DOWN COMMUNIST PRISONERS.

BLOODSHED IN PARIS.

THE capture of Paris by the troops of the Versailles government was marked by the most bloody scenes of vengeance ever witnessed in modern warfare. The troops of the Commune were shot down without mercy, and without even the form of trial, after all resistance had ceased, and it is estimated that nearly twenty thousand of them perished before the slaughter was suspended. Women, and even children, shared the fate of the men, and indeed generally brought it down upon themselves by the ferocity with which they took part in the fighting and in the terrible work of burning the city. The upper sketch on this page shows how the Communists were shot down by the infuriated troops. The lower sketch was taken at the corner of a street where Communist prisoners, captured while fighting, were ranged in rows and "fusilladed" as they stood. The centre figure in the front row was a noted Communist leader of the lowest and most degraded stamp. On his person, after his execution, was found the sum of 150,000 francs, in bank-notes, sewed under the lining of his trowsers. Large sums of money were found upon other Communists, who had been prevented by the Prussians from escaping.

SUMMARY EXECUTIONS IN PARIS—ROWS OF DEAD COMMUNISTS.

Anonymous

Summary Executions in Paris, 1871
Standrechtliche Exekutionen in Paris
Exécutions sommaires à Paris
Wood engraving
From: *Harper's Weekly*,
New York, 8 July 1871

A few weeks after the bloody events of the final week of May, the international press estimated the number of supporters of the Commune who had been shot at 20,000. Most of them, including many women and children, actually died after the fighting had ceased in summary executions.

Bereits wenige Wochen nach der blutigen letzten Maiwoche wurde die Anzahl der erschossenen Kommunarden in der internationalen Presse auf 20 000 geschätzt. Die meisten von ihnen, darunter viele Frauen und Kinder, kamen erst nach den Gefechten bei den standrechtlichen Erschießungen ums Leben.

Quelques semaines après la sanglante dernière semaine de mai, le nombre des communards abattus était déjà estimé à 20 000 dans la presse internationale. La plupart d'entre eux, dont beaucoup de femmes et d'enfants, périrent après les combats au cours d'exécutions sommaires.

J. Ansseau

↑ *View of the Tunnel at Porte Maillot for the Circular Railway, Memorial of the Second Siege*, 1871
Ansicht des Ringbahntunnels an der Porte Maillot, Mahnmal der zweiten Belagerung
Vue du tunnel du chemin de fer de ceinture à la porte Maillot, Mémorial du second siège
Wood engraving
From: Lorédan Larchey, *Mémorial illustré des deux sièges de Paris, 1870–1871*, Paris, 1871

Amidst the ruins of the city stands a photographer, and perhaps his photographs appeared in some of the numerous pictorial volumes and illustrated collections showing the scale of the destruction. In the foreground is a view of the tunnel of the old circular railway, which was used by the first units of the Versailles army to reach the centre of Paris.

Im Zentrum der Ruinenlandschaft steht ein Fotograf. Vielleicht haben seine Aufnahmen Vorlagen für die unzähligen Schmuckbände und Grafikeditionen mit Motiven aus der zerstörten Metropole geliefert. Im Vordergrund öffnet sich ein Blick in den Tunnel der alten Pariser Ringbahn, über den das erste Korps der Versailler Armee ins Zentrum vormaschieren konnte.

Un photographe se tient debout au milieu d'un paysage de ruines. Peut-être ses clichés ont-ils servi de modèles aux innombrables volumes décoratifs et éditions de dessins présentant les motifs de la métropole détruite. Au premier plan, le regard se pose sur le tunnel de la vieille ceinture ferroviaire de Paris, par lequel le premier corps de l'armée versaillaise put s'engouffrer vers le centre.

Arthur Boyd Houghton

The Courts Martial at Versailles – Pétroleuses under Trial, 1871
Die Kriegsgerichte in Versailles – Pétroleuses unter Anklage
Les Conseils de guerre à Versailles – pétroleuses en procès
Wood engraving
From: *The Graphic*, London, 23 September 1871

Arthur Boyd Houghton was in Versailles when a spectacular trial took place for five women from the Commune who were charged with arson. The accusations proved to be unfounded, but the women still received harsh sentences. In his last work as a *special artist*, the obstinate Houghton produced a psychologically dense masterpiece of ambiguous reporting.

Arthur Boyd Houghton war in Versailles bei einem spektakulären Prozess gegen fünf Kommunardinnen zugegen, die der Brandstiftung angeklagt waren. Obgleich sich der Vorwurf als haltlos erwies, wurden drastische Strafen verhängt. Mit seiner letzten Arbeit als *special artist* gelang dem eigensinnigen Künstler ein psychologisch dichtes Meisterwerk doppelbödiger Berichterstattung.

Arthur Boyd Houghton assista à Versailles à un procès spectaculaire contre cinq communardes qui étaient accusées d'incendie criminel. Bien que l'accusation s'avérât sans fondement, de dures sentences furent infligées. Par son dernier travail comme *special*, cet artiste obstiné réussit un chef-d'œuvre d'une grande densité psychologique dans le genre du reportage à double lecture.

Edmond Morin

↑ *Montmartre*
The Night of 25 May in the Cemetery, 1871
Die Nacht des 25. Mai auf dem Friedhof
La Nuit du 25 mai au cimetière
Wood engraving
From: Lorédan Larchey, *Mémorial illustré des deux sièges de Paris, 1870–1871,* Paris, 1871

The scene shows the dead being buried after the battle at Montmartre. Edmond Morin was one of the most versatile press illustrators, and his work was admired by some of the young artists such as Daniel Vierge and Albert Robida who began their careers with reports in this "terrible year". In Van Gogh's opinion, Morin was the equal of the slightly younger Gustave Doré in terms of his ability with artistic illustration.

Die Toten der Schlacht um den Montmartre werden begraben. Edmond Morin war einer der vielseitigsten Pressezeichner, verehrt von jungen Grafikern wie Daniel Vierge und Albert Robida, die mit der Berichterstattung im „furchtbaren Jahr" (*l'année terrible*) ihren Einstand hatten. Van Gogh war der Ansicht, dass Morin als Vertreter der künstlerischen Illustration dem jüngeren Gustave Doré ebenbürtig sei.

Les morts de la bataille de Montmartre vont être enterrés. Edmond Morin était un des dessinateurs de presse les plus éclectiques, ayant l'admiration de jeunes artistes comme Daniel Vierge et Albert Robida qui firent leurs débuts avec la couverture médiatique de «l'année terrible». Selon Van Gogh, Morin était l'égal de Gustave Doré, son cadet, en tant que représentant de l'illustration artistique.

Auguste Lançon & Frederick Moller (sc.)

Prisoners from the Commune at Versailles, 1872
Gefangene aus der Kommune in Versailles
Les Prisonniers de la Commune à Versailles
Wood engraving
From: *L'Illustration,* Paris, 20 January 1872

It was a tragic irony of history that the leading activists of the Commune were made to await their trial in the stables that once belonged to the Sun King. Van Gogh had followed the work of Auguste Lançon, who had himself been active in the Commune, for many years and considered it had a connection with his own work: "Lançon's drawings were wonderful, so manly and so huge" (letter to Theo, 5 May 1885).

Dass die basisdemokratischen Aktivisten der Kommune in den ehemaligen Pferdeställen des Sonnenkönigs auf ihre Prozesse warten mussten, war eine tragische Ironie der Geschichte. Das Werk des Kommunarden Auguste Lançon hat van Gogh über Jahre verfolgt und dabei auch eine Nähe zu seinen eigenen Arbeiten entdeckt. „Lançons Zeichnungen waren bewundernswert, so männlich und so weit" (Brief an Theo, 5. Mai 1885).

Tragique ironie de l'histoire: les activistes de la base démocratique de la Commune durent atttendre leurs procès dans les anciennes écuries du Roi-Soleil. Pendant de nombreuses années, Van Gogh avait suivi les travaux du communard Auguste Lançon et, ce faisant, découvert une analogie avec ses propres œuvres. «Les dessins de Lançon étaient admirables, si virils et si vastes» (lettre à Theo, 5 mai 1885).

Gustave Doré

*Versailles and Paris in 1871 after
the Original Drawings*, Paris, 1907
*Versailles und Paris 1871 nach den
Originalzeichnungen*
*Versailles et Paris en 1871 d'après
les dessins originaux*
Relief etchings

During the Commune uprising in
Paris Gustave Doré fled to Versailles,
where he made drawings at meetings
of the National Assembly and portraits of imprisoned members of the
Commune. He abandoned his idea to
produce a work about the "terrible
year", which he had witnessed while
still in Paris and serving as a volunteer
in the National Guard, and instead
moved on to some reports of London
that he already had in the works (see
ills. pp. 284/285, 286 t., 287).

Gustave Doré war während des
Kommuneaufstands nach Versailles
geflohen. Er zeichnete dort Sitzungen
der Nationalversammlung und Porträts inhaftierter Kommunarden. Den
Plan, ein Werk über das „furchtbare
Jahr" zu produzieren, das er in Paris
als Freiwilliger der Nationalgarde mit-
erlebt hatte, gab er zugunsten einer
bereits geplanten London-Reportage
auf (siehe Abb. S. 284/285, 286 o.,
287).

Gustave Doré avait fui à Versailles
pendant l'insurrection de la Commune.
Il y dessina des séances de l'Assemblée nationale et des portraits de
communards incarcérés. Il abandonna
le projet de produire une œuvre sur
« l'année terrible », qu'il avait vécue à
Paris comme volontaire de la Garde
nationale, au profit d'un reportage
sur Londres qu'il avait déjà prévu (voir
ills. p. 284/285, 286 h., 287).

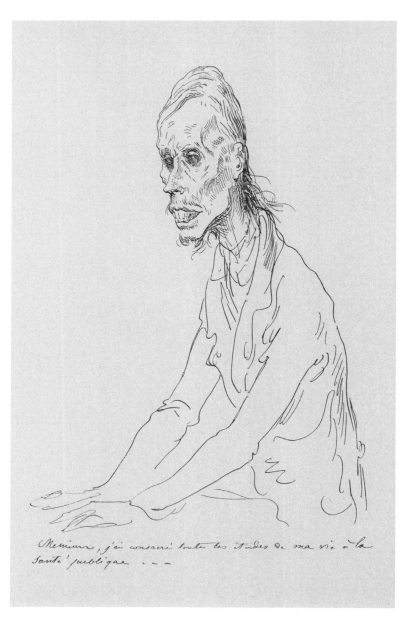

Gustave Doré; Adolphe-François Pannemaker & A. Doms (sc.)

Scripture Reader in a Night Refuge, 1871
Bibelvorleser in einem Nachtasyl
Lecteur de la Bible dans un asile de nuit
Wood engraving
From: Gustave Doré & Blanchard Jerrold, *London: A Pilgrimage*, London 1872

Van Gogh was an admirer of Gustave Doré's report on London and was particularly impressed by this scene in a night shelter. He disagreed when his friends criticised Doré's work for being "illustrative", saying that "If those who disparage him are not able to achieve using both hands what Doré can do with just one finger, then all they say is just arrogance" (letter to A. van Rappard, 19 September 1882).

Van Gogh bewunderte Gustave Dorés London-Report. Besonders war er von dieser Szene im Nachtasyl beeindruckt. Den Vorwurf des „Illustrativen", mit dem van Goghs Künstlerfreunde Doré herabsetzten, ließ er nicht gelten. „Wenn diejenigen, die über ihn schimpfen, mit ihren beiden Händen nicht ein Zehntel davon schaffen, was Doré mit einem Finger kann, dann ist das nichts als Dünkel" (Brief an A. van Rappard, 19. September 1882).

Van Gogh admirait le reportage londonien de Gustave Doré. Il était particulièrement impressionné par cette scène dans l'asile de nuit. Il refusait le terme «illustratif» avec lequel les amis de Van Gogh abaissaient Doré. «Si ceux-là même qui le dénigrent ne sont pas capables de faire avec leurs deux mains un dixième de ce que Doré réussit avec un dòigt, ce n'est alors rien qu'arrogance» (lettre à A. van Rappard, 19 septembre 1882).

Gustave Doré & Stéphane Pannemaker (sc.)

Whitechapel and Thereabouts, 1871
Whitechapel und Umgebung
Whitechapel et ses environs
Wood engraving
From: Gustave Doré & Blanchard
Jerrold, *London: A Pilgrimage*,
London, 1872

Following Blanchard Jerrold's suggestion Gustave Doré spent five years working on his London report, and like Dickens and Henry Mayhew before him he concentrated mostly on the poorest districts in the East End. He was extremely shy, and while out making his sketches he was accompanied by Jerrold, the architectural draughtsman Émile Bourdelin and two plainclothes policemen.

Fünf Jahre arbeitet Gustave Doré auf Einladung seines Freundes Blanchard Jerrold an der London-Reportage. Wie Henry Mayhew und Charles Dickens zuvor widmete er sich dabei bevorzugt dem Elendsviertel des East End. Begleitet wurde der extrem scheue Künstler von seinem Gastgeber sowie dem Architekturzeichner Émile Bourdelin und zwei Polizisten in Zivil.

Gustave Doré travailla pendant cinq ans à son reportage sur Londres sur invitation de son ami Blanchard Jerrold. Comme Henry Mayhew et Charles Dickens avant lui, il se consacra en premier lieu au quartier miséreux d'East End. L'artiste extrêmement timide était accompagné de son hôte ainsi que du dessinateur d'architecture Émile Bourdelin et de deux policiers en civil.

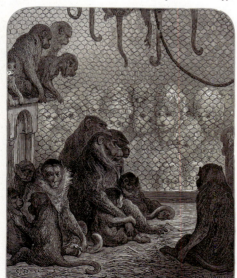

Gustave Doré & A. Doms (sc.)

With the Beasts, 1871
Bei den wilden Tieren
Chez les animaux sauvages
Wood engraving
From: Gustave Doré & Blanchard
Jerrold, *London: A Pilgrimage*,
London, 1872

The great work on London was based on two themes which only came to have any affect on art in about 1900, namely alienation and the class struggle. Doré brought both of these narratives together in his study of the zoo, in which the well-lit world of the upper classes comes up against the dark underworld of the primates. The libidinous connotations with his own visits to observe people in misery are reflected in the blank stares of the crowd as they look in on the animal enclosure.

Das London-Opus gründet auf zwei Themen, die in der Kunst erst um 1900 virulent wurden: Entfremdung und Klassenkonflikt. Im Motiv des Zoos, wo die Lichtwelt der Oberklasse an eine dunkle Unterwelt der Primaten grenzt, führt Gustave Doré beide Narrative zusammen. In den sehnsüchtigen Blicken auf die Zone des Animalischen spiegelt sich die libidinöse Konnotation des eigenen Elendstourismus.

L'œuvre monumentale sur Londres repose sur deux thèmes qui ne gagnèrent en âpreté que vers 1900 : l'aliénation et la lutte des classes. Gustave Doré fait se rejoindre les deux discours dans le motif du zoo, où le monde lumineux de la classe supérieure jouxte les sombres bas-fonds des primates. La connotation libidineuse du tourisme de la misère se reflète dans les regards languissants portés sur la zone des animaux sauvages.

Gustave Doré; Adolphe-François Pannemaker & A. Doms (sc.)

The Bull's Eye, 1871
Mitten ins Schwarze
Plein dans le mille
Wood engraving
From: Gustave Doré & Blanchard
Jerrold, *London: A Pilgrimage*,
London, 1872

The zoo theme was also continued in this scene showing the police checking up on homeless people in the East End. Here it is no longer envy that defines the black and white contrast of the social divide, but state control and coercion. In England, *London: A Pilgrimage* was condemned on all sides, and one of the few foreign editions to appear was published in St. Petersburg in 1882.

Das Motiv des Zoos findet seine Fortführung in der polizeilichen Observation von Obdachlosen im East End. Nicht mehr Sehnsucht bestimmt hier den Helldunkelkontrast der sozialen Kluft, sondern staatlicher Zwang und Kontrolle. In England stieß *London: A Pilgrimage* vorwiegend auf Ablehnung. Eine der wenigen ausländischen Ausgaben erschien 1882 in Sankt Petersburg.

Le thème du zoo trouve sa prolongation dans l'observation par la police de sans-abri à East End. Ce n'est plus l'envie qui détermine ici le contraste en clair-obscur du fossé social, mais la contrainte étatique et le contrôle. En Angleterre, *London: A Pilgrimage* fut largement rejeté. Une des rares éditions étrangères parut à Saint-Pétersbourg en 1882.

SUPPLEMENT, NOVEMBER 9, 1872.] HARPER'S WEEKLY. 881

LONDON: A PILGRIMAGE.

BY GUSTAVE DORÉ AND BLANCHARD JERROLD.

To be Completed in Twelve Parts.—Part 8.

CONTENTS.

CHAPTER XIV.——WORK-A-DAY LONDON
CHAPTER XV.——HUMBLE INDUSTRIES.

ILLUSTRATIONS.

INITIAL LETTER.
THE BEGGAR.
THE MATCH SELLER.
BAKED-POTATO MAN.
THE WORKMEN'S TRAIN.
WAREHOUSING IN THE CITY.

INITIAL LETTER.
THE MONUMENT TO GEORGE PEABODY.
THE ROYAL EXCHANGE.
ORANGE COURT, DRURY LANE.
BILLINGSGATE—LANDING THE FISH.
BILLINGSGATE—EARLY MORNING.

THE RAG MERCHANT'S HOME—COULSTON STREET, WHITECHAPEL.
THE OLD-CLOTHES MAN.
A FLOWER GIRL.
THE GINGER-BEER MAN.
JEWISH BUTCHERS—ALDGATE.
OVER LONDON—BY RAIL.

CHAPTER XIV.

WORK A-DAY LONDON

T work! Before six in the morning, London—winter and summer—is astir. The postmen have already cleared the letter-boxes. It is not a place where the lazy man can lie under the canopy of heaven, and live through a perpetual summer on dishes of macaroni. The *lazzaroni* of Cockayne must needs be a cunning set. If they will not work, and work hard, they must cheat or steal. He who falls from honest, methodical, skilled labor, and the regular travel by the workman's train, must earn his shilling or eighteenpence a day as boardman or dock laborer; or he must withdraw to the work-house, or starve; or shift to the East, and become of that terrible company whose headquarters may be taken to be somewhere about Bluegate Fields. The rigor of the climate, the swiftness of the life, hosts of men with open mouth, the tough hand-to-hand wrestling for every crust, compel that sternness, and produce that care-worn look, which sit upon the poorer classes of London workmen.

Before six in the morning, while the mantle of night still lies over the sloppy streets, and the air stings the limbs to the marrow the shadows of men and boys may be seen, black objects against the deep gloom, gliding out of the side streets to the main thoroughfares. They are the van-guard of the army of Labor, who are to carry forward the marvelous story of London industry another step before sundown: to add a new story to a new terrace, the corner-stone to another building, bulwarks to another frigate, another station to another railway, and tons upon tons of produce from every clime to the mighty stock that is forever packed along the shores of the Thames. As they trudge on their way, the younger and lighter-hearted whistling defiance to the icy wind, the swift carts of fish-mongers, butchers, and green-grocers pass them, and they meet the slow-returning wagons of the market-gardeners, with the men asleep upon the empty baskets. The baked-potato man and the keeper of the coffee stall are their most welcome friends—and their truest, for they sell warmth that sustains and does not poison.

As the day breaks, in winter, the suburbs become alive with shop-boys and shopmen, poor clerks, needle-women of quick and timorous gait, and waiters who have to prepare for the day. The night cabs are crawling home, and the day cabs are being horsed in the steamy mews. The milkmen and women are abroad—first street vocalists of the day. The early omnibus draws up outside the public-house, the bar of which has just been lit up. The bar maid serves—sharp of temper and short in her curl papers. The blinds creep up the windows of the villas. The newsboys shamble along, laden with morning papers, prodigal of chaff, and profuse in the exhibition of comforters. The postman's knock rings through the street; and at the sound every man who has to labor for his bread—whether banker banker's clerk, porter, or vendor of fusees at the Bank entrance—is astir.

Another working-day has fairly opened, and mighty and multiform is the activity. Hasty making of tea and coffee, filling of shaving-pots, brushing of boots and coats and hats, reading of papers, opening of morning letters, kissing of wives and daughters, grasping of reins, mounting of omnibuses, and catching of trains—in every suburb! The start has been made, and the sometime silent City is filling at a prodigious rate. The trim omnibuses from Clapham and Fulham, from Hackney and Hampstead, make a valiant opposition to the suburban lines of railway. The bridges are choked with vehicles. While the City is being flooded with money-making humanity, the West End streets are given up to shop-cleaners and town travelers; and while these early bread-winners are preparing for the fashion of the day, gentlemen who live at ease amble to and fro the early burst in the park; and Her Majesty's civil servants honor the pavement, each looking as though he had just stepped out of a bandbox, and protested somewhat at the stern duty that compelled him to emerge before the day was aired — to use Beau Brummel's delightfully whimsical phrase.

On our way to the City on the tide of Labor we light upon places in which the day is never aired: only the high points of which the sun ever hits. Rents spread with rags, swarming with the children of mothers forever greasing the walls with their shoulders; where there is an angry hopelessness and carelessness painted upon the face of every man and woman, and the oaths are loud, and the crime is continuous; and the few who do work with something like system are the ne'er-do-weels of the great army. As the sun rises the court swarms at once: for here there are no ablutions to perform, no toilets to make—neither brush nor comb delays the outpouring of babes and sucklings from the cellars and garrets. And yet in the midst of such a scene as this we can not miss touches of human goodness, and of honorable instinct making a tooth-and-nail fight against adverse circumstances. Some country wenches, who have

THE MATCH SELLER.

THE BEGGAR.

BAKED-POTATO MAN.

THE WORKMEN'S TRAIN.

Gustave Doré

Gustave Doré & Blanchard Jerrold
London: A Pilgrimage. Part 8:
Work a-Day London, 1872
Werktagslondon | Londres au quotidien
Wood engraving
From: *Harper's Weekly*, New York, 9 November 1872

Blanchard Jerrold's original concept for the project was based on analysing the sum total of goods exchanged and the corresponding flow of money in London on a single and meticulously observed working day. It would thus be an extension of the ethnographic studies conducted by Henry Mayhew, and was probably also influenced by Karl Marx's *Capital* (1867), but this overall plan could not be reconciled with Gustave Doré's narrative interests.

Blanchard Jerrolds ursprüngliche Konzeption ging davon aus, in Erweiterung von Henry Mayhews ethnografischen Studien und wohl auch beeinflusst von Karl Marx' *Kapital* (1867), den gesamten Warenaustausch und Finanzfluss der Metropole anhand eines einzigen, minutiös beobachteten Arbeitstags zu analysieren. Der Plan ließ sich allerdings kaum mit Gustave Dorés narrativen Interessen synchronisieren.

Afin d'étendre les études ethnographiques d'Henry Mayhew et aussi sans doute influencé par *Le Capital* (1867) de Karl Marx, le concept original de Blanchard Jerrold prévoyait d'analyser l'échange intégral des marchandises et les fluctuations financières sur la base d'une seule journée de travail minutieusement observée. Toutefois, ce plan ne put guère coïncider avec les intérêts narratifs de Gustave Doré.

THE GINGER-BEER MAN.

JEWISH BUTCHERS—ALDGATE

OVER LONDON—BY RAIL

Gustave Doré & Adolphe-François Pannemaker (sc.)

Gustave Doré & Blanchard Jerrold
London: A Pilgrimage, 1872
Wood engraving
From: *Harper's Weekly*, New York, 9 November 1872

While *London: A Pilgrimage* was published in England as a separate book edition, in the United State it was serialised in magazines of the press. This celebrated image of a working-class district shows the mark of Émile Bourdelin, but unlike Augustus Pugin and Thomas Rowlandson's *Microcosm of London* (ill. p. 49) the contribution of an

architectural draughtsman went unacknowledged in Doré's case.

Während *London: A Pilgrimage* in England als autonomes Werk erschien, wurde es in Amerika als pressegrafische Serie publiziert. Die berühmte Abbildung einer Arbeitersiedlung trägt die Handschrift von Émile Bourdelin. Anders als in Augustus Pugins und Thomas Rowlandsons *Microcosm of London* (Abb. S. 49) blieb die Mitarbeit des Architekturzeichners hier unerwähnt.

Tandis que *London: A Pilgrimage* paraissait en Angleterre comme œuvre autonome, il fut publié en Amérique sous forme de série de dessins de presse. La fameuse illustration d'une cité ouvrière porte la signature d' Émile Bourdelin. À la différence du *Microcosm of London* d'Auguste Pugin et Thomas Rowlandson (ill. p. 49), la collaboration d'un dessinateur d'architecture n'a pas été mentionnée.

L'ILLUSTRATION, JOURNAL UNIVERSEL. 329

Gavarni à Londres. — A l Opéra.

Gavarni à Londres. — A la Taverne.

qu'une broderie, l'habileté moderne a si bien passé par là qu'elle lui a donné les apparences d'un parc où l'on retrouve toutes les séductions de l'ancien Tivoli, y compris son fameux sorcier qui disait si mal la bonne aventure. On connaît d'ailleurs ses illuminations qui ressemblent tant à des incendies organisés et qui, tous les jeudis et dimanches, donnent aux paisibles habitants de Clignancourt l'idée d'un volcan subitement sorti des carrières Montmartre, tandis que son feu d'artifice leur procure la distraction d'un tintamarre épouvantable.

Quant au Château-des-Fleurs, il est surtout remarquable par sa grille qui est un chef-d'œuvre de serrurerie et l'ouvrage de Lamour, un artiste du bon temps où l'on faisait si bien les grilles. Le Château-des-Fleurs occupe l'emplacement du *Jardin-des-Fées* si célèbre sous le Directoire, et, malgré l'accumulation très-fleurie qu'il offre, nous lui trouvons un défaut, fort joli du reste, je veux dire la prétention de rivaliser avec son voisin le Jardin-d'Hiver. En voilà un qui exhale les suaves haleines de la belle saison et les senteurs embaumées de toutes les plantes du monde connu. Ce jardin d'hiver est bien le plus charmant jardin d'été, et un voyage de long cours dans son enceinte pourrait, à la rigueur, tenir lieu d'un voyage autour du monde. Vous y trouverez la flore des Indes et des deux Amériques mise sous verre et s'épanouissant en vue de Mabille et à la hauteur de l'Hippodrome. L'avantage qu'il a sur ses rivaux, c'est d'offrir aux associations philanthropiques et à la bienfaisance par souscription, la salle de danse la plus vaste et la plus ornée de Paris. Malheureusement il ressemble un peu, et même beaucoup, à ces poëmes des jardins chantés par les poëtes du dix-huitième siècle et dont on disait que pour apercevoir la nature et pouvoir y respirer, il était indispensable de mettre le nez à la fenêtre. Tels sont les paradis perdus hier, retrouvés aujourd'hui, où nos Parisiens vont courir demain, afin d'opposer aux ardentes splendeurs de leur ciel sénégambien, un peu de fraîcheur et d'ombrage, et de substituer, s'il est possible, l'illusion champêtre aux agitations de la grande ville.

Le théâtre promet toujours... ce qu'il n'a pas donné. La Comédie-Française, marchant de reprises en reprises, abuse un peu de ce régime rafraîchissant. Numa a débuté ou va débuter au *Théâtre-Historique* dans le *Chevalier d'Hermenthal*, en attendant *Gulliver*, pièce féerique, variée comme un panorama, fantasque comme la vie, et d'une portée politique et littéraire, comme un journal à quarante francs. Enfin, la Porte-Saint-Martin donne demain l'*Hôtel de la Tête-Noire;* et, à défaut d'un prétexte de compte-rendu théâtral, j'ai bien envie de finir par une page empruntée aux *Causes célèbres*, ce sera autant de gagné sur le bulletin dramatique de la semaine prochaine, et nous n'aurons plus qu'à enregistrer le succès..... ou la chute.

C'est dans cet hôtel de la Tête-Noire, à Saint-Cloud, que fut commis le 30 mai 1823 le crime dont les détails odieux vont revivre dans ce mélodrame. Un jeune homme, Auguste Ballet, arrivé de la veille en compagnie de son ami Castaing, y mourait dans les convulsions du poison. La victime avait fait un testament en faveur de son assassin ; tel fut le motif du crime, dont la procédure retrouva les incidents et dont les débats éclaircirent la ténébreuse horreur jusqu'à l'évidence. Ce procès, qui fit presque autant de bruit que la fameuse affaire Fualdès, s'ouvrit au mois de novembre 1823. Castaing, dit un biographe judiciaire, monta au banc des accusés avec une contenance calme et assurée. Sa grande jeunesse, la douceur de ses traits et son attitude recueillie, tout en lui faisait contraste avec l'horrible crime dont on l'accusait. Dans la prison Castaing ne soutint pas le système de dénégation dans lequel il s'était obstinément renfermé à l'audience; son confident le trahit, et, malgré la déposition favorable des médecins ses collègues, il fut condamné et exécuté. C'est une histoire qui revenait de droit au mélodrame, et l'on vous dira la semaine prochaine le parti que le mélodrame en a tiré.

PH. B.

franchis depuis Trézènes c'est-à-dire Nérac, Phèdre a paru devant les Athéniens de Toulouse appuyée au bras de sa fidèle Œnone. Jamais, s'il faut en croire le témoignage de notre correspondant, la fille de Minos n'avait dit plus naturellement ce vers fameux :

Je ne me soutiens plus : ma force m'abandonne

Bref, la mourante Phèdre avait poussé le dévouement si loin que l'impresario toulousain comprit la nécessité de tourner court au spectacle ; on épargna à Phèdre le désagrément d'avaler la ciguë du dénoûment, et Thésée alla déchausser le cothurne après son invocation à Neptune. Mais, en supprimant un acte tout entier, le directeur avait compté sans les érudits du parterre ; ceux-ci réclamaient impérieusement leur compte alors que les acteurs avaient déjà quitté le théâtre, si bien que pour les calmer le directeur se décida à réduire à deux vers le fameux récit de Théramène, qu'il vint débiter ainsi aux applaudissements de toute la salle :

D'Hippolyte, Seigneur, sachez la triste fin, Il est mort dévoré par un monstre marin.

Une circonstance remarquable de notre été parisien, c'est que depuis longtemps il n'avait affiché de représentations aussi constamment radieuses. Notre soleil n'a point de caprice et ne se permet pas la plus légère fantaisie. Il est en scène depuis cinq heures du matin et il ne s'éclipse jamais avant le soir; aucun nuage importun ne vient intercepter ses rayons. Ce ciel si uniformément bleu et cette situation souriante, quoique un peu trop africaine, ont suggéré la même idée aux entrepreneurs des jardins de plaisance de la capitale et des environs, ils donnent des fêtes à l'unisson. Le parc d'Enghien, qui réalise un coin du fantastique paysage des îles Borromées, est devenu plus que jamais un lieu d'asile pour nos amateurs facilement effarouchés par la chaleur et qui cherchent la fraîcheur des eaux et des ombrages. C'est un but de promenade pour les oisifs de la semaine, et une partie de campagne qui doit tenter les promeneurs agrestes du dimanche. Quant au Château-Rouge... de brique, il offre toujours les mêmes distractions agréables et la foule de ses habitués lui est revenue joyeuse, dansante et non moins légère que par le passé. Peut-être cette végétation vous semblera-t-elle assez maigre, et la verdure de ces parterres un peu suspecte : mais si le jardin n'est

Gavarni à Londres — Économie de loyer pour la nuit.

Paul Gavarni

Gavarni in London, 1849
Gavarni in London | *Gavarni à Londres*
Wood engraving
From: *L'Illustration*, Paris, 21 July 1849

Gustave Doré's reporting on London stirred memories in the English press of an earlier instance of social conditions in England being criticised by another French artist. These were the picturesque depictions of poverty by Paul Gavarni who had visited London on a number of occasions beginning in 1848, and like Doré he too emphasised the growing disparity between the different classes.

Gustave Dorés London-Report rief in der britischen Presse die lange zurückliegende kritische Berichterstattung englischer Sozialverhältnisse eines anderen französischen Künstler in Erinnerung, die pittoresken Elendsschilderungen von Paul Gavarni, der sich ab 1848 wiederholt in London aufgehalten hatte. Wie Doré hatte er den auseinanderdriftenden Klassengegensatz betont.

Le reportage sur Londres de Gustave Doré n'était pas sans rappeler dans la presse britannique les rapports critiques des conditions sociales en Angleterre effectués dans un lointain passé par un autre artiste français : les pittoresques descriptions de la misère de Paul Gavarni, qui à partir de 1848 avait plusieurs fois séjourné à Londres. Comme Doré, il avait souligné le fossé abyssal séparant les classes.

Paul Gavarni

Paris – Forts de la Halle, 1855
Träger in der Markthalle | Forts de la Halle
Wood engraving
From: *The Illustrated London News*, 8 June 1855

Paris – Dames de la Halle, 1855
Damen der Markthalle | Dames de la Halle
Wood engraving
From: *The Illustrated London News*, 8 June 1855

To Van Gogh, Paul Gavarni was a superb if unfathomable artist, and on a par with the much younger English illustrators producing socially realistic works for *The Graphic*. He was especially interested in Gavarni's early Impressionistic depictions of people going about their daily work in the markets of Paris, which had appeared in the *Illustrated London News* in 1855.

Van Gogh hielt Paul Gavarni für einen ebenso großartigen wie abgründigen Künstler, gleichwertig mit den viel jüngeren englischen Sozialrealisten des *Graphic*. Besonderes Interesse zeigte er an Gavarnis frühimpressionistischen Schilderungen des Arbeitsalltags in den Pariser Markthallen, die bereits 1855 in der *Illustrated London News* erschienen waren.

Van Gogh considérait Paul Gavarni comme un artiste aussi extraordinaire qu'insondable, et comme l'égal des bien plus jeunes socio-réalistes anglais du *Graphic*. Il montra un intérêt particulier pour les portraits de l'impressionnisme précoce de Gavarni qui dépeignaient le travail quotidien aux Halles de Paris et qui étaient parus dans les *Illustrated London News* dès 1855.

Georges Montbard & Horace Harral (sc.)

The Communist Refugees' Cooperative Kitchen in Newman Passage, 1872
Die Genossenschaftsküche geflüchteter Kommunisten in der Newman-Passage
La Cuisine coopérative des communistes en exil dans le passage Newman
Wood engraving
From: *The Graphic*, London,
3 February 1872

Together with André Gill and Georges Pilotell, Georges Montbard was one of the most important caricaturists during the time of the Paris Commune. His report on the situation regarding the members of the Commune who had gone into exile, which he produced shortly after fleeing himself to London, was an early example of his inventiveness with illustrations divided into several panels and established his international career as a press artist.

Georges Montbard zählte neben André Gill und Georges Pilotell zu den bedeutensten Karikaturisten der Pariser Kommune. Die Reportage über die Lage der Exilkommunarden, die er kurz nach seiner Flucht nach London aufzeichnete, war ein frühes Beispiel seines Erfindungsreichtums im Bereich der Multipanelgrafik, die seine internationale Karriere als Pressegrafiker begründete.

Avec André Gill et Georges Pilotell, Georges Montbard comptait parmi les plus importants caricaturistes de la Commune de Paris. Le reportage sur la situation des communards exilés, qu'il réalisa après sa fuite à Londres, fut un exemple précoce de sa grande inventivité dans le domaine de l'illustration agencée en cases qui établit sa carrière internationale en tant qu'illustrateur de presse.

Félix Régamey & William James Palmer (sc.)

French Communists in London, 1872
Französische Kommunisten in London
Communistes français à Londres
Wood engraving
From: *The Illustrated London News*,
8 June 1872

Following the defeat of the Commune, the caricaturist Félix Régamey was forced to flee to London since he had been a member of Gustave Courbet's Federation of Artists during the revolt. In the same way as Georges Montbard he was quickly able to establish himself as a *special artist*, to the extent that he was able to support friends such as the poets Arthur Rimbaud and Paul Verlaine who from 1872 had kept company with other former members of the Commune living in exile in London.

Wegen seiner Mitgliedschaft in Gustave Courbets Künstlervereinigung musste der Karikaturist Félix Régamey nach dem Zusammenbruch der Kommune nach London fliehen. Wie Georges Montbard gelang es ihm dort, rasch als *special artist* Fuß zu fassen, sodass er in der Lage war, Freunde wie Paul Verlaine und Arthur Rimbaud zu unterstützen, die seit 1872 Aufnahme in den Kreisen der Londoner Exilkommunarden gefunden hatten.

Le caricaturiste Félix Régamey dut fuir à Londres après après l'effondrement de la Commune pour avoir participé à l'association d'artistes de Gustave Courbet. Comme Georges Montbard, il réussit là-bas à s'établir rapidement comme *special artist*, si bien qu'il fut en mesure de soutenir des amis comme Paul Verlaine et Arthur Rimbaud qui, depuis 1872, avaient été acceptés dans les cercles d'ex-communards exilés à Londres.

Winslow Homer

Station-house Lodgers, 1874
Nachtquartier in einer Bahnhofs-
wartehalle | *Une Nuit dans la salle*
d'attente d'une gare
Wood engraving
From: *Harper's Weekly*, New York,
7 February 1874

Van Gogh paid special attention to the different qualities of American press graphics, although since he didn't start collecting any examples until 1881 he missed the outstanding work of Winslow Homer, who had stopped illustrating for the press in 1875. This illustration is one of his last to appear in the press, and shows a night scene in a railway waiting-room that seems to have been inspired by Velázquez's *Las Meninas*.

Van Gogh hatte ein Auge für die Qualitäten amerikanischer Pressegrafik. Da er dieses Segment allerdings erst ab 1881 sammelte, sind ihm die brillanten Arbeiten von Winslow Homer entgangen. Dieser hatte seine Tätigkeiten für Illustrierte bereits 1875 eingestellt. Das Beispiel seiner späten Pressegrafik, eine Nachtszene in einer Bahnhofswartehalle, scheint von Diego Velázquez' *Las Meninas* inspiriert zu sein.

Van Gogh était très attentif aux qualités des dessins de presse américains. Mais comme il ne collectionnait les estampes que depuis 1881, les brillants travaux de Winslow Homer lui échappèrent. Ce dernier avait cessé ses activités pour les magazines dès 1875. Cet exemple de son dessin de presse tardif, une scène nocturne dans la salle d'attente d'une gare, semble inspiré de l'œuvre de Diego Velázquez *Las Meninas*.

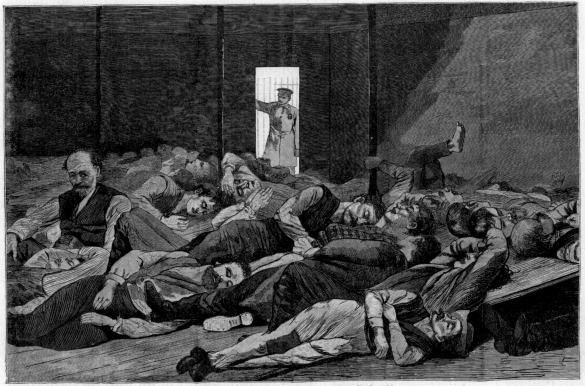

STATION-HOUSE LODGERS.—From a Drawing by Winslow Homer.—[See Page 133.]

AMERICAN SKETCHES: BLACKWELL'S ISLAND PENITENTIARY, NEW YORK—DINING-ROOM.

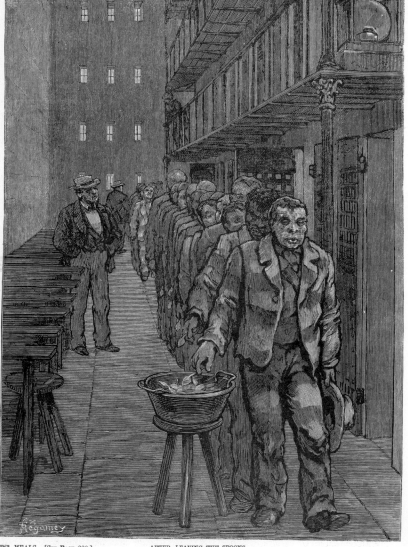

BEFORE—TAKING BREAD. BLACKWELL'S ISLAND—PRISONERS' MEALS.—[SEE PAGE 220.] AFTER—LEAVING THE SPOONS.

Anonymous & Horace Harral (sc.)

Prison Life in England, Parts II and V, 1873
The Career of a Convict, Sketched by Himself
Gefängnisleben in England – Der Werdegang eines Sträflings,
von ihm selbst skizziert
La Vie en prison en Angleterre – La carrière d'un détenu,
esquissé par lui-même

→ *Part II*, 1873
Teil II | chapitre II
Wood engravings
From: *The Graphic*, London, 22 February 1873

↘ *Part V*, 1873
Teil V | chapitre V
Wood engravings
From: *The Graphic*, London, 29 March 1873

When the editor of *The Graphic* decided to dispense for the most part with the schematic illustrations of professional artists on the staff of the magazine, and to encourage more diversity in the pictorial content, an opening was provided for drawings by amateurs to be published. This report of the experiences of a prison inmate was turned into wood engravings with remarkable sensitivity by Horace Harral.

Die Entscheidung des Herausgebers des *Graphic*, weitgehend auf schematisierende Interpretationen professioneller Redaktionszeichner zu verzichten und mehr Diversität in der Pressegrafik zuzulassen, konnte auch den Abdruck von Laienzeichnungen beinhalten. Der Erfahrungsbericht eines Strafgefangenen wurde von Horace Harral auf außerordentlich sensible Weise xylografisch umgesetzt.

La décision de l'éditeur du *Graphic* de largement renoncer aux interprétations schématisantes de dessinateurs professionnels de la rédaction et d'autoriser plus de diversité sur le plan iconographique permettait également l'impression de dessins d'amateurs. Le rapport des expériences d'un détenu fut transposé avec beaucoup de sensibilité en xylographie par Horace Harral.

Félix Régamey & William James Palmer (sc.)

↖ *Blackwell's Island Penitentiary, New York – Dining-room*, 1876
Gefängnis auf Blackwell's Island, New York – Speisesaal
Prison de Blackwell's Island, New York – Réfectoire
Wood engraving
From: *The Illustrated London News*, 4 March 1876

Félix Régamey

← *Blackwell's Island – Prisoners' Meals*, 1876
Blackwell's Island – Häftlingsverpflegung
Blackwell's Island – Repas des prisonniers
Wood engraving
From: *Harper's Weekly*, New York, 11 March 1876

Van Gogh examined Félix Régamey's work closely and was especially fascinated by the "character" of his illustrations of the American prison system. A few months before he died Van Gogh had the idea of copying one of the scenes from this series, but instead decided on a prison scene from Gustave Doré's *London: A Pilgrimage* which he then produced in Régamey's more sculptural style.

Van Gogh beschäftigte sich intensiv mit den Arbeiten Félix Régameys. Besonders fasziniert war er von der „Eigenart" *(character)* seiner Arbeiten über den amerikanischen Strafvollzug. Wenige Monate vor seinem Tod beabsichtigte van Gogh, eine Szene aus dieser Serie zu kopieren, entschied sich dann aber für ein Gefängnismotiv aus Gustave Dorés *London: A Pilgrimage*, das er dann im skulpturalen Stil Régameys interpretierte.

Van Gogh analysa en détail les œuvres de Félix Régamey. Il était surtout fasciné par le « caractère » de ses travaux sur le système pénitentiaire américain. Quelques mois avant sa mort, Van Gogh envisagea de copier une scène de cette série, mais se décida ensuite pour un motif de prison inspiré de l'ouvrage *London: A Pilgrimage* de Gustave Doré, qu'il interpréta dans le style sculptural de Régamey.

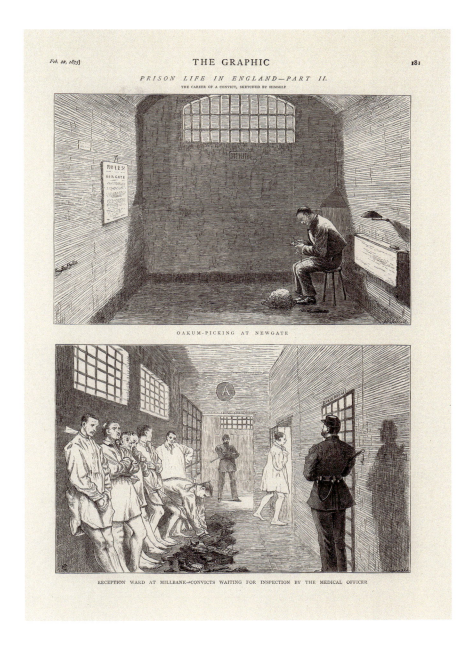

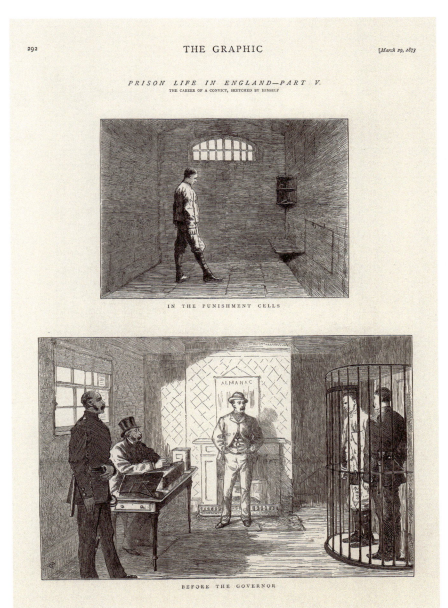

Matthew White Ridley (del. & sc.)

Pitmen Hewing the Coal, 1871
Bergleute beim Kohlehauen
Mineurs taillant du charbon
Wood engraving
From: *The Graphic*, London,
28 January 1871

Matthew White Ridley was a close
friend of James McNeill Whistler's
and specialised in scenes showing
people at work. His illustrations
of coal mining in his native north
England appeared in *The Graphic*,
and to Van Gogh his rough style,
"a solid, straightforward and un-
adorned type of drawing" (letter to
A. van Rappard, 1 November 1882),
was indistinguishable from the older
form of wood engraving he admired.

Matthew White Ridley, ein enger
Freund von James McNeill Whistler,
war auf Motive aus der Arbeitswelt
spezialisiert. Für den *Graphic* zeichnete er Szenen aus dem Steinkohleberg-
bau seiner nordenglischen Heimat.
Sein roher Stil, „diese feste, aufrechte,
ungekünstelte Zeichnung" (Brief an
A. van Rappard, 1. November 1882),
war für van Gogh untrennbar mit der
favorisierten Xylografie alter Schule
verbunden.

Matthew White Ridley, un proche
ami de James McNeill Whistler, se
spécialisa dans les motifs du monde
du travail. Pour le *Graphic*, il dessina
des scènes de mines de charbon
du nord de l'Angleterre, son pays
natal. Son style cru, « ce dessin solide,
honnête, sans artifice » (Lettre à A.
van Rappard, Ier novembre 1882) était
pour Van Gogh indissociable de la
gravure sur bois de la vieille école qui
avait ses faveurs.

Vincent van Gogh

Head of a Peasant Woman with White Cap,
Nuenen, March/April 1885
Kopf einer Bäuerin mit weißer Haube
Tête de paysanne à la coiffe blanche
Oil on canvas
Otterlo, Kröller-Müller Museum

Matthew White Ridley & Eugène Froment (sc.)

Heads of the People VI:
The Miner, 1876
Köpfe des Volkes, VI: Der Bergarbeiter
Têtes du peuple, VI: Le mineur
Wood engraving
From: *Harper's Weekly*, New York,
6 May 1876

There were 11 press illustrations by Matthew White Ridley in Van Gogh's collection, including two copies of this portrait of a miner that was originally published in *The Graphic* in April 1876 in its series of *Heads of the People*. The signs of wear indicate that one of them had been pinned to the wall of Van Gogh's studio, and this illustration was a clear influence on his own work.

Van Gogh besaß elf Pressegrafiken von Matthew White Ridley. Das Porträt eines Minenarbeiters, das ursprünglich im April 1876 im *Graphic* in der Reihe *Heads of the People* erschienen war, lag doppelt vor. Die Gebrauchsspuren deuten darauf hin, dass eine Version an die Atelierwand gepinnt war. Die Grafik hat deutliche Spuren in van Goghs Werk hinterlassen.

Van Gogh possédait onze dessins de presse de Matthew White Ridley. Il avait deux copies du portrait d'un ouvrier minier, qui était paru à l'origine en avril 1876 dans le *Graphic* dans la série *Heads of the People*. Les empreintes d'utilisation révèlent qu'une version était épinglée sur le mur de l'atelier. Ce dessin a laissé des traces manifestes dans l'œuvre de Van Gogh.

Vincent van Gogh

Scenes from Drenthe,
c. 3 October 1883
Drenthe-Szenen | Scènes de Drenthe
Pencil, pen and ink
From: Letter to Theo van Gogh,
Nieuw-Amsterdam, on or about
c. 3 October 1883
Amsterdam, Van Gogh Museum

In order to collate his visual impressions from a recent visit to this northern province of the Netherlands, Van
Gogh used a format with several panels when writing to his brother Theo
that was borrowed from the work of
some of the press illustrators he
admired, such as Georges Montbard
and William Bazett Murray, when a
series of pictorial information had to
be presented in a single image.

Um seine Reiseeindrücke aus der
nordniederländischen Provinz zu visualisieren, griff van Gogh in einem Brief
an seinen Bruder Theo auf eine Multi-
panelkonstruktion zurück, wie sie von
favorisierten Pressezeichnern wie
Georges Montbard und William Bazett
Murray eingesetzt wurde, wenn es
darum ging, eine Reihe von Bildinfor-
mationen zu bündeln.

Afin de visualiser ses impressions
de voyage de la province du nord
des Pays-Bas, Van Gogh recourut
dans une lettre à son frère Theo à
une construction agencée en cases
comme elle était utilisée par ses
dessinateurs de presse préférés,
tels Georges Montbard et William
Bazett Murray, quand il s'agissait
de regrouper une série d'informations en images.

William Bazett Murray

*An Artists' Colony, Fontainebleau,
France*, 1875
Eine Künstlerkolonie
Une Colonie d'artistes
Wood engraving
From: *Harper's Weekly*, New York,
16 October 1875

A year after the Impressionists had triumphed in Paris, William Bazett Murray was commissioned by *The Graphic* to document the daily life of outdoor artists in Barbizon. His report on their unusual, bohemian lifestyle in the forest also appeared in New York, where it inspired a group of artists and illustrators to set up a parody version known as the Tile Club (ill. pp. 300/301).

Ein Jahr nachdem die Impressionisten in Paris reüssiert hatten, erhielt William Bazett Murray vom *Graphic* den Auftrag, den Alltag der Pleinairmaler in Barbizon zu dokumentieren. Sein Bericht vom skurrilen Bohemeleben in den Wäldern erschien auch in New York und inspirierte dort eine Gruppe von Illustratoren und Malern zu der parodistischen Unternehmung des Tile Club (Abb. S. 300/301).

Un an après que les Impressionnistes avaient réussi à Paris, William Bazett Murray reçut du *Graphic* la mission de documenter le quotidien des peintres de plein air à Barbizon. Son rapport d'un style de vie bohème et fantasque parut aussi à New York, où il incita un groupe d'illustrateurs et de peintres à s'embarquer dans la burlesque entreprise du Tile Club (ill. p. 300/301).

OCTOBER 16, 1875.]   HARPER'S WEEKLY.   845

AN ARTISTS' COLONY, FONTAINEBLEAU, FRANCE.

AN ARTISTS' COLONY.

THE pretty little village of Barbizon, a great resort for artists of all nations, is situated on the skirts of the grand forest of Fontainebleau, about forty miles southeast of Paris. ROSA BONHEUR has a house there, where she passes most of her time. The village has two pleasant inns, which are monopolized by brethren of the brush. Sketch No. 1 shows how a wet morning is employed by the fraternity. No. 2, the "Croix du Grand Veneur," is one of the numerous crosses to be found in the forest. This one is a celebrated rendezvous for hunting parties. No. 3 is the picture of a well-known hermit, who has built for himself a Robinson Crusoe hut in the branches

of four trees. He has lived there for several years, subsisting on roots and herbs. In winter he wears a coat made of his own hair, but in summer he has only a short loin cloth for clothing. When the artist saw him he had his beard tied behind his head with a piece of colored ribbon. No. 4 represents a scene which frequently takes place in the billiard-room, the walls of which are covered with silhouettes. No. 5 shows the method of stealing wood. Vipers literally swarm in the forest, and generally high boots are worn as a measure of protection. No. 6 shows an incident that happened lately at Barbizon. The wife of an artist felt a viper coil round her ancle. She had presence of mind to remain still and call for assistance,

and the creature was soon dispatched. On being opened, a whole mouse was found in its interior. She probably owed her escape from a bite to this circumstance, the reptile being gorged. No. 7 is the "salle à manger," or dining-room, the walls of which are paneled and decorated by the visitors.

WHITE ANTS.

THESE remarkable insects have little in common with the small black nuisances of the same name with which we are so familiar, though they resemble them slightly in their social character and habits. Scarcely less wonderful than the bee in their social organization, they differ from

that insect, inasmuch as the labors of the latter are attended with no evil to mankind, but are, on the contrary, productive of an eminently agreeable and useful article of food, while the white ant, so far as naturalists have yet discovered, is productive of nothing but extensive and unmitigated mischief.

These insects live in societies, each of which consists of a countless number of individuals, the large majority of which are wingless. Two individuals only in each society, a male and a female, or, according to some, a king and a queen, are winged, and these alone in the entire society are specimens of the perfect insect. The king and queen are privileged individuals, surrounded with all the respect and consideration, and re-

THE TILE CLUB AT WORK.—

BY C. S. REINHART.—[SEE PAGE 75.]

404   THE TILE CLUB AT WORK.

A TILE IN RELIEF.

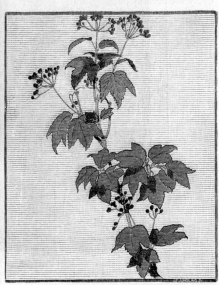

A "MOTIVE" FOR A TILE.

their heads and their hearts, they tried a second. To this, possibly from no nobler motive than curiosity, came doubtfully two more, the "Chestnut" and "Sirius."

Subsequently there appeared and handed in their allegiance the "Obtuse Bard" (whose birthplace was rendered obscure by a bad habit he had of promiscuously begging his bread, for purposes of erasure), the "O'Donoghue," the "Bone," the "Owl,"

seemed to actuate it, and if there ever were any perilous shallows or menacing rocks in its path, it certainly steered clear of them all. There was, to be sure, a dangerous member who desired to change its title to

that of the "Anglo-American-Hibernian Association of Painters on Tiles, limited;" but he was snubbed and suppressed and a title suggestive of an unwholesome ambition and otherwise of a generally inflammatory character was avoided. Another member

COCKATOO TILE.

AN IDEA BY "CADMIUM."

"Polyphemus" (so called from his somewhat obscure resemblance to a gentleman of antiquity who is mentioned in connection with the crude experiments of the oculist, Ulysses), "Cadmium," and the "Marine" and the "Griffin." A certain enthusiasm declared itself, the attendance became regular and the club settled down into a solid, hard-working and self-respecting body. A wise and discriminating spirit

Frederick Juengling (sc.) and others

The Tile Club at Work, 1879
Der Tile Club bei der Arbeit
Le Tile Club au travail
Wood engravings
From: *Scribner's Monthly Magazine*, New York,
January 1879

The series on the Tile Club, which first began appearing in the cultural magazine *Scribner's Monthly* in 1879, was a second coup for its art director Alexander Wilson Drake. Two years earlier he had provoked a heated debate in the American press after he had overseen the publishing of a series of informal wood engravings based on Impressionist sketches. The photoxylographic technique used on that occasion, which had caused such a sensation when it was employed by artists of the New School, was used again here for Drake's new series (ill. p. 233).

Die Tile-Club-Serie, die ab 1879 im Kulturmagazin *Scribner's Monthly* erschien, war der zweite Coup des Artdirectors Alexander Wilson Drake. Zwei Jahre zuvor hatte er mit einer Reihe informeller Holzstiche nach impressionistischen Skizzen eine hitzige Mediendebatte in der amerikanischen Presse ausgelöst. Die Fotoxylografen, die als New School Furore machten, kamen auch hier zum Einsatz (Abb. S. 233).

La série du Tile Club, qui parut dans le magazine culturel *Scribner's Monthly* à partir de 1879, fut le deuxième coup du directeur artistique Alexander Wilson Drake. Deux ans auparavant, il avait déclenché dans la presse américaine un violent débat médiatique avec une série de gravures sur bois informelles d'après des esquisses impressionnistes. Les xylophotographes qui faisaient fureur en tant qu'artistes de la New School furent employés ici aussi (ill. p. 233).

←← **Charles Stanley Reinhart**

The Tile Club at Work, 1880
Der Tile Club bei der Arbeit
Le Tile Club au travail
Wood engraving
From: *Harper's Weekly*, New York,
21 January 1880

"In New York there is at present a group of illustrators who call themselves the Tile Club" Van Gogh told his brother in a letter from 29 March/ 1 April 1883. Many of its members, such as Winslow Homer, were already known as illustrators for the press. They took inspiration from the interdisciplinary emphasis of the Arts and Crafts movement, while at the same time being irritated by its mania for decoration, and at their weekly meetings they painted together on tiles.

„In New York gibt es zurzeit einen Klub von Zeichnern, die sich The Tile Club nennen", teilte van Gogh seinem Bruder in einem Brief vom 29. März/ 1. April 1883 mit. Viele der Mitglieder wie Winslow Homer waren als Pressegrafiker bekannt. Inspiriert vom interdisziplinären Arts-and-Crafts-Impuls, aber auch genervt vom dekorativen Hype der englischen Bewegung, wurden bei den wöchentlichen Treffen gemeinsam Kacheln bemalt.

«À New York en ce moment il y a un club de dessinateurs qui se nomment The Tile Club», annonça Van Gogh en 1883 à son frère dans une lettre du 29 mars/1er avril. Beaucoup de ses membres comme Winslow Homer étaient connus comme illustrateurs de presse. Inspirés par l'élan interdisciplinaire de l'Arts-and-Crafts, mais aussi agacés par l'engouement décoratif du mouvement anglais, ils peignaient ensemble sur des tuiles pendant leurs rencontres hebdomadaires.

Edwin Austin Abbey & Timothy Cole (sc.)

The Tile Club at Play, 1879
Der Tile Club beim Spielen
Le Tile Club au jeu
Wood engravings
From: *Scribner's Monthly Magazine*,
New York, February 1879

In the engravings made by the New School's Tile Club Van Gogh detected "something mechanical, something like a photograph or photogravure" (letter to Theo, 22 December 1882). In this reaction he was concurring with William James Linton's polemical arguments in the American press attacking such illustrations, and statements such as "How can a work that is utterly inexpressive be artistic?", as Linton wrote in June 1879 ("Art in Engraving on Wood").

Van Gogh machte in den Tile-Club-Stichen der New School „etwas Mechanisches" aus, „etwas von einer Fotografie oder Fotogravure" (Brief an Theo, 22. Dezember 1882). Er stimmte darin mit den Polemiken überein, mit denen William James Linton die Grafiken in der amerikanischen Presse überzogen hatte. „Wie kann das vollkommen Ausdruckslose künstlerisch sein?", schrieb dieser im Juni 1879 („Art in Engraving on Wood").

Van Gogh décela «quelque chose de mécanique» dans les gravures du Tile Club de la «New School», «quelque chose d'une photographie ou d'une photogravure» (lettre à Théo, 22 décembre 1882). Il était d'accord avec les polémiques dont la presse américaine avait accablé William James Lintor pour ses dessins. «Comment l'inexpressif absolu peut-il être artistique?», écrivait-il en juin 1879 («Art in Engraving on Wood»).

The "Griffin" at Work, 1879
Der „Griffin" bei der Arbeit
Le «Griffin» au travail

Sketching at East Hampton, 1879
Zeichnen in East Hampton
Dessiner à East Hampton

William Bazett Murray

→ *The International Health Exhibition – Behind the Scenes at the Fountains*, 1884
Die Internationale Gesundheitsausstellung – Hinter den Kulissen an den Brunnen
L'Exposition internationale de la Santé – Derrière les coulisses aux fontaines
Wood engraving
From: *The Illustrated London News*, 2 August 1884

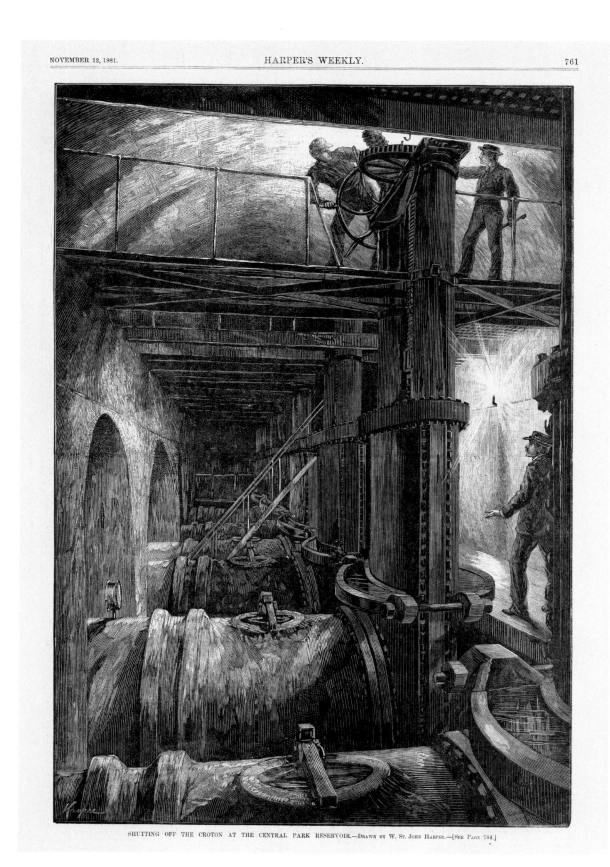

NOVEMBER 12, 1881.   HARPER'S WEEKLY.   761

SHUTTING OFF THE CROTON AT THE CENTRAL PARK RESERVOIR.—DRAWN BY W. ST. JOHN HARPER.—[SEE PAGE 764.]

William St. John Harper

Shutting off the Croton at the Central Park Reservoir, 1881
Abdrehen des Croton-Aquädukts am Wasserreservoir im Central Park
Coupure de l'aqueduc du Croton au réservoir d'eau de Central Park
Wood engraving
From: *Harper's Weekly*, New York, 12 November 1881

William St. John Harper was another illustrator admired by Van Gogh, and was part of a group of Impressionist artists linked with the Art Students League of New York who in the late 1870s gave a new artistic impetus to American press graphics. This is the only illustration by Harper that can definitely be said to have been in Van Gogh's collection.

Der von van Gogh geschätzte William St. John Harper gehörte zu einer Reihe impressionistischer Künstler im Umfeld der Art Students League of New York, die der amerikanischen Pressegrafik in den späten 1870er-Jahren neue malerische Impulse gab. Es handelt sich dabei um die einzige Grafik Harpers, die sich nachweislich in der Sammlung van Goghs befand.

William St. John Harper, pour lequel Van Gogh avait une grande estime, faisait partie d'un groupe d'artistes impressionnistes proches de l'Art Students League of New York, qui à la fin des années 1870 donna un nouvel élan au dessin de presse américain. Il s'agit ici de l'unique dessin d'Harper qui, comme il est prouvé, se trouvait dans la collection de Van Gogh.

BEHIND THE SCENES AT THE FOUNTAINS.

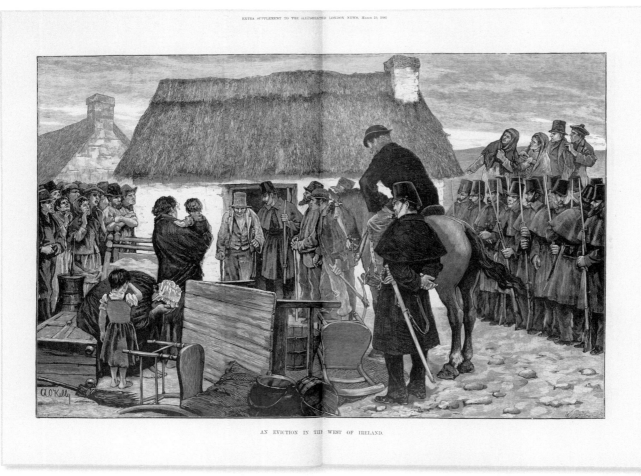

AN EVICTION IN THE WEST OF IRELAND.

THE LAND LEAGUE AGITATION IN IRELAND: SHERIFF'S SALE OF CATTLE, TO PAY RENT.
SEE PAGE 614.

Aloysius O'Kelly & William James Palmer (sc.)

An Eviction in the West of Ireland, 1881
Zwangsräumung im Westen Irlands
Une Expulsion à l'ouest de l'Irlande
Wood engraving
From: *The Illustrated London News*, 19 March 1881

The Land League Agitation in Ireland, 1881
Agitation der Land League in Irland
Agitation de la Land League en Irlande
Wood engraving
From: *The Illustrated London News*, 18 June 1881

Amidst a crowd of protesters, the cattle of an evicted Irish smallholder are being auctioned off. Van Gogh had amassed a collection of over 50 press illustrations about Ireland, which meant he could trace the deteriorating situation as it developed from the time of the Great Famine (see also ill. p. 161) to the Irish National Land League's ongoing struggle for land reform.

Unter massivem Protest findet die Versteigerung des Viehs eines zwangsgeräumten irischen Kleinbauern statt. Das thematische Konvolut von über 50 Drucken, das van Gogh über Irland zusammengetragen hatte, erlaubte es ihm, die Zuspitzung der Krise von der großen Hungersnot (siehe auch Abb. S. 161) bis zum aktuellen Kampf der Irish Land League um Landreformen im Überblick zu studieren.

La vente aux enchères du bétail d'un petit paysan irlandais expulsé a lieu sous de violentes protestations. La collection thématique de plus de 50 gravures, que Van Gogh avait rassemblées sur l'Irlande, lui permit d'étudier dans son ensemble l'aggravation de la crise de la grande famine (voir aussi ill. p. 161) au combat actuel de l'Irish Land League pour des réformes agraires.

Richard Caton Woodville Jr. & W.J. Moses (sc.)

The State of Ireland: Scene outside the Courthouse, Galway, 1880
Der Staat Irland: Szene außerhalb des Gerichtsgebäudes, Galway
L'État d'Irlande : Scène à l'extérieur du palais de justice, Galway
Wood engraving
From: *The Illustrated London News,* 14 February 1880

In this illustration of a population driven to starvation there is a racist stereotyped image likening people to primates, which had been earlier established by caricaturists working for *Punch* such as John Leech and John Tenniel. Van Gogh was deeply impressed by the virtuosity in Richard Caton Woodville's work, a man who was three years his junior and had just embarked on a long career as chief artist for the *Illustrated London News.*

In der Darstellung der hungernden Bevölkerung scheint ein primaten-artiges rassistisches Stereotyp auf, das von den *Punch*-Karikaturisten John Leech und John Tenniel etabliert worden war. Van Gogh war tief beeindruckt von der Virtuosität des drei Jahre jüngeren Richard Caton Woodville, der sich gerade am Beginn einer langen Karriere als Chefzeichner der *Illustrated London News* befand.

Dans la représentation de la population affamée, un stéréotype raciste inspiré des primates et qui avait été établi par les caricaturistes de *Punch* John Leech et John Tenniel fait son apparition. Van Gogh était profondé-ment impressionné par la virtuosité de Richard Caton Woodville, de trois ans son cadet, qui était alors à l'aube d'une longue carrière de dessinateur en chef des *Illustrated London News.*

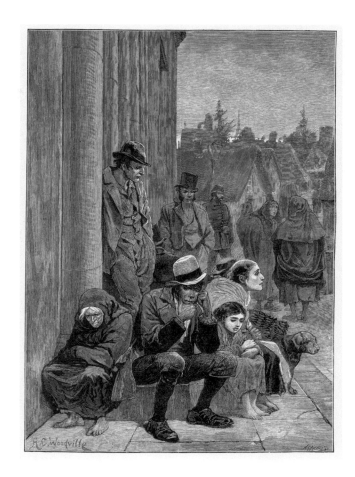

Georges Montbard

Irish Customs – An Eviction, 1874
Irische Sitten – Zwangsräumung
Mœurs irlandaises – Une expulsion
Wood engraving
From: *L'Illustration,* 10 January 1874

Van Gogh's collection on Ireland also included illustrations by Georges Montbard (see also ill. p. 321), who, in the same way as Félix Régamey, had started out as a political caricaturist working in Paris before ending up in London as a member of the Commune in exile. He was then able to establish an international career for himself, and Van Gogh was an admirer of his sensi-tive landscape studies, particularly in his reports from north-west Africa.

In van Goghs Irland-Konvolut befan-den sich auch Grafiken von Georges Montbard (siehe auch Abb. S. 321). Wie Félix Régamey hatte er in Paris als politischer Karikaturist begonnen und war dann als Exilkommunarde in London gelandet. Von dort aus gelang ihm schließlich eine internationale Karriere. Van Gogh schätzte seine ein-fühlsamen Landschaftsstudien, insbe-sondere seine Maghreb-Reportagen.

Dans la collection irlandaise de Van Gogh se trouvaient également des dessins de Georges Montbard (voir aussi ill. p. 321). À l'instar de Félix Régamey, il avait commencé à Paris comme caricaturiste politique et, communard en exil, s'était retrouvé à Londres. De là, il réussit finalement à faire une carrière internationale. Van Gogh admirait ses sensibles études de paysages, en particulier ses repor-tages sur le Maghreb.

220   LE MONDE ILLUSTRÉ

LES MOIS RUSTIQUES. — Les Semailles du printemps. — (Dessin de M. Ryckebusch.)

Philippe Ryckebusch & Édouard Coste (sc.)

Months in the Country – Sowing the Seeds in the Spring, 1879
Ländliche Monate – Die Frühlingsaussaat
Les mois rustiques – Les semailles du printemps
Wood engraving
From: *Le Monde illustré*, Paris, 1879

The French press illustrator Philippe Ryckebusch was the closest to Van Gogh in terms of his choice of subject matter. A worthy successor to Jules Breton and François Bonvin, his popular series of illustrations documenting agricultural work and the decline of various cottage industries were published in *Le Monde illustré* and *L'Illustration*.

Der französische Pressezeichner Philippe Ryckebusch stand van Gogh in der Motivwahl am nächsten. In *Le Monde illustré* und *L'Illustration* veröffentlichte er populäre grafische Folgen, die die Arbeit in der Landwirtschaft und der aussterbenden Heimindustrie in der Nachfolge eines Jules Breton und François Bonvin dokumentierten.

L'illustrateur de presse français Philippe Ryckebusch était le plus proche de Van Gogh dans le choix des motifs. Digne successeur de Jules Breton et de François Bonvin, il publia dans *Le Monde illustré* et *L'Illustration* des séries de dessins fort populaires, qui documentaient le travail agricole et l'industrie artisanale en voie d'extinction.

Paul Renouard & Albert Bellenger (sc.)

↓ *The Industrial Crisis in Lyon – No Work*, 1884
Die Industriekrise in Lyon – Arbeitslos
La crise industrielle à Lyon – Sans travail
Wood engraving
From: *L'Illustration*, Paris, 25 October 1884

This illustration of a group of unemployed weavers brought out Van Gogh's fullest enthusiasm: "there is so much physicality and breadth in it that I feel it could easily stand side by side with works by Millet, Daumier or Lepage" (letter to Theo, 26 January 1885). The sole work by Paul Renouard seemed to Van Gogh to be the main proof that artistic progress can only be made by concentrating exclusively on the study of nature.

Die Darstellung einer Gruppe arbeitsloser Weber hat van Gogh begeistert: „[…] es steckt so viel Körperlichkeit und Weite drin, dass mir scheint, dass sie gut neben einem Millet, Daumier oder Lepage bestehen könnte" (Brief an Theo, 26. Januar 1885). Paul Renouards solitäres Werk schien ihm ein zentraler Beleg dafür zu sein, dass man künstlerisch vorankommt, wenn man sich einzig kompromisslos an die Natur hält.

La représentation d'un groupe de tisserands sans travail a enthousiasmé Van Gogh : «[…] il y a tant de corporéalité et d'ampleur là-dedans, qu'il me semble qu'elle pourrait bien avoir sa place à côté d'un Millet, Daumier ou Lepage» (Lettre à Théo, 26 janvier 1885). L'œuvre solitaire de Paul Renouard lui semblait être la preuve centrale qu'on avance sur le plan artistique quand on s'oriente uniquement et sans compromis vers la nature.

2268. — N. 2174.

L'ILLUSTRATION

25 OCTOBRE 1884

LA CRISE INDUSTRIELLE A LYON
SANS TRAVAIL
Dessin d'après nature de M. Renouard, envoyé spécial de *l'Illustration*

**Henri Toussaint, after Paul Renouard,
& Émile Tilly (sc.)**

Revolutionary Attacks in Lyon, 1882
Die revolutionären Anschläge von Lyon
Les Attentats révolutionnaires de Lyon
Wood engraving
From: *L'Illustration*, Paris, 4 November 1882

The empty restaurant of the Théâtre Bellecour in
Lyon shown here was the scene of a bomb attack
that resulted in a sensational show trial the following
year for a number of notable anarchists, including
Peter Kropotkin, who was enormously influential
amongst the later Impressionist artists. The illustration is by Paul Renouard, whose work became
increasingly important for Van Gogh.

Das leere Nachtcafé des Théâtre Bellecour in Lyon
war Schauplatz eines Bombenattentats, das im
folgenden Jahr einen spektakulären Schauprozess
gegen eine Reihe führender Anarchisten zur Folge
hatte, darunter den in spätimpressionistischen Künstlerkreisen enorm einflussreichen Pjotr Kropotkin. Die
Zeichnung stammt von Paul Renouard, einem Zeichner, der für van Gogh zunehmend wichtig wurde.

Dans le café de nuit vide du Théâtre Bellecour à
Lyon fut perpétré un attentat à la bombe, qui donna
lieu l'année suivante à un sensationnel procès-spec-
tacle contre une série de chefs anarchistes, dont
Pierre Kropotkine qui était extrêmement influent
dans les cercles d'artistes de l'impressionnisme
tardif. Ce dessin est l'œuvre de Paul Renouard,
un dessinateur qui devint de plus en plus important
pour Van Gogh.

Paul Renouard & Albert Bellenger (sc.)

The Industrial Crisis in Lyon, 1884
Die Industriekrise in Lyon
La Crise industrielle à Lyon
Wood engraving
From: *L'Illustration*, Paris, 18 October 1884

A new investigative trend towards a literary style
of naturalism also becomes apparent in Paul
Renouard's psychologically sensitive social illustration work. Renouard's pictorial journalism, which
Van Gogh saw as having no equal, functioned in a
similar manner to Impressionist paintings and was
highly regarded by renowned critics such as Joris-
Karl Huysmans.

In der psychologisch ausdifferenzierten Sozialgrafik
Paul Renouards machte sich eine neue investigative
Tendenz bemerkbar, die am literarischen Naturalis-
mus orientiert war. Renouards bildjournalistische
Kunst, die für van Gogh ein unerreichtes Vorbild blieb,
operierte auf Augenhöhe mit der impressionistischen
Malerei und wurde von namhaften Kritikern wie Joris-
Karl Huysmans hochgeschätzt.

Une nouvelle tendance investigatrice, qui s'orientait
vers le naturalisme littéraire, se manifestait dans les
dessins de portraits socio-psychologiques de Paul
Renouard. L'art journalistique pictural de Renouard,
qui resta pour Van Gogh un modèle inégalé, opérait
à pied d'égalité avec la peinture impressionniste et
fut tenu en haute estime par des critiques de renom
comme Joris-Karl Huysmans.

The Triumph of Caricature

Whereas the caricature movement in France under Charles Philipon had developed in the republican spirit of Bonapartist historical art, the country's second phase of caricatures in the mid-1860s was opposed to the retrograde Bonapartism of Napoleon III. The general outlines for this revised orientation were established by Victor Hugo, who was in exile at the time and brought Napoleon III down to size by depicting him as the ridiculous figure Napoléon le Petit, and by castigating him in his popular poetry collection Les Châtiments (1853). For Hugo, the grotesque was an aspect of the sublime, and caricature was thus one of the highest forms of artistic expression.

The battle with the censors of the Second Empire began with portrait caricature, a genre that had been made more eye-catching by the caricaturist André Gill's poster-style cover illustrations. With the use of this pseudonym and the name of the newspaper he worked for, La Lune, Gill was declaring a journey into the realm of fantasy and an art rooted in eccentricity, which was as far removed as possible from the moderate style of caricatures that appeared in the now well-established magazine Le Charivari. The latter had come to stand for tedious representations of dated customs and a style of illustration that took its lead from academic Classicism. Philipon had even gone as far as dismissing his venerable chief illustrator Honoré Daumier in 1861 for lack of originality.

With his deconstructed Authentic Portrait of Rocambole (see ill. p. 318) in 1867, Gill was launching a direct attack against Napoleon III. He thereby became a star to the anarchists and bohemians in the circle associated with the poet Jules Vallès, a group that went on to become the artistic epicentre during the Paris Commune. Amidst the political turmoil of the Second Empire, the Commune and the stirrings of monarchy in the early years of the Third Republic, and in spite of censorship pressure, Gill and his students developed an exciting pictorial language that anticipated elements of Art Nouveau, Cubism and Agitprop.

The artistic precursor for this reformation of caricature can be traced back to Philipon's early campaigns. From 1875, Gill and his students played a fundamental role in establishing Montmartre as a centre of the arts. The emancipation of the applied arts and their recognition as having equal status with academic disciplines, which had already been recommended by the Commune's Federation of Artists under the leadership of Gustave Courbet, meant they were now pursued with a strong sense of coherence between the various different disciplines. In France, however, this second caricature movement was remembered only reluctantly, since it was so closely linked with memories of the bloody fall of the Commune and the protracted, painful birth of the Third Republic. The fact that its founder, Gill, died in a lunatic asylum in 1885 did not exactly help with its

subsequent popularity. Instead, the art of caricature became depoliticised at the same time as the myth of Daumier the artist was being constructed, which properly began in 1878 with his first retrospective exhibition. By turning Daumier into an outsized monument in this way, one consequence was that the younger artists became marginalised.

Amongst the monarchies in Europe at this time caricature played no significant role, and it was only in republican North America that it reached a similar high point. During the years of rebuilding after the Civil War, a culture of journalistic debate had emerged in which caricature increasingly became a feature. Within a few years, the former picture reporter Thomas Nast presented the first political caricatures almost single-handedly, in a country that had no real tradition of such illustrations. Nast's designs were based chiefly on the graphic work of the Punch illustrator John Tenniel, although he also followed events in France closely and in particular the duels fought over illustrations between André Gill, who was the same age as he was, and the censors. Nast also had the great advantage that in contrast to his colleagues in Europe his illustrations did not appear in satirical reviews, but in the mass-circulation press. As a result their range of effect was vastly greater. His triumphant campaign in the early 1870s against the New York senator William Tweed and his corrupt dealings elevated Nast to the rank of most powerful political commentator in the United States. Moreover, in contrast to social critics who wrote up their views, as an illustrator Nast was able to bring his polemics to the large immigrant population who had little or no ability to read, but whose voices could none the less influence the outcome of elections. No illustrative artist of modern times has had more political influence than Nast, schooled as he was in the radical republican ideals of the revolutions in Europe of 1848.

Nast's influence on American popular culture was no less significant. For example, he was responsible for introducing the use of the two animals that represent the two main parties in politics. He also developed the symbolic figure of Uncle Sam, introduced the graphic symbol for the dollar and popularised Father Christmas in America. Van Gogh, who put together an album of Nast's illustrations, was a fan of his work.

By the mid-1870s, Nast's pictorial style had become increasingly fluid to the point where it resembled the sequential imagery of film-making, as a combined result of the lecture tours he gave about his graphic work and the influence of German illustrated magazines. Even before the pictorial sequences that appeared in the satirical magazine Puck, Nast thus prepared the way for American comic-book culture. Disney's dynamic animal cartoons can be found in essence here, just as much as Robert Crumb's anti-Disney art, which was often inspired by Nast's work (ills. p. 336 t.).

Édouard Manet

Punch | *Pulcinell* | *Polichinelle*, 1874/75
Chromolithograph
Paris, Bibliothèque nationale de France

After the reactionary Marshal Patrice de Mac-Mahon was appointed president of the Third Republic, Manet too took up arms in the battle of caricatures. This lithograph for the republican newspaper *Le Temps*, which was banned from being published,

depicts the former soldier Mac-Mahon, who had ordered the rebellious members of the Commune to be shot down, in the figure of a devious and bullying clown.

Nachdem der reaktionäre Marschall Patrice de Mac-Mahon zum Präsidenten der Dritten Republik ernannt worden war, griff auch Édouard Manet in den Karikaturkampf ein. Die beschlagnahmte Lithografie für die republikanische Zeitung *Le Temps* zeigt den Ex-

Militär, der die Niederschießung des Kommuneaufstands kommandierte, als hinterlistigen Prügelclown.

Après que le maréchal réactionnaire Patrice de Mac-Mahon eut été élu président de la Troisième République, Édouard Manet se jeta aussi dans la bataille de caricatures. La lithographie, confisquée, pour le journal républicain *Le Temps* montre l'ancien militaire, qui ordonna d'abattre les insurgés de la Commune, comme un clown brutal et sournois.

Triumph der Karikatur

Während sich Charles Philipons Karikaturbewegung in Frankreich im republikanischen Geist der alten bonapartistischen Historienkunst entwickelt hatte, positionierte sich die zweite Karikaturwelle in der Mitte der 1860er-Jahre gegen den Retro-Bonapartismus von Napoleon III., einem Neffen Napoleons. Den programmatischen Rahmen lieferte der exilierte Dichter Victor Hugo, der Napoleon II. zur Spottfigur Napoléon le Petit verzwergt hatte und in seinem populären Gedichtzyklus *Les Châtiments* (1853) parodierte. Für Hugo war das Groteske ein Aspekt des Sublimen und die Karikatur dementsprechend eine höchste künstlerische Ausdrucksform.

Der Kampf gegen die Zensoren des Zweiten Kaiserreichs begann auf dem Feld der Porträtkarikatur, ein Format, das durch die posterartigen Titelgrafiken des Cartoonisten André Gill an Attraktivität gewonnen hatte. Gill hatte bereits durch seinen Künstlernamen und den Titel seines Magazins *La Lune* einen Aufbruch ins Fantastische angekündigt, eine Kunst der Exzentrik, die sich im größtmöglichen Gegensatz zum moderaten Karikaturmodus des etablierten *Le Charivari* befand. Der stand mittlerweile für ermüdende Sittenschilderungen und ein Cartooning, das sich an der akademischen Klassik orientierte. Seinen verdienten Chefzeichner Honoré Daumier hatte Philipon bereits 1861 wegen Einfallslosigkeit entlassen.

Mit dem dekonstruierten *Portrait authentique de Rocambole* (Abb. S. 318) unternahm Gill 1867 einen Frontalangriff auf Napoleon III. und stieg damit zum Star einer anarchistischen Bohemeszene um den Dichter Jules Vallès auf, die wenig später das künstlerische Epizentrum der Pariser Kommune bilden sollte. In den politischen Wechselbädern des Kaiserreichs, der Kommune und der monarchistischen Anfangszeit der Dritten Republik entwickelten Gill und seine Schüler unter dem Druck der Zensoren ein aufregendes Bildvokabular, das Elemente von Art nouveau, Kubismus und Agitprop antizipierte.

Die künstlerische Vorreiterrolle dieser Karikaturreformation schloss an Philipons frühe Kampagnen an. Seit 1875 spielten Gill und sein Schülerkreis eine entscheidende Rolle bei der Etablierung der Künstlerszene auf dem Montmartre. Die Emanzipation der angewandten Künste und ihre Gleichstellung mit den akademischen Disziplinen, die unter Gustave Courbet bereits in der Künstlervereinigung der Kommune avisiert worden waren, wurden hier mit großer interdisziplinärer Konsequenz vorangetrieben. In Frankreich blickte man nur ungern auf diese zweite Karikaturbewegung zurück, da sie mit Erinnerungen an den blutigen Zusammenbruch der Kommune und an die langwierigen Geburtswehen der Dritten Republik verbunden war. Dass ihr Begründer André Gill 1885 in der Psychiatrie verstorben war, trug kaum zu ihrer Popularität bei. Stattdessen wurde mit der Konstruktion des Künstlermythos Daumier, die bereits 1878 mit einer ersten retrospektiven Ausstellung eingesetzt hatte, eine Entpolitisierung der Karikatur betrieben. Die Monumentalisierung Daumiers trug wesentlich zur Marginalisierung der jüngeren Bewegung bei.

In den anderen europäischen Monarchien der Zeit spielte die Karikatur keine wichtige Rolle. Einzig im republikanischen Nordamerika gab es eine parallele Hochphase. Während der Aufbaujahre nach dem Bürgerkrieg war dort eine publizistische Streitkultur entstanden, an der zunehmend auch das Cartooning beteiligt war. Innerhalb weniger Jahre wurde die politische Karikatur, die hier auf keine nennenswerte Tradition zurückgreifen konnte, quasi im Alleingang von dem ehemaligen Bildreporter Thomas Nast etabliert. Nast griff dabei vor allem auf die Grafiken des *Punch*-Cartoonisten John Tenniel zurück, hatte aber auch ein waches Auge auf die Entwicklungen in Frankreich, vor allem auf die grafischen Duelle, die sich der gleichaltrige André Gill dort mit den Zensoren lieferte. Von Vorteil war, dass Nasts Cartoons im Gegensatz zu den Arbeiten seiner europäischen Kollegen nicht in satirischen Periodika erschienen, sondern in der auflagenstärksten Nachrichtenillustrierten. Ihr Wirkungsradius war dadurch ungleich höher. Mit seiner triumphalen Kampagne gegen den Korruptionsring des New Yorker Senators William Tweed stieg Nast Anfang der 1870er-Jahre zum mächtigsten politischen Kommentator der Vereinigten Staaten auf. Im Gegensatz zur schreibenden Zunft war der Zeichner Nast in der Lage, mit seinen Polemiken auch die Massen der Einwanderer zu erreichen, die des Lesens kaum oder gar nicht kundig waren, deren Stimmen aber wahlentscheidend sein konnten. Kein visueller Künstler der Neuzeit war politisch einflussreicher als dieser Cartoonist, der von den radikalrepublikanischen Idealen der 1848er-Revolutionen geprägt war.

Nicht weniger fundamental war Nasts Einfluss auf die amerikanische Populärkultur. So gehen beispielsweise die Tieremblebme der beiden großen Parteien auf ihn zurück. Er etablierte die Symbolfigur des Uncle Sam, führte das Dollarzeichen als grafisches Symbol ein und popularisierte Father Christmas in Amerika. Zu seinen Fans zählte offenbar auch Vincent van Gogh, der ein Album mit Nasts Karikaturen zusammenstellt hatte.

Mitte der 1870er-Jahre verflüssigte sich Nasts Cartoonstil unter dem Eindruck seiner grafischen Lecture-Tourneen und dem Einfluss der deutschen Bilderbogenkultur zusehends bis hin zur filmischen Sequenzialität. Noch vor den Bilderfolgen des satirischen *Puck*-Magazins bereitete er der amerikanischen Comickultur den Boden. Disneys dynamische Animal-Cartooning findet sich bei ihm ebenso vorgeprägt wie die Anti-Disney-Kunst von Robert Crumb, der sich wiederholt auf Nasts Vorbild berufen hat (Abb. S. 336 o.).

Draner

A Guardian of Public Order, 1871
Hüter der öffentlichen Ordnung
Gardien de la paix publique
Stencil-coloured relief etching
From: Draner, *Souvenirs du Siège de Paris: Les Défenseurs de la Capitale*, Paris, 1871

Caricatures were sold as single-sheet impressions by vendors on the street and were thus available throughout the city. Hand-coloured copies were often sold as special prints.

Durch die Aushänge der Straßenverkäufer waren die Karikaturblätter im Stadtraum überall präsent.

Handkolorierte Exemplare wurden häufig auch als Sonderdrucke verkauft.

Grâce aux affichages des vendeurs de rue, les feuilles volantes de caricature étaient omniprésentes dans l'espace urbain. Des exemplaires coloriés à la main étaient fréquemment vendus sous forme d'éditions spéciales.

SOUVENIRS DU SIÉGE DE PARIS.

GARDIEN DE LA PAIX PUBLIQUE.
Décidément l'Empire de la liberté est bien
plus rigolo! moins à faire et plus à rire.....

DÉPOSÉ — Tous droits reserves.

Triomphe de la caricature

Alors que le mouvement de caricature de Charles Philipon se développait dans l'esprit républicain de l'ancien art à la gloire de Napoléon, la seconde vague de caricature se positionnait au milieu des années 1860 contre le rétro-bonapartisme de Napoléon III. Victor Hugo, poète alors en exil qui avait réduit Napoléon III au personnage ridicule de Napoléon le Petit dans son cycle lyrique très populaire *Les Châtiments* (1853), en fournit le cadre programmatique. Pour Victor Hugo, le grotesque était un aspect du sublime, et, par conséquent, la caricature une forme d'expression hautement artistique.

Le combat contre les censeurs du Second Empire commença dans le domaine du portrait-charge, un format qui avait gagné en attractivité grâce aux dessins de titre, grands comme des affiches, du caricaturiste André Gill. Par son pseudonyme et le titre de son journal *La Lune*, Gill avait déjà annoncé un voyage dans le fantastique, un art de l'excentricité, qui se situait dans le plus grand contraste possible avec le style de caricature modéré du journal bien établi *Le Charivari*. Celui-ci représentait désormais des scènes de mœurs ennuyeuses et un style de bande dessinée qui se référait au classicisme académique. Dès 1861, Charles Philipon avait licencié son très méritant dessinateur en chef Honoré Daumier pour manque d'originalité.

Avec l'image déconstruite du *Portrait authentique de Rocambole* (ill. p. 318) de 1867, Gill s'attaqua de front à Napoléon III et accéda ainsi au statut de star du milieu bohème et anarchiste dans l'entourage de Jules Vallès, qui devait un peu plus tard former l'épicentre artistique de la Commune de Paris. Dans les aléas politiques du Second Empire, de la Commune et de la phase monarchiste du début de la Troisième République, Gill et ses élèves élaborèrent sous la pression de la censure un langage pictural passionnant qui anticipait les éléments de l'Art nouveau, du cubisme et de l'Agitprop.

Le rôle de précurseur artistique de cette réforme de la caricature s'inspirait des premières campagnes de Philipon. À partir de 1875, Gill et son cercle d'adeptes jouèrent un rôle décisif dans l'implantation de la scène artistique sur la butte Montmartre. L'émancipation des arts appliqués et leur mise à égalité avec les disciplines académiques, qui avaient déjà été avisées dans la Fédération des artistes de la Commune sous la présidence de Gustave Courbet, furent ici promues avec une grande cohérence interdisciplinaire. En France, on ne se penchait que de mauvaise grâce sur ce deuxième mouvement de caricature, qui était associé aux souvenirs de l'effondrement sanglant de la Commune et de la longue et douloureuse naissance de la Troisième République. Le fait que son fondateur André Gill mourût en 1885 dans un hôpital psychiatrique ne contribua guère à sa popularité. Au lieu de cela, une dépolitisation de la caricature fut activée avec la construction du mythe de Daumier comme artiste, qui avait débuté dès 1878 avec une première exposition rétrospective. La survalorisation de Daumier contribua largement à la marginalisation du jeune mouvement.

Dans les autres monarchies européennes de cette époque, la caricature ne jouait aucun rôle important. Seule l'Amérique du Nord républicaine connut, elle aussi, son apogée de la caricature. Pendant les années de reconstruction qui suivirent la guerre civile, une culture de débat journalistique y avait vu le jour dans laquelle le dessin humoristique était de plus en plus présent. En l'espace de quelques années, la caricature politique, qui dans ce pays ne pouvait se référer à aucune tradition notable, s'établit grâce à l'engagement solitaire de l'ancien reporter d'images Thomas Nast. Nast eut surtout recours aux dessins du caricaturiste de *Punch* John Tenniel, mais suivait aussi de très près les événements en France, en particulier les duels par voie de dessins que se livraient André Gill, qui avait le même âge que lui, et les censeurs. Le grand avantage était que les dessins de Nast à l'inverse des travaux de ses collègues européens ne paraissaient pas dans des périodiques satiriques, mais dans des magazines d'information à gros tirage. Ce qui augmentait considérablement leur rayon d'action. Avec sa triomphale campagne contre le cercle de corruption du sénateur new-yorkais William Tweed, Nast avança au rang de commentateur politique le plus puissant des États-Unis au début des années 1870. Contrairement à la corporation des journalistes de plume, le dessinateur Nast pouvait aussi atteindre avec ses polémiques les masses d'immigrants qui ne savaient pas ou à peine lire mais dont les voix pouvaient peser sur le résultat des élections. Aucun artiste de l'image des temps modernes n'eut plus d'influence que ce caricaturiste imprégné des idéaux radicalement républicains des révolutions de 1848.

L'influence de Nast sur la culture populaire américaine ne fut pas moins primordiale. Ainsi, par exemple, les emblèmes des deux grands partis représentant des animaux sont-ils de sa veine. Il imposa le personnage emblématique de l'oncle Sam, instaura le signe dollar comme symbole graphique et popularisa le père Noël en Amérique. Vincent van Gogh faisait manifestement aussi partie de ses adeptes et avait constitué un album avec des caricatures de Nast.

Au milieu des années 1870, le style pictural de Nast se diffracta à vue d'œil en une séquentialité cinématographique, sous l'effet de ses conférences performances où il présentait son travail graphique et sous l'influence des pages illustrées alors populaires en Allemagne. Avant même les séries picturales du magazine satirique *Puck*, il prépara le terrain de la culture américaine de bande dessinée. Le dynamique *animal cartooning* de Disney s'en est autant inspiré que l'art anti-Disney de Robert Crumb, qui s'est souvent réclamé du style de Thomas Nast (ills. p. 336 h.).

Camille Pissarro

Portrait of Cézanne, 1874
Porträt von Cézanne
Portrait de Cézanne
Oil on canvas
London, The National Gallery,
on loan from a private owner

The anarchist Pissarro's portrait of his friend and fellow artist Cézanne is framed by two press graphics. The illustration on the left is by André Gill and relates to a spectacular case of censorship (ill. p. 344), while the one on the right shows the exiled Commune member Gustave Courbet. The painting makes clear how important the revival of political caricature had become for radical artists.

Das Porträt, das der anarchistische Künstler von seinem Freund Paul Cézanne anfertigte, ist von zwei Pressegrafiken eingerahmt. Das linke Blatt von André Gill repräsentiert einen spektakulären Zensurfall (Abb. S. 344), das rechte zeigt den geflohenen Kommunarden Gustave Courbet. Das Gemälde belegt die hohe Bedeutung, die die erneuerte politische Karikatur für radikale Künstlerkreise hatte.

Le portrait que l'artiste anarchiste fit de son ami Paul Cézanne est encadré de deux dessins de presse. Le dessin de gauche, réalisé par André Gill, représente un cas spectaculaire de censure (ill. p. 344), celui de droite montre le communard exilé Gustave Courbet. Le tableau dévoile l'extrême importance que revêtait la caricature politique ravivée dans les cercles d'artistes radicaux.

André Gill & Marchandeau (sc.)

→ *Courbet Painted by Himself and by Gill*, 1867
Courbet, von eigener Hand gemalt und von Gill
Courbet, peint par lui-même – et par Gill
Stencil-coloured relief etching
From: *La Lune*, Paris, 9 June 1867

André Gill's eye-catching cover portraits made *La Lune* the most popular illustrated periodical amidst a wave of caricatures that had begun with a phase of liberalisation towards the end of the Second Empire. However, the fact that the written permission of the person being portrayed had to be displayed, and in this case is even provocatively incorporated into the caricature itself, shows that the actual degree of freedom was somewhat limited.

Mit André Gills attraktiven Titelporträts stieg *La Lune* zum populärsten Journal einer Karikaturwelle auf, die in der Liberalisierungsphase zum Ende des Second Empire einsetzte. Dass es mit den Freiheiten nicht weit her war, macht die schriftliche Erlaubnis des Porträtierten deutlich, die bei Abdruck vorliegen musste und die hier provokanterweise zum Gegenstand der Karikatur wurde.

Avec les attrayants portraits-charge d'André Gill en première page, *La Lune* devint le journal le plus populaire d'un courant de caricature qui prit son essor vers la fin du Second Empire pendant la phase de libéralisation. L'autorisation écrite du personnage croqué, qui devait être présentée et qui devint ici objet de caricature, prouve que les libertés étaient somme toute bien relatives.

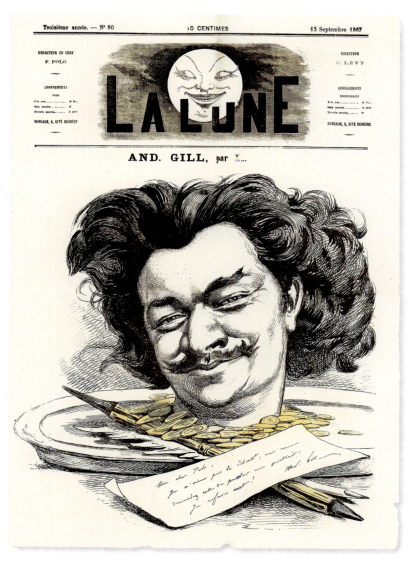

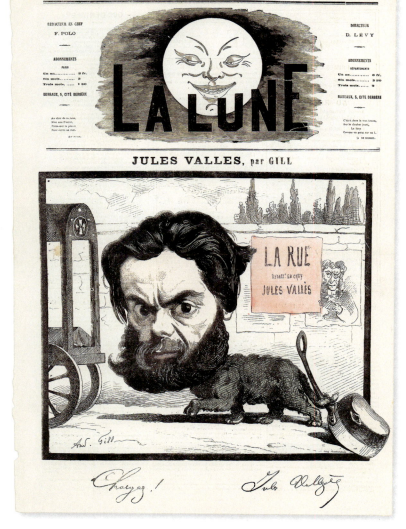

And. Gill, by X…, 1867
And. Gill, von X…
And. Gill, par X…
Stencil-coloured relief etching
From: *La Lune*, Paris,
15 September 1867

André Gill was a well-known personality himself, and Gustave Courbet, who was a friend of his, saw his caricatures as being the equal of academic art. In this self-portrait though Gill depicts himself more as a service provider of illustrations and a victim of the need to earn a living. The writing on the card states that he is no friend of freedom and thus does not give his permission for the portrait to be published.

André Gill war selbst eine Berühmtheit, dessen Karikaturen sein Freund Gustave Courbet als gleichrangig mit akademischer Kunst wertete. In dem Selbstporträt sah Gill sich allerdings eher als grafischen Dienstleister und Opfer monetärer Notwendigkeit. Auf der Karte steht, dass er kein Freund von Freiheit sei und daher auch keine Erlaubnis zur Veröffentlichung erteile.

André Gill était lui-même une célébrité, et son ami Gustave Courbet plaçait ses caricatures à pied d'égalité avec l'art académique. Néanmoins, dans cet autoportrait Gill se voyait davantage comme prestataire de service et victime de la nécessité pécuniaire. Sur la carte il est écrit qu'il n'est pas un ami de la liberté et qu'il ne délivre donc pas d'autorisation de publication.

Jules Vallès by Gill, 1867
Jules Vallès von Gill
Jules Vallès par Gill
Stencil-coloured relief etching
From: *La Lune*, Paris, 14 July 1867

This furious stray dog intent on burying the old Bonapartism amidst the clanging noise of a metal pan is in fact André Gill's colleague Jules Vallès. The anarchist author Vallès used his militant opposition magazine *La Rue* to publish journalism in colloquial language, and its enraged reports lashed out at all and sundry.

Bei dem grimmigen Straßenköter, der mit metallischem Lärm den Bonapartismus zu Grabe trägt, handelt es sich um André Gills Freund Jules Vallès. In seinem oppositionellen Kampfblatt *La Rue* propagierte der anarchistische Dichter einen Journalismus in umgangssprachlicher Diktion, der wütend in alle Richtungen austeilte.

Ce chien de rue hargneux qui porte en terre le bonapartisme dans un vacarme métallique n'est autre que l'ami d'André Gill, Jules Vallès. Dans son journal d'opposition militante, le poète anarchiste propageait dans un langage familier un journalisme qui lançait des critiques au vitriol tous azimuts.

Troisième année. — N° 66.   10 CENTIMES. — Tirage : 41,000   9 Juin 1867

RÉDACTEUR EN CHEF
F. POLO

ABONNEMENTS
PARIS
Un an............. 5 fr.
Six mois....... 3
Trois mois...... 1 50

BUREAUX, 5, CITÉ BERGÈRE

DIRECTEUR
D. LÉVY

ABONNEMENTS
DÉPARTEMENTS
Un an............. 6 fr.
Six mois....... 3 50
Trois mois..... 2

BUREAUX, 5, CITÉ BERGÈRE

Au clair de la lune,
Mon ami Pierrot,
Prête-moi ta plume
Pour écrire un mot.

Air connu.

C'était dans la nuit brune,
Sur le clocher jauni,
La lune
Comme un point sur un I.

(A. DE MUSSET.)

COURBET, peint par lui-même — et par GILL

LA LUNE

N° 89

10 centimes

PORTRAIT AUTHENTIQUE DE ROCAMBOLE
PAR GILL
D'après deux photographies et un grand nombre de documents fournis par **M. le vicomte PONSON DU TERRAIL**, son illustre ami

André Gill & Marchandeau (sc.)

Authentic Portrait of Rocambole, 1867
Authentisches Porträt von Rocambole
Portrait authentique de Rocambole
Stencil-coloured relief etching
From: *La Lune*, Paris, 17 November 1867

Following his attack on state policy regarding Italy, André Gill then launched an offensive against the Emperor himself with such brazen audacity that it spelled the end of *La Lune*, but also made Gill a starring figure in the ranks of the resistance. By likening him to the fictional villain Rocambole, Gill was making allusions to Louis Napoléon's shady past as a former prison inmate and his violent attempts at seizing power, while offsetting that aspect with his later image as a dandy.

Nach dem Angriff auf die Italienpolitik attackierte André Gill den Kaiser frontal mit einer Chuzpe, die das Ende von *La Lune* bedeutete und seinen eigenen Aufstieg zum Star des Widerstands bewirkte. In der Gleichsetzung mit dem Serienhelden Rocambole spielt Gill auf die zwielichtige Vergangenheit des Putschisten und Ex-Sträflings Louis Napoléon an und konterkariert sie mit dessen dandyhaftem Image.

Après son offensive contre sa politique italienne, André Gill attaqua l'empereur de face avec un aplomb qui signifia la fin de *La Lune* et entraîna sa propre ascension comme star de la résistance. En l'assimilant au héros de feuilleton Rocambole, Gill fait allusion au passé nébuleux de putschiste et ancien prisonnier Louis-Napoléon, et démonte ainsi son image de dandy.

The Masked Wrestlers, 1867
Die maskierten Ringer | *Les Lutteurs masqués*
Stencil-coloured relief etching
From: *La Lune*, Paris, 3 November 1867

Gill's illustration of a wrestler in red throwing his tonsured opponent to the ground, having already disarmed him of his religious cudgel, was in defiance of a ban on political caricatures that were against the national interests. The picture refers to the battle for Rome between Garibaldi's republicans and the forces of the Pope, who was supported by Napoleon III, and takes aim at the French Empire's reactionary foreign policy.

Mit der Darstellung eines roten Ringers, der seinen tonsurierten Kontrahenten und dessen sakralen Totschläger zu Boden wirft, übertrat André Gill ein Karikaturverbot für politische Themen von nationalem Belang. Mit der Anspielung auf den Kampf um Rom zwischen Giuseppe Garibaldis Republikanern und dem von Napoleon III. unterstützten Papst zielte er auf die reaktionäre Außenpolitik des Empire.

Avec son portrait d'un lutteur en rouge qui jette au sol son adversaire tonsuré ainsi que son gourdin sacré, André Gill transgressa une interdiction de caricature pour les thèmes politiques d'intérêt national. À travers son allusion à la bataille de Rome entre les républicains de Giuseppe Garibaldi et le pape soutenu par Napoléon III, il visait la politique extérieure réactionnaire de l'Empire.

LA RUE

Ad Gill

André Gill & Marchandeau (sc.)

Untitled, 1867
Ohne Titel | Sans titre
Relief etching
From: *La Rue – Paris pittoresque et populaire*, Paris, 2 November 1867

Death stands at the head of the army as André Gill lampoons the rapid rise of militarism. Jules Vallès, who a few years later became the main publicist for the Commune, brought together for his anti-authoritarian magazine a considerable number of artists who also later supported the Commune's cause, including Gill, Gustave Courbet, Alphonse Lévy, Georges Montbard and Georges Pilotell.

Mit dem Tod, der die Armee regiert, nahm André Gill den grassierenden Militarismus aufs Korn. Jules Vallès, der wenige Jahre später tonangebender Publizist der Pariser Kommune werden sollte, versammelte mit Gustave Courbet, André Gill, Alphonse Lévy, Georges Montbard und Georges Pilotell eine beträchtliche Anzahl von Kommune-Künstlern im Mitarbeiterstab seines antiautoritären Journals.

Avec la mort dirigeant l'armée, André Gill se moque ouvertement du militarisme grandissant. Jules Vallès, qui allait devenir le publiciste majeur de la Commune de Paris quelques années plus tard, réunit avec Gustave Courbet, André Gill, Alphonse Lévy, Georges Montbard et Georges Pilotell un nombre considérable d'artistes de la Commune dans l'équipe de son journal anti-autoritaire.

G. Pilotell

UNE CELLULE DE CONDAMNÉ A MORT

Georges Montbard & Marchandeau (sc.)

Thiers – Berryer – Jules Favre, 1868
Stencil-coloured relief etching
From: *Gulliver, journal hebdomadaire illustré, artistique et comique*, Paris, 20 February 1868

The three political leaders of the bourgeois opposition, the liberal Adolphe Thiers, the monarchist Pierre-Antoine Berryer and the republican Jules Favre, campaigned together against the government of Napoleon III for greater freedom of expression. Georges Montbard's later fondness for montage in his illustration work is already evident here in the confident arrangement of the portrait heads in the colours of the French flag.

Die drei führenden Politiker der großbürgerlichen Opposition, der Liberale Adolphe Thiers, der Monarchist Pierre-Antoine Berryer und der Republikaner Jules Favre, traten unter Napoleon III. gemeinsam für mehr Meinungsfreiheit ein. In der wirkungsvollen Anordnung der trikolorierten Porträts zeigt sich bereits der Hang des Karikaturisten Georges Montbard zur grafischen Montage.

Les trois politiciens de premier plan de l'opposition bourgeoise, le libéral Adolphe Thiers, le monarchiste Pierre-Antoine Berryer et le républicain Jules Favre, s'engagèrent ensemble pour une plus grande liberté d'opinion sous Napoléon III. L'impressionnante disposition des portraits tricolores trahit déjà l'inclination du caricaturiste Georges Montbard pour le montage graphique.

Georges Pilotell & Marchandeau (sc.)

The Prison Cell of a Man Sentenced to Death, 1867
Zelle eines zum Tode Verurteilten
Une Cellule de condamné à mort
Relief etching
From: *La Rue – Paris pittoresque et populaire*, Paris, 30 November 1867

The subject of this night scene was a butcher and highly decorated former soldier who had been convicted of a double murder and was awaiting execution. The illustration was accompanied by a scathing leading article against corruption and militarism written by Jules Vallès which resulted in charges being made against him and *La Rue* being shut down.

Die nächtliche Szene spielt auf die Exekution eines Schlachters und hochdekorierten Militärs an, der des Doppelmords überführt worden war. Der Cartoon führte im Zusammenhang mit einem beißenden Leitartikel von Jules Vallès gegen Korruption und Militarismus zur Verurteilung des Herausgebers und der Einstellung der *La Rue*.

La scène nocturne se réfère à l'exécution d'un boucher et militaire hautement décoré, qui avait été accusé d'un double meurtre. Parallèlement à un éditorial mordant de Jules Vallès contre la corruption et le militarisme, le dessin entraîna la condamnation de l'éditeur et la suppression de *La Rue*.

André Gill

Shall We Make some Pancakes?, 1868
Was wäre, wenn wir Crêpes machen würden?
Si nous faisions des crêpes?
Stencil-coloured relief etching
From: *L'Éclipse*, Paris, 16 August 1868

André Gill's question on the cover of the next issue of *L'Éclipse*, after the one showing *Monsieur X* (see right), was tinged with concern. Would the magazine now be accused of immorality, or even obscenity? For unlike the previous image of the pumpkin this new cover illustration was dealing with a very real obscenity, the immorality of tyranny, and in its variation on the title vignette it showed the sun of freedom being almost entirely eclipsed by the moon of dictatorship.

André Gills Frage auf dem Cover, das dem Umschlag mit *Monsieur X* (siehe rechts) folgt, klingt besorgt.

Würde dieses auch der „Unmoral" und „Obszönität" beschuldigt? Anders als das Kürbisbild dreht sich diese Illustration um eine tatsächliche Obszönität, die Immoralität der Tyrannei, denn das Covermotiv zeigt als Variation auf die Titelvignette die Sonne der Freiheit, wie sie fast vollständig vom Mond der Diktatur verschattet wird.

La question d'André Gill sur la couverture du numéro de L'Éclipse qui suit celu représentant *Monsieur X* (voir à droite) est teintée d'inquiétude. Ce journal serait-il suspect d'«immoralité», voire d'«obscénité»? Contrairement à l'image de la citrouille, cette illustration traite d'une réelle obscénité, l'immoralité de la tyrannie, dans sa variation sur la vignette de titre le motif de la couverture montre le soleil de la liberté qui est presque entièrement assombri par la lune de la dictature.

→ *Monsieur X… ?*, 1868
Stencil-coloured relief etching
From: *L'Éclipse*, Paris, 9 August 1868

In conjunction with Jules Vallès, André Gill had the idea of depicting an object on the cover of his new magazine in which no one could possibly discern any resemblance with anyone. In this pumpkin, however, he hid the facial features of a censor who was widely hated, and who promptly elevated the vegetable to notoriety when he levelled a charge of obscenity against the magazine.

Gemeinsam mit seinem Freund Jules Vallès kam André Gill auf die Idee, auf dem Cover seines neuen Journals einen Gegenstand abzubilden, in dem sich unmöglich irgendjemand wiedererkennen kann. In dem Kürbis verbarg Gill allerdings die Gesichtszüge eines verhassten Zensors, der dem Gemüse prompt durch eine Anklage wegen Obszönität zu notorischer Prominenz verhalf.

Avec son ami Jules Vallès, André Gill eut l'idée d'illustrer la couverture de son nouveau journal avec un objet dans lequel absolument personne ne pourrait se reconnaître. Cependant, Gill dissimula dans la citrouille les traits d'un censeur détesté qui, en portant plainte pour obscénité, assura immédiatement au légume une célébrité notoire.

Première année — N° 29bis
Un numéro : 10 centimes
9 Août 1868

RÉDACTEUR EN CHEF
F. POLO
—
ABONNEMENTS
PARIS
Un an........... 8 fr.
Six mois .... 3 »
Trois mois...... 1 50
—
Bureaux : rue du Croissant, 16

DIRECTEUR
F. POLO
—
ABONNEMENTS
DÉPARTEMENTS
Un an........... 6 fr.
Six mois........ 3 50
Trois mois......2 »
—
Bureaux : rue du Croissant, 16

L'ECLIPSE

MONSIEUR X...? — par GILL

Matt Morgan & Thomas Bolton (sc.)

Tied to the Gun! or, Poor Peace in Danger, 1869
An die Kanone gefesselt! oder Der arme Frieden in Gefahr
Attachée au canon! ou La pauvre paix en danger
Tinted wood engraving
From: *The Tomahawk: A Saturday Journal of Satire*, London, 2 January 1869

As Prussian expansionism and French imperialism made for an increasingly explosive situation in central Europe, the English satirical magazine *The Tomahawk* saw a threat to world peace at the beginning of 1869. Its spectacular engravings with their tonal effects were the work of Thomas Bolton, one of the pioneers of photoxylography.

Angesichts einer durch preußischen Expansionsdrang und französischen Imperialismus zunehmend explosiven Lage in Mitteleuropa sah das englische Satirejournal *Tomahawk* für das neue Jahr 1869 den Weltfrieden in Gefahr. Die spektakulären Chiaroscuro-Tonstiche des *Tomahawk* wurden von Thomas Bolton, dem Pionier der Fotoxylografie, realisiert.

Face à une situation de plus en plus explosive en Europe centrale, due au désir d'expansion prussien et à l'impérialisme français, le journal satirique anglais *Tomahawk* considérait la paix mondiale en danger pour la nouvelle année 1869. Les spectaculaires gravures en clair-obscur du *Tomahawk* ont été réalisées par Thomas Bolton, le pionnier de la xylophotographie.

"Again He Urges on His Wild Career!" or, The Modern Mazeppa, 1869
„Und weiter drängt er auf seinem wilden Lauf!" oder Der moderne Mazeppa
«À nouveau il éperonne sa course sauvage!» ou Le Mazeppa moderne
Tinted wood engraving
From: *The Tomahawk: A Saturday Journal of Satire*, London, 5 June 1869

Matt Morgan here casts the reckless Louis Napoléon, who as Emperor had come under mounting pressure from both the growing power of republicans and a radicalised working class, in the role of Byron's fictional Mazeppa. As punishment for an affair, the Cossack Mazeppa had been tied naked to the back of a wild horse and let loose on a nightmarish ride.

Matt Morgan sah den Hasardeur Louis Napoléon, der als Imperator zunehmend durch die erstarkenden Republikaner und eine radikalisierte Arbeiterschicht unter Druck geraten war, in der Rolle von Lord Byrons Romangestalt Mazeppa. Der Kosake wurde wegen einer Affäre bestraft. Dafür wurde er rücklings auf ein wildes Roß gebunden und durchlebte dort einen Fiebertraum von Ritt.

Matt Morgan voyait le flambeur Louis-Napoléon, qui une fois empereur était de plus en plus sous la pression des républicains en force et d'une classe ouvrière radicalisée, dans le rôle de Mazeppa, personnage de roman de Lord Byron. Le cosaque, châtié pour avoir eu une relation amoureuse, fut ligoté sur le dos sur un cheval sauvage où il endura une cavalcade cauchemardesque.

THE TOMAHAWK, January 2, 1869

TIED TO THE GUN!
POOR PEACE IN DANGER.

THE TOMAHAWK, June 5th, 1869.

"AGAIN HE URGES ON HIS WILD CAREER!"
THE MODERN MAZEPPA.

André Gill & Marchandeau (sc.)

Victor Noir
Life Drawing, 1870
Zeichnung nach der Natur | Dessin d'après nature
Stencil-coloured relief etching
From: *L'Éclipse*, Paris, 16 January 1870

In the course of an argument, the republican journalist Victor Noir had been shot and killed by the
Emperor's great-nephew Pierre Bonaparte. The
event was strongly condemned by a broad swathe
of society and led to many republicans becoming
radicalised, while André Gill's illustration of Noir as
a martyr, which had been published without the
precensor's permission, resulted in him being fined
and sent to prison.

Während eines Streits hatte Pierre Bonaparte, ein
Großneffe des Kaisers, den republikanischen Journalisten Victor Noir erschossen. Das Ereignis hatte
die Bildung einer breiten Opposition und die Radi-
kalisierung vieler Republikaner zur Folge. Da André
Gills Märtyrerbild ohne Genehmigung der Vorzensur
publiziert worden war, wurde der Herausgeber mit
einer Haft- und Geldstrafe belangt.

Pierre Bonaparte, un petit-neveu de l'empereur,
avait tué d'un coup de feu le journaliste républicain
Victor Noir au cours d'une altercation. Cet événement entraîna la formation d'une large opposition et
la radicalisation de nombreux républicains. Comme
l'image de martyr d'André Gill avait été publiée sans
l'autorisation de la précensure, l'éditeur fut emprisonné et dut verser une amende.

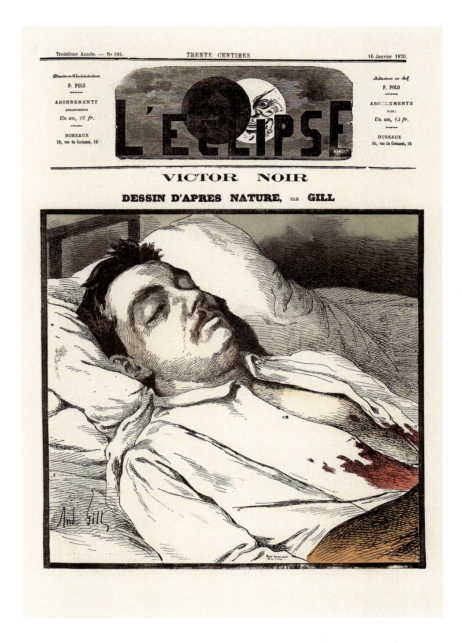

Georges Pilotell

Troppmann – Pierre Bonaparte,
Paris, undated (1870)
Relief etching

The portrait face of Pierre Bonaparte appears in the
pool of Victor Noir's blood, while the wording underneath equates him in the spirit of anti-Bonapartist
exaggeration with the notorious serial killer Jean-
Baptiste Troppmann. Georges Pilotell was one of
the most confrontational caricaturists, and in some of
his more virulent images his style can be seen to be
moving towards an early form of agitprop (see ills.
pp. 320 b., 329 b.).

In der Blutlache Victor Noirs erscheint das Porträt
Pierre Bonapartes, der in antibonapartistischer
Zuspitzung mit dem notorischen Serienmörder
Troppmann gleichgesetzt wird. Georges Pilotell war
einer der konfrontativsten Cartoonisten. Karikatur
ging in manchen seiner pointierten Einblattdrucke
bereits in eine frühe Form des Agitprop über (siehe
Abb. S. 320 u., 329 u.).

Dans la flaque de sang de Victor Noir apparaît le
portrait de Pierre Bonaparte, qui dans l'exaltation
anti-bonapartiste est mis sur le même pied que
Troppmann, le célèbre tueur en série. Georges
Pilotell était l'un des caricaturistes les plus virulents.
Dans quelques-unes de ses feuilles volantes cin-
glantes, la caricature basculait déjà vers une forme
précoce de l'agitprop (voir ills. p. 320 b., 329 b.).

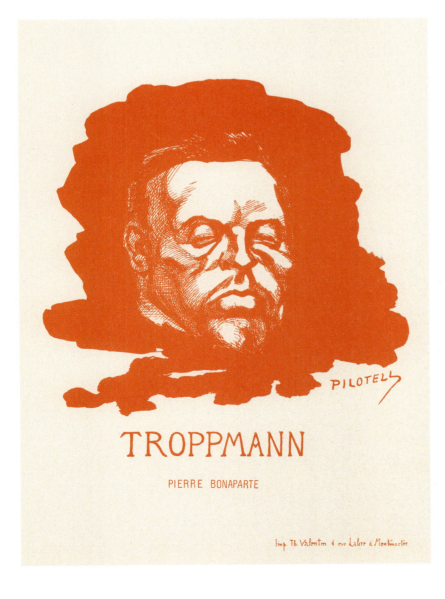

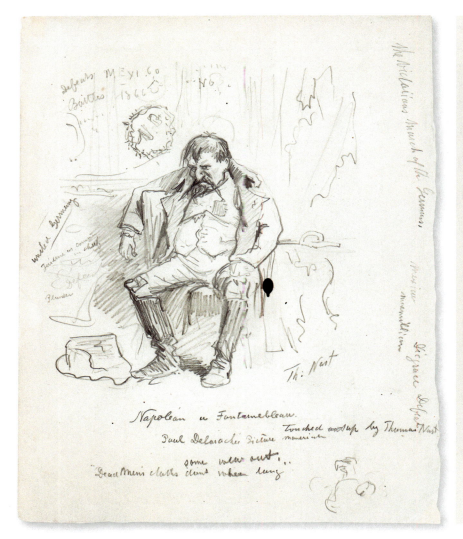

NAPOLÉON
" DEAD MEN'S CLOTHES SOON WEAR OUT. "

Thomas Nast

↑ *Napoleon in Fontainebleau,* 1870
Pencil with ink on paper

After the years Thomas Nast had spent working in pictorial journalism and allegorical propaganda during the Civil War he changed direction to political caricatures, taking his stylistic influence from the work of John Tenniel and Alfred Rethel. Before transferring his illustrations to the wooden blocks, together with detailed instructions to the engraver about the hatching lines that were needed, he prepared his designs in a number of sketches.

Nach den Bürgerkriegsjahren wechselte Thomas Nast unter den stilprägenden Einflüssen von John Tenniel und Alfred Rethel von der grafischen Reportage und der allegorischen Propagandagrafik zum politischen Cartoon. Bevor er seine Zeichnungen detailliert mit allen Schraffurvorgaben für d e Stecher auf die Holzblöcke brachte, bereitete er sie in mehreren Skizzen vor.

Après les années de guerre civile, Thomas Nast, sous l'influence stylistique de John Tenniel et d'Alfred Rethel, passa du reportage illustré et de l'illustration de propagande allégorique à la caricature politique. Avant de déposer sur les blocs ses dessins avec toutes les instructions détaillées de hachures pour les graveurs, il les élaborait en plusieurs esquisses.

↗ *Napoléon*
"Dead Men's Clothes Soon Wear out", 1870
„Die Kleider von Toten tragen sich schnell auf"
« Les habits des morts s'usent vite »
Wood engraving
From: *Harper's Weekly,* New York, 10 September 1870

Following defeat by the German army in the Battle of Sedan, Napoleon III appears here in the same pose as his uncle in a similar situation as depicted in Paul Delaroche's painting *Napoleon at Fontainebleau, 31 March 1814.* On this occasion, however, Thomas Nast suggests there will be no comeback and the compulsion of one Bonaparte to try and repeat the successes of an earlier one will now come to an end as he sits here in the dead man's worn-out uniform.

Der von deutschen Truppen bei Sedan geschlagene Napoleon III. in der Pose, die sein Onkel auf Paul Delaroches Gemälde *Napoléon à Fontainebleau, le 31 mars 1814* in einer vergleichbaren Situation eingenommen hatte. Ein Comeback werde es diesmal allerdings nicht geben, suggeriert Thomas Nast, und der bonapartistische Wiederholungszwang mit dem ausgetragenen Kostüm des Toten nun ein Ende haben.

Napoléon III, vaincu par les troupes allemandes devant Sedan, dans la pose que son oncle avait prise dans une situation analogue sur le tableau de Paul Delaroche *Napoléon à Fontainebleau, le 31 mars 1814.* Mais cette fois, il n'y aura pas de retour, c'est ce que suggère Thomas Nast, et le trouble compulsif de répétition de Bonaparte dans le costume usé du mort aura désormais un terme.

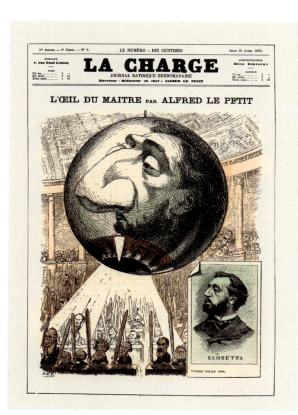

Alfred Le Petit

The Master's Eye, 1870
Das Auge des Meisters | L'Œil du Maître
Stencil-coloured relief etching
From: *La Charge,* Paris, 21 April 1870

The all-seeing eye of the left-wing republican politician Léon Gambetta hovers over the French National Assembly, uniting the forces of the opposition. Gambetta lost the use of his right eye in an accident when he was younger, and the glass ball he then wore in the socket was later used by artists to symbolise his ambiguous political manoeuvring during the Third Republic.

Als allmächtiges Auge schwebt der linksrepublikanische Abgeordnete Léon Gambetta über der französischen Nationalversammlung und bringt die vereinten oppositionellen Kräfte in Stellung. Die Glaskugel, die er seit einem Unfall in der rechten Augenhöhle trug, galt den Zeichnern später als Symbol für seine zwiespältigen politischen Schachzüge zur Zeit der Dritten Republik.

Sous la forme d'un œil tout-puissant, Léon Gambetta, député républicain de gauche, survole l'Assemblée nationale française et positionne les forces unies d'opposition. La boule de verre qu'il portait dans son orbite droit depuis un accident symbolisait pour les dessinateurs ses coups de tactique ambigus à l'époque de la Troisième République.

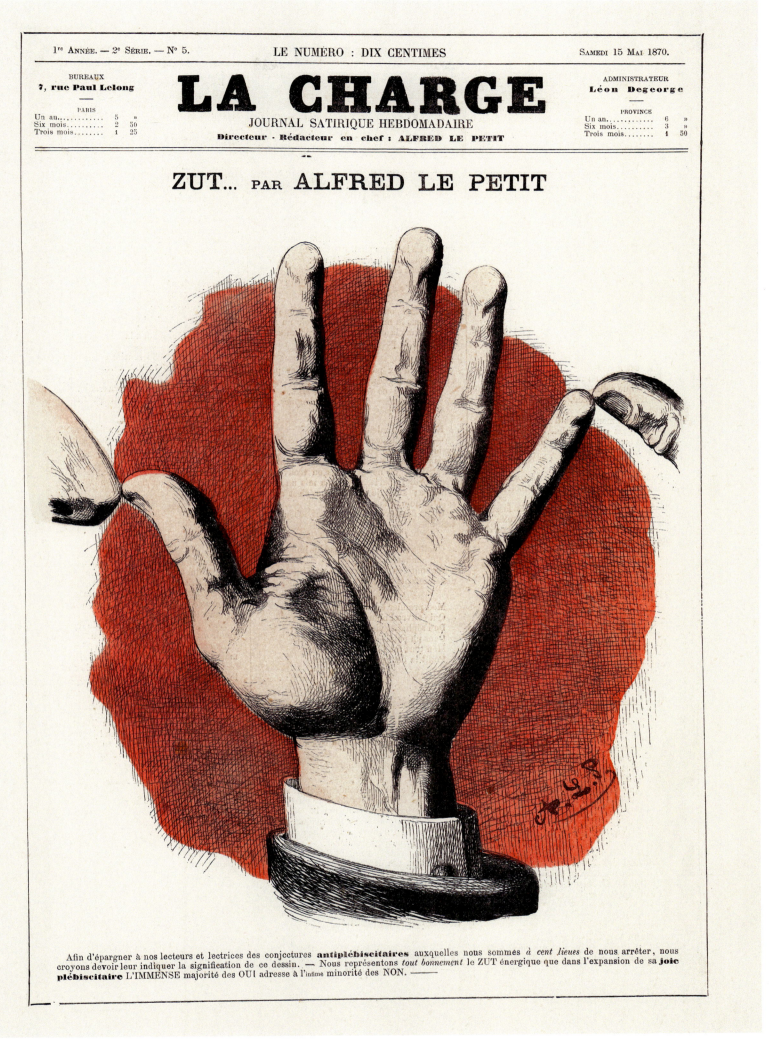

1ʳᵉ Année. – 2ᵉ Série. – N° 5.

LE NUMÉRO : DIX CENTIMES

Samedi 15 Mai 1870.

LA CHARGE

JOURNAL SATIRIQUE HEBDOMADAIRE

Directeur – Rédacteur en chef : ALFRED LE PETIT

BUREAUX
7, rue Paul Lelong

PARIS

Un an............	5	»
Six mois.........	2	50
Trois mois.......	1	25

ADMINISTRATEUR
Léon Degeorge

PROVINCE

Un an............	6	»
Six mois.........	3	»
Trois mois.......	1	50

ZUT... par ALFRED LE PETIT

Afin d'épargner à nos lecteurs et lectrices des conjectures **antiplébiscitaires** auxquelles nous sommes *à cent lieues* de nous arrêter, nous croyons devoir leur indiquer la signification de ce dessin. — Nous représentons *tout bonnement* le ZUT énergique que dans l'expansion de sa **joie plébiscitaire** L'IMMENSE majorité des OUI adresse à l'infime minorité des NON.

Alfred Le Petit

Damn…, 1870
Ach nee… | Zut…
Stencil-coloured relief etching
From: *La Charge*, Paris, 15 May 1870

The Emperor thumbs his nose at the people, following a cleverly worded plebiscite that had been issued to consolidate his power and in the process ended the phase of liberalisation.

With *La Charge*, which was banned on several occasions, Alfred Le Petit stepped out of the shadow of the slightly older André Gill who had been his guide in the profession and distinguished himself as one of the most innovative artists of his day.

Der Kaiser zieht dem Volk eine lange Nase. Um seine Macht zu festigen, hatte er ein trickreich formuliertes

Plebiszit veranstaltet und damit die Phase der Liberalisierung beendet. Mit seinem wiederholt beschlagnahmten Journal *La Charge* trat Alfred Le Petit aus dem Schatten seines nur wenig älteren Mentors André Gill und profilierte sich als einer der innovativsten Künstler der Zeit.

L'empereur fait un pied de nez au peuple. Pour consolider sa puissance,

il avait organisé un plébiscite adroitement formulé et mit fin ainsi à la phase de libéralisation. Avec son journal plusieurs fois suspendu *La Charge*, Alfred Le Petit sortit de l'ombre d'André Gill, son mentor à peine plus âgé que lui, et se profila comme l'un des artistes es plus innovateurs de son époque.

Saïd (Alphonse Lévy) & Coulbeuf (lith.)

It's a Bit Much!…, Paris, undated
(January 1871)
Es ist etwas hoch!…
C'est un peu haut!…
Stencil-coloured lithograph

Under pressure from the German forces besieging Paris, the Republic began to turn more radical and the Prussian foreign minister Bismarck could only bark in vain at the red sun of freedom. After the Treaty of Versailles had been signed a short time later, Honoré Daumier drew an illustration based on a solar eclipse but with the roles reversed (ill. p. 329 t.).

Unter dem Druck der deutschen Belagerung von Paris begann sich die Republik zu radikalisieren. Noch kläfft der preußische Außenminister Bismarck vergeblich gegen die rote Freiheitssonne an. Kurze Zeit später, nach dem Vorfrieden von Versailles, konnte Honoré Daumier das Motiv der Sonnenfinsternis nur noch mit vertauschten Rollen zeichnen (Abb. S. 329 o.).

Sous la pression du siège de Paris par les troupes allemandes, la République commença à se radicaliser. Là, le ministre des Affaires étrangères prussien Bismarck jappe inutilement contre le soleil rouge de la liberté. Peu de temps après, avant le traité de Versailles, Honoré Daumier ne put dessiner le motif de l'éclipse solaire qu'avec les rôles échangés (ill. p. 329 h.).

ACTUALITÉS   336

L'éclipse sera-t-elle totale ?

Honoré Daumier

Actualités
Will This Be a Total Eclipse?, 1871
Wird das eine totale Sonnenfinsternis?
L'éclipse sera-t-elle totale ?
Relief etching
From: *Le Charivari*, Paris, 17 March 1871

Honoré Daumier had been following militaristic Prussia's menacing rise to becoming a German superpower since 1866 through a series of prophetic illustrations. His image of a solar eclipse is one of the best-known examples of the metaphor of light and darkness that permeated political symbolism in France from the time of Louis XIV, the Sun King.

Seit 1866 hatte Honoré Daumier den bedrohlichen Aufstieg des militaristischen Preußen zur deutschen Hegemonialmacht mit einer Reihe hellsichtiger Cartoons begleitet. Seine Sonnenfinsternis-Vision zählt zu den bekanntesten Beispielen einer Licht- und Schatten-Metaphorik, die sich seit der Zeit des Sonnenkönigs Ludwig XIV. durch die politische Emblematik Frankreichs zieht.

Dès 1866, Honoré Daumier avait suivi avec une série de dessins prémonitoires l'ascension menaçante de la Prusse militariste en voie de devenir une puissance hégémoniale allemande. Sa vision de l'éclipse solaire est l'un des plus fameux exemples d'un métaphorisme de clair-obscur qui traverse le symbolisme politique de la France depuis le règne de Louis XIV, le Roi-Soleil.

Georges Pilotell

Actualités 17
Gather Thistles, Expect Prickles, Paris, undated (February/March 1871)
Wer dran rührt, sticht sich | Qui s'y frotte s'y pique
Stencil-coloured relief etching

All those who opposed the social republic failed, whether the Bourbon monarchists in 1830 (fleur-de-lis), the liberal Orléanists in 1848 (rooster) or the Bonapartists in September 1870 (eagle). Georges Pilotell here formulates a historical identity for the Paris Commune at the same time as issuing a warning to those in the executive government of Versailles who sought to oppose it.

Alle, die sich der sozialen Republik entgegengestellt haben, sind gescheitert: 1830 die monarchistischen Bourbonen (Lilienwappen), 1848 die liberalen Orleanisten (Hahn) und im September 1870 die Bonapartisten (Adler). Georges Pilotell formuliert das historische Selbstverständnis der Pariser Kommune und gibt zugleich eine Warnung an ihre Gegner in der Versailler Exekutivregierung aus.

Tous ceux qui se sont opposés à la république sociale ont échoué : en 1830 les Bourbons monarchistes (l'emblème de la fleur de lys), en 1848 les orléanistes libéraux (le coq) et en septembre 1870 les bonapartistes (l'aigle). Georges Pilotell formule l'identité historique de la Commune de Paris et, par la même occasion, émet un avertissement à ses adversaires du gouvernement exécutif de Versailles.

ACTUALITÉS   (17)

REPUBLIQUE OU LA MORT

chez Deforet et César Rue Nle des Petits-champs 64   Imp TALONS Mle St Honoré 19

QUI S'Y FROTTE S'Y PIQUE.

THROWN COMPLETELY INTO THE SHADE.

Thomas Nast

Thrown Completely into the Shade, 1871
Vollständig in den Schatten gestellt
Complètement jeté dans l'ombre
Wood engraving
From: *Harper's Weekly*, New York,
18 March 1871

This sequel to Thomas Nast's adaptation of the Paul Delaroche painting (ill. p. 326 r.) appeared shortly after the German Empire had dictated its humiliating terms for peace to the defeated Republic at Versailles. According to Nast, the shadow cast on the two Bonapartes by the new German empire was "complete", while it can also be seen to imply the fall of the German forces in time as well.

Die Fortsetzung von Thomas Nasts Paul-Delaroche-Adaption (Abb. S. 326 r.) erschien kurz nachdem das Deutsche Reich der besiegten Republik in Versailles seine demütigenden Friedensvereinbarungen diktiert hatte. Der Schatten, in den das neue deutsche Kaisertum die beiden Bonapartes stellt, ist laut Nast „vollständig", das heißt, er schließt als Menetekel auch deren Untergänge mit ein und weist auf das Scheitern des deutschen Kaisertum voraus.

La prolongation de l'adaptation de Paul Delaroche par Thomas Nast (ill. p. 326 d.) parut peu après que l'Empire allemand eut dicté à Versailles à la république vaincue des accords de paix humiliants. L'ombre que le nouvel ordre impérial fait aux deux Bonaparte est «complète», ce qui signifie qu'elle inclut et prédit l'échec de l'Empire allemand.

Honoré Daumier

Actualités
Charlemagne's Successor, 1871
Nachfolger Karls des Großen
Successeur de Charlemagne
Relief etching
From: *Le Charivari*, Paris, 6 April 1871

In Honoré Daumier's image, the newly crowned German emperor rules with an atavistic megalomania over an empire that has failed to keep up with the times. His empire consists of an old bone and a mass of ornate clocks, the favourite loot of German soldiers. The established *Charivari* was the only French satirical periodical that managed to appear continuously throughout the war.

In Honoré Daumiers Vision herrscht der frischgebackene deutsche Kaiser in atavistischem Größenwahn über ein Reich, das aus der Zeit gefallen ist. Es besteht aus einem alten Knochen und einem Meer von Standuhren, dem bevorzugten Beutegut deutscher Soldaten. Der etablierte *Charivari* war das einzige französische Satiremagazin, das während des Kriegs kontinuierlich erscheinen konnte.

Dans la vision d'Honoré Daumier l'empereur allemand frais émoulu règne dans une mégalomanie ataviste sur un empire archaïque. Il consiste en un vieil os et en une mer de pendules, butin favori des soldats allemands. Bien établi dans la place, *Le Charivari* fut le seul journal satirique français qui put paraître sans interruption pendant la guerre.

ACTUALITÉS   348

SUCCESSEUR DE CHARLEMAGNE.

. ACTUALITES .

13

VOS PARATONNERRES NE CONJURERONT PAS L'ORAGE.

Georges Pilotell

Actualités
Your Lightning Conductors Will Not Stop the Storm,
Paris, 1 March 1871
Ihre Blitzableiter halten das Gewitter nicht ab
Vos paratonnerres ne conjureront pas l'orage
Wood engraving

Despite being besieged by Prussian neo-absolutism, the egalitarian storm of a social Republic begins to break over the Place de la Bastille. By featuring the July Column, Georges Pilotell suggests that the new revolutionary social movement aims to complete what the partial revolutions of 1789, 1830 and 1848 had begun.

Trotz der Belagerung durch den preußischen Neo-absolutismus beginnt sich das egalitäre Gewitter einer *République sociale* über der Place de la Bastille zu entladen. Durch den Verweis auf die Revolutions-säule suggeriert Georges Pilotell, dass es der neuen sozialrevolutionären Bewegung um die Vollendung der abgebrochenen Revolutionen von 1789, 1830 und 1848 geht.

Malgré le siège du néo-absolutisme prussien, l'orage égalitaire d'une *République sociale* commence à se déverser sur la Place de la Bastille. Par la référence à la colonne de la Révolution, Georges Pilotell suggère que le nouveau mouvement social révolutionnaire aspire à l'accomplissement des révolutions brisées de 1789, 1830 et 1848.

Chez Deforêt & César, R. Nve des Petits Champs. 64.   Imp. Talons, Paris.

QUELLE TUILE !

ACTULITÉS.

Le Peuple te comprends !.. Vois — sa force...

G. Bar & Barousse (lith.)

Actulités [sic]
"The People Understand!…
See How Strong He Is…", Paris,
undated (March/April 1871)
„Das Volk versteht dich! …
Sieh – seine Stärke…"
«Le Peuple te comprends!…
Vois – sa force…»
Stencil-coloured lithograph

Immediately after the German forces had withdrawn from Versailles, the French executive government felt compelled to install itself there as conflict and unrest began to escalate in Paris. Marx's proletariat appears in the illustration as a giant and sovereign of the people, casting out from the red republic various notable politicians from the bourgeois executive, including Adolphe Thiers, Jules Simon and Jules Favre.

Unmittelbar nach dem Abzug der Deutschen aus Versailles sah sich die französische Exekutivregierung aufgrund der Zuspitzung der Konflikte in Paris gezwungen, dorthin umzuziehen. Es ist Karl Marx' Proletarier, der hier als riesiger Volkssouverän führende Politiker des großbürgerlichen Lagers wie Adolphe Thiers, Jules Simon und Jules Favre aus der roten Republik entfernt.

Juste après le retrait des Allemands de Versailles, vu l'aggravation des troubles à Paris, le gouvernement exécutif français se vit contraint de s'installer dans cette ville. C'est le prolétaire de Karl Marx qui, en immense souverain du peuple, bannit ici de la république rouge les politiciens gouvernants issus de la haute bourgeoisie comme Adolphe Thiers, Jules Simon et Jules Favre.

Saïd (Alphonse Lévy)

Actualités 2
What Bad Luck! Paris, undated
(March/April 1871)
So ein Hammer! | Quelle Tuile!
Stencil-coloured relief etching

The two main politicians in the bourgeois government, Adolphe Thiers (chief of the executive) and Jules Favre (foreign minister, on the left), stand in shock and disbelief as they watch events unfold in the Paris Commune from Versailles when army units tried, and failed, to disarm the National Guard on 18 March.

Ungläubig und schockiert verfolgen die beiden führenden Politker der bürgerlichen Regierung Adolphe Thiers (Chef der Exektive) und links daneben Jules Favre (Außenminister) von Versailles aus das Schauspiel der Pariser Kommune, das mit der gescheiterten Entwaffnung der Nationalgarde am 18. März seinen Ausgang nahm.

Incrédules et choqués, les deux dirigeants politiques du gouvernement bourgeois, Adolphe Thiers (chef de l'exécutif) et à sa gauche Jules Favre (ministre des Affaires étrangères), observent depuis Versailles le spectacle de la Commune de Paris, qui eut pour origine le 18 mars la tentative manquée de désarmer la Garde nationale.

Georges Pilotell & Barousse (lith.)

→ *Sketches of the Revolution: The Commune Stopped by Ignorance and Reaction. In Chorus: It's a Prussian*, Paris, undated (1871)
Revolutionäre Skizzen: Die Kommune, von Ignoranz und Reaktion festgehalten. Im Chor: Das ist ein Preuße
Croquis révolutionnaires : La Commune arrêtée par l'ignorance et la réaction. En chœur : C'est un Prussien
Stencil-coloured lithograph

Georges Pilotell served in a number of different political roles during the time of the Commune but was conscious that its existence was threatened on two fronts. On one side were the military and propaganda reactions of the Versailles government, as represented by the person of Adolphe Thiers, and on the other a type of ignorance by which members of the Commune were denounced as enemies of France and classed as "Prussians".

Georges Pilotell, der in der Kommune in mehreren politischen Ämtern aktiv war, sah deren Existenz doppelt bedroht: durch die militärischen und propagandistischen Reaktionen der Versailler Regierung in Gestalt von Adolphe Thiers und eine Form von Ignoranz, die die Kommunarden als Feinde der Nation, als „Preußen", denunziert.

Georges Pilotell, qui occupa plusieurs postes politiques pendant la Commune, voyait son existence doublement menacée : par les réactions militaires et propagandistes du gouvernement de Versailles dans la silhouette d'Adolphe Thiers et par une forme d'ignorance qui dénonçait les communards comme des ennemis de la nation, comme des « Prussiens ».

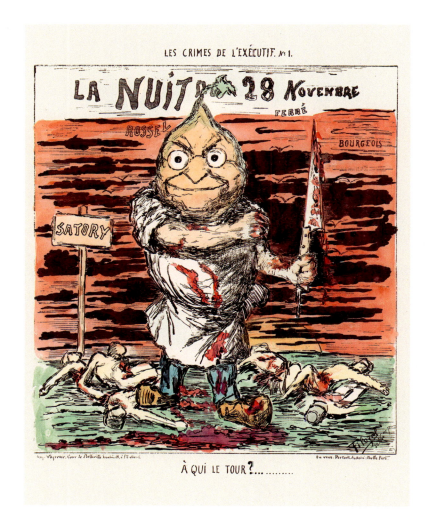

Paul Klenck (Filozel)

The Crimes of the Executive, Paris, undated (December 1871)
Die Verbrechen der Exekutive
Les Crimes de l'exécutif
Stencil-coloured relief etchings

No. 1 – Who's Next?
Wer ist jetzt dran?
À qui le tour ?

When the troops of the executive government in Versailles attacked Paris their actions were especially brutal (see ill. p. 279). Mass shootings without trial and military tribunals towards the end of the year were followed by deportation for thousands of people and numerous executions, including several leading members of the Commune at the Satory camp near Versailles.

Bereits bei der Einnahme von Paris waren die Versailler Truppen mit maßloser Härte vorgegangen (siehe Abb. S. 279). Auf standrechtliche Massenerschießungen folgten nach den Militärtribunalen gegen Ende des Jahres die Deportationen Tausender sowie zahllose Exekutionen, darunter die Erschießung führender Kommunarden auf dem Feld von Satory bei Versailles.

Dès la prise de Paris, les troupes de Versailles avaient sévi avec une brutalité inouïe (voir ill. p. 279). Aux fusillades sommaires de masse et aux tribunaux militaires, vers la fin de l'année, succédèrent la déportation de milliers de personnes ainsi que d'innombrables exécutions, dont la mort de communards de premier rang fusillés au camp de Satory, près de Versailles.

No. 2 – Another One!
Noch einer!
Encore un !

In a series of illustrations of unparalleled savagery and brilliance, the caricaturist Paul Klenck reacted to the army's excesses that were carried out in the name of Adolphe Thiers as chief of the executive government. After he became president during the early years of the Third Republic a blanket of silence was placed over these events.

In einer Zeichnungsfolge von beispielloser Drastik und Brillanz reagierte der Karikaturist Paul Klenck auf die martialischen Exzesse, die der Chef der Exekutive Adolphe Thiers zu verantworten hatte. In den Anfangsjahren der Dritten Republik wurde unter dessen Präsidentschaft ein Mantel des Schweigens über die Ereignisse gelegt.

Dans une série de dessins d'une dureté et d'un éclat sans précédent, le caricaturiste Paul Klenck réagit aux excès militaires dont le chef du gouvernement exécutif Adolphe Thiers s'était rendu responsable. Sous sa présidence durant les premières années de la Troisième République, une chape de silence recouvrit ces événements.

Thomas Nast

Our Artist's Occupation Gone, 1872
Unseres Künstlers Tagwerk ist getan
Notre tâche d'artiste est finie
Wood engraving
From: *Harper's Weekly*, New York,
23 November 1872

Not long after the incumbent president Ulysses S. Grant had won a second term in a triumphant electoral victory over Horace Greeley, part of the success for which was down to Thomas Nast's campaign illustrations on his behalf, the ever bad-tempered pictorial journalist was already seeing his future prospects fading away.

Nachdem der amtierende Präsident Ulysses S. Grant über seinen Gegner Horace Greeley einen triumphalen Wahlsieg errungen hatte, den Thomas Nast durch seine grafische Wahlkampfkampagne mit zu verantworten hatte, sah der ewig mies gelaunte Cartoonist bereits seine Felle davon schwimmen.

Après que le président en fonction, Ulysses S. Grant, eut remporté sur son adversaire Horace Greeley une victoire triomphale, due en partie à la bataille électorale par voie de dessins de presse de Thomas Nast, le caricaturiste perpétuellement de mauvaise humeur voyait déjà ses espoirs s'envoler.

Robert Crumb

*The Real R. Crumb and
He Is Not Pleased!*, July 2003
*Der echte R. Crumb, und er ist
nicht erfreut!*
*Le vrai R. Crumb, et il n'est
pas content!*
Ink
Private collection

Robert Crumb, Interview with
Alex Wood, 2014:

Thomas Nast is one of my favorites, one of my main sources for visual inspiration for my drawing since I was a teenager. [...] You look through these old Harper's Weekly, *or any other 19th century magazines that are full of engraved pictures, and his are by far the strongest.*

Thomas Nast ist einer meiner Lieblingskünstler und seit meiner Jugend eine Hauptquelle visueller Inspiration für Zeichnungen. [...] Wenn man sich die alten Ausgaben von Harper's Weekly *oder anderen Zeitschriften des 19. Jahrhunderts mit vielen Druckgrafiken ansieht, so sind seine bei Weitem die stärksten.*

Thomas Nast est l'un de mes préférés, l'une des sources principales d'inspiration visuelle pour mes dessins, et ce depuis mon adolescence. [...] Vous feuilletez ces vieux Harper's Weekly, *ou n'importe quel autre de ces magazines du XIXᵉ siècle qui regorgent de gravures, et les siennes sont de loin les plus fortes.*

Thomas Nast

The "Brains", 1871
Das „Hirn" | *Le «Cerveau»*
Wood engraving
From: *Harper's Weekly*,
New York, 11 October 1871

The most popular cartoon from Thomas Nast's illustrated campaign against William Tweed compressed the senator's corpulent figure into a symbolic pear shape, representing the rife corruption and plutocratic arrogance associated with his office.

Der populärste Cartoon aus Thomas Nasts grafischer Kampagne gegen William Tweed verdichtete die korpulente Gestalt des Senators in ein birnenförmiges Emblem, das für epidemische Korruption und plutokratische Anmaßung stand.

Le dessin le plus populaire de la campagne par voie de dessins de presse de Thomas Nast contre William Tweed comprima la corpulente stature du sénateur en un emblème en forme de poire qui est censé représenter l'épidémie de corruption et l'arrogance ploutocratique.

HARPER'S WEEKLY

A JOURNAL OF CIVILIZATION.

VOL. XV.—No. 778.]   NEW YORK, SATURDAY, NOVEMBER 25, 1871.   [WITH A SUPPLEMENT. PRICE TEN CENTS.

Entered according to Act of Congress, in the Year 1871, by Harper & Brothers, in the Office of the Librarian of Congress, at Washington.

"WHAT ARE YOU LAUGHING AT? TO THE VICTOR BELONG THE SPOILS."

A GROUP OF VULTURES WAITING FOR THE STORM TO "BLOW OVER."—"LET US *PREY*."

←← Thomas Nast

"What Are You Laughing at? To the Victor Belong the Spoils", 1871
„Was gibt's da zu lachen? Dem Sieger gehört die Beute"
« De quoi riez-vous ? Le butin revient au vainqueur »
Wood engraving
From: *Harper's Weekly*, New York, 25 November 1871

Reports in the newspapers hardly touched "Boss" Tweed, however, since a large number of his constituents were poor immigrants who could not read. The bitter electoral defeat that brought about the downfall of Tammany Hall's Mafia-like organisation was due in large part to the provocative pictorial effect of Thomas Nast's furious illustrative campaign.

Die Zeitungsberichte hatten „Boss" William Tweed kaum tangiert, da seine vor allem aus mittellosen Immigranten bestehende Wählerschaft mehrheitlich illiterat war. Die herbe Wahlniederlage, die das mafiotische Gebäude der Tammany-Hall-Organisation zum Einsturz brachte, war vor allem den suggestiven Bildwirkungen von Thomas Nasts furioser grafischer Kampage geschuldet.

Les articles de journaux n'avaient guère affecté le « Boss » William Tweed, car son électorat composé surtout d'immigrants démunis était en majorité illettré. La cuisante défaite électorale, qui provoqua la chute de la structure mafieuse de l'organisation Tammany Hall, était due avant tout aux effets picturaux suggestifs de la fulgurante campagne par voie de dessins de presse de Thomas Nast.

Thomas Nast

← A Group of Vultures Waiting for the Storm to "Blow Over" – "Let Us Prey", 1871
Eine Gruppe von Geiern warten darauf, dass sich der Sturm „verzieht" – „Lasst uns (beten) Beute machen"
Un Groupe de vautours qui attendent que la tempête « se calme » – « Laissez-nous des proies »
Wood engraving
From: *Harper's Weekly*, New York, 23 September 1871

A violent shitstorm is brewing over a group of vultures involved in picking over the corpse of New York City. In the centre stands senator William Tweed, who had managed to steal from the city's taxpayers as much as $200 million by way of Tammany Hall, a corrupt political organisation that served the Democratic party. The first revelations of wrongdoing had begun to surface in July.

Über einer Gruppe von Geiern, die gerade die Leiche von New York City fleddern, braut sich ein heftiger Shitstorm zusammen. Im Zentrum Stadtrat William Tweed, dem es über Tammany Hall, einer korrupten Organisation der Demokraten, gelungen war, die öffentlichen Haushalte um 200 Millionen Dollar zu erleichtern. Bereits im Juli waren erste Enthüllungen erschienen.

Une houleuse altercation gronde au-dessus d'un groupe de vautours en train de lacérer le cadavre de New York City. Au centre se trouve le conseiller municipal William Tweed qui avait réussi à soutirer du budget public 200 millions de dollars par le biais d'une organisation démocrate véreuse, Tammany Hall. Dès juillet étaient parues les premières révélations.

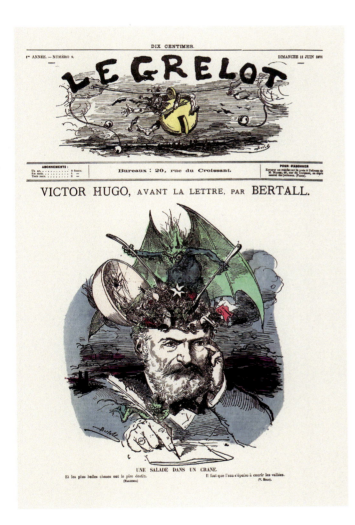

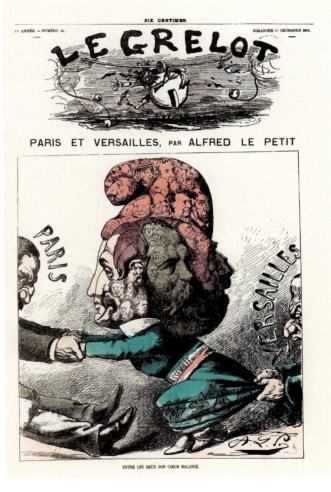

Bertall

Victor Hugo, Ahead of His Time, 1871
Victor Hugo, der Zeit voraus
Victor Hugo, avant la lettre
Stencil-coloured relief etching
From: *Le Grelot*, Paris, 11 June 1871

During the Second Empire in France, the writer Victor Hugo had become a figurehead for republican resistance on the strength of his political views and commitment. While he played no part in the Paris Commune his belief in the ideal of an egalitarian republic was well known; even so, Bertall placed the blame for the uprising with Hugo's inflammatory ideas.

Zur Zeit des Zweiten Kaiserreichs galt der politisch engagierte Dichter Victor Hugo als zentrale Identifikationsfigur des republikanischen Widerstands. An der Kommune hatte er zwar nicht partizipiert, allerdings waren seine Sympathien für das Ideal einer egalitären Republik bekannt. Bertall macht Hugos aufrührerischen „Hirnsalat" für den Ausbruch des Aufstands mit verantwortlich.

Au temps du Second Empire Victor Hugo, poète politiquement engagé, était la figure emblématique de la résistance républicaine. Il n'avait certes pas participé à la Commune, mais sa sympathie pour l'idéal d'une république égalitaire était bien connue. Bertall impute le déclenchement de l'insurrection aux idées enflammées d'Hugo.

Alfred Le Petit

Paris and Versailles, 1871
Paris und Versailles | Paris et Versailles
Stencil-coloured relief etching
From: *Le Grelot*, Paris, 17 December 1871

This composite allegorical image depicts the lack of unity in the National Assembly at the beginning of the Third Republic. The amorphous political head features individuals from the various Republican, Orléanist, Bonapartist and Legitimist factions, who were constitutionally divided between a Chamber of Deputies in Versailles and a Senate in Paris.

Die surreale Allegorie steht für die Zerrissenheit der französischen Nationalversammlung zu Beginn der Dritten Republik: eine politisch

amorphe Masse, bestehend aus republikanischen, orleanistischen, bonapartistischen und legitimistischen Parteiungen, die konstitutionell in eine Abgeordentenkammer in Versailles und einen Senat in Paris gespalten war.

L'allégorie surréelle figure les dissentiments régnant dans l'Assemblée nationale au début de la Troisième République : une masse politique amorphe, mélange de factions républicaines, orléanistes, bonapartistes et légitimistes, qui sur le plan constitutionnel était scindée en une Chambre des députés à Versailles et un Sénat à Paris.

Thomas Nast

The American River Ganges, 1871
Der amerikanische Ganges
Le Gange américain
Wood engraving
From: *Harper's Weekly*, New York,
30 September 1871

William Tweed and his gang are shown
here driving the children out of their
public schools in order to feed them
to the Papist crocodiles. To secure the
votes of the Irish section of the elec-
torate the Tammany Ring had begun
funding Catholic education projects,
using public funds. Thomas Nast,
who had earlier supported Garibaldi
in Italy, viewed this move towards
clericalism as a threat to the country's
liberal constitution.

Will am Tweed und seine Gang treiben
die Kinder aus den öffentlichen Schulen, um sie papistischen Krokodilen
zum Fraß vorzuwerfen. Um irische Wäh-
lerstimmen zu gewinnen, hatte der
Tammany-Ring begonnen, katholische
Bildungsinitiativen mit öffentlichen
Geldern zu finanzieren. Der Garibaldi-
Anhänger Thomas Nast sah im Kle-
rikalismus eine Bedrohung für die
liberale Konstitution der Republik.

William Tweed et sa clique entraînent
les enfants hors des écoles publiques
pour les jeter en pâture à des crocodiles papistes. Afin de gagner des voix
irlandaises aux élections, le Tammany
Ring avait commencé à financer les
initiatives d'éducation catholique avec
des fonds publics. Thomas Nast, parti-
san de Garibaldi, voyait dans le cléri-
calisme une menace pour la constitution libérale du pays.

*Something that Did Blow over –
November 7, 1871*
Auch das zog vorbei
Cela aussi fut balayé
Wood engraving
From: *Harper's Weekly*, New York,
25 November 1871

Thomas Nast responds here to comments made by supporters of the
Tammany Ring who assumed that
the fuss would soon "blow over". The
anti-Tweed campaign boosted the
circulation of *Harper's Weekly* three-
fold, and gave Nast himself phenomenal publicity. In many issues of the
magazine at this time his illustrations
appeared on the cover, as the double-page spread in the centre and
also the cartoon at the back.

Thomas Nast antwortet hier auf Ver-
lautbarungen von Parteigängern des
Rings, die vermuteten, dass die Aufre-
gungen bald wie „weggeblasen" sein
würden. Die Anti-Tweed-Kampage
bescherte *Harper's Weekly* eine Stei-
gerung der Auflage ums Dreifache
und Nast selbst eine phänomenale
Präsenz. In vielen Ausgaben bestritt
er mit seinen Cartoons zugleich das
Cover, die zentrale Doppelseite sowie
den Schlusscartoon.

Thomas Nast répond ici aux déclara-
tions de partisans du Ring, qui présumaient que les turbulences seraient
bientôt comme «balayées». La campagne anti-Tweed assura à *Harper's
Weekly* un tirage trois fois supérieur
à la normale, et à Nast lui-même une
présence phénoménale. Dans de nombreuses éditions il apparaissait à la
fois sur la couverture, sur la double
page centrale et sur le dessin final.

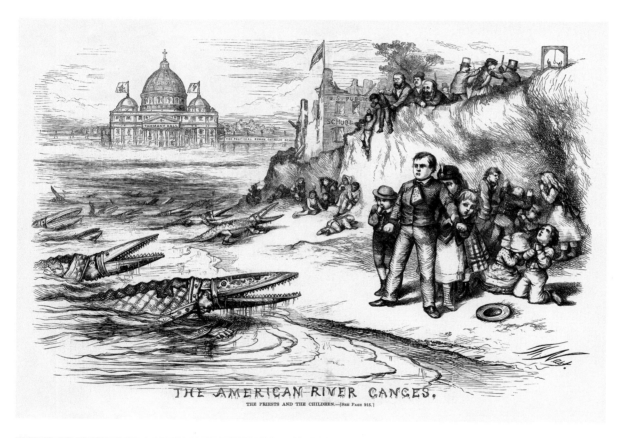

THE AMERICAN RIVER GANGES.
THE PRIESTS AND THE CHILDREN.—[See Page 915.]

SOMETHING THAT DID BLOW OVER—NOVEMBER 7, 1871.

Thomas Nast

Tweed-le-dee and Tilden-dum, 1876
Wood engraving
From: *Harper's Weekly*, New York,
1 July 1876

In December 1875 William Tweed managed to escape during a home visit from jail and fled to Spain, although once again Thomas Nast's drawing of him proved to be his undoing. The cover image showing the "Boss" dressed as a convict and against an allegorically political background was used by the Spanish authorities to identify him, and this spectacular result for an illustration made headlines around the world.

Nachdem William Tweed im Dezember 1875 die Flucht nach Spanien gelungen war, wurde ihm Thomas Nasts Zeichenstift dort ein letztes Mal zum Verhängnis. Nur aufgrund einer Karikatur, die den „Boss" in einem politisch-allegorischen Kontext als Sträfling zeigt, war es den lokalen Behörden gelungen, den Ausbrecher zu identifizieren. Der spektakuläre Cartoon-Event sorgte weltweit für Schlagzeilen.

Après que William Tweed eut réussi à fuir en Espagne en décembre 1875, le crayon de Thomas Nast lui fut une dernière fois fatal. Grâce à la seule caricature qui montre le « Boss » comme un détenu dans un contexte politico-allégorique, les autorités locales purent identifier le fugitif. Cet événement spectaculaire du monde de la caricature fit la une des journaux du monde entier.

Charles Jay Taylor

The Ring Frauds – Trial of "Boss" Tweed, 1873
Der Betrügerring – Prozess gegen „Boss" Tweed
Le Cercle des fraudeurs – Procès du « boss » Tweed
Wood engraving
From: *The Daily Graphic*, New York,
12 November 1873

In late November 1873, Tweed was sentenced to 12 years in prison for theft and corruption. The trial was covered by *The Daily Graphic*, and in fact this first illustrated daily newspaper was founded earlier in the year very much as a result of Thomas Nast's triumphant campaign, which stimulated an increased interest in pictorial journalism.

Ende November 1873 wurde William Tweed wegen Diebstahls und Korruption zu zwölf Jahren Haft verurteilt. Das Verfahren wurde vom *Daily Graphic* begleitet. Die Gründung dieser ersten täglichen Nachrichtenillustrierten zu Anfang des Jahres war nicht zuletzt Thomas Nasts triumphaler Kampagne zu verdanken, die einen gesteigerten Hunger nach Bildjournalismus zur Folge hatte.

Fin novembre 1873, William Tweed fut condamné à douze ans de prison pour vol et corruption. Le procès fut couvert par le *Daily Graphic*. La création de ce premier magazine quotidien illustré au début de l'année est notamment due à la triomphale campagne de Thomas Nast qui éveilla un appétit accru pour le journalisme illustré.

André Gill

→ *Ambush*, 1872
Umlauert | Guet-apens
Stencil-coloured relief etching
From: *L'Éclipse,* Paris, 17 March 1872

The French Republic sits threatened here on all sides, surrounded by three factions of the National Assembly – the monarchist Legitimists (fleur-de-lis) and Orléanists (pear), together with the Bonapartists (tricorne) who held the majority but were divided on the question of the king – and the German Empire (spiked helmet), which had annexed Alsace-Lorraine and continued to occupy parts of France until 1873.

Die bedrohte französische Republik, umstellt vom monarchistischen Lager aus Legitimisten (Lilie), Orleanisten (Birne) und Bonapartisten (Dreispitz), das in der Nationalversammlung zwar überwog, in der Königsfrage jedoch uneins war, sowie vom Deutschen Reich (Spitzhelm), das neben der Annexion von Elsass-Lothringen noch bis 1873 Teile Frankreichs unter Besatzung hielt.

La République française menacée, encerclée par le camp monarchiste des légitimistes (fleur de lys), orléanistes (poire) et bonapartistes (tricorne) qui, s'il avait la majorité dans l'Assemblée nationale, n'était pas uni pour autant quant à la question du monarque, et par l'Empire allemand (casque à pointe) qui en plus de l'annexion de l'Alsace-Lorraine occupa encore des territoires français jusqu'en 1873.

"HOME AGAIN."
MATT MORGAN'S RETURN, WITH HIS GAMEBAG FULL OF CARTOONS—OPENING OF THE FALL CAMPAIGN.

THE GREAT POLITICAL ECLIPSE.

Matt Morgan

"Home Again" – Matt Morgan's Return, 1873
„Wieder zu Hause"– Matt Morgans Rückkehr
«À nouveau chez soi» – Le Retour de Matt Morgan
Wood engraving
From: *Frank Leslie's Illustrated Newspaper*, New York, 11 August 1873

After *The Tomahawk* went bankrupt, the English caricaturist Matt Morgan was hired in 1870 by Frank Leslie to work for him in the United States. Leslie was looking for an artist who would have the same appeal as the mighty Thomas Nast at the rival *Harper's Weekly*, but after several attempts to establish himself as a star cartoonist in Nast's style Morgan changed to pictorial journalism.

Nach dem Bankrott des *Tomahawk* nahm der britische Karikaturist Matt Morgan Ende 1870 ein Angebot von Frank Leslie an. Leslie war auf der Suche nach einem Zeichner, der sich gegenüber dem übermächtigen Thomas Nast vom Rivalen *Harper's Weekly* behaupten konnte. Nachdem wiederholte Anläufe gescheitert waren, ihn als Starcartoonisten à la Nast zu etablieren, verlegte sich Morgan auf grafische Sozialreportagen.

Après la faillite du *Tomahawk*, le caricaturiste britannique Matt Morgan accepta une offre de Frank Leslie, fin 1870. Leslie était à la recherche d'un illustrateur qui puisse s'imposer face au tout-puissant Thomas Nast du journal concurrent *Harper's Weekly*. Après plusieurs tentatives manquées de s'établir comme caricaturiste vedette à la Nast, Morgan se lança dans le reportage illustré à portée sociale.

Joseph Keppler

The Great Political Eclipse, 1874
Die große politische Sonnenfinsternis
La grande éclipse politique
Wood engraving
From: *Frank Leslie's Illustrated Newspaper*, New York, 14 November 1874

In late 1872 Frank Leslie added the Viennese caricaturist Joseph Keppler to his stable to provide reinforcements against Thomas Nast. Keppler had already made a name for himself when he founded two short-lived satirical journals in St. Louis, but it was only when he launched *Puck* there that he was able to establish a significant political counterpoint to Nast's Republican line (see ill. pp. 362/363).

Ende 1872 holte Frank Leslie den Wiener Karikaturisten Joseph Keppler als Verstärkung gegen Thomas Nast in den Ring. Keppler hatte sich durch die Gründung zweier kurzlebiger Satireblätter in St. Louis einen Namen gemacht. Allerdings gelang es Keppler erst mit der Etablierung eines weiteren eigenen Magazins, *Puck*, einen gewichtigen politischen Kontrapunkt zu Nasts republikanischer Linie zu setzen (siehe Abb. S. 362/363).

Fin 1872, Frank Leslie plaça dans le ring le caricaturiste viennois Joseph Keppler en renfort contre Thomas Nast. Keppler s'était fait un nom à St. Louis grâce à la création de deux journaux satiriques qui furent de courte durée. Néanmoins, Keppler ne réussit qu'avec le lancement d'un autre magazine, *Puck*, à faire un contrepoint politique de poids à la ligne républicaine de Nast (voir ill. p. 362/363).

Cinquième année — N° 177   Un numéro : **10** centimes. — Tirage, **31,000**   Dimanche 17 Mars 1872

RÉDACTEUR EN CHEF
F. POLO
—o—
ABONNEMENTS
PARIS
52 numéros . . . . 6 fr.
26 numéros . . . . 3 —
Les abonnements partent du
1er de chaque mois
BUREAUX
16, rue du Croissant, 16

DIRECTEUR
F. POLO
—o—
ABONNEMENTS
DEPARTEMENTS
52 numéros . . . . 8 fr.
26 numéros . . . . 5 —
—o—
ANNONCES
Fermage exclusif de la publicité
ADOLPHE EWIG
10, rue Taitbout, 10

GUET-APENS, PAR GILL

André Gill & Ferdinand Lefman (sc.)

→ *Split Decisions*, 1873
Spagat | Grand écart
Stencil-coloured relief etching
From: *L'Éclipse*, Paris, 20 April 1873

On the eve of elections for the French government the various opposing parties were threatening to split the Republic apart, and even a wily old player such as Adolphe Thiers could hardly manage to hold all the cards at once. After a vote of no confidence he resigned as president and was replaced by Marshal Patrice de Mac-Mahon, who had previously been in charge of the Versailles army that defeated the Commune.

Am Vorabend der Parlamentswahlen drohten die auseinanderstrebenden Kräfte, die Republik zu zerreißen. Selbst einem trickreichen Spieler wie Adolphe Thiers konnte es kaum mehr gelingen, das Blatt zu halten. Nach einem Misstrauensantrag wurde der Liberalkonservative durch Marschall Patrice de Mac-Mahon ersetzt, der den Oberbefehl über die Niederschlagung der Kommune hatte.

À la veille des élections parlementaires, les forces divergentes menaçaient de déchirer la République. Même un joueur aussi ingénieux qu'Adolphe Thiers ne pouvait guère réussir à tenir toutes les cartes en main. Après une motion de censure, le politicien libéral conservateur fut remplacé par le maréchal Patrice de Mac-Mahon qui avait eu le commandement suprême pour écraser la Commune.

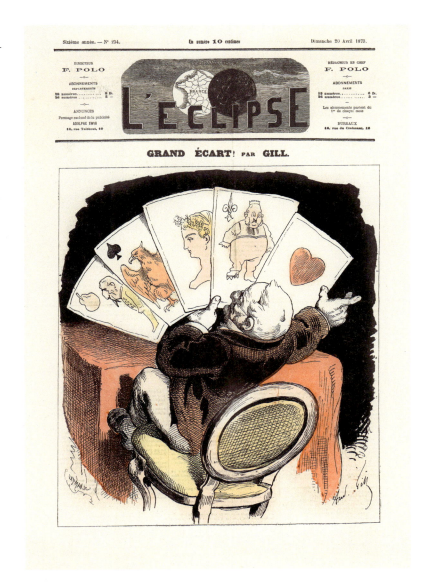

André Gill

Split Decisions, 1873
Spagat | Grand écart
Watercolour with gouache and pencil

Unlike his American colleague Thomas Nast, André Gill did not have to do the work of transferring his designs directly on to the wooden blocks for printing since they were instead produced by chemigraphic etching. The watercolour originals were used as a reference for the stencil colouring, even if the finished results, as shown by the example seen here, could differ considerably.

André Gill musste nicht wie sein amerikanischer Kollege Thomas Nast direkt auf die Druckstöcke zeichnen. Seine Entwürfe wurden chemigrafisch als Strichätzung übersetzt. Die aquarellierten Vorlagen enthielten auch Anhaltspunkte für die Schablonenkolorierungen, die allerdings, wie das Beispiel zeigt, erheblich vom Entwurf abweichen konnten.

À l'inverse de son collègue américain Thomas Nast, André Gill ne devait pas dessiner directement sur les blocs d'imprimerie. Ses ébauches étaient transposées comme gravures au trait au moyen de la chimigraphie. Les modèles aquarellisés contenaient aussi des indications pour les coloriages au pochoir, qui pouvaient toutefois nettement se différencier de l'ébauche, comme en témoigne cet exemple.

André Gill & Ferdinand Lefman (sc.)

← *Safely Delivered*, 1872
Die Entbindung | La Délivrance
Stencil-coloured relief etching
From: *L'Éclipse*, Paris, 4 August 1872

President Adolphe Thiers proudly holds up the reparations that were to be paid to the German Empire, which have just been delivered to him. The fact that the money was collected in such a surprisingly short time helped to stabilise the fragile Republic, and also rebuffed those on the side of the Monarchists. Because of censorship these figures are hidden by the clouds, but they could easily be identified by their footwear.

Stolz präsentiert Präsident Adolphe Thiers die Geburt der Reparationssumme, die an das Deutsche Reich zu leisten war. Dass ihm die Kollekte in überraschend kurzer Zeit gelungen war, stabilisierte die fragile Republik und brüskierte die Repräsentanten des monarchistischen Lagers. Die waren wegen der Zensur unter Wolken versteckt, ließen sich aber leicht am Schuhwerk identifizieren.

Très fier, le président Adolphe Thiers présente la naissance de la somme des réparations qui devaient être versées à l'Empire allemand. Le fait que l'argent ait été collecté en étonnamment peu de temps stabilisa la fragile République et heurta les représentants du camp monarchiste. Ils étaient cachés sous les nuages à cause de la censure mais étaient faciles à identifier à cause de leurs souliers.

2ᵉ ANNÉE. — Nᵒ 63   DIX CENTIMES   DIMANCHE 23 JUIN 1872

RÉDACTION
20, RUE DU CROISSANT, 20
PARIS
—
ABONNEMENT
Un an.................... 8 fr.
Six mois 4
Trois mois............... 2

ADMINISTRATION
20, RUE DU CROISSANT, 20
PARIS
—
ABONNEMENT
Un an.................... 8 fr.
Six mois 4
Trois mois............... 2

A CHOISIR! PAR ALFRED LE PETIT

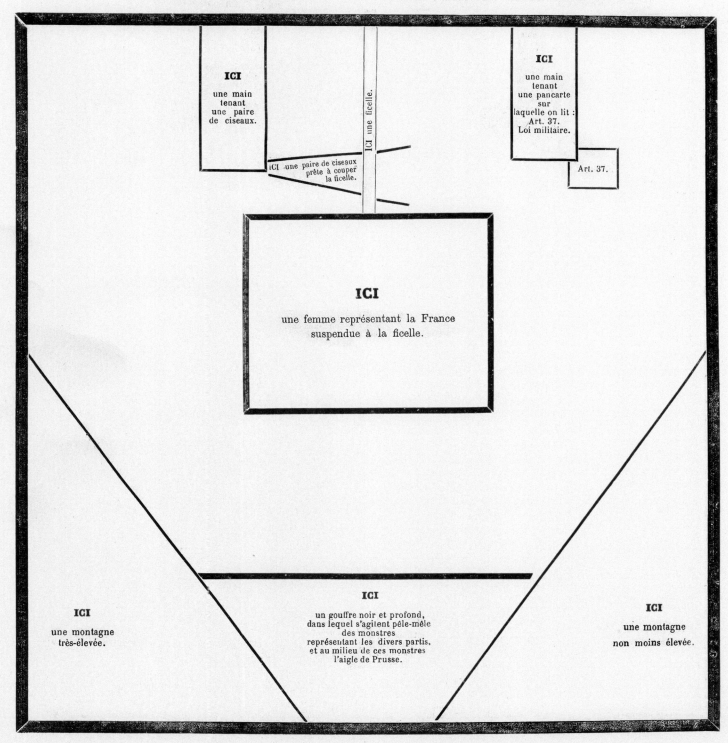

La Censure a autorisé la semaine dernière à l'un de nos confrères un dessin dont elle n'avait certainement pas compris la portée et que la plupart des journaux ont vivement critiqué. Afin de réparer la faute commise, et pour faire un exemple, elle interdit aujourd'hui — du même coup — les quatre dessins que lui avait soumis le *Grelot*. C'est de la bonne justice...

Le temps nous manquant pour en faire d'autres, le *Grelot* se contente de décrire l'un de ses quatre dessins refusés — afin que le public puisse se convaincre que ce dessin n'avait rien de contraire aux lois, ni aux mœurs, ni au respect qu'on doit aux autorités établies quoique provisoires.

Alfred Le Petit

← *You Can Choose!* 1872
Bitte auswählen! | *À choisir!*
Relief etching
From: *Le Grelot*, Paris, 23 June 1872

Censorship rules regularly meant that inventive solutions had to be found for certain illustrations (see ills. pp. 115, 360, 361). When precensors rejected a caricature that questioned the French army's ability to defend itself against the German Empire, Alfred Le Petit reduced the picture to its compositional elements and replaced the pictorial details with short descriptive texts.

Zensurauflagen provozierten immer wieder kühne bildnerische Lösungen (siehe Abb. S. 115, 360, 361). Als die Vorzensur eine Karikatur zurückgewiesen hatte, die die Wehrfähigkeit der französischen Armee gegenüber dem Deutschen Reich in Zweifel zog, minimierte Alfred Le Petit die Darstellung auf ihr kompositorisches Skelett und ersetzte die Bildsymbolik durch einen deskriptiven Text.

Des lois de censure provoquaient régulièrement des solutions audacieuses en images (voir ills. p. 115, 360, 361). Après que la précensure eut rejeté une caricature qui mettait en doute la capacité de défense de l'armée française face à l'Empire allemand, Alfred Le Petit réduisit l'image à une structure de squelette et remplaça les symboles picturaux par un texte descriptif.

Ball and Chain, 1873
Der Klotz | *Le Boulet*
Stencil-coloured relief etching
From: *Le Grelot*, Paris, 20 July 1873

As chief illustrator for the major republican satirical magazine *Le Grelot*, Alfred Le Petit was constrained from two directions. For one, the stringent censorship measures under Mac-Mahon held him back like a ball and chain, while he also had to put up with in-house controls set in place by his conservative publisher Madre. The second situation was the more onerous since there was no way of communicating it to his readership.

Der Chefzeichner des führenden republikanischen Satiremagazins *Le Grelot* stand unter doppeltem Druck. Alfred Le Petit hatte nicht nur die rigiden Zensurmaßnahmen unter Marschall Mac-Mahon als Klotz am Bein, er war auch noch einer hauseigenen Kontrolle durch den konservativen Verleger Madre unterworfen. Die war insofern gravierender, als er sie seinem Publikum nicht kommunizieren konnte.

L'illustrateur en chef du plus important journal satirique républicain *Le Grelot* était sous pression à double titre. Alfred Le Petit ne traînait pas seulement les rigides mesures de censure sous le maréchal Mac-Mahon comme un boulet, il était de surcroît soumis aussi à un contrôle interne en la personne de l'éditeur conservateur Madre. Ce joug était d'autant plus pesant qu'il ne pouvait pas le faire savoir à son public.

Alfred Le Petit & Ferdinand Lefman (sc.)

This Is How It Is!, 1873
So ist das! | *C'est comme ça!*
Stencil-coloured relief etching
From: *Le Grelot*, Paris,
28 December 1873

Alfred Le Petit protested strenuously against the proposed introduction of precensorship rules that would impose the same restrictions on words (the quill pen seen here) as already applied to pictures (the pencil tied to the post). Adding his cartoon signature at the bottom, he was making his case to the censors that word and image are inseparable.

Mit persönlichem Nachdruck protestierte Alfred Le Petit gegen die Einführung einer geplanten Vorzensur, die dem Wort (in Gestalt einer Feder) die gleichen Restriktionen auferlegen würde wie dem Bild (im Emblem der gemarterten Zeichenkreide). Mit dem Signaturen-Cartoon am unteren Bildrand gab er den Zensoren zu verstehen, dass Wort und Bild untrennbar sind.

Alfred Le Petit protesta personnellement avec énergie contre l'instauration d'une précensure prévue, qui imposerait à la parole (sous forme d'une plume) les mêmes restrictions qu'à l'image (symbolisée par la craie martyrisée). Avec son effigie signée au bas de l'image il faisait comprendre aux censeurs que parole et image sont indissociables.

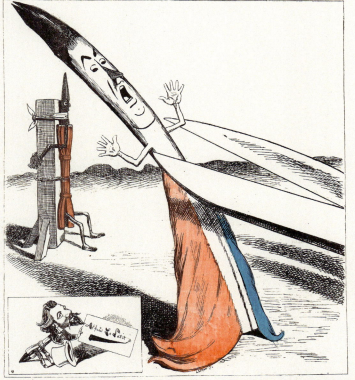

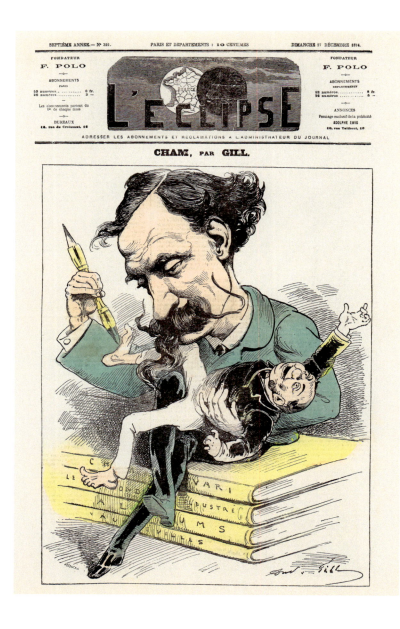

André Gill & Ferdinand Lefman (sc.)

The Journalism of the Future, 1875
Der Journalismus der Zukunft
Le Journalisme de l'avenir
Stencil-coloured relief etching
From: *L'Éclipse*, Paris,
5 December 1875

December 1875 marked the end of
a year of intense repression for the
press illustrators of the Third Republic,
during which 225 illustrations had
been banned, including 17 caricatures
for *L'Éclipse*. The prospects for the
future under Mac-Mahon's regime of
"moral order" seemed very bleak.

Im Dezember 1875 ging für die Pressegrafiker der Dritten Republik ein
Jahr größter Repressionen zu Ende.
225 Illustrationen waren verboten
worden, davon 17 Karikaturen für
L'Éclipse. Die Zukunftsperspektiven
unter Marschall Mac-Mahons Regime
der „Ordre moral" schienen düster.

En décembre 1875 se terminait une
année de répressions massives pour
les dessinateurs de presse de la
Troisième République. 225 dessins
avaient été interdits, dont 17 caricatures pour *L'Éclipse*. Les perspectives
d'avenir sous le régime de l'«Ordre
moral» du maréchal Mac-Mahon
s'annonçaient lugubres.

→ *Conquering Heroes of the
Salon*, 1876
Die Triumphatoren des Salons
Les Triomphateurs du Salon
Stencil-coloured relief etching
From: *L'Éclipse*, Paris, 14 May 1876

Édouard Manet's presence overshad-
owed the Salon of 1876 even though
he was not involved in any way after
his paintings were scandalously
rejected. The portrait of him as the
triumphant hero echoes the features
of the jovial drinker in his painting
Le Bon Bock (*A Good Glass of Beer*),
which celebrates the Société du Bon
Bock, a club co-founded the year
before by André Gill and from which
the early avant-garde artists' culture in
Montmartre developed (see ill. p. 501).

Édouard Manet überstrahlte den Salon 1876 durch Abwesenheit, denn
seine Werke waren skandalöserweise
zurückgewiesen worden. Das Porträt
des Triumphators trägt Züge des
jovialen Trinkers auf Manets Gemälde
Le Bon Bock, des Programmbilds
der im Jahr zuvor von André Gill mit
begründeten Société du Bon Bock,
aus der sich die frühavantgardistische
Künstlerklubkultur des Montmartre
entwickelte (siehe Abb. S. 501).

Édouard Manet brilla par son absence
au Salon de 1876, car ses œuvres
avaient été scandaleusement refusées.
Le portrait du triomphateur a les traits
d'un buveur jovial sur le tableau de
Manet *Le Bon Bock*, illustration du
programme de la Société du Bon Bock
co-fondée par André Gill un an plus
tôt, d'où allait irradier la culture de club
des premiers artistes avant-gardistes
de Montmartre (voir ill. p. 501).

André Gill

Cham, 1874
Stencil-coloured relief etching
From: *L'Éclipse*, Paris,
27 December 1874

Cham was the most popular cartoonist in France, and since 1839 he
had established a wide readership
of all ages for caricatures as a genre
by way of numerous collections of
illustrations and appearances in illustrated newspapers and magazines.
In the rather forced way in which the
aristocratic Cham is making the small
bourgeois figure laugh here it is also
possible to read André Gill's criticism,
from the perspective of a political
caricaturist, of using press illustrations
simply to entertain.

Cham war der populärste französische Cartoonist. Seit 1839 hatte er
in zahllosen Alben und Illustrierten-
beiträgen einem breiten Publikum,
das quer durch alle Altersschichten
ging, das Comicgenre erschlossen. In
der forcierten Weise, wie der aristo-
kratische Zeichner einen Bourgeois
zum Lachen bringt, scheint eine Kritik
des Politcartoonisten André Gill am
grafischen Entertainment durch.

Cham était le caricaturiste français le
plus populaire. Depuis 1839, dans d'innombrables albums et suppléments
illustrés de journaux, il avait diffusé
le genre de la caricature à un vaste
public, toutes générations confondues.
Une critique du caricaturiste politique
André Gill à l'adresse du divertissement par voie de dessins de presse
transparaît dans la manière forcée
avec laquelle le dessinateur aristo-
crate fait rire un bourgeois.

LES TRIOMPHATEURS DU SALON, PAR GILL.

Detaille : *La Reconnaissance*, ou le triomphe de Meissonier. — **Firmin-Girard** : *Le Marché aux Fleurs*, ou le triomphe de l'adresse et de la photographie. — **Carolus Duran & Vibert** : *La Marquise* et *la Banquière*, ou le triomphe des escaliers chics. — **Clairin** : *Sarah-Bernhardt*, ou le triomphe de la levrette. — **Feyen-Perrin** : *Les Cancalaises*, ou le triomphe de la grâce. — **Jean Béraud** : (441) *La Sortie du cimetière*, ou le triomphe de l'esprit. — **G. Doré** : *L'Entrée à Jérusalem*, ou le triomphe de la dimension et de la tapisserie. — **Bastien Lepage** : *M. Wallon*, ou le triomphe de la sincérité. — **EDOUARD MANET**, ou le triomphe de l'absence.

„Wenn Sie mit Ihrem schwächlichen leidenden Körper ein Held geworden sind, Suwarow," entgegnete die schöne muthige Frau, weshalb soll ich mit meinem kräftigen und gesunden nicht mindestens ein guter Soldat sein?"

„Ich bin ein Mann, Gräfin."

„Und ich ein Weib, das ist noch mehr."

„Wie Sie glauben."

Suwarow setzte sich hierauf zu Pferde und ritt, unbekümmert um die türkischen Vorposten, welche wiederholt Feuer auf ihn gaben, ganz nahe an die feindliche Stellung, er überzeugte sich, daß dieselbe stark verschanzt sei und daß die Türken auf seinen beiden Flanken vorrückten.

„Sie wollen uns umgehen," murmelte er, „gut, sehr gut, ich möchte nur wissen, welcher Dummkopf sie kommandirt."

(Schluß folgt.)

Die fromme Helene.

Von W. Busch.

XIII.

„Oh, Franz!" — spricht Lene — und sie weint —
„Oh, Franz! Du bist mein einz'ger Freund!"

„Ja!" — schwört der Franz mit mildem Hauch —
„Ich war's, ich bin's und bleib es auch!"

„Nun gute Nacht! Schon tönt es Zehn!
Willsgott! Auf baldig Wiederseh'n!"

Die Stiegen steigt er sanft hinunter.
Schau, schau! Die Kathi ist noch munter.

Das freut den Franz. — Er hat nun mal
'n Hang für's Küchenpersonal.

Der Jean, der heimlich näher schlich,
Bemerkt die Sache zorniglich.

Vor großer Eifersucht erfüllt,
Hebt er die Flasche rasch und wild.

Und — Kracks! — Es dringt der scharfe Schlag
Bis tief in das Gedankenfach.

's ist aus! — der Lebensfaden bricht.
Helene naht. — Es fällt das Licht. —

XIV.

Ach, wie ist der Mensch so sündig!
Lene, Lene! Gehe in dich! —

Und sie eilt tieferschüttert
Zu dem Schranke schmerzdurchzittert.

Fort! Ihr falschgesinnten Zöpfe!
Schminke und Pomadetöpfe!

Fort! Du Apparat der Lüste,
Hochgewölbtes Herzgerüste!

Fort vor allem mit dem Uebel
Dieser Lust- und Sündenstiebel!

Trödelkram der Eitelkeit,
Fort, und sei der Gluth geweiht!!

O, wie lieblich sind die Schuhe
Demuthsvoller Seelenruhe!! —

Sieh, da geht Helene hin,
Eine schlaue Büßerin!

(Fortsetzung folgt.)

„Thäten Sie nicht besser," fragte eine ältere Dame einen bequemen Junggesellen, „sich für die weite Fahrt auf dem Ozean des Lebens eine Gesellschafterin zu erkiesen?" — „Wenn ich die Gewißheit hätte, daß dieser Ozean dann auch ein „stilles Meer" wäre!" erwiderte der Gefragte mit seiner Ironie.

Wie man Graf und Hauptmann wird. Bei einer Revue sagte Paul I. von Rußland plötzlich in seiner gewöhnlich barschen Weise zu einem Unterleutnant, namens Krasanow: „Haben Sie auch etwas gelernt, um Offizier zu sein?" — „Ich weiß Alles, Majestät." sagte der Leutnant unerschrocken. — „So, so, wollen sehen. Wie viele Stiche mußte der Schneider machen, als er Ihre Uniform verfertigte?" — „Zweiundzwanzig Tausend einhundert und vierzehn, Majestät." — „Ist das die genaue Anzahl?" — „Sicherlich, sonst würde ich nicht gewagt haben, es Euer ajestät zu sagen." — „Brav, ich habe gern Antworten auf meine Fragen. Ein Offizier soll Alles wissen, gerade wie der Kaiser eines Reiches, der auch Alles weiß." — „Auch wie ich heiße?" wagte Krasanow zu fragen. — „Auch das," erwiderte der Kaiser ohne zu zürnen. „Ihr heißt Graf Balowski." — „Und mein Rang?" — „Hauptmann in der Garde." So wurde der Unterleutnant Krasanow durch seine Geistesgegenwart und die Laune des Selbstherrschers Graf und Hauptmann.

Thomas Nast

By Inflation You Will Burst, 1873
Bei Inflation platzt du | En cas d'inflation, tu explodes
Wood engraving
From: *Harper's Weekly*, New York,
20 December 1873

When the financial crisis in the United States hit the stock exchange in September, President Grant enacted a hard-currency policy to inject cash into the system. Thomas Nast applauded him for his decision not to bow to pressure from the business lobby and to increase the amount of money in circulation, and in his view inflation would only result in a final financial collapse.

Im Zuge der Finanzkrise, die im September auf die amerikanischen Börsenplätze übergesprungen war, vertrat US-Präsident Ulysses S. Grant eine Politik der harten Währung. Thomas Nast applaudierte ihm zu seiner Entscheidung, sich nicht dem Druck der Wirtschaftslobby zu beugen und keine Vermehrung der Geldmenge zuzulassen. Inflation würde laut Nast nur den finalen Finanzkollaps zur Folge haben.

En conséquence de la crise financière qui avait atteint les places boursières américaines en septembre, le président américain Ulysses S. Grant préconisait une politique de monnaie forte. Thomas Nast l'applaudit pour sa décision de ne pas céder à la pression du lobby économique et de n'autoriser aucune augmentation de l'offre monétaire. Selon Nast, une inflation ne ferait qu'entraîner l'effondrement financier final.

DECEMBER 20, 1873.]   HARPER'S WEEKLY.   1141

BY INFLATION YOU WILL BURST.
UNCLE SAM. "You stupid Money-Bag! there is just so much Money in you; and you can not make it any more by blowing yourself up!"

LET WELL ENOUGH ALONE, AND DON'T MAKE IT WORSE.
Money is *tight*, but let it recover itself naturally, and then it will stand on a *Sounder Basis*.   Stimulants or *Inflation* only bring *final collapse*.

Wilhelm Busch

← *Helen Who Couldn't Help It*,
1872/73
Die fromme Helene | La Pieuse Hélène
Relief etching
From: *Frank Leslie's Illustrirte Zeitung*,
New York, 1 February 1873

The illustrated novel *Die fromme Helene*, which was filled with aspects of Prussia's anti-clerical domestic policy, was the last in a series of political parables by the satirical draughtsman Wilhelm Busch. It was published in the mass-circulation German edition of *Frank Leslie's Illustrated Newspaper* amidst growing demand in the United States for the illustrated work of Kaspar Braun (ill. p. 174).

Der Bilderroman *Die fromme Helene*, der die antiklerikale preußische Innenpolitik flankierte, stand am Ende einer Reihe politischer Parabeln Wilhelm Buschs. Der Abdruck in der auflagenstarken deutschsprachigen Ausgabe von *Frank Leslie's Illustrated Newspaper* erfolgte im Zusammenhang mit einer wachsenden Nachfrage nach Kaspar Brauns Bilderbogenkultur (Abb. S. 174) in Amerika.

Le roman illustré *Die fromme Helene*, empreint de la politique intérieure anticléricale de la Prusse, était la dernière d'une série de parables politiques signées Wilhelm Busch. La publication dans l'édition germanophone à grand tirage du *Frank Leslie's Illustrated Newspaper* eut lieu dans le contexte d'une demande croissante, aux États-Unis, pour les pages illustrées popularisées par Kaspar Braun (ill. p. 174).

→→ Thomas Nast

The Biggest Scare and Hoax Yet! – The Wild Animals Let Loose Again by the Zoomorphism Press, 1875
Allergrößte Panikmache und Zeitungsente! – Erneut wilde Tiere von der Zoomorphismus-Presse losgelassen
La plus grande panique et un canular ! – À nouveau des animaux sauvages sont lâchés par la presse de zoomorphisme
Wood engraving
From: *Harper's Weekly*, New York,
6 February 1875

A spectacular hoax report about animals escaping from the zoo in Central Park and running freely through the city provided the backdrop for Thomas Nast's complex criticism of what he considered to be the blind attacks by the press on the annual report to Congress by the lion-hearted President. The zoomorphic imagery in Nast's political cartoons prepared the way for the later work of Walt Disney.

Eine spektakuläre Falschmeldung über den Ausbruch einer Horde wilder Tiere im Central Park bildete den Hintergrund von Thomas Nasts komplexer Kritik an den seiner Ansicht nach blinden Attacken der Presse auf den Jahresbericht des löwenmutigen Präsidenten, den dieser dem Kongress vorlegte. Der Boden für Walt Disneys zoomorphes Cartooning wurde durch Nasts politische Karikaturen vorbereitet.

Un canular spectaculaire selon lequel une horde d'animaux sauvages en fuite serait à Central Park forma la toile de fond de la critique complexe de Thomas Nast à l'égard des attaques, selon lui, aveugles de la presse contre le rapport annuel que le président, avec un courage de lion, avait présenté au Congrès. Les caricatures politiques de Nast préparèrent le terrain pour les dessins zoomorphes de Walt Disney.

"STILL ANOTHER OUTRAGE."

MORE GNAWING TO BE DONE.

THE BIGGEST SCARE AND HOAX YET!—THE WILD

LET LOOSE AGAIN BY THE ZOOMORPHISM PRESS.

Thomas Nast

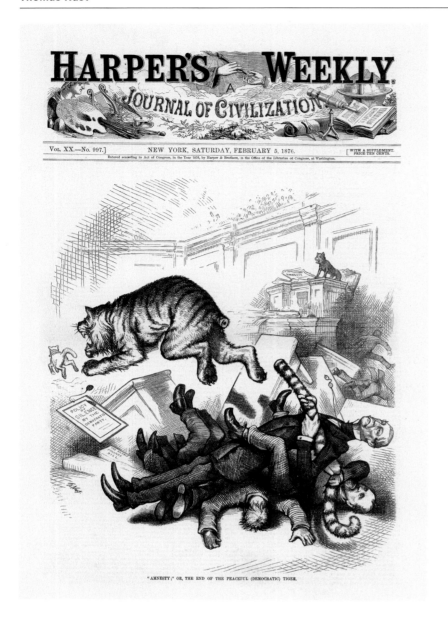

"Amnesty", or, the End of the Peaceful (Democratic) Tiger, 1876
„Amnestie" oder Das Ende des friedlichen (demokratischen) Tigers
«Amnestie» ou la fin du tigre pacifique (démocratique)
Wood engraving
From: *Harper's Weekly*, New York, 5 February 1876

As debates in Congress continued on the subject of granting pardons to hundreds of Secessionist leaders, old rifts from the time of the Civil War opened up again between Democrats and Republicans. In the heated discussions that ensued, Thomas Nast saw the predatory nature of the Democratic tiger break out, first of all in pursuit of the Republican lamb before a few months later, maddened with rage, smashing into its own reflection.

Während der Debatten um die Begnadigung Hunderter führender Sezessionisten öffneten sich im Kongress alte Bürgerkriegsgräben zwischen Demokraten und Republikanern. Thomas Nast sah in den hitzigen Diskussionen die Raubtiernatur des demokratischen Tigers durchbrechen, der zuerst dem republikanischen Lamm nachsetzt, um dann Monate später tollwütig am eigenen Spiegelbild zu zerschellen.

Pendant les débats menés pour la grâce de centaines de chefs sécessionnistes, les vieux clivages datant de la guerre civile entre Démocrates et Républicains ressurgirent au Congrès. Dans ces discussions enflammées, Thomas Nast voyait percer la nature de prédateur du tigre démocrate qui d'abord poursuit l'agneau républicain, avant de s'écraser, fou de rage, devant son propre reflet dans le miroir quelques mois plus tard.

The Democratic Tiger Gone Mad, 1876
Der demokratische Tiger hat den Verstand verloren
Le tigre démocratique a perdu la raison
Wood engraving
From: *Harper's Weekly*, New York, 20 May 1876

Right from the beginning, Thomas Nast's work as a political cartoonist made use of arguments spread across the separate instalments of a series, on the model of the campaigning graphic work of William Hone and Charles Philipon. The development from showing single events to sequential narratives can be traced back to the picture stories that first appeared in early broadsheets and to Nast's experience from the lecture tours he started making in 1873 where he drew illustrations as part of his performance.

Von Anfang an ist Thomas Nast als politischer Cartoonist nach dem Vorbild der Kampagnen William Hones und Charles Philipons in argumentativen Abfolgen vorgegangen. Der Übergang zu sequenziellen Verdichtungen geht auf den Einfluss der Bilderbogenkultur zurück sowie auf Nasts Erfahrungen als Zeichenperformer, die er seit 1873 bei seinen Vortragstourneen machte.

Dès le début, Thomas Nast a procédé en tant que caricaturiste politique en séries argumentatives d'après le modèle des campagnes de William Hone et de Charles Philipon. Le passage à une intensification séquentielle remonte à l'influence de la culture des pages illustrées ainsi qu'aux expériences de Nast comme illustrateur performant pendant les tournées de conférences qu'il effectua à partir de 1873.

Thomas Nast

No Rest for the Wicked –
Sentenced to More Hard Labor, 1876
Keine Ruhe für die Gottlosen –
Zu weiterer Zwangsarbeit verurteilt
Pas de repos pour les méchants –
Condamnés à plus de travaux forcés
Wood engraving
From: *Harper's Weekly*, New York, 2 December 1876

During the election campaigning of 1876, Thomas
Nast, a Republican, was unable on this occasion to
damage the Democratic candidate's reputation to
the point where the outcome of the voting would be
guaranteed. Amidst the nerve-racking stalemate
that followed the election, he emerged as a committed supporter of civil rights and cast a particularly
critical eye on voters in the South.

Während des Wahlkampfs war es dem Republikaner
Thomas Nast diesmal nicht gelungen, den demokra-
tischen Kandidaten so weit zu demontieren, dass
es zu einem eindeutigen Ergebnis gekommen wäre.
In der nervenaufreibenden Pattsituation bringt Nast
sich als bewährten Streiter für Bürgerrechte in
Erinnerung und stellt besonders den Wahlblock der
Südstaaten unter seine kritische Beobachtung.

Pendant la campagne électorale, le Républicain
Thomas Nast n'était pas parvenu cette fois à démon-
ter le candidat démocrate au point d'obtenir un
résultat sans équivoque. Dans l'éprouvante situation
d'impasse, Nast réapparaît comme un défenseur
confirmé des droits civiques et observe d'un œil critique les électeurs des États du Sud en particulier.

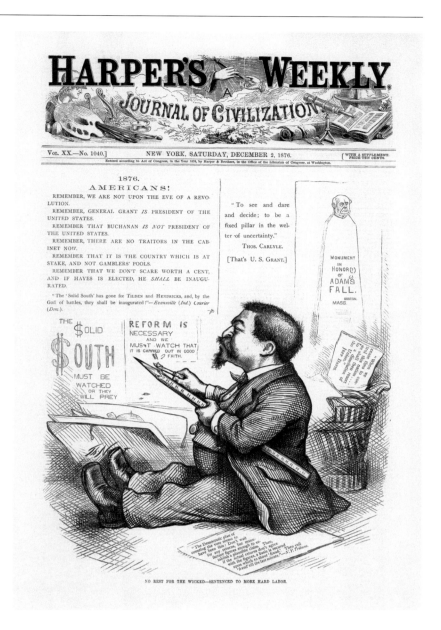

"Nay, Patience, or We Break the Sinews", 1877
„Geduldet Euch doch, oder wir brechen [ihm] den Hals"
« Patience, ou nous lui cassons les reins »
Wood engraving
From: *Harper's Weekly*, New York, 5 May 1877

The concessions made to the southern states by
the new Republican President Rutherford B. Hayes
set Thomas Nast at odds for the first time with his
party's line, and with his magazine. When the founding publisher fell ill Nast felt unsupported, and reluctantly decided to lay down arms temporarily to give
national interests a chance, here shown in the guise
of Uncle Sam.

Die Konzessionen, die der neue republikanische Präsident Rutherford B. Hayes dem Südstaatenblock
zugestand, brachte Thomas Nast erstmals auf Kon-
frontationskurs gegen die Linie seiner Partei und
seines Journals. Da ihm, nachdem der Verleger vor
seinem Tod schwer erkrankt war, die Rückendeckung
fehlte, entschied er sich widerwillig für ein vorläufi-
ges Stillhalteabkommen zugunsten der Staatsräson
in der Gestalt von Uncle Sam.

Les concessions que le nouveau président républicain Rutherford B. Hayes fit au bloc des États du
Sud placèrent Thomas Nast pour la première fois
en situation de conflit avec la ligne de son parti et
de son journal. Comme l'éditeur tomba gravement
malade, puis mourut, et que Nast manquait de soutien, il se décida à contrecœur pour un accord mora-
toire provisoire en faveur de la raison d'État sous la
forme d'Oncle Sam.

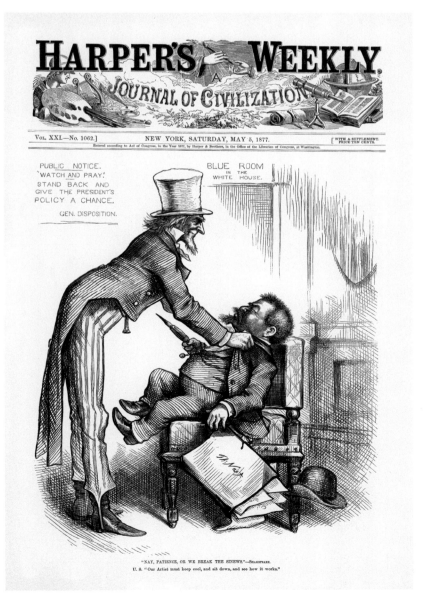

MON COCHER — PAR GILL

André Gill; Yves & Barret (sc.)

My Coachman, 1877
Mein Kutscher | *Mon Cocher*
Stencil-coloured relief etching
From: *La Lune rousse*, Paris,
9 September 1877

Anyone who had assumed that mass-printed caricature portraits were exclusively of well-known figures would have been surprised in September 1877 if they looked in at the kiosks and displays of street vendors in Paris. André Gill's first such starring portrait showed the concierge of his building, followed a little later by his coachman and then the man who brought his coal.

Wer bislang davon ausgegangen war, dass das karikierte Konterfei in Massenauflage ein Privileg Prominenter sei, der erlebte im September 1877 an den Kiosken und Aushängen der Straßenverkäufer eine Überraschung. André Gill veröffentlichte zuerst ein Starporträt seines Hauswarts, wenig später folgte der Kutscher und schließlich der lokale Kohlenlieferant.

Ceux qui jusqu'à présent présumaient que le portrait-charge était le privilège des célébrités eurent en septembre 1877 une belle surprise devant les kiosques et affichages des vendeurs de rue. André Gill publia d'abord un portrait de star de son concierge, un peu plus tard ce fut le tour du cocher et finalement du charbonnier local.

MON CHARBONNIER — PAR GILL

André Gill; Yves & Barret (sc.)

My Coal Merchant, 1877
Mein Kohlenhändler | Mon Charbonnier
Stencil-coloured relief etching
From: *La Lune rousse*, Paris,
23 September 1877

André Gill's series of different workers appeared just before an election that was critical for the future of the Third Republic. The portraits weren't naturalistic case studies, but represented types with an egalitarianism that evoked the suppressed ideals of the Commune in such a comical and burlesque manner that the censors were left with no grounds on which to object.

André Gills Arbeiterserie erschien kurz vor einer Wahl, von der das Schicksal der Dritten Republik abhing. Die Porträts zeigen keine naturalistischen Fallstudien. Sie repräsentieren einen ikonischen Egalitarismus, der die verdrängten Ideale der Pariser Kommune auf eine so joviale und burleske Weise wachrief, dass er den Zensoren keinerlei Angriffsfläche bot.

La série de Gill sur les métiers parut juste avant une élection dont dépendait le sort de la Troisième République. Les portraits ne montrent pas d'études naturalistes de cas. Ils représentent un égalitarisme iconique qu' évoquaient les idéaux réprimés de la Commune de Paris d'une manière si joviale et si burlesque qu'il ne présentait aux censeurs aucune surface d'attaque.

Cramponne-toi, Gugusse, v'la que ça recommence ! — par GILL

La Censure

André Gill; Yves & Barret (sc.)

Hold on Tight, Silly Billy, It's Starting Again!, 1877
Halt dich gut fest, dummer August, es geht schon wieder los!
Cramponne-toi, Gugusse, v'la que ça recommence!
Stencil-coloured relief etching
From: *La Lune rousse*,
Paris, 4 March 1877

Afte*r* *L'Éclipse*'s publisher decided to reduce the journal's format, André Gill launched his own periodical in which he could expand his work to illustrations the size of a poster. Soon afterwards, selling publications on the street was banned temporarily by the authorities, but once the Republicans secured a majority in the elections for the National Assembly Gill felt the powers of the censors were in decline.

Nachdem der Verleger von *L'Éclipse* das Format reduziert hatte, gründete André Gill ein eigenes Magazin, in dem er sich zu postergroßen Dimensionen aufschwingen konnte. Die Behörden verboten daraufhin zeitweise den Straßenverkauf. Als die Republikaner bei den Wahlen für die französische Abgeordnetenkammer die Mehrheit gewannen, sah Gill bereits die Macht der Zensoren schwinden.

Après que l'éditeur de *L'Éclipse* en eut réduit le format, André Gill lança son propre journal dans lequel il pouvait obtenir des dimensions d'affiche. À la suite de quoi, les autorités interdirent provisoirement la vente dans la rue. Quand les Républicains emportèrent la majorité aux élections de l'Assemblée nationale, Gill vit dès lors la puissance des censeurs diminuer.

UN DESSIN DE GILL — PAR GILL

Pauvre Anastasie, tu seras donc toujours la même!

André Gill; Yves & Barret (sc.)

A Picture of Gill, 1878
Eine Zeichnung von Gill
Un dessin de Gill
Stencil-coloured relief etching
From: *La Lune rousse*, Paris,
27 January 1878

However, André Gill was celebrating too soon, and despite the left-wing majority arbitrary repression continued just as before. Madame Anastasie, the symbolic figure of ever-renewing censorship, was created by Gill and Alfred Le Petit based on similar designs by Nicolas-Toussaint Charlet, Eugène Delacroix and Grandville (see ill. p. 109). She took the form of an evil governess who, in her short-sightedness, even takes fright at childish scribbles.

André Gill hatte sich zu früh gefreut. Trotz linker Mehrheiten hielten die will-kürlichen Repressionen an. Madame Anastasie, die Symbolgestalt der ewig wiederauferstehenden Zensur, wurde von Gill und Alfred Le Petit nach Vor-lagen von Nicolas-Toussaint Charlet, Eugène Delacroix und Grandville ent-wickelt (siehe Abb. S. 109). Sie er-scheint als böse Gouvernante, die in ihrer Blindheit selbst über kindische Kritzeleien erschrickt.

André Gill s'était réjoui trop tôt. Malgré les majorités de gauche, les répressions arbitraires se poursui-virent. Madame Anastasie, la figure symbolique de la censure toujours ressuscitée, a été élaborée par Gill et Alfred Le Petit d'après de modèles de Nicolas-Toussaint Charlet, Eugène Delacroix et Grandville (voir ill. p. 109). Elle apparaît sous les traits d'une méchante gouvernante, qui, dans son aveuglement, s'effraie même de gri-bouillages enfantins.

→→ Charles Gilbert-Martin

Give Us Back Our Pictures!, 1877
Geben Sie das Bild zurück!
Rendez le cadre!
Stencil-coloured relief etching
From: *Le Don Quichotte*, Bordeaux,
13 July 1877

In Bordeaux, the caricaturist Charles Gilbert-Martin became involved in a spectacular duel with a local admin-istrator called Jacques de Tracy. The popular cartoonist responded to the latter's repeated precensorship and banning of illustrations by declaring that his newspaper would go on a picture strike until de Tracy was no longer in office. Instead of showing illustrations he resorted to covers that used only words, with content that attacked the censor (see ill. p. 115).

In Bordeaux lieferte sich der Karika-turist Charles Gilbert-Martin ein spek-takuläres Duell mit einem lokalen Präfekten namens Jacques de Tracy. Auf dessen wiederholte Vorzensuren reagierte der populäre Cartoonist mit der Ankündigung, sein Magazin werde so lange in einen Bilderstreik treten, bis de Tracy aus dem Amt sei. Statt Bilder zu zeigen, wich er auf typografi-sche Titel aus, in denen er den Zensor attackierte (siehe Abb. S. 115).

À Bordeaux, le caricaturiste Charles Gilbert-Martin se livra à duel specta-culaire avec un préfet local du nom de Jacques de Tracy. Aux précensures répétées de ce dernier le dessinateur populaire réagit en annonçant que son journal ne publierait pas d'illustra-tions jusqu'à ce que De Tracy quitte ses fonctions. Au lieu de montrer des images, il eut recours à des titres typographiques dans lesquels il atta-quait le censeur (voir ill. p. 115).

4ᵐᵉ ANNÉE. — Nº 160 PARIS ET DÉPARTEMENTS : 15 CENTIMES 13 JUILLET 1877.

LE DON QUICHOTTE

Rédacteur en Chef : Ch. GILBERT-MARTIN.

BORDEAUX
—
BUREAUX et ATELIERS :
RUE CABIROL, 7.
—
ABONNEMENTS :
POUR LA FRANCE & L'ALGÉRIE
UN AN .... 10 fr.
SIX MOIS .... 5 »
ÉTRANGER, le port en sus.

Les Abonnements doivent être adressés à
BORDEAUX, au bureau du Journal.

PARIS
—
DÉPOT GÉNÉRAL & VENTE
Chez M. S. COSTE
20, rue du Croissant

Envois en province aux Libraires et
Marchands de journaux directement
et par l'entremise du Petit Journal.

POUR PARIS
Les Annonces sont reçues
chez M. J.-B. CHANARD,
41, boulevard Saint-Germain,
seul autorisé.

RENDEZ LE CADRE !

M. de Tracy se révèle tous les jours sous un nouvel aspect qui le rend plus séduisant.

Nous venons d'apprendre qu'en 1870, il embrasait le département de l'Allier par ses professions de foi républicaines. Dans une lettre adressée à la *Gironde*, il déclare que *ses sentiments sont toujours les mêmes*. Cette lettre, nous assure-t-on, va être mise en musique par Offenbach.

Le dernier exploit de M. de Tracy laisse derrière lui tous les autres. Ne pouvant plus saisir les dessins du *Don Quichotte*, par la raison bien simple que le *Don Quichotte* ne publie plus de dessins, il vient de saisir chez M. Mendes, marchand de tableaux, une aquarelle que j'y avais mise en vente. Il faut absolument qu'il saisisse quelque chose. C'est un tic.

Cette aquarelle représentait un saltimbanque essayant de soulever un poids. M. de Tracy a sans doute trouvé à mon personnage une forte ressemblance avec celui dont il a empêché la publication dans le *Don Quichotte*.

Mais il ne s'agissait plus ici ni de journal, ni de dessin politique. Il n'y avait qu'un objet d'art. On n'y voyait ni légende, ni inscription, ni emblème d'aucune sorte.

L'œuvre du journaliste était tributaire de M. le Préfet, qui s'en est donné à tire-larigot pendant quelques semaines, mais l'œuvre du peintre était inviolable. Ce saltimbanque n'avait rien de particulier ; il ressemblait à tous les saltimbanques, qui sont nombreux, comme chacun sait. L'administration ne nous persuadera jamais qu'elle prenne ombrage des saltimbanques.

Il faut donc que M. le Préfet de la Gironde ait eu des raisons spéciales en s'appropriant ce tableau, qui représente une valeur marchande et pour lequel plusieurs acquéreurs s'étaient présentés. On en offrait bon prix. Je me refuse à croire que M. de Tracy veuille le mettre aux enchères pour couvrir une partie des frais de sa candidature, qu'il va de nouveau poser dans l'Allier (*toujours avec les mêmes sentiments*). Ce serait trop d'honneur pour moi.

M. Mendes n'a pu préserver de la confiscation que la ficelle qui retenait le tableau, en objectant avec énergie que cette ficelle était sa propriété.

Si M. le Préfet de la Gironde tient à posséder une de mes œuvres, je la lui abandonne d'autant plus volontiers qu'il met trop de délicatesse dans l'expression de son désir.

Mais, au moins, qu'il se contente de la peinture, sans exiger le cadre que je n'ai pas encore payé et que mes moyens ne me permettent pas de lui abandonner. Je jure sur ma tête que ce cadre n'est pas séditieux.

M. de Tracy, rendez le cadre !

RENDEZ LE CADRE !!

RENDEZ LE CADRE !!!

Ch. GILBERT-MARTIN.

Charles Gilbert-Martin

↓ *This Is the Picture!!!*, 1877
Hier ist das Bild!!! | *Voici le cadre!!!*
Stencil-coloured relief etching
From: *Le Don Quichotte*, Bordeaux,
10 August 1877

The sparring over the empty picture frame excited great attention and gave a phenomenal boost in circulation to Charles Gilbert-Martin's *Don Quichotte*. The series of abstract covers came to an end after four months when the hated de Tracy lost in local elections amidst accusations that he had abused his authority in relation to the *Don Quichotte* affair.

Der Schlagabtausch um den leeren Bilderrahmen wurde legendär und bescherte Charles Gilbert-Martins *Don Quichotte* fantastische Auflagensteigerungen. Die Serie abstrakter Cover endete nach vier Monaten, nachdem der verhasste Präfekt nach Vorwürfen wegen Amtsanmaßung, die man ihm im Zusammenhang mit der *Don-Quichotte*-Affäre machte, bei den Kommunalwahlen unterlegen war.

La joute verbale à laquelle le cadre vide donna lieu devint légendaire et fournit au *Don Quichotte* de Charles Gilbert-Martin de fantastiques hausses de tirage. La série de couvertures abstraites cessa après quatre mois, lorsque le préfet détesté fut battu aux élections communales après des accusations d'usurpation de pouvoir qu'il dut affronter en relation avec l'affaire *Don Quichotte*.

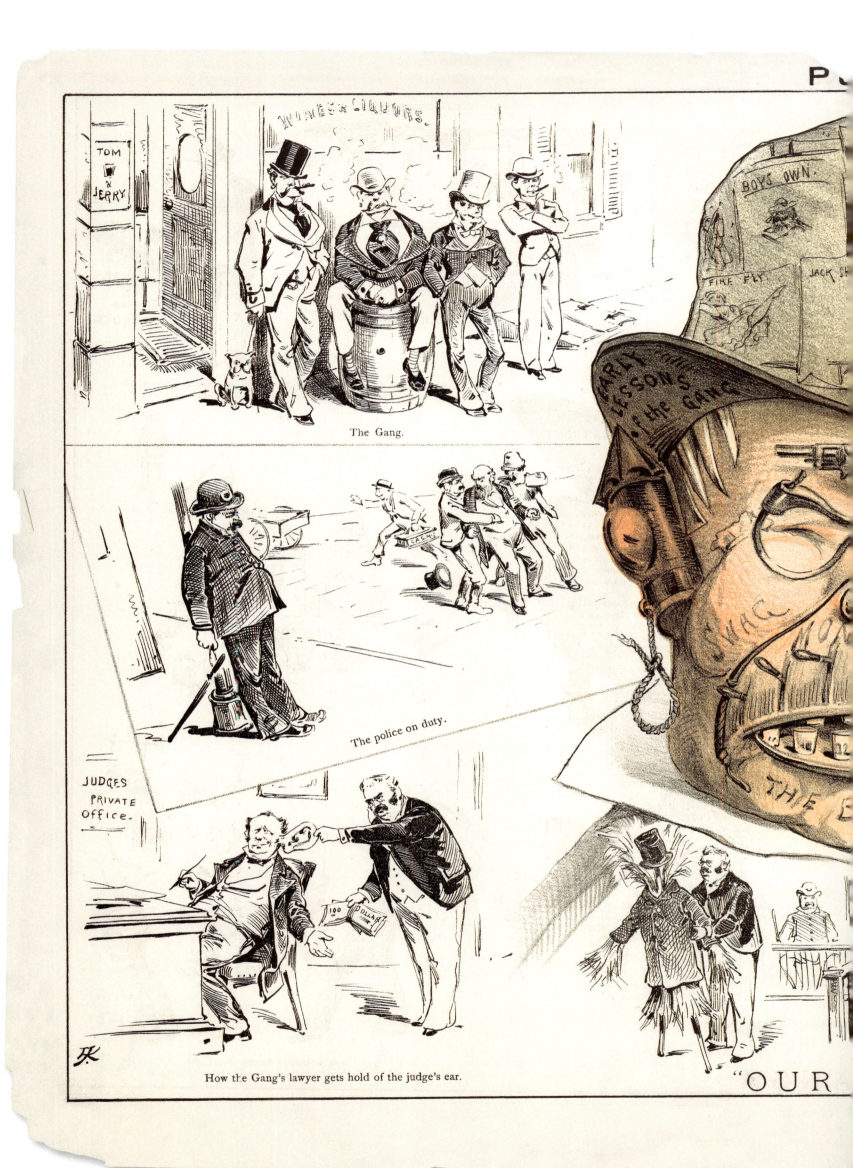

The Gang.

The police on duty.

How the Gang's lawyer gets hold of the judge's ear.

How car-conductors and the police *prevent* car-robberies in broad-daylight.

ENCOURAGEMENT.
How our manly citizens look on, but don't interfere—as it's "none of their business!"

How Mr. Straw, the bail-man, gets them out of court.

SIMPLE *IMPRISONMENT* NO CURE.
The only prevention lies in the cat-o'-nine-tails.

←←**Joseph Keppler**

Our Gangs, 1878
Unsere Banden | Nos Bandes
Tinted lithograph
From: *Puck*, New York, 28 August 1878

During the Gilded Age in the United States, street crime and corruption ran rampant in the big cities. Inspired by the colour illustrations in the French press, Joseph Keppler put great faith in the effects of colour when he relaunched *Puck* in New York He experimented initially with applying individual colours in selected areas for the first year of *Puck* in its English edition, before moving on to multi-coloured lithographs.

In Amerikas Metropolen zur Zeit des Gilded Age waren Straßenkriminalität und Korruption epidemisch. Inspiriert von der kolorierten französischen Karikaturpresse, setzte Joseph Keppler in seinem neu aufgelegten Magazin *Puck* in New York auf die Wirkung der Farbe. Bevor er zu mehrfarbigen Tonlithografien überging, experimentierte er im ersten Jahr der englischsprachigen Ausgabe des *Puck* mit dem Einsatz einzelner Sonderfarben.

Dans les métropoles américaines au temps du Gilded Age, la criminalité de rue et la corruption étaient endémiques. Inspiré par la presse de caricature française mise en couleur, Joseph Keppler misa sur les effets de la couleur quand il relança son magazine *Puck* à New York. Avant de passer aux lithographies en plusieurs couleurs, il expérimenta l'utilisation de couleurs spéciales et individuelles pendant la première année de l'édition anglaise de *Puck*.

Bernhard Gillam

→ *Hopelessly Bound to the Stake*, 1883
Hoffnungslos an den Scheiterhaufen gefesselt
Attaché sans espoir au bûcher
Tinted lithograph
From: *Puck*, New York, 15 August 1883

A contrasting viewpoint of the workers' struggle is provided by the illustrations of Bernhard Gillam. The worker who is unattached to any organisation appears here helpless and at the mercy of the infernal hustle and bustle of big business. In particular, railroad tycoons such as Jay Gould and the Vanderbilts added to his misery by attempting to keep him in an early-industrial version of serfdom.

Bernhard Gillam lieferte eine entgegengesetzte Perspektive auf den Arbeitskampf. Der unorganisierte Arbeiter erscheint hier hilflos dem infernalischen Treiben des Großkapitals ausgeliefert. Vor allem Tycoons des Eisenbahngewerbes wie Jay Gould und die Vanderbilts heizen ihm ein, indem sie ihn in einer frühindustriellen Form der Leibeigenschaft zu halten versuchen.

Bernhard Gillam fournit une perspective opposée sur la lutte des ouvriers. L'ouvrier désorganisé apparaît ici livré sans recours à l'agitation infernale du grand capital. En particulier les tycoons du secteur du chemin de fer comme Jay Gould et les Vanderbilt l'excitent en essayant de l'assujettir dans une forme de servage des débuts de l'industrie.

THE "INTERNATIONALISTS" ARE TO MAKE THE WORLD ALL ONE MILLENNIUM—(CHAOS).

Thomas Nast

The "Internationalists" Are to Make the World All One Millennium – (Chaos), 1878
Die „Internationalisten" werden ein ganzes Jahrtausend in die Welt bringen – (Chaos)
Les « internationalistes » vont apporter tout un millénaire dans le monde – (Chaos)
Wood engraving
From: *Harper's Weekly*, New York, 1 June 1878

Following the events of the Paris Commune, Thomas Nast launched a campaign in 1871 against the unions, which he considered to be synonymous with communism and anarchism. When a socialist workers' party was established in the United States he responded with this vision of a global inferno, using picturesque effects inspired by Gustave Doré's Neo-Romantic illustrations.

1871 hatte Thomas Nast im Anschluss an die Ereignisse der Pariser Kommune eine Kampagne gegen die Gewerkschaften gestartet, die er als Synonym für Kommunismus und Anarchie betrachtete. Die Gründung einer sozialistischen Arbeiterpartei in Amerika kommentierte er mit dieser Vision eines gobalen Infernos, dessen malerische Wirkung von den neuromantischen Illustrationen Gustave Dorés inspiriert war.

En 1871, à la suite des événements de la Commune de Paris, Thomas Nast avait lancé une campagne contre les syndicats qu'il considérait comme synonymes de communisme et d'anarchisme. Il commenta la fondation d'un parti socialiste d'ouvriers en Amérique avec la vision d'un enfer global, dont l'effet pittoresque était inspiré des illustrations néoromantiques de Gustave Doré.

HOPELESSLY BOUND TO THE STAKE.

PUCK.

THE RIOTERS' RAILROAD

Anonymous

The Rioters' Railroad to Ruin, 1877
*Der Schienenweg der Aufständischen
ins Verderben*
La Voie ferrée des rebelles vers la ruine
Tinted lithograph
From: *Puck*, New York, 1 August 1877

During the recession that followed the financial crisis of 1873 (see ill. p. 351) huge numbers of workers were laid off or had their wages cut, especially in the railroad companies. A series of strikes followed, and the situation was only brought under control after federal troops were sent in. The bourgeois press was unanimous in seeing a spirit of destruction behind the emerging workers' movement.

In der Rezession, die auf den Crash von 1873 folgte (siehe Abb. S. 351), war es vor allem bei den amerikanischen Eisenbahngesellschaften zu Massenentlassungen und Lohnkürzungen gekommen. Eine Serie von Streiks konnte erst durch den Einsatz von Bundestruppen beendet werden. Die bürgerliche Presse vermutete einhellig einen Geist der Zerstörung hinter der sich formierenden Arbeiterbewegung.

Pendant la dépression qui suivit le krach de 1873 (voir ill. p. 351) il y eut des licenciements massifs et des baisses de salaires, en particulier dans les compagnies de chemin de fer américaines. Une série de grèves ne put être interrompue que par l'intervention des troupes fédérales. La presse bourgeoise était unanime à voir un esprit de destruction derrière le mouvement ouvrier naissant.

TERROR.

RUIN.

Émile Cohl

→ *An Election Fantasy*, 1881
Wahlfantasie | Fantaisie électorale
Stencil-coloured relief etching
From: *La Nouvelle Lune*, Paris,
4 September 1881

This illustrated digest of recent elections for the National Assembly in France shows the victorious Republican Léon Gambetta at the top after he had defeated the radicals, and below him the long-necked hopefuls and long-nosed losers. Émile Cohl's sketchy style generates an incoherent ensemble of people's voices and comments, alongside sequences that are cinematic and the simultaneous actions that appear on the stage.

Das grafische Resümee der zurückliegenden Parlamentswahlen zeigt im oberen Segment den siegreichen Republikaner Léon Gambetta als Bezwinger der Radikalen und weiter unten langhalsige Aspiranten und langnasige Verlierer. Émile Cohls loser Strich generiert ein inkohärentes Kontinuum aus Stimmen, Kommentaren, filmischer Abfolge und bühnenraumartigem Simultangeschehen.

Le résumé illustré des élections parlementaires passées montre tout en haut le Républicain victorieux Léon Gambetta comme le vainqueur des radicaux et, en dessous, des aspirants au long cou et des perdants au long nez. Le leste coup de crayon d'Émile Cohl génère un continuum incohérent de voix, de commentaires, de séquences de films et d'actions simultanées comme sur une scène.

The Nouvelle Lune *Prize*, 1880
Die Auszeichnungen der Nouvelle-Lune
Les Prix de la Nouvelle-Lune
Stencil-coloured relief etching
From: *La Nouvelle Lune*, Paris,
22 August 1880

In France, the last battles against censorship of the press were fought under the Republican President Jules Grévy, although Émile Cohl was able to react more flexibly to the threat of illustrations being banned in *La Nouvelle Lune* because of the new possibilities that were available with photomechanical relief etching. Here, for example, he replaced one of the scenes on the cover that had been objected to with a cheeky remark about Madame Anastasie, the symbolic figure of censorship (see ill. p. 359).

In der französischen Presse wurden unter dem republikanischen Präsidenten Jules Grévy letzte Gefechte gegen die Zensur geführt. Émile Cohl von *La Nouvelle Lune* war dank der neuen Möglichkeiten der fotomechanischen Hochätzung in der Lage, flexibel auf die Verbote zu reagieren. Hier ersetzte er beispielsweise ein beanstandetes Panel durch eine freche Ansprache an Madame Anastasie, die Symbolgestalt der Zensur (siehe Abb. S. 359).

Dans la presse française, les derniers combats contre la censure furent menés sous le président républicain Jules Grévy. Grâce aux nouvelles possibilités de gravure en relief photomécanique, Émile Cohl de *La Nouvelle Lune* fut en mesure de réagir avec souplesse aux interdits. Ici par exemple, il remplaça une vignette qui était objet de réclamations par un discours insolent à Madame Anastasie, la figure symbolique de la censure (voir ill. p. 359).

For the Sculpture Exhibition, 1880
Für die Skulpturenausstellung bestimmt
Destiné à l'exposition de sculpture
Stencil-coloured relief etching
From: *La Nouvelle Lune*, Paris,
2 May 1880

Émile Cohl's later, pioneering interest in the metamorphic processes used in animated films shows through here in this anti-Jesuit fantasy. The previous year he had been invited by his tutor André Gill to join the Hydropaths, a group of artists, writers, press cartoonists and actors, which opened up new interdisciplinary horizons for him.

In der antijesuitischen Fantasie scheint bereits das Interesse des späteren Pioniers des Animationsfilms an metamorphotischen Abläufen durch. Émile Cohl war im Jahr zuvor über seinen Lehrer André Gill in den Künstlerklub Les Hydropathes aufgenommen worden, einen Zusammenschluss von Literaten, Pressegrafikern und Schauspielern, der ihm neue interdisziplinäre Horizonte eröffnete.

Dans l'imaginaire anti-jésuite transparaît déjà l'intérêt du futur pionnier du film d'animation pour les processus métamorphotiques. Un an plus tôt, Émile Cohl avait été admis par l'intermédiaire de son professeur André Gill dans le club d'artistes Les Hydropathes, une association d'hommes de lettres, de dessinateurs de presse et de comédiens, qui lui ouvrit de nouveaux horizons interdisciplinaires.

FANTAISIE ÉLECTORALE, par Em. Cohl.

André Gill & Émile Cohl

Two Drawings of And. Gill, 1882
Zwei Zeichnungen von And. Gill
Deux dessins de And. Gill
Stencil-coloured relief etching
From: *La Nouvelle Lune*, Paris, 1 January 1882

André Gill himself hardly appeared at all in the journal that continued with the popular format established with *La Lune*, but the mystery was solved when a couple of cartoons were published showing him under lock and key. The general arrangement of the pictures was reminiscent of those in early pictorial journalism (see ill. p. 123 t.), although it wasn't the case that he had been sent to prison but to a mental asylum following a series of breakdowns.

André Gill war in diesem Nachfolgemagazin seines populären *La-Lune*-Formats selbst kaum vertreten. Das Rätsel löste sich, als er sich mit Cartoons meldete, die ihn in Gefangenschaft zeigten. Sie erinnerten an Motive des frühen Bildjournalismus (siehe Abb. S. 123 o.). Allerdings handelte es sich nicht um ein Gefängnis, sondern um eine psychiatrische Anstalt, in die er nach mehreren Krisen eingeliefert worden war.

André Gill était à peine représenté dans le journal qui succéda à son format populaire *La Lune*. Le mystère fut levé lorsqu'il réapparut avec des dessins qui le représentait en détention. Ils n'étaient pas sans rappeler les motifs usités dans les débuts de la presse illustrée (voir ill. p. 123 h.). Gill ne se trouvait pourtant pas en prison, mais dans un asile psychiatrique où il avait été interné après plusieurs crises.

New Sketches by André Gill
Schnelle Skizzen von André Gill
Nouveaux croquis d'André Gill, 1883
Stencil-coloured relief etching
From: *La Nouvelle Lune*, Paris, 4 March 1883

The drawings by André Gill that Émile Cohl used for the cover of *La Nouvelle Lune* just over a year later were intended to show the senior artist as he gradually recovered. Never before had a loss of artistic control been presented as a subject of popular journalism, and while the fragile nature of Gill's brilliance was evident, the long-term "ability" was just as present as it had always been.

Die Zeichnungen von André Gill, die sein Schüler Émile Cohl ein Jahr später auf dem Titel von *La Nouvelle Lune* platzierte, sollten die fortschreitende Genesung des Meisters dokumentieren. Nie zuvor war ein künstlerischer Kontrollverlust Gegenstand der Populärpublizistik gewesen. Demonstriert wurde hier auch die Fragilität von Virtuosität. Das „Können" stand umfassend zur Disposition.

Les dessins d'André Gill que son élève Émile Cohl plaça un an plus tard sur la couverture de *La Nouvelle Lune* devaient documenter le rétablissement progressif du maître. Jamais auparavant une perte de contrôle artistique n'avait été autant exposée auprès du public. Ici, c'était aussi la fragilité de la virtuosité qui était mise en avant. Le «savoir-faire» était livré à tous.

Émile Cohl

Serious Advice Given with a Smile, 1882
Ernsthafter Rat mit einem Lächeln
Un conseil sérieux en riant
Stencil-coloured relief etching
From: *La Nouvelle Lune*, Paris,
27 August 1882

As censorship came to an end, Émile Cohl turned more and more to ways of including cryptic messages in his illustrations, and his coded political works duly became an informal competition for his readership. Whoever was able to solve the calligraphic riddle of this Punch character was also decoding the identity of the clown himself. In this case it was former president Mac-Mahon, who in 1876 had banned Manet's drawing of a clown (see ill. p. 311) on the grounds that he thought it was him being represented.

Mit dem Ende der Zensur wandte sich Émile Cohl verstärkt Techniken der Codierung zu. Aus politischer Kryptografie wurde ein Gewinnspiel für die Leser. Wer das kalligrafische Rätsel des *Polichinelle* löst, hat auch die Identität des Prügelkaspers erraten. Es handelt sich um den Ex-Präsidenten Patrice Mac-Mahon, der 1876 Édouard Manets Clowngrafik verbieten ließ (siehe Abb. S. 311), weil er sich darin zu erkennen glaubte.

Avec la fin de la censure, Émile Cohl se tourna davantage vers des procédés de codage. Sa cryptographie politique devint un concours pour les lecteurs. Celui qui résout l'énigme calligraphique de *Polichinelle* a aussi deviné l'identité du Guignol. Il s'agit de l'ancien président Patrice Mac-Mahon, qui fit interdire le dessin de clown d'Édouard Manet en 1876, parce qu'il croyait s'y reconnaître (voir ill. p. 311).

TROISIÈME ANNÉE. — N° 35.   Un numéro hebdomadaire : 10 Centimes   DIMANCHE 27 AOUT 1882.

ADMINISTRATION ET RÉDACTION
167, rue Montmartre
DIRECTEUR
S. HEYMANN
ABONNEMENTS
Un an .... 8 francs
Six mois ..... 4 —

LA NOUVELLE LUNE

UN CONSEIL SÉRIEUX EN RIANT, PAR EM. COHL

Émile Cohl

QUESTION DU JOUR. — Les deux premiers devineurs qui auront débrouillé l'affiche de Polichinelle et divulgué son secret, auront droit chacun à un abonnement d'un an à la *NOUVELLE LUNE*.

(Voir les détails à la deuxième page).

→→ **Émile Cohl**

Charles Lullier – Paul de Cassagnac Two Fine Friends, 1882
Die beiden Kumpane
Les Deux Compères
Stencil-coloured relief etching
From: *La Nouvelle Lune*, Paris,
26 February 1882

The former general during the Paris Commune, Charles Lullier, and his arch-enemy, the pro-Bonapartist Paul de Cassagnac, are shown here facing off like a couple of snarling dogs. Inspired by Guignol puppet shows and spurred on by his experiments with collage techniques (which he continued to develop later in his animated films), Émile Cohl briefly succeeded in reviving the rather worn-out tradition of portrait caricature.

Wie zwei tollwütige Hunde stehen sich der Ex-General der Pariser Kommune Charles Lullier und sein Intimfeind, der bonapartistische Publizist Paul de Cassagnac, gegenüber. Inspiriert vom Guignol-Theater und Experimenten mit Techniken der Collage, die er später in seinen Trickfilmen fortführen sollte, gelang es Émile Cohl für kurze Zeit, die ermüdete Tradition der Porträtkarikatur neu zu beleben.

L'ancien général de la Commune de Paris, Charles Lullier, et son ennemi intime, le publiciste bonapartiste Paul de Cassagnac, se font face tels deux chiens enragés. Inspiré par le théâtre de Guignol et les expériences avec les méthodes de collage, qu'il devait poursuivre plus tard dans ses dessins animés, Émile Cohl réussit pour quelque temps à faire revivre la tradition éteinte du portrait-charge.

Dix centimes

LA NOUVELLE LUNE

LES DEUX COMPÈRES

Charles LULLIER

LA NOUVELLE LUNE   Dix centimes

par Émile COHL

Paul de CASSAGNAC

Adolphe Willette & Charles Gillot (sc.)

→ *Page of Artist's Sketches*, 1885
Skizzenblatt eines Künstlers | *Page de croquis d'artiste*
Relief etching
From: *Le Courrier français*, Paris,
17 May 1885

At the same time as André Gill's condition was growing worse, his colleagues and supporters founded the Incoherents, an anti-art association that, amongst other things, held exhibitions featuring works "by people who couldn't draw". A craze for doodles began to appear in press illustrations, which foreshadowed the unconscious aspect of the automatic writing of the 20th century and also the interest in Art Brut.

Während André Gills Zustand sich verschlechterte, gründeten seine Anhänger *Les Arts Incohérents*, eine Antikunst-Assoziation, deren Ausstellungen damit warben, dass sie Zeichnungen zeigten „von Leuten, die nicht wissen, wie man zeichnet". Es etablierte sich ein pressegrafischer Kult der Kritzelei, der den Boden bereitete für die Anschauungen der Écriture automatique im 20. Jahrhundert und für die Art brut.

Tandis que l'état de santé d'André Gill s'aggravait, ses adeptes fondèrent Les Arts incohérents, une association anti-art dont les expositions vantaient la présentation de «dessins exécutés par des gens qui ne savent pas dessiner». Un culte du gribouillage s'établit dans le dessin de presse, qui prépara le terrain aux concepts d'écriture automatique au XXᵉ siècle et à l'Art brut.

Émile Cohl

Exhibition of Incoherent Arts, 1886
Ausstellung der Arts Incohérents
Exposition des Arts Incohérents
Relief etching
Cover of: Jules Lévy (ed.), *Catalogue de l'Exposition des Arts incohérents*, Paris, 1886

By 1886 the Incoherents had reached the height of their popularity. After André Gill, the chief artist of *La Lune*, had died the previous year, everyone involved in the exhibition must have been aware that the moon on the catalogue cover through which the movement's founder Jules Lévy is passing symbolises not only a foolish kind of madness but also a certain pathological danger.

1886 befand sich die Gruppierung der *Incohérents* auf dem Zenit ihrer Popularität. Dass der Mond durch den der Initiator der Bewegung, der Schriftsteller Jules Lévy, auf dem Ausstellungscover hindurchgeht, nicht nur närrische Verrücktheit symbolisierte, sondern auch eine pathologische Gefährdung, musste allen Beteiligten nach dem Tod des Meisters von *La Lune,* André Gill, klar gewesen sein.

En 1886, les Incohérents étaient au zénith de leur popularité. Que la lune à travers laquelle passe l'initiateur du mouvement, l'écrivain Jules Lévy, sur la couverture du catalogue d'exposition ne symbolise pas seulement la folie bouffone, mais aussi une menace pathologique dut avoir été évident pour tous les intéressés après le décès du maître de *La Lune,* André Gill.

→→ Kawanabe Kyōsai

Sketch | *Skizze* | *Esquisse*, c. 1880
Woodblock print with ink and colour

In terms of imaginative range, the illustration work of Kawanabe Kyōsai exceeded the fantastic designs drawn by Hokusai. During the upheavals of the Meiji Restoration he established the genre of political cartoons in Japan, despite opposition from the censors, while his work first became known in France in 1881 through an account written by the artist, traveller and former member of the Commune Félix Régamey.

Kawanabe Kyōsai übersteigerte die Fantastik Katsushika Hokusais ins Bodenlose. Während der Umbrüche der Meiji-Restauration begründete er gegen alle Widerstände der Zensur das politische Cartooning in Japan. Durch einen Bericht des Ex-Kommunarden und Reisezeichners Félix Régamey wurde Kyōsais Werk 1881 erstmals in Frankreich bekannt.

Kawanabe Kyōsai surpassa l'imagination de Katsushika Hokusai. Pendant les bouleversements de la Restauration de Meiji, il inaugura en dépit de toutes les oppositions de la censure le genre de la caricature politique au Japon. C'est un reportage de l'ancien communard et illustrateur voyageur Félix Régamey qui fit connaître l'œuvre de Kyōsai en France en 1881.

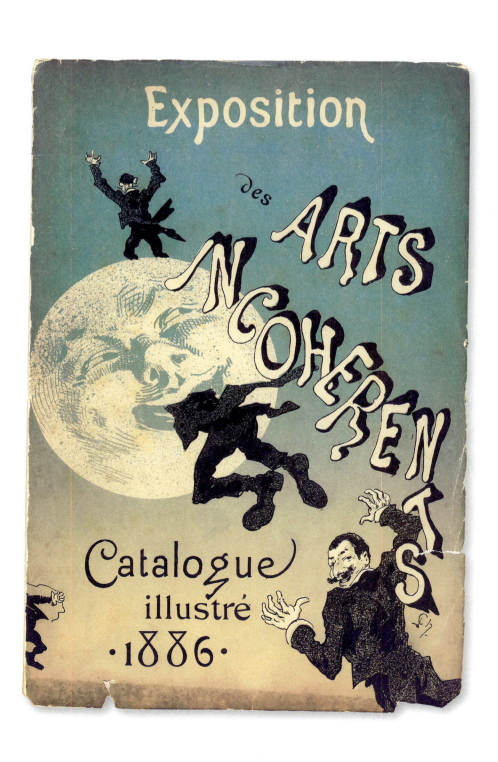

Page de Croquis d'artiste, par A. Willette, indiquant le développement de son talent depuis son plus bas âge jusqu'à ce jour.

Thomas Nast

New York in a Few Years from Now, 1881
New York in wenigen Jahren
New York dans quelques années
Relief etching
From: *Harper's Weekly*, New York, 27 August 1881

In contrast to the fantastic visions of the future described by Jules Verne and Albert Robida, Thomas Nast's view was straightforward and pessimistic. He also associated it with a criticism of North American megalomania, and a campaign against pollution which he had started following a number of deaths at industrial sites at Hunter's Point in New York.

Im Gegensatz zu den fantastischen Visionen eines Jules Verne und Albert Robida war Thomas Nasts Blick in die Zukunft lapidar und pessimistisch. Er verband ihn mit einer Kritik an der nordamerikanischen Megalomanie und einer Kampagne gegen Umweltverschmutzung, die er im Zusammenhang mit Todesfällen bei den Industrieanlagen von Hunter's Point gestartet hatte.

Contrairement aux visions fantastiques d'un Jules Verne ou d'un Albert Robida, le regard que porte Thomas Nast sur le futur était lapidaire et pessimiste. Il y joignait une critique de la mélagomanie de l'Amérique du Nord et une campagne contre la pollution, qu'il avait lancée suite aux décès survenus sur le site industriel d'Hunter's Point.

A View from the Niagara as It May Be a Few Years Hence | *Ansicht des Niagara-Flusses, wie er in wenigen Jahren aussehen kann* | *Vue du fleuve Niagara, comme il sera peut-être dans quelques années*, 1883
Relief etching
From: *Harper's Weekly*, New York, 13 January 1883

→→**Albert Robida**

The Drrrrrrama!!!, 1881
Das Drrrrrrama!!! | *Le Drrrrrrame!!!*
Stencil-coloured relief etching
From: *La Caricature*, Paris,
29 October 1881

The bustling energy of Albert Robida's illustrations reflects the spirit of optimism in France during the Belle Époque that followed in the wake of Mac-Mahon's overly moralising presidency. Robida was the editor and chief illustrator of a new edition of *La Caricature*, although unlike its celebrated predecessor its content was now mostly apolitical and directed more at simple entertainment.

Die exaltierten Illustrationen von Albert Robida spiegeln die Aufbruchstimmung der Belle Époque, die in Frankreich auf das Ende der moralinsauren Präsidentschaft Mac-Mahons folgte. Robida war Herausgeber und Hauptzeichner einer Neuauflage von *La Caricature*, die im Gegensatz zum legendären Vorgänger weitgehend apolitisch und auf Unterhaltung aus war.

Les illustrations exaltées d'Albert Robida reflètent l'atmosphère de renouveau de la Belle Époque qui suivit en France la fin de la présidence moralisatrice de Mac-Mahon. Robida était l'éditeur et le principal dessinateur d'une réédition du journal *La Caricature*, qui contrairement à son prédécesseur légendaire était largement apolitique et tourné vers le divertissement.

Albert Robida

Boarding Platform for Airships, 1883
Anlegebrücke für Luftschiffe
Embarcadère des aéronefs
Relief etching
From: Albert Robida, *Le Vingtième Siècle*,
Paris, 1883

The success of Albert Robida's science fiction trilogy
Le Vingtième Siècle (1883–1890) resulted in him
becoming one of the most imitated press illustrators
of the late 19th century. In contrast to Jules Verne,
for Robida progress was not reserved solely for the
elite, while his method of foreseeing the future was
based on the principle used by his role model George
Cruikshank, that is exaggerating the present state of
society through caricature. Predictions that appeared
in this first instalment included the rise of a leisure
society, the emancipation of women, mass tourism,
rapid transportation, telephones, television, cinema
and media wars.

Mit seiner Science-Fiction-Trilogie *Le Vingtième
Siècle* (1883–1890) stieg Albert Robida zu einem
der meistadaptierten Pressegrafiker der Jahrhundertwende auf. Im Gegensatz zu Jules Verne war
Fortschritt bei ihm nicht das Werk von Eliten. Seine
Methode der Prognostik basierte wie die seines
Vorbilds George Cruikshank auf einer karikaturesken Zuspitzung des gesellschaftlichen Status quo.
Zu den Prognosen des ersten Bands zählten: Frei-
zeitgesellschaft, Frauenemanzipation, Massentou-
rismus, Schnellverkehr, Telefonie, Television, Kino
und Medienkrieg.

Avec sa trilogie de science-fiction *Le Vingtième
Siècle* (1883–1890), Albert Robida devint l'un des
dessinateurs de presse les plus imités au tournant
du siècle. À l'inverse de Jules Verne, le progrès
chez lui n'était pas l'œuvre des élites. Sa méthode
de pronostic, comme celle de son modèle George
Cruikshank, était fondée sur une exagération caricaturale du statu quo de la société. Parmi les pro-
gnostics du premier volume comptaient : la société
de loisirs, l'émancipation des femmes, le tourisme
de masse, les transports rapides, le téléphone, la
télévision, le cinéma et la guerre des médias.

EMBARCADÈRE DES AÉRONEFS.

Emotions during the Civil War, 1883
Die Emotionen des Bürgerkriegs
Les Émotions de la guerre civile
Relief etching
From: Albert Robida, *Le Vingtième Siècle*,
Paris, 1883

For this burlesque vision of the media wars of the
future Robida used his experiences as a *special
artist* during the unrest of the Paris Commune.

Albert Robida verarbeitete in dieser burlesken Vision
über den Medienkrieg der Zukunft seine Erfahrungen als *special artist* während der Kämpfe um die
Pariser Kommune.

Dans cette vision burlesque de la guerre des médias
du futur, Albert Robida tira parti de son expérience
de *special artist* au cours des combats menés pour
la Commune de Paris.

LES ÉMOTIONS DE LA GUERRE CIVILE

LE DRRRRRRRA

— Épouse criminelle, je vous broierai, vous et votre infâme complice... cette lettre! il me faut cette lettre!!!

— Il me saisit par les cheveux, brisant mes faibles mains, tordant mes bras... d'une voix épouvantable il me cria: Isabelle je t'aime!... et alors...
— Et alors?
— Et alors, je m'évanouis!

LE RAVIN.

Décor sauvage et terrible, rochers pointus, pont jeté sur l'abîme. C'est là que Ruffio, le bandit au service du duc de Carriñoli, doit assassiner la malheureuse marquesa pour lui voler sa fille.

LA PLAT

Créneaux sur Créneaux; dans le f premier plan, coups d'épée et coups c

LE DRAME SCIENTIFIQUE ET VOYAGEUR.

Tigres et serpents à sonnettes! Les infortunées jeunes filles, ont des désagréments avec les habitants des Jungles; poursuivies par les peaux rouges, les arabes et les gauchos, menacées d'être sacrifiées à la déesse Kali ou coupées en morceaux et mangées par les Niams-Niams, ennuyées par les hommes, les moustiques, les crocodiles et les serpents à sonnettes...
—Heureusement Dumaine est là! Vite, vite, sauvez-là, sauvez-les!... Grand Dieu, faites qu'il arrive à temps, grâce pour elles!!!

— Nous reconnais-tu?
— Aaah!!!

LES MILLE ET UN TRAVAU

Un rude travailleur! En cinq heures il lui faut: faire de la gymnastique s quatre coups de feu au premier acte; estocader avec douze spadassins et en t sième acte; s'évader de la Bastille et emporter la j une première évanouie da ver la jeune femme et courir avec elle se jeter aux pieds de son vieux père....

— Le danger et moi nous sommes frères, mais je suis l'aîné.

— Pit-é, monseigneur, pitié. Voyez, je me traîne à vos pieds, pitié!... Vous avez tué mon père et ma mère, mais si vous faites grâce à mon amant, je vous bénirai, monseigneur!

— Trop tard!!!

L'EXPIATION.

— Elle était pure, elle était innocente, vous n'avez pas eu pitié de ses prières, de ses larmes, de ses sanglots!... Misérable, qu'as-tu fait de Marguerite?

Sur les longues barres rouges d'un féroce coucher de soleil, le bourreau de Bethune lève son glaive... laissez passer la justice de Dieu!

LA C

Pour drames de famille: empoiso mort parle!

— Ta potion sentait la mort aux r

— par A. ROBIDA

L'ÉTANG DE PLOUGASTEL.

...re et la silhouette du donjon. Au ...tage et massacre !

Pour drames bretons et chouans. La malheureuse jeune fille s'est jetée à l'eau. Les bretons lèvent les bras au ciel et les arbres tordent désespérément leurs branches.

— Perdue ! je suis perdue !!!... Ah, Leonora Galigaï, je reconnais là ton infernale habileté !

— Cent ducats par coup de dague, c'est pour rien, monseigneur...
— Tu en auras cinq cents !
— Faudra-t-il qu'il souffre pour la somme ?

LE BALLET.

Le malheureux chevalier, après avoir brillamment défendu la jeune fille contre une armée de reîtres et de lansquenets, est tombé entre les mains de son féroce rival qui se demande s'il doit le faire pendre ou écorcher ! C'est le moment de placer un petit ballet de riLaudes pour ramener un aimable sourire sur les lèvres des spectateurs chauves de l'orchestre... que la fête commence, on repleurera ensuite !

L'ENFANT DE LA MALHEUREUSE BARONNE.

Au prologue.
Une livre de carton.

Au premier acte.
78 kilos ! et pas en carton
je vous prie de le croire !

— Malédiction ! c'est la tasse que j'avais préparée pour la duchesse !... Ah, satan, je suis perdue... Ah ! le doigt de Dieu ! couic !

— C'était, il y a scize ans ! une jeune fille crut aux serments d'un homme beau, noble et perfide... elle l'aima, le misérable, et il l'abandonna, le lâche, avec six enfants !..... cet homme, c'était vous, cette jeune fille, c'était ma sœur !!!

...MIER DE DRAME.
...arracher la jeune première des bras d'un prince perfide, recevoir ...nd acte ; supporter la question ordinaire et extraordinaire au troi...ilos), au quatrième ; reestocader au cinquième avec la garde. resau-

...AIRE.
substitutions et autres peccadilles. La
...assassin !

LE CARREFOUR DE LA TRUIE QUI FILE.

Enlèvement de la jeune baronne au sortir d'une fête chez le régent.

YVES & BARRET

— Voilà 35 ans que je gémis dans ce cachot... à force de patience j'ai déjà scié un barreau de la fenêtre... et il y en a encore six !

— Je lui résistais, il m'a assassinée !

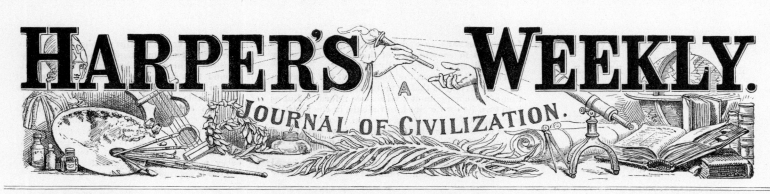

VOL. XXX.—No. 1527.
Copyright, 1886, by HARPER & BROTHERS.

NEW YORK, SATURDAY, MARCH 27, 1886.

TEN CENTS A COPY.
$4.00 PER YEAR, IN ADVANCE.

OUR *SYSTEM* OF FEATHERING NESTS BREEDS TWEEDS ALL OVER THE LAND.

Syd B. Griffin (del.) & J. Ottmann (lith.)

*The Evil Spirits of the
Modern Daily Press*, 1888
*Die bösen Geister der modernen
Tagespresse*
*Les Mauvais Esprits de la presse
quotidienne moderne*
Tinted lithograph
From: *Puck*, New York,
21 November 1888

The evil spirits emerging from the
rotary printing press represent the sensationalist style of pictorial journalism
that was chiefly associated with Joseph
Pulitzer's *New York World*. From 1895
its Sunday supplement became one of
the first newspapers to publish comic
strips, which developed into such a
major part of American culture (see ills.
pp. 526/527, 529). *Puck* was the
model for these cartoons, and as early
as 1884 Pulitzer had even tried to buy
his way in to Joseph Keppler's satirical
magazine.

Die bösen Geister aus den Rotations-
pressen repräsentieren einen illustrierten Sensationsjournalismus, den man
vor allem mit Joseph Pulitzers *New
York World* verband. In deren Sonntagsbeilage etablierte sich ab 1895 die
amerikanische Comickultur (siehe
Abb. S. 526/527, 529). Vorbild für
Pulitzers Cartoonpublizistik war *Puck*.
Bereits 1884 hatte sich der Freund
Joseph Kepplers in das Satiremagazin
einzukaufen versucht.

Les mauvais esprits des rotatives
représentent une presse illustrée à
sensation qui était surtout associée au
New York World de Joseph Pulitzer.
À partir de 1895, son supplément
du dimanche accueillit les traditionnelles caricatures américaines (voir
ills. p. 526/527, 529). Le modèle de
Pulitzer fut *Puck*. Dès 1884, l'ami de
Joseph Keppler avait essayé d'acheter
son entrée dans le journal satirique.

THE EVIL SPIRITS OF THE MODERN DAILY PRESS.

Thomas Nast

*Our System of Feathering Nests
Breeds Tweeds all over the Land*,
1886
*Unser System der Kuckuckseier
brütet im ganzen Land Tweeds aus
Notre système de coucous dans le nid
fait éclore des Tweed dans tout le pays*
Relief etching
From: *Harper's Weekly*, New York,
27 March 1886

Towards the end of his association
with *Harper's Weekly*, Thomas Nast
came to the sobering realisation that
the great victory over the Tweed Ring
had been only cosmetic, and had
not brought about any real political
changes. Corruption and patronage
were no longer occasional outbreaks
but had become inherent parts of
a system in which the main element
was not the people, but money.

Gegen Ende seines Engagements
bei *Harper's Weekly* musste Thomas
Nast ernüchtert feststellen, dass der
große Triumph über den Tweed-Ring
nur der Kosmetik gedient hatte, nicht
der politischen Läuterung. Korruption
und Patronage waren mittlerweile
kein Makel mehr, sondern einem System immanent, das kaum mehr *res
publica*, sondern Plutokratie war.

Vers la fin de sa coopérat on avec
Harper's Weekly, Thomas Nast, dé-
sabusé, dut constater que le grand
triomphe remporté sur le Tweed-Ring
n'avait eu qu'un effet cosmétique
sans renouvellement politique. Entre-
temps, la corruption et le népotisme
n'étaient plus des défauts, mais partie intégrante d'un système qui était
davantage une ploutocratie qu'une
res publica.

The Golden Age of Illustrated Journalism

The period from the founding of the German Empire in 1871 to the end of the First World War is marked by the fundamental contradiction between revolutionary social and technical progress on the one hand, and on the other the straitjacket of neo-absolutist rule into which many nations forced themselves. From the perspective of the Western world, the years beginning with the 1880s were a time of prosperity, the Golden Age of the Belle Époque. However, even a cursory glance at the news pictures of the day is sufficient to show that while an extended era of peace and affluence existed within Europe, there was constant warring elsewhere in the world. Before the European empires turned their guns on each other in 1914 they were pointed at the populations of Africa and Asia in the competition for colonial conquests, with Britain the main power. Most of the 24 wars reported on from 1873 onwards by the style-defining *special artist* Melton Prior for the globally distributed *Illustrated London News* were British colonial wars.

Prior's groundbreaking style of illustration gave people the feeling of being directly involved in the events being depicted, while no other artist at the time expressed so forcefully the changes that were increasingly affecting the communication sector. His drawings, reproduced by means of chemigraphy, displayed the same sense of modernity that had been identified by Baudelaire and by the Impressionists in the earlier works of Constantin Guys, Prior's predecessor, but which seldom showed through in the schematic printed versions. Prior also maintained an ethos of authenticity in his work, although this meant that the content of some of his illustrations could unwittingly play into the hands of critics of colonialism (see ills. pp. 402, 422 b.). The situation was quite different though with his rival Richard Caton Woodville Jr., who reproduced pictures for the same wars in his London studio based on sketches drawn up by *special artists*. Woodville represented the theatrical side of pictorial journalism, and like his younger French colleague Georges Scott he had trained as a history painter. These two chroniclers of European Imperial expansionism, Prior and Woodville, called the tune at this time, and would light their last fireworks with the First World War.

Since photography and halftones fell short in certain ways this meant that new opportunities for working in the press were still possible for artists with academic training. They were used, for instance, as photo painters to transfer the blurred tones in the photographic originals into high-contrast templates for printing. An experienced history painter such as Louis Sabattier was able to employ a method of skilful montages to adapt the photographic templates into pictorial narratives that were as detailed as they were charged with atmosphere.

The new mass press was also affected by a strange collision between the theatricality of traditional historical art and the new dynamic emphasis on factual reporting. Founded in 1863 by Moïse Polydore Millaud, *Le Petit Journal* introduced a new form of sensationalist journalism. Its low price and the fact that it was sold openly on the street quickly made the newspaper a market leader that was bought by a broad range of readers who went beyond the educated middle-class subscribers of the traditional press.

Sales of the illustrated Sunday edition of *Le Petit Journal*, which first appeared in 1884, depended to a great extent on its attractive colour front page, and to obtain the most striking results the history painters let fly with a barrage of visual and narrative tricks and devices in the last years before photomechanical production took over for good. Facts and fantasy were brought together in the most startling fashion to illustrate the "Faits Divers" sections (Miscellaneous Items), and the Surreal qualities of these illustrations appealed not only to visual artists such as Max Ernst but also the art critic Félix Fénéon, who used them as an anarchist form of expression — within the space of one year he managed to place 1,111 false reports (see examples on pp. 448, 449, 456, 491) in the daily newspaper *Le Matin*, which in spite of their absurdity could not be distinguished from the genuine items.

In the 1890s, the success of the French sensationalist press was taken up in the United States by the two media moguls Joseph Pulitzer and William Randolph Hearst. Meanwhile, the *Berliner Illustrirte Zeitung* shook up the press landscape in Germany during the reign of Kaiser Wilhelm II with its unconventional layout and policy of direct, open sales. At the same time, within these newspapers of the mass press new forms of investigative reporting were becoming established. The picture reporters of this "muckraking journalism" included Jacob Riis, who took his camera into the slum areas of New York's Lower East Side, and the illustrator Fritz Koch-Gotha, who mingled with striking miners in the Ruhr for his reports for the *Berliner Illustrirte Zeitung* and also went undercover to visit Russian night shelters.

N° 200   Supplément illustré du Petit Journal

UN LION EN AUTOMOBILE

Anonymous

A Lion Travelling by Car, 1909
Ein Löwe im Automobil | *Un Lion en automobile*
Coloured relief etching
From: *Le Petit Journal*, Paris, 20 May 1909

Surrealistic images could be found in France from one week to the next on the news-stand displays.

Der Surrealismus fand in Frankreich Woche für Woche an den Auslagen der Kioske statt.

Le surréalisme était présent en France, semaine après semaine, sur les affiches des kiosques.

Glanzzeit des Bildjournalismus

Die Epoche, die 1871 mit der deutschen Reichsgründung einsetzte und mit dem Ersten Weltkrieg endete, ist gekennzeichnet von dem fundamentalen Widerspruch zwischen revolutionärem sozialem und technischem Fortschritt und einem neoabsolutistischen Korsett, in das sich die meisten Nationen zwängten. Aus westlicher Perspektive stellte sich der Zeitraum seit den 1880er-Jahren als eine Phase der Prosperität dar, als Belle Époque oder Gilded Age. Allein ein flüchtiger Blick auf die Bildnachrichten der Zeit genügt jedoch, um zu erkennen, dass diese lange Periode innereuropäischen Friedens und Wohlstands von permanentem Krieg außerhalb Europas begleitet war. Bevor die europäischen Imperien ab 1914 ihre Kanonen gegeneinander feuerten, waren diese im kolonialem Wettstreit auf die Völker Afrikas und Asiens gerichtet. Führend war hier nach wie vor Großbritannien. Die Mehrzahl der 24 Kriegseinsätze, von denen der stilprägende *special artist* Melton Prior seit 1873 für die global verbreitete *Illustrated London News* berichtete, waren englische Kolonialkriege.

Priors seismografischer Zeichenmodus gab dem Leser das Gefühl, unmittelbar am Geschehen beteiligt zu sein. Kein anderer Künstler der Zeit brachte die zunehmende Dynamisierung der Kommunikation prägnanter zum Ausdruck. In seinen chemiegrafisch reproduzierten Zeichnungen manifestierte sich jene *modernité*, die Charles Baudelaire und die Impressionisten in den originalen Skizzen von Constantin Guys, Priors Vorgänger, ausgemacht hatten, die sich aber anhand der schematisierten Pressegrafiken nur selten nachweisen ließ. Priors Ethos der Authentizität brachte es mit sich, dass die Inhalte einiger seiner Zeichnungen ungewollt auch den Kolonialkritikern in die Hände spielen konnten (siehe Abb. S. 402, 422 u.). Ganz anders verhielt es sich mit den Arbeiten seines Konkurrenten Richard Caton Woodville Jr., der die gleichen Kriege nach den Vorlagen der *special artists* in seinem Londoner Atelier nachstellte. Woodville vertrat die theatrale Seite des Bildjournalismus. Wie sein jüngerer französischer Kollege Georges Scott war er ein ausgebildeter Historienmaler. Die beiden tonangebenden Chronisten des imperialen Expansionismus sollten ihr letztes Feuerwerk im Ersten Weltkrieg abbrennen.

Auch die Unzulänglichkeiten der Fotografie und Autotypie eröffneten akademisch ausgebildeten Künstlern neue Betätigungsfelder bei den Zeitungen. Sie wurden als Fotomaler gebraucht, um die verschwommenen Tonwerte der Lichtbilder in kontrastreiche Druckvorlagen zu übersetzen. Ein ausgebildeter Historienmaler wie Louis Sabattier war in der Lage, fotografische Vorlagen durch geschickte Montagen in ebenso komplexe wie atmosphärisch dichte Bilderzählungen zu übersetzen.

Zu einem bizarren Zusammentreffen zwischen der Theatralik tradierter Historienkunst und der dynamischen Faktizität des Nachrichtenwesens kam es im Bereich der neuen Massenpresse. Moïse Polydore Millauds 1863 gegründetes *Le Petit Journal* war bahnbrechend für eine neue Form des Sensationsjournalismus. Mit Niedrigpreisen und einem offenen Vertrieb über den Straßenverkauf hatte das marktführende Blatt eine breite Käuferschicht jenseits der bildungsbürgerlichen Klientel der herkömmlichen Abonnentenpresse erschlossen.

Da der Absatz der seit 1884 erscheinenden illustrierten Sonntagsausgabe des *Petit Journal* wesentlich von der Attraktion der farbigen Titelgrafik abhing, eröffneten die Historienmaler hier am Vorabend fotomechanischer Hegemonie ein Trommelfeuer visueller und narrativer Reize. Fakten und Fantasie gingen bei der Illustrierung der „Faits divers" (verschiedenen Meldungen) die abenteuerlichsten Verbindungen ein. Nicht nur bildende Künstler wie Max Ernst waren von den surrealen Qualitäten der „Faits divers" überzeugt. Der Kunstkritiker Félix Fénéon nutzte sie als anarchistisches Ausdrucksmedium und platzierte in der Tageszeitung *Le Matin* im Verlauf eines Jahres 1111 Falschmeldungen (Beispiele siehe S. 448, 449, 456, 491), die in ihrer Absurdität nicht von den regulären „Faits divers" zu unterscheiden waren.

In den 1890er-Jahren schlossen die beiden amerikanischen Medienmagnaten Joseph Pulitzer und William Randolph Hearst an den Erfolg der französischen Sensationspresse an. In Deutschland mischte die *Berliner Illustrirte Zeitung* mit offenem Direktverkauf und einem unkonventionellen Layout die wilhelminische Presselandschaft auf. Im Schoß dieser Massenpressen etablierten sich neue Formen der investigativen Reportage. Zu den Bildreportern dieses „muckraking journalism" (Missstände aufdeckenden Journalismus) zählten auch der Sozialreformer Jacob Riis, der mit seiner Kamera die Slums der New Yorker Lower East Side inspizierte, und der Illustrator Fritz Koch-Gotha, der sich für die *Berliner Illustrirte Zeitung* unter streikende Bergarbeiter im Ruhrgebiet mischte und undercover aus russischen Nachtasylen berichtete.

Maurice Radiguet

Miscellaneous Items: The Press Is the Main Source of Education, 1906
Vermischtes. Die Presse ist die große Erziehung
Faits divers. La presse est la grande éducatrice
Coloured relief etching
From: *L'Assiette au Beurre*, Paris, 8 September 1906

The sensationalist *Faits divers* news items are seen here from the pessimistic cultural viewpoint of the satirical press.

Die sensationsheischenden *Faits divers* aus der kulturpessimistischen Sicht der satirischen Presse.

Les *Faits divers* avides de sensations vus sous l'angle culturel pessimiste de la presse satirique.

Splendeur du journalisme illustré

L'époque qui commença par la fondation de l'Empire allemand en 1871 et se termina par la Première Guerre mondiale est marquée par la contradiction fondamentale entre le progrès révolutionnaire et technique et un corset néo-absolutiste que s'imposèrent la plupart des nations. D'un point de vue occidental, la période débutant à partir des années 1880 constitua une phase de prospérité, connue sous le nom de Belle Époque ou encore d'Âge d'or. Cependant, un bref regard sur les informations en images de l'époque suffit pour découvrir que cette longue période de paix à l'intérieur de l'Europe et de confort matériel était accompagnée de guerres permanentes hors d'Europe. Avant que les empires européens n'allument leurs canons les uns contre les autres à partir de 1914, ces derniers étaient dirigés contre les peuples d'Afrique et d'Asie dans la concurrence coloniale. Dans ce contexte, la Grande-Bretagne était comme toujours au premier rang. La plupart des 24 conflits guerriers, sur lesquels le très influent *special artist* Melton Prior effectua dès 1873 des reportages pour le journal distribué dans le monde entier *Illustrated London News*, étaient des guerres coloniales anglaises.

Le style de dessin séismographique de Prior donnait au lecteur le sentiment de participer en direct à l'événement. Aucun autre artiste contemporain n'exprima avec autant de force la dynamique qui s'amplifiait dans le secteur de la communication. Dans ses dessins reproduits selon le procédé chimigraphique se manifestait cette *modernité* que Charles Baudelaire et les impressionnistes avaient perçue dans les esquisses originales de Constantin Guys, le prédécesseur de Prior, mais qui ne transparaissait que rarement à travers les dessins de presse schématisés. L'éthique d'authenticité prônée par Prior eut pour conséquence que le contenu de certains de ses dessins pouvait aussi involontairement faire le jeu des opposants au colonialisme (voir ills. p. 402, 422 b.). Il en allait tout autrement des travaux de son rival Richard Caton Woodville Jr. qui, dans son atelier londonien, reconstituait les mêmes guerres d'après les modèles des *specials*. Woodville incarnait la face théâtrale du journalisme illustré. À l'instar de son plus jeune collègue Georges Scott, il avait suivi une formation de peintre d'histoire. Ces deux chroniqueurs de l'expansionnisme impérial donnaient le ton et allumèrent leur dernier feu d'artifice au cours de la Première Guerre mondiale.

Les insuffisances de la photographie et de la similigravure ouvrirent à des artistes de formation académique de nouveaux champs d'activité auprès des journaux. Ils étaient recherchés comme peintres photographes pour transposer les valeurs tonales des photographies en modèles d'impression contrastés. Un peintre d'histoire professionnel comme Louis Sabattier était en mesure de transposer par des montages élaborés des modèles photographiques en narrations graphiques d'une grande complexité et d'une atmosphère intense.

Dans la branche de la jeune presse de masse, il se produisit une bizarre interférence entre le théâtralisme de l'art académique ancestral et la dynamique factualité du secteur de l'information. *Le Petit Journal*, fondé en 1863 par Moïse Polydore Millaud, fut révolutionnaire pour une nouvelle forme de sensationnalisme. Grâce à des prix modiques et à une distribution en vente libre sur la voie publique, le journal de premier plan avait conquis un large lectorat au-delà des abonnés bourgeois et cultivés de la presse traditionnelle.

Comme la vente de l'édition illustrée dominicale du *Petit Journal*, qui paraissait depuis 1884, dépendait largement de l'attractivité du dessin en couleurs figurant à la une, les peintres d'histoire déclenchèrent à la veille de l'hégémonie photomécanique une rafale de charmes visuels et narratifs. Dans l'illustration des « faits divers », événements réels et fantasmes se confondèrent dans les combinaisons les plus aventureuses. Les artistes des beaux-arts, tel Max Ernst, n'étaient pas les seuls à apprécier les qualités surréelles des « faits divers ». Le critique d'art Félix Fénéon les utilisa comme medium d'expression anarchiste et, en l'espace d'un an, inséra dans le quotidien *Le Matin* 1 111 fausses nouvelles (exemples voir p. 448, 449, 456, 491), qui dans leur absurdité ne pouvaient pas être distinguées des « faits divers » réguliers.

Dans les années 1890, les deux magnats des médias américains Joseph Pulitzer et William Randolph Hearst prolongèrent le succès de la presse française à sensation. En Allemagne, le *Berliner Illustrirte Zeitung* bouscula le paysage médiatique wilhelminien par une vente libre et directe ainsi qu'une mise en page inconventionnelle. Au sein de ces presses de masse s'établirent de nouvelles formes du reportage d'investigation. Parmi les reporters photographes de ce « *muckraking journalism* » (journalisme dénonçant les scandales) comptaient également Jacob Riis qui, muni de son appareil photo, inspecta les quartiers insalubres du Lower East Side à New York ainsi que le dessinateur Fritz Koch-Gotha, qui se mêla à des mineurs en grève pour le *Berliner Illustrirte Zeitung* et effectua des reportages clandestins dans des asiles de nuit russes.

Anonymous (photo.)

Mr. R. Caton Woodville Jr. at Work in His Studio, 1895
Mr R. Caton Woodville Jr. bei der Arbeit in seinem Atelier
M. R. Caton Woodville Jr. au travail dans son atelier
Relief etching
From: *The Illustrated London News,* 7 December 1895

Richard Caton Woodville Jr. was one of the most influential artists in the transitional period between history painting and cinematography (see ills. pp. 421, 472 b., 517). The illustrator of jingoistic nationalism is shown here with his extensive arsenal of props, which he used when painting his devotional images of Empire based on the reports of various correspondents.

Richard Caton Woodville Jr. war einer der einflussreichsten Künstler im Übergang zwischen Historienkunst und Kinematografie (siehe Abb. S. 421, 472 u., 517). Hier fixiert der Illustrator des Jingoismus sein üppiges Requisitenarsenal, mit dem er aus den diffusen Nachrichten der Korrespondenten imperiale Andachtsbilder komponierte.

Richard Caton Woodville Jr. était l'un des artistes les plus influents au moment de la transition entre peinture d'histoire et cinématographie (voir ills. p. 421, 472 b., 517). L'illustrateur du jingoïsme donne à voir ici son volumineux arsenal d'accessoires avec lequel il réalisait des images pieuses de l'Empire à partir d'informations diffuses fournies par des correspondants.

William Simpson

*The Lava Beds, Lake Tule, California
The Scene of the Modoc Indian
War*, 1873
*Die Szene aus dem Modoc-Krieg
La scène de la guerre des Modocs*
Wood engraving
From: *The Illustrated London News*,
7 June 1873

In the course of a trip round the world
during which he travelled from Beijing
to San Francisco, William Simpson
also witnessed a number of guerrilla-
warfare attacks by Modoc Indians on
units of the U.S. army. He described
the somewhat hallucinatory encounter
in the lava beds region in his travel
account *Meeting the Sun*, the excerpts
from which that appeared in the press
being almost certainly used by Jules
Verne as source material for *Around
the World in Eighty Days*.

Auf einer Reise um die Erde, die ihn
von Beijing nach San Francisco führte, wurde William Simpson Zeuge des
Guerillakriegs, den die Modoc gegen
die US-Armee führten. Die halluzina-
torische Szene in den Lava Beds
erwähnte er auch in seinem Reise-
buch *Meeting the Sun*, dessen Vorab-
druck Jules Verne wohl zu seinem
Roman *In 80 Tagen um die Welt*
inspirierte.

Dans son voyage autour du monde qui
l'a mené de Beijing à San Francisco,
William Simpson devint le témoin de
la guérilla que les Indiens Modocs
menaient contre l'armée américaine.
Il évoqua aussi la scène hallucinatoire
dans les Lava Beds dans son récit
de voyage *Meeting the Sun*, dont la
prépublication inspira sans doute
Jules Verne pour son roman *Le Tour
du monde en 80 jours*.

→ *Exploration of Jerusalem:
Rock-cut Cistern under the Site
of Solomon's Temple*, 1872
*Erkundung von Jerusalem:
In den Fels gehauene Zisterne unter
dem Tempel Salomos
Exploration de Jérusalem:
citerne percée dans la roche sous
le site du temple de Salomon*
Wood engraving
From: *The Illustrated London News*,
13 April 1872

William Simpson's growing reputation
as a researcher and watercolourist
brought new respectability to the profession of pictorial journalism, and
this situation also benefited the press
illustrators who worked in later years.
At the same time, wood engravers
appreciated the quality of his original
artwork since it was always well laid
out with a wash that could easily
be transferred, while being clear and
exact in the details.

Mit seiner wachsenden Anerkennung
als Forscher und Aquarellkünstler ver-
schaffte William Simpson dem bildjournalistischen Gewerbe einen Grad
von Respektabilität, von der etliche
seiner Nachfolger profitieren konnten.
Bei den Xylografen waren seine Vorlagen besonders geschätzt. Sie waren
offen in der lavierten Anlage und dabei
sehr präzise und bestimmt im Detail.

Grâce à sa renommée croissante
comme chercheur et aquarelliste,
William Simpson conféra à la branche
du journalisme illustré un degré de
respectabilité dont bon nombre de
ses successeurs purent profiter. Ses
modèles étaient particulièrement
appréciés des xylographes. Ils étaient
à la fois clairement composés en lavis
et très nets et précis dans les détails.

William Simpson

The Rock-cut Tunnel near the Fountain of the Virgin, Nazareth, Palestine, 1869
In den Fels gehauener Gang nahe der Marienquelle, Nazareth, Palästina
Le Tunnel percé dans la roche près de la fontaine de la Vierge, Nazareth, Palestine
Pencil and ink with wash

An interest in archaeological subjects in William Simpson's work can be traced back to his earlier expeditions to India and present-day Ethiopia. The watercolours showing the excavation work that he painted on behalf of the Palestine Exploration Fund were reproduced in the press and also featured in a large exhibition.

Bereits bei den Expeditionen nach Indien und Abessinien (heute Äthiopien) hatte sich ein zunehmendes Interesse William Simpsons an archäologischen Themen herauskristallisiert. Die Aquarelle, die er auf Einladung des Palestine Exploration Fund von deren Grabungsarbeiten angefertigt hatte, wurden in der Presse reproduziert und in einer umfangreichen Ausstellung gezeigt.

L'intérêt croissant de William Simpson pour les thèmes archéologiques remontait à des expéditions en Inde et en Abyssinie (l'actuelle Éthiopie). L'aquarelle représentant les travaux de fouilles et qu'il avait réalisée à la demande du Palestine Exploration Fund fut reproduite dans la presse et montrée dans une vaste exposition.

144

MELTING STEEL.

LEVÉE.

PUDDLING IRON.

VIEW FROM MONUMENT HILL.

ON THE MONONGAHELA RIVER

COAL FLOTILL

VIEWS ABOUT PITTSBURG, PENNSYLVANIA.—DRAWN BY C. S. REINHAR

145

BLOWING GLASS

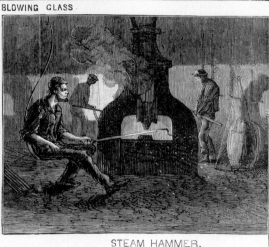

STEAM HAMMER.

OHIO RIVER

GE 147.]

Charles Stanley Reinhart

Views about Pittsburgh, Pennsylvania, 1871
Ansichten von Pittsburgh in Pennsylvania
Vues de Pittsburgh, Pennsylvanie
Wood engraving
From: *Harper's Weekly*, New York,
18 February 1871

Charles Stanley Reinhart's impressions of
the booming steel industry in his home town
of Pittsburgh are some of the most engaging
composite press graphics of the time. Along
with Winslow Homer, Edwin Austin Abbey
and Frederic Remington, Reinhart was one of
the new rank of young American artists who
owed their start in the profession to the art
director Charles Parsons.

Charles Stanley Reinharts Impressionen über
die boomende Stahlindustrie seiner Heimatstadt Pittsburgh gehören zu den eindrucks-
vollsten pluralen Pressegrafiken der Zeit.
Neben Winslow Homer, Edwin Austin Abbey
und Frederic Remington zählte Reinhart zu
der Riege junger amerikanischer Künstler,
die ihren Aufstieg dem Artdirector Charles
Parsons verdankten.

Les impressions de Charles Stanley Reinhart
sur l'industrie sidérurgique en pleine expansion de sa ville natale Pittsburgh comptent parmi les plus fascinantes mosaïques de dessins
de presse de l'époque. Avec Winslow Homer,
Edwin Austin Abbey et Frederic Remington
Reinhart faisait partie de l'équipe de jeunes
artistes américains qui devaient leur promotion
au directeur artistique Charles Parsons.

→→ **Henry François Farny**

*Hog-slaughtering and Pork-packing in
Cincinnati*, 1873
*Schweineschlachtung und Schweinezerlegung
in Cincinnati*
Abattage et découpage de porcs à Cincinnati
Wood engraving
From: *Harper's Weekly*, New York,
6 September 1873

Industrial mass production in North America
first became established with the slaughtering of animals. The technology of production
lines, which was developed in the slaughter-
houses of Cincinnati from the late 1840s, was
a source of fascination for press illustrators
because of its association with violence and
death, and it duly became a popular subject
for documentary illustrations in multi-panel
formats (see also ill. pp. 416/417).

Die industrielle Massenproduktion hatte in
Nordamerika ihren Ausgang im Bereich der
Tierschlachtung genommen. Die Fließbandtechnologie, die ab den späten 1840er-Jahren
in den Schlachthöfen Cincinnatis entwickelt
wurde, faszinierte die Pressezeichner in ihrer
Verbindung mit Gewalt und Tod und wurde
zu einem beliebten Motiv dokumentarischer
Multipanelgrafik (siehe auch Abb. S. 416/417).

La production industrielle de masse avait pris
son essor en Amérique du Nord dans le secteur de l'abattage d'animaux. La technologie de
chaînes de production qui fut développée dans
les abattoirs de Cincinnati dès la fin des années
1840 fascinait l'illustrateur de presse dans sa
relation avec la violence et la mort et devint un
motif favori du dessin documentaire en plusieurs
cases (voir aussi ill. p. 416/417).

CLUTCHING.   SLAUGHTERING AND BLEEDING.   SCALDING-VAT.   PICKING.

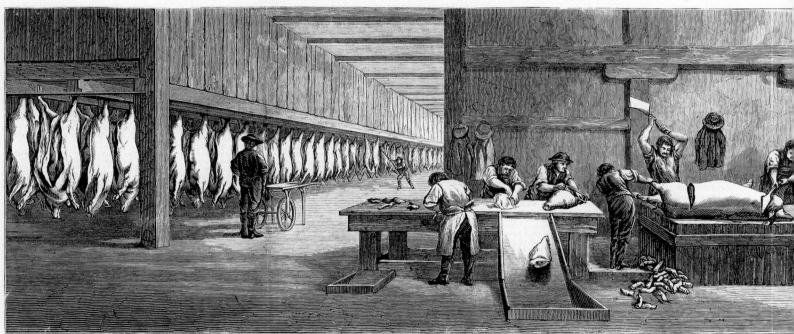

DRYING-ROOM.   TRIMMING-TABLE.

THE CURING-CELLARS.

HOG-SLAUGHTERING AND PORK-PACKING IN CH

EKLY.

777

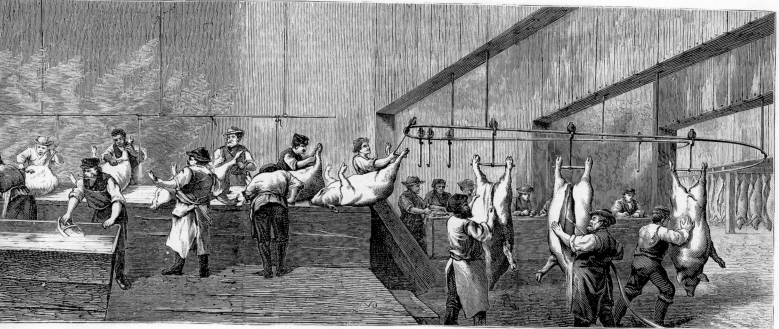

SCRAPING AND SHAVING.　　　　THE GAMBRELS.　　　　DISEMBOWELING AND WASHING.

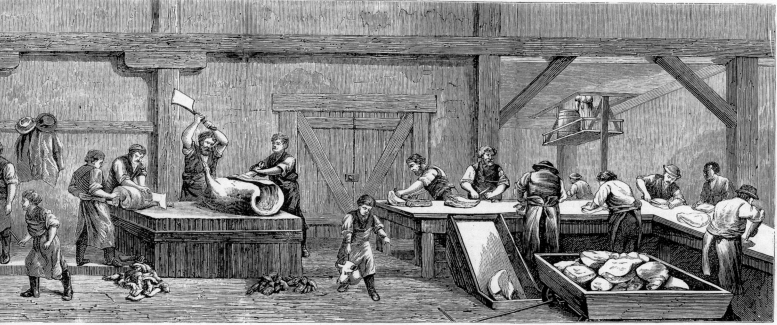

CUTTING-BLOCKS.　　　　TRIMMING-TABLES.

LARD-RENDERING.　　　　PRESSING.　　　　"STEAM LARD" TANKS.

ATI.—FROM DRAWINGS BY H. F. FARNY.—[SEE PAGE 778.]

Melton Prior

↓ *The Ashantee War – Sketches by Our Special Artist*, 1874
Der Ashanti-Krieg – Skizzen unseres special artist | *La Guerre ashanti – Esquisses de notre* special artist
Wood engravings
From: *The Illustrated London News*, 31 January 1874

During the third Ashanti war, Melton Prior was given his first appointment as a picture correspondent as the British Empire sought to consolidate its economic interests on the then Gold Coast of West Africa. He went on to cover 23 further war assignments up until 1904. In the first picture below he is shown sketching, surrounded by a number of Fante locals.

Im dritten Aschanti-Krieg, mit dem das britische Königreich seine ökonomischen Interessen an der westafrikanischer Goldküste weiter zu sichern suchte, wurde Melton Prior erstmals als grafischer Kriegskorrespondent engagiert. 23 weitere Kriegseinsätze sollten bis 1904 folgen. Im oberen Bild ist er selbst beim Skizzieren zu sehen, umringt von Angehörigen der Ethnie der Fante.

Le dessinateur Melton Prior fut engagé pour la première fois comme correspondant de guerre au cours de la troisième guerre anglo-ashanti, avec laquelle l'Empire britannique cherchait à sécuriser ses intérêts économiques sur la côte ouest-africaine, jadis nommée Côte-de-l'Or. 23 interventions militaires devaient suivre jusqu'en 1904. Sur l'image du haut, on le voit dessiner, entouré de membres de l'ethnie des Fanti.

→ *The Ashantee War: Advancing on Coomassie, Facsimile of a Sketch by our Special Artist*, 1874
Der Ashanti-Krieg: Vorrücken auf Coomassie, Faksimile einer Skizze unseres special artist
La Guerre ashanti: avancée sur Coomassie, fac-similé d'une esquisse réalisée par notre special artist
Wood engraving
From: *The Illustrated London News*, 28 March 1874

While William Simpson's reporting is characterised by its ethnographic detail and objectivity, the dynamic sketches made by Melton Prior, who was 22 years younger, suggest an authentic degree of engagement. Indeed, in the course of the military action depicted here Prior himself killed two Ashanti warriors.

Während sich William Simpsons Reportagen durch eine ethnografische Detailtreue und Distanzierung auszeichneten, suggerierten die dynamischen Skizzen des 22 Jahre jüngeren Kollegen Melton Prior Engagement und Authentizität. Im Verlauf der gezeichneten Kampfhandlungen tötete er selbst zwei Aschanti-Krieger.

Alors que les reportages de William Simpson se distinguaient par le souci ethnographique du détail et la distanciation, les esquisses dynamiques de son collègue Melton Prior, de vingt-deux ans son cadet, suggéraient l'engagement et l'authenticité. Au cours des opérations de combat qu'il a représentées, il tua lui-même deux guerriers ashanti.

THE ILLUSTRATED LONDON NEWS, JAN. 31, 1874. — 97

THE ASHANTEE WAR.—SKETCHES BY OUR SPECIAL ARTIST.

FETISH TREE IN A VILLAGE NEAR CAPE COAST CASTLE.

↘ *Sketches from Coomassie, by our Special Artist: The King's Slaughtering Place*, 1874
Skizzen aus Coomassie, von unserem special artist: *Der Schlachtplatz des Königs*
Esquisses de Coomassie par notre special artist: *la place de tuerie du roi*
Wood engraving
From: *The Illustrated London News*, 25 April 1874

As the punitive expedition reached the heart of the Ashanti Empire, the British troops came upon the fabled city of Kumasi but found it deserted. Melton Prior's illustration of the "King's Slaughtering Place", with human remains lying all around, was published as a double-page spread. It thus helped to justify the controversial colonial war, which included the looting and destruction of Kumasi.

Bei ihrer Strafexpedition ins Innere des Aschanti-Reichs fanden die britischen Truppen die sagenumwobene Hauptstadt Kumasi verlassen vor. Der von Melton Prior skizzierte „Schlachtplatz des Königs" mit den Überresten menschlicher Opfer wurde doppelseitig abgedruckt. Er diente der Legitimation des umstrittenen Kolonialkriegs inklusive der Plünderung und Zerstörung Kumasis.

Pendant leur expédition punitive à l'intérieur de l'empire ashanti, les troupes britanniques trouvèrent la légendaire capitale Kumasi abandonnée. La «place de tuerie du roi» dessinée par Melton Prior avec les restes mortels de victimes humaines fut imprimée en double page. Elle servit à la légitimation de la guerre coloniale controversée, y compris le pillage et la destruction de Kumasi.

CAPTAIN GLOVER'S HEAD-QUARTERS AT ADDAH.

THE ASHANTEE WAR: ADVANCING ON COOMASSIE, FACSIMILE OF A SKETCH BY OUR SPECIAL ARTIST.

SKETCHES FROM COOMASSIE, BY OUR SPECIAL ARTIST: THE KING'S SLAUGHTERING PLACE.

THE ILLUSTRATED LONDON NEWS.

REGISTERED AT THE GENERAL POST-OFFICE FOR TRANSMISSION ABROAD.

No. 2158.—VOL. LXXVII.   SATURDAY, OCTOBER 9, 1880.   WITH TWO SUPPLEMENTS } SIXPENCE BY POST, 6½D.

ENGLISH SPECIAL CORRESPONDENTS GOING TO THE MONTENEGRIN CAMP: A GOOD BIT OF ROAD.—SEE PAGE 350.
FROM A SKETCH BY CAPTAIN J. W. GAMBIER, R.N.

Johann Nepomuk Schönberg, after Captain J.W. Gambier

*English Special Correspondents Going to the
Montenegrin Camp*, 1880
*Englische Sonderberichterstatter begeben sich
zum montenegrinischen Lager*
*Correspondants spéciaux anglais se rendant
au camp de Montegrino*
Wood engraving
From: *The Illustrated London News*, 9 October 1880

The action associated with the Serbian and Bulgarian
independence movements, and the ensuing Russo-
Turkish War, meant that the Balkans were a subject
for international reporting for some time. Johann
Schönberg worked as a *special artist* in the field for
a number of international journals, and in this example the versatile artist has worked up a sketch originally drawn by a soldier.

Der Balkan stand im Zug der serbischen und bul-
garischen Unabhängigkeitsbewegungen und des
daraus folgenden Russisch-Türkischen Kriegs lange
Zeit im Fokus der internationalen Berichterstattung.
Johann Schönberg war als *special artist* für mehrere
internationale Illustrierte vor Ort. Hier interpretiert
der vielseitige Künstler die Skizze eines Militärs.

En raison des mouvements d'indépendance serbes
et bulgares et de la guerre russo-turque qui en
découla, les Balkans furent longtemps le point de
mire des reportages internationaux. En tant que
special artist, Johann Schönberg se trouva sur place
pour le compte de plusieurs magazines illustrés
internationaux. Ici, l'artiste aux talents polyvalents
interprète le dessin d'un militaire.

Eugène Burnand & Ch. P. Arbanz (sc.)

Heading for the High Plateaux, 1879
Auf dem Weg ins Hochland
En route pour les Hauts Plateaux
Wood engraving
From: *Le Tour du Monde*, no. 38, Paris, 1879

The monthly magazine *Le Tour du Monde* combined
the impulse of European expansionism with high-
quality literary travel accounts, alongside pictures
by some of the most accomplished illustrators and
engravers of the day. The Swiss painter Eugène
Burnand was known for his striking depictions of
animals in picturesque settings.

Das Monatsmagazin *Le Tour du Monde* flankierte
den europäischen Expansionismus mit literarisch
hochwertigen Reiseberichten, die von einigen der
hervorragendsten Illustratoren und Xylografen ins
Bild gesetzt wurden. Der Schweizer Maler Eugène
Burnand war für seine dynamischen Tierdarstel-
lungen in pittoresken Umgebungen bekannt.

Le magazine mensuel *Le Tour du Monde* encou-
rageait l'expansionisme européen par des récits
de voyage de haute qualité littéraire, qui étaient
mis en images par quelques-uns des plus remarquables illustrateurs et xylographes. Le peintre
suisse Eugène Burnand était connu pour ses
représentations dynamiques d'animaux dans des
décors pittoresques.

Journal des Voyages

ET DES AVENTURES DE TERRE ET DE MER

Nº 1. — Prix 15 centimes	Bureaux : 7, rue du Croissant.
Abonnements avec Primes. — PARIS, 10 fr. — DÉPARTEMENTS, 12 fr.	

TEXTE. — Avis de l'éditeur. — Aventures périlleuses d'un marin français dans la Nouvelle-Guinée. — Une Course de taureaux à Madrid. — Christophe Colomb, sa vie et ses découvertes. — Un Drame au fond de la mer. — Géographie du département de l'Ain. — Le Tour de la Terre en quatre-vingts récits. — Curiosités géographiques. — Chronique.

ILLUSTRATIONS. — Châtiment des criminels à la Nouvelle-Guinée. — Les courses de taureaux (trois dessins). — Christophe Colomb exposant son plan devant les moines. — Un drame au fond de la mer (le crime). — Carte du département de l'Ain. — La Terre dans l'espace.

AVENTURES PÉRILLEUSES D'UN MARIN FRANÇAIS DANS LA NOUVELLE-GUINÉE. — CHÂTIMENT DES CRIMINELS.

Horace Castelli & A. Leray (sc.)

Criminal Punishment, 1877
Bestrafung der Verbrecher
Châtiment des criminels
Wood engraving
From: *Journal des Voyages*, no. 1,
Paris, 1877

In the *Journal des Voyages*, the sensationalist style of journalism that had been flourishing since the mid-1860s was applied to travel reporting. Its innovative mixture of xenophobic fantasy and ethnographic facts made this weekly journal a rival to the popular science magazine *Le Tour du Monde*.

Das *Journal des Voyages* übertrug die Parameter eines seit Mitte der 1860er-Jahre florierenden Sensationsjournalismus auf das Genre der Reisereportage. Mit einer innovativen Mischung aus xenophober Fantastik und ethnografischen Fakten konkurrierte das Unterhaltungsblatt im Wochenrhythmus mit dem populärwissenschaftlichen Magazin *Le Tour du Monde*.

Journal des Voyages transféra les codes d'un journalisme sensationnaliste florissant depuis le milieu des années 1860 vers le genre du reportage de voyage. Avec un mélange novateur de fantasmes xénophobes et de faits ethnographiques, le journal de loisirs hebdomadaire faisait concurrence au magazine populaire et scientifique *Le Tour du Monde*.

Journal des Voyages

ET DES AVENTURES DE TERRE ET DE MER

Nº **61**. — Prix : **15** centimes.	Bureaux : 7, rue du Croissant.
Abonnements. — PARIS, 8 fr. — DÉPARTEMENTS, 10 fr. — Dimanche 8 Septembre 1878.	

TEXTE. — L'Arbre anthropophage. — Le Volcan dans les glaces (suite). — Trouville. — A travers l'Australie (suite). — Il ne faut pas juger de l'arbre par l'écorce (suite). — Le Livre de Stanley (fin). — Chronique.

ILLUSTRATIONS. — L'Arbre anthropophage : ce fut alors une épouvantable orgie. — A travers l'Australie : son confrère d'Angleterre ne voulait y voir qu'un vulgaire os à moelle. — Trouville : la ville vue de la mer ; l'église ; la plage.

L'ARBRE ANTHROPOPHAGE. — Ce fut alors une épouvantable orgie. (Page 132.)

61

Horace Castelli & Jean-Achille Pouget (sc.)

The Man-eating Tree, 1878
Der Menschenfresserbaum
L'Arbre anthropophage
Wood engraving
From: *Journal des Voyages*, no. 61, Paris, 1878

The strange and often outlandish illustrations by Horace Castelli represent an important link between the late-Romantic dream images of artists such as Gustave Doré and the later artists of the *Faits divers* news items, including Henri Meyer, Osvaldo Tofani and Achille Beltrame.

Horace Castelli war mit seinen bizarren Kolportageillustrationen ein wichtiges Bindeglied zwischen der spätromantischen Traumfabrikation eines Gustave Doré und Künstlern der *Faits divers* wie Henri Meyer, Osvaldo Tofani oder Achille Beltrame.

Avec ses illustrations bizarres et triviales, Horace Castelli constitua un lien important entre l'usine à rêves du romantisme tardif d'un Gustave Doré et les artistes des *Faits divers* comme Henri Meyer, Osvaldo Tofani ou Achille Beltrame.

OUR SPECIAL ARTIST'S ADVENTURES IN ZULULAND.—SEE PAGE 366.

Melton Prior

Our Special Artist's Adventures in Zululand, 1879
Abenteuer unseres special artist *in Zululand*
Les Aventures de notre special artist *au Zoulouland*
Wood engraving
From: *The Illustrated London News*, 18 October 1879

Melton Prior's somewhat slapstick adventures during the Zulu War in South Africa are followed by the scene in the last panel on this page which shows Prior and another *special artist* in the act of setting fire to an indigenous dwelling. In the accompanying commentary, however, he criticised the military command for ordering such retaliation on the grounds that it was not "particularly elegant or dignified".

Die slapstickartigen Abenteuer Melton Priors während des Kriegs gegen das südafrikanische Volk der Zulu münden im letzten Bild des Multipanels in der Zerstörung einer indigenen Behausung durch Prior und einen weiteren *special artist*. In seinem Begleitkommentar kritisierte Prior allerdings derartige von der militärischen Führung angeordnete Vergeltungsmaßnahmen als nicht „besonders elegant und würdig".

Les aventures bouffonnes de Melton Prior pendant la guerre contre le peuple des Zoulous en Afrique du Sud finissent, sur la dernière scène de la planche composée de plusieurs dessins, par la destruction d'une habitation d'indigènes par Prior et un autre *special*. Cependant, dans son commentaire d'accompagnement Prior critiquait de tels actes de représailles ordonnés par le commandement militaire comme n'étant ni «particulièrement élégants ni décents».

Frederic Villiers

The War in the East – With the Army of the Drina, 1876
Der Krieg im Osten – Bei der Drina-Armee
La Guerre à l'Est – avec l'armée de la Drina
Wood engraving
From: *The Graphic*, London, 21 October 1876

Serbia's war of independence against the Ottoman Empire was Frederic Villiers's first assignment for *The Graphic*, and he and Johann Schönberg were the main picture correspondents for this crisis in the Balkans for the Western press. His illustrations were good at capturing the atmosphere but more awkward in their representation of anatomy and perspective, and as a result they often had to be reworked.

Der Unabhängigkeitskrieg Serbiens gegen das Osmanische Reich war der erste Einsatz von Frederic Villiers für *The Graphic*. Neben Johann Schönberg war er der wichtigste Bildreporter der Balkankrise aus westlicher Perspektive. Seine Skizzen waren atmosphärisch präzise, aber anatomisch und perspektivisch ungelenk. Sie mussten daher oft erheblich überarbeitet werden.

La guerre d'indépendance de Serbie contre l'Empire ottoman fut la première intervention de Frederic Villiers pour *The Graphic*. Avec Johann Schönberg il était le principal reporter d'images de la crise des Balkans vue sous l'angle occidental. Ses dessins rendaient avec précision l'atmosphère, mais étaient maladroits en termes d'anatomie et de perspective. Pour cette raison, ils devaient fréquemment subir d'importantes retouches.

Anonymous

Pictorial News, 1880
Bildnachrichten | *Nouvelles illustrées*
Wood engravings
From: *The Graphic*, London, 19 June 1880

→→ **Anonymous**

Cormorant Nests in the Strait of Magellan, 1871
Kormorannester in der Magellanstraße
Les Nids de cormorans dans le détroit de Magellan
Wood engraving
From: *L'Univers illustré*, Paris, 11 November 1871

This scene showing a colony of breeding cormorants in Tierra del Fuego was engraved for the *Illustrated London News* in 1869. It was then re-used by a number of periodicals around the world because it was such a remarkable image.

Die Szene mit den brütenden Kormoranen auf Feuerland wurde 1869 für die *Illustrated London News* gestochen und wegen ihrer fantastischen Anmutung von einer Vielzahl internationaler Periodika übernommen.

La scène des cormorans en train de couver sur la Terre de Feu fut gravée en 1869 pour l'*Illustrated London News* et reprise par une multitude de périodiques internationaux pour sa superbe élégance.

LES NIDS DE CORMORANS DANS L[...]

TROIT DE MAGELLAN. — Voir page 447.

Frank Dadd

The Queen's Return from the Highlands, Her Majesty Crossing Tay Bridge, Dundee, 1879
*Rückfahrt der Königin aus den Highlands, Ihre Majestät überquert die Brücke über den Tay, Dundee,
Retour de la reine des Highlands, Sa Majesté traverse le pont sur le Tay, Dundee*
Wood engraving
From: *The Illustrated London News*, 5 July 1879

On the return journey from her summer residence in Scotland, Queen Victoria is shown here crossing the more than three km of the Tay Bridge and giving a thoughtful look at the recently opened structure. The magical qualities of wood-engraving illustrations such as this were an inspiration in later years to Max Ernst in creating his Surrealist collage novels.

Auf der Rückfahrt von ihrer schottischen Sommerresidenz überquert Queen Victoria die mehr als drei Kilometer lange Tay Bridge und wirft einen melancholischen Blick auf das erst kürzlich eröffnete Bauwerk. Die magischen Qualitäten solcher Tonstichillustrationen inspirierten später Max Ernst zu seinen surrealen Bilderromanen.

Pendant son voyage de retour de sa résidence d'été écossaise, la reine Victoria traverse le Tay Bridge, long de plus de trois kilomètres, et jette un regard mélancolique sur l'édifice récemment inauguré. Les qualités magiques de telles illustrations xylographiques inspirèrent plus tard Max Ernst pour ses romans-collages surréels.

Francis H. Schell & Thomas Hogan

A Promenade in Mid-air — The Brooklyn Ascent to the Bridge Tower, 1877
*Eine Promenade in der Luft – Der Brooklyner Anstieg zum Brückenturm
Une promenade en l'air – la montée vers la tour du pont de Brooklyn*
Wood engraving
From: *Harper's Weekly*, New York, 31 March 1877

A PROMENADE IN MID-AIR—THE BROOKLYN ASCENT TO THE BRIDGE TOWER.—Drawn by Schell and Hogan.—[See Page 254.]

THE INTERCOLLEGIATE BOAT-RACE—CORNELL WINS.—From Sketches and Instantaneous Photographs.—[See Page 61]

Anonymous

The Intercollegiate Boat-race –
Cornell Wins – from Sketches and
Instantaneous Photographs, 1875
Die Ruderregatta der Hochschulen –
Cornell siegreich – nach Skizzen
und Momentaufnahmen
La Régate d'aviron des collèges –
Cornell décroche la victoire –
d'après des esquisses et des clichés
momentanés
Wood engraving
From: *Harper's Weekly*, New York,
31 July 1875

Cornell University was victorious on
this occasion in the annual rowing
regatta of the intercollegiate competition. The composite image — which
features illustrated documentation,
typographic notations, interpretative
wood-engraving and use of the new
technique of chronophotography,
which had only recently been introduced by Eadweard Muybridge (see
ill. p. 512) — gives an idea of the possibilities for pictorial synthesis that
could still be achieved by the use
of chemigraphy, after it was first introduced in the middle of the 19th
century (see ills. pp. 247, 248/249).

Die Cornell University war dieses Mal
der Gewinner der jährlichen Ruderregatta zwischen den Colleges. Das
Kompositum aus zeichnerischer Dokumentation, typografischer Notation,
xylografischer Interpretation und der
Technik der Chronofotografie, die erst
kürzlich durch Eadweard Muybridge
eingeführt worden war (siehe Abb.
S. 512), lässt erahnen, welche Möglichkeiten bildnerischer Synthesen
die seit Mitte des 19. Jahrhunderts
genutzte Chemiegrafie demnächst
noch eröffnen würde (siehe Abb.
S. 247, 248/249).

Cette fois, c'est la Cornell University
qui remporta la régate annuelle d'aviron intercollégiale. La composition
de documentation graphique, de notation typographique, d'interprétation
xylographique et de technicue de
chronophotographie, qui venait tout
juste d'être lancée par Eadweard
Muybridge (voir ill. p. 512), laisse de-
viner quelles possibilités de synthèses
picturales la chimigraphie, utilisée
depuis le milieu du XIXe siècle, allait
bientôt présenter (voir ills. p. 247,
248/249).

→→ **Anonymous**

Concluding Sketches of the Afghan
War, 1879
Abschlussskizzen aus dem
Afghanischen Krieg
Esquisses finales de la guerre afghane
Wood engraving
From: *The Graphic*, London,
12 July 1879

After a treaty agreement which relin-
quished control of Afghan foreign
affairs to the British, it appeared that
the Second Anglo-Afghan War had
come to an end. The illustration demonstrates an increasingly innovative
use of the multi-panel format, and in
this case the floating arrangement
of the rounded segments in particular
above the main scene showing the
river crossing creates a gentle and
almost dreamlike impression of space.

Nachdem sich die Briten vertraglich
die Kontrolle über die Außenpolitik Afghanistans gesichert hatten,
schien der zweite angloafghanische
Krieg beendet. Das Blatt demonstriert einen zunehmend innovativen
Umgang mit dem Multipanelformat.
Durch die schwebende Anordnung
blasenförmiger Segmente über dem
Zentralmotiv einer Flussdurchque-
rung entsteht ein weicher, traum-
artiger Raumeindruck.

Un fois que les Britanniques se furent
assuré le contrôle de la politique extérieure de l'Afghanistan. la seconde
guerre anglo-afghane semblait termi-
née. Cette planche démontre une
approche de plus en plus innovatrice
du format multi-cases. L'agencement
flottant de vignettes en forme de
bulles au-dessus du motif central de
la traversée d'un fleuve engendre une
impression spatiale douce et onirique.

1. FORDING THE RIVER CABUL AT GOSHTIA.—2. AFTER A HOT DAY'S WORK JELLALABAD.—3. PREPARING FO

CONCLUDING SKETCH

DE: THE TAILOR IN CAMP.—4. THE GUARD RELIEVED.—5. A GUEST HOUSE: THE PESHAWUR CHURCH MISSION.

OF THE AFGHAN WAR

WEST GOTHAM COURT, CHERRY STREET.

STAGE OF THE OLD CHATHAM STREET THEATRE, NOW USED AS A STABLE.

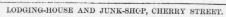

LODGING-HOUSE AND JUNK-SHOP, CHERRY STREET.

ENTRANCE TO AN ALLEYWAY, CHERRY STREET.

TENEMENT LIFE IN NEW YORK—SKETCHES IN THE FOURTH WARD.—DRAWN BY CHARLES GRAHAM.—[SEE PAGE 246.]

William Allen Rogers

*Tenement Life in New York – Sketches
in "Bottle Alley"*, 1879
*Leben in den Mietskasernen New Yorks –
Skizzen in der „Bottle Alley"*
*Vivre en location à New York – Esquisses
dans la «Bottle Alley»*
Wood engraving
From: *Harper's Weekly*, New York,
22 March 1879

Campaigns in the illustrated press for improving
housing and sanitation were as important in
American society as elsewhere. The animated
sketches drawn by William Rogers provide a glimpse
of life in one of the most infamous areas of New
York's impoverished Five Points district. A decade
later, Jacob Riis (ills. p. 431) contributed to the
demolition of this neglected neighbourhood through
his documentary photographic work.

Auch in Amerika spielten Kampagnen der Illustrierten zur Verbesserungen der Wohn- und Sani-
tärverhältnisse eine wichtige Rolle. William Rogers
karikatureske Skizzen bieten Einblicke in eine der
berüchtigtsten Zonen des New Yorker Slumquar-
tiers Five Points. Eine Dekade später trug Jacob
Riis mit seinen fotografischen Dokumentationen
dazu bei, dass diese Hinterhofgegend abgerissen
wurde (Abb. S. 431).

En Amérique aussi, les campagnes menées par
les magazines illustrés jouèrent un rôle majeur
dans l'amélioration des conditions de logement et
de confort sanitaire. Les esquisses caricaturales de
William Rogers permettent de jeter un regard dans
l'une des zones les plus mal famées de Five Points,
un quartier pauvre de New York. Dix ans plus tard,
Jacob Riis (ills. p. 431) contribuera avec sa documentation photographique à la démolition de cette
zone d'arrière-cours.

TENEMENT LIFE IN NEW YORK—SKETCHES IN "BOTTLE ALLEY."—Drawn by William A. Rogers.—[See Page 226.]

Charles Graham

← *Tenement Life in New York –
Sketches in the Fourth Ward*, 1879
*Leben in den Mietskasernen New
Yorks – Skizzen im vierten Bezirk*
*Vivre en location à New York –
Esquisses dans le quatrième
arrondissement*
Wood engraving
From: *Harper's Weekly*, New York,
29 March 1879

The documentary reports that were
published about the run-down district
of New York's Lower East Side
appeared in relation to the new tenement reform law that was supposed to
ensure access to light and air in tenement housing by enforcing stricter
building regulations. While William
Rogers (above) sketched on site,
Charles Graham's illustrations are
clearly based on photographs.

Die Dokumentationen über die Slum-
quartiere in der New Yorker Lower
East Side standen im Zusammenhang
mit einem neuen Mietgesetz, das
durch verschärfte Bauauflagen für
bessere Klima- und Lichtverhältnisse
in den Mietshäusern sorgen sollte.
Während William Rogers (oben) wohl
vor Ort skizziert hatte, sind Charles
Grahams Grafiken offensichtlich weitgehend nach Fotografien entstanden.

La documentation sur les zones
miséreuses du quartier Lower East
Side à New York est liée à une nouvelle législation relative aux locations
qui, par des règlements plus stricts,
devait améliorer les conditions de
chauffage et d'éclairage. Tandis que
William Rogers (en haut) avait dessiné sur place, les dessins de Charles
Graham sont manifestement réalisés
à partir de photographies.

→→ Jules Férat & Frederick Moeller (sc.)

*The Ruins of Rue Béranger before
It Was Cleaned up*, 1878
*Schutthaufen in der Rue Béranger
vor den Aufräumarbeiten*
*Les Ruines de la rue Béranger avant
le déblaiement*
Wood engraving
From: *Le Monde illustré*, Paris,
25 May 1878

The scene shows an explosion in a toy
shop in which 15 people died and two
houses were destroyed. Jules Férat,
who had made a name for himself
illustrating the stories of Jules Verne,
working here with Frederick Moeller, a
wood engraver who had been an early
interpreter of Manet designs, has succeeded in adapting a straightforward
photographic original into a dramatic
three-dimensional image filled with
narrative detail. The scene's disturbing
effect was greatly increased when it
was printed at right angles in landscape format.

Eine Explosion in einem Spielwarenla-
den forderte 15 Menschenleben und
zerstörte zwei Häuser. Dem Zeichner
Jules Férat, der sich einen Namen mit
Jules-Verne-Illustrationen gemacht
hatte, war es hier gemeinsam mit dem
Xylografen Frederick Moeller, einem
frühen Interpreten Édouard Manets,
gelungen, eine lapidare Fotovorlage in
einen dramatischen Tiefenraum mit
einer romanhaften Detailfülle zu übersetzen. Der Abdruck im Querformat
trug wesentlich zu dem verstörenden
Eindruck bei.

Une explosion dans un magasin de
jouets causa la mort de 15 personnes
et détruisit deux maisons. Le dessinateur Jules Férat, qui s'était fait un
nom avec les illustrations de Jules
Verne, réussit ici en collaboration avec
Frederick Moeller, xylographe et interprète de la première heure d'Édouard
Manet, à traduire un modèle de photographie concis en un profond espace
dramatique à l'aide d'une foule de
détails narratifs. C'est surtout la reproduction en format oblong qui crée un
effet troublant.

LES RUINES DE LA RUE BÉRANGER AVANT LE DÉBLAIEMENT

Fac-simile de la photographie exécutée par les soins de la Préfecture de police le lendemain du sinistre. — Reproduction de M. Férat.

**Adrien Marie
& Charles Gillot (sc.)**

*Théâtre de l'Ambigu-Comique
L'Assommoir*, 1879
Der Totschläger | L'Assommoir
Relief etching
From: *L'Illustration*, Paris,
1 February 1879

The investigative journalism that became more popularised with the emergence of the tabloid press was also the starting point for Émile Zola's literary and theatrical naturalism. The illustrations here show a key scene from the stage adaptation of his most successful novel, *L'Assommoir* (1877).

Der investigative Journalismus, der mit dem Aufstieg der Boulevardpresse populär wurde, war der Ausgangspunkt von Émile Zolas literarischem und theatralem Naturalismus. Die Illustrationen zeigen eine Schlüsselszene aus der Adaption seines erfolgreichsten Romans *L'Assommoir* (1877).

Le journalisme d'investigation qui devint populaire avec la montée de la presse à sensation fut le point de départ du naturalisme littéraire et théâtral d'Émile Zola. Les illustrations montrent une scène centrale de l'adaptation de son roman le plus populaire, *L'Assommoir* (1877).

**Frédéric de Haenen
& Charles Baude (sc.)**

→ *Le Théâtre illustré*
Le Pavé de Paris, 1883
Play by | Drama von | drame de
Adolphe Belot
Wood engraving
From: *Le Monde illustré*, Paris,
14 April 1883

The war scene in Adolphe Belot's play occurs in a dream as Madame Delaunay lies on stage at the Théâtre de la Porte Saint-Martin. The illustrations in the series *Le Théâtre illustré* were intent on confusion of this kind between different levels of reality, and it was often hard to tell what belonged to the original theatrical scenes and what was part of the later illustrations in the press.

Die Kriegsszene in dem Drama von M. Adolphe Belot spielt sich im Traum einer Madame Delaunay ab, die auf der Bühne des Boulevardtheaters Théâtre de la Porte Saint-Martin liegt. Die Grafiken der Reihe *Le Théâtre illustré* waren auf solche Verwischungen von Realitätsebenen aus. Eine Unterscheidung zwischen der Wirklichkeit der Theaterszenen und den dokumentarischen Pressegrafiken war oft kaum auszumachen.

Dans le drame de M. Adolphe Belot la scène de guerre a lieu dans un rêve de Madame Delaunay, qui gît sur la scène du théâtre de boulevard de la Porte Saint-Martin. Les dessins de la série *Le Théâtre illustré* visaient à ce genre de confusions des niveaux de réalité. Il était souvent difficile de faire une différence entre la réalité des scènes théâtrales et les dessins de presse à visée documentaire.

Jules Férat & Regnier (sc.)

*Théâtre de l'Ambigu-Comique
L'Assommoir*, 1879
Der Totschläger | L'Assommoir
Wood engraving
From: *Le Monde illustré*, Paris, 25 January 1879

Max Klinger

A Mother I, 1883
Eine Mutter I | Une mère I
Etching with aquatint
From: Max Klinger, *Dramen, Opus IX,* 1883
Kupferstichkabinett, Staatliche Museen zu Berlin

Max Klinger's six-part cycle of etchings was dedi-
cated to Émile Zola, and constitutes a multifaceted
tribute to the culture of press graphics. The section
entitled *A Mother* consists of three illustrations, and
was based on a number of reports about life in
working-class Berlin; its starting point was a notice
in the press about the attempted suicide of a woman
who had been suffering abuse.

Max Klingers sechsteiliger Radierzyklus ist Émile
Zola gewidmet und stellt eine facettenreiche Hommage an die Kultur der Pressegrafik dar. Bei der
aus drei Grafiken bestehenden Folge *Eine Mutter*
handelt es sich um eine Metareportage aus dem
Berliner Arbeitermilieu. Ausgangspunkt war eine
Pressenotiz über den Selbstmordversuch einer
misshandelten Frau.

Le cycle de gravures en six parties de Max Klinger
est dédié à Émile Zola et constitue un hommage
aux multiples facettes à la culture du graphisme
de presse. La série *Une m*ère, composée de trois
dessins, est un méta-reportage sur le milieu ouvrier à
Berlin. Le point de départ en fut une notice de presse
sur la tentative de suicide d'une femme maltraitée.

**Frédéric Lix &
Frederick Moeller (sc.)**

*Inside the Chamber of Deputies,
11 November 1880
In der Abgeordnetenkammer
À la Chambre des députés*
Wood engraving
From: *Le Monde illustré*, Paris,
20 November 1880

This tumultuous crowd scene was a
regular occurrence in the Chamber
of Deputies during the confrontational
early period of the Third Republic in
France. As president of the Chamber,
Léon Gambetta has ordered one
of the Legitimist deputies, who has
worked himself up into a fury, to be
seized and taken away to a room
specially set aside for such disruptive
individuals to calm down.

Die tumultartige Massenszene gibt
ein charakteristisches Ereignis in der
französischen Abgeordnetenkammer
während der explosiven Anfangsphase einer republikanisch regierten
Dritten Republik wieder. Kammerprä-
sident Gambetta lässt einen tobenden
legitimistischen Abgeordneten ergrei-
fen und in einen eigens dafür einge-
richteten Beruhigungsraum bringen.

Cette scène de masse tumultueuse
représente un événement caractéristique de la Chambre des députés française pendant la période explosive
de la Troisième République. Gambetta,
le président de la Chambre, fait saisir
un député légitimiste et, afin qu'il se
calme, le fait transporter dans une
pièce spécialement meublée à cet
effet.

Theodore R. Davis

→ *The Transportation of Dressed Beef
from the West – Chicago Cattle Yards
and Slaughter-houses*, 1882
*Der Transport von Rindfleisch aus
dem Westen – Chicagoer Vieh- und
Schlachthöfe | Le Transport de viande
de bœuf venant de l'Ouest – Enclos
de betail et abattoirs à Chicago*
Wood engraving
From: *Harper's Weekly*, New York,
28 October 1882

By the late 1870s, Chicago had
become the world's slaughterhouse
on the strength of its well-connected
transportation network and the invention of the refrigerator car, seen here
in diagram form. The use of improved
assembly-line technology (see also ill.
pp. 394/395) also went on to become
the model for mass production in the
automotive industry.

Aufgrund seines dichten Transportnet-
zes und der Erfindung des Eisenbahn-
kühlwagens, der in diagrammatischer
Ansicht wiedergegeben ist, entwickelte sich Chicago seit Ende der 1870er-
Jahre zum Schlachthof der Welt. Die
verbesserte Fließbandtechnologie
(siehe auch Abb. S. 394/395) wurde
zum Vorbild für die industrielle Monta-
gefertigung in der Automobilindustrie.

Grâce à un dense réseau de transport et à l'invention du wagon frigo-
rifique, représenté ici sous forme de
diagramme, Chicago devint dès la
fin des années 1870 l'abattoir du
monde. La technologie de chaîne de
montage (voir aussi ill. p. 394/395)
servit de modèle à la production d'assemblage dans l'industrie automobile.

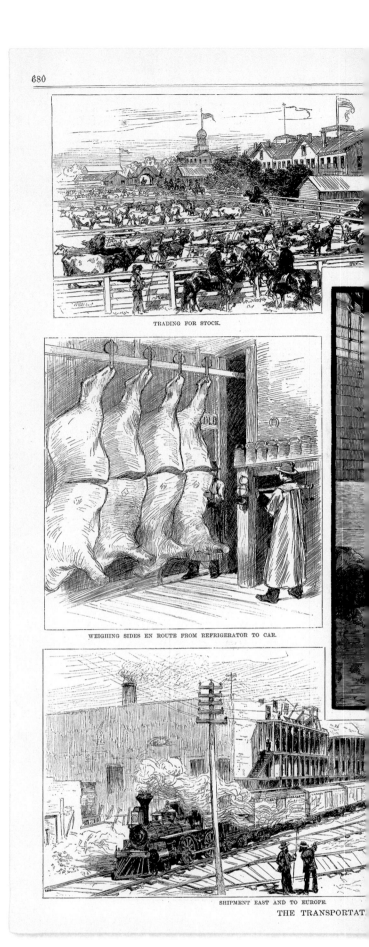

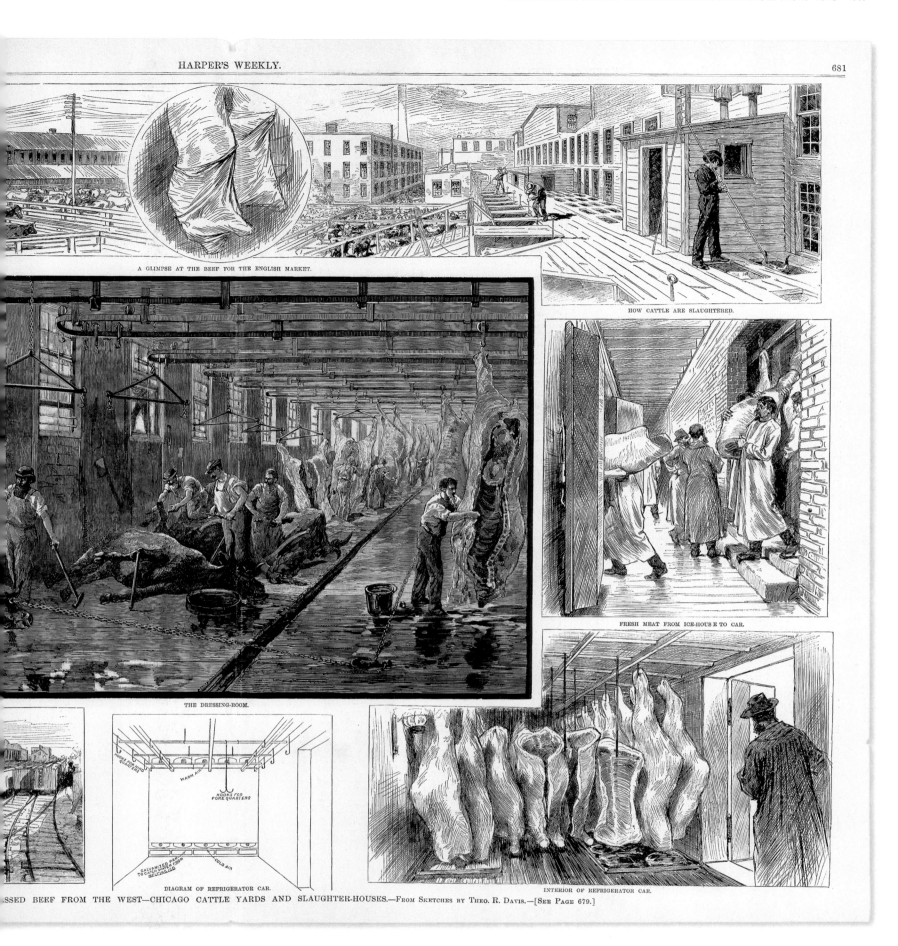

HARPER'S WEEKLY.

681

A GLIMPSE AT THE BEEF FOR THE ENGLISH MARKET.

HOW CATTLE ARE SLAUGHTERED.

THE DRESSING-ROOM.

FRESH MEAT FROM ICE-HOUSE TO CAR.

DIAGRAM OF REFRIGERATOR CAR.

INTERIOR OF REFRIGERATOR CAR.

...SSED BEEF FROM THE WEST—CHICAGO CATTLE YARDS AND SLAUGHTER-HOUSES.—From Sketches by Theo. R. Davis.—[See Page 679.]

→→ **Daniel Vierge, after Henri Scott**

The Mer de Glace above Saumur, 1880
Das Eismeer stromaufwärts von Saumur
La Mer de glace en amont de Saumur
Wood engraving
From: *Le Monde illustré*, Paris, 24 January 1880

The freezing winter of 1880 transformed a stretch of the Loire river near Saumur into a picturesque sea of ice. At the time, Daniel Vierge was at the height of his career as a press illustrator, but the following year he was forced to learn how to draw with his opposite

hand after suffering a stroke. In terms of innovative ability and prolific output, he was the only press artist who could be compared with Gustave Doré.

Der arktische Winter 1880 hatte die Loire bei Saumur in ein pittoreskes Eismeer verwandelt. Daniel Vierge befand sich, kurz bevor er wegen einer halbseitigen Lähmung gezwungen war, die Zeichenhand zu wechseln, im Zenit seiner pressegrafischen Karriere. Vierge war der Einzige, der es in puncto Innovationskraft und Produktivität mit Gustave Doré aufnehmen konnte.

L'hiver arctique de 1880 avait transformé la Loire en une pittoresque mer de glace près de Saumur. Juste avant d'être contraint de changer de main pour dessiner à cause d'une hémiplégie, Daniel Vierge était au zénith de sa carrière d'illustrateur. Vierge était le seul à pouvoir concurrencer Gustave Doré en termes de force d'innovation et de productivité.

Ile de Souzay.   Dampierre.   Saumur.   Villeberm

LA MER DE GLACE EN AMONT DE SAUMUR. — Vue prise de la cale de Panvigne, au-dessus de Villebe

s menacé.

Levée de la Loire dont la rupture peut inonder la vallée d'Orléans.

curieux sur la levée de la Loire. — (Dessin de M. Vierge, d'après le croquis de M. Scott, envoyé spécialement par le *Monde illustré.*)

EXTRA SUPPLEMENT TO THE ILLUSTRATED LONDON NEWS, Aug. 5, 1882.—155

THE WAR IN EGYPT: FACSIMILE OF OUR ARTIST'S SKETCHES.

THE ILLUSTRATED LONDON NEWS, Aug. 5, 1882.—156

THE WAR IN EGYPT: FACSIMILE OF OUR ARTIST'S SKETCHES.

456—THE ILLUSTRATED LONDON NEWS, Oct. 14, 1882.—400

STORMING THE TRENCHES OF TEL-EL-KEBIR.

FACSIMILE OF A SKETCH BY OUR SPECIAL ARTIST.

Melton Prior

← The War in Egypt, 1882
Der Krieg in Ägypten | La Guerre en Égypte
Relief etchings
From: *The Illustrated London News*, 5 August 1882

Following nationalist revolts in Egypt against foreign financial control and attacks on the European
quarter of Alexandria, the latter city was occupied
by British troops in July 1882. The finished illustrations from the zinc etchings based on Melton Prior's
sketches show a spy after being arrested and the
execution of a suspected arsonist.

Nachdem es in Ägypten zu nationalistischen Erhe-
bungen gegen die ausländische Finanzkontrolle
gekommen war und in Alexandria Übergriffe auf
das Ausländerviertel stattgefunden hatten, wurde
die Stadt im Juli 1882 von britischen Truppen eingenommen. Die überarbeiteten Zinkätzungen nach
Melton Priors Skizzen zeigen einen festgenomme-
nen Spion und die Exekution eines mutmaßlichen
Brandstifters.

Après que des révoltes nationalistes contre le contrôle étranger des finances avaient secoué l'Égypte
et que des attaques du quartier étranger d'Alexandrie
avaient eu lieu, la ville fut occupée par les troupes
britanniques en juillet 1882. Les gravures au zinc
retouchées d'après les esquisses de Melton Prior
montrent un espion arrêté et l'exécution d'un incen-
diaire présumé.

↙ Storming the Trenches of Tel-el-Kebir, 1882
Erstürmung der Schützengräben von Tel-el-Kebir
Assaut des tranchées de Tel-el-Kebir
Relief etching
From: *The Illustrated London News*,
14 October 1882

The decisive battle between the invading British
army and the soldiers of the nationalist Urabi movement was fought in the Egyptian desert on 13 September 1882. In this illustration Melton Prior has
captured the moment when the Highland Brigade
made its bayonet charge, although the chemigraphic
reproduction of his sketch was not in fact published
until a month after the event took place.

Am 13. September 1882 kam es in der ägyptischen
Wüste zur Entscheidungsschlacht zwischen der britischen Invasionsarmee und den Soldaten der nationalistischen Urabi-Bewegung. Melton Prior hielt den
Moment fest, als die Highland-Brigade zum Bajonett-
angriff überging. Die chemiegrafische Reproduktion
seiner Skizze wurde erst einen Monat nach dem
Ereignis publiziert.

La bataille décisive entre l'armée d'invasion britannique et les soldats du mouvement nationaliste urabi
se déroula dans le désert égyptien le 13 septembre
1882. Melton Prior dessina le moment où la brigade
de Highland passa à l'attaque à la baïonnette. La
reproduction en photogravure de son esquisse ne
fut publiée qu'un mois après l'événement.

Richard Caton Woodville Jr.

*↓ Battle of Tel-el-Kebir: The Charge at the
Bayonet's Point*, 1882
*Schlacht von Tel-el-Kebir: Der Angriff mit
aufgepflanztem Bajonett*
*Bataille de Tel-el-Kebir : L'attaque à la pointe
de la baïonnette*
Wood engraving
From: *The Illustrated London News*, 7 October 1882

Richard Caton Woodville's version of Melton Prior's
sketch (ill. p. 420 b.) was done in the photorealistic
style of historical art of the time. Where the original
drawing showed a general overview of the action, for
his painting Woodville chose a subjective viewpoint
that leads the eye into the scene. The engraving produced from this gouache was then published a week
before Prior's sketch appeared.

Richard Caton Woodvilles Version von Melton Priors
Skizze (Abb. S. 420 u.) ist in der fotorealistischen
Manier der zeitgenössischen Historienkunst gehalten. Während die zeichnerische Vorlage die Kampf-
handlung im Überblick zeigt, wählt die Malerei eine
subjektive Perspektive, die den Betrachter in das
Geschehen hineinzieht. Die Xylografie nach Woodvilles Gouachemalerei wurde eine Woche vor der
Skizze Priors publiziert.

La version de Richard Caton Woodville de l'esquisse
de Melton Prior (ill. p. 420 b.) est réalisée dans le
style photoréaliste de la peinture d'histoire contemporaine. Alors que le dessin d'origine montre les
combats dans leur ensemble, le peintre choisit une
perspective subjective qui entraîne l'observateur
dans l'action. Cette xylographie exécutée d'après la
peinture à la gouache de Woodville fut publiée une
semaine avant l'esquisse de Prior.

BATTLE OF TEL-EL-KEBIR: THE CHARGE AT THE BAYONET'S POINT.
FROM A SKETCH BY OUR SPECIAL ARTIST.

Melton Prior

↑ *Departure of Baker Pasha and Staff from Suez for*
Suakin Soudan on SS Mansourah, December 1883
Aufbruch Baker Paschas und seines Stabs auf de
SS Mansourah *von Sues nach Suakin im Sudan*
Départ du pacha Baker et de sa suite de Suez pour
Suakin au Soudan sur le paquebot Mansourah
Ink with wash

The British occupation of Egypt added fuel to the
Islamic Mahdist Revolt in the provinces of Sudan
that broke out in 1881. When the Sudanese port
city of Suakin was besieged by jihadist forces, a
huge army of various Egyptian units was assembled in Suez in late 1883 and placed under the control of the English general Valentine Baker. In the
same way as other well-known *special artists*, Melton
Prior often made several different versions of his
drawings, and these could then be sold or used for
display purposes.

Die britische Okkupation Ägyptens hatte in den
Sudan-Provinzen den 1881 ausgebrochenen isla-
mistischen Mahdi-Aufstand befeuert. Um die von
den Dschihadisten belagerte Hafenstadt Suakin
zu befreien, wurde Ende 1883 in Sues eine riesige
Armee aus disparaten ägyptischen Einheiten unter
der Führung des englischen Generals Valentine
Baker zusammengestellt. Wie andere prominente
special artists fertigte Melton Prior von seinen Zeichnungen oft mehrere Fassungen an, die für Verkaufs-
und Ausstellungszwecke genutzt werden konnten.

L'occupation britannique de l'Égypte avait attisé
l'insurrection Mahdi islamiste qui avait éclaté dans
les provinces du Soudan en 1881. Fin 1883, une
gigantesque armée fut constituée d'unités égyptiennes disparates à Suez, sous le commandement
du général anglais Valentine Baker, pour libérer
la ville portuaire de Suakin occupée par les djiha-
distes. Comme d'autres *specials* renommés, Melton
Prior exécutait souvent plusieurs versions de ses
dessins qui pouvaient être utilisées pour être ven-
dues ou exposées.

↑ *The War in the Soudan: Sketches by our*
Special Artist, 1884
Der Krieg im Sudan: Skizzen unseres special artist
La Guerre au Soudan : esquisses réalisées par
notre special artist
Wood engraving
From: *The Illustrated London News*,
12 January 1884

Anonymous

→ *Lecture on the Egyptian War, by Mr. Melton Prior before the Prince of Wales at the Savage Club*, 1883
Vortrag über den Ägyptenkrieg von Mr Melton Prior vor dem Prinzen von Wales im Savage Club
Conférence sur la guerre d'Égypte de M. Melton Prior devant le prince de Galles au Savage Club
Wood engraving
From: *The Illustrated London News*, 3 March 1883

Anonymous

↘ *"A War Artist's Experiences during the Last Decade", Lecture by Mr. F. Villiers, Special Artist of* The Graphic, *at Willis's Rooms*, 1887
„Erlebnisse eines Kriegsmalers im vergangenen Jahrzehnt", Vortrag von Mr F. Villiers, special artist des Graphic, in den Willis's Rooms
«Expériences d'un dessinateur de guerre durant la dernière décennie», conférence par M. F. Villiers, special artist pour The Graphic, dans les Willis's Rooms
Wood engraving
From: *The Graphic*, London, 17 December 1887

Specials such as William Simpson, Melton Prior and his rival Frederic Villiers were stars in their own right, and in between war assignments they presented their work in exhibitions and with magic lanterns in the course of lecture tours. Meanwhile, their travel accounts, war reports and memoirs often became bestsellers.

Special artists wie William Simpson, Melton Prior und dessen Rivale Frederic Villiers waren Stars, die ihre Arbeit zwischen den Kriegseinsätzen in Ausstellungen und in Vorträgen mittels Laterna-magica-Projektoren präsentierten. Ihre Reisebücher, Kriegsreportagen und Memoiren waren meist Bestseller.

Des *specials* comme William Simpson, Melton Prior et son rival Frederic Villiers étaient des stars qui, entre les opérations de guerre, présentaient leur travail dans des expositions et dans des conférences au moyen de projecteurs de lanterne magique. Leurs livres de voyage, reportages de guerre et mémoires étaient la plupart du temps des best-sellers.

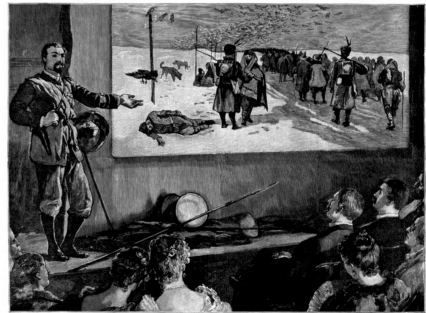

Melton Prior

← *The War in the Soudan: Battle of El-Teb*, 1884
Der Krieg im Sudan: Schlacht von El-Teb
La Guerre au Soudan : bataille d'El-Teb
Relief etching
From: *The Illustrated London News*, 22 March 1884

General Baker's Egyptian units were annihilated by the Mahdi's soldiers, but British troops then became involved in further fighting at the end of February. Melton Prior's detailed depiction of the battle, which showed British soldiers bayoneting wounded Mahdists in the trenches, provoked protests at home and heated debates in Parliament.

Nachdem die ägyptischen Einheiten unter General Baker von den Mahdisten vernichtend geschlagen worden waren, kam es Ende Februar zu einer weiteren Schlacht mit britischen Truppen. Melton Priors akurate Darstellung der Kampfhandlungen, die britische Soldaten beim Bajonettieren verwundeter Mahdisten in den Schützengräben zeigt, führte im britischen Parlament zu Protesten und heftigen Debatten.

Une fois que les unités égyptiennes commandées par le général Baker eurent essuyé des mahdistes une cuisante défaite, une nouvelle bataille eut lieu fin février contre les troupes britanniques. La représentation précise que Melton Prior fait des combats et qui montre les soldats britanniques tuant des mahdistes blessés à la baïonnette dans les tranchées provoqua des protestations et de violentes discussions au Parlement britannique.

L'ILLUSTRATION
JOURNAL UNIVERSEL

PRIX DU NUMÉRO : 75 CENTIMES
Collection mensuelle : **3** fr. — Volume semestriel : **18** fr.
Les demandes d'abonnement doivent être affranchies et accompagnées d'un mandat-poste ou d'une valeur à vue sur Paris au nom du Directeur-Gérant.

42ᵉ ANNÉE. — VOL. LXXXIV. — Nᵒ 2171.
SAMEDI 4 OCTOBRE 1884
BUREAUX : 13, RUE ST-GEORGES, PARIS

PRIX D'ABONNEMENT
PARIS & DÉPARTEMENTS : 3 mois, **9** fr.; 6 mois, **18** fr.; un an, **36** fr.
ÉTRANGER : Pour tous les pays faisant partie de l'Union postale :
3 mois, **11** francs; 6 mois, **22** francs; un an, **44** francs

L'AÉROSTAT ÉLECTRIQUE DIRIGEABLE DE MM. TISSANDIER FRÈRES

LA NACELLE ET LE MOTEUR

D'après une photographie.

Jules Férat & Auguste Tilly (sc.)

*The Tissandier Brothers' Steerable
Electric Airship*, 1884
*Das lenkbare elektrische Luftschiff
der Gebrüder Tissandier
L'Aérostat électrique dirigeable
de MM. Tissandier frères*
Wood engraving
From: *L'Illustration*, Paris,
4 October 1884

Having already illustrated works by
Jules Verne, Jules Férat was ideally
suited for depicting the trip made
by the Tissandier brothers in their
electric airship. The original photograph he used, which has since disappeared, was probably a studio shot
which was then combined with one
or more aerial photographs. The unusual sharpness achieved by the wood
engraving makes a further contribution to the overall fantastic result.

Als Illustrator von Jules Vernes Werken war Jules Férat bestens qualifi-
ziert, die Reise der Brüder Tissandier
in ihrem elektrischen Luftschiff ins
Bild zu setzen. Bei der verschollenen
fotografischen Vorlage handelte es
sich vermutlich um eine Studioaufnah-
me, die Férat dann mit einem Luftbild
kombinierte. Zu der fantastischen
Wirkung trägt auch die Überschärfe
des technischen Tonstichs bei.

En tant qu'illustrateur des œuvres
de Jules Verne, Jules Férat était parfaitement qualifié pour mettre en
images le voyage des frères Tissandier
dans leur aérostat dirigeable électrique. La photographie qui servit de
modèle a disparu. Il s'agit probablement d'un cliché de studio que Férat
combina ensuite avec une photographie aérienne. L'extrême netteté de la
xylographie technique contribue aussi
à produire un remarquable effet.

Anonymous

*The Earthquake on the Island
of Ischia*, 1883
*Das Erdbeben auf der Insel Ischia
Le Tremblement de terre de l'île
d'Ischia*
Wood engraving
From: *L'Illustration*, Paris,
18 August 1883

The engravings produced from the
direct exposure of photographs generally differ from wood engravings,
which were based on graphic interpretations of photographs, by their more
two-dimensional appearance and lack
of depth.

Die durch direkte Aufbelichtungen
von Fotografien entstandenen Stiche unterschieden sich in der Regel
durch einen flächigeren Eindruck
beziehungsweise eine mangelnde
Raumtiefe von Xylografien, die zeichnerische Interpretationen von Fotografien zur Grundlage hatten.

Les gravures réalisées par l'exposition directe de photographies se
différenciaient en général des xylographies, qui étaient basées sur des
interprétations graphiques de photographies, par une impression plus
plate ou encore un manque de profondeur spatiale.

Henri Meyer, after Anonymous (photo.), & Fortuné Méaulle (sc.)

*The Mystery of the Rue du Vert-
Bois*, 1886
*Das Rätsel von der Rue du Vert-Bois
Le Mystère de la rue du Vert-Bois*
Wood engraving
From: *Le Journal illustré*, Paris,
15 August 1886

The emerging tabloid press exploited
the possibilities of photography in a
much more confrontational and experimental way than the illustrated magazines of the middle classes. Shortly
after the appearance of Henri Meyer's
shocking reproduction of a police
photograph showing the dead body
of an unidentified child, *Le Journal
illustré* then published Nadar's first
photographic report, reproduced by
chemigraphy, together with a series
of interviews also using photographs
(see ills. pp. 514/515).

Die neue Boulevardpresse ging mit
den Möglichkeiten der Fotografie
wesentlich konfrontativer und experimenteller um als die bürgerlichen
Illustrierten. Kurze Zeit nach Henri
Meyers schockierender Wiedergabe
des Polizeifotos einer nicht identifi-
zierten Kinderleiche veröffentlichte
Le Journal illustré mit einer Fotointer-
viewstrecke Nadars erste chemiegrafisch reproduzierte Fotoreportage
(siehe Abb. S. 514/515).

La nouvelle presse à sensation utilisa
les possibilités de la photographie de
façon plus provocante et plus expérimentale que les magazines illustrés
bourgeois. Peu de temps après la
publication choquante par Henri Meyer
d'un cliché de police représentant le
cadavre non identifié d'un enfant, *Le
Journal illustré* publia le premier reportage photo de Nadar en photogravure
avec une série d'interviews-photos
(voir ills. p. 514/515).

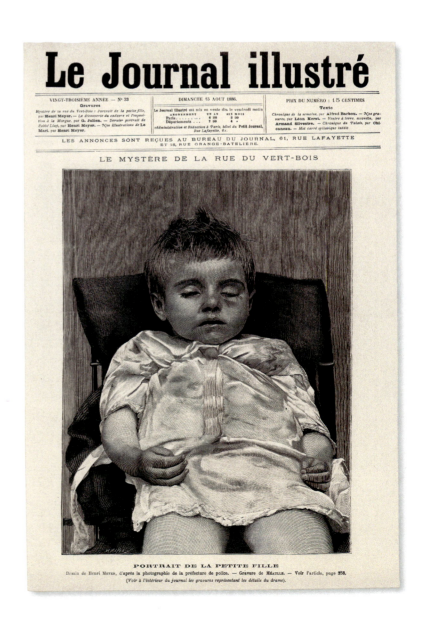

Wu Youru

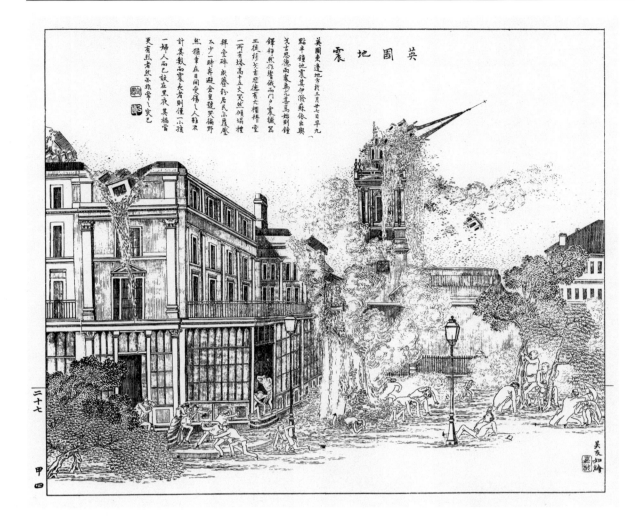

An Earthquake in England, 1884
Ein Erdbeben in England
Un tremblement de terre en Angleterre
Lithograph
From: *Dianshizhai huabao*, Shanghai,
vol. 1, January –June 1884

When reporting on international news
in China the local *special artists* had
to rely on pictures that were already
available to produce their illustrations.
The resulting synthetic style, combin-
ing Eastern tradition with Western
influences, had a formative effect on
the development of Chinese picture
books (*Lianhuanhua*), which became
popular under Mao Zedong.

Bei internationalen Meldungen waren
die chinesischen *special artists* auf
Vorlagen angewiesen. Der syntheti-
sche Stil aus östlicher Tradition und
westlichen Einflüssen wurde prägend
für die Entwicklung der chinesischen
Bildergeschichten (*Lianhuanhua*), die
unter Mao Zedong populär waren.

En ce qui concerne les nouvelles internationales, les *specials* chinois étaient
tributaires de modèles. Le style synthétique fait de tradition orientale et
d'influences occidentales marqua
l'évolution des histoires imagées chinoises (*Lianhuanhua*), qui eurent beaucoup de succès sous Mao Zedong.

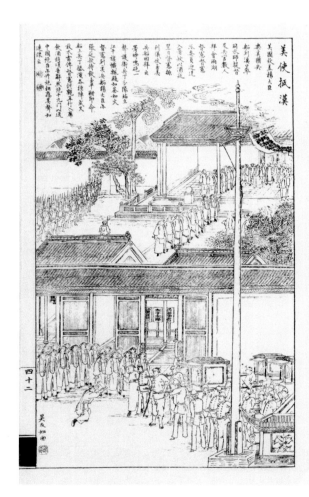

*The American Consul Arrives at Hankou –
A White Elephant from Siam*, 1884
*Der amerikanische Konsul trifft in Hankou
ein – Ein weißer Elefant aus Siam*
*Le consul américain arrive à Hankou –
Un éléphant blanc de Siam*
Lithograph
From: *Dianshizhai huabao*, Shanghai,
vol. 1, January – June 1884

The first illustrated news journal to be
published in China appeared in Shanghai
in April 1884. The lithographic workshop
established in Shanghai by the publisher
and businessman Ernest Major experimented from an early date with photo-
lithography, and this new technique was
used to reproduce the two wood engravings shown here from *Harper's Weekly*,
facing a lithograph of Wu Youru's brush
design.

Ab April 1884 erschien in Schanghai die
erste chinesische Nachrichtenillustrierte.
Die lithografische Anstalt des Verlegers
und Kaufmanns Ernest Major experimentierte früh mit der Fotolithografie. Mit
dieser neuen Technik wurden die beiden
Fotoxylografien aus *Harper's Weekly*
reproduziert, die den lithografischen Pin-
selzeichnungen von Wu Youru gegenübergestellt sind.

Le premier magazine illustré chinois parut
à Shangaï à partir d'avril 1884. L'établissement lithographique de l'éditeur et
homme d'affaires Ernest Major expérimenta très tôt la photolithographie. Les
deux xylophotographies du *Harper's
Weekly*, qui sont présentées en contraste
avec les dessins au pinceau de Wu Youru,
furent reproduites à l'aide de cette nouvelle technique.

Charles Upham & Julian Rice

South Carolina – The Terrible Earthquake at Charleston, 1886
South Carolina – Das verheerende Erdbeben in Charleston
Caroline du Sud – Le terrible tremblement de terre à Charleston
Wood engraving
From: *Frank Leslie's Illustrated Newspaper*, New York,
11 September 1886

As camera shutter speeds increased in the late 1870s it became possible to experiment with the use of snapshots, which resulted in a clear shift towards more dynamic images and not only in cartoons but also in documentary press illustrations.

Die Anschauung der Momentfotografie, die seit Ende der 1870er-Jahre durch kurze Kameraverschlüsse möglich wurde, bewirkte nicht nur im Cartooning, sondern auch in der dokumentarischen Pressegrafik eine merkliche Tendenz zur Dynamisierung.

L'expérimentation du cliché instantané, qui devint possible dès la fin des années 1870 grâce aux vitesses d'obturation rapides des chambres photographiques, entraîna non seulement dans la caricature, mais aussi dans le dessin de presse documentaire une nette tendance à la dynamisation.

James Forman

Illinois
The Frightful Railway Massacre, 1887
Die furchtbare Eisenbahnkatastrophe
L'effroyable déraillement de train
Wood engraving
From: *Frank Leslie's Illustrated Newspaper*, New York,
20 August 1887

As the result of a bridge having been weakened by fire near to Chatsworth, Illinois, a horrific train crash occurred in which at least 81 people died.

Eine durch ein Feuer beschädigte Eisenbahnbrücke bei Chatsworth, Illinois, verursachte ein verheerendes Zugunglück mit 81 Toten.

Un pont de chemin de fer endommagé par un incendie près de Chatsworth, Illinois, provoqua un effroyable accident ferroviaire où 81 passagers trouvèrent la mort.

Anonymous

The Riot in Trafalgar Square, 1887
Der Aufstand auf dem Trafalgar Square
La Révolte à Trafalgar Square
Wood engravings
From: *The Graphic*, London, 19 November 1887

The first "Bloody Sunday" in history dates from 13 November 1887, when a large demonstration organised by the Irish National League and a federation of socialist groups marched in protest against conditions in Ireland. Despite a ban, the marchers converged on Trafalgar Square in London, where fighting broke out until the gathering was violently dispersed by police and army units.

Der 13. November 1887 ging als erster Bloody Sunday in die Annalen ein. Eine Großdemonstration der Irish National League und verschiedener sozialistischer Gruppen gegen die Unterdrückung Irlands war trotz eines Verbots auf den gesperrten Trafalgar Square in London gezogen und dort von Polizei- und Armeeeinheiten niedergeschlagen worden.

Le 13 novembre 1887 passa dans les annales comme le premier Bloody Sunday. Une manifestion massive de l'Irish National League et de divers groupements socialistes contre l'oppression de l'Irlande avait marché en direction du Trafalgar Square fermé, malgré une interdiction, et avait été réprimée par des unités de la police et de l'armée.

Anonymous

Fight at the Bottom of Parliament Street between the Police and Contingents from South London and Battersea, 1887
Kampf am Ende der Parliament Street zwischen der Polizei und Aufgeboten aus Südlondon und Battersea
Combat au bout de Parliament Street entre la police et des contingents du sud de Londres et de Battersea
Wood engraving
From: *The Graphic*, London, 19 November 1887

Among those taking part in the demonstration were Annie Besant, George Bernard Shaw and the two founders of the socialist Arts and Crafts movement, William Morris and Walter Crane.

Zu den Demonstrationsteilnehmern zählten Annie Besant, George Bernard Shaw sowie die beiden Begründer der sozialistisch orientierten Arts-and-Crafts-Bewegung, William Morris und Walter Crane.

Parmi les participants à la manifestation se trouvaient Annie Besant, George Bernard Shaw ainsi que les deux fondateurs du mouvement Arts-and-Crafts à tendance socialiste, William Morris et Walter Crane.

Christian Wilhelm Allers

→ *Mine Host at Mindelang/The Opium-smoker*, 1897
Mein Wirt in Mindelang/Der Opiumraucher
Mon Hôte à Mindelang/Le fumeur d'opium
Relief etchings
From: *The Graphic*, London, 4 October 1902

C.W. Allers was the most well-known German pictorial journalist of his day and based his style in part on that of *special artists* such as Melton Prior, although he himself never actually worked for any of the illustrated press. His numerous documentary images of everyday life in Germany under Kaiser Wilhelm II were published exclusively as independent portfolios, beginning in 1885, but Allers's artistic career was brought to an abrupt end in 1902 when he was charged with pederasty.

Obwohl er sich stilistisch an *special artists* wie Melton Prior orientierte, arbeitete der bekannteste deutsche Zeichenreporter der Zeit, C.W. Allers, nie für Illustrierte. Seine zahllosen Dokumentationen des Alltagslebens im wilhelminischen Reich sind ab 1885 ausschließlich als autonome Mappenwerke erschienen. 1902 endete seine Karriere abrupt wegen des Vorwurfs der Päderastie.

Bien qu'il s'inspirât du style de *special artists* comme Melton Prior, C.W. Allers, le plus célèbre dessinateur de presse allemand de son époque, ne travailla jamais pour un magazine. Ses innombrables documentations de la vie quotidienne dans l'Empire wilhelminien sont parus à partir de 1885 exclusivement sous forme de portfolios. Des accusations de pédérastie mirent brutalement fin à sa carrière en 1902.

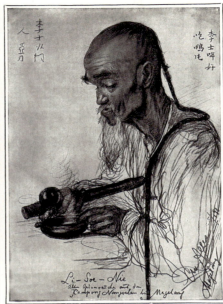

MINE HOST AT MINDELANG
DRAWN BY C. W. ALLERS

THE OPIUM-SMOKER
DRAWN BY C. W. ALLERS

Emil Limmer

The Duke of Anhalt's Salt Mine, 1889
Das herzogl. anhaltische Salzbergwerk
La Mine de sel du duc d'Anhalt
Wood engraving
From: *Illustrirte Zeitung*, Leipzig, 7 September 1889

Emil Limmer was one of the most versatile and prolific illustrators for the German press, and his depictions of people at work were especially outstanding. From 1883 he worked mostly for the *Illustrirte Zeitung*, the main German illustrated news magazine (see also ills. p. 467).

Emil Limmer war einer der vielseitigsten und produktivsten deutschen Pressegrafiker. Herausragend waren seine Darstellungen des Arbeitslebens. Seit 1883 arbeitete er hauptsächlich für die *Illustrirte Zeitung*, die marktführende deutsche Nachrichtenillustrierte (siehe auch Abb. S. 467).

Emil Limmer fut l'un des illustrateurs de presse allemands les plus éclectiques et les plus prolifiques. Il réalisa d'excellentes représentations de la vie au travail. À partir de 1883, il travailla surtout pour l'*Illustrirte Zeitung*, le magazine illustré allemand de premier plan (voir aussi ills. p. 467).

1. Fahrt in die Tiefe. 2. Bergschwerter in der 13. Etage. 3. Förbert. 4. Unterirdische Fettreißbetr- und Wasserhaltungsmaschine, IX. Etage. 5. Salzfluß Nr. 4, I. Etage. 6. Glauber zu einer Salzfluß, 13. Etage. 7. Einfahrtsfluß Nr. 6, I. Etage. 8. Bergzimmervorlage. 9. Großer Saal in der 5. Etage. 10. Wieder Tageslicht.
Das herzogl. anhaltische Salzbergwerk Leopoldshall. Originalzeichnung von E. Limmer.

Amédée Forestier, after Julius Mendes Price & R. Taylor (sc.)

↓ *Prison Life in Siberia: The Governor Visiting the Men's Prison in Yeniseisk*, 1891
Gefängnisleben in Sibirien: Der Gouverneur besucht die Männerhaftanstalt in Jenisseisk
Vie de prisonnier en Sibérie : Le gouverneur visite la prison pour hommes à Ienisseïsk
Wood engraving
From: *The Illustrated London News*, 28 February 1891

Julius Price took over the position of travel and war correspondent for the *Illustrated London News* that had previously been the responsibility of William Simpson. His account of a journey from Siberia to northern China appeared first in the newspaper, before later being published in book form. He was particularly interested in prisons along his route, and in Yeniseisk he found no political prisoners, only ordinary criminals.

Julius Price übernahm die Position des Reise- und Kriegskorrespondenten William Simpson bei der *Illustrated London News*. Sein Bericht über eine Expedition von Sibirien nach Nordchina war zuerst in der Zeitschrift und im Anschluss als Buch erschienen. Sein Interesse galt besonders den örtlichen Gefängnissen. In Jenisseisk fand er keine politischen, sondern ausschließlich kriminelle Straftäter vor.

Julius Price remplaça William Simpson comme correspondant de voyage et de guerre, aux *Illustrated London News*. Son reportage sur une expédition menant de Sibérie au nord de la Chine était d'abord paru dans la revue, puis sous forme de livre. Il s'intéressait particulièrement aux prisons locales. À Ienisseïsk, il ne trouva pas de prisonnniers politiques, mais uniquement des criminels.

Frederic Remington

Prospectors in the Sierra Madre, 1890
Schürfer in der Sierra Madre
Prospecteurs dans la Sierra Madre
Relief etching
From: *Harper's Weekly*, New York, 26 April 1890

Frederic Remington had reported on the last wars with the Indians for *Harper's Weekly* since 1886, and through his glorification of the Wild West he shaped its iconography and the myth of the cowboy like no other artist. The phenomenal success of his artistic illustrations was only achieved because of the possibilities made available by the new techniques of photomechanical reproduction.

Frederic Remington hatte für *Harper's Weekly* seit 1886 von den letzten Indianerkriegen berichtet. Mit seinen Glorifizerungen der American Frontier prägte er wie kein anderer die Ikonografie des Western und den Mythos des Cowboys. Der durchschlagende Erfolg seiner malerischen Illustrationen wurde erst durch die neuen fotomechanischen Reproduktionstechniken ermöglicht.

À partir de 1886, Frederic Remington avait effectué des reportages sur les dernières guerres indiennes pour *Harper's Weekly*, il influença comme nul autre l'iconographie de l'Ouest et le mythe du cow-boy. Le sensationnel succès de ses illustrations pittoresques ne fut possible que grâce aux nouvelles techniques de reproduction photomécaniques.

Kenyon Cox, after Jacob Riis (photo.)

Jacob Riis

↑ *How the Other Half Lives: Poverty in a West Twenty-eighth Street Tenement – An English Coal-heaver's Home*, 1889
Wie die andere Hälfte lebt: Armut in einer Miets-wohnung in der West Twenty-Eighth Street – Zuhause eines englischen Kohleträgers
Comment vit l'autre moitié : pauvreté dans un appartement locatif de West Twenty-Eighth Street – l'intérieur d'un soutier anglais
Wood engraving
From: *Scribner's Monthly Magazine*, New York, July–December 1889

↗ *How the Other Half Lives: Lodgers in a Crowded Bayard Street Tenement – "Five Cents a Spot"*, 1889
Wie die andere Hälfte lebt: Untermieter in einer überfüllten Mietswohnung in der Bayard Street – „Fünf Cent der Schlafplatz"
Comment vit l'autre moitié : sous-locataires dans un appartement locatif surpeuplé de Bayard Street – « Cinq cents la couchette »
Relief etching
From: *Scribner's Monthly Magazine*, New York, July–December 1889

↓ *"Five Cents a Spot" – Unauthorized Lodgings in a Bayard Street Tenement*, 1889
„Fünf Cent der Schlafplatz" – Nicht zugelassene Unterkünfte in einer Mietswohnung in der Bayard Street
« Cinq cents la couchette » – Hébergements illicites dans un appartement locatif de Bayard Street
Photograph
New York, Museum of Modern Art

In the late 1870s Jacob Riis began working as a police reporter in New York, with special interest in the run-down areas of the Lower East Side. His commitment to this cause was influenced by the campaigns for social reform started by *The Graphic* in London some years previously (see ills. p. 258), and in order to be able to document visually and fully the miserable conditions in the tenement buildings he began experimenting with flash photography. The 16-page report that appeared in *Scribner's Monthly* featured a selection of Riis's photographs, as adapted for publication by established artists such as the painter Kenyon Cox. The article with its accompanying striking illustrations was a resounding success, and when an expanded version was published in book form it had a decisive effect on changing housing conditions in the slums.

Als Polizeireporter hatte sich Jacob Riis in den späten 1870er-Jahren auf Berichte aus den Slums der New Yorker Lower East Side spezialisiert. Geprägt war sein Engagement von den sozialreformatori-schen Kampagnen der frühen Londoner Zeitschrift *The Graphic* (siehe Abb. S. 258). Um die Misere in den Mietskasernen visuell belegen zu können, begann Riis mit der Blitzlichtfotografie zu experimentieren. Für den 16-seitigen Beitrag in *Scribner's Monthly* wurde eine Auswahl von Riis' Aufnahmen durch renommierte Künstler wie den Maler Kenyon Cox zeichnerisch interpretiert. Der wirkungsvoll illustrierte Artikel hatte einen durchschlagenden Erfolg. Die Publikation einer erweiterten Buchfassung trug schließlich entscheidend zur Reformierung der Wohnverhältnisse in den Slums bei.

Comme reporter de police, Jacob Riis s'était spécialisé à la fin des années 1870 dans les articles sur les quartiers miséreux du Lower East Side de New York. Son engagement était imprégné des campagnes de réformes sociales de la revue londonienne de la première heure *The Graphic* (voir ills. p. 258). Afin de fournir des preuves visuelles de la misère régnant dans les cités-casernes, Riis commença à expérimenter la photographie avec flash. Pour le rapport de 16 pages paru dans le *Scribner's Monthly*, une sélection des clichés de Riis fut l'objet d'interprétations graphiques par des artistes de renom, tel le peintre Kenyon Cox. L'article encadré d'illustrations frappantes eut un succès retentissant. La publication d'une version livresque étendue eut une influence décisive sur le changement des conditions de logement dans les quartiers miséreux.

HOTEL DE TREVISE
RUE DE BERRI

HOTEL DE SAGAN
RUE SAINT-DOMINIQUE

BOULEVARD SAINT-GERMAIN
ANTICHAMBRE DU 1ᵉʳ ÉTAGE

LA DYNAMITE A PARIS
RUE DE CLICHY
VUE EXTÉRIEURE DE LA MAISON

CASERNE LOBAU
INTÉRIEUR DU RÉFECTOIRE

Anonymous

↑ *Dynamite in Paris*, 1892
Dynamit in Paris
La Dynamite à Paris
Coloured relief etching
From: *Le Petit Journal*, Paris,
16 April 1892

Anonymous (sc.), after R. Alt (photo.)

*The Effects of the Dynamite Explosion in
the Rue de Clichy*, 1892
*Die Auswirkungen der Dynamitexplosion
in der Pue de Clichy | Les Effets de l'explosion
de dynamite dans la rue de Clichy*
Wood engravings
From: *L'Illustrazione Italiana,* Milan,
10 April 1892

In March 1892, three bomb attacks shook Paris
as action was taken in revenge for a massacre
that resulted when the army opened fire on a
May Day demonstration in northern France the
previous year. The series of violent anarchist
attacks corresponded to the strategy of "propaganda by deed", and the Paris Commune itself
can be seen as an early form of the same ideas.

Die drei Bombenattentate, die Paris im März
1892 erschütterten, waren eine Vergeltung
für ein Massaker, das Militärs bei der Niederschlagung einer Maidemonstration in der nord-
französischen Provinz angerichtet hatten. Die
anarchistische Gewaltserie war Ausdruck der
aktionistischen „Propaganda der Tat", als deren
frühe Manifestation die Pariser Kommune galt.

Les trois attentats à la bombe qui secouèrent
Paris en mars 1892 constituaient des représailles pour un massacre que l'armée avait perpétré dans une province du nord de la France
afin de réprimer une manifestation de mai. La
série d'actes de violence anarchique était l'expression de la stratégie d'action «Propagande
par le fait», dont la Commune de Paris fut la
manifestation précoce.

Parigi. — EFFETTI DELLO SCOPPIO DI DINAMITE DI VIA CLICHY (da fotografie inviateci dal nostro corrispondente R. Alt).

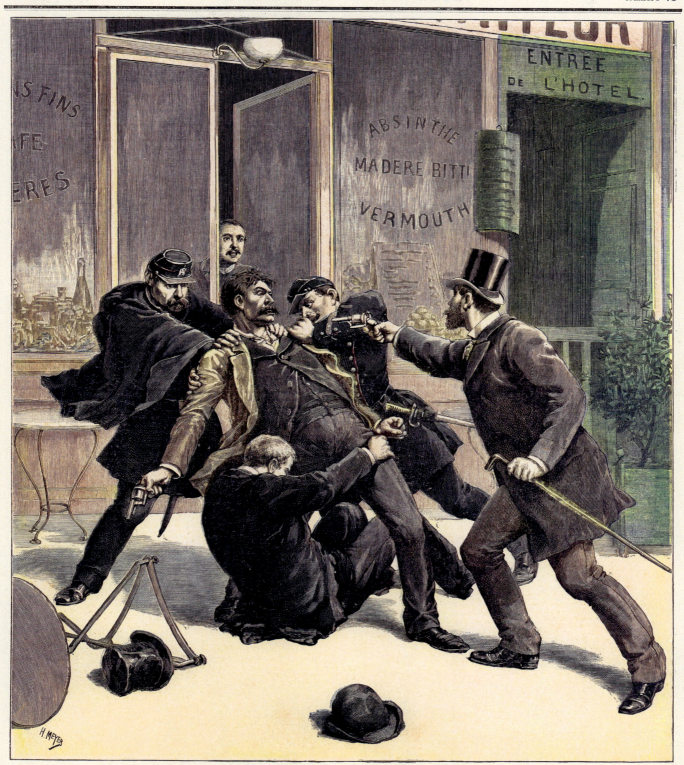

Henri Meyer & Fortuné Méaulle (sc.)

Ravachol Arrested, 1892
Die Verhaftung Ravachols
L'Arrestation de Ravachol
Coloured relief etching
From: *Le Petit Journal*, Paris,
16 April 1892

Three days after the last attack the bomber, the French anarchist Ravachol, was caught and arrested. He was executed by guillotine, and duly became a martyr for the cause of "propaganda by deed" and an idol for bohemian artists and writers. Ravachol was a cult figure not only in Montmartre, however, but also amongst the anarchists and artists in Barcelona, where Picasso was a young student a few years later.

Drei Tage nach dem letzten Anschlag konnte der Urheber, der französische Anarchist Ravachol, verhaftet werden. Nach seiner Hinrichtung durch die Guillotine wurde er zum Märtryrer der „Propaganda der Tat" und zum Idol der Künstlerboheme. Nicht nur auf dem Montmartre wurde Ravachol Kult, sondern auch unter Anarchisten und Künstlern in Barcelona, zu denen unter anderem wenige Jahre später der junge Picasso angehörte.

Trois jours après le dernier attentat, son auteur, l'anarchiste français Ravachol, put être arrêté. Après son exécution par la guillotine, il devint le martyr de la « Propagande par le fait » et l'idole de la bohème artistique. Ravachol devint une figure de culte non seulement à Montmartre, mais aussi parmi les anarchistes et les artistes de Barcelone, dont fit partie quelques années plus tard, entre autres, le jeune Picasso.

Henri Lanos

The Monument of London, 1891
Das Monument in London
Le Monument de Londres
Wood engraving
From: *The Graphic*, London,
12 December 1891

In terms of style, the work of Henri
Lanos was inspired by that of Paul
Renouard, and like him he also worked
for both *L'Illustration* in France and
The Graphic in England, beginning in
the late 1880s.

Henri Lanos orientierte sich stilistisch
an Paul Renouard. Wie dieser arbeitete er seit den späten 1880er-Jahren
sowohl für das französische Magazin
L'Illustration als auch für die englische
Zeitschrift *The Graphic*.

Henri Lanos s'inspira du style de
Paul Renouard. Comme ce dernier, il
travailla à partir de la fin des années
1880 non seulement pour le magazine français *L'Illustration*, mais aussi
pour la revue anglaise *The Graphic*.

Dante Paolocci

↓ *Rome – The New Slaughter-
house*, 1892
Rom – Der neue Schlachthof
Rome – Le Nouvel Abattoir
Wood engraving
From: *L'Illustrazione Italiana*, Milan,
7 February 1892

Dante Paolocci was one of the most
prolific pictorial journalists to work
for *L'Illustrazione Italiana*, the leading
illustrated news journal in Italy that
had been founded in 1873. In the
same way as many of his fellow illustrators Paolocci increasingly made
use of photography, which in the
example shown here probably supplied the external views of the new
slaughterhouse in Rome.

Dante Paolocci zählte zu den produktivsten Bildjournalisten von
L'Illustrazione Italiana, der 1873
gegründeten marktführenden Illustrierten Italiens. Wie viele seiner
Kollegen griff Paolocci zunehmend
auf Fotografie zurück, die in diesem
Fall wohl die Grundlage bildete für
die grafischen Außenansichten des
neuen Schlachthofs in Rom.

Dante Paolocci était l'un des reporters d'images les plus productifs de
L'Illustrazione Italiana, le magazine
illustré fondé en 1873 et dominant
en Italie. Comme bon nombre de ses
collègues, Paolocci eut de plus en
plus recours à la photographie, qui
dans ce cas précis constitua la base
des dessins des vues extérieures du
nouvel abattoir de Rome.

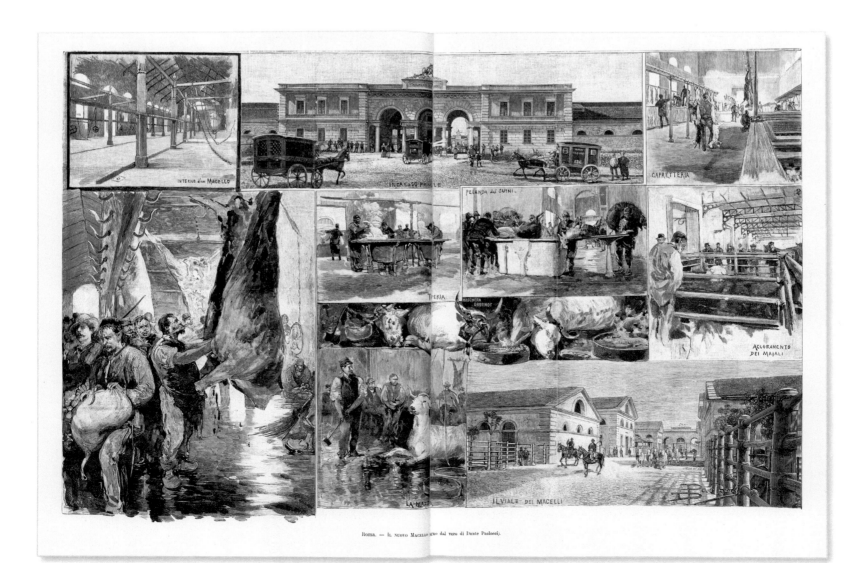

Édouard Zier

The Serpentine Dance: Loie Fuller and Her Transformations, 1892
Der Schlangentanz. Loie Fuller und ihre Verwandlungen
La Danse serpentine. Loie Fuller et ses transformations
Gouache with ink

The American dancer Loie Fuller made an impression on many artists in Art Nouveau Paris with her "serpentine dance" routine, while her early films were a source of inspiration to the Cubists. She began her international career in 1892 at the Folies Bergère cabaret in Paris. Édouard Zier's original artwork for *L'Illustration* includes the use of collage to produce the different panels for the design.

Die amerikanische Tänzerin Loie Fuller beeindruckte mit ihrem Schlangentanz viele Künstler des Art nouveau und inspirierte über den frühen Film auch Positionen des Kubismus. 1892 hatte sie im Pariser Varieté Folies Bergère ihre Weltkarriere gestartet. Édouard Ziers originale Druckvorlage für das Magazin *L'Illustration* demonstriert den Einsatz von Collage beim Aufbau einer Multipanelgrafik.

La danseuse américaine Loie Fuller impressionna beaucoup d'artistes de l'Art nouveau avec sa danse serpentine et inspira aussi les cubistes à travers ses premiers films. Elle avait entamé sa carrière internationale au théâtre des Folies Bergère en 1892. Le modèle d'impression original réalisé par Zier pour le magazine *L'Illustration* démontre l'utilisation du collage dans le montage de l'image composée de plusieurs vignettes.

48.—THE ILLUSTRATED

Meisenbach

LADIES' MEETING OF THE TOXOPF

WS, JULY 14, 1894.—49

SOCIETY, REGENT'S PARK, JULY 11.

Frederic Villiers

"The Great War of 1892": A Forecast
„Der Große Krieg von 1892":
Eine Vorhersage
«La Grande Guerre de 1892»:
Une prédiction

←*Extraordinary Scene in the*
Place de la Concorde, 1892
Ungewöhnliche Szene auf der
Place de la Concorde
Scène extraordinaire sur la place
de la Concorde
Wood engraving
From: *Black and White*, London,
16 January 1892

↓*The Bombardment of Varna*, 1892
Die Bombardierung von Varnam
Le Bombardement de Varna
Relief etching
From: *Black and White*, London,
9 April 1892

←←**Lucien Davis**

Ladies' Meeting of the Toxophilite
Society, Regent's Park, 1894
Damentreff der Toxophilite Society
Réunion de dames de la Toxophilite
Society
Relief etching
From: *The Illustrated London News*,
14 July 1894

As an illustrator, Lucien Davis specialised in representing the upper classes
during the Victorian era, and London's
West End was his main area of interest for receptions, society balls, clubs
and sporting activities. His use of a
back-lighting effect, which gave his
subjects an ethereal quality, was a
characteristic feature of his work.

Lucien Davis hatte sich als Illustrator auf die Repräsentation der viktorianischen Oberschicht spezialisiert.
Das Londoner West End war seine
Domäne: Empfänge, Bälle, Klubs
und Sport. Signifikant war der Gegen-
lichteffekt, durch den er seine Sujets
ätherisch entrückte.

Lucien Davis s'était spécialisé comme
illustrateur dans la représentation
de la haute société de l'époque victorienne. Le quartier West End de Londres était son domaine: les réceptions,
les bals, le club et le sport. L'effet de
contre-jour, par lequel il faisait apparaître ses sujets comme éthérés, était
caractéristique.

Stanley Llewellyn Wood, after Frederic Villiers

"The Great War of 1892": A Forecast
„Der Große Krieg von 1892":
Eine Vorhersage
«La Grande Guerre de 1892»:
Une prédiction

Battle of Alexandrovo by the Electric
Light between the German and
Russian Forces, 1892
Schlacht von Alexandrowo bei elek-
trischem Licht zwischen deutschen
und russischen Streitkräften
Bataille d'Alexandrovo sous lumière
électrique entre les forces allemandes
et russes
Relief etching
From: *Black and White*, London,
23 January 1892

As a *special artist*, Frederic Villiers was one of the most important people involved in a group of experts on military strategy who plotted the highly regarded scenario for the illustrated weekly *Black and White* of a great war that was forecast to take place "probably in the near future". The predicted world war would be provoked by an attempted assassination in the Balkans, and when France, in a spirit of revenge, then intervened in the fighting between the German Empire and Russia a chain reaction was started that closely resembled the course of the real world war that broke out 22 years later. The destructive power of weapons technology in the future was difficult to foresee, however, in this early work of modern documentary fiction which was published as a series of simulated reports from the front.

Frederic Villiers gehörte als *special artist* zu den prominentesten Mitgliedern eines militärstrategischen Expertenteams, das für die Illustrierte *Black and White* das viel beachtete Szenario eines großen Kriegs erarbeitete, von dem es hieß, dass er „wahrscheinlich in nächster Zukunft" stattfinden werde. Ausgelöst würde dieser angekündigte Weltkrieg durch ein Attentat auf dem Balkan. Als sich Frankreich in revanchistischer Absicht in den darauf folgenden Konflikt zwischen Deutschem Reich und Russland einmischt, kommt es zu einer Kettenreaktion, die dem Ablauf des mit 22-jähriger Verspätung stattfindenden realen Weltkriegs nahekommt. Schwer vorherzusehen war für diese erste moderne Dokufiktion, die als Abfolge simulierter Frontberichte publiziert wurde, die Vernichtungskraft zukünftiger Waffentechnik.

En tant que *special artist*, Frederic Villiers comptait parmi les membres les plus connus de l'équipe d'experts en stratégie militaire qui élabora pour le magazine *Black and White* le très remarqué scénario d'une grande guerre, dont il était dit qu'elle aurait lieu «probablement dans un proche avenir». Cette guerre mondiale annoncée serait déclenchée par un attentat dans les Balkans. Lorsque la France dans un esprit de revanche intervient dans le conflit qui oppose l'Empire allemand à la Russie, une réaction en chaîne se produit, qui ressemble au déroulement de la guerre mondiale qui eut lieu réellement vingt-deux ans plus tard. Cette première fiction documentaire moderne, publiée en feuilleton sous forme de rapports de front fictifs, pouvait difficilement prévoir la force de destruction de la future technologie de l'armement.

Anonymous (sc.), after José Gómez de la Carrera (photo.)

Manzanillo
A Crossing on the River Yara, 1895
Ein Übergang über den Fluss Yara
Une traversée du fleuve Yara
Wood engraving
From: *La Ilustración Española y Americana*, Madrid,
30 May 1895

In publishing such excellent engravings as this, made from a photograph by the pioneer of photojournalism in Cuba, José Gómez de la Carrera, Spain's most popular illustrated news magazine sought to introduce its readers to the natural landscapes of the eastern part of the island. At the same time, however, this was the very area from which the Cuban independence movement first began before the insurrection in February 1895 spread the uprising to the rest of the country.

Mit den exzellenten Xylografien nach Aufnahmen von José Gómez de la Carrera, dem Pionier des kubanischen Fotojournalismus, wollte die verbreitetste spanische Illustrierte ihren Lesern nicht nur ostkubanische Natur nahebringen. Es handelte sich dabei um die Ausgangsorte der kubanischen Unabhängigkeitsbewegung, die sich seit Februar 1895 mit landesweiten Aufständen gerade machtvoll in Erinnerung brachte.

Avec les excellentes xylographies réalisées d'après des photographies de José Gómez de la Carrera, le pionnier cubain du photojournalisme, la revue illustrée la plus diffusée en Espagne ne voulait pas mettre à la portée de ses lecteurs seulement les paysages naturels de l'est de Cuba. Il s'agissait ici des lieux d'où s'amplifia le mouvement d'indépendance cubain, qui à partir de février 1895 se rappela à la mémoire du public par des insurrections dans tout le pays.

Manzanillo
Remains of La Demajagua Sugar Factory, from which
the First Calls for Independence Were Heard
on 10 October 1868, 1895
Ruinen der Zuckermühle von La Demajagua, aus der
am 10. Oktober 1868 der erste Schrei nach
Unabhängigkeit erschallte
Ruines du moulin à sucre de La Demajagua
dans lequel résonna le premier cri séparatiste,
le 10 octobre 1868
Wood engraving
From: *La Ilustración Española y Americana*, Madrid,
30 May 1895

Seen here partly overgrown by plants are pieces of the abandoned machinery from the sugar factory run by Carlos Manuel de Céspedes that was destroyed by Spanish troops. In October 1868 Céspedes had rung the bell outside the factory to call for resistance to Spanish rule and for an end to slavery, which eventually led to the War of Independence that broke out in 1895 and ended, temporarily, in 1898 after the United States intervened.

Die überwucherten Maschinenrelikte gehörten zu der von spanischen Truppen zerstörten Zuckerfabrik von Carlos Manuel de Céspedes, der dort im Oktober 1868 zum Widerstand gegen die Sklaverei und die spanische Fremdherrschaft aufgerufen hatte und damit 1895 einen Befreiungskrieg initiierte, der mit der US-amerikanischen Intervention 1898 nur vorläufig beendet war.

Les restes de machines envahis d'herbes appartenaient à la sucrerie de Carlos Manuel de Céspedes, que des unités espagnoles avait détruite. En octobre 1868, ce dernier avait au même endroit appelé à la résistance contre l'esclavage et la domination espagnole, et ainsi conduit en 1895 à une guerre d'indépendance, qui prit fin provisoirement en 1898 grâce à l'intervention américaine.

José Guadalupe Posada (del. & sc.)

The Attempted Assassination of the President
of the Republic, General Porfirio Díaz, 1897
Das Attentat auf den Präsidenten der Republik,
General Porfirio Díaz
L'Attentat à la vie du président de la République,
le général Porfirio Díaz
Lead engraving

The attempted assassination by a lone anarchist
of the dictatorial ruler of Mexico, Porfirio Díaz, took
place on the Republic's Independence Day. The
popular and versatile illustrator José Guadalupe
Posada used a photograph of the event which he
then engraved in his characteristic bold style on
a lead plate using a burin shaped like a comb.

Der anarchistische Attentatversuch auf den mexikanischen Diktator Díaz fand am republikanischen
Unabhängigkeitstag statt. Der populäre und vielseitige Illustrator José Guadalupe Posada griff in
der Darstellung des Ereignisses auf eine Fotografie
zurück, die er in der ihm eigenen robusten Manier
unter Verwendung eines kammartigen Stichels in
eine Bleiplatte stach.

La tentative anarchiste d'assassinat du dictateur
mexicain Díaz eut lieu le jour de l'indépendance
républicaine. Le populaire et éclectique illustrateur
José Guadalupe Posada représenta l'événement
en utilisant une photographie qu'il incrusta selon
sa rude méthode habituelle dans une plaque de
plomb à l'aide d'un burin en forme de peigne.

EL ATENTADO CONTRA EL PRESIDENTE DE LA REPUBLICA,
General Don Porfirio Diaz
la mañana del 16 de Septiembre de 1897 al entrar al Parque de la Alameda por el ángulo sudeste.

Momento en que fue aprehendido Arnulfo Arroyo.

Copia de un magnífico grabado publicado por EL MUNDO Ilustrado.

William Glackens

↓ *The Ford of San Juan – "The Bloody Bend", 1898*
Die Furt von San Juan – „Die blutige Biegung"
Le Gué de San Juan – «Le tournant sanglant»

↘ *The "Rough Riders" Charging up the*
San Juan Hill, 1898
Die „Rough Riders" stürmen den Hügel
von San Juan hinauf
Les «Rough Riders» prennent d'assaut
la colline de San Juan

Relief etchings
From: *McClure's Magazine*, New York, October 1898

After George Luks had reported from Havana in
1895 on the early part of the Cuban struggle for
independence from Spain, William Glackens worked
as a *special artist* in Cuba three years later at the
time the United States intervened to bring about an
end to the war. Both artists were members of the
Ashcan School of painting, and for the progressive
McClure's Magazine Glackens depicted realistic
scenes from the decisive battle for San Juan Hill,
near Santiago.

1895 hatte George Luks aus Havanna vom kubanischen Unabhängigkeitskampf gegen Spanien
berichtet. Mit William Glackens war drei Jahre später
im Verlauf der nordamerikanischen Intervention ein

weiterer Exponent der Ashcan School als *special
artist* in Kuba tätig. Für das progressive Periodikum
McClure's Magazine hielt er Szenen aus der Entscheidungsschlacht um den San-Juan-Hügel bei
Santiago fest.

En 1895, George Luks avait effectué à La Havane
des reportages sur la lutte des Cubains pour l'indépendance contre l'Espagne. Trois ans plus tard,
au cours de l'intervention nord-américaine William
Glackens, lui aussi un représentant de l'Ashcan
School, travaillait à Cuba en tant que *special*. Pour
le périodique progressiste *McClure's Magazine*, il
fixa des scènes de la bataille décisive de la colline
de San Juan près de Santiago.

The Battle of the Jungle.—This Issue Contains a Large Number of Remarkable Photographs of the Recent Bloody Engagements Around Manila.

AWFUL SLAUGHTER OF THE FILIPINOS.

HOW THEIR DEAD BODIES FILLED THE TRENCHES AFTER THE BATTLE OF CALOOCAN.—From a Photograph of the Fearful Scene Taken by "Leslie's Weekly's" Special Correspondent.

Anonymous (photo.)

Awful Slaughter of the Filipinos, 1899
Das schreckliche Massaker an den Filipinos
L'Affreux Massacre des Filipinos
Relief etching
From: *Leslie's Weekly*, New York,
13 April 1899

The American war against the Philippines after the island state had declared its independence was accompanied by a campaign on the home front against the expansionist policies of the emerging world power that was supported in the press by reports of war atrocities. This famous cover photo showing a mass grave owes part of its impact to the excellent work of preparing the image for publication.

Der US-amerikanische Krieg gegen die Philippinen nach der Unabhängigkeitserklärung des Landes war an der Heimatfront von einer Kampagne gegen den Expansionismus der aufsteigenden Weltmacht begleitet, die von Berichten über Kriegsgräuel unterstützt wurde. Das legendäre Titelfoto mit einem Massengrab verdankt seine emblematische Wirkung auch einer hervorragenden pressegrafischen Nachbearbeitung.

La guerre menée par les Étas-Unis contre les Philippines après la déclaration d'indépendance du pays était accompagnée au pays d'une campagne contre l'expansionisme de la puissance mondiale émergente, étayée par des rapports sur les atrocités de guerre. La légendaire photographie en une représentant un charnier doit aussi son effet emblématique à un excellent traitement de l'illustration.

Thomas Nast

⬐ *Hail, Free Cuba!*, 1898
Sei gegrüßt, freies Kuba!
Salut, Cuba libre!
Relief etching
From: *Leslie's Weekly*, New York,
1 December 1898

Thomas Nast's symbolic depiction of Cuba freed from the yoke of Spanish colonial rule was based on a design by his fellow illustrator William Rogers. While Nast had supported Garibaldi, he seems to have had little doubt about the moral legitimacy of the United States intervening in Central and South America, and a few years later he accepted the post of Consul General in the Republic of Ecuador.

Thomas Nasts symbolische Darstellung eines vom spanischen Kolonialjoch befreiten Kuba geht auf eine

Grafik seines Kollegen William Rogers zurück. Als Anhänger Garibaldis hatte er offenbar wenig Zweifel an der moralischen Legitimation der US-Interventionen in Mittel- und Südamerika. Kurze Zeit später nahm Nast einen Posten als Generalkonsul in der Republik Ecuador an.

La représentation symbolique que réalise Thomas Nast de Cuba libéré du joug colonial espagnol repose sur un dessin de son collègue William Rogers. Fervent admirateur de Garibaldi, il avait manifestement peu de doute quant à la légitimation morale de l'intervention des États-Unis en Amérique centrale et en Amérique du Sud. Peu de temps après, Nast accepta d'occuper le poste de consul général dans la République d'Équateur.

The Awful Tale of Starvation and Death at El Caney, Illustrated in This Number.

HAIL, FREE CUBA!
FROM OUR MARTYRED DEAD ARISE LIFE AND LIBERTY TO THE LONG-OPPRESSED ISLE.—By Thomas Nast.

CUBA LIBRE!

12　NEW YORK JOURNAL COLORED SUPPLEMENT, SUNDAY, AUGUST 21, 1898.

CUBA'S DAILY DRAMA

ACT I.—BROUGHT IN WOUNDED FROM THE FIELD.

ACT II.—IN THE HOSPITAL TENT AWAITING AMPUTATION.

ACT III.—IN THE FOLDS OF OLD GLORY HE AWAITS BURIAL.

ACT IV.—"EACH IN HIS NARROW CELL FOREVER LAID!"

THE TRAGEDY OF WAR—EACH ACTOR A HERO.

William Allen Rogers

Henry Brevoort Eddy

← *Free Cuba!*, 1898
Freies Kuba! / Cuba libre !
Relief etching
From: *Harper's Weekly*, New York,
30 April 1898

Cuba's Daily Drama: The Tragedy of War – Each Actor a Hero, 1898
Kubas tägliches Drama. Die Tragödie des Krieges – Jeder Mitwirkende ein Held
Drame quotidien à Cuba. La tragédie de la guerre – Chaque acteur, un héros
Coloured relief etching
From: *New York Journal*,
21 August 1898

The wave of anti-Spanish hysteria that contributed to the American intervention in the Cuban War of Independence was itself fuelled by a circulation war,

between the media moguls William Randolph Hearst and Joseph Pulitzer and their newspapers the *New York Journal* and *New York World*. The vivid yellow from which the American term "yellow journalism" is derived was not restricted to the cartoon pages.

Die antispanische Hysterie, die zur Intervention in den kubanischen Unabhängigkeitskrieg führte, war im Zug eines Auflagenkriegs zwischen den Medienmogulen William Randolph Hearst und Joseph Pulitzer von deren Blättern *New York Journal* und *New York World* geschürt worden. Das

knallige Gelb, das den Begriff des *yellow journalism* prägte, kam nicht nur auf den Comicseiten zum Einsatz.

L'hystérie anti-espagnole qui provoqua l'intervention dans la guerre d'indépendance cubaine avait été attisée dans le contexte d'une guerre de distribution entre les géants médiatiques William Randolph Hearst et Joseph Pulitzer par leurs journaux respectifs *New York Journal* et *New York World*. Le jaune tape-à-l'œil qui engendra la notion de *yellow journalism* ne fut pas seulement utilisé dans les pages de bandes dessinées de manière significative.

←←**Samuel Begg, after Karl August Thiele (photo.)**

The Gladstone Memorial Service in Hyde Park
on Sunday, 5 June, 1898
Die Trauerfeier für Gladstone am Sonntag,
den 5. Juni, im Hyde Park
La Cérémonie funèbre de Gladstone le dimanche
5 juin, à Hyde Park
Relief etching
From: *The Illustrated London News*, 11 June 1898

Samuel Begg was a master at producing illustrations from photographs. Since the quality that could be achieved in reproductions did not approach the soft tonal values of a photograph, *special artists* were increasingly employed to paint high-contrast versions of the photographic originals. These were often classed as independent works and credited to the artist whose name appeared in the signature, as in the present case.

Samuel Begg war ein Meister der Fotomalerei. Da die Reproduktionsqualität den weichen Tonwerten der Fotografie nicht gerecht wurde, waren *special artists* vermehrt damit beschäftigt, kontraststarke Versionen von fotografischen Vorlagen zu malen.

Nicht selten wurden diese, wie hier, durch die Signatur als eigenständige künstlerische Leistungen kenntlich gemacht.

Samuel Begg était un maître de la peinture d'après photo. Comme la qualité de reproduction ne correspondait pas aux douces nuances de ton de la photographie, de plus en plus de *specials* s'employaient à peindre des versions contrastées de modèles photographiques. Celles-ci étaient souvent classées comme œuvres artistiques indépendantes par la signature de l'auteur, comme c'est le cas ici.

Henry Charles Seppings Wright, after Frederic Villiers

The Battle of Omdurman:
The Khalifa's Army Attacking the
Sirdar's Forces at Keriri, 1898
Die Schlacht von Omdurman:
Die Kalifenarmee greift die
Streitkräfte des Sirdar in Keriri an
La Bataille d'Omdurman:
Les armées du calife attaquent les
forces armées du Sirdar à Keriri
Relief etching
From: *The Illustrated London News*,
24 September 1898

Although the Mahdists had been defeated at El-Teb (see ill. p. 422 b.), they had still managed to establish an autonomous caliphate in Sudan with Omdurman as its capital. On 2 September 1898 they suffered a crushing defeat there at the hands of an army of British and Egyptian soldiers led by Major General Kitchener and backed by modern weapons. Frederic Villiers recorded the events from a nearby gunboat, in drawings as well as photographs.

Den Mahdisten war es trotz ihrer Niederlage bei El-Teb (siehe Abb. S. 422 u.) gelungen, im Sudan ein autonomes Kalifat mit Omdurman als Hauptstadt zu errichten. Dort wurden sie am 2. September 1898 von angloägyptischen Truppen unter Major General Kitchener mit moderner Waffentechnik vernichtend geschlagen. Frederic Villiers hielt das Geschehen von einem Kanonenboot aus mit Filmkamera und Zeichenstift fest.

Malgré leur défaite près d'El-Teb (voir ill. p. 422 b.), les mahdistes étaient parvenus à instaurer au Soudan un califat autonome avec Omdurman pour capitale. Le 2 septembre 1898, ils y essuyèrent une cinglante défaite contre des troupes anglo-égyptiennes commandées par le général de division Kitchener et équipées d'une technologie d'armement moderne. Frederic Villiers fixa l'événement depuis une cannonière avec un appareil photo et un crayon à dessin.

Winsor McCay

→ *Confusion*, 1899
Verwirrung | Confusion
Relief etching
From: *Life*, New York, 27 April 1899

The creator of the lavish comic strip *Little Nemo* first appeared in print on a national level with a series of anti-imperialist cartoons for the light-entertainment magazine *Life*. In Winsor McCay's imaginative criticism of the hubris of Western civilisation and the megalomania of the United States, which became recurring themes in his later work (see ills. p. 477), he was continuing in the tradition of Thomas Nast and Albert Robida.

Der Schöpfer des opulenten Comicopus *Little Nemo* trat überregional erstmals mit einer Reihe antiimperialistischer Cartoons für das Humormagazin *Life* in Erscheinung. In seiner fantasiereichen Kritik an der Hybris der westlichen Zivilisation und der US-amerikanischen Megalomanie, die sein weiteres Werk leitmotivisch durchzog (siehe Abb. S. 477), knüpfte Winsor McCay an die Arbeit von Thomas Nast und Albert Robida an.

Le créateur de l'opulente bande dessinée *Little Nemo* fit sa première apparition suprarégionale avec une série de dessins anti-impérialites pour le magazine humoristique *Life*. Dans son imaginative critique de l'hybris de la civilisation et de la mégalomanie américaine qui traversa son œuvre suivante comme un leitmotiv (voir ills. p. 477), Winsor McCay rejoignait les travaux de Thomas Nast et d'Albert Robida.

Le Petit Journal

Le Petit Journal
CHAQUE JOUR 5 CENTIMES

Le Supplément illustré
CHAQUE SEMAINE 5 CENTIMES

SUPPLÉMENT ILLUSTRÉ
Huit pages : CINQ centimes

ABONNEMENTS

	SIX MOIS	UN AN
SEINE ET SEINE-ET-OISE	2 fr.	3 fr. 50
DÉPARTEMENTS	2 fr.	4 fr.
ÉTRANGER	2 50	5 fr.

Dixième année   DIMANCHE 1ᵉʳ JANVIER 1899   Numéro 424

Epouvantable accident rue des Apennins

Carrey & Fortuné Méaulle (sc.)

Terrible Accident, Rue des Apennins, 1899
Schreckliches Unglück | Épouvantable accident
Coloured relief etching
From: *Le Petit Journal*, Paris, 1 January 1899

"In Bordeaux a gas explosion occurred at the Larrieu family house. He was injured. His mother-in-law's hair caught fire. The ceiling fell in."

„Gasexplosion bei Larrieu aus Bordeaux. Er wurde verletzt. Das Haar seiner Schwiegermutter stand in Fammen. Die Decke brach ein."

«Une explosion de gaz chez les Larrieu à Bordeaux. Il fut blessé. Les cheveux de sa belle-mère flambèrent. La plafond creva.»

From: Félix Fénéon, *Nouvelles en trois lignes*, no. 151, *Le Matin*, 1906

384   Supplément illustré du Petit Journal

DÉRAILLEMENT DU SUD-EXPRESS
Le wagon-restaurant

Anonymous

Express to the South Derailed, 1900
Entgleisung des Sud-Express
Déraillement du Sud-Express
Coloured relief etching
From: *Le Petit Journal*, Paris, 2 December 1900

"Two toddlers from Nangis (Seine-et-Marne), Fassiot and Valot, were playing and put some logs on the line: a train was derailed."

„Die Jungen Fassiot und Valot aus Nangis (Seine-et-Marne) hatten Baumstämme auf die Schienen gelegt: Ein Zug entgleiste."

«Les bambins Fassiot et Valot, de Nangis (Seine-et-Marne) avaient gaiement mis des troncs sur les rails : un train marchand dérailla.»

From: Félix Fénéon, *Nouvelles en trois lignes*, no. 573, *Le Matin*, 1906

Anonymous

Hot-air Balloon Tethered at Porte Maillot Carried off by a Storm: The Landing in the Rue du Parc, Clichy, 1904
Fesselballon an der Porte Maillot vom Sturm fortgerissen. Landung in Clichy, Rue du Parc
Le Ballon captif de la Porte Maillot emporté par la tempête. L'atterrissage à Clichy, rue du Parc
Relief etching
From: *L'Illustration*, Paris, 30 July 1904

During a storm at an airfield near Paris a hot-air balloon broke free of its moorings and was carried away with nine people still in its basket. The moment when it later crash-landed was reconstructed by an editorial illustrator using a sketch made by an eye witness to the event and also statements from those who had been on board. The resulting illustration was then approved by the balloon's usual pilot.

Auf einem Pariser Flugplatz hatte sich während eines Sturms ein Fesselballon losgerissen und war mit neun Passagieren an Bord davongeflogen. Aufgrund einer Augenzeugenskizze und der Aussagen der Passagiere wurde der Moment der Bruchlandung von einem Redaktionszeichner rekonstruiert. Das pressegrafische Resultat wurde schließlich vom Piloten des Ballons zertifiziert.

Sur un aérodrome parisien un ballon captif s'était détaché pendant une tempête et s'était envolé avec neuf passagers à bord. Un dessinateur de rédaction reconstruisit le moment de l'atterrissage forcé à l'aide de dessins de témoins et de témoignages des passagers. Le résultat graphique fut finalement certifié par le pilote du ballon.

Henri Meyer

Disaster at Halle: A Hot-air Balloon Explodes, 1895
Die Katastrophe von Halle – Explosion eines Ballons
La Catastrophe de Hal – Explosion d'un ballon
Coloured relief etching
From: *Le Petit Journal*, 29 September 1895

→ *Suicide at the Arc de Triomphe*, 1898
Ein Freitod am Triumphbogen
Un suicide à l'Arc de Triomphe
Relief etching
From: *Le Petit Journal*, Paris, 8 May 1898

Henri Meyer's brilliant work in press illustration ranged from political caricatures and fantastic illustrations to photographic reproductions and designs to accompany the "Miscellaneous Items" news sections. In this instance, reports of a balloon accident near the Belgian city of Halle inspired him to create an unusual composition in which, as was typical in the popular press, the element of horror was the main focus.

Das pressegrafische Spektrum des brillanten Henri Meyer reichte von der politischen Karikatur über Fantasy-Illustrationen bis zur Fotografik und der „Faits divers"-Malerei. Hier hatte

ihn die Meldung eines Flugunglücks in der belgischen Stadt Halle zu einer bizarren Komposition angeregt, bei der, wie im boulevardesken Genre üblich, das Grauen im Vordergrund zu stehen hatte.

La palette de dessins de presse du brillant Henri Meyer allait de la caricature politique à la photo graphique et à la peinture de faits divers en passant par les illustrations fantastiques. Ici, l'annonce d'un accident aérien dans la ville belge de Hal lui inspira une composition étrange, dans laquelle l'horreur devait être au premier plan, comme il était courant dans le genre populaire.

UN SUICIDE A L'ARC DE TRIOMPHE

Journal des Voyages

ET DES AVENTURES DE TERRE ET DE MER

(SUR TERRE ET SUR MER; MONDE PITTORESQUE; TERRE ILLUSTRÉE réunis)

DIMANCHE 19 JANVIER 1902.

Journal hebdomadaire. ⚓ ABONNEMENTS : UN AN : PARIS, SEINE ET SEINE-&-OISE, 8 fr. — DÉPARTEMENTS, 10 fr. — UNION POSTALE, 12 fr. ⚓ *rue Saint-Joseph, 12, Paris, 2e.*

| Nº 268 2e SÉRIE | LA FIN DU MONDE | LE DÉLUGE DE GLACE | PAR VICTOR FORBIN | PRIX 15 c. |

Au premier choc de l'avalanche, l'orgueilleuse Tour de trois cents mètres s'écroulera comme un château de cartes. (P. 131, col. 3.)

Nº 268. *(Deuxième série.)*   Nº 1280 *de la collection.*

Louis Tinayre

The End of the World – Engulfed by Ice, by Victor Forbin, 1902
Das Ende der Welt – Der Eishagel, von Victor Forbin
La Fin du monde – Le déluge de glace par Victor Forbin
Wood engraving
From: *Journal des Voyages*, Paris, 19 January 1902

Carrey & Fortuné Méaulle (sc.)

Disaster in Nesdal (Norway)
A Cliff Collapses – Dozens Dead, 1906
Die Katastrophe von Nesdal (Norwegen)
Eine Felswand bricht ab – Zahlreiche Opfer
La Catastrophe de Nesdal (Norvège)
Une falaise qui s'écroule – Nombreuses victimes
Coloured relief etching
From: *Le Petit Parisien*, 5 February 1906

48   Supplément Littéraire Illustré du " Petit Parisien "

La Catastrophe de Nesdal (Norvège)
UNE FALAISE QUI S'ÉCROULE. — NOMBREUSES VICTIMES

JOURNAL DES VOYAGES

LA VALLÉE DE YOSEMITI

Sur cette plate-forme les excursionnistes qui ne sont pas sujets au vertige dominent la vallée de Yosemiti. (P. 311, col. 3.)

Anonymous

Yosemite Valley, 1902
Das Yosemite-Tal | La Vallée de Yosemiti
Wood engraving
From: *Journal des Voyages*, Paris,
28 September 1902

Vittorio Sella (photo.)

*In the Bernese Oberland – The Aletsch Glacier,
the Largest in Europe*, 1904
*Im Berner Oberland – Der Aletschgletscher,
der größte Europas*
*Dans l'Oberland bernois – Le glacier d'Aletsch,
le plus grand d'Europe*
Coloured relief etching
From: *L'Illustration*, Paris, 20 August 1904

(Phot. V. Sella).

DANS L'OBERLAND BERNOIS. — Le glacier d'Aletsch, le plus grand d'Europe.

Le glacier d'Aletsch, le plus grand des Alpes, prend naissance sur le versant sud-est de la Jungfrau, à environ 3.000 mètres d'altitude. Par une coulée gigantesque d'une vingtaine de kilomètres, il vient finir, à 1.700 mètres, dans la chaîne qui borde la haute vallée du Rhône. Sa largeur moyenne atteint 2 kilomètres.

La partie supérieure forme, avec les glaciers convergents, un immense bassin circonscrit par les trois géants des Alpes bernoises (Finsteraarhorn, 4.275 mètres ; Aletschhorn, 4.182 mètres ; Jungfrau, 4.167 mètres) et présentant un rond-point central, nommé *Place de la Concorde*, où l'on peut, des fenêtres d'un hôtel accroché à un rocher perdu dans cette masse de glace, s'offrir un des plus étonnants réveils que nous ménagent les Alpes. L'accès est facile, car les régions mouvementées comme celle que montre notre gravure alternent avec des surfaces très plates.

Osvaldo Tofani

The Adventures of a Carriage Horse, 1896
Abenteuer eines Droschkenpferdes | Les Exploits d'un cheval de fiacre
Coloured relief etching
From: *Le Petit Journal*, Paris, 9 February 1896

"A pair of horses galloped off through Versailles. Sergeant Michaud of the 27th Dragoons attempted to stop them. His skull was fractured."

„Zwei Pferde galoppierten durch Versailles. Unteroffizier Michaud vom 27. Dragoner-Regiment wollte sie aufhalten. Er erlitt einen Schädelbruch."

«Deux chevaux traversent Versailles au galop. Le sous-officier Michaud du 27e régiment de dragons voulait les arrêter. Il subit une fracture du crâne.»

From: Félix Fénéon, *Nouvelles en trois lignes*, no. 738, *Le Matin*, 1906

Henri Meyer

A Terrible Kicking, 1898
Schreckliches Auskeilen | Terrible ruade
Coloured relief etching
From: *Le Petit Journal*, Paris, 3 July 1898

Georges Scott

An Accident on the Elevated Railroad in New York, 1905
Unfall der New Yorker Hochbahn
L'Accident de l'«elevated» métropolitain aérien de New York
Relief etching
From: *L'Illustration*, Paris, 23 September 1905

The press photo of an accident on the elevated railroad in Manhattan that was used for this complex illustration, with its several points of focus, showed only the derailed carriages. The part at the bottom where the medical teams and bystanders can be seen is an added extra. Georges Scott's talent for dramatising the pictorial space was particularly evident in his reports from the front during the First World War.

Das Pressefoto eines Hochbahnunglücks in Manhattan, das dieser polyfokalen Montagemalerei zugrunde liegt, gibt nur die Situation der derangierten Züge wieder. Der untere Bereich mit den Sanitätern und die Zuschauer am Bildrand wurden hinzugefügt. Georges Scotts Begabung für die Dramatisierung von Räumen kam vor allem in seinen Frontberichten des Ersten Weltkriegs zum Tragen.

La photo de presse d'un accident du métro aérien à Manhattan qui servit de modèle à cette scène de montage polyfocale ne représente que la situation des trains déraillés. La partie inférieure où apparaissent les ambulanciers et les badauds au bord de l'image est un rajout. Le penchant de Georges Scott à la dramatisation d'espaces était particulièrement évident dans ses rapports du front de la Première Guerre mondiale.

Carrey

New York
Accident on the Elevated Railroad, 1905
Unfall der Hochbahn
Accident sur le Chemin de fer aérien
Coloured relief etching
From: *Le Petit Parisien*, 1 October 1905
Private collection

In his depiction of this accident on the elevated railroad in New York the press illustrator for *Le Petit Parisien* strayed noticeably further from the original documentary material than his fellow artist at *L'Illustration* (see ill. p. 456).

Weit mehr als sein Kollege von *L'Illustration* entfernte sich der Grafiker des *Le Petit Parisien* bei der Visualisierung des New Yorker Hochbahnunglücks von dem zugrunde liegenden Dokumentationsmaterial (siehe Abb. S. 456).

Dans sa visualisation de l'accident du métro aérien de New York, le dessinateur du *Petit Parisien* s'est nettement plus éloigné du matériel de documentation que son collègue de *L'Illustration* (voir ill. p. 456).

320   Supplément Littéraire Illustré du " Petit Parisien "

A NEW-YORK
Accident sur le Chemin de fer aérien. — Un Train qui tombe dans la rue. Nombreuses Victimes

№ 416   Supplément illustré du Petit Journal

CRIME DU KREMLIN-BICÊTRE
Le cadavre brûlé (Scène reconstituée d'après les aveux de l'assassin)

Henri Meyer

A Crime in Le Kremlin-Bicêtre, 1897
Verbrechen von Kremlin-Bicêtre | Crime du Kremlin-Bicêtre
Coloured relief etching
From: *Le Petit Journal*, Paris, 26 December 1897

Anonymous

L'APACHE EST LA PLAIE DE PARIS
Plus de 30,000 rôdeurs contre 8,000 sergents de ville

↓ *The Apache Way: Horrific Revenge against a Night-prowler*, 1907
Sitten der Apachen. Schreckliche Rache an einem Herumtreiber
Mœurs d'Apaches. Atroce vengeance sur un rôdeur
Coloured relief etching
From: *Le Petit Journal*, Paris, 19 May 1907

← *The Apaches – the Plague of Paris*,
1907 | *Der Apache ist die Wunde von
Paris* | *L'Apache est la plaie de Paris*
Coloured relief etching
From: *Le Petit Journal*, Paris,
20 October 1907

Paris in the grip of Apaches! There
were 30,000 of these violent young
criminals, and only 8,000 police
officers. The street gangs and their
culture had been a noted phenomenon in the press since 1904, where
they appeared with provocative
expressions and a dress code that
resembled the clothes worn by London costermongers (see ill. p. 185 t. l.).
As "savages" in Paris they can also
be seen as forerunners of the wider
culture of hooligans and rockers,
amongst others.

Paris in den Händen der Apaches!
30 000 jugendlichen Kriminellen stün-
den nur 8000 Polizisten gegenüber.
Seit 1904 machte das Phänomen der
Kultur der Straßengangs Furore, die
mit provokanten Ausdrucksformen und
einem Dresscode auftraten, der an die
Londoner Costermonger angelehnt
war (siehe Abb. S. 185 o. l.). Die Pariser
„Wilden" waren Vorreiter der Halbstar-
ken- und Rockerkultur.

Paris aux mains des Apaches! Seulement 8 000 policiers affrontaient
30 000 jeunes délinquants. À partir
de 1904, le phénomène d'une culture
de bandes de rue faisait fureur. Ils
apparaissaient avec des formes d'expression provocantes et un code
vestimentaire inspiré des marchands
de quatre-saisons de Londres (voir ill.
p. 185 h. g.). Les «sauvages» parisiens furent les précurseurs de la
culture de voyous et de rockers.

↓ *How They Treat Apaches Abroad:
"Hard Labour" and the "Cat-o'-Nine-
Tails" in England*, 1907
*Wie man mit den Apachen im Ausland
umgeht. Die „hard labour" und die
„neunschwänzige Katze" in England*
*Comment on traite les Apaches à
l'étranger. Le «hard labour» et le «chat
à neuf queues» en Angleterre*
Coloured relief etching
From: *Le Petit Journal*, Paris,
3 November 1907

The press campaign against the
Apaches gained momentum quickly
amidst criticism that the lax French
penal system was incapable of dealing with the problem of juvenile delin-
quency on such an epidemic scale.
The solution recommended in the
press was to adopt the British system,
setting offenders to hard labour on
treadmills and whipping those who
were unrepentant.

Die Pressekampagne gegen die
Apaches kam in Fahrt: Der laxe französische Strafvollzug werde des
Problems epidemischer Jugendkrimi-
nalität nicht Herr, hieß es. Als Antidot
empfahl man das britische System
mit harter Zwangsarbeit an den Tret-
mühlen und der Auspeitschung von
Unverbesserlichen.

La campagne de presse contre les
Apaches prit de l'ampleur : le système pénitentiaire français laxiste
ne maîtrisait soi-disant pas la délin-
quance juvénile. Comme antidote,
il était recommandé de suivre le système britannique prônant les épuis-
sants travaux forcés et la flagellation
des irréductibles.

MŒURS D'APACHES
Atroce vengeance d'un rôdeur

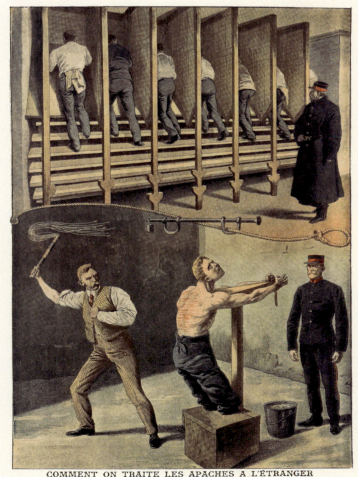

COMMENT ON TRAITE LES APACHES A L'ÉTRANGER
Le « hard labour » et le « chat à neuf queues » en Angleterre

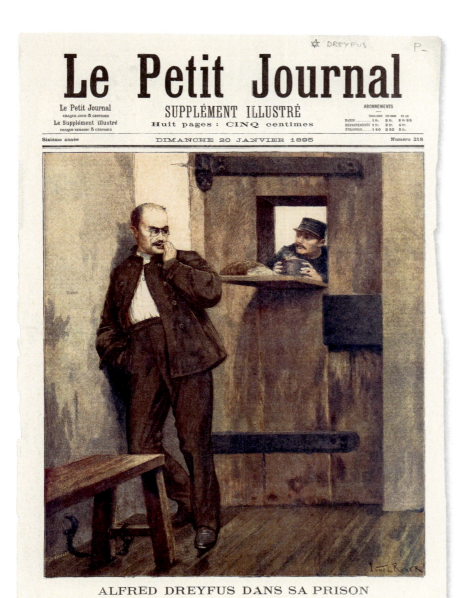

ALFRED DREYFUS DANS SA PRISON

Lionel Royer & Fortuné Méaulle (sc.)

Alfred Dreyfus in His Cell, 1895
Alfred Dreyfus im Gefängnis
Alfred Dreyfus dans sa prison
Wood engraving
From: *Le Petit Journal*, Paris, 20 January 1895

The Jewish army officer Alfred Dreyfus was sentenced in 1894 to life imprisonment for treason, and *Le Petit Journal* had played a prominent part in the anti-Semitic campaign that had pushed the Ministry of War to conduct a hasty trial despite the lack of clear evidence. In his illustration Lionel Royer gave the imprisoned Dreyfus grotesque and almost devilish features, as his hair seems to suggest two horns.

Der jüdische Offizier Alfred Dreyfus war 1894 wegen Landesverrats zu lebenslanger Haft verurteilt worden. *Le Petit Journal* hatte sich bei der antisemitischen Kampagne hervorgetan, die das Kriegsministerium trotz zweifelhafter Beweislage zu einem übereilten Verfahren gedrängt hatte. Lionel Royer verlieh dem Häftling durch die hörnerartigen Haarpartien geradezu groteske luziferische Züge.

En 1894, l'officier juif Alfred Dreyfus avait été condamné à la prison à perpétuité pour haute trahison. *Le Petit Journal* s'était particulièrement distingué dans la campagne antisémite qui avait poussé le ministère de la Guerre à un procès précipité malgré des éléments de preuve douteux. Lionel Royer affubla le prisonnier de traits grotesques et diaboliques par des mèches de cheveux ressemblant à des cornes.

Melton Prior

The Dreyfus Trial at Rennes: Scene in the Courtyard of the Lycée at 10 a.m., 1899
Der Dreyfus-Prozess in Rennes: Szene im Hof des Lycée um 10 Uhr morgens
Le Procès de Dreyfus à Rennes: scène dans la cour du lycée à 10 heures du matin
Relief etching
From: *The Illustrated London News*, 26 August 1899

After evidence showing that Dreyfus was innocent was made public, and following Émile Zola's intervention in the case and the social and political earthquake it precipitated throughout France, the retrial became an international media spectacle (see ills. pp. 538, 539 t.). Melton Prior was one of the accredited picture reporters, and filed illustrations of the trial as well as the general setting.

Nachdem Beweise für Dreyfus' Unschuld publik geworden waren und Émile Zola mit seiner Intervention ein gesellschaftliches und politisches Erdbeben in Frankreich ausgelöst hatte, geriet die Wiederaufnahme des Verfahrens zu einem internationalen Medienspektakel (siehe Abb. S. 538, 539 o.). Zu den akkreditierten Bildreportern zählte Melton Prior. Er zeichnete sowohl den Prozess als auch das Umfeld.

Après que les preuves de l'innocence de Dreyfus avaient été rendues publiques et qu'Émile Zola avait provoqué un séisme sociétal et politique en France, la révision du procès se transforma en un spectacle médiatique international (voir ills. p. 538, 539 h.). Melton Prior faisait partie des reporters illustrateurs accrédités. Il fit des esquisses du procès, mais aussi du décor alentour.

THE ILLUSTRATED LONDON NEWS, Aug. 26, 1899.—272

THE DREYFUS TRIAL AT RENNES: SCENE IN THE COURTYARD OF THE LYCÉE AT 10 A.M. WHEN THE COURT RISES FOR A REST.
Facsimile of a Sketch by our Special Artist, Melton Prior.

M. le greffier Coupois lisant l'arrêt de la Cour de cassation. Au fond, le colonel Jouaust, président du Conseil de guerre.   Généraux Billot, Mercier et Zurlinden.   M. Hanotaux.

AFFAIRE DREYFUS A RENNES. — La première audience du conseil de guerre. [Dessin d'après nature de notre collaborateur M. Sabattier.] — Voir l'article, page 59

Louis Sabattier & Albert Bellenger (sc.)

↑ *The Dreyfus Affair at Rennes – The First Hearing*
of the Council of War, 1899
Die Dreyfus-Affäre in Rennes – Die erste Anhörung
des Kriegsrats
Affaire Dreyfus à Rennes – La première audience
du conseil de guerre
Wood engraving
From: *L'Illustration*, Paris, 12 August 1899

Louis Sabattier's illustration captures the tense
atmosphere of this trial of the century with extraordinary subtlety. The visual tour of the courtroom,
assembled from details observed separately, also
suggests the results achieved by the rival forms
of media, photography and cinema.

Louis Sabattiers Zeichnung gibt die angespannte
Atmosphäre dieses Jahrhundertprozesses auf außerordentlich subtile Weise wieder. Die aus pointierten
Einzelbeobachtungen montierte grafische Fahrt
durch den Gerichtssaal vergegenwärtigt auch eine
mediale Konkurrenz durch Fotografie und Film.

Le dessin de Louis Sabattier rend l'atmosphère
tendue de ce procès du siècle de manière extraordinairement subtile. Le travelling graphique à
travers la salle d'audience, résultat d'observations
isolées et tranchantes, rend aussi palpable la
concurrence médiatique de la photographie et
du cinéma.

Gerschel (photo.)

The Judges and Defence Examine Alphonse
Bertillon's Dossier, 1899
Richter und Verteidigung prüfen die Unterlagen
von Monsieur Alphonse Bertillon
Les juges et la défense examinant le dossier
de M. Alphonse Bertillon
Relief etching
From: Louis Rogès, *Cinq semaines à Rennes.*
Deux cents photographies de Gerschel, Paris, 1899

Although cameras were not permitted in the courtroom, Gerschel succeeded in taking photographs of
several different phases of the trial with the aid of a
small camera he had managed to smuggle in. While
the hearing was still under way, the Dreyfus affair
became the subject of the first documentary drama
series, filmed by Georges Méliès.

Obgleich im Gerichtssaal keine Kameras erlaubt
waren, gelang es dem Fotografen Gerschel, verschiedene Phasen des Prozesses mit einer ein-
geschmuggelten Kleinkamera abzulichten. Der
Fall Dreyfus wurde noch während der Verhand-
lungen zum Gegenstand eines ersten filmischen
Dokudramas von Georges Méliès.

Bien que les caméras ne fussent pas autorisées
dans la salle d'audience, le photographe Gerschel
parvint à photographier diverses phases du procès à l'aide d'un petit appareil photo dissimulé. Au
cours même de l'audience, l'affaire Dreyfus devint
l'objet du premier drame documentaire, filmé par
Georges Méliès.

Paul Renouard

10   SPECIAL NUMBER OF THE GRAPHIC   SEPTEMBER 14, 1899

MAITRE LABORI
(M. Zola's Counsel)

M. ZOLA

M. CLÉMENCEAU

THE TRIAL OF M. ZOLA IN THE ASSIZE COURT, PARIS

The Trial of M. Zola in the Assize Court, Paris, 1899
*Der Prozess gegen Monsieur Zola im Schwur-
gericht, Paris*
Le Procès de M. Zola à la cour d'assises, Paris
Relief etching
From: *The Graphic* (special number), London,
14 September 1899

After the case against Dreyfus had been reviewed
Émile Zola was put on trial and charged with libel for
his open letter *J'Accuse…!*, in which he condemned
the first Dreyfus trial as a deliberate miscarriage
of justice. The three main protagonists appear here
combined to symbolise the proceedings: Zola's
lawyer, Fernand Labori, Zola himself and behind him
Georges Clemenceau, who had published Zola's
letter on the front page of the newspaper he owned,
L'Aurore.

Auf die Dreyfus-Revision folgte das Verfahren
gegen Émile Zola, der wegen seines offenen Briefes
J'accuse…!, in dem er die Verurteilung als Justiz-
irrtum und Intrige angeprangert hatte, der Verleum-
dung angeklagt war. Auf ikonische Weise sind hier
die drei Hauptprotagonisten vereint: Zolas Anwalt
Fernand Labori, Zola selbst und im Hintergrund
Georges Clemenceau, der den Brief Zolas auf der
Titelseite seiner Zeitung *L'Aurore* abdruckte.

La révision de l'affaire Dreyfus fut suivie du procès
atté à Émile Zola, accusé de calomnie pour sa
lettre ouverte *J'accuse…!* dans laquelle il dénonçait
la condamnation comme une erreur de justice et
une intrigue. Comme sur une icône, les trois protagonistes sont ici réunis : Fernand Labori, l'avocat
de Zola, Zola lui-même et, en arrière-plan, Georges
Clemenceau, qui publia la lettre de Zola dans son
journal *L'Aurore*.

The Lawyer Labori II, 1899/1905
Rechtsanwalt Labori II | Maître Labori II
Etchings with drypoint
From: Paul Renouard, *Mouvements, gestes,
expressions*, Paris, 1905

Paul Renouard made a number of sketches of Émi e
Zola's charismatic lawyer as he pleaded his case
at various different stages during the trial, and
later included some of these illustrations in a monumental portfolio he published that documented
his 20-year interest in sequential movement. He
had been inspired to undertake this work, entirely
on his own, by Hokusai's collection of *Manga*
sketches (ill. p. 53 b.).

Paul Renouard hatte das Plädoyer von Émile Zolas
charismatischem Anwalt in verschiedenen Phasen
festgehalten und in ein monumentales Mappenwerk aufgenommen, das sein seit über 20 Jahren
anhaltendes Interesse an sequenziellen Abläufen
dokumentierte. Inspiriert zu dem solitären Unternehmen hatte ihn Katsushika Hokusais *Manga*-
Opus (Abb. S. 53 u.).

Paul Renouard avait consigné le plaidoyer du cha-
rismatique avocat d'Émile Zola dans ses phases
diverses et l'avait archivé dans un monumental port-
folic, qui documentait l'intérêt qu'il porta pendant
plus de vingt ans aux processus séquentiels. L'œuvre
de Katsushika Hokusai *La Manga* l'avait inspiré pour
réaliser cette entreprise solitaire (ill. p. 53 b.).

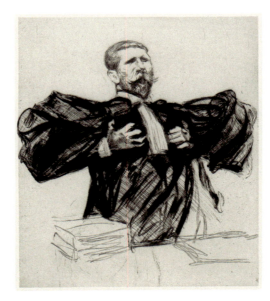

L'AFRIQUE CENTRALE ACCESSIBLE AUX TOURISTES. — Les passagers de l'« Abbas-Pacha » visitant un village de Shilouks sur la rivière Sobat, qui se jette dans le Nil Blanc près de Fachoda.
D'après les photographies de M. de Guerville. — Voir son article à la page 442.

Louis Sabattier, after Amédée Baillot de Guerville (photo.)

Central Africa Opens up to Tourists, 1905
Zentralafrika für Touristen zugänglich
L'Afrique centrale accessible aux touristes
Relief etching
From: *L'Illustration,* Paris, 30 December 1905

A group of English tourists is shown here visiting a Shilluk settlement in southern Sudan near Fashoda (now Kodok), a name that would have been familiar to French readers since it had been the site of a recent international incident following a colonial and territorial dispute between France and Britain. Louis Sabattier interpreted the glib promise of geographical access in the title with an illustration depicting the evident sense of mutual alienation.

Eine Gruppe englischer Touristen besucht eine Siedlung der Schilluk, die sich im Südsudan unweit von Faschoda (heute: Kodok) befand. Der Ort war französischen Leser bekannt, denn hier war es erst kurz zuvor zu einem internationalen Zwischenfall

gekommen, dem ein kolonialer und territorialer Konflikt zwischen England und Frankreich folgte. Der geografischen Erreichbarkeit, die der Titel versprach, entgegnete Louis Sabattier mit einer pointierten Darstellung bilateraler Fremdheit.

Un groupe de touristes anglais chez les Shilluk. La colonie située au sud du Soudan se trouvait près de Fachoda (l'actuel Kodok), bien connu des lecteurs français. À cet endroit même, peu auparavant, un incident international était survenu et avait entraîné un conflit territorial et colonial entre l'Angleterre et la France.. Louis Sabattier opposa à l'accessibilité géographique que le titre promettait une représentation acerbe de l'étrangeté bilatérale.

→→ Louis Sabattier

The World's Fair – Performers from Eastern Theatre Troupes Arriving at the Trocadéro, 1900
Weltausstellung – Die orientalischen Theaterkünstler begeben sich zum Trocadéro
Exposition universelle – Les artistes des théâtres orientaux se rendant au Trocadéro
Coloured relief etching
From: *L'Illustration*, Paris, 1 September 1900

The soft-focus effect in Louis Sabattier's paintings from photographs often also conveyed ambiguous messages of cultural criticism. This scene from the World's Fair held in Paris in 1900, for example, can be interpreted as a criticism of the Eurocentric perspective inherent in the Orientalist painting tradition of Sabattier's teachers Jean-Léon Gérôme and Gustave Boulanger.

Die weichgezeichneten Fotomalereien von Louis Sabattier transportierten nicht selten doppelbödige kulturkritische Inhalte. Die Szene aus dem Umfeld der Pariser Weltausstellung kann als Kritik an der

eurozentrischen Perspektive der orientalistischen Malereitradition seiner Lehrer Jean-Léon Gérôme und Gustave Boulanger gelesen werden.

Les photos peintures en flou artistique de Louis Sabattier transportaient souvent des messages ambigus de critique culturelle. La scène représentant les alentours de l'Exposition universelle de Paris peut être interprétée comme une critique à la perspective eurocentrique de la peinture orientaliste de ses professeurs Jean-Léon Gérôme et Gustave Boulanger.

EXPOSITION UNIVERSELLE. — Les artistes d

héâtres orientaux se rendant au Trocadéro.

František Kupka

↓ *The Mysteries of the Building Work on the Paris Métro*, 1905
Die Geheimnisse des Pariser Metrobaus
Les Mystères de la construction du métropolitain
Relief etching
From: *L'Illustration*, Paris, 25 November 1905

The esoteric aspect of František Kupka's art was apparent even in his illustrations for the satirical press, but it also played a significant part in his documentary work for *L'Illustration* and the *Berliner Illustrirte Zeitung*. In the building work for the tunnels of the Paris Métro he sensed the presence of atavistic earth forces at a depth of eight metres below the Seine, in a world that belonged to Cyclopes and Nibelungs.

Die esoterische Dimension von František Kupkas Kunst war in seinen Arbeiten für die satirische Presse offensichtlich. Sie spielte allerdings auch in seinen dokumentarischen Grafiken für *L'Illustration* und die *Berliner Illustrirte Zeitung* eine Rolle. Bei den Tunnelarbeiten für die Pariser Metro spürte er acht Meter unter der Seine atavistische Erdkräfte am Werk, eine Welt der Zyklopen und Nibelungen.

La dimension ésotérique de l'art de František Kupka était manifeste dans ses travaux pour la presse satirique. Toutefois, elle jouait aussi un grand rôle dans ses dessins documentaires pour *L'Illustration* et la *Berliner Illustrirte Zeitung*. Dans les chantiers souterrains du métro parisien à huit mètres au-dessous de la Seine, il sentait vibrer les forces ataviques de la terre, un monde de cyclopes et de Nibelungen.

Emil Limmer

→ *Foundry at the Ückingen Steelworks*, 1901
Gießhalle in den Ückinger Werken
Salle de fonderie dans les aciéries d'Uckange
Coloured relief etching
From: *Illustrirte Zeitung*, Leipzig, 11 April 1901

↘ *Rolling Mill*, 1901
Blockwalzwerk | *Laminoir dégrossisseur*
Coloured relief etching
From: *Illustrirte Zeitung*, Leipzig, 11 April 1901

To mark the occasion of the death of Carl Ferdinand von Stumm-Halberg, the German industrialist and influential politician, the *Illustrirte Zeitung* published a special issue about the Stumm family's long-established Saarland mining business together with coloured views of men at work in the company's ironworks at Neunkirchen and the blast furnaces at Ückingen.

Anlässlich des Todes des politisch äußerst einflussreichen deutschen Großindustriellen Carl Ferdinand von Stumm-Halberg widmete die *Illustrirte Zeitung* dem traditionsreichen saarländischen Montanunternehmen der Familie Stumm eine Sondernummer mit kolorierten Einblicken in die Arbeitswelten des Eisenwerks in Neunkirchen und der Hochofenanlage in Ückingen.

À l'occasion du décès de Carl Ferdinand von Stumm-Halberg, un grand industriel allemand extrêmement influent en politique, l'*Ilustrirte Zeitung* consacra à l'entreprise minière traditionnelle de la famille Stumm en Sarre un numéro exceptionnel enrichi de vues en couleurs dans le monde du travail de l'usine sidérurgique à Neunkirchen et les hauts fourneaux d'Uckange.

LES MYSTÈRES DE LA CONSTRUCTION DU MÉTROPOLITAIN : LE CHANTIER SOUS LA SEINE, EN AMONT DU PONT AU CHANGE

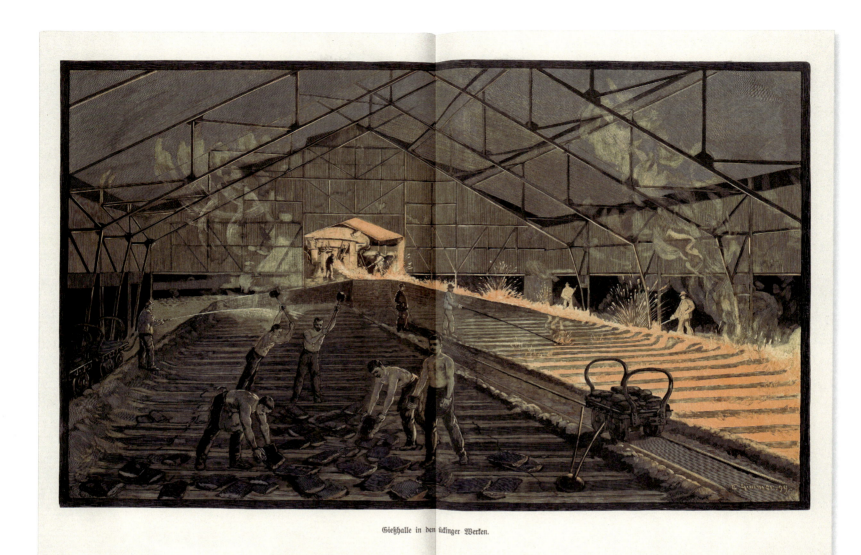

Gießhalle in den Rückinger Werken.

Blockwalzwerk.

Anonymous (photo.)

→ *A German Machinist*, 1907
Deutscher Maschinenarbeiter
Ouvrier sur machine allemand
Colour-tinted wood engraving
From: *Nimm mich mit*, no. 7,
Berlin, 1907

→→ *A German Blacksmith*, 1906
Ein deutscher Schmied
Un forgeron allemand
Colour-tinted wood engraving
From: *Nimm mich mit,* no. 18,
Berlin, 1906

The liberal socialist weekly *Nimm mich mit* was the main periodical in Germany for "Miscellaneous Items" news features. The series of workers' portraits it published in support of the workers' movement are excellent examples of early photographic studies of the subject, which would later be picked up in earnest by photographers associated with the New Objectivity movement in the 1920s, such as August Sander.

Das sozialliberale Wochenblatt *Nimm mich mit* war die führende deutsche „Faits divers"-Illustrierte. Bei der Porträte he, die sie zur Unterstützung der Gewerkschaftsbewegung publizierte, handelte es sich um hervorragende Beispiele einer frühen Arbeiterfotografie, an die in den 1920er-Jahren Exponenten der Neuen Sachlichkeit wie August Sander anküpfen konnten.

L'hebdomadaire socio-libéral *Nimm mich mit* était le magazine illustré allemand le plus important dans le domaine des faits divers. La série de portraits qu'il publia en soutien au mouvement syndical présentait des exemples exceptionnels de la photographie ouvrière à ses débuts, à laquelle les exposants de la Nouvelle Objectivité comme August Sander purent se référer dans les années 1920.

No. 18.   II. Jahrg. 1906.

Nimm mich mit

Ein buntes Blatt   für 5 Pfennig   für Alle und Alles

„Nimm mich mit" kann durch alle Buch= und Zeitschriftenhandlungen, Kol= porteure u. durch die Post bezogen werden.

Einzelpreis 5 Pfge., frei ins Haus ge= liefert 6 Pfge. — pro Quartal (13 Nr.) 65 Pfge., Bestellgeld 12 Pfge.

Ein deutscher Schmied.

Der Zentralverband der Schmiede wird die nächste außerordentliche Generalversammlung in Berlin abhalten. Dann wird man im Berliner Gewerkschaftshause Hunderte der pracht= vollsten Arbeitergestalten sehen können. Eine wahre Augenweide, ein kerndeutscher Arbeitertypus ist der märkische Schmied, den wir nach einer Photographie im ol igen Bilde bringen.

Louis Sabattier

← Automobile Life – the "Breakdown", 1904
Das automobile Leben – Die „Panne"
La Vie automobile – La «Panne»
Relief etching
From: *L'Illustration*, Paris, 17 August 1904

Turning to post-Orientalist subjects, Louis Sabattier regularly found an exotic appeal in the early years of motorised transport. In this example, a car has broken down and the incident has led to a confrontation between the gentleman driver and his passengers, in their protective clothing, and the lower-class peasantry standing around with a sense of suspicion. Indeed, in rural areas at this time it was not uncommon for motorists to be jeered at or even physically attacked.

Wiederholt beschäftigte sich der Postorientalist Louis Sabattier mit der Exotik des frühen Automobilverkehrs. Eine Panne führt zur Konfrontation der in Schutzkleidung gehüllten Kaste bourgoiser Herrenfahrer mit einer argwöhnischen bäuerlichen Ethnie. Im ländlichen Raum waren Proteste und tätliche Übergriffe auf die Automobilisten keine Seltenheit.

Une fois de plus, le post-orientaliste Louis Sabattier tourne son attention vers l'exotisme de la circulation automobile à ses tout débuts. Une panne provoque la confrontation entre la classe de conducteurs bourgeois portant des vêtements de protection et la classe de paysans pour le moins méfiants. Dans les régions rurales, protestations et attaques physiques étaient plutôt fréquentes.

Samuel Begg, after G.H. Jones (photo.)

The Duke and Duchess of York at the Dinorwic Slate Quarries, Carnarvonshire, 1899
Der Herzog und die Herzogin von York im Schiefersteinbruch von Dinorwic, Carnarvonshire
Le Duc et la Duchesse d'York dans les carrières d'ardoise de Dinorwic, Carnarvonshire
Relief etching
From: *The Illustrated London News*, 6 May 1899

A visiting group of royals is shown here ascending an incline at a slate quarry in Wales. The differences were enormous between the flatness of halftone printed images and illustrations such as this, where photographs have been worked up as paintings and the surface has been broken up.

Mitglieder der königlichen Familie im Aufzug eines walisischen Schiefersteinbruchs. Die Differenzen zwischen der Monotonie eines autotypischen Druckbilds und solchen flächig aufgelösten Fotomalereien waren enorm.

Membres de la famille royale britannique dans l'ascenseur d'une ardoisière au pays de Galles. Les différences entre la monotonie d'une image imprimée en modulation d'amplitude et de telles photos peintures dissoutes en surface étaient énormes.

Samuel Begg, after Dr. Arthur Stark

The Sketcher Sketched: Mr. Melton Prior Sketching under Fire at Nicholson's Nek, 1899
Der gezeichnete Zeichner: Mr Melton Prior zeichnet unter Beschuss am Nicholson's Nek
Le Dessinateur dessiné: M. Melton Prior dessinant sous le feu de la bataille de Nicholson's Nek
Relief etching
From: *The Illustrated London News*, 16 December 1899

After covering 20 war assignments Melton Prior was at the height of his popularity during the Second Boer War in South Africa. Samuel Begg's photorealistic illustration based on the sketch of an eye witness shows the veteran artist calmly working away on a sketch of the battle while the British positions were being bombarded by artillery fire from the enemy behind him.

Nach 20 Kriegseinsätzen war Melton Prior im zweiten englischen Krieg gegen die südafrikanischen Burenrepubliken auf dem Zenit seiner Popularität angelangt. Samuel Beggs fotorealistische Interpretation einer Augenzeugenskizze zeigt, wie der coole Veteran unterhalb der feindlichen Artilleriestellungen an einer Vedute der bombardierten britischen Stellungen arbeitet.

Après 20 interventions de guerre, Melton Prior était parvenu au zénith de sa popularité dans la seconde guerre menée contre les républiques boers d'Afrique du Sud. L'interprétation photographique réaliste par Samuel Begg d'une esquisse fournie par un témoin montre le vétéran installé sous les positions d'artillerie ennemies et en train de travailler calmement à une vue des positions britanniques bombardées.

THE ILLUSTRATED
LONDON NEWS

REGISTERED AT THE GENERAL POST OFFICE AS A NEWSPAPER.

No. 3133.—VOL. CXIV.   SATURDAY, MAY 6, 1899.   WITH SUPPLEMENT: ROYAL ACADEMY PICTURES   SIXPENCE. BY POST, 6½D.

THE DUKE AND DUCHESS OF YORK AT THE DINORWIC SLATE QUARRIES, CARNARVONSHIRE: THE ROYAL PARTY ASCENDING ONE OF THE INCLINES.

FROM A PHOTOGRAPH BY G. H. JONES, PORT DINORWIC.

The Duke and Duchess are seated in the front carriage of the two, together with Mrs. Assheton Smith and Lord Carrington.

LE SIEGE DE PORT-ARTHUR. — La pyramide humaine.

« ...Devant la batterie du fort Zaredoutni se dressait un haut mur de pierre qu'e les Japonais, une fois, firent le miracle d'escalader. Le capitaine Lebedief, commandant les marins, se posta à la crête de la muraille, le revolver d'une main, le sabre de l'autre, et tua ou blessa 22 Japonais qui, faisant la pyramide humaine, essayaient de remonter l'escalade. Après le troisième assaut, le capitaine Lebedief, exténué, s'anait été fut écrasé par un obus... »

Dépêche d'un correspondant de guerre.

Georges Scott

The Siege of Port Arthur – The Human Pyramid, 1904
Die Belagerung von Port Arthur – Die Menschenpyramide
Le Siège de Port Arthur – La pyramide humaine
Relief etching
From: *L'Illustration*, Paris, 10 September 1904

Following a surprise attack by the Japanese on the Chinese port of Lüshunkou (Port Arthur), which was being used as a naval base for the Russian fleet, a war broke out with Japan that had catastrophic consequences for the Tsarist Empire. This illustration, showing a mounted attack being resisted by a single Russian soldier, is of course a highly imaginative interpretation of the original war correspondent's report.

Ein japanischer Angriff auf die als russischer Marinestützpunkt fungierende chinesische Hafenstadt Lüshunkou (Port Arthur) leitete einen für das Zarenreich katastrophalen Krieg mit Japan ein. Bei der Darstellung einer Attacke, die von einem einzigen russischen Offizier zurückgeschlagen wird, handelt es sich um eine fantastiereiche Visualisierung eines Korrespondentenberichts.

Une attaque japonaise de la ville portuaire chinoise de Lüshunkou (Port Arthur), qui servait de base à la marine russe, déclencha une guerre avec le Japon qui s'avéra catastrophique pour l'Empire tsariste. Cette représentation d'une attaque refoulée par un seul officier russe est en fait la visualisation très fantaisiste du rapport d'un correspondant.

Richard Caton Woodville Jr.

On the Walls of the Chinese Fortress, 1900
Auf den Mauern der chinesischen Festung
Sur les murs de la forteresse chinoise
Relief etching
From: *Rodina*, St. Petersburg, 8 October 1900

Russia was one of the eight allied nations that had invaded the Chinese Empire in June 1900 as an expeditionary army to put down the nationalist uprising of the Yihetuan movement (otherwise known as the Boxer Rebellion). This article in Russia's most popular news magazine, *Rodina*, featured a cover illustration by Richard Caton Woodville that had originally appeared in the *Illustrated London News*.

Russland zählte zu den acht alliierten Staaten, die im Juni 1900 mit einem sogenannten Expeditionsheer in das Kaiserreich China eindrangen, um dort den Aufstand der nationalistischen Yihetuan-Bewegung (Boxeraufstand) niederzuschlagen. Der Bericht in der populärsten russischen Illustrierten *Rodina* wurde mit einer von der *Illustrated London News* übernommenen Grafik Richard Caton Woodvilles eingeleitet.

La Russie faisait partie des huit États alliés qui envahirent la Chine impériale en juin 1900 avec une armée expéditionnaire pour y mater la révolte du mouvement nationaliste des Yihétuan (révolte des Boxers). L'article paru dans le magazine russe le plus populaire *Rodina* était précédé d'un dessin de Richard Caton Woodville, repris des *Illustrated London News*.

НА СТѢНАХЪ КИТАЙСКОЙ КРѢПОСТИ. Рисунокъ художника К. Вудвиль.

William Hatherell & Frédéric de Haenen

The Moment of Tragedy: The Grand Duke's Carriage Blown up by a Bomb in the Senate Square, the Kremlin, Moscow, 1905
Der Moment der Tragödie: Die Kutsche des Großfürsten, von einer Bombe auf dem Senatsplatz im Moskauer Kreml in die Luft gesprengt
Le Moment de la tragédie : La calèche du grand-duc, pulvérisée par une bombe sur la place du Sénat au Kremlin de Moscou
Relief etching
From: *The Graphic*, London, 25 February 1905

The Tsarist regime was shaken by economic recession, defeat in the war with Japan and a massacre of demonstrating workers in St. Petersburg. As the first Russian Revolution broke out in 1905, Grand Duke Sergei Alexandrovich was assassinated in Moscow in a bomb attack. The event was depicted using eye-witness sketches by the genre artist William Hatherell working with the illustrator of action scenes Frédéric de Haenen.

Wirtschaftsrezession, der katastrophale Krieg gegen Japan und ein Massaker gegen demonstrierende Arbeiter in Sankt Petersburg hatten die Grundfesten des Zarismus erschüttert. Im Zug der revolutionären Ereignisse war es zu einem Attentat auf den Großfürsten gekommen. Das Ereignis wurde mit einer Zeugenskizze gemeinschaftlich von dem Genrekünstler William Hatherell und dem Actiongrafiker Frédéric de Haenen rekonstruiert.

La récession économique, la désastreuse guerre contre le Japon et le massacre d'ouvriers manifestant à Saint-Pétersbourg avaient ébranlé les fondations du tsarisme. Dans le trouble des événements révolutionnaires, le grand-duc de Moscou avait été victime d'un attentat. L'événement fut reconstruit à partir de dessins d'un témoin par l'artiste de genre William Hatherell en collaboration avec le dessinateur d'actions Frédéric de Haenen.

Carrey & Fortuné Méaulle (sc.)

In Moscow – Assassination of Grand Duke Sergei, 1905
In Moskau – Ermordung des Großfürsten Sergei
À Moscou – Assassinat du grand-duc Serge
Coloured relief etching
From: *Le Petit Parisien*, 5 March 1905

Carrey's illustration depicted the force of the bomb's explosion that claimed the lives of the Tsar's son and his coachman with greater dramatic effect than his fellow artists at *The Graphic*. Because of the large number of anarchist attacks in France, the artists of the country's "Miscellaneous Items" news sections had become rather proficient at illustrating explosions.

Effektvoller als seine Kollegen vom *Graphic* hatte Carrey die Wucht der Nitroglyzerinbombe in Szene gesetzt, die das Mitglied der Zarendynastie und seinen Kutscher das Leben gekostet hatte. Aufgrund der Vielzahl anarchistischer Attentate hatten es die Künstler der „Faits divers" zu einer wahren Meisterschaft in der Visualisierung von Explosionen gebracht.

Carrey avait mis en scène la violence de la bombe nitroglycérine qui avait coûté la vie au membre de la dynastie tsariste et à son cocher de façon plus efficace que ses collègues du *Graphic*. Vu le grand nombre des attentats anarchistes, les artistes des faits divers étaient passés maîtres dans la visualisation des explosions.

Nr. 10   Berliner Illustrirte Zeitung.   149

Russische Bettlertypen.   Zeichnung nach dem Leben von Fritz Koch.

Das Leben für den Zaren.

Skizzen unseres nach Rußland entsandten Zeichners Fritz Koch·

Leben und Treiben in einer russischen Kneipe, genannt »Traktir«.
Im Vordergrund die in jedem Traktir unvermeidliche Katze.

Typische Figur eines Dienst-
mädchens, barfuß servierend.

134   Berliner Illustrirte Zeitung.   Nr. 9

Frauen vor dem Massenquartier,
die für die »besser situierten Mieter« Kleider und Decken feilbieten.

Ein halbes Zimmer als Wohnung für eine Arbeiterfamilie.
Den hinteren Teil des Zimmers (hinter der Gardine) bewohnt eine zweite Familie. An der Wand eine Madonna und ein Geschirrbord.

Mittagessen im Asyl aus nur einem Napf für alle dienenden Eßnapf.

Der Wirt des Asyls.

Ein Korridor als Arbeiterwohnung.
Die angrenzenden Zimmer, aus denen allein das Licht hereinfällt, sind von andern Familien bewohnt.

Arme, die Einlaß ins Asyl erbitten,
und oft stundenlang in der Kälte warten müssen.

Fritz Koch-Gotha

Life for the Tsar, 1905
Das Leben für den Zaren | La Vie pour le tsar
Relief etchings
From: *Berliner Illustrirte Zeitung*

← 5 March 1905
↙ 26 February 1905

For his first picture-reporting assignment Fritz Koch-Gotha had mingled with striking miners in the Ruhr, and not long afterwards he was sent to Russia by the progressive editorial staff of his newspaper, the *Berliner Illustrirte Zeitung*. This resulted in important developments for modern picture reporting since his material was gathered while he was undercover in night shelters and the homes of working people.

Für seine erste Zeichenreportage hatte sich Fritz Koch-Gotha unter streikende Minenarbeiter im Ruhrgebiet gemischt. Wenig später wurde er von der progressiven Redaktion der *Berliner Illustrirten Zeitung*, die innovativ auf die Entwicklung der modernen Bildreportage einwirkte, nach Russland geschickt, um dort undercover aus Nachtasylen und Arbeiterheimen zu berichten.

Pour son premier reportage pictural, Fritz Koch-Gotha s'était mêlé à des mineurs en grève dans la Ruhr. Un peu plus tard, il fut envoyé en Russie par la rédaction progressiste de la *Berliner Illustrirte Zeitung*, qui exerçait une influence novatrice sur le développement du reportage illustré moderne, afin d'écrire clandestinement des articles sur les asiles de nuit et les foyers d'ouvriers.

Achille Beltrame

→ *The Revolution in Odessa*, 1905
Die Revolution in Odessa | La Révolution à Odessa
Colour-tinted wood engraving
From: *Nimm mich mit*, no. 11, Berlin, 1905

Odessa was a key location during the Russian Revolution of 1905 and was the scene of fighting between mutinous units of the Black Sea Fleet, with support from striking workers, and the reactionary troops of the Russian army. The illustration here is an early work by Achille Beltrame, the leading light of "Miscellaneous Items" painting work, who from 1899 to 1945 supplied weekly illustrations for the sensationalist reports of the Italian newspaper *La Domenica del Corriere*.

Odessa war ein Brennpunkt der russischen Revolution von 1905. Meuternde Einheiten der Schwarzmeerflotte und aufständische Arbeiter lieferten sich hier Kämpfe mit den Truppen der Reaktion. Es handelt sich um eine frühe Arbeit des Champions der „Faits divers"-Malerei, Achille Beltrame. Von 1899 bis 1945 illustrierte er wöchentlich Sensationsmeldungen für die italienische Illustrierte *La Domenica del Corriere*.

Odessa était l'un des points chauds de la révolution russe de 1905. Des unités de la flotte de la mer Noire en mutinerie et des ouvriers en rébellion s'y livrèrent des combats contre les troupes réactionnaires. Il s'agit ici d'un des premiers travaux du champion de la peinture de faits divers, Achille Beltrame. De 1889 à 1945, il illustra chaque semaine les nouvelles à sensation pour la revue italienne *La Domenica del Corriere*.

Die Revolution in Odessa.

Das Zarenmanifest hat seine Wirkung nicht, oder doch nicht überall im russischen Reiche geübt. Die erhoffte Beruhigung ist n i c h t eingetreten, und die Revolution erhob nur noch kühner ihr Haupt. Die wüstesten Szenen spielten sich ab und in fast allen Städten des Reiches kam es und kommt es noch immer zu Straßenkämpfen und Meuchelmorden. Ein Hauptherd der Revolution und der Gegenrevolution war auch Odessa. Hier kam es an ver= schiedenen Orten zu Barrikadenkämpfen. Die Straßenbahnen wurden zerstört, die Wagen umgeworfen und als Deckung benutzt, und blutige Schlachten wurden zwischen Volk und Soldaten geschlagen.

Fritz Koch-Gotha & Lyonel Feininger

← *Rapid Transportation*, 1905
Schnellverkehr | Transport rapide
Relief etchings
From: *Berliner Illustrirte Zeitung*, 10 December 1905

Lyonel Feininger & the Brown Brothers (photo.)

↙ *Rapid Transportation in the Future – The Ostrich at a Trot*, 1905
Schnellverkehr der Zukunft – Der Strauß als Traber
Transport rapide de l'avenir – L'Autruche comme trotteur
Relief etchings
From: *Berliner Illustrirte Zeitung*, 10 December 1905

Alongside Fritz Koch-Gotha, who was six years his junior, Lyonel Feininger was one of the main press illustrators in Germany at the turn of the 20th century. He specialised in political cartoons and also various imaginative utopian illustrations in the style of Albert Robida and Winsor McCay.

Lyonel Feininger zählte mit dem sechs Jahre jüngeren Fritz Koch-Gotha zu den führenden deutschen Pressegrafikern der Jahrhundertwende. Neben dem politischen Cartooning gehörte das burleske utopische Genre à la Albert Robida und Winsor McCay zu seinen Spezialitäten.

Avec Fritz Koch-Gotha de six ans son cadet, Lyonel Feininger comptait parmi les plus éminents dessinateurs de presse allemands du tournant du siècle. En plus de la caricature politique, le genre utopique burlesque à la manière d'Albert Robida et de Winsor McCay était une de ses spécialités.

Winsor McCay

↗ *The Spectrophone: The Imperial City of Philyorgo*, 1904
The Spectrophone: Die Kaiserstadt Philyorgo
The Spectrophone: La ville impériale de Philyorgo
Relief etching
From: *Los Angeles Herald*, 4 March 1904

→ *The Spectrophone: The Last Day of Manhattan*, 1905
The Spectrophone: Der letzte Tag von Manhattan
The Spectrophone: Le dernier jour de Manhattan
Relief etching
From: *New York Herald*, 26 February 1905

At the height of his career as a cartoonist Winsor McCay produced some delightful illustrations for the humorous futuristic series *The Spectrophone*, written by the satirist John Kendrick Bangs. Set in the 44th century, it featured the vast trading metropolis of the universe, Philyorgo, that had been formed by merging together the big cities of the east coast of the United States before eventually succumbing to over-expansion and collapsing into the sea.

Auf dem Höhepunkt seiner Karriere als Comickünstler begleitete Winsor McCay die humoreske Zukunftsserie *The Spectrophone* des Satirikers John Kendrick Bangs mit kongenialen Illustrationen. Die amerikanische Ostküste hat sich im 44. Jahrhundert zu Philyorgo zusammengeschlossen, der Handelsmetropole des Universums, die schließlich an ihrer Hypertrophie zugrunde geht und im Meer versinkt.

Au faîte de sa carrière comme artiste de bandes dessinées, Winsor McCay dota la série futuriste et humoristique *The Spectrophone* du satiriste John Kendrick Bangs d'illustrations congéniales. Au 44e siècle, la côte est des États-Unis s'est unie pour former Philyorgo, la métropole commerciale de l'univers, qui finit par mourir d'hypertrophie et sombre dans la mer.

A STRANDED FLORODORA COMPANY WALKING HOME FROM THE NORTH POLE

"CARRYING MY BUREAU ALL THE ELECTRIC LIGHT FIXTURES AND GRAND PIANO ALONG WITH IT"

"AT THIS POINT," CRIED THE MEGAPHONE BRED PILOT "WE SEE THE SOUTHERN EXPOSURE OF THE CITY OF PHILYORGO"

"DIRECTLY BENEATH US, DEEPER IN WATER THAN IT EVER WAS BEFORE IN HISTORY LIES WHAT WAS ONCE KNOWN AS WALL STREET."

L'explosion

Le Prologue du Drame

Le siege du garage

Un acte d'heroism

La colère de la foule

HONNEUR AUX BRAVÉS

Bonnot est pris !

Le Gerant : A. Chatelain.

Corbeil. — Imp. Crêté

Anonymous

Gunfire at Choisy-le-Roi, 1912
Die Schießerei von Choisy-le-Roi
La Fusillade de Choisy-le-Roi
Coloured relief etching
From: *L'Œil de la police*, no. 175, Paris, 1912

Seen here in the French pulp crime magazine is the story of the dramatic shootout with the anarchist gang member Jules Bonnot as told in the form of a comic strip. Bonnot, who had worked as a chauffeur for Arthur Conan Doyle, kept the whole of France in suspense as he and his fellow gang members committed several robberies with the innovative use of

a getaway car. The lawless provocation of these "Automobile Apaches" (see ill. p. 459 t.) was a source of fascination to many avant-garde artists.

Das Kriminalkolportage-Magazin zeigte die dramatische Festnahme des anarchistischen Gangsters Jules Bonnot in comicstripartiger Rekonstruktion. Der ehemalige Chauffeur Conan Doyles hatte

ganz Frankreich mit etlichen Raubüberfällen, die er mit seiner motorisierten Bande verübte, in Atem gehalten. Die provokante Gesetzlosigkeit der „Automobil-Apachen" (siehe Abb. S. 459 o.) übte eine starke Faszination auf avantgardistische Künstlerkreise aus.

Le magazine spécialisé dans les histoires criminelles de bas niveau montrait l'arrestation dramatique du gangster anarchiste Jules Bonnot dans une reconstruction caricaturale. L'ancien chauffeur de Conan Doyle avait tenu la France entière en haleine par de nombreux hold-ups qu'il commettait avec sa bande motorisée. Le refus provocant de toute loi des

«Apaches en automobile» (voir ill. p. 459 h.) exerça une grande fascination sur les cercles d'artistes d'avant-garde.

Anonymous

*A Redskin Encampment on a Hotel
Roof in New York*, 1913
*Ein Lager der Rothäute auf einem
Hoteldach in New York*
*Un campement de peaux rouges
sur le toit d'un hôtel à New York*
Coloured relief etching
From: *Le Petit Journal*, Paris,
20 April 1913

When 10 members of the Blackfoot
Confederacy were invited to visit New
York by the railroad president Louis
W. Hill, in a scheme to promote tourism, they set up camp and pitched
their teepees on the roof of the Hotel
McAlpin, at the time the largest hotel
in the world. The illustration, which was
composed using a number of photographs, omits all the female members
of the visiting party.

Die zehn Mitglieder der Blackfeet-
Konföderation, die der amerikanische
Eisenbahnmagnat Louis W. Hill für
eine Tourismusshow nach New York
City eingeladen hatte, schlugen ihre
Zelte auf dem Dach des damals welt-
größten Hotels McAlpin auf. In der
Grafik, die aus mehreren Fotografien
kompiliert worden war, wurden die
weiblichen Vertreter der Konföderation nicht gezeigt.

Les dix membres de la confédération
des Pieds-Noirs, qui avait invité le
magnat américain des chemins de
fer Louis W. Hill pour un show touristique dans la ville de New York,
installèrent leurs tentes sur le toit de
l'hôtel McAlpin, à l'époque le plus
grand hôtel du monde. Sur le dessin,
compilé à partir de plusieurs photographies, les représentantes féminines
de la confédération sont complètement absentes.

Anonymous

The Redskins and the Phonograph,
1913
Die Rothäute und der Phonograph
Les Peaux Rouges et le phonographe
Coloured relief etching
From: *Le Petit Journal*, Paris,
25 May 1913

The anonymous illustrator once again took liberties with this reproduction of a photograph showing the Blackfoot being recorded on a phonograph. To create a warlike impression he gave one of them a spear, and as they speak into the phonograph horn their facial features have been grotesquely exaggerated.

Auch bei der Wiedergabe einer Fotografie, die Vertreter der Blackfeet bei einer fonografischen Aufnahme zeigt, nahm sich der Illustrator beträchtliche interpretative Freiheiten. Um einen kriegerischen Eindruck zu vermitteln, wurde der Gruppe ein Speer hinzugefügt und die Gesichtszüge wurden ins Groteske gesteigert.

Dans la reproduction de la photographie montrant les représentants des Pieds-Noirs pendant un enregistrement de phonographe, l'illustrateur s'est octroyé de grandes libertés d'interprétation. Pour créer une atmosphère belliqueuse, il a muni le groupe d'une lance et exagéré les traits du visage de façon grotesque.

420

THE GRAPHIC, OCTOBER 2, 1915

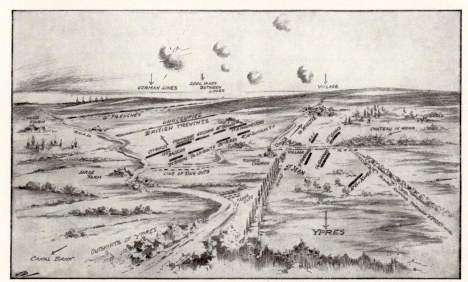

HOW GERMAN TRENCHES ARE STORMED
AS SEEN AND DRAWN BY FRENCH AND BRITISH SOLDIERS

BRITISH TRENCH POSITIONS: YPRES BEFORE A RECENT ATTACK NEAR ST. JEAN AND WIELTJE

Copyrighted in the United States and Canada.

A FRENCH ASSAULT: CARRYING A NETWORK OF GERMAN TRENCHES IN CHAMPAGNE

The top sketch, made by an Indian officer, shows part of the system of British trenches before Ypres, once more the scene of heavy fighting, just before an attack. The lower sketch, by a French soldier, gives an idea of the extraordinary network of German trenches which the French have just penetrated in the Champagne advances. In wood-fighting the Germans regard the French as "very devils."

Anonymous

How German Trenches Are Stormed, 1915
Wie deutsche Schützengräben gestürmt werden
Comment les tranchées allemandes sont prises d'assaut
Relief etchings
From: *The Graphic*, London, 2 October 1915

Ralph Cleaver

Where the British "Break-through" Took Place, 1915
Wo der britische „Durchbruch" erfolgte
Où la «percée» britannique eut lieu
Relief etching
From: *The Graphic*, London, 2 October 1915

During the First World War, independent reporting from the front was almost impossible. The British press, unlike the German and French, was not subject to direct military control, but even so journalists were typically denied access to areas where fighting was taking place. The Western Front in particular seemed to be almost hermetically sealed off, and while experienced *special artists* such as Frederic Villiers managed to send reports from there to begin with, they soon became frustrated and turned their attention elsewhere. For this reason generally, sketches by army personnel were often used by the press, which were either reproduced photomechanically or, as in this case, worked up by press illustrators.

Unabhängige Frontberichterstattung war im Ersten Weltkrieg kaum möglich. Die britische Presse war zwar anders als die deutschen und französischen Medien keiner direkten militärischen Kontrolle unterworfen, allerdings war den Journalisten in der Regel der Zugang zu den Kriegsschauplätzen verwehrt. Vor allem die Westfront schien hermetisch abgeriegelt. Erfahrenen *special artists* wie Frederic Villiers gelangen anfangs zwar einige Dokumentationen, sie wichen allerdings schon bald frustriert auf andere Fronten aus. Häufig wurde daher auf Zeichnungen von Militärs zurückgegriffen, die entweder fotomechanisch reproduziert oder wie hier von Pressegrafikern interpretiert wurden.

Une couverture médiatique indépendante du front pendant la Première Guerre mondiale n'était guère possible. À l'inverse des médias français et allemands, la presse britannique n'était soumise à aucun contrôle militaire direct, mais l'accès aux champs de bataille était généralement interdit aux journalistes. Le front de l'Ouest surtout semblait hermétiquement bouclé. Si des *specials* expérimentés comme Frederic Villiers réussirent au début à produire quelques documentations, ils se tournèrent très tôt, frustrés, vers d'autres fronts. C'est pourquoi il fallait souvent avoir recours aux dessins des militaires, qui étaient soit reproduits par procédé photomécanique soit, comme ici, interprétés par les dessinateurs de presse.

WHERE THE BRITISH "BREAK-THROUGH" TOOK PLACE
THE EARLY MORNING ATTACK ON THE MINING VILLAGE OF LOOS

Copyrighted in the United States and Canada.

Drawn by Ralph Cleaver.

Our great attack was made south of La Bassée, where we carried the German trenches over a front of five miles, penetrating their lines in some places to a depth of 4000 yards. In this advance our men captured the village of Loos and the mining works round it. It was here that we took nearly all our prisoners, the town being surrounded on three sides, and the Germans caught in a trap. The most noticeable features of the landscape, as our picture shows, are the numerous slag heaps, all of which had been converted into strongholds. On the horizon is seen the famous "Tower Bridge," a mass of pit machinery which the Germans used as an observation station,

François Flameng

While *L'Illustration* had to operate during the war under strict military control, it still managed to publish a spectacular series of pictures in the tradition of Napoleonic history painting. With these brilliant open-air studies of the damage done by war and the everyday life of soldiers in the trenches, the established history painter François Flameng and his student Charles Hoffbauer provided something of a prosaic counterpoint to scenes of war and conflict, and the newspaper continued to publish them for the duration of the war.

Unter strikter Militärkontrolle brannte *L'Illustration* während des Krieges ein letztes Feuerwerk in der Tradition bonapartistischer Historienkunst ab. Einen prosaischen Kontrapunkt zu den Kriegs- und Kampfszenen bot die Serie brillanter Pleinairstudien von Kriegsschäden und vom Schützengrabenalltag des renommierten Historienmalers François Flameng und seines Schülers Charles Hoffbauer, die das Magazin über die Dauer des Kriegs publizierte.

Sous strict contrôle militaire, *L'Illustration* alluma, pendant la guerre, un dernier feu d'artifice dans la tradition de l'art de l'épopée napoléonienne. La série de brillantes études en plein air offrait un contre-point prosaïque aux scènes de guerre et de combat et au quotidien des tranchées du peintre d'histoire de renom François Flameng et de son élève Charles Hoffbauer, que le magazine publia pendant toute la durée de la guerre.

A Gutted House in a Street in Arras, 1915
Zerstörtes Haus in einer Straße von Arras
Maison éventrée dans une rue d'Arras
Coloured relief etching
From: *L'Illustration*, Paris, 11 December 1915

*A Fire at Arras
Cathedral*, 1915
*Brand der Kathedrale
von Arras*
*Incendie de la
cathédrale d'Arras*
Coloured relief etching
From: *L'Illustration*, Paris,
11 December 1915

№ 19   Berliner Illustrirte Zeitung.   265

AUS DER RIESENSCHLACHT IM WESTEN

Aus der Riesenschlacht im Westen: Anstürmende Engländer, vom Maschinengewehrfeuer in der Flanke gefaßt.
Zeichnung von Fritz Koch-Gotha.

Bei Arras erbeuteter englischer Tank-Panzerwagen.   Phot. A. Groß.

Fritz Koch-Gotha

From the Great Battle in the West: Attacking English Troops, Caught on the Flank by Machine-gun Fire, 1917
Aus der Riesenschlacht im Westen: Anstürmende Engländer, vom Maschinengewehrfeuer in der Flanke gefasst
Grande bataille à l'Ouest : Anglais à l'attaque, pris sous le feu des mitraillettes sur le flanc

← Pencil with ink and wash
↙ Relief etching
From: *Berliner Illustrirte Zeitung*, 13 May 1917

The *Berliner Illustrirte Zeitung* received no preferential treatment from the military command because as a mass-market weekly its line was one of liberal socialism. As a result, Fritz Koch-Gotha was given no pictorial material from any German sources and had to rely on foreign sources instead. His illustrations show a patriotic sympathy, but also present a sense of distance and at times featured a hint of satire. Koch-Gotha worked with clear tonal values which he used to subtle effect in conjunction with freely drawn contour lines, although he also had to take into account the inevitable darkening and loss of middle tones that was produced by the coarse resolution that resulted from having to use cheap paper.

Die *Berliner Illustrirte* gehörte als sozialliberales Massenblatt nicht zu den Medien, die von der Militärführung bevorzugt behandelt wurden. Mangels heimischen Bildmaterials musste Fritz Koch-Gotha oft auf ausländische Quellen zurückgreifen. Seine Grafiken folgten zwar der patriotischen Linie, aber oft mit distanziertem und nicht selten satirischem Unterton. Koch-Gotha arbeitete mit klaren Tonwerttrennungen, die er durch einen lockeren Einsatz von Konturlinien zu nuancieren wusste. Dabei musste er berücksichtigen, dass die grobe Rasterung, die durch die Verwendung von billigem Papier notwendig war, eine Verdunklung und den Verlust von Zwischentönen zur Folge hatte.

Journal à grand tirage socio-libéral, la *Berliner Illustrirte* ne faisait pas partie des médias jouissant d'un traitement de faveur de la part des militaires. Faute de recevoir du matériel graphique de son pays, Fritz Koch-Gotha dut souvent avoir recours à des sources étrangères. Ses dessins s'inscrivaient dans la ligne patriotique, mais étaient souvent teintés d'une certaine distance, parfois même d'une note satirique. Koch-Gotha travaillait avec de nettes valeurs tonales qu'il savait nuancer par l'utilisation désinvolte des lignes de contour. Pourtant, il devait tenir compte du fait que le tramage grossier, dû à l'utilisation d'un papier à bon marché, avait pour effet un assombrissement et la perte des tons intermédiaires.

Fritz Koch-Gotha

*A German Landwehr Cavalry Officer
Causes a Stir in Liège*, 1915
*Deutscher Landwehr-Kürassier als
Lütticher Sehenswürdigkeit
Cuirassier allemand de la Landwehr présenté
comme une attraction à Liège*
Relief etching
From: *Berliner Illustrirte Zeitung*, 7 February 1915

Open criticism, such as the boorish and arrogant
manner of this German soldier in occupied Belgium
in an illustration by the *Berliner Illustrirte Zeitung*'s
popular chief artist, was very much the exception
to the rule.

Offene Kritik, wie sie der populäre Chefillustrator
der *Berliner Illustrirten* am groben und selbstherr-
lichen Auftritt deutscher Militärs im besetzten
Belgien übte, war die Ausnahme.

La critique ouverte, comme le populaire illustrateur en chef de la *Berliner Illustrirte* l'exprime à
travers le comportement grossier et arrogant des
militaires allemands dans la Belgique occupée,
était l'exception.

Paul Renouard

*Those Who Learn How to Be
Blind*, 1915
*Die, die lernen, blind zu sein
Ceux qui apprennent à être aveugles*
Relief etching
From: *L'Illustration*, Paris, 22 May 1915

Paul Renouard's empathetic style
of art was largely ill suited to the
nationalistic context of an illustrated
magazine reporting on the war. In this
picture of the wounded, the 70-year-
old pioneer of impressionistic pictorial journalism made a visual reference
to Bruegel the Elder's painting *The
Blind Leading the Blind*, although the
massed presence of angelic nurses
does not distract completely from the
grim subject matter.

Die empathische Kunst Paul
Renouards fügte sich nur schwer in
den chauvinistischen Kontext einer
Kriegsillustrierten. Bei dieser Inva-
lidendokumentation arbeitete der
mittlerweile 70-jährige Pionier impressionistischer Zeichenreportage mit
einer Anspielung auf Pieter Bruegels
Blindensturz. Der düstere Gehalt ließ
sich auch durch die massive Anwe-
senheit engelgleicher Pflegerinnen
nicht neutralisieren.

L'art empathique de Paul Renouard
s'accordait plutôt mal au contexte
chauviniste d'un magazine de guerre
illustré. Dans sa documentation sur
les invalides, le pionnier du reportage
imagé, alors âgé de 70 ans, se référa
dans son travail à l'œuvre de Pieter
Bruegel *La Parabole des aveugles*.
Le sordide contenu ne se laissait pas
neutraliser par la présence massive
d'angéliques infirmières.

CEUX QUI APPRENNENT A ÊTRE AVEUGLES

André Devambez

Attacking in Waves, 1916
Die Angriffswellen
Les Vagues d'assaut
Relief etching
From: *L'Illustration*, Paris,
17 June 1916

André Devambez had a virtuoso
talent for choreographing illustrations
of mass movement, in the tradition
of Jacques Callot and Auguste Raffet,
and specialised in battle scenes. He
was an influential illustrator, and his
obsession with high-angle views of
military action resulted in him being
appointed later on as official artist of
the French Air Ministry.

André Devambez hatte sich als Vir-
tuose grafischer Massenchoreogra-
fie in der Tradition Jacques Callots
und Auguste Raffets auf virtuelle
Schlachtenszenen spezialisiert. Seine
Obsession für militärperspektivische
Aufsichten trug dem einflussreichen
Illustrator später die Ernennung zum
offiziellen Künstler des französischen
Luftfahrtministeriums ein.

Virtuose de la chorégraphie de masse,
André Devambez s'était spécialisé
dans ces scènes de batailles virtuelles,
fidèle à la tradition de Jacques Callot
et d'Auguste Raffet. Son obsession
des vues dans la perspective militaire
valut plus tard à l'influent illustrateur
d'être nommé artiste officiel du ministère français de l'Aviation.

LES VAGUES D'ASSAUT
Dessin d'ANDRÉ DEVAMBEZ.

Georges Scott

Behind the Battle Line, 1916
Hinter der Kampflinie
Derrière la ligne de bataille
Relief etching
From: *L'Illustration*, Paris,
11 March 1916

Georges Scott's dynamic representation of an endless French supply line
to the "blood pump" of Verdun became
a celebrated and famous propaganda
image for the war: "Photography, which
was neither technically equipped for
shots at night nor capable of producing exciting narratives on the model of
cinema, could not compete with illustration" (Keller 2013, *Verdun*).

Georges Scotts dynamische Darstellung der endlosen französischen
Nachschublinie zur „Blutpumpe" Verdun wurde zu einer Ikone der Weltkriegspropaganda: „Die technisch
besonders für Nachtaufnahmen gar
nicht gerüstete und durch das Film-
Paradigma noch nicht zum spannen-
den Erzählen animierte Fotografie
konnte hier nicht konkurrieren"
(Keller 2013, *Verdun*).

La représentation dynamique par
Georges Scott de l'interminable
convoi de ravitaillement français en
direction de Verdun, la «pompe à
sang», devint une icône de la propagande pendant la Première Guerre
mondiale : «La photographie, qui
n'était ni équipée sur le plan technique
pour des prises de vue nocturnes ni
animée pour des récits captivants par
les paradigmes cinématographiques,
n'était pas une concurrence ici»
(Keller 2013, *Verdun*).

ENLÈVEMENT D'UNE JEUNE DÉTENUE

Pierre Yrondy

Kidnapping a Young Prisoner, 1901
Entführung einer jungen Strafgefangenen
Enlèvement d'une jeune détenue
Relief etching
From: *Le Petit Parisien*, 26 April 1905

Supplément illustré du Petit Journal   189

CYCLISTES ATTAQUÉS DANS LE BOIS DE VINCENNES

Anonymous

Cyclists Attacked in the Bois de Vincennes, 1901
Radfahrer im Wald von Vincennes angegriffen
Cyclistes attaqués dans le bois de Vincennes
Coloured relief etching
From: *Le Petit Journal*, Paris, 16 June 1901

"More than 30 hotheads have been running riot in
Bondy and Pantin. 18 have been arrested; one of
them had just stabbed a passer-by."

„Gut 30 Heißsporne lärmten durch Bondy und Pantin. 18 wurden verhaftet; einer hatte soeben einen
Passanten niedergestochen."

«Plus de 30 forcenés sèment le trouble à Bondy et
Pantin. 18 furent arrêtés ; l'un d'eux venait de poign-
arder un passant.»

From: Félix Fénéon, *Nouvelles en trois lignes*, no. 185,
Le Matin, 1906

The Illustration Revolution

In the course of an interview with Pierre Cabanne, Marcel Duchamp replied to a question about his artist's training in Montmartre with the surprising admission that he had hardly had any contact with painters while he was there, but mostly illustrators instead. He also added that at the time even artists such as Juan Gris worked as illustrators (Cabanne 1971, p. 22). Indeed, in Paris at the turn of the century almost every artist involved with the avant-garde had had some experience working with press graphics. Duchamp's brother, the Cubist painter Jacques Villon, affirmed in an interview with Dora Vallier the central importance of the illustrated press: "In this period, the influence of the journals on art is incontestable. Thanks to them, painting was liberated more rapidly from academicism" (Leighten 2013, p. 31). However, the influence of press graphics ran much deeper and was more complex than the simple encounter with the realities of daily life that Villon went on to refer to. For example, the daily newspaper Le Courrier français, for which both Duchamp and Villon did most of their illustration work (see ill. p. 507), was previously the main outlet for the Incoherents art movement. In the 1880s, the artists in this group, which was closely bound up with press graphics, marked the decisive transition from the traditional artistic parodies found in Salon caricatures to art as a form of revolution through the series of experimental exhibitions they staged. Critics at the time hailed this anti-academic opposition with visionary clarity, with one writer claiming that "In the future, art will either be incoherent or it will cease to exist" (Le Voltaire, 15 October 1883).

This awakening in the arts was also helped by the abolition of censorship in France in 1881, which as far as caricatures were concerned led to a reflective phase in the media and an openness to interdisciplinary work. These developments coincided with new techniques for chemigraphic reproduction, which were of great service in making the Incoherents' stylistic device of montage into a regular mode of illustration in press graphics. Before deconstruction and collage became essential aspects in creating Cubist art, they had already been long since established for their use in newspapers and magazines. Indeed, illustrations made with pasted paper or free methods of photomontage had been employed in the press from the 1890s (see ill. p. 534 t.).

Modernism's classic orientation towards an original and uncontrolled expression was preceded by a caricatural period of incubation with the Incoherents' provocative dilettantism. The playful primitivism of the group, with their creative methods of free association in an early Dadaist spirit, passed almost without interruption into ideologically motivated forms of graphic crudeness, such as those that appeared in the anarchist newspaper Le Père peinard (1889–1900; see ills. p. 537). The editorial staff for this weekly included the Neo-Impressionist artists Lucien Pissarro and Maximilien Luce, as well as the Incoherent illustrator Adolphe Willette, a friend of Villon's and Duchamp's who was a key figure in the art world of Montmartre, which first came to life when the famous literary cabaret Le Chat Noir was founded there in 1881. With his dreamlike illustrations infused with a sense of pantomime, Willette left his mark on the magazine Le Chat noir that was launched in 1883 by the cabaret's owner Rodolphe Salis and which ushered in the avant-garde magazine culture of fin-de-siècle Paris (see ills. p. 506). In a style that resembled chronophotography, Willette's successor Théophile Steinlen began to adapt Willette's silent sequence of images into a more cinematic format. Steinlen also introduced urban realism to cartoons (see ill. p. 510), a few years before Richard Outcault's series The Yellow Kid first appeared in Pulitzer's New York World in 1895, the same year the first moving pictures were screened. However, it is not as a comic-book pioneer that he is chiefly remembered but as a pioneer of modern socialist art, on the basis of his later work for anarchist trade-union newspapers. He was an influential figure for many of the important artists in the Berlin Secession and the American Ashcan School, such as Käthe Kollwitz and John Sloan, and indeed the pre-Cubist Picasso. Last but not least, the founding of the trend-setting satirical magazine Simplicissimus (1896–1944) in Munich owed a debt to its publisher Albert Langen's liking for Steinlen's socially critical pictorial journalism.

The success of the large-format illustrations in Simplicissimus and the Art Nouveau magazine Jugend (1896–1940), which was also founded in Munich and in the same year, encouraged the Paris publisher Samuel Schwarz a few years later to publish L'Assiette au beurre, a satirical newspaper which, apart from its picture captions, relied exclusively on the effect of its graphic work (see ill. p. 493). By giving his illustrators free rein with regard to content as well as design, Schwarz succeeded in bringing together the most experimental artists of the time under the general banner of satirical illustration, including Naturalist artists, Symbolists, Aesthetic artists, Synthetists, Nabis, Fauves, aspiring Cubists and, in the person of František Kupka, a future abstract artist. The 600 themed and individually edited issues of L'Assiette au beurre, published between 1901 and 1912, stand as monumental proof of Jacques Villon's remark that press graphics helped to set art free. While a libertarian arts magazine it was nevertheless banned in many countries because of its

Édouard Bernard

The "Fifteen Thousand", 1907
Die „Fünfzehntausend"
Les « quinze mille »
Coloured relief etching
From: *L'Assiette au Beurre*, Paris,
2 November 1907

The title of the satirical magazine *L'Assiette au Beurre* has the literal meaning of a "plate of butter" but is also an expression for the appropriation of state income at local levels to obtain various advantages. In the illustration a member of the French Assembly is shown greedily consuming his own government allowance, which had almost doubled since November of the previous year.

Der Titel des Satiremagazins *L'Assiette au Beurre* bedeutet wörtlich „der Butterteller", bezeichnete aber auch die unrechtmäßige Aneignung von Staatseinnahmen auf lokaler Ebene zum eigenen Vorteil. Ein Abgeordneter ist beim Verzehr seiner Diäten zu sehen, die im November des vergangenen Jahres um fast das Doppelte angehoben wurden.

Le titre du magazine satirique *L'Assiette au Beurre* est une référence aux recettes illégales de l'État, réalisées au niveau local pour le bénéfice personnel. Un député est ici en train de dévorer ses diètes, qui ont presque doublé au mois de novembre de l'année passée.

anarcho-syndicalist stance, yet it could still reach a circulation of between 40,000 and 250,000 copies beyond the borders of the Third Republic. Alongside *Simplicissimus* it was one of the main examples of pictorial journalism for the Russian Revolution of 1905 and also the various reformist movements in Muslim countries in the early 20th century. Furthermore, the fact that the controversial magazines of the modern caricature movement in France, *Hara-Kiri* (1960–1970) and *Charlie Hebdo* (since 1970), can still refer to how radical *L'Assiette au beurre* was visually is a clear testament to its explosive power.

One further important association between artistic modernism and pictorial journalism occurred with the propaganda produced during the First World War. The same combination reached a high point a little later with the pictorial news distributed by the Bolshevik telegraph agency Rosta (1919–1922),

under the direction of the painter and poet Vladimir Mayakovsky (see ills. pp. 586–589). His poem "Order of the Day to the Army of the Arts" (1918), which called for "Street-brooms [to be] our brushes, / and the public squares our palettes" (Duwakin 1975, p. 37), also connected Rosta's posters with the caricature campaigns of William Hone, Charles Philipon and the Paris Commune. However, Mayakovsky's hope of a "revolution of artistic taste" (1930, "Ich bitte um Worte"; Duwakin 1975, p. 66), in relation to pictorial journalism, proved to be an illusion in the decades that followed. After the First World War, artistic modernism increasingly turned to isolation and autonomy, and much of the culture associated with it was marked by segregation and elitism. The Rosta posters did not then represent the beginnings of an era of art as intervention, but the end of the age of avant-garde press graphics.

Revolution der Illustration

Marcel Duchamp verblüffte seinen Interviewpartner Pierre Cabanne auf dessen Frage nach seiner künstlerischen Lehrzeit auf dem Montmartre mit der Feststellung, dass er dort kaum mit Malern, sondern vor allem mit Cartoonisten in Kontakt gestanden habe. Und er fügte hinzu, dass damals selbst ein Künstler wie Juan Gris Illustrator gewesen sei (Cabanne 1971, S. 22). Tatsächlich gab es zur Jahrhundertwende in Paris kaum einen Protagonisten der bildnerischen Avantgarde, der keine Berührung mit der Pressegrafik hatte. Im Interview mit Dora Vallier unterstrich der kubistische Maler Jacques Villon, Duchamps Bruder, die zentrale Bedeutung der illustrierten Presse. „Ihr Einfluss auf die Kunst war konkurrenzlos und trug dazu bei, die Befreiung der Malerei vom Akademismus zu beschleunigen" (Leighten 2013, S. 31). Die pressegrafischen Impulse waren allerdings weitaus tiefgreifender und vielschichtiger als die bloße Konfrontation mit der Alltagswirklichkeit, auf die Villon auch anspielte. So handelte es sich beispielsweise bei dem Journal *Le Courrier français*, für das die beiden Brüder hauptsächlich zeichneten (siehe Abb. S. 507), um das ehemalige Zentralorgan von *Les Arts Incohérents*. Diese pressegrafisch geprägte Bewegung hatte in den 1880er-Jahren mit einer Reihe experimenteller Ausstellungen den entscheidenden Übergang von der kunstparodistischen *Salon-caricatural*-Tradition zur Kunstrevolution markiert. Die zeitgenössische Kritik hatte diese antiakademische Opposition damals mit einer hellsichtigen Prognose begrüßt: „Die Kunst wird in Zukunft entweder inkohärent sein, oder sie wird nicht mehr sein" (*Le Voltaire*, 15. Oktober 1883).

Zu verdanken war dieser künstlerische Aufbruch auch der Aufhebung der Zensur in Frankreich 1881, die im Bereich der Karikatur eine Phase der medialen Reflexion und der interdisziplinären Öffnung eingeleitet hatte. Hinzu kamen die neuen chemiegrafischen Reproduktionsmöglichkeiten, mit deren Hilfe das inkohärente Stilmittel der Montage in den pressegrafischen Vordergrund rückte. Bevor Dekonstruktion und Montage wesentlich für die Bildfindungen der Kubisten wurden, hatten sie sich bereits als wichtige Stilmittel in der Pressegrafik durchgesetzt. Das „papier collé", eine frühe Form der Collage, und die offene Fotomontage wurden dort seit den 1890er-Jahren eingesetzt (siehe Abb. S. 534 o.).

Die Orientierung der klassischen Moderne am originären, unkontrollierten Ausdruck hatte im provokanten Dilettantismus der *Incohérents* eine karikatureske Inkubationsphase durchlaufen. Der spielerische Primitivismus dieser frühdadaistischen Gruppierung mit ihren kreativen Techniken des freien Assoziierens ging fast nahtlos über in ideologisch motivierte Formen grafischer Roheit, wie sie beispielsweise von dem anarchistischen Journal *Le Père peinard* (1889–1900) propagiert wurden (siehe Abb. S. 537). Zu dessen wichtigsten Mitarbeitern zählten neben den neoimpressionistischen Künstlern Lucien Pissarro und Maximilien Luce auch der *Incohérent* Adolphe Willette. Der Freund Villons und Duchamps gilt als Schlüsselfigur der Künstlerszene des Montmartre, die 1881 mit der Gründung des legendären literarischen Cabarets Le Chat noir ihren Ausgang genommen hatte. Willette prägte mit pantomimischen Traumcomics das gleichnamige Magazin, das der Betreiber des Cafés Rodolphe Salis 1883 begründet hatte und das bahnbrechend für die avantgardistische Zeitschriftenkultur des Fin de Siècle werden sollte (siehe Abb. S. 506). Analog zur Chronofotografie begann Willettes Nachfolger Théophile Steinlen dessen Format der stummen Bilderfolgen kinematografisch zu verflüssigen. Einige Jahre vor Richard Outcaults *Yellow-Kid*-Serie, die 1895 in Joseph Pulitzers *New York World* zeitgleich mit den ersten Filmvorführungen startete, führte Steinlen auch den urbanen Realismus im Comicgenre ein (siehe Abb. S. 510). Er ging jedoch nicht als Pionier des Comicstrips in die Annalen ein, sondern aufgrund seiner nachfolgenden Arbeiten für anarchistische Gewerkschaftszeitungen als Wegbereiter moderner sozialistischer Kunst. Führende Vertreter der Berliner Secession und der amerikanischen Ashcan School wie Käthe Kollwitz und John Sloan standen ebenso unter seinem Einfluss wie der vorkubistische Picasso. Nicht zuletzt ist auch die Gründung des stilprägenden Münchener Satiremagazins *Simplicissimus* (1896–1944) einer Vorliebe von Steinlens Verleger Albert Langen für seine sozialkritische Bildpublizistik zu verdanken.

Der Erfolg der großflächigen Grafik des *Simplicissimus* und des ebenfalls 1896 in München gegründeten Jugendstil-Magazins *Jugend* (1896–1940) motivierte einige Jahre später wiederum den Pariser Verleger Samuel Schwarz zur Herausgabe von *L'Assiette au Beurre*, einer Satirezeitung, die bis auf vereinzelte Bildunterschriften ausschließlich auf die Wirkung der Grafik setzte (siehe Abb. S. 493). Indem er seinen Illustratoren die größtmöglichen inhaltlichen und gestalterischen Freiheiten ließ, gelang es Schwarz, die experimentierfreudigsten Künstler der Zeit unter dem Dach des Cartooning zu versammeln: Naturalisten, Symbolisten, Ästhetizisten, Synthetisten, Nabis, Fauves, angehende Kubisten und mit František Kupka auch einen zukünftigen abstrakten Künstler. Die 600 Themen- und Autorenhefte von *L'Assiette au Beurre*, die von 1901 bis 1912 erschienen sind, können als monumentaler Beleg für Jacques Villons These von der Befreiung der Kunst durch die Pressegrafik gelten. Obgleich das libertäre Künstlermagazin wegen seiner

Charles Léandre & Bordie (sc.)

Rodolphe Salis
The "Chat Noir" Goes for a
Stroll, 1895
Die „Chat noir" auf Streifzug
Le « Chat noir » se ballade
Relief etching
From: *Le Rire*, no. 41, Paris,
17 August 1895

The artist and author Rodolphe Salis,
the founder and host of the artistic
cabaret Le Chat Noir and publisher of
the magazine of the same name, also
took the role of narrator with his powerful voice in the cabaret's elaborate
productions of shadow theatre. In this
example he is shown improvising for a
performance of Caran d'Ache's historical play about Napoleon, *L'Épopée*,
which he also accompanied when the
show went out on tour.

Der Maler und Dichter Rodolphe
Salis, Betreiber des Künstlercabarets
Le Chat noir und Herausgeber der
gleichnamigen Zeitung, fungierte
bei den aufwendigen Schattenthea-
terproduktionen als stimmgewaltiger
Rezitator. Hier improvisiert er zu
einer Aufführung von Caran d'Aches
napoleonischem Historienspektakel
L'Épopée, mit dem er auch auf Tour-
nee ging.

Le peintre et poète Rodolphe Salis,
patron du cabaret d'artistes Le Chat
noir et éditeur du journal éponyme,
faisait fonction de récitant à la voix
sonore dans des productions raffi-
nées de théâtre d'ombres. Là, il impro-
visait pour une représentation du
spectacle *L'Épopée* de Caran d'Ache,
consacré à l'épopée napoléonienne,
avec lequel il partait aussi en tournée.

anarchosyndikalistischen Orientierung in den meisten Ländern verboten war, konnte es mit einer Auflagenhöhe zwischen
40 000 und 250 000 Exemplaren über die Grenzen der Dritten
Republik ausstrahlen. Neben dem *Simplicissimus* zählte es zu
den zentralen Vorbildern der Bildpublizistik der russischen Revolution von 1905 und der Reformbewegungen in muslimischen
Ländern zu Beginn des 20. Jahrhunderts. Dass sich auch die
umstrittenen Journale der jüngsten französischen Karikaturbewegung, *Hara-Kiri* (1960–1970) und *Charlie Hebdo* (seit 1970),
auf die visuelle Drastik von *L'Assiette au Beurre* berufen können,
zeugt von der ungebrochenen Brisanz dieses Magazins.

Ein weiteres wichtiges Feld für die Auseinandersetzung der
künstlerischen Moderne mit dem Bildjournalismus war die
Propaganda im Ersten Weltkrieg. Einen späten Höhepunkt
repräsentiert die Bildnachrichtenunternehmung der bolschewistischen Telegrafenagentur ROSTA (1919–1922) unter der

Leitung des Malers und Dichters Wladimir Majakowski (siehe
Abb. S. 586–589). Sein Gedicht *Tagesbefehl an die Kunstarmee*,
in dem er 1918 schrieb, dass „Straßenbesen [...] unsere Pinsel"
und „Plätze unsere Paletten (Duwakin 1975, S. 37) seien,
verband die Aushänge der ROSTA-Plakate mit den Karikaturkampagnen William Hones, Charles Philipons und der Pariser
Kommune. Majakowskis Hoffnung auf eine bildjournalistische
„Revolutionierung des Kunstgeschmacks", die er 1930 in seinem
Gedicht *Ich bitte um Worte* äußerte (Duwakin 1975, S. 66), sollte
sich allerdings in den folgenden Jahrzehnten als trügerisch
erweisen. Die künstlerische Moderne war nach dem Ersten
Weltkrieg zunehmend auf Abschottung und Autonomie aus.
Segregation und Elitarismus bestimmten den Kulturbetrieb. So
markierten die ROSTA-Plakate nicht den Anfang einer interventionistischen Kunstepoche, sondern das Ende eines Zeitalters pressegrafischer Avantgarde.

Révolution de l'illustration

Au cours d'une interview, Marcel Duchamp étonna son interlocuteur Pierre Cabanne, qui l'interrogeait sur sa période d'apprentissage artistique à Montmartre, par l'affirmation qu'il n'avait guère de contact avec les peintres, mais surtout avec les dessinateurs humoristiques. Et il ajouta qu'à l'époque même un artiste comme Juan Gris était illustrateur (Cabanne 1971, p. 22). En effet, à Paris, au tournant du siècle, il n'y avait guère un protagoniste de l'avant-garde artistique qui ne fût en relation avec le dessin de presse. Dans une interview avec Dora Vallier, le peintre cubiste Jacques Villon, frère de Duchamp, souligna l'importance centrale de la presse illustrée. «À cette époque, l'influence des journaux sur l'art était incontestable. Grâce à eux, la peinture a été libérée plus rapidement de l'académisme» (Leighten 2013, p. 31). Les stimulations déclenchées par le dessin de presse furent cependant beaucoup plus profondes et complexes que la simple confrontation avec la réalité quotidienne à laquelle Villon faisait allusion en conclusion. Ainsi, par exemple, le journal Le Courrier français, pour lequel les deux frères dessinaient principalement (voir ill. p. 507), était l'ancien organe central du mouvement des Arts incohérents. Dans les années 1880, ce mouvement influencé par le dessin de presse avait marqué le passage décisif de la tradition de parodie artistique propre au Salon caricatural à la révolution de l'art par une série d'expositions expérimentales. Les critiques contemporains avaient alors salué l'opposition anti-académique dans un pronostic visionnaire : «L'art sera incohérent ou ne sera pas (Le Voltaire, 15 octobre 1883).»

Ce renouveau artistique était aussi dû à l'abolition de la censure en France en 1881 qui, dans le domaine de la caricature, avait marqué le début d'une phase de réflexion médiatique et d'ouverture interdisciplinaire. À cela s'ajoutèrent les nouvelles techniques chimigraphiques de reproduction à l'aide desquelles la méthode stylistique incohérente du montage était placée au premier plan dans le secteur du dessin de presse. Avant que la déconstruction et le montage ne deviennent incontournables pour la création d'images des cubistes, ils s'étaient déjà imposés comme méthodes de style fondamentales dans le dessin de presse. Le papier collé et le montage photographique libre y furent utilisés dès les années 1890 (voir ill. p. 534 h.).

L'orientation du modernisme classique à l'expression originelle, incontrôlée, avait traversé aussi une phase d'incubation caricaturesque dans le dilettantisme provocant des Incohérents. Le primitivisme ludique de ce groupe de dadaïstes précoces avec ses techniques créatrices d'association libre passa presque sans transition à des formes motivées idéologiquement de rudesse graphique, comme elles étaient notamment propagées par le journal anarchiste Le Père peinard (1889–1900 ; voir ills. p. 537). Aux côtés des artistes néo-impressionnistes Lucien Pissarro et Maximilien Luce l'Incohérent Adolphe Willette en était un des principaux membres de rédaction. L'ami de Villon et de Duchamp est considéré comme une figure majeure de la scène artistique de Montmartre, qui avait pris son essor en 1881 avec la fondation du légendaire cabaret littéraire Le Chat noir. Avec ses dessins rêveurs évoquant la pantomime, Willette marqua de son empreinte le magazine éponyme que le patron du café, Rodolphe Salis, avait créé en 1883 et qui devait se révéler novateur pour la culture de revue avant-gardiste de la fin de siècle (voir ills. p. 506). De façon analogue à la chronophotographie, le successeur de Willette, Théophile Steinlen commença à convertir cinématographiquement son format de séries de clichés muets. Quelques années avant la série Yellow Kid de Richard Outcault, qui fut lancée en 1895 dans le New York World de Joseph Pulitzer en même temps que les premières projections de films, Steinlen introduisit le réalisme urbain dans le genre de la bande dessinée (voir ill. p. 510). Néanmoins, il n'entra pas dans les annales comme pionnier du comic strip, mais grâce à ses travaux ultérieurs pour des journaux anarchistes de syndicats comme précurseur de l'art socialiste moderne. Des représentants majeurs de la Sécession berlinoise et de l'Ashcan School américaine comme Käthe Kollwitz et John Sloan subirent son influence tout autant que le peintre précubiste Picasso. Et la création du magazine satirique munichois dominant Simplicissimus (1896–1944) est aussi en grande partie due au penchant de l'éditeur de Steinlen, Albert Langen, pour son journalisme illustré socio-critique.

Quelques années plus tard, le succès des dessins grand format de Simplicissimus et du magazine d'Art nouveau fondé également à Munich la même année, Jugend (1896–1940), encouragea l'éditeur parisien Samuel Schwarz à la publication de L'Assiette au Beurre, un journal satirique qui, à part quelques légendes isolées, misait exclusivement sur l'effet des dessins (voir ill. p. 493). En laissant à ses illustrateurs la plus grande liberté possible quant au contenu et au design, Schwarz réussit à rassembler les artistes les plus friands d'expériences de l'époque sous le label du dessin satirique : des naturalistes, des symbolistes, des esthétistes, des synthétistes, des nabis, des fauves, des cubistes en herbe et, avec František Kupka, un futur artiste abstrait. Les 600 numéros de thèmes et d'auteurs de L'Assiette au Beurre, parus de 1901 à 1912, peuvent être considérés comme la preuve monumentale de la thèse de Jacques

Anonymous (photo.)

Vladimir Mayakovsky, Moscow, February 1930

Vladimir Mayakovsky is shown here standing in front of a display of posters from Rosta's series of pictorial news. The photograph is from a retrospective exhibition that revealed his disagreement with Stalin's cultural policy, and was taken only a few months before he committed suicide.

Wladimir Majakowski vor Plakaten der ROSTA-Bildnachrichtenserie. Die Aufnahme entstand wenige Monate vor seinem Freitod in einer retrospektiven Ausstellung, die den Dissens mit der stalinistischen Kulturpolitik offenkundig machte.

Vladimir Maïakovski devant des affiches de la série d'informations en images ROSTA. Ce cliché a été pris, quelques mois seulement avant son suicide, dans une exposition rétrospective qui mettait en évidence sa dissension avec la politique culturelle de Staline.

Villon soulignant la libération de l'art par le dessin de presse. Bien que le magazine artistique libertaire fût interdit dans la plupart des pays à cause de son orientation anarcho-syndicaliste, il put se flatter d'un tirage allant de 40 000 à 250 000 exemplaires au-delà des frontières de la Troisième République. Avec le *Simplicissimus*, il fut l'une des principales références pour le journalisme illustré de la révolution russe de 1905 et des mouvements réformateurs dans les pays musulmans au début du XXe siècle. Le fait que les journaux controversés du mouvement contemporain de caricature en France, *Hara-Kiri* (1960–1970) et *Charlie Hebdo* (depuis 1970), puissent se réclamer de la radicalité visuelle de *L'Assiette au Beurre* démontre que ce journal a gardé intacte sa force explosive.

Un autre champ de débat entre le modernisme artistique et le journalisme illustré fut la propagande pendant la Première Guerre mondiale. Plus tard, la diffusion de nouvelles en images par l'agence télégraphique bolchévique ROSTA (1919–1922) sous la direction du peintre et poète Vladimir Maïakovski constitua une apogée (voir ills. p. 586–589). Son «Ordre du jour à l'armée de l'art» (1918), que «les rues… soient nos pinceaux» et «les places, nos palettes» (Duwakin 1975, p. 37), liait les affichages des fenêtres ROSTA aux campagnes de caricature de William Hone, de Charles Philipon et de la Commune de Paris. L'espoir de Maïakovski d'une «révolution du goût artistique» dans le domaine du journalisme illustré, qu'il exprima en 1930 dans son poème *Ich bitte um Worte* (Duwakin 1975, p. 66), s'avéra toutefois illusoire au cours des décennies suivantes. Après la Première Guerre mondiale, le modernisme artistique tendit de plus en plus à l'isolation et l'autarcie. La ségrégation et l'élitisme dominèrent le milieu culturel. Ainsi, les affiches ROSTA ne marquèrent pas le début d'une époque artistique interventionniste, mais la fin d'une ère d'avant-garde du dessin de presse.

1. Entrance to the Gorge.   3. Higher up the Grosse Enge.   5. The Passage opens wider.   7. Upper Outlet of the Aar-Schlucht.
2. The Grosse Enge.   4. A Narrow Gangway.   6. The Schräibach Waterfall.   8. Village of Meiringen.

SKETCHES IN THE AAR-SCHLUCHT, MEIRINGEN, SWITZERLAND.

Anonymous

*Sketches in the Aar-Schlucht,
Meiringen, Switzerland,* 1889
*Skizzen in der Aar-Schlucht,
Meiringen, Schweiz*
*Esquisses dans les gorges de l'Aar,
Meiringen, Suisse*
Wood engraving
From: *The Illustrated London News*,
28 September 1889

Montages made up of typographical
elements, drawings, photographs and
prints were collected by people as
a hobby in the form of scrapbooks.
The aesthetics of this popular cultural
form of saving memories were also
adopted in press graphics for illustrations featuring several views.

Montagen aus typografischen Elementen, Zeichnungen, Fotografien
und Drucken in sogenannten Scrapbooks zu sammeln, war ein beliebtes
Hobby. Die Ästhetiken dieser populären Memorabilienkultur strahlte in
besonderer Weise auch auf die plu-
rale Illustriertengrafik aus.

La collection de montages faits
d'éléments typographiques, de dessins, de photographies et d'imprimés sous forme de «scrapbooking»
devint un hobby. L'esthétique de
cette culture populaire du souvenir
influença aussi particulièrement
le pluralisme des illustrations dans
les magazines illustrés.

Anonymous

Leaflet | *Faltblatt* | *Dépliant,* 1881
Wood engravings
From: *The Illustrated London News*, 2 July 1881 (left);
30 April 1881 (right)

The patchwork patterns of sections from large folded graphics, that
were bound in to the better-quality illustrated magazines on special
occasions, also corresponded to a new aesthetics of incoherence.

Auch die Patchworkmuster der zusammengefalteten Großgrafiken,
die zu besonderen Anlässen in den bürgerlichen Illustrierten einge-
bunden waren, spiegelten eine neue Ästhetik der Inkohärenz.

Les motifs de patchwork des dessins pliés et à grand format, qui
étaient intégrés aux illustrés bourgeois lors d'occasions particu-
lières, reflétaient eux aussi la nouvelle esthétique de l'incohérence.

Émile Cohl

Incoherents Exhibition, 1886
Ausstellung der Incohérents
Exposition des Incohérents
Relief etching
From: *Le Charivari*, Paris, 22 October 1886

The Incoherents, some of whom used the pseudonym Dada and long before the word was taken up by the Dadaists themselves, consisted mostly of writers along with artists who also worked as press illustrators. The experimental flair and energy they employed to counter the limitations of the established arts prompted the euphoric prediction from one critic that in the future "art will either be incoherent or it will cease to exist" (*Le Voltaire*, 15 October 1883).

Die Incohérents, von denen Einzelne bereits lange vor den Dadaisten das Pseudonym Dada verwendeten, setzten sich hauptsächlich aus Pressegrafikern und Dichtern zusammen. Der experimentelle Elan, mit dem sie den Limitierungen der etablierten Künste entgegneten, veranlasste einen Kritiker zu der euphorischen Prognose: „Die Kunst wird entweder inkohärent sein, oder sie wird nicht mehr sein" (*Le Voltaire*, 15. Oktober 1883).

Les Incohérents, dont certains membres utilisèrent le pseudonyme de Dada longtemps avant les dadaïstes, se composaient principalement de dessinateurs de presse et de poètes. L'élan expérimental avec lequel ils s'opposaient aux limites des arts établis, suscita chez un critique un pronostic euphorique : « L'art sera incohérent ou ne sera pas » (*Le Voltaire*, 15 octobre 1883).

Joseph Faverot

Café des Incohérents
An Exhibition by the Real Incoherents, 1886
Die Ausstellung der wahren Incohérents
L'Exposition des véritables Incohérents
Relief etching
From: *Le Courrier français*, Paris,
14 November 1886

The main techniques used in the artistic parodies of the Incoherents were montage, coded references and free association. The group presented a series of popular exhibitions in Paris that also toured in the provinces, and together with their catalogues, numerous newspaper articles, costume balls and running a café in their own name, they asserted themselves vigorously in France in the years from 1882 to 1893 (see also ills. pp. 374, 375).

Montage, Codierung und freies Assoziieren waren Haupttechniken der kunstparodistischen Gruppierung der Arts Incohérents. Mit einer Reihe populärer Ausstellungen in Paris, Tourneen durch die Provinz,

Katalogen, zahllosen Zeitungsartikeln, Kostümbällen und einem eigenen Künstlercafé war die Bewegung von 1882 bis 1893 überaus präsent in Frankreich (siehe auch Abb. S. 374, 375).

Montage, codification et association libre étaient les principales techniques des Arts incohérents, un groupe qui s'adonnait à la parodie artistique. Grâce à une série d'expositions populaires à Paris, à des tournées en province, à des catalogues, à d'innombrables articles de journaux, à des bals masqués et à un café d'artistes, le mouvement fut extrêmement présent en France de 1882 à 1893 (voir aussi ills. p. 374, 375).

LE COURRIER FRANÇAIS

L'Exposition des véritables Incohérents, au Café des Incohérents, rue Fontaine-Saint-Georges, 16bis
(ENTRÉE GRATUITE)

Dessin de J. FAVEROT.

Alfred Le Petit

Holy Relics (fragments), 1886
Heilige Reliquien (Fragmente)
Reliques saintes (fragments)
Relief etching
From: Jules Lévy (ed.), *Catalogue de l'Exposition des Arts incohérents,*
Paris, 1886

In 1883, Alfred Le Petit began to incorporate collaged materials and found objects into his *Journal parlé* (Spoken Journal) performances at the Théâtre de l'Athénée in Paris. The following year, at the annual exhibition of Incoherent Arts, he presented a sculpture consisting of an umbrella and a broom with the enigmatic title *Parapluie pour spectacle* (An Umbrella Displayed), and two years later followed that up with this miscellaneous collection of peculiar relics.

1883 begann Alfred Le Petit im Rahmen seiner *Journal-parlé*-Performances im Théâtre de l'Athénée, Materialcollagen und Objets trouvés zu entwickeln. 1884 präsentierte er in der Jahresausstellung der Incohérents unter dem enigmatischen Titel *Parapluie pour spectacle* eine skulpturale Kombination aus Regenschirm und Besen. Zwei Jahre später war er mit einem Sammelsurium absurder Reliquien vertreten.

En 1883, Alfred Le Petit commença à développer des collages de matériaux et d'objets trouvés dans le cadre de ses performances du *Journal parlé* au Théâtre de l'Athénée. Lors de l'exposition annuelle de 1884 des Incohérents, il présenta une combinaison sculpturale à partir d'un parapluie et d'un balai sous le titre énigmatique *Parapluie pour spectacle.* Deux ans plus tard, il était représenté avec un bric-à-brac d'absurdes reliques.

Eugène Mesplès

The Honest Woman and the Other One, 1884
Die anständige Frau und die andere
L'Honnête Femme et l'autre
Relief etching
From: Jules Levy (ed.), *Catalogue illustré de l'Exposition des Arts incohérents en 1884,* Paris, 1884

In this work by Eugène Mesplès the Incoherents' delight in language and wordplay was taken to an unprecedented degree of minimalism. His typographic and geometric evocation of sexual attraction anticipated not only the mechanical narrative between the sexes in Marcel Duchamp's *Large Glass* but also the references to Tantric geometry exercises used by James Joyce in writing *Finnegans Wake.*

Eugène Mesplès trieb die inkohärente Lust an Reden und Sprachspielen auf eine ungekannte minimalistische Höhe. Seine typografisch-geometrische Evokation sexueller Anziehung antizipierte nicht nur den technischen Geschlechtermythos von Marcel Duchamps *Grand Verre,* sondern auch die tantrische Geometrieaufgabe, die James Joyce' Dichtung *Finnegans Wake* zugrunde liegt.

Eugène Mesplès porta l'incohérente envie de discours et de jeux de mots à un summum minimaliste jusqu'alors inconnu. Son évocation géométrique et typographique de l'attirance sexuelle n'anticipe pas seulement le mythe technique des sexes du *Grand Verre* de Marcel Duchamp, mais aussi l'exercice tantrique de géométrie qui est à la base de l'œuvre de James Joyce *Finnegans Wake.*

Alphred Ko-S'Inn-Hus

Venus Demi-lot, or, the Husband of Venus de Milo, 1886
Die Venus demi-lot oder Der Gemahl der Venus von Milo
Le Vénus demi-lot ou le mari de la Vénus de Milo
Relief etching
From: Jules Lévy (ed.), *Catalogue de l'Exposition des Arts Incohérents,* Paris, 1886

The sculpture shown here by Alfred Caussinus, who used a phonetic variation of his name as a pseudonym for this work, is the sort of conglomeration of artistic parody, wordplay (*Venus Demi-lot* – Venus's Other Half – is homophonically equivalent to the title of the original statue, *Venus de Milo*) and found object that appealed to the Incoherents. A few decades later, Marcel Duchamp described his own more prosaic version of using found objects in a somewhat Incoherent style as "readymades".

Die Skulptur von Alfred Caussinus, der für dieses Werk das Pseudonym Alphred Ko-S'Inn-Hus verwendet, repräsentiert ein Konglomerat aus Kunstparodie, phonetischem Sprachspiel (*Venus demi-lot,* Venus' andere Hälfte klingt phonetisch wie der Titel der Originalstatue, *Vénus de Milo*) und Objet trouvé, das bei den Incohérents beliebt war. Jahrzehnte später belegte Marcel Duchamp seine etwas prosaischere Variante inkohärenter *bricolage* mit dem Begriff des Readymade.

La sculpture d'Alfred Caussinus, qui utilise pour cette œuvre le pseudonyme Alphred Ko-S'Inn-Hus, représente un conglomérat de parodie artistique, de jeu phonétique (*Venus demi-lot,* l'autre moitié de Vénus, sonne phonétiquement comme le nom de la statue originale, *Vénus de Milo*) et d'objet trouvé, qui était fort apprécié chez les Incohérents. Des décennies plus tard, Marcel Duchamp créa sa version quelque peu plus prosaïque de *bricolage* incohérent sous le terme de ready-made.

Marc Sonal

Cruel Enigma!!! Charming!!!, 1886
Grausames Rätsel!!! Charmant!!!
Cruelle énigme!!! Charmant!!!
Relief etching
From: Jules Lévy (ed.), *Catalogue de l'Exposition des Arts incohérents,* Paris, 1886

Marc Sonal's beauty unmasked became a key image for the Incoherents. The illustration was also later published by Georges Bataille in the Surrealist magazine *Documents,* which served as a reminder to artists in 1930 of the importance of the Incoherents as a pioneering movement for the liberation of art.

Marc Sonals demaskierte Schönheit wurde zur Ikone der Arts Incohérents. Durch den Abdruck dieser Grafik in der Surrealistenzeitung *Documents* erinnerte Georges Bataille seine Künstlerkollegen 1930 an die Bedeutung dieser Vorläuferbewegung für die Befreiung der Kunst.

La beauté démasquée de Marc Sonal devint l'icône des Arts incohérents. En imprimant ce dessin dans le journal surréaliste *Documents,* Georges Bataille rappela en 1930 à ses collègues artistes l'importance de ce mouvement précurseur de la libération de l'art.

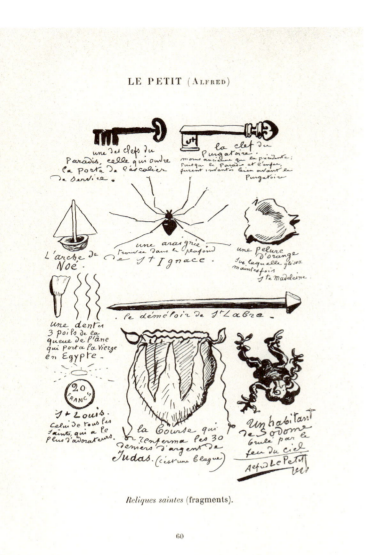

Reliques saintes (fragments).

60

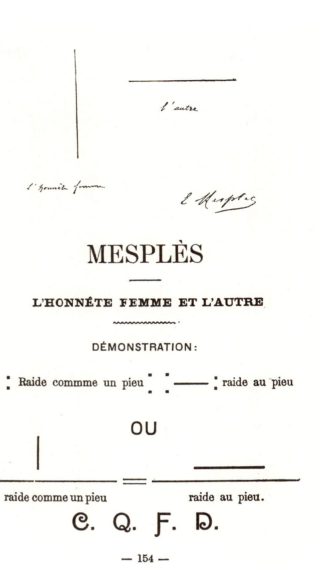

154

Le mari de la Vénus de Milo.

61

Cruelle énigme!!! Charmant!!!

37

Eugène Bataille (Sapeck)

← *Mona Lisa Smoking a Pipe*, 1887
Die Mona Lisa, Pfeife rauchend
La Joconde fumant la pipe
Relief etching
From: Coquelin Cadet, *Le Rire*,
Paris, 1887

The satirical artist Sapeck, one of André Gill's last students, was the most radical of the Incoherents. He was a very early performance artist who walked around Paris with his head painted blue, and had himself pulled through the streets in a cart as the "World-famous Sapeck". Long before Marcel Duchamp's *L.H.O.O.Q.*, in this illustration Sapeck applied a masculine attribute to the famous portrait of the Mona Lisa, in the process degrading her mysterious ideal of beauty to the level of a stuffy old pipe-smoker.

Der Karikaturist Sapeck, ein später Schüler André Gills, war der radikalste Incohérent. Als Pionier der Aktionskunst flanierte er mit himmelblauem Kopf durch Paris und ließ sich als „weltberühmter Sapeck" in einem Karren über die Boulevards ziehen. Lange vor Marcel Duchamp in *L.H.O.O.Q.* applizierte er dem Porträt der sogenannten Mona Lisa ein männliches Attribut und degradierte das rätselhafte Schönheitsideal zum „Pfeifenkopf".

Le caricaturiste Sapeck, un élève tardif d'André Gill, fut l'Incohérent le plus radical. Pionnier de l'art d'action, il flâna avec une tête bleu azur à travers Paris et se fit tirer dans une brouette sur les boulevards comme le « mondialement célèbre Sapeck ». Longtemps avant Marcel Duchamp dans *L.H.O.O.Q.*, il affubla la fameuse Mona Lisa d'un attribut masculin et dégrada le mystérieux idéal de beauté au rang de « tête de pipe ».

Émile Cohl

Portrait of Léon Cladel, 1885
Woodburytype
From: L.-G. Mostrailles, *Têtes de pipes, avec 21 photographies par Émile Cohl*, Paris, 1885

Together with his fellow caricaturists Nadar, Bertall and Alfred Le Petit, Émile Cohl was an early exponent of experimental photography. As in-house photographer for the Incoherents he provided two symbolic portraits for a book on famous writers. This enigmatic ear was used to represent the novelist Léon Cladel, who had been described by Jules Vallès as nothing but a "shepherd with cotton wool in his ears".

Émile Cohl zählte ebenso wie die Karikaturistenkollegen Nadar, Bertall und Alfred Le Petit zu den Exponenten experimenteller Fotografie. Für einen Band über prominente Literaten lieferte der Hoffotograf der Incohérents zwei Beispiele symbolischer Porträtkunst ab. Die rätselhafte Ohrmuschel repräsentiert den Dichter Léon Cladel, der von Jules Vallès als „Hirte mit Watte in den Ohren" bezeichnet wurde.

Émile Cohl faisait partie au même titre que ses collègues caricaturistes Nadar, Bertall et Alfred Le Petit des artistes exposants de la photographie expérimentale. Pour un ouvrage sur des figures célèbres de la littérature, le photographe attitré des Incohérents produisit deux exemples d'art symbolique du portrait. L'énigmatique pavillon de l'oreille représente le poète Léon Cladel que Jules Vallès désigna comme « berger avec du coton dans les oreilles ».

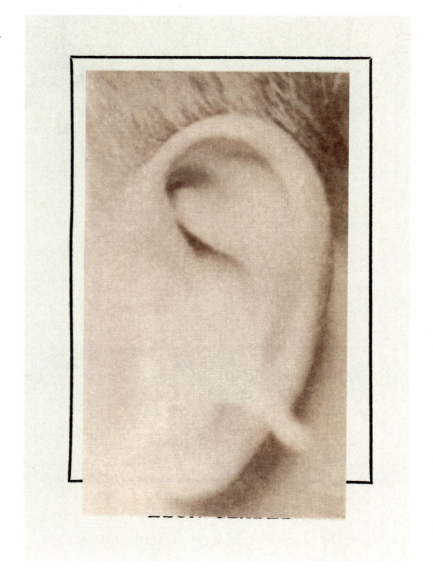

COMBAT DE NÈGRES DANS UNE CAVE, PENDANT LA NUIT
(Reproduction du célèbre tableau.)

7

Alphonse Allais

"Negroes" Fighting in a Cellar at Night, 1897
Kampf der „Neger" im Keller, während der Nacht
Combat de « nègres » dans une cave, pendant la nuit
Relief etching
From: Alphonse Allais, *Album primo-avrilesque*, Paris, 1897

Alphonse Allais was editor of the *Chat noir* magazine and a key figure in the artistic milieu of Montmartre at the time. His work was highly regarded later on by the Dadaists, amongst others, while in 2015 an X-ray examination of Kazimir Malevich's *Black Square* revealed an inscription that had been painted over and which suggested that this key work of modernism, the iconic "zero point of painting", had in fact been created in direct response to Allais's black rectangle and its racist connotations.

Der Dichter Alphonse Allais zählte als Chefredakteur des Magazins *Le Chat noir* zu den Schlüsselfiguren der Szene auf dem Montmartre. Sein Werk wurde nicht nur von Dadaisten hochgeschätzt. 2015 brachte eine Röntgenanalyse von Kasimir Malewitsch' *Schwarzem Quadrat* eine übermalte Inschrift zum Vorschein, die darauf schließen lässt, dass dieses Schlüsselwerk der Moderne, dieser ikonische Nullpunkt der Malerei, in direkter Auseinandersetzung mit Allais' rassistisch konnotiertem schwarzen Rechteck entstand.

Rédacteur en chef du magazine *Le Chat noir*, le poète Alphonse Allais était une des figures emblématiques de la scène montmartroise. Ses travaux n'étaient pas estimés que par les dadaïstes. En 2015, une analyse aux rayons X du *Carré noir* de Kasimir Malevitch révéla une inscription recouverte de peinture qui laisse supposer que cette œuvre clé de l'art moderne, ce zéro iconique de la peinture, fut créé en réponse directe au carré noir d'Allais et à ses connotations racistes.

← **Adolphe Willette**

Pierrot Wins the Jackpot, 1884
Pierrot hat das große Los gezogen
Pierrot a gagné le gros lot
Relief etching
From: *Le Chat noir*, Paris, 21 March 1884

The Chat Noir cabaret run by Rodolphe Salis, who was himself also an artist and performer, was the birthplace of avant-garde culture in Montmartre. From January 1882 the artists' club published its own magazine, which became well known for Adolphe Willette's comic-strip series *Pierrot fumiste*, whose protagonist personified the life of a bohemian, and sometimes melancholy artist.

Geburtsstätte der avantgardistischen Montmartre-Kultur war das von dem Maler und Performer Rodolphe Salis betriebene Kabarett Le Chat noir. Seit Anfang 1882 brachte dieser Künstlerklub eine eigene Zeitung heraus, die von Adolphe Willettes Comicreihe um den *Pierrot fumiste*, eine Personifikation des melancholischen Künstlerbohemien, bestimmt wurde.

Le cabaret Le Chat noir, dirigé par le peintre et poète Rodolphe Salis, fut le berceau de la culture avant-gardiste de Montmartre. Dès le début de 1882, ce club publia son propre journal qui était défini par la série de bandes dessinées d'Adolphe Willette autour du *Pierrot fumiste*, personnification du bohémien artiste et mélancolique.

The Romance of the Rose, 1883
Der Rosenroman | Le Roman de la rose
Relief etching
From: *Le Chat noir*, Paris, 5 May 1883

The cartoon historian David Kunzle rated Adolphe Willette as one of the "great masters of expressive gestures" (Kunzle 1990), on a par with Toulouse-Lautrec and Aubrey Beardsley. Furthermore, he also saw the somewhat oblique dream world of Willette's Pierrot as a precursor to the more fantastic cartoon situations seen later in *Little Nemo* and *Krazy Kat*.

Der Comichistoriker David Kunzle stellt den Zeichner Adolphe Willette als einen „der Großmeister ausdruckshafter Gestik (Kunzle 1990)" in eine Reihe mit den nachfolgenden Toulouse-Lautrec und Aubrey Beardsley. In der kryptischen Traumwelt von Willettes Pierrot sieht Kunzle die fantastischen Comicszenarien von *Little Nemo* und *Krazy Kat* vorweggenommen.

L'historien de bandes dessinées David Kunzle classe le dessinateur Adolphe Willette comme un «grand maître de la gestique expressive (Kunzle 1990)» au même rang que Toulouse-Lautrec et Aubrey Beardsley. Dans le monde de rêves cryptique du Pierrot de Willette, Kunzle voit l'anticipation des scénarios de bandes dessinées fantastiques comme *Little Nemo* et *Krazy Kat*.

Where Do You Get the Money from?, 1889
Woher kommt das Geld? | D'où vient l'argent?
Relief etching
From: *Le Pierrot*, Paris, 22 February 1889

In 1885 Adolphe Willette left *Le Chat noir* and began supplying illustrations to various anarchist publications, as well as founding his own short-lived magazine in 1888, *Le Pierrot*. His use of comic strips without words, which he had developed for *Le Chat noir* based on Kaspar Braun's earlier pictorial work (see ill. p. 174), now became increasingly marked by political commentary.

1885 verließ Adolphe Willette *Le Chat noir*, um für eine Reihe anarchistischer Journale zu zeichnen. 1888 gründete er ein eigenes kurzlebiges Magazin, *Le Pierrot*. Das Format des stummen Strips, das er in *Le Chat noir* nach dem Vorbild von Kaspar Brauns Bilderbögen (siehe Abb. S. 174) etabliert hatte, durchsetzte er nun zunehmend mit politischen Kommentaren.

En 1885, Adolphe Willette quitta *Le Chat noir* afin de dessiner pour une série de journaux anarchistes. En 1888, il fonda son propre magazine *Le Pierrot*, qui fut de courte durée. Désormais, il enrichit de commentaires politiques le format de bandes dessinées muettes, qu'il avait établi dans *Le Chat noir* d'après le modèle des pages illustrées de Kaspar Braun (voir ill. p. 174).

Jacques Villon

At the Cabaret du Néant, 1897
Im Cabaret du Néant | Au Cabaret du Néant
Relief etching
From: *Le Courrier français*, Paris, 10 October 1897

Jacques Villon's sequence of images relating to Loïe Fuller's "serpentine dance" (see ill. p. 435) shows the influence of his fellow artist Adolphe Willette's cartoons, while his own development towards Cubist abstraction can be seen in the way he has examined the paradoxical area that lies between representations of space and of time. The enigmatic parallelism of different elements, as later used by his brother Marcel Duchamp, also seems to be foreshadowed here.

Jacques Villons Bilderfolge mit Anspielung auf Loïe Fullers Schlangentanz (siehe Abb. 435) verrät den Einfluss der Comics seines Freundes Adolphe Willette. In der Beschäftigung mit Paradoxien im Grenzbereich zwischen Raum- und Zeiterfahrung kündigt sich bereits Villons Entwicklung zur kubistischen Abstraktion hin an. Auch der enigmatische Elementarparallelismus seines Bruders Marcel Duchamp scheint hier antizipiert.

La série d'images de Jacques Villon avec une allusion à la danse serpentine de Loïe Fuller (voir ill. p. 435) souligne l'influence des bandes dessinées de son ami Adolphe Willette. Dans son analyse des paradoxes à la lisière entre expérience spatiale et temporelle se révèle déjà l'évolution de Villon vers l'abstraction cubiste. Ici, il semble aussi anticiper le parallélisme élémentaire et énigmatique de son frère Marcel Duchamp.

LE COURRIER FRANÇAIS   5

Au Cabaret du Néant

Dessin de JACQUES VILLON.

Oui, monsieur, ça va commencer.

... L'ombre de celle que vous aimez va apparaître.

... La voici.

Mais soyons convenables, pfutt... elle a disparu...

— Dites donc..... Quand donnez-vous ça,... sans coupures ?

Théophile Steinlen

LE CHAT NOIR

Dessin de Steinlen.

To His Friend A. Allais, 1887
Seinem Freund A. Allais
À son ami A. Allais
Relief etching
From: *Le Chat noir*, Paris,
12 March 1887

Beginning in early 1884, the Swiss-born illustrator Théophile Steinlen continued with Adolphe Willette's format of comic strips without words in *Le Chat noir*, but in a manner that was more sequential and more closely resembled chronophotography. He found great success initially with cartoons of playful cats, but a few years on and influenced by Émile Zola's writings he changed his subject matter to social themes.

Seit Anfang 1884 führte der Schweizer Grafiker Théophile Steinlen in *Le Chat noir* Adolphe Willettes Format des stummen Comics fort, allerdings auf eine sequenziellere Weise, die an der Chronofotografie orientiert war. Großen Erfolg hatte Steinlen anfangs mit verspielten Katzenmotiven. Nach einigen Jahren wurden diese jedoch unter dem Eindruck der Schriften Émile Zolas von sozialen Themen verdrängt.

À partir du début de 1884, le dessinateur suisse Théophile Steinlen reprit dans *Le Chat noir* le format d'Adolphe Willette des bandes dessinées sans paroles, mais de façon plus séquentielle et orientée vers la chronophotographie. Au début, Steinlen obtint un grand succès avec des motifs ludiques de chat. Mais, après quelques années, sous l'influence des œuvres d'Émile Zola, ceux-ci furent supplantés par des thèmes sociaux.

→ *The Sensitive Horse*, 1890
Das empfindsame Pferd
Le Cheval susceptible
Relief etching
From: *Le Chat noir*, Paris,
7 June 1890

While the absence of words in Adolphe Willette's comic strips carried a sense of poetry, in Théophile Steinlen's hands it seemed heavy and laden with menace. It is also significant that the only character able to break through this wall of non-communication here is a "sensitive" animal, which in its indignation hurls a mouthful at the interfering bourgeois as shown in the speech bubble: "Hey, you useless idiot! Mind your own business!"

Während die Stille in Adolphe Willettes Bilderfolgen poetisch konnotiert war, wirkte sie bei Théophile Steinlen bleiern und bedrohlich. Bezeichnenderweise ist es ein „empfindsames" Tier, dem es als einzigem Wesen gelingt, die Mauer der Kommunikationslosigkeit zu durchbrechen. Empört schleudert es dem intervenierenden Bourgeois eine harsche Sprechblase entgegen: „Hey Penner! Kümmer dich um deinen eigenen Kram!"

Alors que le silence dans les séries d'images d'Adolphe Willette avait acquis des connotations poétiques, il semble de plomb et lourd de menaces chez Théophile Steinlen. De manière significative, un «animal susceptible» est la seule créature qui réussisse à percer le mur de l'incommunication. Indigné, il adresse au bourgeois qui tente d'intervenir une rude remontrance: «Hé! Feignant! Mêle-toi de tes affaires!»

Le Cheval susceptible, — dessin de Steinlen.

LE CHAT NOIR

A monsieur Georges Ohnet, pour l'encourager.

Flagrants délits : Outrage à la morale, — dessin de Steinlen.

Théophile Steinlen

Caught in the Act: A Moral Outrage, 1889
In flagranti: Verstoß gegen die Sittlichkeit
Flagrants délits : Outrage à la morale
Relief etching
From: *Le Chat noir*, Paris, 2 November 1889

For Théophile Steinlen, public spaces were scenes of social conflict. He was the first illustrator to give such areas a cinematic quality, and just like the shadow-theatre performances at the Chat Noir cabaret the shadows themselves played an important role by suggesting surveillance and the maintenance of public order.

Für Théophile Steinlen war der öffentliche Raum ein Ort sozialer Konflikte. Er war der Erste, der ihn auf eine filmische Weise durchdrang. Eine große Rolle spielte dabei, analog zu dem populären Théâtre d'ombres des Chat noir, die Herrschaft der Schatten, die als Instanzen der Überwachung und der Reglementierung fungieren.

Pour Théophile Steinlen l'espace public était un lieu de conflits sociaux. Il fut le premier à lui insuffler un esprit cinématographique. Comme dans le populaire théâtre d'ombres du Chat noir, la domination des ombres qui servaient d'instances de surveillance et de réglementation y jouait un rôle capital.

Franklin Morris Howarth

→ *Fair vs. Fare.*
A Street-car Tragedy of Every Day, 1892
Eine Alltagstragödie in der Straßenbahn | *Une tragédie quotidienne dans le tramway*
Coloured relief etching
From: *Puck*, New York, 1892

At this date Franklin Howarth, a pioneer of American comic strips, was working without the use of speech bubbles, and his series of urban scenes from everyday life in an Art Nouveau style appeared in several popular illustrated magazines and also as an early comic book. The narrative, which resembles that in a stage play, cannot be understood by the pictures alone but relies on the captions underneath.

Sprechblasenfrei operierte zu dieser Zeit der Pionier des amerikanischen Comicstrips Franklin Morris Howarth. Seine Serie urbaner Alltagsszenen im Art-nouveau-Stil erschien in mehreren populären Magazinen sowie als frühes Comicbook. Die bühnenartige Narration erschließt sich nicht bildnerisch, sondern allein über die dialogischen Begleittexte.

À cette époque, Franklin Morris Howarth le pionnier du *comic strip* américain, travaillait sans bulle de texte. Sa série de scènes urbaines quotidiennes parut dans le style de l'Art nouveau dans plusieurs magazines populaires ainsi que comme l'un des premiers livres de bande dessinée. La narration, digne d'une scène de théâtre, ne peut être comprise à travers les images, mais seulement grâce aux dialogues qui l'accompagnent.

PUCK.

Mrs. Grinne } Oh, I'm so glad to meet you! and you are going
Mrs. Barrett } my way, too.

Mrs. Grinne } Well, as I live! There is the conductor waiting
Mrs. Barrett } for his fare, and I had forgotten all about it.

Mrs. Grinne.— Now, let *me* pay the fare.
Mrs. Barrett.— No, indeed! *I'm* going to do it.

Mrs. Grinne— Well, I must *insist*, for I have the change right here.
Mrs. Barrett.— And I have two fives always handy.

Mrs. Grinne.— Here is the fare, conductor — Oh, good gracious!
there! I've dropped it.
Mrs. Barrett.— This for both, conductor.

Mrs. Grinne.— You need n't growl, conductor. If the cars did n't
have these gratings on the floor you would n't have so much bother
in finding dropped money. Thanks.

Mrs. Grinne } So glad to have met you. We had a delightful
Mrs. Barrett } adventure; did n't we? Good-by, dear.

Mrs. Barrett *(going East)*.— The mean thing. I know she just dropped
that money in order to make me pay her fare.
Mrs. Grinne *(going West)*.— She tried her *best* to make me pay her fare,
but that *accident* happened at a fortunate time.

FAIR *VS.* FARE.
A Street-car Tragedy of Every Day.

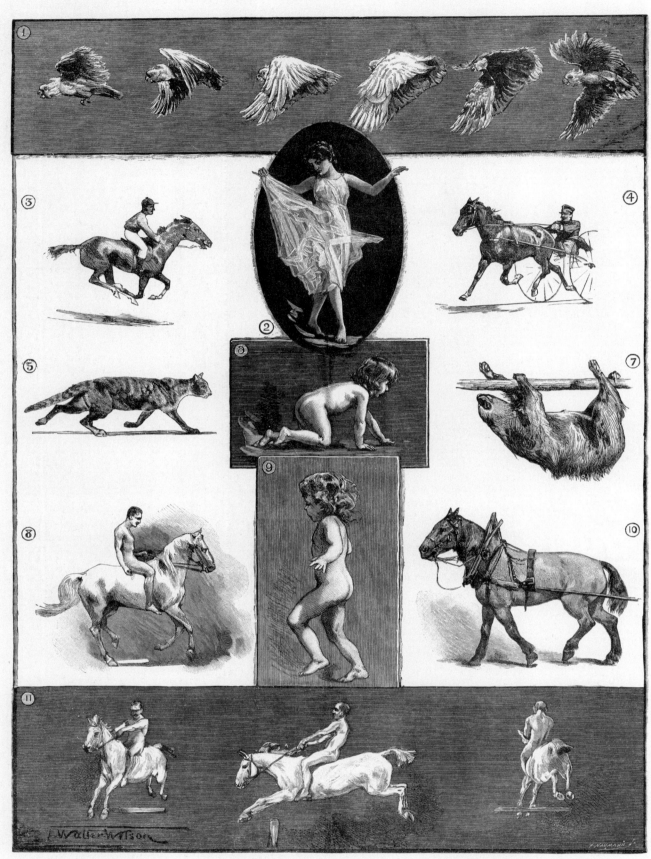

THE ILLUSTRATED LONDON NEWS, May 25, 1889.— 648

1. A selection of six phases in the stroke of a bird's wing (cockatoo), illustrating independent action of the primary feathers.   2. A phase in the action of a dancing-girl.   3. A phase occurring in the gallop.
4. A phase of fast trotting.   5. A phase of a cat trotting.   6. A phase in the crawling of a child.   7. A phase in the motion of a sloth clinging to a pole.   8. Phase of the canter; almost identical with
figure of Greek sculpture on the frieze of the Parthenon.   9. Phase of a child running.   10. Phase in the walk of a draught-horse.   11. Phase of leaping, as seen simultaneously from three points of view.

MOTIONS OF ANIMALS ILLUSTRATED BY THE INSTANTANEOUS PHOTOGRAPHS OF MR. MUYBRIDGE.

Thomas Walter Wilson & Paul Hermann Naumann (sc.)

*Motions of Animals Illustrated by
the Instantaneous Photographs of
Mr. Muybridge*, 1889
*Tierbewegungen, illustriert durch die
Momentaufnahmen von Mr Muybridge
Mouvements d'animaux, illustrés par
les clichés instantanés de M. Muybridge*
Wood engraving
From: *The Illustrated London News*,
25 May 1889

Decades before the invention of cinematography, moving images had taken
their first steps with the aid of rotat-
ing cylinders. Based on this principle
a device called a praxinoscope was
developed in 1877 which animated a
series of images, allowing early chro-
nophotographers such as Eadweard
Muybridge to present their sequences
of still photographs at the speed of
normal film.

Bereits Jahrzehnte vor der Kinematografie hatten die Bilder mittels
drehbarer Bildertrommeln das Laufen
gelernt. 1877 wurde auf Grundlage
dieses Prinzips ein Gerät, das Praxi-
noskop, entwickelt, mit dem frühe Chro-
nofotografen wie Eadweard Muybridge
ihre Fotosequenzen in Filmgeschwin-
digkeit vorführen konnten.

Des décennies avant le cinémato-
graphe, les images avaient déjà
appris à marcher à l'aide de disques
rotatifs. En 1877, un appareil fut mis
au point sur la base de ce principe,
le praxinoscope, avec lequel les premiers chronophotographes comme
Eadweard Muybridge purent présenter leurs séquences de photos à la
vitesse d'un film.

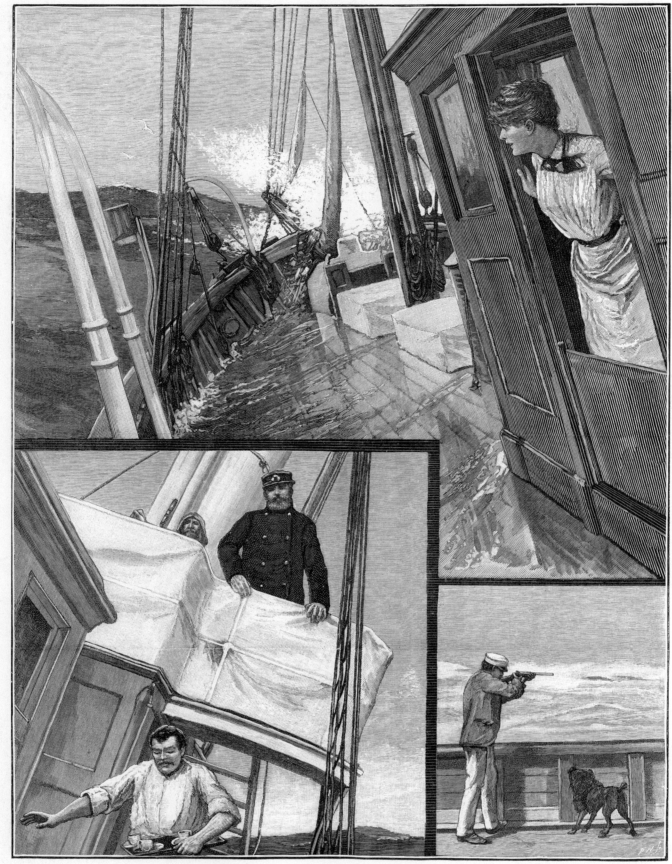

THE ILLUSTRATED LONDON NEWS, SEPT. 7, 1889.— 316

ROUGH WEATHER IN THE BAY OF BISCAY.

A GOOD ROLL.

YACHTING SKETCHES.

A SHOT AT A WHALE.

Anonymous

Yachting Sketches, 1889
Skizzen aus dem Segelsport
Esquisses de nautisme
Wood engraving
From: *The Illustrated London News*,
7 September 1889

By the late 1880s a style of cinematic montage was regularly being used in illustrations made up of several panels. The dynamics of these images were not necessarily based on chronological succession, as in the earlier pictorial broadsheets and strip cartoons, but might represent combinations of different viewpoints or angles.

In den späten 1880er-Jahren etablierte sich im Bereich der Multipanelgrafik ein filmischer Montagemodus, dessen Dynamik nicht auf dem zeitlichen Nacheinander der Bilderbogen und des frühen Comicstrips basierte, sondern auf einer Kombination unterschiedlicher Perspektiven und Blickwinkel.

Vers la fin des années 1880, un mode de montage cinématographique s'établit dans le secteur des planches dessinées composées de plusieurs cases, dont la dynamique ne reposait pas sur la succession temporelle de séries d'images et sur les premières bandes dessinées, mais sur une combinaison de perspectives et de champs de vision différents.

LE JOURNAL ILLUSTRÉ

284 — 5 SEPTEMBRE 1886 — Nᶜ 36 — PRIX : 15 CENTIMES   PRIX : 15 CENTIMES — Nᵒ 36 — 5 SEPTEMBRE 1886 — *284*

1. « — Et que voulez-vous que j'écrive sur votre album? »..

2. « — Je vois a cette page le nom de M. Pasteur. C'est au-dessous du sien que je mettrai mon nom. M. Pasteur est l'un des plus grands génies de notre époque : parce que nos savants étant partis, jusqu'alors, des phénomènes *connus* pour arriver à l'inconnu, il a, lui, procédé inversement. Je dois vous avouer que l'école scientifique à laquelle j'ai appartenu m'avait fait considérer cette nouveauté comme un non-sens. »

3. « — Je vais vous écrire mon premier principe philosophique. Ce n'est pas moi qui l'ai formulé : c'est Malebranche. J'ai bien cherché; je n'ai pas trouvé mieux. »

LE JOURNAL ILLUSTRÉ

285 — 5 SEPTEMBRE 1886 — Nº 36 — PRIX : 15 CENTIMES PRIX : 15 CENTIMES — Nº 36 — 5 SEPTEMBRE 1886 — 285

5. « — Je n'ai jamais bu que de l'eau et pourtant, je suis président de la Société des vins d'Anjou, — mais président honoraire seulement ! »

6. « — C'est là l'inconvénient de cette philosophie du jour, de cette philosophie de rhéteurs, de grands diseurs de riens. On se contente de mots et de paroles creuses... »

7. « — Remarquez que je suis loin de blâmer ce que je ne puis expliquer ; mais je vous dirai qu'il faut qu'on me prouve, *qu'il faut que je voie.* »

8. « — Alors, puisqu'ils nous affirment qu'ils dirigent, à leur volonté, leur ballon, qu'ils viennent me prendre ici, à cette fenêtre, tous les jours de séance à l'Institut et qu'ils me ramènent ! Cela m'évitera de descendre et de monter mes deux étages d'escaliers. »

1. The Commercial Traveller makes himself agreeable   3. Hands up, or die!   6. Shoot away!
   to the Passengers   4. The old Broker swears most horribly   7. Stop that Engine or down you go
2. Another gentleman of pleasing manner   5. He objects to "Shell out "   8. The robbers stand on the line till the train disappears

A TRAIN ROBBERY IN COLORADO

Anonymous

A Train Robbery in Colorado, 1891
Ein Zugüberfall in Colorado
L'Attaque d'un train dans le Colorado
Wood engraving
From: *The Graphic*, London,
8 August 1891

The illustrator for *The Graphic* has succeeded here in turning a straightforward news item about a train robbery into an exciting storyboard as if for a film. The third scene foreshadows the famous close-up for Edwin Porter's early Western *The Great Train Robbery* (1903), with the actor Justus D. Barnes shooting right ahead of him and into the audience.

Dem Zeichner des *Graphic* war es gelungen, eine prosaische Pressemeldung über einen Zugüberfall in ein spannendes Storyboard zu übersetzen. Szene 3 antizipiert den legendären Close-up in Edwin Porters bahnbrechendem Western *The Great Train Robbery* (1903), in dem der Schauspieler Justus D. Barnes frontal ins Publikum feuert.

L'illustrateur du *Graphic* parvint à transformer un article de presse prosaïque sur l'attaque d'un train en un scénarimage plein de suspense. La scène n° 3 anticipe le légendaire gros plan du western précurseur d'Edwin Porter *The Great Train Robbery* (1903), dans lequel l'acteur Justus D. Barnes tire de face sur le public.

←← Paul Nadar (photo.) & Stanislas Krakow (sc.)

Interview I and II, 1886
Three Conversations with Monsieur Chevreul | Drei Gespräche mit Monsieur Chevreul | Trois entretiens avec Monsieur Chevreul
Relief etchings
From: *Le Journal illustré*, Paris,
5 September 1886

The combined techniques of photographic snapshots and halftone engraving enabled Félix Nadar, the inventor of the political strip cartoon, to develop his interest in sequential narratives but told now through photography. His three interviews with the 100-year-old chemist and colour theorist Eugène Chevreul were photographed by Nadar's son Paul, and are a milestone in photo reporting.

Die Techniken der Momentaufnahme und der Autotypie erlaubten es dem Erfinder des politischen Comicstrips Félix Nadar, sein Interesse an sequenzieller Erzählweisen mit der Fotografie zu verbinden. Die drei Fotointerviews, die er mit dem 100-jährigen Chemiker und Farbtheoretiker Eugène Chevreul führte, wurden von Nadars Sohn Paul aufgenommen und gelten als Meilenstein der Fotoreportage.

Les techniques du cliché momentané et de la similigravure permirent à l'inventeur de la bande dessinée politique Félix Nadar d'associer son intérêt pour les narrations séquentielles à la photographie. Les trois interviews avec photos qu'il mena avec le chimiste et théoricien centenaire de la couleur Eugène Chevreul furent enregistrées par le fils de Nadar Paul et sont considérées comme une pierre angulaire du reportage photographique.

Richard Caton Woodville Jr. & H.F. Davey (sc.)

→ *After Rocky Mountain Sheep*, 1890
Auf der Jagd nach dem Rocky-Mountain-Schaf
À la poursuite du mouflon des Rocheuses
Wood engraving
From: *The Illustrated London News*,
10 May 1890

It has been well established that early pioneers of cinematographic montage such as D.W. Griffith and Sergei Eisenstein were inspired in the ways they edited their sequences of scenes by the narrative techniques used in 19th-century serial novels. There can be little surprise then that a genre of proto-cinematic storyboards was likewise first developed in the illustrations of press graphics.

Pioniere der cinematografischen Montage wie D.W. Griffith und Sergei Eisenstein ließen sich in ihren Schnittfolgen bekanntlich von den filmischen Erzähltechniken der Feuilletonromane des 19. Jahrhunderts inspirieren. Dass sich im pressegrafischen Milieu ein Genre des protocineastischen Storyboards entwickelte, sollte daher kaum verwundern.

Il est établi que des pionniers du montage cinématographique comme D.W. Griffith et Sergueï Eisenstein se sont inspirés dans leurs séquences de montage par les techniques narratives des romans-feuilletons du XIXᵉ siècle. Il n'est donc guère étonnant que le genre du scénarimage proto-cinéastique se développât dans le milieu du dessin de presse.

THE ILLUSTRATED LONDON NEWS, MAY 10, 1890.— 597

1. A Search.   2. Stalking.   3. Success.

AFTER ROCKY MOUNTAIN SHEEP.

" As Christmas Day approaches there **are evidences** of a coming festival **on** every side ; evidences which almost a blind man can see. On the day before Christmas these evidences a

CHRISTMAS SHOPPI

SCENE ON AN UP-TOWN TRAIN

LESLIE'S WEEKLY.

...l that he is a marked man who has not a bundle or so under his arm and whose pockets do not bulge with mysterious packages.   On the elevated cars they are especially apparent."

HOMEWARD BOUND.

NEW YORK ELEVATED RAILROAD.

L.L. Roush

Perils and Difficulties in Reaching Klondike Gold-fields Illustrated.

LESLIE'S WEEKLY
☆ILLUSTRATED☆

Vol. LXXXV.—No. 2186.
Copyright, 1897, by ARKELL WEEKLY CO., No. 119 Fifth Avenue.
All Rights Reserved.

NEW YORK, AUGUST 5, 1897.

[PRICE, 10 CENTS. $4.00 YEARLY.
12 WEEKS $1.00.
Entered as second-class matter at the New York post-office.

A SUMMER NIGHT IN NEW YORK.

There are nights in July and August when it is impossible for the people to sleep in the crowded tenements in which the poor are lodged like rabbits in a warren. Then many of them take their mattresses to the roofs and endeavor to find rest in the open air.

A Summer Night in New York, 1897
Eine Sommernacht in New York
Une nuit d'été à New York,
Relief etching
From: *Leslie's Weekly*, New York,
5 August 1897

In his press illustrations on the symphony of life in big cities, L.L. Roush aligned himself with the Progressive Era's ideals for social reform. A number of his pictorial subjects were taken up soon after in the paintings and drawings of the newly established Ashcan School of artists, whose work was also concerned with social criticism (see ills. p. 528).

In seiner pressegrafischen Großstadtsinfonie folgte L.L. Roush den sozialreformatorischen Idealen der progressivistischen Ära. Einige seiner Motive fanden sich wenig später auch in den Malereien und Grafiken der sich gerade formierenden sozialkritischen Ashcan School (siehe Abb. S. 528).

Dans sa symphonie de la grande ville présentée en dessins de presse, L.L. Roush s'orienta vers les idéaux de réformes sociales caractéristiques de l'ère progressiste. Plusieurs de ses motifs apparurent un peu plus tard dans les peintures et dessins de l'Ashcan School qui était en train de se former et s'orientait vers la critique sociale (voir ills. p. 528).

→ *The Rally 'round the Ice-wagon,* 1897
Die Versammlung um den Eiswagen
Le Rassemblement autour du marchand de glaces
Relief etching
From: *Leslie's Weekly*, New York,
2 September 1897

In terms of their design, the condensed arrangement of elements from staged and documentary photography, careful retouching and the visual traces of wood engraving all corresponded to a new and pulsating attitude to life in the melting pots of American cities.

Gestalterisch entsprach das synkopische Gefüge aus Elementen inszenierter und dokumentarischer Fotografie, lockerer Retuschmalerei und akzentuierender Xylotypogravur einem neuen pulsierenden Lebensgefühl der amerikanischen „melting pots".

Sur le plan du design, cet assortiment syncopé d'éléments de photographie mise en scène et de photographie documentaire, de retouches désinvoltes et d'accents de gravure xylotypique correspondait à un nouveau style de vie du «melting pot» américain.

←←**L.L. Roush**

Christmas Shoppers Homeward Bound
Weihnachtseinkäufer auf dem Weg
nach Hause
Clients rentrant chez eux après
les emplettes de Noël, 1895
Relief etching
From: *Leslie's Weekly*, New York,
12 December 1895

L.L. Roush's series of scenes from American city life began in the same year in which cinema was born, and marked a decisive stage in the development of photomontage. Composite photographic processes had been in use for more than 30 years by this date, especially for pictorialist works, but in ways that were less overt and more concerned with some manipulation of the image.

L.L. Roush' Serie mit Szenen aus dem amerikanischen Großstadtleben startete im Geburtsjahr des Films und markiert einen Meilenstein in der Entwicklung der Fotomontage. Fotografische Kompositverfahren wurden zwar bereits seit mehr als 30 Jahren praktiziert, vor allem im Piktorialismus, allerdings auf eine verdeckte, manipulative Weise.

La série de L.L. Roush représentant des scènes de la vie quotidienne dans les métropoles américaines démarra l'année où le cinéma vit le jour et marque une étape décisive dans l'évolution du montage photographique. Certes, des procédés composites de photographie étaient utilisés depuis plus de trente ans, en particulier dans le pictorialisme, mais de manière dissimulée et manipulatrice.

Leslie's Weekly

★ILLUSTRATED★

Vol. LXXXV.—No. 2190.
Copyright, 1897, by ARKELL WEEKLY CO., No. 110 Fifth Avenue.
All Rights Reserved.

NEW YORK, SEPTEMBER 2, 1897.

PRICE, 10 CENTS. $4.00 YEARLY.
13 WEEKS $1.00.
Entered as second-class matter at the New York Post-office.

THE RALLY 'ROUND THE ICE-WAGON.

Ice becomes a common necessity of life in the torrid season between June and October. If the demand for it in our crowded cities is enormous, the supply is inexhaustible, and its cheapness places it within the reach of all. For the very poor, who cannot afford to buy, in New York, there is the Free Ice Fund of one of the great daily newspapers, whose proprietor generously devotes to the good work a portion of the money intrusted to him by charitable subscribers for that purpose. The ice-wagon, cool and dripping, is a cherished American institution, and its daily passage through the tenement district is hailed with delight by the entire population, as shown in the accompanying picture.

LE PROMENOIR DES FOLIES-BERG
(PHOTOGRAPHIE INSTANTANÉE)

Sonntagvormittag   in Halensee.

7

E. Lagrange

E. Lagrange

The Floor of the Folies Bergère, 1896
Das Foyer in den Folies Bergère
Le Promenoir des Folies Bergère
Relief etching
From: *Le Panorama. La journée
de la Parisienne,* no. 2, Paris, 1896

At the same time as L. L. Roush's illustrations were appearing in New York, the French photographer E. Lagrange was working on a series of candid montages about the sights of Paris and its places of entertainment. The first of these views appeared in 1896, under the general title *Le Panorama*, and millions of copies were printed for the influential press publisher Ludovic Baschet.

Während L. L. Roush' Illustrationen in New York publiziert wurden, arbeitete der französische Fotograf E. Lagrange an einer Serie offener Montagen über Pariser Sehenswürdigkeiten und Vergnügungsstätten. Sie erschien seit 1896 in Millionenauflage in der Reihe *Le Panorama* des bedeutenden Grafik- und Zeitungsverlags Ludovic Baschet.

Tandis que les illustrations de L. L. Roush étaient publiées à New York, le photographe français E. Lagrange travaillait à une série de montages ouverts sur les curiosités et lieux de divertissement de Paris. Elle parut à partir de 1896 à des millions d'exemplaires dans la collection *Le Panorama* et fut publiée par l'influent éditeur d'estampes et de journaux Ludovic Baschet.

Georg August Busse

Sunday Morning in Halensee, 1900
Sonntagvormittag in Halensee
Dimanche matin à Halensee
Relief etching
From: *Berliner Leben. Zeitschrift für
Schönheit und Kunst*, Berlin, 1900

Seemingly influenced by the work of E. Legrange and L. L. Roush, in 1900 the Berlin artist and photographer Georg August Busse turned to a similar style of montage. His scenes of typical daily life in the Prussian capital were published in the *Berliner Leben.*

Offenbar unter dem Einfluss von E. Lagrange und L. L. Roush wandte sich der Berliner Fotograf und Maler Georg August Busse seit 1900 der offenen Montage zu. Seine repräsentativen Szenen aus der preußischen Hauptstadt erschienen in dem Periodikum *Berliner Leben.*

Visiblement sous l'influence d'E. Lagrange et de L. L. Roush, le photographe et peintre berlinois Georg August Busse se tourna vers le montage ouvert à partir de 1900. Ses scènes représentatives de la capitale prussienne sont parues dans le périodique *Berliner Leben.*

Original-Aufnahme für „Berliner Leben" von Georg Busse, Berlin.

LESLIE'S WEEKLY.

ON THE DECK OF A NORTH-ATLANTIC STEAMSHIP.

IN THE STOKE-HOLE OF A NORTH-ATLANTIC STEAMSHIP.

SOME OF THOSE WHO GO DOWN TO THE SEA IN SHIPS.

L.L. Roush

Some of Those Who Go down to the Sea in Ships, 1897
Einige von denen, die auf dem Meer in Schiffen einfahren | *Certains de ceux qui embarquent sur des bateaux*
Relief etchings
From: *Leslie's Weekly*, New York,
19 August 1897

The rhythmical sense of composition in this representation of two classes of society aboard a luxury ocean-liner can be seen as an early form of the critical montages that would come to be used by John Heartfield and Sergei Eisenstein. The photographic illustration was also distributed in Europe, after it was published in the Belgian magazine *Le Patriote illustré*. It was part of a series by L.L. Roush that appeared in *Leslie's Weekly* up until 1897, after which it resumed four years later in the Sunday supplement of Joseph Pulitzer's *New York World* under the title "Photo-scenes from Real Life".

Die rhythmisch komponierte Darstellung einer Zwei-klassengesellschaft im Bild eines Luxusdampfers kann als frühes Beispiel einer kritischen, auf John Heartfield und Sergei Eisenstein vorausweisenden Form der Montage gelten. Über einen Abdruck in der belgischen Illustrierten *Le Patriote illustré* war diese Fotografik auch in Europa präsent. L.L. Roush' Serie in *Leslie's Weekly* endete 1897 und wurde vier Jahre später in der Sonntagsbeilage von Joseph Pulitzers *New York World* als „Photo-Scenes from Real Life" fortgesetzt.

La représentation composée de façon rythmique d'une société à deux classes sur l'image d'un paquebot de luxe peut être considérée comme un exemple précoce d'une forme de montage critique annonçant les travaux de John Heartfield et de Sergueï Eisenstein. Ce dessin photographique fut diffusé aussi en Europe après avoir été imprimé dans le magazine belge *Le Patriote illustré*. En 1897, la série de L.L. Roush cessa de paraître dans *Leslie's Weekly* et fut ensuite reprise quatre ans plus tard comme «Photo-Scenes from Real Life» dans le supplément du dimanche du *New York World* de Joseph Pulitzer.

Georgina A. Davis

→ *A Harbinger of Spring on the East Side, New York*, 1895
Ein Frühlingsbote in der New Yorker East Side
Un signe avant-coureur du printemps dans le quartier East Side de New York
Relief etching
From: *Leslie's Weekly*, New York, 28 March 1895

This springtime scene from New York's East Side, filled with the joys of life, shows Georgina Davis, who had been working as the first in her role of "Our Lady Artist" at *Leslie's Weekly* since 1880, setting a deliberate counterpoint to the focus on "slumming" in the work of artists such as Jacob Riis (see ills. p. 431). Her illustration corresponds to the progressive spirit of the time, and declared a more differentiated perspective on the living conditions of the poor.

Mit dieser lebenslustigen Frühlingsszene aus der New Yorker East Side setzte Georgina A. Davis, die seit 1880 als erste „Our Lady Artist" für *Leslie's Weekly* arbeitete, einen programmatischen Kontrapunkt zum deklassierenden „slumming" eines Jacob Riis (siehe Abb. S. 431). Die Grafik entsprach dem progressivistischen Zeitgeist und kündigte eine differenziertere Perspektive auf die schlechten Lebensverhältnisse an.

Avec cette scène printanière débordante de joie de vivre, croquée dans le quartier East Side de New York, Georgina A. Davis, qui travaillait depuis 1880 comme la première «Our Lady Artist» pour *Leslie's Weekly*, plaça un contrepoint programmatique au «slumming» déclassant d'un Jacob Riis (voir ills. p. 431). Le dessin correspondait à l'esprit du temps progressiste et annonçait une perspective plus différenciée des mauvaises conditions de vie.

NEXT WEEK, "THE NAVIES OF THE WORLD."

Leslie's Weekly
∗ILLUSTRATED∗

Vol. LXXX.—No. 2063.
Copyright, 1895. Published Weekly by Arkell Weekly Co.,
No. 110 Fifth Avenue. All Rights Reserved.

NEW YORK, MARCH 28, 1895.

[Price, 10 Cents. $4.00 Yearly.
13 Weeks, $1.00.
Entered as second-class matter at the New York post-office.

As the spring advances and street life in the city takes on its more busy and enlivening forms, the organ-grinder once more seeks his accustomed haunts on the East Side, and finds eager welcome from the children of the poor. Our picture shows a scene on Hester Street, near Allen—the centre of the most densely populated district in the world—on one of the brighter days in early March. In pleasant summer days, hundreds of children in this district engage in sidewalk dances to the music of barrel-organs.

A HARBINGER OF SPRING ON THE EAST SIDE, NEW YORK.—Drawn by Miss G. A. Davis.

A WILD POLITICAL FIGHT IN HO...

A MEASURE OF ECONOMY.	EVIDENCE OF WEALTH.	ROOM FOR IMPROVEMENT.	BOTH ARE SHARP FELLOW...
Bunting—You are not cutting your own grass this year, I see, Larkin. Larkin—No. It is cheaper for me to hire it done than to buy lawn mowers to lend to the neighbors.	"Oh, he is immensely wealthy." "How do you know?" "Why, I saw him draw a check on the bank the other day, and there was a whole lot of checks left in his book."	"That young man who occupies the first floor, front, has some tough-looking callers." "Yes, his room is better than his company."	"I'm the machine that can get a h... of human beings," boasted the Gu... tine. "Well, I sometimes take a hand ... self," replied the Buzz Saw, modest...

HIS TIME HAD COME.

"Ha! ha!" sardonically cried the
eavy villain in the fourth act, "now
y time has come." And then the supe
me on and handed him the property
atch.

GOOD CHANCE FOR A JOB.

Tramp—Kind madam, I hain't hed
nuthin' t' eat for two weeks——
Woman at the door—Wait till I call
my husband; he's a dime museum man-
ager, and may give you a fasting job.

A SURE CURE FOR DUMBNESS.

Mr. Gabbleton—Oh, doctor, my wife
has suddenly lost the power of speech
—can't utter a word!
Eminent Physician (laconically)—Take
her to the opera.

AT THE END OF THE LESSON.

He—But I promised my wife I would
never marry again.
She—And will you cast me off because
of a promise to a dead woman?
He—Ah, but she isn't dead yet.
She—(Faints.)

George Luks

Studies from the Lower East Side, undated
Studien aus der Lower East Side
Études de Lower East Side
Pencil

Alongside pictorial reporters such as John
Sloan and William Glackens (see ills. p. 571 t.;
441 b. l. and b. r.), George Luks was one of
the main artists in the socially critical Ashcan
School. Some of the later offshoots of this
influential American art movement included
Edward Hopper and Ben Shahn, while the
group's illustrations for the press showed
close connections with the contemporaneous
"gutter" art being created by artists of the
Berlin Secession.

George Luks gehörte zusammen mit grafi-
schen Reportern wie John Sloan und William
Glackens (siehe Abb. S. 571 o.; 441 u.l. und
u.r.) zum Kern der sozialkritischen Ashcan
School. Edward Hopper und Ben Shahn zähl-
ten zu den späten Ausläufern dieser tonange-
benden amerikanischen Kunstbewegung.
Vergleichbar eng waren die pressegrafischen
Verzahnungen mit der parallelen deutschen
„Rinnstein"-Kunst der Berliner Secession.

Avec des reporters illustrateurs comme John
Sloan et William Glackens (voir ills. p. 571 h.;
441 b.g. et b.d.) George Luks constituait
le noyau de l'Ashcan School à tendance
socio-critique. Edward Hopper et Ben Shahn
comptaient parmi les dérivés tardifs de cet
influent mouvement artistique américain. Il y
avait une interaction comparablement étroite
du dessin de presse avec l'art de «gouttière»
allemand, parallèle, de la Sécession berlinoise.

←← Richard Felton Outcault & George Luks

*A Wild Political Fight in Hogan's
Alley,* 1896
*Ein wilder politischer Kampf in
Hogan's Alley*
*Un sauvage combat politique dans
Hogan's Alley*
Coloured relief etching
From: *The World on Sunday, Comic
Weekly,* New York, 2 August 1896
Ohio State University, Billy Ireland
Cartoon Library & Museum

In May 1895, Richard Outcault's
comic strip *Hogan's Alley,* featuring
the Yellow Kid, ushered in the age of
American comic books. The hidden-
picture style of illustration, set in the
run-down districts of New York,
harked back to William Hogarth's use
of the socially critical grotesque, while
the use of various signs and placards
to convey written content was derived
from Thomas Nast's political cartoons.

Im Mai 1895 läutete Richard Out-
caults Serie *Hogan's Alley* mit dem
Yellow Kid als Protagonisten die Ära
des amerikanischen Comics ein. Die
Wimmelbilder aus den New Yorker
Slums schlossen an William Hogarth's
Tradition sozialkritischer Groteske an.
Die Verwendung von Reklametafeln
als Träger von Kommentaren war hin-
gegen von Thomas Nasts politischen
Cartoons inspiriert.

En mai 1895, la série de Richard
Outcault *Hogan's Alley* avec le Yellow
Kid comme protagoniste sonna l'ère
de la bande dessinée américaine.
Les images fourmillant de détails des
bidonvilles new-yorkais renouent
avec la tradition de grotesque critique
sociale de William Hogarth. En
revanche, l'utilisation de panneaux
publicitaires comme supports de commentaires étaient inspirés des caricatures politiques de Thomas Nast.

THE OPEN-AIR SCHOOL IN HOGAN'S ALLEY.

George Luks

The Open-air School in Hogan's Alley, 1896
Die Freiluftschule in Hogan's Alley
L'École en plein air dans Hogan's Alley
Coloured relief etching
From: *The World on Sunday, Comic Weekly*, New York, 18 October 1896
Ohio State University, Billy Ireland Cartoon Library & Museum

After his media rival William Randolph Hearst poached Richard Outcault, the creator of the Yellow Kid, for the *New York Journal*, Joseph Pulitzer continued with the comic strip with the young artist George Luks replacing Outcault in 1896. Luks already had much experience as a press illustrator, and the socially realistic settings of the cartoons matched his own artistic tendencies.

Nachdem sein Konkurrent William Randolph Hearst Richard Outcault, den Erfinder des Yellow Kid, für das *New York Journal* abgeworben hatte, ließ Joseph Pulitzer die Serie ab 1896 kurzerhand von dem jungen Maler George Luks fortführen, der bereits vielfältige Erfahrungen als Pressegrafiker hatte. Der sozialrealistische Hintergrund der Comicserie kam Luks künstlerischen Interessen entgegen.

Après que son concurrent William Randolph Hearst eut débauché Richard Outcault, le créateur du Yellow Kid, pour le *New York Journal*, Joseph Pulitzer continua sans plus attendre la série à partir de 1896 avec le jeune peintre George Luks, qui avait déjà accumulé de nombreuses expériences comme illustrateur de presse. Le contexte de réalisme social de la série de bande dessinée correspondait aux inclinations artistiques de Luks.

A SAINT-LAZARE

Chanson, par ARISTIDE BRUANT *

Ritournelle. Mod°

mf

Chant.

C'est · de · d'la · pri-son que j'é-cris, Mon pauvr' Po-ly-te, Hi-er, je n'sais pas c'qui m'a pris, A la vi-si-te; C'est des ma-la-di's qui s'voient pas, Quand ça s'dé-cla-re, N'em-pêch' qu'au-jour-d'hui j'suis dans l'tas à Saint-La-za-re!

Ritournelle

II

Mais pendant c' temps-là, toi, vieux chien,
   Quéqu' tu vas faire ?
Je n' peux t'envoyer rien de rien,
   C'est la misère.
Ici tout le monde est décavé,
   La braise est rare ;
Faut trois mois pour faire un linvé
   A Saint-Lazare.

III

Vrai d' te savoir comm' ça, sans l' sou,
   Je m' fais un' bile !...
T' es capabl' de faire un sal' coup,
   J' suis pas tranquille.
T'as trop d' fierté pour ramasser
   Des bouts d' cigare
Pendant tout l' temps que j' vas passer
   A Saint-Lazare.

IV

Va-t'en trouver la grand' Nana,
   Dis que j' la prie
D' casquer pour moi, j'y rendrai ça
   A ma sortie.
Surtout, n'y fais pas d' boniments,
   Pendant qu' je m' marre
Et que j' bois des médicaments
   A Saint-Lazare.

V

Et puis, mon p'tit loup, bois pas trop,
   Tu sais qu' t'es teigne
Et quand t' as un p'tit coup d' sirop
   Tu fous la beigne.
Si tu t' faisais coffrer, un soir,
   Dans un' bagarre,
Y a pus personn' qui viendrait m' voir
   A Saint-Lazare.

VI

J' finis ma lettre en t'embrassant,
   Adieu, mon homme.
Malgré qu' tu soy' pas caressant
   Ah! j' t'ador' comme
J'adorais l' bon Dieu comm' papa,
   Quand j'étais p'tite,
Et qu' j'allais communier à
   Saint' Marguerite.

(Dessin de Steinlen)

Les deux précédentes chansons publiées par GIL BLAS ILLUSTRÉ : " LES PETITS JOYEUX " et " A SAINT-OUEN " sont aussi de M. ARISTIDE BRUANT, le chansonnier si connu des bas-fonds de Paris.

Théophile Steinlen & Rougeron-Vignerot (sc.)

*At Saint-Lazare, a Song by
Aristide Bruant,* 1891
*In Saint-Lazare, ein Lied von
Aristide Bruant*
*À Saint-Lazare, chanson par
Aristide Bruant*
Relief etching
From: *Gil Blas illustré*, Paris,
9 August 1891

To accompany the sharp social comment in the songs of Aristide Bruant, the famous cabaret singer and performer of Montmartre, Théophile Steinlen developed a somewhat melancholic style of illustration for *Gil Blas illustré* with prostitutes and day labourers as the main characters. Shortly after this scene from the Saint-Lazare women's prison was published, Picasso began visiting there to find subjects for his Blue Period works.

Begleitend zu den sozialkritischen Chansons des Montmartre-Stars Aristide Bruant etablierte Théophile Steinlen im *Gil Blas illustré* einen melancholischen Illustrationsstil mit Prostituierten und Tagelöhnern als Protagonisten. Kurze Zeit nach der Veröffentlichung der Szene aus dem Frauengefängnis Saint-Lazare begann Picasso, dort Motive für seine Blaue Periode zu rekrutieren.

En accompagnement des chansons teintées de critique sociale de la star de Montmartre Aristide Bruant, Théophile Steinlen introduisit dans le *Gil Blas illustré* un style d'illustration mélancolique en prenant pour protagonistes des prostituées et des travailleurs journaliers. Peu après la publication de la scène de la prison pour femmes à Saint-Lazare, Picasso commença à y glaner des motifs pour sa période bleue.

Pablo Picasso (Ruiz)

A Question of Breeding, 1902
Eine Frage der Vorfahren
Question d'ancêtres
Relief etching
From: *Le Frou-Frou*, Paris,
18 January 1902

Unlike most of his fellow artists, Picasso avoided working as an illustrator in France, and in the few French press graphic works by him that are known his style is similar to that used by Constantin Guys or Toulouse-Lautrec. The illustrations he produced at this time for the Madrid magazine *Arte Joven* and Barcelona's daily newspaper *El Liberal*, however, were more idiosyncratic and were signed with his artist's name.

Im Gegensatz zu den meisten seiner Künstlerfreunde mied es Picasso, in Frankreich als Illustrator in Erscheinung zu treten. In seinen wenigen Pressegrafiken imitierte er Constantin Guys und Toulouse-Lautrec. Eigenwilliger und mit Künstlernamen signiert waren hingegen seine zeitgleichen Arbeiten für das Madrider Kunstmagazin *Arte Joven* und die Barceloner Tageszeitung *El Liberal*.

À l'inverse de la plupart de ses amis artistes, Picasso évitait de se produire comme illustrateur en France. Dans ses rares dessins de presse, il imitait Constantin Guys et Toulouse-Lautrec. En revanche, ses travaux contemporains pour le magazine d'art madrilène *Arte Joven* et le quotidien barcelonais *El Liberal* étaient originaux et signés de son nom d'artiste.

1100

Question d'ancêtres

— Eh! bien, monsieur le... marquis? Tu es marquis, je crois?
— Oui, mes aïeux étaient croisés...
— Ah!... Les miens étaient de race pure...

CHOCOLAT DANSANT DANS UN BAR

Sois bonne ô ma chère inconnue !

Dessin de H. de TOULOUSE-LAUTREC.

Henri de Toulouse-Lautrec

Chocolat Dancing in a Bar, 1896
Chocolat, in einer Bar tanzend
Chocolat dansant dans un bar
Coloured relief etching
From: *Le Rire*, Paris, 28 March 1896

Toulouse-Lautrec's work as a picture reporter in bohemian Paris began at around the same time he met Vincent van Gogh and Émile Bernard. His first illustrations for the press appeared in late 1886 in *Le Courrier français*, although his work appeared mostly in *Le Rire*, the most popular satirical magazine in France at the time.

Der Beginn von Toulouse-Lautrecs Tätigkeit als grafischer Reporter der Pariser Bohemeszene fiel mit seiner Bekanntschaft mit Vincent van Gogh und Émile Bernard zusammen. Ende 1886 waren dann erste Pressegrafiken im *Le Courrier français* erschienen. Die größte Verbreitung fanden Toulouse-Lautrecs Arbeiten in *Le Rire*, dem populärsten französischen Karikaturmagazin der Zeit.

Le début de l'activité de Toulouse-Lautrec comme reporter illustrateur de la scène de la bohème parisienne coïncida avec sa rencontre avec Vincent van Gogh et Émile Bernard. Fin 1886, ses premiers dessins de presse étaient parus dans *Le Courrier français*. Les travaux de Toulouse-Lautrec connurent leur plus grande diffusion dans *Le Rire*, le magazine satirique français le plus populaire.

Émile Bernard

Vincent van Gogh, 1891
Coloured relief etching
From: *Les Hommes d'aujourd'hui*,
Paris, 17 June 1891

Not long after Van Gogh's death, this iconic illustration by Émile Bernard for the monographic periodical founded by André Gill represented the first step in the canonisation of his fellow artist. However, Bernard's view that Van Gogh had been exceptionally self-aware and logical in his work as an artist did not gain much acceptance since the latter was widely taken to have been insane.

Mit seinem ikonischen Beitrag für das von André Gill begründete monografische Periodikum leitete Émile Bernard kurze Zeit nach van Goghs Tod die Kanonisierung des Künstlerfreunds mit ein. Bernards Ansicht, dass der als verrückt geltende Maler künstlerisch außergewöhnlich reflektiert und folgerichtig vorgegangen sei, konnte sich allerdings nicht durchsetzen.

Par sa contribution iconique au périodique monographique fondé par André Gill, Émile Bernard initia, peu de temps après la mort de Van Gogh, la canonisation de son ami artiste. Le point de vue de Bernard, selon lequel le peintre qui passait pour fou avait agi de manière réfléchie et logique, ne put toutefois pas s'imposer.

LE COURRIER FRANÇAIS   5

Etude de M.ᵉ BINON, huissier
Avenue des Ternes, 2.

VENTE
PAR AUTORITÉ DE JUSTICE
à Paris rue du faubourg Saint honoré 233

Dessin de J.-L. Forain.

L'Affiche de Vente.   *Aux mânes de MM. Vercoutère et Gouffé.*

Jean-Louis Forain & Charles Decaux (sc.)

Notice of Sale, 1890
Das Verkaufsplakat | L'Affiche de Vente
Relief etching
From: *Le Courrier français*, Paris, 2 February 1890

The announcement of a forced sale of household goods breaks up the framework of the pictorial narrative with a force that refers back to the early montage work of Jules Bourdet as much as it looks ahead to the Cubist dissecting technique of papier collé. Jean-Louis Forain's work was well known by Picasso and his circle, while Ambroise Vollard, Picasso's dealer and also Cézanne's, showed some of Forain's paintings. The critic and poet Guillaume Apollinaire considered him one of the most important artists working at the time.

Die Wucht, mit der die Annonce einer Zwangsversteigerung den bildnarrativen Rahmen aufsprengt, bezieht sich auf die frühen Montagen Jules Bourdets und antizipiert zugleich die zergliedernde Technik des kubistischen „papier collé". Jean-Louis Forains Werk war im Kreis Picassos bestens bekannt. Ambroise Vollard, der Händler Paul Cézannes und Picassos, vertrat seine Malereien, und der Kunstkritiker und Dichter Guillaume Apollinaire hielt ihn für einen der bedeutensten Künstler.

La puissance, avec laquelle l'annonce d'une vente forcée fait éclater le cadre de la narration en images, se réfère aux premiers montages de Jules Bourdet et préfigure en même temps la technique de découpage du «papier collé» cubiste. L'œuvre de Jean-Louis Forain était parfaitement connu dans le cercle de Picasso. Ambroise Vollard, le marchand d'art de Paul Cézanne et de Picasso, exposait ses peintures, et le critique d'art et poète Guillaume Apollinaire le considérait comme l'un des artistes majeurs.

Jules Grandjouan

The Passport, 1906
Der Pass | Le Passeport
Coloured relief etching
From: *L'Assiette au Beurre*, Paris,
4 August 1906

Six years before the use of collage was formally adopted in art, Jules Grandjouan shook up the illusory pictorial space of printed graphics by integrating a real passport page into this illustration in a special issue of *L'Assiette au Beurre* about the idiocies of increasing bureaucratisation. The anarchist magazine was a favourite of the artists who met in the Cubist seedbed of the Bateau-Lavoir.

In einer Sondernummer von *L'Assiette au Beurre* über Bürokratisierungswahn irritierte Jules Grandjouan sechs Jahre vor der kanonischen Einführung der Collage in der Kunst den illusionistischer Bildraum durch die Integration eines Passdokuments. Das anarchistische Magazin war eine bevorzugte Illustrierte der Künstler der kubistischen Urzelle Bateau-Lavoir.

Six ans avant l'introduction canonique du collage dans l'art, Jules Grandjouan bousculait l'espace pictural illusionniste par l'intégration d'un passeport dans un numéro exceptionnel de *L'Assiette au Beurre* sur le délire de la bureaucratisation. Le magazine anarchiste était l'un des magazines préférés des artistes de la cité d'artistes cubistes du Bateau-Lavoir.

LE PASSEPORT
— Visage rond... Ce n'est pas vous !
— Ce n'est plus moi...

Vos Papiers

Bruno Paul

Jugend, 1896
Coloured relief etching
From: *Jugend*, Munich, 29 August 1896

The illustrator, designer and architect Bruno Paul embodied the universality of Art Nouveau or Jugendstil more than any other artist. His first illustrations for *Jugend*, the magazine from which the art movement took its name, reveal the influence of the Nabis in France, specifically in the cloisonnist separation of colours. Soon after this date Paul went to work as a political cartoonist for the satirical magazine *Simplicissimus*, which was also founded in 1896.

Der Illustrator, Designer und Architekt Bruno Paul verkörperte wie kein anderer Künstler den universellen Anspruch des Jugendstils. Pauls frühe Grafik für das Magazin, dem die Bewegung ihren Namen verdankt, weist den cloisonnistischen Einfluss der französischen Nabis auf. Wenig später wechselte Paul als politischer Cartoonist zum ebenfalls 1896 gegründeten Satiremagazin *Simplicissimus*.

L'illustrateur, designer et architecte Bruno Paul incarnait comme aucun autre artiste l'exigence universelle du Jugendstil. Les premiers dessins de Paul pour le magazine, auquel le mouvement doit son nom, trahit l'influence cloisonniste des Nabis français. Un peu plus tard, Paul passa comme caricaturiste politique au magazine satirique *Simplicissimus*, également fondé en 1896.

Jacques Villon

Untitled, 1901
Ohne Titel | Sans titre
Coloured relief etching
From: *Cocorico*, Paris, 1 April 1901

Jacques Villon's cover design for the important Art Nouveau magazine *Cocorico*, founded in 1898 by the artists Paul-Émile Boutigny and Alphonse Mucha, follows in the tradition of the poster art of Jules Chéret and Toulouse-Lautrec.

Jacques Villons Titelgrafik für das tonangebende Art-nouveau-Magazin *Cocorico*, das 1898 von den Künstlern Paul-Émile Boutigny und Alfons Mucha initiiert worden war, steht in der Nachfolge der Plakatkunst eines Jules Chéret und Toulouse-Lautrec.

Le graphique de titre réalisé par Jacques Villon pour le très influent magazine d'Art nouveau *Cocorico*, fondé par Paul-Émile Boutigny et Alfons Mucha en 1898, s'inscrit dans la tradition de l'art de l'affiche d'artistes comme Jules Chéret et Toulouse-Lautrec.

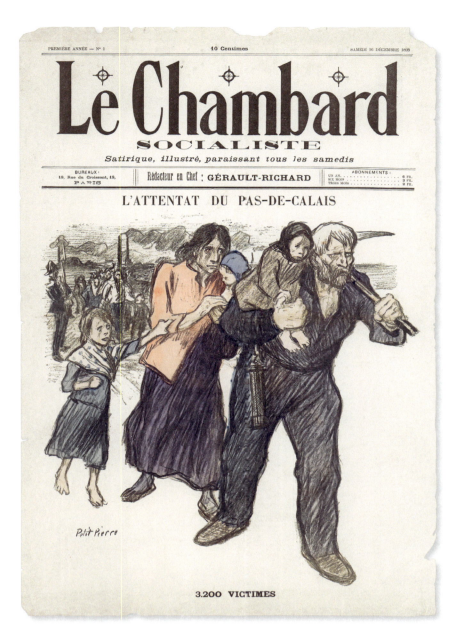

Théophile Steinlen (Petit Pierre)

Outrage in the Pas-de-Calais, 1893
Der Anschlag im Pas-de-Calais
L'Attentat du Pas-de-Calais
Coloured relief etching
From: *Le Chambard socialiste*, Paris,
16 December 1893

Théophile Steinlen's first work for the weekly journal *Le Chambard socialiste*, which aligned itself with the revolutionary syndicalism of the workers' movement, marked the beginning of a long career as a political artist. With his heroic depictions of workers, which followed in the tradition of the political illustrations of Philippe-Auguste Jeanron (see ill. p. 102), Charles-Joseph Traviès and Honoré Daumier, Steinlen left his own stamp on socialist art.

Théophile Steinlens erste Arbeit für das Wochenblatt *Le Chambard socialiste*, das dem revolutionären Syndikalismus der Gewerkschaftsbewegung nahestand, markierte den Beginn einer langjährigen Tätigkeit als Politkünstler. Mit seinen heroischen Arbeitersujets, die auf frühe Politgrafiken eines Philippe-Auguste Jeanron (siehe Abb. S. 102), Charles-Joseph Traviès und Honoré Daumier zurückgreifen, prägte er die sozialistische Kunst wie kein Zweiter.

Le premier travail de Théophile Steinlen pour l'hebdomadaire *Le Chambard socialiste*, qui était proche du syndicalisme révolutionnaire du mouvement syndical, marqua le début d'une longue période d'activité comme artiste politique. Avec ses sujets héroïques d'ouvriers, qui se réfèrent aux premiers dessins politiques de Philippe-Auguste Jeanron (voir ill. p. 102), Charles-Joseph Traviès et Honoré Daumier, il influença l'art socialiste comme aucun autre.

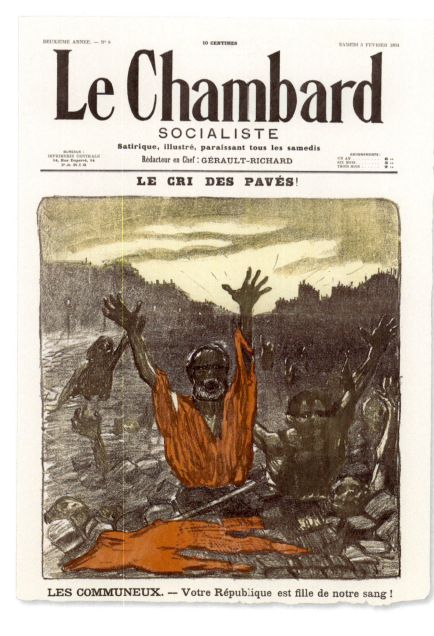

The Pavements Cry Out!, 1894
Der Schrei des Pflasters!
Le Cri des pavés!
Coloured relief etching
From: *Le Chambard socialiste*, Paris,
3 February 1894

By the mid-1880s, memories of the ideals the Paris Commune had stood for began to shape the way in which the growing workers' movement in France presented itself. Théophile Steinlen's vision of former members of the Commune, as dead bodies in the cellars of the Third Republic (see ills. pp. 279, 281 t.) clawing their way upwards to the light of a freedom that had yet to be gained, became an enduring symbol of the class struggle in France.

Ab Mitte der 1880er-Jahre begann die Erinnerung an die Ideale der Pariser Kommune eine konstitutive Rolle für das Selbstverständnis der erstarkenden französischen Arbeiterbewegung zu spielen. Théophile Steinlens Vision der Kommunarden, die als Leichen im Keller der Dritten Republik (siehe Abb. S. 279, 281 o.) zum Licht einer noch zu erkämpfenden Freiheit streben, wurde zur Ikone des französischen Klassenkampfs.

Vers le milieu des années 1880, le souvenir des idéaux de la Commune de Paris commença à jouer un rôle fondamental dans la conception du mouvement ouvrier français en pleine expansion. La vision de Théophile Steinlen des communards qui, cadavres dans la cave de la Troisième République (voir ills. p. 279, 281 h.), aspirent à la lumière d'une liberté encore à conquérir, devint l'icône de la lutte des classes en France.

Maximilien Luce

*What Do the Common People Want for the
Boaraucrats?… "Down the Sewers!"*, 1898
*Was wünscht das Volk den Schuftokraten? …
„Ab in den Gulli!"*
*Ce que le populo souhaite aux chameaucrates?…
Le « Tout-à l'Égout!»*
Relief etching
From: *Le Père peinard*, Paris, 2 January 1898

The symbolic figure of Peinard the cobbler wants
the whole ruling body of the Third Republic to be
sent down below. The weekly paper carried journalism rooted in oral culture in the tradition previously
established by Jules Vallès (see ill. p. 316 r.), and its
main illustrators were the Neo-Impressionist artists
Lucien Pissarro and Maximilien Luce. By contributing more than 100 illustrations, Luce had a major
influence on shaping the appearance of this anarchist journal.

Die Symbolfigur des Schusters Peinard wünscht den
gesamten Herrschaftsapparat der Dritten Republik
zur Hölle. Das Wochenblatt stand in der Nachfolge
des an der Oralität orientierten Journalismus von
Jules Vallès (siehe Abb. S. 316 r.). Hauptzeichner
waren die neoimpressionistischen Künstler Lucien
Pissarro und Maximilien Luce. Letzterer prägte das
Erscheinungsbild des Undergroundmagazins mit
über 100 Beiträgen.

La figure symbolique du savetier Peinard veut
envoyer au diable toute l'élite gouvernementale de
la Troisième République. L'hebdomadaire s'inscri-
vait dans la tradition orale du journalisme de Jules
Vallès (voir ill. p. 316 d.). Les principaux illustrateurs
étaient les artistes néoimpressionnistes Lucien
Pissarro et Maximilien Luce. Ce dernier marqua de
son empreinte l'apparence du magazine activiste
avec plus de 100 croquis.

Ce que le populo souhaite aux chameaucrates?.... Le " TOUT-A-L'ÉGOUT! "

Anonymous

Their Sword and How They Use It, 1898
Ihr Schwert und die Art, wie sie es benutzen
Leur épée et leur manière de s'en servir
Relief etching
From: *Le Père peinard*, Paris, 22 May 1898

This cartoon served as a reminder that in May 1871
the French army was only in fact able to turn its
weapons against its own people after consent from
the occupying German forces. Being an anarchist
publication, *Le Père peinard* was one of the main targets during the new wave of repressions, although
its purposely crude style of illustration, which was a
match for the language used in the written reports,
was an influence later on for the artists of the
Fauvist movement.

Der Cartoon erinnert daran, dass das französische
Militär im Mai 1871 seine Waffen nur mit Billigung
der deutschen Besatzer gegen das eigene Volk
richten konnte. Das anarchistische Wochenblatt *Le
Père peinard* war ein Hauptziel der neuen Strafver-
folgungswelle. Die betont krude Bildpublizistik der
Zeitschrift, die dem rohen Slang der Texte entsprach,
hat die Kunst des Fauvismus inspiriert.

La caricature rappelle qu'en mai 1871 l'Armée
française n'avait pu pointer ses armes sur ses com-
patriotes qu'avec l'assentiment des occupants
allemands. L'hebdomadaire anarchiste fut la cible
principale de la nouvelle vague de répression. Le
journalisme pictural délibérément rude du *Père
peinard*, qui correspondait au jargon cru des textes,
a inspiré l'art du fauvisme.

Leur épée et leur manière de s'en servir.

Théophile Steinlen

Striking Arguments, 1898
Schlagende Argumente | *Arguments frappants*
Relief etching
From: *La Feuille*, Paris, 21 January 1898

Théophile Steinlen's image of a mob hungry for pictures and roused to fury appeared in the anarchist and journalist Zo d'Axa's magazine *La Feuille* only a few days after Émile Zola's open letter *J'Accuse…!* had been published. The prospect of a review of the sentence passed on the Jewish officer Alfred Dreyfus (see ills. p. 460) opened up ideological rifts amongst the population of France and led to several anti-Semitic attacks.

Théophile Steinlens Vision eines bildwütigen Mobs war in dem Autorenblatt des anarchistischen Literaten Zo d'Axa nur wenige Tage nach der Veröffentlichung von Émile Zolas Pamphlet *J'accuse …!* erschienen. Die Aussicht auf eine Revision der Verurteilung des jüdischen Hauptmanns Alfred Dreyfus (siehe Abb. S. 460) hatte ideologische Gräben aufgerissen und zu zahllosen antisemitischen Übergriffen geführt.

La vision de Théophile Steinlen d'une populace déchaînée était parue dans le journal de l'écrivain anarchiste Zo d'Axa, quelques jours seulement après la publication du pamphlet de Zola *J'accuse… !*. La perspective d'une révision de la condamnation du capitaine juif Alfred Dreyfus (voir ills. p. 460) avait réveillé des clivages idéologiques et provoqué d'innombrables attaques antisémites.

Caran d'Ache

The Review, 1898
Die Revision | *La Révision*
Relief etching
From: *Psst… !*, Paris, 3 September 1898

After Émile Zola had intervened in the Dreyfus affair, a number of politically confrontational journals were founded to respond to the case as well. The two anti-Dreyfusards Jean-Louis Forain and Caran d'Ache launched a weekly illustrated magazine, *Psst…!*, which ran to 85 issues, and in this illustration Caran d'Ache made clear with his bold outlines the only kind of review that could be of interest to him.

Nach Émile Zolas Intervention wurden mehrere politisch konfrontative Periodika gegründet, die sich des Falls Dreyfus annahmen. Das grafische Wochenblatt *Psst…!* der beiden Anti-Dreyfusianer Jean-Louis Forain und Caran d'Ache brachte es auf 85 Nummern. Welche Art der Revision er sich im Fall Dreyfus wünschte, brachte Caran d'Ache hier in cloisonistischer Deutlichkeit zum Ausdruck.

Après l'intervention d'Émile Zola, plusieurs périodiques d'opinion politique opposée furent créés et se saisirent de l'affaire Dreyfus. L'hebdomadaire satirique *Psst… !* des deux anti-dreyfusards Jean-Louis Forain et Caran d'Ache publia jusqu'à 85 numéros. Caran d'Ache démontre ici avec une netteté cloisonniste le genre de révision qu'il souhaitait pour l'affaire Dreyfus.

Maximilien Luce

Girls for the Soldiers. For Forain, Former Member of the Commune, and Corporal Poiré, Known as Caran d'Ache, 1898
Soldatenmädchen. An den Ex-Kommunarden Forain und Korporal Poiré, genannt Caran d'Ache
Filles à soldats. À Forain, ex-communard et au caporal Poiré, dit Caran d'Ache
Relief etching
From: *Le Père peinard*, Paris, 2 October 1898

The Dreyfus affair divided the bohemian art world into two camps, and Maximilien Luce, for one, was appalled at the loyalist U-turn made by Jean-Louis Forain, a former member of the Commune who had sided with André Gill as well as the poets Arthur Rimbaud and Paul Verlaine. In the typical rough style of illustration favoured by *Le Père peinard* he depicted the two editors of the inflammatory hate-mongering *Psst…!* as a pair of prostitutes offering their services to the army and the Church.

Der Fall Dreyfus entzweite die künstlerische Boheme. Maximilien Luce zeigte sich entsetzt über die loyalistische Wende des Ex-Kommunarden Jean-Louis Forain, der mit André Gill, Paul Verlaine und Arthur Rimbaud sympathisiert hatte. In der gewohnten Drastik des *Père peinard* stellte er die beiden Herausgeber des revanchistischen Hetzblatts *Psst…!* als Prostituierte dar, die sich dem Militär und der Kirche anbieten.

L'affaire Dreyfus divisa la bohème artistique en deux camps. Maximilien Luce était indigné par le retournement loyaliste de l'ancien communard Jean-Louis Forain qui avait sympathisé avec André Gill, Paul Verlaine et Arthur Rimbaud. Avec la rudesse habituelle du *Père peinard*, il représenta les deux éditeurs du journal de propagande revancharde *Psst…!* en prostituées qui s'offrent à l'armée et à l'Église.

A Forain, ex-communard et au caporal Poiré, dit Caran d'Ache.

Dessin de Vallotton.

L'Europe : Ce n'est rien, on égorge un homme

Félix Vallotton

Europe: It's Nothing, They're just Cutting a Man's Throat, 1900
Europa: Das ist nichts, sie schlachten nur einen Menschen ab
L'Europe : Ce n'est rien, on égorge un homme
Relief etching
From: *Le Cri de Paris*, Paris, 25 March 1900

With this two-dimensional depiction of a murder, which represented Britain's colonial war against the Boers in South Africa, Félix Vallotton was keeping true to his minimalist style of wood engravings. He designed the covers for *Le Cri de Paris* for several years, a political weekly in turn closely associated with *La Revue blanche*, the art and literature journal that was sympathetic to anarchism and popular with the Nabis.

In der flächigen Auffassung der Mordszene, die auf den Krieg Großbritanniens gegen die südafrikanischen Burenrepubliken anspielt, blieb Félix Vallotton seiner minimalistischen Holzschnittmanier treu. Mehrere Jahre gestaltete er die Cover von *Le Cri de Paris*. Das politische Wochenblatt war eng mit *La Revue blanche* assoziiert, dem anarchistischen Kulturmagazin um die Künstlergruppe der Nabis.

Dans l'interprétation plate d'une scène de meurtre, qui fait allusion à la guerre de la Grande-Bretagne contre les républiques boers d'Afrique du Sud, Félix Vallotton resta fidèle à son style minimaliste de xylographie. Plusieurs années durant, il a conçu les couvertures du *Cri de Paris*. L'hebdomadaire politique était étroitement associé à *La Revue blanche*, le magazine culturel anarchiste du groupe d'artistes des Nabis.

N° 315. 7ᵉ année. 17 Novembre 1900. Prix exceptionnel : 50 centimes

KRUGER LE GRAND
et John Bull le Petit
par CARAN D'ACHE
Numéro spécial publié par **Le Rire**

Caran d'Ache

Kruger the Great and the Little John Bull, 1900
Kruger der Große und John Bull der Kleine
Kruger le Grand et John Bull le Petit
Coloured relief etching
From: *Le Rire*, Paris,
17 November 1900

The Boer War was also the subject of a special issue of the humorous magazine *Le Rire*. As a special author's issue, meanwhile, it can be seen as the prototype for the satirical magazine *L'Assiette au Beurre*, which was founded soon afterwards. There were 24 pages of illustrations, with no text apart from the picture captions, and a cover image showing the Boer president Paul Kruger.

Der Burenkrieg war auch Gegenstand eines Sonderhefts des Humormagazins *Le Rire*. Die einmalige Autorennummer kann als Prototyp für das wenig später gegründete Satiremagazin *L'Assiette au Beurre* gelten. Sie bestand aus einer 24-seitigen Bildstrecke und enthielt außer den Bildunterschriften keine weiteren Texte. Das Cover zeigt den Burenpräsidenten Paul Kruger.

La guerre des Boers fit aussi l'objet d'une édition spéciale du magazine humoristique *Le Rire*. Le numéro unique d'auteurs peut être considéré comme le prototype du magazine satirique *L'Assiette au Beurre* fondé un peu plus tard. Il consistait en une galerie d'illustrations de 24 pages et ne présentait aucun texte en dehors des légendes. La couverture montre le président des Boers Paul Kruger.

Caran d'Ache

Mr. Cecil Rhodes – Money is Made from the Blood of Others, 1900
Mr Cecil Rhodes – Das Geld wird mit dem Blut der anderen gemacht
M. Cecil Rhodes – L'argent, c'est le sang des autres
Coloured relief etching
From: *Le Rire*, Paris,
17 November 1900

The diamond magnate Cecil Rhodes, who encouraged British intervention in South Africa as a result of his political and sometimes illicit manoeuvrings, is presented here as being responsible for the subsequent guerrilla warfare and heavy losses of human life. Caran d'Ache's uncompromising use of bold outlines and single colours found an echo in the art of the Nabis while also foreshadowing by many years the later style of comic-book art.

Der Diamantenmagnat Cecil Rhodes, der die britische Intervention in Südafrika durch eine Reihe abenteuerlicher Winkelzüge eingeleitet hatte, wird als Urheber des verlustreichen Guerillakriegs in Szene gesetzt. Caran d'Aches herausfordernder Einsatz von Konturlinie und Farbe korrespondierte mit der Kunst der Nabis und wies weit auf die Kunst des Comics voraus.

Le magnat du diamant Cecil Rhodes, qui avait initié l'intervention britannique en Afrique du Sud par une série de manœuvres aventureuses, est présenté comme l'instigateur de la guérilla qui fut lourde de pertes. L'utilisation provocatrice de lignes de contour et de couleurs par Caran d'Ache correspondait à l'art des Nabis et annonçait longtemps à l'avance l'art de la bande dessinée.

L'Impudique Albion

Jean Veber

Shameless Albion, 1901
Unzüchtiges Albion
L'Impudique Albion
Coloured relief etching
From: *L'Assiette au Beurre*,
Paris, 28 September 1901

The disrespectful portrait of Edward VII on the back cover of Jean Veber's anti-British issue of *L'Assiette au Beurre* caused it to be banned from being sold on the street, although this only led to an increase in sales to 250,000 copies, an unprecedented total in the era before the world wars. As 12 new editions were published, the bared bottom of the symbolic figure of Albion was gradually covered up with different undergarments.

Dass es Jean Vebers anglophobes Album bereits vor den Weltkriegen auf eine beispiellose Auflage von 250 000 Exemplaren bringen konnte, lag an einem Straßenverkaufsverbot, das wegen des despektierlichen Porträts des englischen Monarchen Eduard VII. auf der Rückseite des Hefts verhängt worden war. In den folgenden zwölf Neuauflagen wurde das Gesäß der englischen Symbolfigur Albion mit wechselnden Dessous verdeckt.

Suite à une interdiction de vente dans la rue qui avait été imposée à cause du portrait irrespectueux du monarque anglais Édouard VII sur le dos de couverture du magazine, l'album anglophobe de Jean Veber put atteindre le tirage sans précédent de 250 000 exemplaires, bien avant les guerres mondiales. Au cours des douze nouvelles éditions suivantes, le postérieur de la figure symbolique Albion fut recouverte de divers dessous.

Jean Veber

Reconcentration Camps 1901
Rekonzentrationslager
Les Camps de reconcentration,
Coloured relief etching
From: *L'Assiette au Beurre*,
Paris, 28 September 1901

The British army reacted to the guerrilla warfare attacks by the Boers by setting up a series of centrally located internment camps. The illustration highlights reports of the inhuman conditions, in which thousands of women and children died, while this special issue of the magazine on the horrors of Britain's concentration camps was later used by the Germans as propaganda during both world wars.

Die britische Armee begegnete dem burischen Guerillakampf mit der Einrichtung zentraler Internierungslager. Die Grafik illustriert Meldungen über die katastrophalen Haftbedingungen, durch die Tausende Frauen und Kinder umkamen. Das Themenheft über den Horror britischer Konzentrationslager wurde in den beiden Weltkriegen von der deutschen Seite als Propagandamaterial eingesetzt.

L'armée britannique réagit à la guérilla des Boers en construisant des camps d'internement. Le dessin illustre les articles décrivant les conditions catastrophales de détention à la suite desquelles des milliers de femmes et d'enfants périrent. Cette édition spéciale sur l'horreur des camps de concentration britanniques fut utilisée par les Allemands comme matériel de propagande pendant les deux guerres mondiales.

LES CAMPS DE RECONCENTRATION

..... Grâce à la bonne organisation des camps de reconcentration l'abondance et la santé y règnent. C'est un véritable plaisir de voir les enfants courir et jouer innocemment entre les tentes sous l'œil souriant de leurs mères qui oublient ainsi un moment la mélancolie de leur position .....
..... Les mesures de précaution que nous avons prises ont abaissé la mortalité des enfants à 380 pour mille.

(Rapport officiel au War Office.)

414

František Kupka

The Madmen, Paris, 1899
Die Verrückten | *Les Fous*
Tinted lithograph

In this neutral space where all are equal a group of madmen are marking out a patriotic zone with the blessing of the Church. František Kupka's image of what lies in store for societies inclined to militant nationalism helped to establish a new form of satirical illustration that was occult as well as being based on fantasy. The print, with its elements resembling collage work, was shown at the World's Fairs in Paris and St. Louis and also published in the cultural magazine *Cocorico*.

Im egalitären Niemandsraum zirkelt eine Gruppe Irrsinniger unter dem Segen der Kirche eine patriotische Zone ab. Mit seiner Vision über das Verhängnis hochgerüsteter Nationalismen begründete František Kupka eine neue Form okkult-fantastischer Satire. Der collageartige Druck wurde auf den Weltausstellungen in Paris und St. Louis ausgestellt und in dem Kulturmagazin *Cocorico* abgedruckt.

Dans le no man's land égalitaire, un groupe de fous prend les mesures d'une zone patriotique avec la bénédiction de l'Église. Par cette vision du désastre de nationalismes armés jusqu'aux dents, František Kupka créa une nouvelle forme de satire occulte et fantastique. La gravure fut exposée aux Expositions universelles de Paris et de St. Louis, et imprimée dans le magazine culturel *Cocorico*.

František Kupka

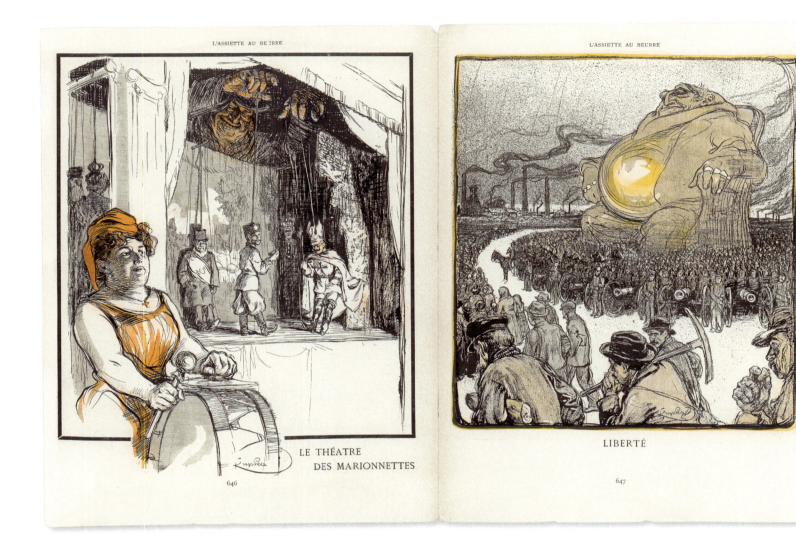

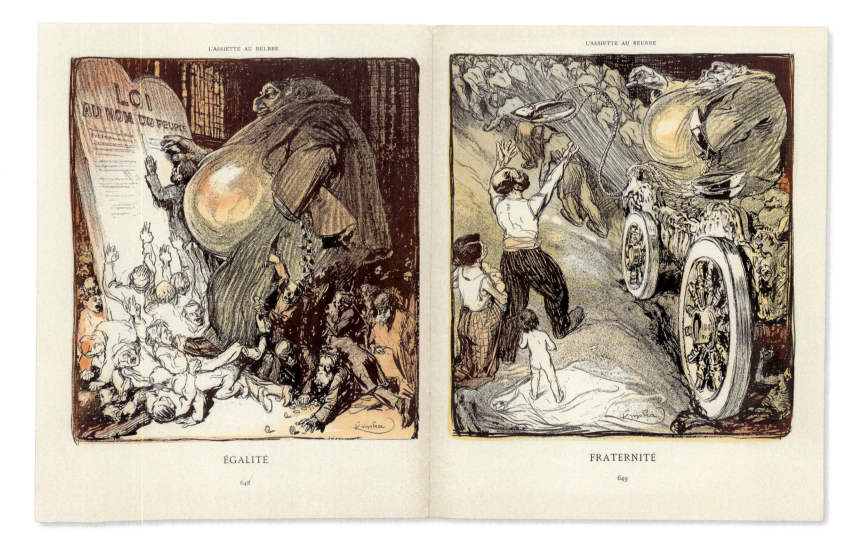

František Kupka

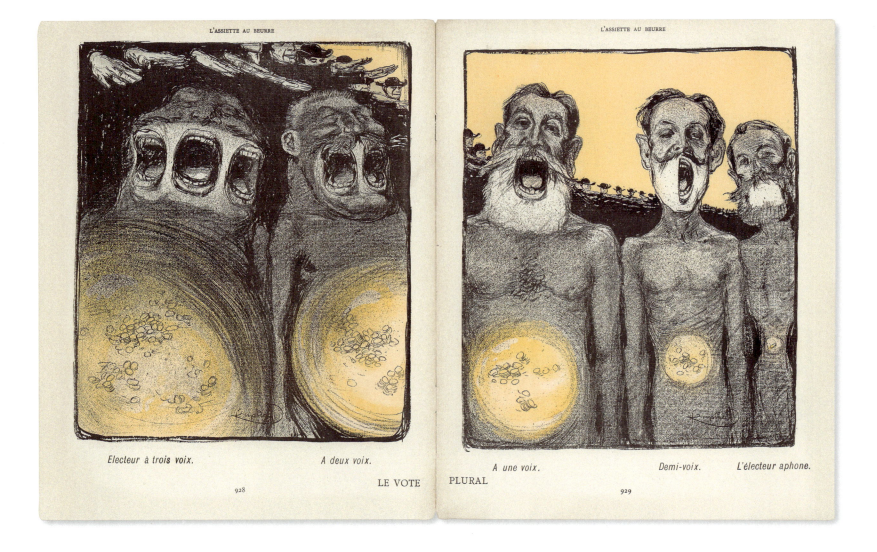

L'ASSIETTE AU BEURRE

Electeur à trois voix. A deux voix.

LE VOTE

928

L'ASSIETTE AU BEURRE

A une voix. Demi-voix. L'électeur aphone.

PLURAL

929

L'Argent (Money) was the first of three themed issues of *L'Assiette au Beurre* illustrated by František Kupka. Traces of his interest in theosophy are evident at various points, along with the influence of the two anarchist writers and polymaths Peter Kropotkin and Élisée Reclus.

L'Argent (Geld) hieß das erste von drei Themenheften, die František Kupka unter dem Eindruck theosophischer Lehren und der Schriften der beiden anarchistischen Universalgelehrten Pjotr Kropotkin und Élisée Reclus für *L'Assiette au Beurre* zeichnete.

L'Argent était le titre du premier de trois numéros thématiques que František Kupka dessina pour *L'Assiette au Beurre* sous l'impression des doctrines théosophiques et des ouvrages des deux anarchistes et savants universels Pierre Kropotkin et Élisée Reclus.

↖↖ *The Puppet Theatre*, 1902
Das Marionettentheater
Le Théâtre des Marionnettes

↖ *Liberty*, 1902
Freiheit | Liberté
Coloured relief etchings
From: *L'Assiette au Beurre*,
Paris, 11 January 1902

While the symbolic figure of Marianne stands proudly in the foreground proclaiming the three values of the motto of the Republic, in the background it is Capital that governs the action on the political stage. Liberty, the first Republican value, has been corrupted to mean the freedom of Capital to enslave the poor.

Während im Vordergrund die französische Symbolfigur Marianne stolz das dreifache Motto der Republik verkündet, ist es das Kapital, das im Hintergrund das Spiel auf der politischen Bühne dirigiert. *Liberté*, das erste republikanische Motto, ist zur Freiheit des Kapitals pervertiert, die Besitzlosen zu versklaven.

Tandis qu'au premier plan Marianne, la figure symbolique de la France, proclame fièrement la triple devise de la République, en arrière-plan c'est le capital qui mène le jeu sur la scène politique. *Liberté*, la première valeur républicaine, est détournée en liberté du capital pour réduire les pauvres en esclavage.

← ← *Equality*, 1902
Gleichheit | Égalité

← *Fraternity*, 1902
Brüderlichkeit | Fraternité
Coloured relief etchings
From: *L'Assiette au Beurre*,
Paris, 11 January 1902

In similar fashion Equality, the second Republican value, has been perverted into a system of justice determined by class and once again governed by Mammon. Fraternity meanwhile, the third value, has been distorted into a gesture of condescending pity which in fact puts the poor right under the yoke of oppression.

Égalité (Gleichheit), das zweite republikanische Motto, ist unter der Macht des Mammons in Klassenjustiz umgeschlagen. *Fraternité (Brüderlichkeit)*, das dritte Ideal, ist zu einer Geste mitleidiger Herablassung pervertiert, mit der das Kapital den Bedürftigen ein Joch der Unterdrückung zuwirft.

Égalité, la seconde devise républicaine, a été pervertie en justice de classe sous l'emprise de Mammon. *Fraternité*, le troisième idéal, est dénaturée en un geste de condescendance apitoyée avec lequel le capital met les démunis sous le joug de l'oppression.

Plural Voting, 1902
Die Mehrstimmenwahl
Le Vote plural
Coloured relief etchings
From: *L'Assiette au Beurre*,
Paris, 3 May 1902

In this satirical allegory on Belgium's use of plural voting, a pseudodemocratic system that was graded according to social status and income, František Kupka's developing interest in the kinetic and amorphous possibilities of illustration are already becoming apparent. As his art moved towards abstraction, both of these aspects played an increasingly important role.

In der satirischen Allegorie auf das pseudodemokratische Mehrstimmenwahlrecht in Belgien, das nach Status und Einkommen gestaffelt war, kündigte sich bereits ein verstärktes Interesse František Kupkas an kinetischen und amorphen Phänomenen an. Auf seinem Weg in die Abstraktion spielten diese beiden Aspekte eine zentrale Rolle.

Dans l'allégorie satirique du pseudodémocratique vote plural en Belgique, qui était échelonné en fonction du statut social et du revenu, František Kupka manifesta un intérêt croissant pour les phénomènes cinétiques et amorphes. Sur son chemin vers l'abstraction, ces deux aspects jouèrent un rôle central.

Théophile Steinlen

Hugo's Vision, 1902
Die Vision Hugos | *La Vision de Hugo*
Coloured relief etching
From: *L'Assiette au Beurre*, Paris, 26 February 1902

Following the influence of František Kupka's visionary allegories, Théophile Steinlen produced a blood-soaked panorama of the horrors of imperial policy across six double pages with no captions. The sequence was marked by a free association of apocalyptic images, and was published on the occasion of the centenary of Victor Hugo's birth. The colonial scene here relates to Belgian atrocities in the Congo.

Auf sechs wortlosen Doppelseiten entwarf Théophile Steinlen unter dem Eindruck von František Kupkas visionären Allegorien ein blutgetränktes Panorama imperialen Schreckens. Anlass für die frei assoziierende apokalyptische Bildfolge war der 100. Geburtstag Victor Hugos. Die Kolonialszene spielt auf die Gräuel Belgiens im Kongo an.

Sous l'influence des allégories visionnaires de František Kupka, Théophile Steinlen conçut sur six doubles pages sans commentaires un panorama ensanglanté des horreurs impérialistes. Le centenaire de Victor Hugo fournit l'occasion pour la réalisation de cette libre association d'images apocalyptiques. Cette scène coloniale fait allusion aux atrocités perpétrées par les Belges au Congo.

9. Jahrgang   **Luxus-Ausgabe**   Nummer 4

Simplicissimus

Abonnement vierteljährlich 3 Mk. 50 Pfg.   Illustrierte Wochenschrift   Bayr. Post-Zeitungsliste: No. 885

(Alle Rechte vorbehalten)

Die afrikanische Gefahr

(Zeichnung von Th. Th. Heine)

Es ist höchste Zeit, daß die Regierung mit aller Macht gegen die Hereros vorgeht, sonst kommen die schwarzen Bestien schließlich noch nach Deutschland und heben bei uns die Sklaverei auf.

Thomas Theodor Heine

The African Peril, 1904
Die afrikanische Gefahr
Le Péril africain
Coloured relief etching
From: *Simplicissimus*, Munich,
19 April 1904

Together with Bruno Paul, Thomas Theodor Heine left a decisive mark on the graphic appearance of Germany's most important satirical magazine, *Simplicissimus*. In this illustration he associated the uprising of the Herero people in Germany's colony in southwest Africa with the socialist agenda of the workers' movement at home.

Thomas Theodor Heine, der zusammen mit Bruno Paul entscheidend das grafische Erscheinungsbild des wichtigsten deutschen Satiremagazins *Simplicissimus* prägte, verknüpfte hier den Aufstand des südwestafrikanischen Volks der Herero in der deutschen Kolonie mit der sozialistischen Agenda der Arbeiterbefreiung im eigenen Land.

Thomas Theodor Heine, qui avec Bruno Paul influença de manière décisive l'apparence graphique du plus important magazine satirique allemand *Simplicissimus*, combina ici la révolte des Hétéros, peuple du Sud-Ouest africain dans la colonie allemande, avec l'agenda socialiste de la libération des ouvriers dans son pays.

Félix Vallotton

Crime and Punishment, 1902
Verbrechen und Strafe | *Crimes et châtiments*
Tinted lithographs
From: *L'Assiette au Beurre*, Paris, 1 March 1902

→ *You Can Shout Your Head off in there!…*, 1902
Da drinnen kannste rumschreien!…
Là-dedans tu pourras gueuler!…

↘ *Drinking Day Is Here!…*, 1902
Der Tag des Alkoholtrinkens ist gekommen!…
Le jour de boire est arrivé!…

Félix Vallotton's themed author's issue of *L'Assiette au Beurre* on "Crime and Punishment" was hard to outdo in terms of its crudeness, and in effect it resembled an early kind of punk zine with 23 lithographic pages loosely fixed together. Its sweeping libertarian attacks on authoritarian social conditions in France were in the same spirit as the enraged autobiographical writings of Jules Vallès and the sarcastic criticisms of writers such as Octave Mirbeau.

Félix Vallottons Autorenheft *Crimes et châtiments* war an Roheit kaum zu überbieten: ein frühes grafisches Punkzine, bestehend aus 23 zusammengehefteten lithografischen Blättern. Der libertäre Rundumschlag gegen die autoritären sozialen Verhältnisse korrespondierte mit Jules Vallès' wütender Autobiografie und den sarkastischen Schriften eines Octave Mirbeau.

Le numéro spécial illustré par Félix Vallotton *Crimes et châtiments* était, en termes de crudité, difficile à surpasser: un des premiers punkzines graphiques consistant en 23 lithographies détachables. Ce coup de balai libertaire dénonçant les conditions sociales autoritaires était de la même veine que la féroce autobiographie de Jules Vallès et que les écrits sarcastiques d'Octave Mirbeau.

Là-dedans tu pourras gueuler!…

Le jour de boire est arrivé!…

LES GARDIENS DE LA PAIX

Gustave-Henri Jossot

The Keepers of the Peace, 1904
Die Ordnungshüter
Les Gardiens de la paix
Coloured relief etching
From: *L'Assiette au Beurre*,
Paris, 13 February 1904

In response to the two-dimensional and somewhat garish art of the Pont-Aven School and also the style of Félix Vallotton's illustrations, Gustave-Henri Jossot developed an individual form of cloissonist caricature. His uncompromising approach was a model for artists in the modern caricature movement in France such as Cabu and Charb, both of whom were killed in January 2015 in the attack on the offices of the satirical magazine *Charlie Hebdo*.

In der Auseinandersetzung mit der grellen Flächenkunst der Schule von Pont-Aven und den Grafiken Félix Vallottons entwickelte Gustave-Henri Jossot eine unverwechselbare Art cloisonnistischer Karikatur. Jossots kompromissloser Zugriff wurde vorbildhaft für Exponenten der jüngsten französischen Karikaturbewegung wie Cabu und Charb. Beide wurden im Januar 2015 bei dem Anschlag auf die Redaktion von *Charlie Hebdo* ermordet.

Dans son analyse de l'art planaire et criard de l'École de Pont-Aven et des dessins de Félix Vallotton, Gustave-Henri Jossot développa une forme incomparable de caricature cloisonniste. L'approche intransigeante de Jossot servit de modèle à des représentants de la caricature contemporaine en France, tels Cabu et Charb. Tous deux furent assassinés en janvier 2015 lors de l'attentat contre la rédaction de *Charlie Hebdo*.

Gustave-Henri Jossot

Untitled (Cra), 1902
Ohne Titel (Cra) | *Sans titre (Cra)*
Coloured relief etching
From: *L'Assiette au Beurre*, Paris,
17 May 1902

This line of priests walking in single file alongside a similar line of geese implies that there is a connection between piety and conformist conditioning. Gustave-Henri Jossot's best-known press illustration was published in a special issue of *L'Assiette au Beurre* on the political influence of Catholic orders, and indeed caricatures played an important role in the bid to establish secularism in France

Die Priester im Gänsemarsch suggerierten einen Zusammenhang zwischen konformistischer Konditionierung und Frömmigkeit. Gustave-Henri Jossots bekannteste Pressegrafik war in einem Sonderheft der *L'Assiette au Beurre* über den politischen Einfluss katholischer Orden erschienen. Im Ringen um die Durchsetzung des Laizismus in Frankreich spielte die Karikatur eine wichtige Rolle.

Les prêtres qui marchent au pas de l'oie suggèrent une connexion entre le conditionnement conformiste et la religiosité. Le dessin de presse le plus connu de Gustave-Henri Jossot avait été publié dans un numéro spécial de *L'Assiette au Beurre*, consacré à l'influence politique des ordres catholiques. La caricature joua un rôle majeur dans la lutte visant à instaurer la laïcité en France.

Gustave-Henri Jossot

All Is Lost, even Honour…, 1907
Alles ist verloren, sogar die Ehre …
Tout est perdu, même l'honneur…
Coloured relief etching
From: *L'Assiette au Beurre*,
Paris, 1 June 1907

Before he emigrated to Tunisia in 1911 and converted temporarily to Islam, Gustave-Henri Jossot produced 18 themed author's issues for *L'Assiette au Beurre* in which he made mocking attacks against the whole corrupt foundations of authoritarian late-bourgeois society, including hypocrisy, prudery, vanity, opportunism, the mania for law and order and the obsession with discipline.

Bevor Gustave-Henri Jossot 1911 nach Tunesien auswanderte und vorübergehend zum Islam konvertierte, nahm er für *L'Assiette au Beurre* in 18 Autorenheften sämtliche korrupten Grundfeste der autoritären spätbürgerlichen Gesellschaft – wie Hypokrisie, Prüderie, Ordnungswahn, Disziplinierungswut, Eitelkeit und Opportunismus – aufs Korn.

Avant d'émigrer en Tunisie en 1911 et de se convertir pour un temps à l'islam, Gustave-Henri Jossot tourna en dérision pour *L'Assiette au Beurre*, dans 18 numéros illustrés par lui seul, l'ensemble des fondements corrompus de la société autoritaire et bourgeoise – comme l'hypocrisie, la pruderie, la maniaquerie, la rage de discipline, la vanité et l'opportunisme.

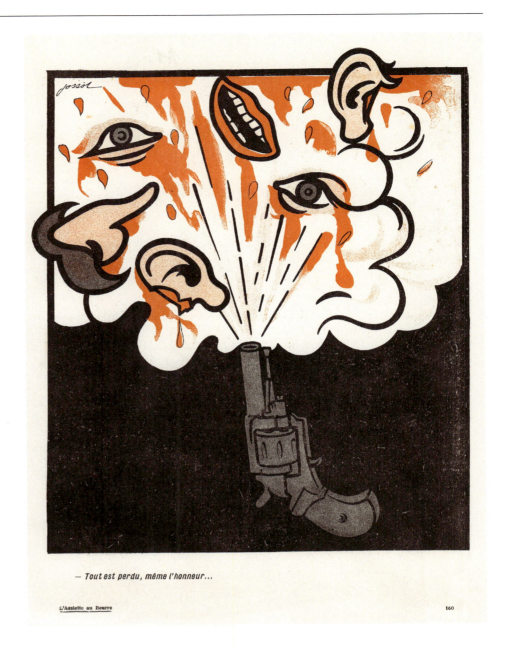

— *Tout est perdu, même l'honneur…*

L'Assiette au Beurre

160

L'ASSIETTE AU BEURRE

Raphael Bordallo Pinheiro

Disturbance in the Chamber, 1904
Unruhen in der Kammer
Tumultes à la Chambre
Coloured relief etching
From: *A Parodia*, Lisbon,
4 February 1904

In the last illustrated magazine he founded, *A Parodia*, Raphael Bordallo Pinheiro marshalled all his remarkable skills as a creative and satirical artist. His dental fantasy, which bears a resemblance to the sculptural qualities of his prize-winning ceramic work, was prompted by a remark from the speaker in parliament about the running laughter of his fellow members.

In seinem letzten Karikaturmagazin *A Parodia* zog Raphael Bordallo Pinheiro die Summe seiner überragenden gestalterischen und satirischen Fähigkeiten. Die Bemerkung eines Redners in der portugiesischen Abgeordnetenkammer über das Gelächter seiner Kollegen inspirierte ihn zu dieser dentalen Fantasie, die den plastischen Qualitäten seiner preisgekrönten Keramiken nahesteht.

Dans son dernier magazine satirique *A Parodia*, Raphael Bordallo Pinheiro mit à profit la somme de ses talents exceptionnels de créateur et d'humoriste. La remarque d'un orateur à la Chambre des députés du Portugal sur le ricanement de ses collègues lui inspira cette fantaisie dentale qui est proche des qualités esthétiques de ses céramiques primées.

O DELIRIO DOS EMPENHOS

Ratos, ratos e mais ratos!

RAPHAEL BORDALLO PINHEIRO - IMIT.

Raphael Bordallo Pinheiro

Mice, Mice and still more Mice!, 1902
Mäuse, Mäuse und noch mehr Mäuse!
Des souris, des souris et encore plus de souris!
Coloured relief etching
From: *A Parodia*, Lisbon,
26 March 1902

The overworked Portuguese prime minister Ernesto Rodolfo Hintze Ribeiro can see the politicians in the two main parties as nothing but a mass of annoying mice trying to dance about on his head. Many of the cartoons by Raphael Bordallo Pinheiro, the most popular Art Nouveau artist in Portugal, are characterised by his inventive use of ornament.

Der überanstrengte portugiesische Ministerpräsident Ernesto Rodolfo Hintze Ribeiro nimmt die Abgeordneten der beiden dominierenden Parteien nur noch als enervierende Mäuse wahr, die ihm auf dem Kopf herumtanzen. Viele Cartoons von Raphael Bordallo Pinheiro, dem populärsten Art-nouveau-Künstler Portugals, zeichnen sich durch einen erfindungsreichen Umgang mit der Ornamentik aus.

Surmené, le Premier ministre portugais Ernesto Rodolfo Hintze Ribeiro ne voient dans les députés des deux partis dominants que des souris énervantes qui virevoltent au-dessus de sa tête. Un grand nombre des dessins humoristiques de Raphael Bordallo Pinheiro, l'artiste le plus populaire de l'Art nouveau au Portugal, se distinguent par une utilisation inventive de l'ornement.

Paul Iribe

→ *To M. Chauchard, a Rich Man*, 1903
An M. Chauchard, einen reichen Mann
À M. Chauchard, homme riche

↘ *What Else is there for My Poor Fellow Artists if They Don't Have the Beautiful Subjects I Have?*, 1903
Was machen nur meine armen Kollegen, die keine solch schönen Sujets vor Augen haben?
Comment font mes pauvres confrères qui n'ont pas d'aussi beaux sujets sous les yeux?

Coloured relief etchings
From: *L'Assiette au Beurre* (*Esthètes!*), Paris,
25 April 1903

Before going on to a dazzling career as a graphic designer, Paul Iribe started out with illustrations for *L'Assiette au Beurre*. His work not only for the press but also in fashion, film and ceramics was of key importance for the Art Deco movement (see ill. p. 578 t.), although in this themed author's issue of the magazine on "Aesthetes!" he satirised those who would later be his patrons along with their high-society tastes.

Mit Illustrationen für *L'Assiette au Beurre* begann Paul Iribes steile Karriere als Grafikdesigner. Seine Arbeiten für Presse, Mode, Film und Keramikindustrie waren wegweisend für die Art-déco-Bewegung (siehe Abb. S. 578 o.). In dem Themenheft *Esthètes!* zum Ästhetizismus der Hautevolee nahm Iribe seine spätere Klientel aufs Korn.

La fulgurante carrière de designer graphiste de Paul Iribe démarra avec des illustrations pour *L'Assiette au Beurre*. Ses travaux pour la presse, la mode, le cinéma et l'industrie de la céramique furent déterminants pour le mouvement de l'Art déco (voir ill. p. 578 h.). Dans le numéro *Esthètes!* consacré à l'esthétique de haute volée, Iribe tourna sa clientèle en dérision.

A M. Chauchard, homme riche.
— *Évidemment, il est très joli... mais, vraiment, ce n'est pas assez cher... pour moi.*

L'Éditeur-Imprimeur-Gérant : SCHWARZ, 9, rue Sainte-Anne, Paris. — Imp. spéciale de *l'Assiette au beurre*, 9, rue Sainte-Anne, Paris. — Abonnements : un an, Paris, 21 fr. ; département, 22 fr. ; étranger, 23 fr. — La reproduction des dessins est formellement interdite tant en France qu'à l'étranger — Les manuscrits et dessins ne sont pas rendus.

Bruno Paul

← *The Gordon Bennett Race*, 1904
Gordon Bennett-Rennen | Course Gordon-Bennett
Coloured relief etching
From: *Simplicissimus*, Munich, 14 June 1904

The first automobile race to be held in Germany involved 18 drivers from seven different countries. *Simplicissimus* devoted a special issue to this major social event, for which the illustrators took special cares to depict the strange outfits worn by those taking part and the automobiles themselves as killing machines.

Das erste Autorennen auf deutschem Boden wurde von 18 Teilnehmern aus sieben Nationen bestritten. Das gesellschaftliche Großereignis war dem *Simplicissimus* eine Sondernummer wert, in der die Zeichner vor allem auf die bizarren Kostümierungen der Teilnehmer und auf das Automobil als Mordmaschine abhoben.

La première course automobile sur le sol allemand eut lieu avec 18 participants issus de sept nations. *Simplicissimus* jugea ce grand événement sociétal digne d'un numéro exceptionnel, dans lequel les illustrateurs firent surtout ressortir les curieux costumes des participants et l'automobile comme une machine meurtrière.

— *Comment font mes pauvres confrères qui n'ont pas d'aussi beaux sujets sous les yeux?*

1827   Esthètes!

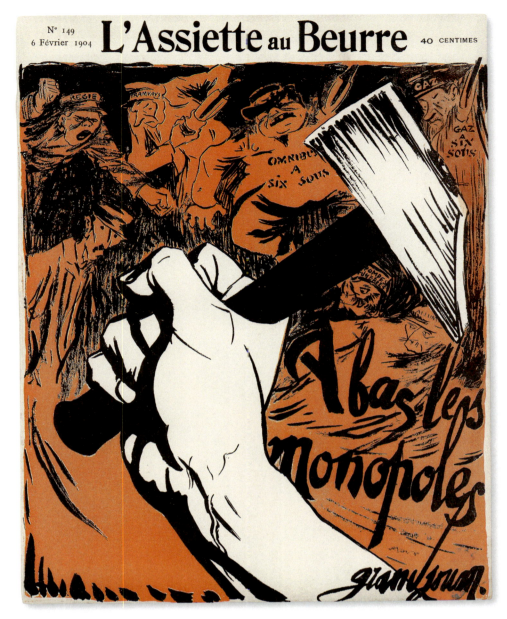

Jules Grandjouan

Down with Monopolies, 1904
Nieder mit den Monopolen | À bas les monopoles
Coloured relief etching
From: *L'Assiette au Beurre*, Paris, 6 February 1904

Jules Grandjouan was one of the most versatile and productive artists who worked for *L'Assiette au Beurre*, and considered himself a propagandist for the anarcho-syndicalist workers' movement before later becoming active on behalf of the Communist Party. His graphic style was much more immediate and energetic than that of his role model Théophile Steinlen, and anticipated the art of agitprop.

Jules Grandjouan war einer der vielseitigsten und produktivsten Künstler von *L'Assiette au Beurre*. Er verstand sich als Propagandist des anarcho-syndikalistischen Gewerkschaftsbunds und war später in der kommunistischen Partei aktiv. Mit einem grafischen Zugriff, der weitaus apodikti-scher und energetischer war als der seines Vor-bilds Théophile Steinlen, antizipierte Grandjouan die Kunst des Agitprop.

Jules Grandjouan fut l'un des artistes les plus éclectiques et les plus prolixes de *L'Assiette au Beurre*. Il se considérait comme un propagandiste de la confédération syndicale à tendance anar-chiste et fut par la suite un membre actif du parti communiste. Grandjouan anticipa l'art de l'Agit-prop par une approche graphique nettement plus démonstrative et plus énergique que son modèle Théophile Steinlen.

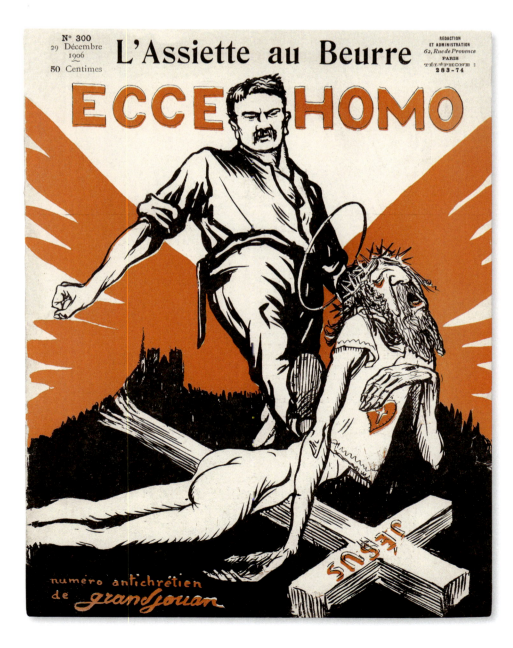

Ecce Homo
Anti-Christian Issue, 1906
Antichristliche Ausgabe | Numéro antichrétien
Coloured relief etching
From: *L'Assiette au Beurre*, Paris,
29 December 1906

Jules Grandjouan's fundamental criticism of Christian morality can be associated as much with atheistic left-wing Hegelianism as with Nietzsche's later philosophy.

Jules Grandjouans Fundamentalkritik der christlichen Moral konnte sich sowohl auf den atheistischen Linkshegelianismus als auch auf die Spätphilosophie Friedrich Nietzsches berufen.

La critique fondamentale de Jules Grandjouan à l'égard de la morale chrétienne pouvait s'ap-puyer aussi bien sur l'hégélianisme athéiste de gauche que sur la philosophie tardive de Friedrich Nietzsche.

Félix Nadar

A Horse's Misery, 1905
Elend des Pferdes | Misère du cheval
Coloured relief etching
From: *L'Assiette au Beurre*,
Paris, 10 June 1905

This sad cover illustration, about the unhappy lives of the horses that were gradually being retired from working on the streets as motorised transport became established, was Nadar's final work. He was 85 at the time, and thus ended his prolific career as a pictorial journalist in the same form of media in which he had started out 57 years previously, with work for Charles Philipon's *Le Charivari*.

Der melancholische Titelcartoon über das Elend der Pferde, die allmählich als Fortbewegungsmittel gegenüber der motorisierten Konkurrenz ins Hintertreffen gerieten, war die letzte Arbeit Nadars. Der 85-Jährige beendete damit seine reiche bildpublizistische Laufbahn in demselben Medium, in dem er sie 57 Jahre zuvor mit Arbeiten für Charles Philipons *Le Charivari* begonnen hatte.

Le mélancolique dessin de couverture sur la misérable condition des chevaux, qui comme moyen de transport étaient peu à peu supplantés par la concurrence motorisée, fut la dernière œuvre de Nadar. Âgé de 85 ans, il termina ainsi sa prolifique carrière de journaliste d'illustration dans le média dans lequel il avait commencé cinquante-sept ans plus tôt en travaillant pour *Le Charivari* de Charles Philipon.

Olaf Gulbransson

The Blind Tsar, 1905
Der blinde Zar | Le Tsar aveugle
Coloured relief etching
From: *Simplicissimus*, Munich,
21 February 1905

Blithely unaware, Tsar Nicholas II
wades through the blood of his subjects. The recent Bloody Sunday in
St. Petersburg, when the army fired
on a peaceful demonstration by workers in front of the Tsar's palace, sent
waves of horror through the liberal
press right around the world. A month
later, *Simplicissimus* in Munich devoted
a special issue to the event.

Ahnungslos watet Zar Nikolaus II.
durch das Blut seiner Untertanen.
Der Petersburger Blutsonntag, bei
dem die Armee eine friedliche Arbeiterdemonstration vor der Zarenresi-
denz zusammengeschossen hatte,
löste eine Welle des Entsetzens in
der liberalen Weltpresse aus. Der
Münchner *Simplicissimus* widmete
dem Ereignis einen Monat später
eine Sondernummer.

Sans se douter de rien, le tsar
Nicolas II patauge dans le sang de
ses sujets. Le Dimanche rouge de
Saint-Pétersbourg, au cours duquel
l'armée tira sur une manifestation
pacifique d'ouvriers depuis la résidence du tsar, souleva une vague d'indignation à travers la presse libérale
du monde entier. Un mois plus tard,
le *Simplicissimus* de Munich consacra
un numéro spécial à l'événement.

Boris Kustodiev

→ *Invasion*, 1905
Coloured relief etching
From: *Zhupel*, no. 2,
St. Petersburg, 1905
Private collection

Boris Kustodiev was a student of the
painter Ilya Repin's, and this depiction
by him of the horrors of the events
in St. Petersburg became a classic
image of the first Russian Revolution
as well as being printed in many foreign illustrated magazines.

Boris Kustodijew war ein Student
des Malers Ilja Repins. Seine Darstellung des Horrors der Petersburger
Ereignisse wurde zur Ikone der ersten
Russischen Revolution und in zahl-
reichen ausländischen Illustrierten
abgedruckt.

Boris Koustodiev fut un élève du
peintre Ilia Répine. Sa représentation de l'horreur des événements
de Saint-Pétersbourg devint une
icône de la première révolution russe
et fut imprimée dans de nombreux
magazines étrangers.

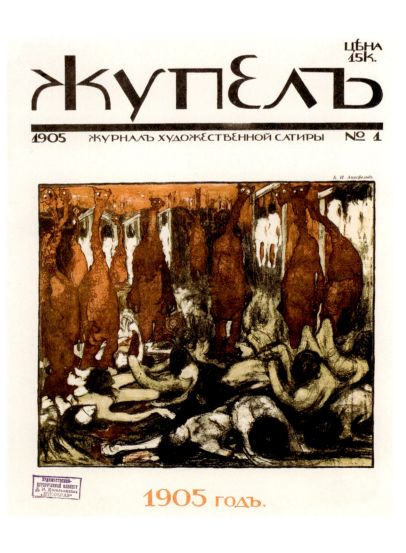

Mstislav Dobuzhinsky

←← *October Idyll*, 1905
Oktoberidyll | Idyllle d'Octobre
Coloured relief etching
From: *Zhupel*, no. 1,
St. Petersburg, 1905
Private collection

Of the hundreds of satirical journals that emerged in Russia in October 1905 with the relaxation of censorship, the illustrated magazine *Zhupel* had the greatest impact abroad. In common with most of its contributing artists, Mstislav Dobuzhinsky, who had found his inspiration in the illustrations in *Simplicissimus*, was involved with the influential Russian Art Nouveau movement Mir Iskusstwa.

Von den Hunderten satirischen Periodika, die in Russland im Oktober 1905 nach der Lockerung der Zensur aus dem Boden geschossen waren, erfuhr das Karikaturmagazin *Zhupel* die größte internationale Resonanz. Der von Zeichnern des *Simplicissimus* inspirierte Mstislaw Dobuschinski zählte wie die meisten Mitarbeiter des *Zhupel* zur einflussreichen russischen Art-nouveau-Gruppe Mir Iskusstwa.

Parmi les centaines de périodiques satiriques qui émergèrent en Russie en octobre 1905 après le relâchement de la censure, le magazine de caricature *Zhupel* obtint la plus grande résonance internationale. Mstislav Doboujinski, sous l'inspiration des dessinateurs du *Simplicissimus*, appartenait à l'influent groupe russe d'Art nouveau Mir iskousstva, comme la plupart des collaborateurs du *Zhupel*.

Boris Anisfeld

← *The Year 1905*
Das Jahr 1905 | L'Année 1905
Coloured relief etching
From: *Zhupel,* no. 1,
St. Petersburg, 1905
Los Angeles, University of Southern California, Libraries

Many of the artists who worked for *Zhupel* had trained at the Academy of Fine Arts in St. Petersburg, from where the massacre committed in front of the Tsar's palace was clearly visible. Boris Anisfeld had studied in the masters class taught by the major Russian realist painter Ilya Repin, although his press illustration work tended more towards the mystical Symbolism of Mikhail Vrubel.

Viele Künstler des *Zhupel* kamen aus dem Umfeld der Petersburger Kunstakademie, von wo aus man das Massaker vorm Zarenpalast in Sichtweite miterleben konnte. Boris Anisfeld hatte in der Meisterklasse des führenden russischen Realisten Ilja Repin studiert, tendierte in seiner Grafik allerdings eher zu dem mystischen Symbolismus eines Michail Wrubel.

De nombreux artistes du *Zhupel* sortaient du milieu de l'Académie des beaux-arts de Saint-Pétersbourg, d'où ils purent suivre sur le vif le massacre perpétré devant le palais du tsar. Boris Anisfeld avait étudié dans la classe de maître de la figure emblématique du réalisme en Russie Ilia Répine, mais tendait plutôt dans ses dessins vers le symbolisme de Mikhaïl Vroubel.

Kresba od STRIMPLA.

Dessin de STRIMPL.

Maďar. — Drahý otče, prokázal jste tolik dobrých služeb věci maďarské, že, jak doufám, zbarví se vaše fialové roucho purpurově.

L'Assiette au Beurre

Le Magyar. — Cher père, vous avez rendu tant de services à la cause hongroise que i'espère voir votre robe violette se teindre de rouge.

404

Gabriele Galantara

→ *The Awakening*, 1906
Das Erwachen | Le Réveil
Coloured relief etching
From: *L'Assiette au Beurre*,
Paris, 10 February 1906

As seen here, the awakening Fourth Estate brings about the collapse of the autocratic edifice of Tsarism. The abolition of serfdom in Russia in 1861 made little difference to the dependent relations of the ordinary people, and the key demand for land reform had also not been fulfilled by the first Russian Revolution. Gabriele Galantara was the most important political cartoonist in Italy.

Der erwachende vierte Stand bringt das autokratische Gebäude des Zarismus zum Einsturz. Die Aufhebung der Leibeigenschaft in Russland 1861 hatte die Abhängigkeitsverhältnisse kaum verändert. Der zentralen Forderung nach einer Landreform wurde auch im Zuge der ersten Russischen Revolution nicht entsprochen. Gabriele Galantara war der bedeutendste politische Cartoonist Italiens.

Le quart-état en ébullition provoque l'effondrement de l'édifice autocrate du tsarisme. En 1861, l'abolition du servage en Russie n'avait guère modifié les relations de dépendance. Dans le sillage de la première révolution russe, la revendication centrale d'une réforme agraire n'avait pas été satisfaite. Gabriele Galantara fut le caricaturiste politique majeur en Italie.

Ludvík Strimpl

← *The Magyar*, 1908
Der Magyar | Le Magyar

→ *The Hungarian Bucephalus*, 1908
Der ungarische Bukephalos
Le Bucéphale hongrois

Coloured relief etching
From: *L'Assiette au Beurre*
(*Les Slaves*), Paris,
9 September 1908

The theme for this special bilingual issue of *L'Assiette au Beurre* entitled "The Slavs" was the marginalisation of ethnic Slovak groups as the result of a policy of Magyarisation put in place by the Hungarian aristocracy, which was internationally condemned following a massacre at Černová in 1907. The illustration on the left relates to the question of the Catholic clergy's responsibility.

Zentrales Thema der zweisprachigen Spezialausgabe mit dem Titel *Les Slaves* war die ethnische Ausgrenzung der slowakischen Bevölkerungsgruppen durch die Magyanisierungspolitik der ungarischen Aristokratie, die durch das Massaker von Černová international am Pranger stand. Die Abbildung links spielt auf die Verantwortung katholischer Kleriker an.

Le thème central de l'édition spéciale et bilingue portant le titre *Les Slaves* était l'exclusion ethnique des communautés slovaques par la politique de magyarisation de l'aristocratie hongroise, que l'opinion internationale avait clouée au pilori à cause du massacre de Černová. L'image de gauche fait allusion à la responsabilité du clergé catholique.

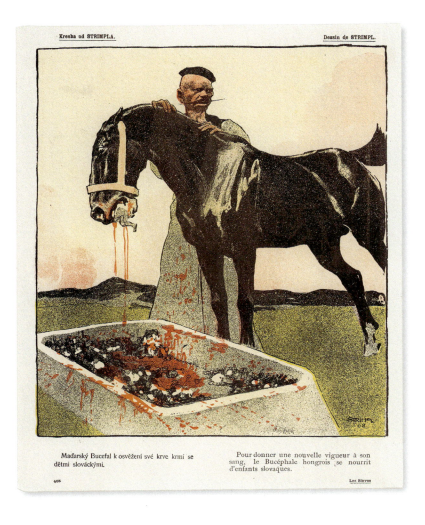

Kresba od STRIMPLA.   Dessin de STRIMPL.

Maďarský Bucefal k osvěžení své krve krmí se dětmi slováckými.

Pour donner une nouvelle vigueur à son sang, le Bucéphale hongrois se nourrit d'enfants slovaques.

LE RÉVEIL

L'Assiette au Beurre   Vive la Russie

Интеллигент. мусульманинъ съ женой

Въ своемъ имѣніи на Кавказѣ

Въ Парижѣ

Qafqazda öz kəndində   Müsəlman intiligenti və xanımı   Parijdə

Josef Rotter

An Educated Muslim with His Wife in the Caucasus and in Paris, 1909
Ein gebildeter Muslim mit seiner Gemahlin im Kaukasus und in Paris
Un musulman cultivé avec sa femme dans le Caucase et à Paris
Coloured relief etching
From: *Molla Nasreddin*, Tbilisi, 1909

The new freedom of the press under the Tsar was also a benefit to the multi-ethnic population of Transcaucasia. The polyglot Azerbaijani satirical magazine *Molla Nasreddin* was read by educated members of society throughout the Muslim world, and its main topics of journalistic inquiry included education reform, the fight against religious intolerance and the emancipation of Muslim women.

Von der neuen zaristischen Pressefreiheit profitierte auch das multiethnische Transkaukasien. Das polyglotte aserbaidschanische Satiremagazin *Molla Nasreddin* wurde von bildungsbürgerlichen Schichten in der gesamten muslimischen Welt gelesen. Zentrale journalistische Anliegen waren die Reformierung des Bildungssystems, der Kampf gegen religiöse Intoleranz und die Emanzipation der Muslimas.

La Transcaucasie multiethnique profita aussi de la nouvelle liberté de presse tsariste. Le magazine satirique polyglotte d'Azerbaïdjan *Molla Nasreddin* était lu par les classes bourgeoises cultivées dans l'ensemble du monde mulsulman. Le principal object f journalistique était la réforme du système éducatif, la lutte contre l'intolérance religieuse et l'émancipation des femmes musulmanes.

→→ Aristide Delannoy

Liberty – Equality – Fraternity
Dr. Clemenceau – Health for Everyone, 1908
Freiheit – Gleichheit – Brüderlichkeit
Dr Clemenceau – Gesundheit für alle
Liberté – Egalité – Fraternité
Docteur Clemenceau – La Santé pour tous
Coloured relief etching
From: *L'Assiette au Beurre*, Paris, 31 October 1908

The left-wing republican prime minister Georges Clemenceau oversaw harsh repressive measures against both the press and the workers' movement. One of the prisoners he is guarding, with his grim expression, is the illustrator of the image itself,

Aristide Delannoy, who appears on the extreme right having recently been sentenced to a year's imprisonment for insulting the army. While in prison he contracted tuberculosis, and died as a result in 1911.

Der linksrepublikanische Ministerpräsident Georges Clemenceau war für rigide Repressionen gegenüber der Presse und den Gewerkschaften verantwortlich. Unter den Gefangenen, die er hier grimmig bewacht, befand sich rechts außen auch der Autor der Grafik, Aristide Delannoy. Dieser war kürzlich wegen Beleidigung des Militärs zu einer einjährigen Haftstrafe verurteilt worden. Im Gefängnis verstarb er dann 1911 an Tuberkulose.

Le Premier ministre républicain de gauche Georges Clemenceau fut responsable de sévères répressions touchant la presse et les syndicats. Parmi les prisonniers, qu'il surveille ici farouchement, se trouvait à l'extrême droite l'auteur du dessin, Aristide Delannoy. Ce dernier avait été condamné à un an de prison pour insulte à l'armée. Atteint de tuberculose, il mourut en prison en 1911.

Josef Rotter

The End of the Macedonian Problem, or
The Turks Cast out of Europe – The Turks in
Anatolia, c. 1912 (?)
Das Ende der makedonischen Geschehnisse
oder die Vertreibungen der Türken aus Europa –
Die Türken in Anatolien
La Fin des événements de Macédonie ou les
expulsions des Turcs hors d'Europe – Les Turcs
en Anatolie
Coloured relief etching
From: *Molla Nasreddin*, Tbilisi, c. 1912

Jalil Mammadguluzadeh, the founder and editor of *Molla Nasreddin,* assembled a group of brilliant illustrators in Tbilisi who were every bit the equal of their fellow artists working for *Simplicissimus* or *L'Assiette au Beurre*. The map shows the critical geopolitical situation in the Balkans that had developed after the Ottoman geese were sent back to their homeland in Anatolia.

Jalil Mammadguluzadeh, der Herausgeber des *Molla Nasreddin,* versammelte in Tiflis eine Reihe brillanter Grafiker, die ihren Kollegen vom *Simplicissimus* und von *L'Assiette au Beurre* auf Augenhöhe begegnen konnten. Die Karte veranschaulicht die kritische geopolitische Lage auf dem Balkan, die durch die Vertreibung der osmanischen Gänse in ihr anatolisches Kerngebiet entstanden war.

Jalil Mammadguluzadeh, l'éditeur du *Molla Nasreddin* réunit à Tbilissi une pléiade de brillants dessinateurs, qui n'avaient rien à envier à leurs collègues du *Simplicissimus* et de *L'Assiette au Beurre*. La carte concrétise la situation géopolitique critique des Balkans qui avait résulté du refoulement des oies ottomanes vers leur pays, l'Anatolie.

— Est-ce que vous n'êtes pas toujours libres de penser ? Tout ce qu'on vous demande, c'est de

Dessin de DELANNOY.

Dessin de JUAN GRIS.

Avec la liberté de la Presse, de puissants quotidiens se fonderont et apprendront aux Turcs à marcher... avec le progrès.

L'instruction sera gratuite et obligatoire. On enseignera aux enfants le respect de la loi et les faits glorieux des ancêtres.

L'Assiette au Beurre   342

Juan Gris

The Regenerated Turkey, 1908
Die erneuerte Türkei | *La Turquie régénérée*
Relief etchings
From: *L'Assiette au Beurre* (*La Turquie régénérée*),
Paris, 29 August 1908

These exaggerated depictions of outdated autocratic conditions in the Ottoman Empire, by Juan Gris and the anarchist writer Charles Malato in the themed issue of the magazine on the Young Turk Revolution, were also taking an indirect swipe at atavistic standards in the supposedly enlightened French Republic. This included the restrictions placed on the press under Georges Clemenceau (see ill. pp. 566/567) and the continued use of beheading for the death penalty.

Mit ihren überspitzten Darstellungen der überholten autokratischen Zustände im Osmanischen Reich zielten Juan Gris und der anarchistische Autor Charles Malato in ihrem Themenheft zur jungtürkischen Revolution indirekt auch auf die Atavismen der aufgeklärten französischen Republik. Dazu zählten die Gängelung der Presse unter Georges Clemenceau (siehe Abb. S. 566/567) und die Todesstrafe durch Enthauptung.

Avec ses représentations exagérées des conditions autocrates archaïques de l'Empire ottoman, Juan Gris et l'auteur anarchiste Charles Malato visaient indirectement les atavismes de la République française éclairée dans leur édition spéciale sur la révolution des Jeunes-Turcs, notamment le musèlement de la presse sous Georges Clemenceau (voir ill. p. 566/567) et la peine de mort par décapitation.

Dessin de JUAN GRIS.

Guidés par un besoin d'expansion propre à toute nation civilisée, les Turcs iront dans les pays sauvages, porter les procédés de civilisation.

ABONNEMENTS: Un an, Paris, 25 fr.; Dep., 26 fr.; Etrang., 28 fr. La reprod. des dessins est formellement interdite en France et à l'Etranger.—Les manus. et dessins ne sont pas rendus.
Rédaction et Administration, 67, Rue de Provence, Paris
E. VICTOR, Imprimerie spéciale de l'Assiette au Beurre, 62, rue de Provence, Paris.   L'Imprimeur-Gérant : E. VICTOR.

The Regenerated Turkey, 1908
Die erneuerte Türkei | *La Turquie régénérée*
Relief etching
From: *L'Assiette au Beurre* (*La Turquie régénérée*),
Paris, 29 August 1908

In the same spirit, this scene of barbaric slaughter was aimed less at Turkey's colonial excesses than at France's involvement in black Africa and the critical situation in the Congo. In the art historian Patricia Leighten's view, the illustration with its use of silhouettes is Juan Gris's most powerful political image and probably "the most uncompromising cartoon published in Paris in the pre-war period".

Auch das Bild eines barbarischen Gemetzels zielte weniger auf türkische Kolonialexzesse als auf das französische Engagement in Schwarzafrika und die Kongo-Affäre. Die Kunsthistorikerin Patricia Leighten hält die scherenschnittartige Szene für Juan Gris' kraftvollste politische Arbeit und für den wahrscheinlich „krassesten Cartoon, der im Paris der Vorkriegszeit veröffentlicht wurde".

De même, le tableau d'un barbare carnage visait moins les excès coloniaux des Turcs que l'engagement français en Afrique noire et l'affaire du Congo. L'historienne d'art Patricia Leighten considère la scène représentée en forme de découpage comme l'œuvre politique de Juan Gris la plus puissante et comme sans doute la « caricature la plus violente qui fût publiée dans le Paris d'avant-guerre ».

Juan Gris

*New Year's Gifts: Thank You, Mister Fifteengrand,
and See You Next Year, if the Butter Hasn't Melted
by then…*, 1910
*Die Neujahrsgaben: Danke, Herr Fünfzehntausend,
und dann bis nächstes Jahr, falls die Butter nicht
geschmolzen ist …*
*Les Étrennes: Merci, m'sieu Quinzemille, et à l'année
prochaine, si le beurre n'est pas fondu…*
Coloured relief etching
From: *L'Assiette au Beurre*, Paris, 1 January 1910

An ominous-looking pastry chef is shown here
bringing a minister his bloated parliamentary allowance from the rapidly dwindling state budget. In this
themed issue about New Year's gifts, Juan Gris produced his last work as a satirical illustrator for the
press before later turning more seriously to painting
under the influence of Picasso and Georges Braque.

Ein unheilvoller Konditor überbringt dem Abgeord-
neten seinen fetten Diätenanteil aus dem schnell
dahinschmelzenden Staatshaushalt. Mit diesem
Themenheft über Neujahrsgeschenke beendete
Juan Gris seine Tätigkeit als satirischer Presse-
grafiker, um sich wenig später unter dem Einfluss
Georges Braques und Picassos verstärkt der
Malerei zuzuwenden.

Un inquiétant pâtissier apporte au député sa grasse
part de diète provenant du budget de l'État qui fond
comme du beurre. Avec ce numéro thématique sur
les étrennes du Nouvel An, Juan Gris termina son
activité de dessinateur de presse satirique pour, un
peu plus tard, se consacrer avec plus d'intensité
à la peinture sous l'influence de Georges Braque et
de Picasso.

— Merci, m'sieu Quinzemille, et à l'année prochaine, si le beurre n'est pas fondu..

New Year's Gifts, 1910
Die Neujahrsgaben | Les Étrennes
Coloured relief etching
From: *L'Assiette au Beurre*, Paris, 1 January 1910

A ministerial official informs the two plumbers that
they will not be receiving any New Year's bonus, on
the grounds that in future he will only relieve himself
at the ministry. In the extreme flatness of his illustrations, together with their sparsely rhythmic use of
lines and the geometrical arrangement of the pictorial space, Juan Gris was already making use of the
essential characteristics of his later Cubist art.

Ein Ministerialbeamter verweigert seinen Sanitärar-
beitern die Neujahrsgratifikation mit dem Argument,
dass er sein Geschäft zukünftig nur noch auf dem
Amt verrichten werde. Mit der extremen Flächigkeit,
dem verknappten rhythmischen Lineament und der
geometrischen Verschränkung des Bildraums antizipierte Juan Gris in seinen Cartoons bereits wesentliche Merkmale seiner kubistischen Kunst.

Un fonctionnaire ministériel refuse à ses plombiers
leurs étrennes du Nouvel An sous prétexte qu'à
l'avenir il ne fera ses besoins qu'au ministère. Par
l'extrême planéité, le linéament rythmique réduit et
l'interconnexion géométrique de l'espace pictural,
Juan Gris anticipait déjà dans ses croquis les caractéristiques majeures de son art cubiste.

— Comment, pas d'étrennes, sous prétexte que vous n'allez jamais au petit endroit !…
— Non, mes amis, je n'aime que ceux du Ministère !

L'AVORTÉE
— Pour ce que vous en auriez fait à vingt ans !

(Dessin de A. Willette.)

Adolphe Willette

The Abortion 1903
Die Abtreibung | *L'Avortée*
Coloured relief etching
From: *L'Assiette au Beurre*,
retrospective issue, Paris,
20 January 1922

As a pioneering artist of comic strips (see ills. p. 506) and teacher of Théophile Steinlen, Marcel Duchamp and his brother Jacques Villon, Adolphe Willette was an important catalyst for the culture of the avant-garde. With the intention of exposing certain double standards in France's legal system he made a direct comparison, in this illustration, between abortion and execution decreed by the State, according to a line of strictly deterministic logic and with the accused woman responding to those judging her by saying "It's only what you'd have done when you were 20!"

Als Pionier des Comicstrips (siehe Abb. S. 506) und Mentor von Théophile Steinlen sowie der Brüder Marcel Duchamp und Jacques Villon zählte Adolphe Willette zu den Katalysatoren der Avantgardekultur. Um die Doppelmoral der Justiz zu entlarven, konfrontierte er hier in milieudeterministischer Konsequenz die Praxis der Abtreibung mit dem Akt staatlicher Tötung. „Das hätten Sie im Alter von 20 Jahren daraus gemacht!", entgegnet die Angeklagte ihren Richtern.

Pionnier de la bande dessinée (voir ills. p. 506) et mentor de Théophile Steinlen ainsi que des frères Marcel Duchamp et de Jacques Villon, Adolphe Willette était l'un des catalysateurs de la culture d'avant-garde. Afin de dénoncer la double morale de la justice, il confronta ici la pratique de l'avortement à l'acte d'exécution au nom de l'État dans une logique rigoureuse de milieu. «Pour ce que vous en auriez fait à vingt ans!», rétorque l'accusée à ses juges.

Käthe Kollwitz

Pictures of Misery I, 1909
Bilder vom Elend I | *Images de la misère I*
Relief etching
From: *Simplicissimus*, Munich, 31 May 1909

The series of illustrations that Käthe Kollwitz produced for *Simplicissimus* marked a shift in her work as an artist away from her previous style of history painting to depicting instead the living conditions of poor workers in her own day. Her approach was based on Théophile Steinlen's socially conscious graphic work (see ill. p. 536 t.) and also corresponded to the magazine's general ethos, which had itself taken Steinlen's pictorial journalism as its model when it was founded.

Die Grafikserie, die Käthe Kollwitz für den *Simplicissimus* schuf, markierte eine Wende im Werk der bislang historisierend arbeitenden Künstlerin hin zur Beschreibung zeitgenössischer proletarischer Verhältnisse. Ihre an der Sozialgrafik Théophile Steinlens (siehe Abb. S. 536 o.) orientierte Haltung entsprach dem Ethos dieses Satiremagazins, das sich bei seiner Gründung Steinlens Bildpublizistik zum Vorbild nahm.

La série de dessins que Käthe Kollwitz réalisa pour le *Simplicissimus* constitue un tournant dans l'œuvre de l'artiste, qui travaillait jusqu'alors dans le style de la peinture d'histoire et se consacra à la description des conditions de vie contemporaines des prolétaires. Sa position, orientée vers le dessin à visée sociale de Théophile Steinlen (voir ill. p. 536 h.), correspondait à l'éthique de ce magazine satirique qui prit dès sa création le journalisme illustré de Steinlen pour modèle.

Bilder vom Elend

I

(Käthe Kollwitz)

— 515 —

John Sloan

Class War in Colorado, 1914
Klassenkrieg in Colorado
Guerre des classes dans le Colorado
Coloured relief etching
From: *The Masses*, New York,
June 1914
Beinecke Rare Book & Manuscript
Library, Yale University

The Masses was New York's bohemian artists' answer to the socially
critical illustrated press of Montmartre.
Its art editor was the founding Ashcan
School artist John Sloan, and his
cover illustration of a miner resisting
the National Guard during the massacre of striking miners at Ludlow,
Colorado, became a key image for the
American workers' movement.

The Masses war die Antwort der New
Yorker Künstlerboheme auf die sozialkritischen Bildpressen der Montmartre-
Szene. Als Artdirector fungierte der
führende Ashcan-Künstler John Sloan.
Seine Darstellung eines Minenarbeiters, der sich während des Massakers
an streikenden Minenarbeitern in
Ludlow (Colorado) gegen die Nationalgarde erhebt, wurde zur Ikone der
amerikanischen Arbeiterbewegung.

The Masses fut la réponse des artistes
de la bohème new-yorkaise à la presse
illustrée teintée de critique sociale de
la scène montmartroise. John Sloan,
l'artiste Ashcan majeur, en était le
directeur artistique. Sa représentation
d'un mineur se révoltant contre la
Garde nationale lors du massacre perpétré contre des mineurs en grève à
Ludlow (Colorado) devint l'icône du
mouvement ouvrier américain.

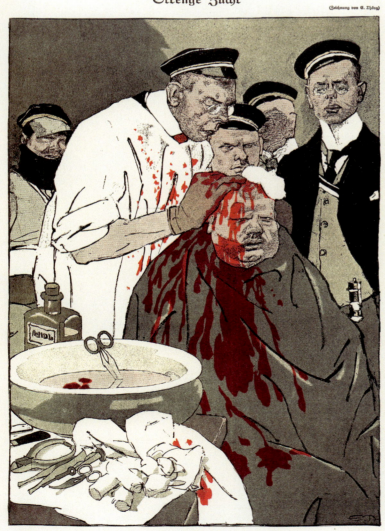

Eduard Thöny

Harsh Punishment, 1914
Strenge Zucht | *Sévère punition*
Coloured relief etching
From: *Simplicissimus*, Munich, 8 June 1914

Eduard Thöny, whose illustration here shows a
fencing wound being treated, was one of the most
influential artists who worked for *Simplicissimus*.
His Art Nouveau style, created using collage, scraping and spraying, was widely imitated, although
during both world wars the critical distance of his
bourgeois social and military scenes was replaced
by an emphasis on nationalistic propaganda.

Eduard Thöny, dessen Zeichnung hier die Ver-
sorgung einer Mensurwunde zeigt, zählte zu den
einflussreichsten Grafikern des *Simplicissimus*.
Sein mittels Collage,- Schabe- und Spritztechni-
ken erzeugter Art-nouveau-Stil fand international
Nachahmer. In den Weltkriegen schlug dann der
Modus seiner bourgeoisen Gesellschafts- und
Militärszenen von kritischer Distanzierung in natio-
nalistische Propaganda um.

Eduard Thöny, dont le dessin ci-contre représente
les soins donnés à une plaie d'escrime, était l'un des
dessinateurs les plus influents du *Simplicissimus*.
Son style Art nouveau, obtenu à l'aide de techniques
de collage, de raclage et de pulvérisation, trouva de
nombreux imitateurs dans le monde. Pendant les
guerres mondiales, son style de scènes bourgeoises
de la société et de l'armée mua d'une distanciation
critique à la propagande national-socialiste.

WILLIBALD KRAIN, KRIEG

5. DIE FRAUEN

Art. Institut Orell Füssli, Zürich

Willibald Krain

The Women, 1916
Die Frauen | Les Femmes
Coloured relief etching
From: Willibald Krain, *Krieg*, Zurich, 1916

The German writer and journalist Kurt
Tucholsky emphasised Willibald Krain's
position as an exceptional artist who
courageously swam "against the tide
of blood" during the war by issuing
collections of pacifist illustrations.

These works, which could only be
published in neutral Switzerland
because of military censorship at
home, established Krain's career
as a socially critical press illustrator
whose images appeared to widespread acclaim all round the world.

Der Schriftsteller und Journalist
Kurt Tucholsky hob Willibald Krains
Stellung als Ausnahmekünstler her-
vor, der mit seinem pazifistischen

Mappenwerk noch während des
Kriegs mutig „gegen den Blutstrom"
geschwommen sei. Das Opus, das
wegen der Militärzensur nur in der
neutralen Schweiz erscheinen konnte,
begründete Krains Karriere als sozialkritischer Pressegrafiker, dessen Werk
international rezipiert wurde.

L'écrivain et journaliste Kurt Tucholsky
souligna la position de Willibald Krain
comme artiste d'exception qui, avec

son portfolio pacifiste, avait coura-
geusement «nagé contre la marée
de sang» pendant la guerre. Ces travaux, qui ne purent paraître que dans
la Suisse neutre à cause de la censure militaire, établit la carrière de
Krain comme dessinateur de presse
sociocritique dont l'œuvre obtint une
acceptance internationale.

Max Liebermann

"Now Let's Thrash Them!"
(The Emperor), 1914
„Jetzt wollen wir sie dreschen!"
(Der Kaiser)
« Maintenant nous voulons les battre !»
(L'empereur)
Lithograph
From: *Kriegszeit. Künstlerflugblätter*,
Berlin, 7 September 1914

In Germany, as in other countries, artists who had previously been critical of the regime were suddenly gripped by a rush of patriotism as the First World War began. Max Liebermann was one such who supported the Kaiser's war policy with large numbers of illustrations expressing hatred and revenge. At the same time though, since *Kriegszeit* had also been founded by Liebermann's dealer Paul Cassirer, his steady supply of work for the newspaper enabled him to assert a dominant position within the Berlin Secession group.

Nicht nur in Deutschland wurden vormals regimekritische Künstler zu Weltkriegsbeginn von Wallungen des Patriotismus erfasst. Max Liebermann unterstützte den Kriegskurs des Kaisers mit zahllosen revanchistischen Grafiken. Die Beteiligung an der Kriegszeitung seines Galeristen Paul Cassirer bot ihm auch die Möglichkeit, seine dominante Stellung im Gefüge der Berliner Sezession zu behaupten.

Ce n'est pas seulement en Allemagne que des artistes, auparavant critiques vis-à-vis du régime au début de la guerre, furent transportés d'élans patriotiques. Max Liebermann a soutenu la politique belliqueuse du Kaiser par de nombreux dessins revanchards. La collaboration au journal de guerre de son galeriste Paul Cassirer lui fournit l'occasion de consolider sa position dominante au sein de la Sécession berlinoise.

Marcel Capy

A Shell Has Knocked the Arc de Triomphe out of l'Étoile! (The Hun Press), 1918
Eine Granate hat den Triumphbogen vom l'Étoile gerückt! (Die deutschen Zeitungen)
Un obus a déplacé l'Arc de triomphe de l'Étoile! (Les journaux boches)
Coloured relief etching
From: *La Baïonnette*, Paris,
20 June 1918

From the end of March 1918, Paris came under bombardment from three long-range German guns. This illustration of a shell hitting the Arc de Triomphe depicts the German desire to be able to secure a direct hit of strategic importance despite the lack of accuracy of their long-range weaponry. Marcel Capy was one of a number of French illustrators who left their mark on the classic comic-strip style of pictures during the First World War.

Ab Ende März 1918 wurde Paris von drei deutschen Ferngeschützen unter Beschuss genommen. Der Granateneinschlag im Triumphbogen visualisiert das Wunschdenken des Gegners, mit dem unpräzisen Langstreckenbombardement einen strategischen Volltreffer landen zu können. Marcel Capy zählte zu einer Reihe französischer Zeichner, die während des Ersten Weltkriegs den klassischen Bande-dessinée-Stil prägten.

À partir de la fin mars 1918, Paris fut bombardé par trois canons allemands à longue portée. Le coup ayant frappé l'Arc de triomphe visualise le souhait profond de l'adversaire de pouvoir toucher au cœur un point stratégique par un bombardement imprécis à longue portée. Marcel Capy fut l'un des dessinateurs français qui marquèrent de leur empreinte le style de bande dessinée pendant la Première Guerre mondiale.

LA BAIONNETT

(Dessin d'Ancrenaz.)

LE CHŒUR DES BOCHES :
— Ciel! qu'arriverait-il, s'il se mettait tout debout?...

Imprimerie CRÉTÉ, Corbeil (S.-et-O.).   *Le Gérant :* F. TINESSE.

Paul Ancrenaz

← *The Hun Chorus: Good Heavens!*
What Would It Be like if He Stood
Right up?…, 1916
Der Chor der boches: *Himmel! Was*
passiert erst, wenn der aufsteht? …
Le Chœur des Boches : Ciel !
qu'arriverait-il, s'il se mettait tout
debout ?…
Coloured relief etching
From: *La Baïonnette*, Paris,
20 July 1916

In France, news of the Russian bear's
first victories against the German
army on the Eastern Front was celebrated with a sense of euphoria and
as relief from the trench warfare at
Verdun. The satirical war magazine
La Baïonnette recruited several artists
who had worked for *L'Assiette au
Beurre*, and continued its tradition of
experimentation by developing innovative new styles of illustration.

In Frankreich feierte man die ersten
Erfolge des russischen Bären gegen
die deutsche Armee an der Ostfront
euphorisch als Entlastung des Stel-
lungskriegs bei Verdun. Das satirische
Kriegsmagazin *La Baïonnette* griff
auf viele Mitarbeiter von *L'Assiette
au Beurre* zurück und setzte dessen
experimentelle Tradition mit neuen
innovativen Positionen fort.

En France, on fêtait euphoriquement
les premières victoires de l'ours russe
contre l'armée allemande sur le front
de l'Est comme un soulagement
de la guerre de tranchées à Verdun.
Le magazine de guerre satirique *La
Baïonnette* fit appel à de nombreux
collaborateurs de *L'Assiette au Beurre*
et prolongea leur tradition expérimentale avec des positions innovantes.

↓ *Their Factories of War: And Is this*
just Macaroni then?, 1916
Ihre Rüstungsbetriebe. Und das da,
sind das Makkaroni?
Leurs usines de guerre. Et ça,
est-ce des macaronis ?
Coloured relief etching
From: *La Baïonnette*, Paris,
14 September 1916

At the end of August 1916, the
French press welcomed Italy's decla-
ration of war against Germany as a
new ally against the Axis powers. Paul
Ancrenaz, who continued in his own
manner with the cloissonist cartoon
style of Caran d'Ache and Gustave-
Henri Jossot (see ills. pp. 541, 552),
countered the feelings of prejudice
about Italy's supposed lack of military
strength by referring to its powerful
war industry.

Ende August 1916 konnte die französische Presse mit dem Kriegseintritt
Italiens einen neuen Verbündeten
gegen die Achsenmächte begrüßen.
Paul Ancrenaz, der in eigenwilliger
Weise die Tradition des cloisonnistischen Comic eines Caran d'Ache und
Gustave-Henri Jossot (siehe Abb.
S. 541, 552) fortschrieb, entgegnete
hier dem Vorurteil einer militärischen
Impotenz des italienischen Partners
mit einem Verweis auf dessen mächtige Kriegsindustrie.

Fin août 1916, avec l'entrée en guerre
de l'Italie, la presse française pouvait
saluer un nouvel allié contre les forces
de l'Axe. Paul Ancrenaz, qui poursuivait à sa manière personnelle la tradition de bande dessinée cloisonniste
de Caran d'Ache et de Gustave-Henri
Jossot (voir ills. p. 541, 552), ripos-
tait ici au préjugé de l'impuissance
militaire du partenaire italien par une
référence à sa puissante industrie
de guerre.

LA BAIONNETTE

LEURS USINES DE GUERRE
— Et ça, est-ce des macaronis ?
— 588 —

(Dessin d'Ancrenaz.)

Zyg Brunner

← *Their Latest Fashion: Portrait, from Life, of a "Pioneer of Civilisation and Culture"*, 1916
Ihr letzter Schrei: Porträt nach der Natur von einem „Pionier der Civilisation und Kultur"
Leur dernier cri : Portrait, d'après nature, d'un «Pionnier der Civilisation und Kultur»
Coloured relief etching
From: *La Baïonnette*, Paris,
11 May 1916

In a special issue of *La Baïonnette* on machines of war the German use of chemical weapons (left) was contrasted with the seemingly supernatural workings of Nemesis on the French side (right) whereby an enemy could be annihilated by a lightning bolt striking from the ether. The variation between the two-dimensional linear aesthetics of Art Nouveau and the related style of cartoons was characteristic of the satirical press in France during the war.

In einem Themenheft von *La Baïonnette* über Kriegsmaschinen wurde dem deutschen Einsatz chemischer Waffen (links) auf der französischen Seite (rechts) das überirdische Wirken der Nemesis gegenübergestellt, die den Feind in der Form eines

Pierre Legrain

→ *An Enemy Company Has Been Destroyed by Our Deadly Hertzian Waves*, 1916
Eine feindliche Kompanie durch unsere Radioblitzwellen vernichtet
Une compagnie ennemie a été anéantie par nos ondes herziennes foudroyantes
Coloured relief etching
From: *La Baïonnette*, Paris,
11 May 1916

ätherischen Blitzstrahls zu Fall bringt. Das Oszillieren zwischen den verwandten flächig-linearen Ästhetiken von Art nouveau und Comic war typisch für die satirische Kriegspresse Frankreichs.

Dans un numéro spécial de *La Baïonnette* consacré aux machines de guerre, l'utilisation par les Allemands d'armes chimiques (à gauche) est juxtaposée à l'action supraterrestre de Némésis du côté français (à droite), qui fait tomber l'ennemi sous forme d'un éclair éthéré. L'oscillation entre les esthétiques analogues linéaires et planaires de l'Art nouveau et de la bande dessinée fut caractéristique de la presse de guerre satirique en France.

LA BAÏONNETTE

(Dessin de P. Legrain.)

Pierre Legrain

COMMUNIQUÉ DU...
Une compagnie ennemie a été anéantie par nos ondes herziennes foudroyantes.

— 293 —

Georges Goursat (Sem)

←*England Does Its Part*, 1916
Der Beitrag Englands | *La Part de l'Angleterre*
Coloured relief etching
From: *La Baïonnette*, Paris, 15 June 1916

Tommy Atkins, symbolising the British army, is shown here striding across the English Channel to hurry to the aid of his French allies on the embattled Western Front. Sem was a popular chronicler of scenes from Parisian high society, and went on to become one of the French army's most effective and committed pictorial propagandists during the First World War.

Im Stechschritt überquert Tommy Atkins, der symbolische Repräsentant der britischen Armee, den Ärmelkanal, um seinem französischen Verbündeten an der bedrängten Westfront zu Hilfe zu eilen. Sem, der populäre Chronist der Pariser Hautevolee, war während des Ersten Weltkriegs einer der effektivsten und engagiertesten Bildpropagandisten der französischen Armee.

Tommy Atkins, le représentant symbolique de l'armée britannique, traverse la Manche au pas de l'oie pour voler au secours de ses alliés français en difficulté sur le front de l'Ouest. Sem, le chroniqueur populaire de la haute société parisienne, fut l'un des propagandistes d'images les plus efficaces et les plus engagés de l'armée française pendant la Première Guerre mondiale.

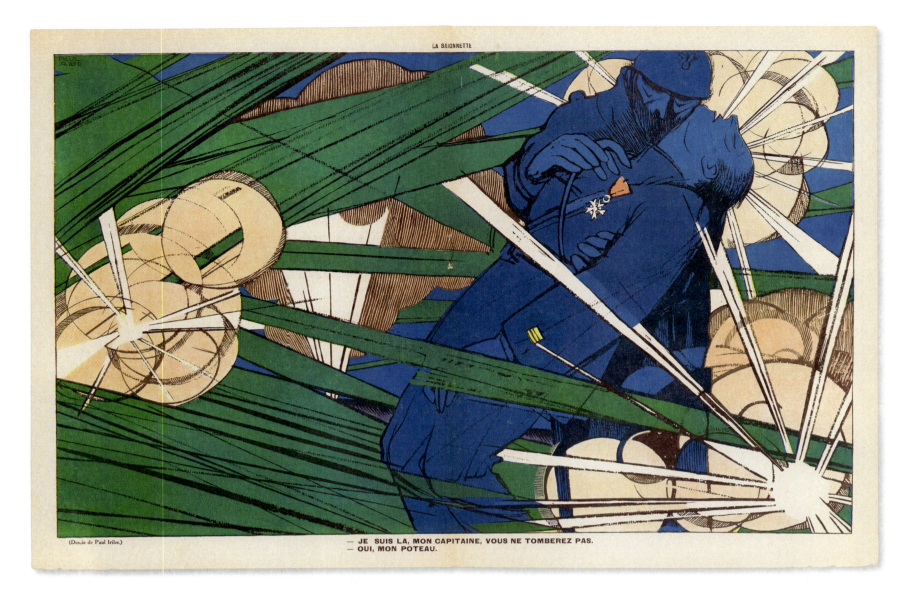

LA BAIONNETTE

(Dessin de Paul Iribe.)

— JE SUIS LA, MON CAPITAINE, VOUS NE TOMBEREZ PAS.
— OUI, MON POTEAU.

LA BAIONNETTE

(Dessin de Paul Iribe.)

DEBOUT LES MORTS !

Paul Iribe

← *"I'm here, Captain, You Won't Fall. –
Thanks, Mate"*, 1917
„*Ich bin da, Herr Hauptmann, Sie fallen nicht. –
Ja, Kamerad*"
« *Je suis là, mon capitaine, vous ne tomberez pas. –
Oui, mon poteau* »
Coloured relief etching
From: *La Baïonnette*, Paris, 5 July 1917

Paul Iribe's stylistic fusion of Art Nouveau with a futuristic adaptation of the Cubist dissection of space was groundbreaking for the later aesthetics of Art Deco.

Paul Iribes stilistische Fusion aus Art nouveau und futuro-kubistischer Raumzergliederung erwies sich als wegweisend für die Ästhetik des Art déco.

La fusion stylistique conçue par Paul Iribe, qui consistait en une fusion d'Art nouveau et une dissection futuro-cubiste de l'espace, ouvrit la voie de l'esthétique de l'Art déco.

↙ *"Dead Men, on Your Feet!"*, 1917
„*Ersteht auf von den Toten!*" | « *Debout les morts!* »
Coloured relief etching
From: *La Baïonnette*, Paris, 26 July 1917

A ghostly army of fallen soldiers is here being called to attention by a heroic leader. The eerie scene is thought to have inspired Abel Gance's famous surrealistic ending to his anti-war film *J'Accuse* (1919), and indeed Paul Iribe's talent for scenography was also recognised by Cecil B. DeMille who invited him to Hollywood soon after the war.

Eine Geisterarmee gefallener Soldaten wird von einem mythischen Führer zu den Waffen gerufen. Die gespenstische Szene hat wohl Abel Gance zu der berühmten surrealen Schlusssequenz seines Antikriegsfilms *J'accuse* (1919) inspiriert. Paul Iribes szenografisches Talent wurde auch von Cecil B. DeMille erkannt, der den Künstler kurz nach Kriegsende nach Hollywood einlud.

Une armée fantomatique de soldats morts au combat est exhortée par un chef mythique à prendre les armes. Cette scène spectrale a probablement inspiré Abel Gance pour la fameuse séquence finale et surréelle de son film contre la guerre *J'accuse* (1919). Le talent scénographique de Paul Iribe a été aussi reconnu par Cecil B. DeMille qui invita l'artiste à Hollywood juste après la guerre.

↓ *"… The Way Zeppelins Fly Is very Different
from the Way ze Birds Fly…"*, 1915
„*… Der Zeppelinflug unterscheidet sich deutlich
vom Flug der Vögel …*"
« *… Le vol du Zeppelin diffère beaucoup du vol
des Zoiseaux…* »
Relief etching
From: *Le Mot*, Paris, 3 April 1915

Anti-aircraft searchlights have here chanced upon a group of menacing-looking Zeppelins, which were greatly feared because of their silent attacks by night. After *Le Témoin*, the avant-garde war journal *Le Mot* was Paul Iribe's second venture into publishing, and the new standards he set for artistic illustration were of considerable influence right across the world.

Suchscheinwerfer der Flugabwehr haben eine Gruppe grimmiger Zeppeline aufgeschreckt, deren lautlose Nachtangriffe gefürchtet waren. Die avantgardistische Kriegszeitung *Le Mot* war nach *Le Témoin* das zweite Periodikum, das Paul Iribe selbst herausgab. Der neue Standard, den er damit im Bereich der künstlerischen Illustration gesetzt hatte, strahlte international aus.

Des projecteurs de la défense aérienne ont surpris un groupe de farouches zeppelins dont les silencieuses attaques nocturnes étaient redoutées. La revue patriotique avant-gardiste *Le Mot* fut après *Le Témoin* le deuxième périodique que Paul Iribe édita. Le nouveau standard, qu'il avait ainsi positionné dans le domaine de l'illustration artistique, eut un rayonnement international.

" ... Le vol du Zeppelin diffère   beaucoup   du   vol des zoiseaux... "   (MŒURS DES ZEPPELINS, PAGE 2).

LA CROIX DE FER.

Paul Iribe

The Iron Cross, 1915
Das Eiserne Kreuz | *La Croix de fer*
Coloured relief etching
From: *Le Mot*, Paris 1 July 1915

With a childish spirit of nonsense Paul Iribe here undermines the sacred aura associated with the Iron Cross. The imaginative designs that appeared in the final issue of *Le Mot* exemplified the magazine's eclectic mix of styles, which ranged from various types of cartoon to geometric abstraction and lyrical doodling.

Mit kindischem Nonsens unterminiert Paul Iribe hier die hieratische Aura des Eisernen Kreuzes. Die fantasievolle Grafik in der letzten Ausgabe von *Le Mot* stand exemplarisch für den Stilmix aus Comic, geometrischer Abstraktion und lyrischem Gekritzel, der das Erscheinungsbild dieses Magazins bestimmte.

Avec un sens puéril de l'absurde, Paul Iribe démonte ici l'aura hiératique de la Croix de fer. Le dessin fantaisiste du dernier numéro de la revue *Le Mot* est exemplaire pour le mélange de styles fait de bande dessinée, d'abstraction géométrique et de gribouillage lyrique, qui déterminait l'apparence de ce magazine.

Jean Cocteau (Jim)

"It Seems this Giant, Hindenburg, Is Going to Surrender on the Western Front" (Berliner Tageblatt), 1915
„Hindenburg, dieser Riese, wird wohl an die westliche Kriegsfront gehen"
«Hindenbourg, ce géant, va, paraît-il, se rendre sur le front occidental de la guerre»
Coloured relief etching
From: *Le Mot*, Paris, 1 July 1915

Paul Iribe's most notable fellow artist at *Le Mot* was the multi-talented Jean Cocteau, who was six years his junior and signed his playful war cartoons with the name of his dog, Jim. The head of the defeated giant belongs to Paul von Hindenburg, the supreme commander of the German army.

Paul Iribes wichtigster Mitstreiter bei *Le Mot* war das sechs Jahre jüngere Multitalent Jean Cocteau, der seine martialisch-verspielten Cartoons mit dem Namen seines Hunds Jim unterzeichnete. Der Kopf des besiegten Riesen gehört dem Oberbefehlshaber der deutschen Armee, Paul von Hindenburg.

Le collègue le plus important de Paul Iribe à la revue *Le Mot* était Jean Cocteau, un multitalent de six ans son cadet, qui signait ses dessins à fois ludiques et martiaux du nom de son chien Jim. La tête du géant terrassé est celle du commandant suprême de l'armée allemande, Paul von Hindenburg.

le mot.

N° 20. — 1re Année.   30 Centimes.   1er Juillet 1915.

DESSIN DE JIM.

Hindenbourg, ce géant, va, paraît-il, se rendre sur le front occidental de la guerre.
(Berliner Tageblatt.)

Jacques Lehmann (Nam)

The Camouflage Unit, 1917
Die Tarnmaler | *Les Camoufleurs*
Coloured relief etching
From: *La Baïonnette*, Paris,
23 August 1917

Military camouflage painting, which was developed in 1915 by the French army's specialist camouflage unit, was also suited to introducing a patriotic public that was used to the illusions of history painting to the more expansive aesthetics of Modernism.

Die militärische Tarnmalerei, die 1915 in der Section de Camouflage der französischen Armee entwickelt wurde, war geeignet, ein an den Illusionismus der Historienkunst gewohntes patriotisches Publikum mit den dispersiven Ästhetiken des Modernismus vertraut zu machen.

La peinture de camouflage militaire, qui fut développée dans la section de camouflage de l'armée francaise en 1915, était appropriée pour familiariser un public patriote accoutumé à l'illusionnisme de la peinture d'histoire aux esthétiques dispersives du modernisme.

Auguste Roubille

Disillusioned, 1917
Ernüchtert | *Désenchanté*
Coloured relief etching
From: *La Baïonnette*, Paris,
23 August 1917

Military camouflage painting was based on the techniques of Synthetic Cubism, and amongst the many avant-garde artists who were employed as camouflage painters were the established Cubists Fernand Léger and Jacques Villon, together with the cartoonist, former member of the Commune and early Cubist Jean-Louis Forain.

Die militärische Camouflagemalerei war am Vorbild des synthetischen Kubismus orientiert. Zu den vielen avantgardistischen Künstlern, die als Tarnmaler eingesetzt wurden, zählten neben Erzkubisten wie Fernand Léger und Jacques Villon auch der exkommunardische Cartoonist und Frühkubist Jean-Louis Forain.

La peinture de camouflage militaire était inspirée du modèle du cubisme synthétique. Parmi les nombreux artistes d'avant-garde qui furent employés comme peintres de camouflage, il y avait en plus de Fernand Léger et de Jacques Villon, profondément cubistes, le caricaturiste, ex-communard et cubiste de la première heure Jean-Louis Forain.

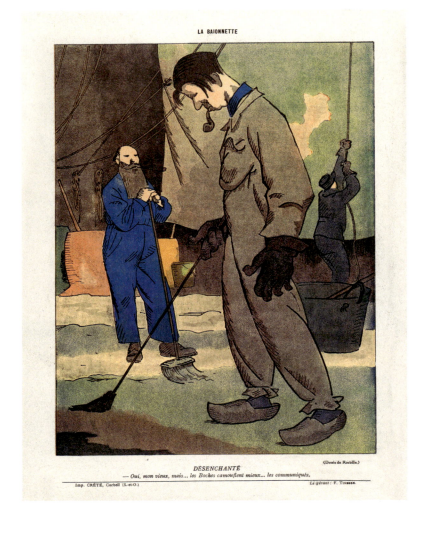

Albert Gleizes

Return, 1915
Heimkehr | Retour
Coloured relief etching
From: *Le Mot*, Paris, 1 July 1915

By including work by Fauvist and Cubist artists such as Raoul Dufy, André Lhote and Albert Gleizes in his illustrated magazine, Paul Iribe succeeded in bringing out the affinity between caricature and the pictorial techniques of modern art. Moreover, through Lhote, Gleizes and particularly Léon Bakst a connection was established with the Russian avant-garde.

Durch die Einbindung von fauvistischen und kubistischen Künstlern wie Raoul Dufy, André Lhote und Albert Gleizes in sein Cartoonmagazin gelang es Paul Iribe, die Affinität zwischen Karikatur und modernistischen Bildstrategien hervorzuheben. Über Lhote, Gleizes und Léon Bakst bestanden außerdem enge Anbindungen an die russische Avantgardeszene.

Par l'implication d'artistes fauvistes et cubistes comme Raoul Dufy, André Lhote et Albert Gleizes dans sa revue de bandes dessinées, Paul Iribe réussit à faire ressortir l'affinité entre caricature et stratégies picturales modernistes. De plus, par l'intermédiaire de Lhote, Gleizes et de Léon Bakst existaient d'étroites relations avec la scène d'avant-garde russe.

RETOUR.

→ → Kazimir Malevich & Vladimir Mayakovsky

"Our French Allies Have a Cart Full of Defeated German Soldiers / Their English Brothers Are Carrying Baskets Packed with More Ragged German Soldiers", 1914
„Die französischen Alliierten haben einen Korb voller besiegter deutscher Soldaten / Die englischen Brüder tragen eine Wanne mit zerfetzten deutschen Soldaten"
« Les alliés français ont une charrette pleine de soldats allemands vaincus / Les frères anglais portent corbeille avec des soldats allemands en lambeaux »
Segodnyashny Lubok Publishers, Moscow, 1914
Colour lithograph
London, The British Library

This series of 23 cartoons produced by two members of the Russian avant-garde as propaganda during the First World War was based on the tradition of Russian folk prints (*lubok*). For the poet and artist Vladimir Mayakovsky his work in illustration marked the beginnings of his confrontational activities, whereas for Kazimir Malevich it signalled the end of his period of Cubist and Neo-Primitivist painting.

Die Serie von 23 Cartoons, mit der sich die russische Avantgarde an der Weltkriegspropaganda beteiligte, war an die Tradition der populären russischen Bilderbogenkultur (Lubok) angelehnt. Während das illustratorische Unternehmen für den Maler und Dichter Wladimir Majakowski den Beginn seiner interventionistischen Aktivitäten bedeutete, markierte es für Kasimir Malewitsch das Ende seiner kubistischen und neoprimitivistischen Malerei.

La série de 23 dessins, avec laquelle l'avant-garde russe participa à la propagande de la guerre mondiale, était liée à la tradition d'estampes populaires russes (loubok). Alors que pour le peintre et poète Vladimir Maïakovski les travaux d'illustration signifièrent le début de ses activités interventionnistes, ils marquèrent pour Kasimir Malevitch la fin de sa peinture cubiste et néo-primitiviste.

Типо-Литографія С. М. Мухарскаго, Москва.

У союзниковъ французовъ
Битыхъ нѣмцевъ полный кузовъ,

А у братцевъ англичанъ
Драныхъ нѣмцевъ цѣлый чанъ.

1)

РАНЬШЕ НАШИ ЗАВОДЫ
ГОТОВИЛИ ОРУЖИЯ ЭТИ,

Rosta Collective (Mikhail Cheremnykh)

Between 1919 and 1922, a collective of Russian artists under the leadership of Vladimir Mayakovsky produced thousands of posters illustrated with pictorial news on behalf of the Bolshevik telegraph agency Rosta. The posters were reproduced by hand using stencils, and were displayed nationwide in shop windows to provide information about the Civil War as well as political and economic developments. On stylistic grounds the series *GPP 81* about Lenin's new market economy can be attributed to the founder of this Rosta initiative, Mikhail Cheremnykh, who before Communism and cartoons became separated by ideology had developed an exciting fusion of late Cubist abstraction with a comic-strip style, which looked ahead even to the artistic attitudes of the 1960s and 1970s.

Von 1919 bis 1922 produzierte ein Kollektiv russischer Künstler unter der Leitung Wladimir Majakowskis Tausende von Bildnachrichten in Plakatform für die bolschewistische Telegrafenagentur Rosta. Es handelte sich um Plakate, die mittels Schablonen handreproduziert wurden. Sie kamen als Tableaus landesweit in Schaufenstern zum Aushang und informierten über den Bürgerkrieg und über politische und wirtschaftliche Kampagnen. Stilistisch kann die Folge *GPP 81* über Lenins neue Marktwirtschaft dem Begründer der Rosta-Initiative, Michail Tscheremnych, zugeordnet werden. Bevor Kommunismus und Comic ideologisch auseinanderdividiert wurden, hatte der russische Cartoonist eine spannende Fusion aus spätkubistischer Abstraktion und Comicstil entwickelt, die bereits auf künstlerische Positionen der 1960er- und 1970er-Jahre vorausweist.

De 1919 à 1922, un collectif d'artistes russes sous la direction de Vladimir Maïakovski produisit des milliers d'informations illustrées sous forme d'affiches pour l'agence télégraphique bolchévique Rosta. Il s'agissait d'affiches reproduites à la main au moyen d'un pochoir. Elles étaient exposées à travers tout le pays comme tableaux dans des vitrines et fournissaient des informations sur la guerre civile et les campagnes politiques et économiques. D'un point de vue stylistique, la série *GPP 81* sur la nouvelle économie de marché de Lénine peut être attribuée au fondateur de l'initiative Rosta, Mickaïl Tcheremnych. Avant que le communisme et la bande dessinée ne soient strictement séparés, l'illustrateur russe avait développé une passionnante fusion d'abstraction de cubisme tardif et de style de bande dessinée, qui préfigure déjà les positions artistiques des années 1960 et 1970.

GPP 81, March 1921
Hand-made stencil prints
Berlin, Galerie Thomas Flor

*1) In the Past, Our Factories Produced Weapons
such as This
Ursprünglich produzierten unsere Fabriken diese Waffen
Autrefois, nos usines fabriquaient ces armes*

*2) Now We Have New Weapons
Jetzt haben wir eine neue Waffe
Maintenant nous avons une arme nouvelle*

*3) And We Are ready for the Spring
Sodass wir für den Frühling gewappnet sind
Si bien que nous sommes équipés pour le printemps*

Rosta Collective (Mikhail Cheremnykh)

GPP 81, March 1921
Hand-made stencil prints
Berlin, Galerie Thomas Flor

4) The Harrow and Plough Must Be Looked after
Egge und Pflug müssen gewartet werden
La herse et la charrue doivent être réparées

5) Workers! There Is a New Front now
Arbeiter! Eine neue Front ist eröffnet
Travailleurs ! Un nouveau front est ouvert

6) Faster, on with the Work of Agricultural Reconstruction!
Schneller, vorwärts mit der landwirtschaftlichen Umstrukturierung!
Plus vite, en avant avec la restructuration agricole !

Скорей
за сельскохозяйственный
ремонт!

STUPEUR DE JEUNES RECRUES APERCEV

O MÉDIT

Appendix

Bibliography

General Literature
Allgemeine Publikationen
Littérature générale

Acevedo-Valdés, Esther & Agustín Sánchez González, *Historia de la caricatura en México*, Lleida, 2011.

Altick, Richard, *The English Common Reader: A Social History of the Mass Reading Public, 1800–1900* (1957), Columbus, Ohio, 1998.

Anderson, Patricia, *The Printed Image and the Transformation of Popular Culture, 1790–1860*, Oxford, 1991.

Bann, Stephen, *Parallel Lines: Printmakers, Painters, and Photographers in Nineteenth-Century France*, New Haven, 2001.

Bayard, Émile, *L'Illustration et les illustrateurs*, Paris, 1898.

Bayard, Émile, *La Caricature et les caricaturistes*, Paris, 1901.

Bellander, Claude (ed.), *Histoire générale de la presse française*, Paris, 1969–1976 (5 vols.).

Berg, Stephan, Ulrike Groos, Clemens Krümmel & Alexander Roob (eds.), *Diving Trips. Drawing as Reportage / Tauchfahrten. Zeichnung als Reportage*, Düsseldorf, 2005.

Bryant, Mark, *The World's Greatest War Cartoonists and Caricaturists (1792–1945)*, London, 2011.

Charle, Christophe, *Le Siècle de la presse (1830–1939)*, Paris, 2004.

Cilleßen, Wolfgang & Rolf Reichardt (eds.), *Revolution und Gegenrevolution in der europäischen Bildpublizistik 1789–1889*, Hildesheim, 2010.

Cornell University Library, *The Making of America* (ebooks.library.cornell.edu/m/moa/; accessed 9 February 2022)

Daniel, Ute (ed.), *Augenzeugen. Kriegsberichterstattung vom 18. zum 21. Jahrhundert*, Göttingen, 2006.

Daniel, Ute & Wolfram Siemann (eds.), *Propaganda, Meinungskampf, Verführung und politische Sinnstiftung, 1789–1989*, Frankfurt, 1994.

Daniels, Dieter, *Kunst als Sendung. Von der Telegrafie zum Internet*, Munich, 2002.

Davidson, Marshall B., *The Drawing of America: Eyewitnesses to History*, New York, 1983.

De la Motte, Dean & Jeannene M. Przyblski, *Making the News: Modernity & the Mass Press in Nineteenth-Century France*, Boston, 1999.

Dewitz, Bodo von & Robert Lebeck, *Kiosk. Eine Geschichte der Fotoreportage / A History of Photojournalism (1839–1973)*, Göttingen, 2001.

Dixmier, Michel, *Quand le crayon attaque: Images satiriques et opinion publique en France (1814–1918)*, Paris, 2007.

Doyle, Susan, Jaleen Grove & Whitney Sherman, *History of Illustration*, New York & London, 2018.

Dyos, Harold James & Michael Wolff (eds.), *The Victorian City: Images and Realities*, London, 1973 (2 vols.).

Faulstich, Werner, *Medienwandel im Industrie- und Massenzeitalter (1830–1900)*, Göttingen, 2004.

Fox, Celina, *Londoners*, London, 1987.

Fox, Celina, *Metropole London. Macht und Glanz einer Weltstadt 1800–1840*, Recklinghausen, 1992.

Fox, Paul & Gil Pasternak (eds.), *Visual Conflicts: On the Formation of Political Memory in the History of Art and Visual Cultures*, Newcastle, 2011.

Frankel, Oz, *States of Inquiry: Social Investigation and Print Culture in Nineteenth-Century Britain and the United States*, Baltimore, 2006.

Gaehtgens, Barbara (ed.), *Genremalerei. Zur Geschichte einer klassischen Bildgattung und ihrer Theorie*, Berlin, 2002.

Gaehtgens, Thomas W., *Historienmalerei. Zur Geschichte einer klassischen Bildgattung und ihrer Theorie*, Berlin, 1996.

Ganz, David & Felix Thürlemann (eds.), *Das Bild im Plural*, Berlin, 2010.

Gascoigne, Bamber, *How to Identify Prints: A Complete Guide to Manual and Mechanical Processes from Woodcut to Ink Jet*, New York, 2004.

Germer, Stefan & Michael F. Zimmermann (eds.), *Macht der Bilder – Bilder der Macht. Zeitgeschichte in Darstellungen des 19. Jahrhunderts*, Munich & Berlin, 1997.

Gluck, Mary, *Popular Bohemia: Modernism and Urban Culture in Nineteenth-Century Paris*, Cambridge, Massachusetts, 2005.

González Ramírez, Manuel, *La caricatura política*, Mexico City, 1955.

Gretton, Tom, "The Pragmatics of Page Design in Nineteenth-Century General-Interest Weekly Illustrated News Magazines in London and Paris", *Art History*, no. 4, vol. 33, September 2010, pp. 680–709.

Grivel, Charles, André Gunthert & Bernd Stiegler (eds.), *Die Eroberung der Bilder. Photographie in Buch und Presse. 1816–1914*, Munich, 2006.

Hamerton, Philip, *The Graphic Arts: A Treatise on the Varieties of Drawing, Painting, and Engraving*, London, 1882.

Hanebutt-Benz, Eva-Maria, Frieder Schmidt & Walter Wilkes (eds.), *Die Buchkultur im 19. Jahrhundert*, vol. 1: *Technische Grundlagen*, Hamburg, 2010.

Harrington, Peter, *British Artists and War: The Face of Battle in Paintings and Prints, 1700–1914*, London, 1993.

Harrison, Stanley, *Poor Men's Guardians: A Record of the Struggles for a Democratic Newspaper Press, 1763–1973*, London, 1974.

Haynes, Christine, *Lost Illusions: The Politics of Publishing in Nineteenth-Century France*, Cambridge, Massachusetts, 2010.

Hill, Jason E. & Vanessa R. Schwartz (eds.), *Getting the Picture: The Visual Culture of the News*, London & New York, 2015.

Hodgson, Pat, *The War Illustrators*, New York, 1977.

Hofmann, Werner, *Die Karikatur von Leonardo bis Picasso* (1956), Hamburg, 2007.

Hogarth, Paul, *The Artist as Reporter* (1967), London, 1986 (enlarged edition).

Hollweck, Ludwig, *Karikaturen. Von den Fliegenden Blättern bis zum Simplicissimus, 1844–1914*, Herrsching, 1973.

Hornung, Clarence P. & Fridolf Johnson, *200 Years of American Graphic Art: A Retrospective Survey of the Printing Arts and Advertising since the Colonial Period*, New York, 1976.

Houfe, Simon, *The Dictionary of 19th Century Book Illustrators* (1978), Woodbridge, Suffolk, 1996.

Jackson, Mason, *The Pictorial Press: Its Origin and Progress*, London, 1885.

Jobling, Paul & David Crowley, *Graphic Design: Reproduction and Representation since 1800*, Manchester & New York, 1996.

Kaenel, Philippe & Rolf Reichardt (eds.), *Interkulturelle Kommunikation in der europäischen Druckgraphik im 18. und 19. Jahrhundert / The European Print and Cultural Transfer in the 18th and 19th Centuries / Gravure et communication interculturelle en Europe aux 18e et 19e siècles*, Hildesheim, Zurich & New York, 2007.

Kasper, Josef, *Belichtung und Wahrheit. Bildreportage von der Gartenlaube bis zum Stern*, Frankfurt & New York, 1982.

Kessemeier, Siegfried (ed.), *Ereignis-Karikaturen. Geschichte in Spottbildern, 1600–1930*, Münster, 1983.

Knightley, Philip, *The First Casualty: The War Correspondent as Hero and Myth-Maker from the Crimea to Iraq*, Baltimore, 2004.

Kunzle, David, *The History of the Comic Strip: The Nineteenth Century*, Berkeley, 1990.

Kutschmann, Theodor, *Geschichte der deutschen Illustration vom ersten Auftreten des Formschnittes bis in die Gegenwart*, Goslar & Berlin, 1899.

Landow, George P. (ed.), *The Victorian Web: Literature, History & Culture in the Age of Victoria* (victorianweb.org; accessed 9 February 2022)

Langemeyer, Gerhard, Gerd Unverfehrt, Herwig Guratzsch & Christoph Stölzl (eds.), *Karikatur. Bild als Waffe. Mittel und Motive der Karikatur in fünf Jahrhunderten*, Munich, 1984.

Linley, Margaret (ed.), *Media, Technology, and Literature in the Nineteenth Century* (2011), London & New York, 2016.

Lucie-Smith, Edward, *The Art of Caricature*, London, 1981.

Maidment, Brian, *Reading Popular Prints, 1790–1870*, Manchester, 2001.

Martin, Michele, *Images at War: Illustrated Periodicals and Constructed Nations*, Toronto, 2006.

Mathews, Joseph James, *Reporting the Wars*, Minneapolis, 1957.

Maurice, Arthur Bartlett & Frederic Taber Cooper, *The History of the Nineteenth Century in Caricature* (1904), New York, 1971.

Mayor, A. Hyatt, *Prints and People: A Social History of Printed Pictures*, Princeton, 1980.

Melton Prior Institute for Reportage Drawing & Printing Culture (meltonprior-institut.org; accessed 9 February 2022).

Miller, Henry, *Politics Personified: Portraiture, Caricature and Visual Culture in Britain, c. 1830–80*, Manchester, 2015.

Möbius, Hanno, *Montage und Collage. Literatur, bildende Künste, Film, Fotografie, Musik, Theater bis 1933*, Munich, 2000.

Nochlin, Linda, *Misère: The Visual Representation of Misery in the 19th Century*, New York, 2018.

Paul, Gerhard (ed.), *Bilder des Krieges – Krieg der Bilder: Die Visualisierung des Krieges in der Moderne*, Paderborn, 2004.

Pennell, Joseph, *Pen Drawing and Pen Draughtsmen*, London & New York, 1889.

Pennell, Joseph, *Modern Illustration*, London, 1895.

Pilz, Georg (ed.), *Sozialistische deutsche Karikatur, 1848–1978. Von den Anfängen bis zur Gegenwart*, Berlin, 1978.

Ray, Gordon N., *The Illustrator and the Book in England from 1790 to 1914*, New York, 1976.

Reichardt, Rolf (ed.), *Französische Presse und Pressekarikaturen 1789–1992*, Mainz, 1992.

Roob, Alexander, *Our Artist*, Cologne, 2006.

Roob, Alexander, "Keine Nachrichten von Nirgendwo. Henry James unter den Illustratoren", in: Michael Glasmeier & Alexander Roob (eds.), *Henry James: Bild und Text*, Vienna, 2016, pp. 216–306.

Schmidt-Burkhardt, Astrit, *Stammbäume der Kunst. Zur Genealogie der Avantgarde*, Berlin, 2005.

Shikes, Ralph, *The Indignant Eye: The Artist as Social Critic in Prints and Drawings from the 15th Century to Picasso*, Boston, 1969.

Shikes, Ralph, *The Art of Satire: Painters as Caricaturists and Cartoonists from Delacroix to Picasso*, New York, 1984.

Smolderen, Thierry, *The Origins of Comics: From William Hogarth to Winsor McCay*, Jackson, Mississippi, 2000.

Tucker, Amy, *The Illustration of the Master: Henry James and the Magazine Revolution*, Stanford, California, 2010.

Unger, Arthur W., *Die Herstellung von Büchern, Illustrationen, Akzidenzen usw.*, Halle, 1910.

Wilkinson-Latham, R.J., *From Our Special Correspondent: Victorian War Correspondents and Their Campaigns*, London, 1979.

Wrigley, Richard (ed.), *The Flâneur Abroad: Historical and International Perspectives*, Newcastle, 2014.

Early Illustrated News
Frühe Bildnachrichten
Premières informations en images

Alpers, Svetlana, *The Art of Describing: Dutch Art in the Seventeenth Century*, Chicago, 1983.

Andrews, Malcolm, *The Search for the Picturesque: Landscape Aesthetics and Tourism in Britain, 1760–1800*, Aldershot, 1989.

Antal, Frederick, *Hogarth and His Place in European Art*, New York, 1962.

Barrell, John, *The Spirit of Despotism: Invasions of Privacy in the 1790s*, Oxford, 2006.

Bauer, Jens-Heiner (ed.), *Daniel Nikolaus Chodowiecki. Das druckgraphische Werk*, Hanover, 1982.

Beall, Karen F., *Kaufrufe und Straßenhändler. Eine Bibliographie / Cries and Itinerant Trades. / A Bibliography*, Hamburg, 1975.

Benedict, Philip, *Graphic History: The Wars, Massacres and Troubles of Tortorel and Perrissin*, Geneva, 2007.

Bindman, David, *Hogarth and His Times*, London, 1997.

Boime, Albert, *A Social History of Modern Art*, vol. 1: *Art in an Age of Revolution, 1750–1800*, Chicago, 1987.

Boime, Albert, *A Social History of Modern Art*, vol. 2: *Art in an Age of Bonapartism, 1800–1815*, Chicago, 1990.

Bonn, Robert L., *Painting Life: The Art of Pieter Bruegel, the Elder*, New York, 2006.

Bouquillard, Jocelyn & Christophe Marquet, *Hokusai, First Manga Master*, New York, 2007.

Brothers, Ann (ed.), *Worlds in Miniature: The Etchings of Jacques Callot and Wenceslaus Hollar*, Sydney, 1998.

Bruntjen, Sven Hermann Arnold, *John Boydell: A Study of Art Patronage and Publishing in Georgian London*, New York, 1985.

Bugler, Caroline (ed.), *The Image of London: Views by Travellers and Emigrés, 1550–1920*, London, 1987.

Busch, Werner, *Nachahmung als bürgerliches Kunstprinzip. Ikonographische Zitate bei Hogarth und in seiner Nachfolge*, Hildesheim & New York, 1977.

Buschhoff, Anne & Alexander Roob (eds.), *William Hogarth. Die Kunst der Zeitgenossenschaft*, Bremen, 2014.

Bußmann, Klaus & Heinz Schilling (eds.), *1648. Krieg und Frieden in Europa*, Münster & Osnabrück, 1999.

Büttner, Nils, *Die Erfindung der Landschaft. Kosmographie und Landschaftskunst im Zeitalter Bruegels*, Göttingen, 2000.

Champfleury, Jules, *Histoire de l'imagerie populaire*, Paris, 1869.

Champfleury, Jules, *Histoire de la Caricature sous la République, l'Empire et la Restauration*, Paris, 1874.
Cilleßen, Wolfgang (ed.), *Krieg der Bilder. Druckgraphik als Medium politischer Auseinandersetzung im Europa des Absolutismus*, Berlin, 1997.
Clayton, Tim & Sheila O'Connell, *Bonaparte and the British: Prints and Propaganda in the Age of Napoleon*, London, 2015.
Collenberg-Plotnikov, Bernadette, *Klassizismus und Karikatur. Eine Konstellation der Kunst am Beginn der Moderne*, Berlin, 2008.
Collison, Robert Lewis, *The Story of Street Literature: Forerunner of the Popular Press*, Oxford, 1973.
Copley, Stephen & Peter Garside, *The Politics of the Picturesque: Literature, Landscape and Aesthetics since 1770*, Cambridge, 1994.
Darnton, Robert, *The Business of Enlightenment: A Publishing History of the Encyclopédie, 1775–1800*, Cambridge, Massachusetts, 1979.
Donald, Diana, *The Age of Caricature: Satirical Prints in the Reign of George III*, London & New Haven, 1996.
Eaves, Morris, *The Counter-Arts Conspiracy: Art and Industry in the Age of Blake*, Ithaca & London, 1992.
Eisenstein, Elizabeth L., *The Printing Press as an Agent of Change*, Cambridge, Massachusetts, 1979.
Faulstich, Werner, *Die bürgerliche Mediengesellschaft (1700–1830)*, Göttingen, 2002.
Femmel, Gerhard, *Die Franzosen. Goethes Grafiksammlung. Katalog und Zeugnisse*, Leipzig, 1980.
Fischer, Erik, *Melchior Lorck, Catalogue Raisonné*, Copenhagen, 2009 (4 vols.).
Fischer, Ernst & Wilhelm Haefs (eds.), *Von Almanach bis Zeitung. Ein Handbuch der Medien in Deutschland 1700–1800*, Munich, 1999.
Ford, John, *Ackermann (1783–1983): The Business of Art*, London, 1983.
Fort, Bernadette & Angela Rosenthal (eds.), *The Other Hogarth: Aesthetics of Difference*, Princeton, 2001.
Füssel, Stephan (ed.), *Georg Braun und Franz Hogenberg. Civitates Orbis Terrarum – Städte der Welt*, Cologne, 2011.
Godfrey, Richard T., *Wenceslaus Hollar: A Bohemian Artist in England*, New Haven & London, 1994.
Godfrey, Richard T. & Mark Hallett (eds.), *James Gillray: The Art of Caricature*, London, 2001.
Guratzsch, Herwig (ed.), *James Gillray. Meisterwerke der Karikatur*, Stuttgart, 1986.
Hale, Meredith McNeill, *The Birth of Modern Political Satire: Romeyn de Hooghe and the Glorious Revolution*, Oxford, 2020.
Hallett, Mark, "The Medley Print in Early Eighteenth-Century London", *Art History*, no. 2, vol. 20, June 1997, pp. 214–237.
Hallett, Mark, *The Spectacle of Difference: Graphic Satire in the Age of Hogarth*, New Haven, 1999.
Hallett, Mark & Christine Riding (eds.), *Hogarth*, London, 2006.
Hampe, Theodor (ed.), *Das Trachtenbuch des Weiditz von seinen Reisen nach Spanien (1529) und den Niederlanden (1531/32)* (1927); reprint: Christoph Weiditz, *Authentic Everyday Dress of the Renaissance: All 154 Plates from the "Trachtenbuch"*, New York, 1994.
Harms, Wolfgang (ed.), *Illustrierte Flugblätter aus den Jahrhunderten der Reformation und der Glaubenskämpfe*, Coburg, 1983.
Haywood, Iain, *Romanticism and Caricature*, Cambridge, 2013.
Hellwig, Fritz (ed.), *Franz Hogenberg – Abraham Hogenberg: Geschichtsblätter*, Nördlingen, 1983.
Herding, Klaus & Rolf Reichardt (eds.), *Die Bildpublizistik der französischen Revolution*, Frankfurt, 1989.
Hitchcock, Tim, *Down and Out in Eighteenth-Century London*, Hambledon & London, 2004.
Hofmann, Werner (ed.), *Goya. Das Zeitalter der Revolutionen, 1789–1830*, Munich, 1980.
Hofmann, Werner (ed.), *Luther und die Folgen für die Kunst*, Munich & Hamburg, 1983.
Jaime, Ernest (ed.), *Musée de la caricature, ou recueil des caricatures les plus remarquables publiées en France depuis le XIVe siècle jusqu'à nos jours*, Paris, 1838 (2 vols.).
Kohle, Hubertus & Rolf Reichardt (eds.), *Visualizing the Revolution: Politics and Pictorial Arts in Late Eighteenth-Century France*, Chicago, 2008.
Kremers, Anorthe & Elisabeth Reich (eds.), *Loyal Subversion? Caricatures from the Personal Union between England and Hanover (1714–1837)*, Göttingen, 2014.
Kunzle, David, *The Early Comic Strip: Narrative Strips and Picture Stories in the European Broadsheet from c. 1450 to 1825*, Berkeley, 1973.
Landwehr, John, *Romeyn de Hooghe, the Etcher: Contemporary Portrayal of Europe, 1662–1707*, Leyden & New York, 1973.
Langemeyer, Gerhard, *"Aesopus in Europa": Bemerkungen zur politisch-satirischen Graphik des Romeyn de Hooghe (1645–1706)*, Münster, 1974.
Langemeyer, Gerhard (ed.), *Bilderwelten. Französische Illustrationen des 18. und 19. Jahrhunderts aus der Sammlung Von Kritter*, Dortmund, 1985.
Lieure, Jules (ed.), *Jacques Callot: Catalogue raisonné de l'œuvre gravé / The Complete Etchings & Engravings*, San Francisco, 1988/89 (2 vols.).
Mair, Victor H., *Painting and Performance: Chinese Picture Recitation and Its Indian Genesis*, Honolulu, 1988.
Mee, Jon, *Print, Publicity, and Popular Radicalism in the 1790s*, Cambridge, 2016.
Nierop, H.V., E. Grabowsky, A. Janssen, H. Leeflang & G. Verhoeven (eds.), *Romeyn de Hooghe. De verbeelding van de late Gouden Eeuw*, Amsterdam, 2008.
Oettingen, Wolfgang von, *Daniel Chodowiecki. Ein Berliner Künstlerleben im achtzehnten Jahrhundert*, Berlin, 1895.
Paulson, Ronald, *Breaking and Re-Making: Aesthetic Practice in England, 1700–1820*, New Brunswick, New Jersey, 1989.
Paulson, Ronald, *Hogarth*, New Brunswick, New Jersey & London, 1991–93 (3 vols.).
Pennington, Richard, *A Descriptive Catalogue of the Etched Work of Wenceslaus Hollar, 1607–1677*, Cambridge, 1982.
Rauser, Amelia, *Caricature Unmasked: Irony, Authenticity, and Individualism in Eighteenth-Century English Prints*, Newark, 2008.
Rees, Joachim, *Die Kultur des Amateurs. Studien zu Leben und Werk von Anne Claude Philippe de Thubières, Comte de Caylus 1692–1765*, Weimar, 2006.
Rees, Joachim, *Die verzeichnete Fremde. Formen und Funktionen des Zeichnens im Kontext europäischer Forschungsreisen 1770–1830*, Paderborn, 2015.
Rice, Anthony, *Der verzauberte Blick. Das Naturbild berühmter Expeditionen aus drei Jahrhunderten*, Munich, 1999.
Riggs, Timothy A., *Hieronymus Cock, Printmaker and Publisher*, New York, 1977.
Roob, Alexander, *Auch ich in Verdun. Zu den Ansichten und Zeichnungen des Kriegsreisenden Goethe*, Cologne, 2008.
Roob, Alexander, "Exkursion, Trivia und Montage. Zur englischen Früh-Flanerie", in: Volker Adolphs & Stephan Berg (eds.), *Der Flaneur. Vom Impressionismus bis zur Gegenwart*, Cologne, 2018, pp. 229–255.
Satterfield, Andrea McKenzie, *The Assimilation of the Marvelous Other: Reading Christoph Weiditz's Trachtenbuch (1529) as an Ethnographic Document*, graduate thesis, University of South Florida, 2007.
Savoy, Bénédicte (ed.), *Napoleon und Europa. Traum und Trauma*, Munich, 2010.
Scheffler, Ernst, Sabine Scheffler & Gerd Unverfehrt, *So zerstieben geträumte Weltreiche. Napoleon I. in der deutschen Karikatur*, Stuttgart, 1995.
Schilling, Michael, *Bildpublizistik der frühen Neuzeit. Aufgaben und Leistungen des illustrierten Flugblatts in Deutschland bis um 1700*, Tübingen, 1990.
Schnurr, Eva-Maria, *Religionskonflikt und Öffentlichkeit. Eine Mediengeschichte des Kölner Kriegs*, Cologne, 2009.
Schroeder, Thomas, *Jacques Callot. Das gesamte Werk*, Munich, 1971 (2 vols.).
Schulze Altcappenberg, Heinrich (ed.), *Disegno. Der Zeichner im Bild der frühen Neuzeit*, Berlin & Florence, 2008.
Shesgreen, Sean, *Images of the Outcast: The Urban Poor in the Cries of London*, London, 2002.
Smiles, Sam, *Eye Witness: Artists and Visual Documentation in Britain, 1770–1830*, Aldershot, 2000.
Sommer, Monika (ed.), *Hieronymus Löschenkohl. Sensationen aus dem alten Wien*, Vienna, 2009.
Song, Yingxing, E-Tu Zen Sun & Shiou-Chuan Sun (eds.), *T'ien-Kung K'ai-Wu: Chinese Technology in the Seventeenth Century*, University Park, Pennsylvania, 1966.
Spaans, Joke, *Graphic Satire and Religious Change: The Dutch Republic, 1676–1707*, Amsterdam, 2011.
Traeger, Jörg, *Goya. Die Kunst der Freiheit*, Munich, 2000.
Van Grieken, Joris (ed.), *Hieronymus Cock: The Renaissance in Print*, Brussels, 2013.
Wagner, Peter, *Reading Iconotexts: From Swift to the French Revolution*, Chicago, 1997.
Weißbrich, Thomas, *Höchstädt 1704. Eine Schlacht als Medienereignis. Kriegsberichterstattung und Gelegenheitsdichtung im Spanischen Erbfolgekrieg*, Amsterdam, 2015.
Wolf, Reva, *Goya and the Satirical Print in England and on the Continent, 1730 to 1850*, Boston, 1991.

The Industrial Turn
Die industrielle Wende
Le tournant industriel

Bain, Ian (ed.), *Thomas Bewick: My Life* ("A Memoir of Thomas Bewick Written by Himself", 1862), London, 1981.
Bain, Ian (ed.), *The Watercolours and Drawings of Thomas Bewick and His Workshop Apprentices*, London, 1981 (2 vols.).
Becker, Ingeborg, "Friedrich über Alles. Menzel und die Buchillustration", in: Lucius Grisebach (ed.), *Adolph Menzel. Zeichnungen, Druckgraphik und illustrierte Bücher*, Berlin, 1984, pp. 44–51.
Blachon, Remi, *La Gravure sur bois au XIXe siècle. L'âge du bois debout*, Paris, 2001.
Dohmen, Walter, *Die Lithographie. Geschichte, Kunst, Technik*, Cologne, 1982.
Gusman, Pierre, *La Gravure sur bois en France au XIXe siècle*, Paris, 1929.
Hanebutt-Benz, Eva-Maria, *Studien zum deutschen Holzstich im 19. Jahrhundert*, Frankfurt, 1984.
Hanebutt-Benz, Eva-Maria, Frieder Schmidt & Walter Wilkes (eds.), *Die Buchkultur im 19. Jahrhundert*, vol. 1: *Technische Grundlagen*, Hamburg, 2010.
Jackson, John, W.A. Chatto & G. Bohn, *A Treatise on Wood Engraving (with a New Chapter on the Artists of the Present Day)*, London, 1861.
Kainen, Jacob, *Why Bewick Succeeded: A Note in the History of Wood Engraving*, Washington, 1959.
Kristeller, Paul, *Holzschnitt und Kupferstich in vier Jahrhunderten*, Berlin, 1905.
Linton, William James, *The Masters of Wood Engraving*, New Haven & London, 1889.
Masjutin, Wassili N., *Thomas Bewick. Sein Leben und sein Werk. Eine Untersuchung über die technischen Grundlagen des Holzschnittes nebst einer kritischen Würdigung des Schaffens Th. Bewicks*, Berlin, 1923.
Ruskin, John, *Ariadne Florentina: Six Lectures on Wood and Metal Engraving*, Orpington, 1872.
Tattersfield, Nigel (ed.), *The Complete Illustrative Work of Thomas Bewick*, London; New Castle, Delaware, 2011.
Uglow, Jenny, *Nature's Engraver: A Life of Thomas Bewick*, London, 2006.
Watkins, Jonathan (ed.), *Thomas Bewick: Tale-Pieces*, Birmingham, 2009.
Welz, Reinhard (ed.), *Geschichte der Lithographie: Spiegelwelt – Gespiegelte Welt*, Mannheim, 2007.
William James Linton Archive, *A Guideline through the Interwoven Histories of Radical Culture* (meltonpriorinstitut.org/pages/linton.php5; accessed 9 February 2022).

Realism and Caricature
Realismus und Karikatur
Réalisme et la caricature

Ashraf, Phyllis Mary, *The Life and Times of Thomas Spence*, Newcastle, 1983.
Athanassoglou-Kallmyer, Nina Maria, *Eugène Delacroix: Prints, Politics and Satire, 1814–1822*, New Haven, 1991.
Balzer, Wolfgang, *Der junge Daumier und seine Kampfgefährten. Politische Karikatur in Frankreich 1830–1835*, Dresden, 1956.
Beaumont, Matthew (ed.), *Adventures in Realism*, New York, 2008.
Belchem, John, *Popular Radicalism in Nineteenth-Century Britain*, London, 1996.
Bezucha, Robert J. (ed.), *The Art of the July Monarchy: France, 1830 to 1848*, Columbia, Missouri & London, 1990.
Boime, Albert, *Art in an Age of Counterrevolution, 1815–1848*, Chicago, 2004.
Bosch-Abele, Susanne, *La Caricature 1830–1835: Opposition mit dem Zeichenstift*, Gelsenkirchen, 2000.
Brückmann, Remigius (ed.), *Politische Karikaturen des Vormärz (1815–1848)*, Karlsruhe, 1984.
Champfleury, Jules, *Histoire de la Caricature moderne*, Paris, 1865.
Contensou, Martine, *Balzac et Philipon associés, grands fabricants de caricatures en tous genres*, Paris, 2001.
Davis, Michael T. (ed.), *Radicalism and Revolution in Britain, 1775–1848: Essays in Honour of Malcolm I. Thomis*, Houndmills, 2000.
Day-Hickman, Barbara Ann, *Napoleonic Art: Nationalism and the Spirit of Rebellion in France (1815–1848)*, Newark, 1999.
Dayot, Armand, *Charlet et son œuvre*, Paris, 1892.

De Goncourt, Edmond & Jules De Goncourt, *Gavarni, L'Homme et l'œuvre*, Paris, 1873.

Farwell, Beatrice, *The Cult of Images: Baudelaire and the 19th-Century Media Explosion*, Santa Barbara, 1977.

Farwell, Beatrice, *The Charged Image: French Lithographic Caricature, 1816–1848*, Santa Barbara, 1989.

Forbes, Amy Wiese, *The Satiric Decade: Satire and the Rise of Republicanism in France, 1830–1840*, Lanham, Maryland, 2010.

Fox, Celina, *Graphic Journalism in England during the 1830s and 1840s*, New York & London, 1988.

Giacomelli, Hector, *Raffet. Son œuvre lithographique et ses eaux-fortes*, Paris, 1862.

Goldstein, Robert Justin, *Censorship of Political Caricature in Nineteenth-Century France*, Kent, Ohio, 1989.

Guilbaut, Serge (ed.), *Théodore Géricault: The Alien Body / Tradition in Chaos*, Vancouver, 1997.

Hackwood, Frederick W., *William Hone: His Life and Times*, London, 1912.

Hannoosh, Michele, *Baudelaire and Caricature: From the Comic to an Art of Modernity*, University Park, Pennsylvania, 1992.

Harrison, Stanley, *Poor Men's Guardians: A Record of the Struggles for a Democratic Newspaper Press, 1763–1973*, London, 1974.

Haywood, Iain, *The Revolution in Popular Literature: Print, Politics and the People, 1790–1860*, Cambridge, 2004.

Hiekisch-Picard, Sepp, "Künstler und Illustratoren um Charles Philipon und das Verlagshaus Aubert", in: Gerhard Langemeyer (ed.), *Bilderwelten. Französische Illustrationen des 18. und 19. Jahrhunderts. Aus der Sammlung von Kritter*, Dortmund, 1985, pp. 140–144.

Hone, William, *The Three Trials of William Hone, for Publishing Three Parodies*, London, 1876.

Jerrold, William Blanchard, *The Life of George Cruikshank: In Two Epochs*, London & New York, 1882.

Kerr, David S., *Caricature and French Political Culture, 1830–1848: Charles Philipon and the Illustrated Press*, Oxford, 2000.

Kleinert, Annemarie, *Die frühen Modejournale in Frankreich. Studien zur Literatur der Mode von den Anfängen bis 1848*, Berlin, 1980.

Knight, Charles, *Knowledge Is Power: A View of the Productive Forces of Modern Society, and the Results of Labour, Capital and Skill*, London, 1859.

Knight, Charles, *Passages of a Working Life during Half a Century*, London, 1863–1865 (3 vols.).

Koch, Ursula E. & P.-P. Sagave, *Le Charivari: Die Geschichte einer Pariser Tageszeitung im Kampf um die Republik*, Cologne, 1983.

Krümmel, Clemens, "The Raft of the Historical Image", in: Dierk Schmidt, *SIEV-X: On a Case of Intensified Refugee Politics; An Image Cycle in Three Parts, Conversations and Texts*, Berlin, 2005, pp. 82–89.

Ladoue, Pierre, *Un peintre de l'épopée française, Raffet*, Paris, 1946.

Lauster, Martina, *Sketches of the Nineteenth Century: European Journalism and Its Physiologies, 1830–50*, London, 2007.

Ledger, Sally, *Dickens and the Popular Radical Imagination*, New York, 2007.

Lhomme, Francois, *Nicolas-Toussaint Charlet. 1792–1845*, Paris, 1892.

Maidment, Brian, *Comedy, Caricature and the Social Order, 1820–50*, Manchester, 2013.

McCalman, Iain, *Radical Underworld: Prophets, Revolutionaries, and Pornographers in London, 1795–1840*, New York, 1988.

Neuschäfer, Hans-Jörg (ed.), *Der französische Feuilletonroman, die Entstehung der Serienliteratur im Medium der Tageszeitung*, Darmstadt, 1986.

Noack, Dieter & Lilian Noack (eds.), *The Daumier Register* (daumier-register.org; accessed 9 February 2022).

O'Brien, David, *After the Revolution: Antoine-Jean Gros, Painting and Propaganda*, University Park, Pennsylvania, 2006.

Patten, Robert L., *George Cruikshank's Life, Times and Art*, vol. 1: *1792–1835*, New Brunswick, New Jersey, 1992.

Patten, Robert L. (ed.), *George Cruikshank: A Revaluation*, Princeton, 1992.

Quideau, Florence & Édouard Papet, *Honoré Daumier & La Maison Aubert: Political and Social Satire in Paris, 1830–1860*, New Brunswick, New Jersey, 2008.

Renonciat, Annie, *La Vie et l'œuvre de J. J. Grandville*, Paris, 2000.

Robichon, Francois & Jean Tulard, *Raffet: 1804–1860*, Paris, 1999.

Roob, Alexander, "Wider Daumier. Eine Revision der frühen französischen Karikaturbewegung und Sozialgrafik", in: Andreas Strobl (ed.), *Monsieur Daumier. Ihre Serie ist reizvoll! Die Stiftung Kames*, Munich & Berlin, 2012, pp. 26–39.

Roob, Alexander, "Die frühe Wertzeichenagitation am Beispiel der Mulready-Ganzsache", in: Michael Glasmeier (ed.), *Sichtagitation Briefmarke. KP Brehmer – Aby Warburg*, Hamburg, 2020.

Rousseau, Madeleine & Marie-Martine Dubreuil, *La Vie et l'œuvre de Philippe-Auguste Jeanron*, Paris, 2000.

Schrenk, Klaus (ed.), *J. J. Grandville. Karikatur und Zeichnung. Ein Visionär der französischen Romantik*, Ostfildern, 2000.

Shesgreen, Sean, *Images of the Outcast: The Urban Poor in the Cries of London*, London, 2002.

Siegfried, Susan L., *The Art of Louis-Leopold Boilly: Modern Life in Napoleonic France*, New Haven & London, 1995.

Smith, Francis Barrymore, *Radical Artisan: William James Linton, 1812–97*, Manchester, 1973.

Tiedemann, Rolf (ed.), *Walter Benjamin. Das Passagen-Werk*, Frankfurt, 1983 (2 vols.).

Unverfehrt, Gerd, *La Caricature. Bildsatire in Frankreich 1830–1835 aus der Sammlung von Kritter*, Göttingen, 1980.

Vogler, Richard A. (ed.), *Graphic Works of George Cruikshank*, London, 1980.

Walker, Susannah Lucy, *Order and Pleasure in the Lithographic Work of Nicolas-Toussaint Charlet (1792–1845)*, doctoral thesis, University College London, 2012.

Wechsler, Judith, *A Human Comedy: Physiognomy and Caricature in 19th-Century Paris*, Chicago, 1982.

Weisberg, Gabriel P., *The Realist Tradition: French Painting and Drawing, 1830–1900*, Cleveland, 1980.

Weisberg, Gabriel P., "Early Realism", in: Robert J. Bezucha (ed.), *The Art of the July Monarchy: France, 1830 to 1848*, Columbia, Missouri & London, 1990, pp. 101–115.

Weisberg, Gabriel P., "The Coded Image: Agitation in Aspects of Political and Social Caricature" in: Robert J. Bezucha (ed.), *The Art of the July Monarchy: France, 1830 to 1848*, Columbia, Missouri & London, 1990, pp. 148–191.

Wilson, Ben, *The Laughter of Triumph: William Hone and the Fight for a Free Press*, London, 2005.

Wood, Marcus, *Radical Satire and Print Culture, 1790–1822*, Oxford, 1994.

Worrall, David, *Radical Culture: Discourse, Resistance and Surveillance, 1790–1820*, Detroit, 1992.

Yousif, Keri, *Balzac, Grandville, and the Rise of Book Illustration*, Farnham, 2012.

Zbinden, Rolf & Juerg Albrecht, *Honoré Daumier. Rue Transnonain, le 15 avril 1834. Ereignis-Zeugnis-Exempel*, Hamburg, 1989.

The Rise of Illustrated Journalism
Der Aufstieg des Bildjournalismus
L'Essor des nouvelles illustrées

Acevedo, Esther, *Constantino Escalante. Una mirada irónica*, Mexico City, 1996.

Allen, Joan & Owen R. Ashton, *Papers for the People: A Study of the Chartist Press*, London, 2005.

Archer, Mildred (ed.), *Visions of India: The Sketchbooks of William Simpson, 1859–62*, London, 1986.

Bätschmann, Oskar, *Edouard Manet. Der Tod des Maximilian*, Frankfurt, 1993.

Baudelaire, Charles & Constantin Guys, *Le peintre de la Vie moderne*, Paris (1863) 1923.

German edition *see* Kemp, Friedhelm & Claude Pichois

Baudelaire, Charles & Jonathan Mayne (ed.), *The Painter of Modern Life and Other Essays*, London, 1964.

Beam, Philip C., *Winslow Homer's Magazine Engravings*, New York, 1979.

Begley, Adam, *The Great Nadar: The Man behind the Camera*, New York, 2017.

Boime, Albert, *Art in an Age of Civil Struggle, 1848–1871: A Social History of Modern Art*, vol. 4, Chicago, 2007.

Bory, Jean-François (ed.), *Nadar*, vol. 2: *Dessins et écrits*, Paris, 1979.

Briggs, Jo, *Novelty Fair: British Visual Culture between Chartism and the Great Exhibition*, Manchester, 2016.

Brückmann, Remigius (ed.), *Politische Karikaturen des Vormärz. (1815–1848)*, Karlsruhe, 1984.

Buchanan-Brown, John, *The Illustrations of William Makepeace Thackeray*, London, 1979.

Buchinger-Früh, Marie Luise, *Karikatur als Kunstkritik: Kunst und Künstler in der Salonkarikatur des "Charivari" zwischen 1850 und 1870*, Bern, 1989.

Bucklow, Spike & Sally Woodcock (eds.), *Sir John Gilbert: Art and Imagination in the Victorian Age*, Farnham, 2011.

Busch, Werner, *Adolph Menzel. Auf der Suche nach der Wirklichkeit*, Munich, 2015.

Carlebach, Michael L., *The Origins of Photojournalism in America*, Washington & London, 1992.

Carlisle, Janice, *Picturing Reform in Victorian Britain*, Cambridge, 2012.

Chabanne, Thierry (ed.), *Les Salons caricaturaux*, Paris, 1990.

Clark, Timothy J., *The Absolute Bourgeois. Artists and Politics in France 1848–1851*, London 1973.

Clark, Timothy J., *Image of the People: Gustave Courbet and the 1848 Revolution* (1973), London, 1982.

Dalziel, George & Edward Dalziel, *The Brothers Dalziel: A Record of Work, 1840–1890*, London, 1901.

De Mare, Eric, *The Victorian Woodblock Illustrators*, London, 1980.

Doosry, Yasmin & Rainer Schoch (eds.), *1848: Das Europa der Bilder*, vol. 1: *Der Völker Frühling*; vol. 2: *Michels März*, Nuremberg, 1998.

Du Maurier, George, "The Illustration of Books from the Serious Artist's Point of View.", part I, *Magazine of Art*, London, August 1890, pp. 349–353.

Duflo, Pierre, *Constantin Guys, Fou de dessin, Grand reporter, 1802–1892*, Paris, 1988.

Eichler, Ulrike, *Münchener Bilderbogen*, Munich, 1974.

Elberfield, John, *Manet and the Execution of Maximilian*, New York, 2007.

Eyre-Todd, George (ed.), *The Autobiography of William Simpson* (1903), London, 2007.

Fischer, Hubertus (ed.), *Jahrbuch Forum Vormärz Forschung: Europäische Karikaturen im Vor- und Nachmärz*, Bielefeld, 2006.

Fletcher, Ian & Natalia Ishchenko (eds.), *War in the Crimea: An Illustrated History*, Stroud, 2014.

Fox, Celina, *Graphic Journalism in England during the 1830s and 1840s*, New York & London, 1988.

Gagel, Hanna & Arbeitsgruppe Kunst der bürgerlichen Revolution (eds.), *Kunst der bürgerlichen Revolution von 1830 bis 1848/49*, Berlin, 1972.

Gambee Jr., Budd Leslie, *Frank Leslie and His Illustrated Newspaper, 1855–1860*, Ann Arbor, 1964.

Gassen, Richard W. (ed.), *Liberalnichtoftsky und der deutsche Michel: Die Karikatur in der Revolution von 1848*, Heidelberg, 1988.

Goldman, Paul, *Beyond Decoration: The Illustrations of John Everett Millais*, London, 2005.

Guernsey, Alfred H. & Henry Mills Alden, *Harper's Pictorial History of the Civil War*, New York, 1894 (2 vols.).

Guratzsch, Herwig & Gerd Unverfehrt (eds.), *Gustave Doré. Illustrator. Maler. Bildhauer.* vol. 1: *Beiträge zu seinem Werk*, Dortmund, 1982.

Hartwig, Helmut & Karl Riha (eds.), *Politische Ästhetik und Öffentlichkeit. 1848 im Spaltungsprozess des historischen Bewusstseins*, Wismar, 1974.

Haywood, Iain, *The Revolution in Popular Literature: Print, Politics and the People, 1790–1860*, Cambridge, 2004.

Herbert, Christopher, *Culture and Anomie: Ethnographic Imagination in the Nineteenth Century*, Chicago, 1991.

Hibbert, Christopher, *The Illustrated London News' Social History of Victorian Britain*, London, 1975.

Hoffmann, Horst, *Theodor Kaufmann (1814–1896). Freiheitskämpfer und Historienmaler aus Uelzen*, Uelzen, 2001.

Houfe, Simon, *John Leech and the Victorian Scene*, London, 1984.

Humpherys, Anne, *Travels into the Poor Man's Country: The Work of Henry Mayhew*, Athens, Georgia, 1977.

Jacobson, Doranne, *The Civil War in Art: A Visual Odyssey*, New York, 1996.

Jerrold, Douglas, *The Life of George Cruikshank: In Two Epochs*, London & New York, 1882.

Kaenel, Philippe, *Le Métier d'illustrateur (1830–1880): Rodolphe Töpffer, J. J. Grandville, Gustave Doré*, Paris, 1996.

Katz, Harry L. & Vincent Virga, *Civil War Sketch Book: Drawings from the Battlefront*, New York, 2012.

Keller, Ulrich, *The Ultimate Spectacle: A Visual History of the Crimean War*, London, 2001.

Kelly, Richard, *The Art of George du Maurier*, London, 1996.

Kemp, Friedhelm & Claude Pichois (eds.), *Charles Baudelaire, Sämtliche Werke*, vol. 1, Munich, 1977.

Koch, Ursula E., *Der Teufel in Berlin. Von der Märzrevolution bis zu Bismarcks Entlassung. Illustrierte politische Witzblätter einer Metropole. 1848–1890*, Cologne, 1991.

Kunzle, David, "Cham and Daumier: Two Careers, Two Reputations, Two Audiences" (1980), meltonpriorinstitut. org, feature, September 2010 (accessed 23 May 2018).

Kunzle, David, *Father of the Comic Strip: Rodolphe Töpffer*, Jackson, Mississippi, 2007.

Kushner, Marylin S., *Winslow Homer: Illustrating America*, New York, 2000.

Lagarde-Fouquet, Annie, *Édouard Charton et le combat contre l'ignorance*, Rennes, 2006.

Lindner, Rolf, *Walks on the Wild Side: Eine Geschichte der Stadtforschung*, Frankfurt & New York, 2004.

Lindner, Rolf, "Henry Mayhew, Stadt-ethnograph", *Berliner Blätter. Ethnographische und ethnologische Beiträge*, special issue 35/2005: *Die Zivilisierung der urbanen Nomaden*, pp. 8–24.

Mainardi, Patricia, *Art and Politics of the Second Empire: The Universal Expositions of 1855 and 1867*, New Haven, 1987.

Marchandiau, Jean-Noël, *L'Illustration: vie et mort d'un journal, 1843–1944*, Toulouse, 1987.

Morris, Frankie, *Artist of Wonderland: The Life, Political Cartoons, and Illustrations of Tenniel*, Charlottesville, Virginia, 2005.

Paine, Albert Bigelow, *Thomas Nast: His Period and His Pictures*, New York, 1904.

Pankhurst, Richard (ed.), *Diary of a Journey to Abyssinia, 1868: The Diary and Observation of William Simpson*, Newburyport, Massachusetts, 2002.

Patten, Robert L., *George Cruikshank's Life, Times and Art*, vol. 2: *1835–1878*, New Brunswick, New Jersey, 1992.

Pellissier, Pierre, *Émile de Girardin, Prince de la Presse*, Denoël, 1985.

Prager, Arthur, *The Mahogany Tree: An Informal History of Punch*, New York, 1979.

Probst, Hansjörg & Karin v. Welck (eds.), *Mit Zorn und Eifer. Karikaturen aus der Revolution 1848/49*, Mannheim, 1998.

Ray, Frederic E., *Our Special Artist: Alfred R. Waud's Civil War*, New York, 1974.

Ribeyre, Félix, *Cham – sa vie et son œuvre*, Paris, 1884.

Riha, Karl & Gerhard Rudolph (eds.), *Düsseldorfer Monatshefte (1847–1849)*, Düsseldorf, 1979.

Roob, Alexander, "Thomas Nast & Theodor Kaufmann: Higher Forms of Hieroglyph", meltonpriorinstitut.org, feature, November 2012 (accessed 23 May 2018).

Roob, Alexander, "Absturz an den Klippen Albions, William James Lintons 'English Republic'", *Zeitschrift für Ideengeschichte*, XIII/2, Munich, 2019, pp. 87–106.

Schmidt, Katharina (ed.), *Nadar! Karikaturist – Fotograf – Aeronaut*, Düsseldorf, 1976.

Simpson, Roger, *Sir John Tenniel: Aspects of His Work*, Madison, New Jersey, 1994.

Simpson, William, *Meeting the Sun: A Journey all round the World*, London, 1874.

Sinnema, Peter, *Dynamics of the Pictured Page: Representing the Nation in the Illustrated London News*, Aldershot, 1998.

Slater, Michael, *Douglas Jerrold: A Life*, London, 2002.

Smith, Karen W., *Constantin Guys: Crimean War Drawings, 1854–1856*, Cleveland, 1978.

Spielmann, Marion Harry, *The History of "Punch"*, London, Paris & Melbourne, 1895.

Stoll, André (ed.), *Die Rückkehr der Barbaren. Europäer und "Wilde" in der Karikatur Honoré Daumiers*, Hamburg, 1985.

Taithe, Bertrand, *The Essential Mayhew: Representing and Communicating the Poor*, London, 1996.

Tatham, David, *Winslow Homer and the Pictorial Press*, Syracuse, New York, 2003.

Thackeray, William Makepeace, *The Paris Sketch Book (1840) and Art Criticisms*, London, 1922.

Van Doren Stern, Philip, *They Were There: The Civil War in Action as Seen by Its Combat Artists*, New York, 1959.

Vizetelly, Henry, *Glances Back through Seventy Years: Autobiographical and Other Reminiscences*, London, 1893 (2 vols.).

Weber, Wolfgang, *Johann Jakob Weber: Der Begründer der illustrierten Presse in Deutschland*, Leipzig, 2003.

White, Gleeson, *English Illustration: "The Sixties": 1855–70*, London, 1903.

Wood, Martin T., *George du Maurier, the Satirist of the Victorians*, London, 1913.

The Turn of Chemigraphy
Die chemiegrafische Wende
Le tournant chimigraphique

Anthony, A.V., Timothy Cole, John P. Davis, Frederick Juengling, Richard A. Müller & John Tinkey, "A Symposium of Wood-Engravers", *Harper's New Monthly Magazine*, vol. 60, no. 357, February 1880, pp. 442–453.

Anthony, A.V., Timothy Cole & Elbridge Kingsley, *Three Essays by Three Engravers*, New York, 1916.

Beegan, Gerry, "The Mechanization of the Image: Facsimile, Photography, and Fragmentation in Nineteenth-Century Wood Engraving", *Journal of Design History*, no. 8, 1995, pp. 257–274.

Beegan, Gerry, *The Mass Image: A Social History of Photomechanical Reproduction in Victorian London*, Houndmills & New York, 2008.

Blachon, Remi, *La Gravure sur bois au XIXᵉ siècle. L'âge du bois debout*, Paris, 2001.

Brandt, William H., *Interpretive Wood-Engraving: The Story of the Society of American Wood-Engravers*, New Castle, Delaware, 2000.

Cate, Phillip D., *The Graphic Arts and French Society, 1871–1914*, New Brunswick, New Jersey, 1988.

Cole, Timothy, *Considerations on Engraving*, New York, 1921.

Essick, Robert N., *William Blake: Printmaker*, Princeton, 1980.

Federation of Master Process Engravers, *The Process Engraver's Compendium for Users of Photo-Process Engraving*, London, 1932.

Fraipont, Gustave, *Les Procédés de reproduction en relief. Manière d'exécuter les dessins pour la photogravure et la gravure sur bois*, Paris, 1895.

Frid, Jenya, *Gillotage: The Lost History of an Influential Technique*, master's thesis, Hunter College, New York, 2013.

Gretton, Tom, "Difference and Competition: The Imitation and Reproduction of Fine Art in a Nineteenth-Century Illustrated Weekly News Magazine", *Oxford Art Journal*, vol. 23, no. 2, 2000, pp. 145–162.

Gretton, Tom, "Signs for Labour-Value in Printed Pictures after the Photomechanical Revolution: Mainstream Changes and Extreme Cases around 1900", *Oxford Art Journal*, no. 28, 2005, pp. 371–390.

Gusman, Pierre, *La Gravure sur bois en France au XIXᵉ siècle*, Paris, 1929.

Hanebutt-Benz, Eva-Maria, *Studien zum deutschen Holzstich im 19. Jahrhundert*, Frankfurt, 1984.

Hanebutt-Benz, Eva-Maria, Frieder Schmidt & Walter Wilkes (eds.), *Die Buchkultur im 19. Jahrhundert*, vol. 1: *Technische Grundlagen*, Hamburg, 2010.

Harris, Neil, *Cultural Excursions: Marketing Appetites and Cultural Tastes in Modern America*, Chicago, 1990.

Hayden, Arthur, *Chats on Old Prints*, London, 1906.

Hinton, Alfred Horsley, *A Handbook of Illustration*, New York, 1894.

Houfe, Simon, *Phil May: His Life and Work, 1864–1903*, Ashgate, 2002.

Ivins Jr., William M., *How Prints Look: Photographs with a Commentary*, New York, 1943.

Ivins Jr., William M., *Prints and Visual Communication*, Cambridge, Massachusetts, 1953 (new edition: New York, 1969).

Jussim, Estelle, *Visual Communication and the Graphic Arts: Photographic Technologies in the Nineteenth Century*, New York & London, 1974.

Ketelsen, Thomas & Alexander Roob, *Chinesische Methode. Die Fotografik der New School of Wood Engraving*, Cologne, 2012.

Koehler, Sylvester Rosa, "Friedrich Juengling und der moderne Holzstich", *Zeitschrift für Bildende Kunst*, 1891, new series, vol. 2, pp. 81–90, 112–122.

Linton, William James, "Art in Engraving on Wood", *The Atlantic Monthly*, vol. 43, 1879, pp. 705–715.

Linton, William James, *Some Practical Hints on Wood-Engraving*, New Haven, 1879.

Linton, William James, *The History of Wood-engraving in America*, Boston, 1882.

Linton, William James, *Wood-engraving: A Manual of Instruction*, New Haven, 1884.

Lützow, Carl von (ed.), *Der Holzschnitt der Gegenwart in Europa und Nord-Amerika*, Vienna, 1887.

Osborn, Max, *Der Holzschnitt*, Bielefeld & Leipzig, 1905.

Pennell, Joseph, *Modern Illustration*, London, 1895.

Pettit, James, *Modern Reproductive Graphic Processes*, New York, 1884.

Rice, Stephen P., "Photography in Engraving on Wood: On the Road to a Halftone Revolution", common-place.org, vol. 7, no. 3, April 2007 (accessed 23 May 2018).

Roob, Alexander, "Art or Craft: William James Linton vs. William Morris; A Posthumous Dispute", meltonpriorinstitut. org, feature, May 2009 (accessed 23 May 2018).

Roob, Alexander, "Adolph Menzel: *Der Zerbrochne Krug* & Henry Wolf: *Destroyed*", in: Alexander Roob, *Anti-Porter*, Stuttgart, 2013, pp. 26–41.

Sander, David M., *Wood Engraving: An Adventure in Printmaking*, New York, 1982.

Sandweiss, Martha A., *Print the Legend: Photography and the American West*, New Haven, 2002.

Smith, Ralph Clifton, *Life and Works of Henry Wolf*, Champlain, New York, 1927.

Unger, Arthur W., *Die Herstellung von Büchern, Illustrationen, Akzidenzen usw.*, Halle, 1910.

Viscomi, Joseph, *Blake and the Idea of the Book: The Production, Editing, and Dating of Illuminated Books*, Princeton, 1993.

Wakeman, Geoffrey, *Victorian Book Illustration: The Technical Revolution*, Detroit, 1973.

Weitenkampf, Frank, *American Graphic Art*, New York, 1912.

Van Gogh's "Bible for Artists"
Van Goghs Künstlerbibel
La bible pour artistes de Van Gogh

Aragon, Louis, *L'Exemple de Courbet*, Paris, 1952.

Bakker, Nienke, Andreas Blühm, Sjraar van Heugten, Leo Jansen & Chris Stolwijk, *Vincent's Choice: The Musée imaginaire of Van Gogh*, Amsterdam, 2003.

Boime, Albert, *Art and the French Commune: Imagining Paris after War and Revolution*, Princeton, 1995.

Boime, Albert, "Van Gogh and Thomas Nast", in: Joseph D. Masheck (ed.), *Van Gogh 100*, Westport, Connecticut, 1996.

Clayton, Hollis, *Paris in Despair: Art and Everyday Life under Siege (1870–71)*, Chicago, 1986.

De Mare, Eric, *The Victorian Woodblock Illustrators*, London, 1980.

Druillet, Philippe, Côme Fabre, Philippe Kaenel, Erika Dolphin & David Kunzle, *Gustave Doré: Master of Imagination*, Paris, 2014.

Edwards, Lee McCormick, *Herkomer: A Victorian Artist*, Aldershot, 1999.

Erpel, Fritz (ed.), *Vincent van Gogh, Die Rohrfederzeichnungen*, Munich, 1990.

Farner, Konrad, *Gustave Doré, der Industrialisierte Romantiker* (1962), Munich, 1975.

Herding, Klaus, *Realismus als Widerspruch. Die Wirklichkeit in Courbets Malerei*, Frankfurt, 1987.

Hogarth, Paul, *Arthur Boyd Houghton*, London, 1981.

Housman, Laurence, *Arthur Boyd Houghton: A Selection from His Work in Black and White*, London, 1896.

Jansen, Leo, Hans Luijten & Nienke Bakker, *Vincent van Gogh: The Letters* (vangoghletters.org/vg/letters.html; accessed 9 February 2022).

Jerrold, Blanchard, *The Life of Gustave Doré*, London, 1891.

Kitton, Frederic G., *Dickens and His Illustrators*, London, 1899.

Korda, Andrea, *Printing and Painting the News in Victorian London: The Graphic and Social Realism, 1869–1891*, Ashgate, 2015.

Koven, Seth, *Slumming: Sexual and Social Politics in Victorian London*, Princeton, 2006.

Marks, John George, *Life and Letters of Frederick Walker, A.R.A.*, London & New York, 1896.

Milner, John, *Art, War and Revolution in France, 1870–1871: Myth, Reportage and Reality*, New Haven, 2000.

Nochlin, Linda, "Van Gogh, Renouard, and the Weavers' Crisis in Lyons", in: Linda Nochlin, *The Politics of Vision: Essays on Nineteenth-Century Art and Society*, New York, 1989, pp. 95–119.

Nord, Philip, *Impressionists and Politics: Art and Democracy in the Nineteenth Century*, New York, 2000.

O'Sullivan, Niamh, *Aloysius O'Kelly: Art, Nation, Empire*, Dublin, 2010.

Pickvance, Ronald, *English Influences on Vincent van Gogh*, London, 1974.

Pisano, Ronald G., *The Tile Club and the Aesthetic Movement in America*, New York, 1999.

Quilter, Harry, "Some Graphic Artists", *Universal Review*, no. 2, September 1888, pp. 94–104.

Roob, Alexander, "Xylographism Unbound – The Influence of Illustrated Journal Graphics on the Art of Vincent van Gogh", meltonpriorinstitut.org, feature, July 2007 (accessed 23 May 2018).

Roob, Alexander, "Van Gogh's Favorites II: Hubert Herkomer and the School of English Social Realism", meltonpriorinstitut.org, feature, September 2007 (accessed 23 May 2018).

Roob, Alexander, "Arthur Boyd Houghton – Our One-Eyed Artist in America", meltonpriorinstitut.org, feature, August 2008 (accessed 23 May 2018).

Roob, Alexander, "Paul Renouard, the Zola of Drawing", meltonpriorinstitut.org,

feature, September 2008 (accessed 23 May 2018).
Roob, Alexander, "Die Tradition der doppelten Indifferenz. Andy Warhol, der Tile Club und der New School", in: Annette Geiger & Michael Glasmeier (eds.), *Kunst und Design. Eine Affäre*, Hamburg, 2012, pp. 65–78.
Roob, Alexander, "William James Linton und sein politisches Lehrstück Cetewayo and Dean Stanley", in: Alexander Roob, *Anti-Porter*, Kunstmuseum Stuttgart, 2013.
Roob, Alexander, "London, ein Meta-Report. Über Gustave Dorés *London. A Pilgrimage*", in: Michael Glasmeier (ed.), *Strategien der Zeichnung. Kunst der Illustration*, Hamburg, 2014, pp. 125–153.
Roob, Alexander, "Empty Chairs or Xylographism Unbound", in: Bice Curiger (ed.), *Van Gogh – Pre-Pop*, Fondation Vincent van Gogh, Arles, 2018.
Roosevelt, Blanche, *Life and Reminiscences of Gustave Doré*, London & New York, 1885.
Ross, Kristin, *Communal Luxury: The Political Imaginary of the Paris Commune*, London, 2015.
Sánchez, Gonzalo J., *Organizing Independence: The Artists Federation of the Paris Commune and Its Legacy, 1871–1889*, Lincoln, Nebraska, 1997.
Scheler, Lucien (ed.), *Albert Robida. Album du siège et de la Commune: Paris 1870–1871*, Paris, 1971 (2 vols.).
Schmandt, Peter, *Armenhaus und Obdachlosenasyl in der englischen Graphik und Malerei (1830–1880)*, Marburg, 1991.
Schrenk, Klaus (ed.), *Auf den Barrikaden von Paris. Alltag der Pariser Kommune*, Berlin, 1979.
Thomas, William Luson, "The Making of the Graphic", *Universal Review*, no. 2, September 1888, pp. 80–93.
Tillier, Bertrand, *La Commune de Paris, révolution sans image? – Politique et représentations dans la France républicaine, 1871–1914*, Seyssel, 2004.
Treuherz, Julian, *Hard Times: Social Realism in Victorian Art*, Manchester, 1987.
Van Heugten, Sjraar, *Van Gogh Drawings: Influences & Innovations*, Arles, 2015.
Vizetelly, Henry, *Paris in Peril*, London, 1882 (2 vols.).

The Triumph of Caricature
Triumph der Karikatur
Triomphe de la caricature

Adler, John & Draper Hill, *Doomed by Cartoon: How Cartoonist Thomas Nast and the New York Times Brought Down Boss Tweed and His Ring of Thieves*, New York, 2008.
Banta, Martha, *Barbaric Intercourse: Caricature and the Culture of Conduct, 1841–1936*, Chicago, 2002.
Berleux, Jean, *La Caricature politique en France pendant la guerre, le siège de Paris et la Commune*, Paris, 1890.
Boime, Albert, "Thomas Nast and French Art", *American Art Journal*, vol. 4, no. 1, 1972, pp. 43–65.
Bork, Angela et al. (ed.), *Die politische Lithographie im Kampf um die Pariser Kommune*, Cologne, 1976.
Courtet-Cohl, Pierre, Bernard Génin & Isao Takahata, *Émile Cohl: L'inventeur du dessin animé*, Sophia Antipolis, 2008.
Crafton, Donald, *Émile Cohl, Caricature, and Film*, Princeton, 1990.
Dewey, Donald, *The Art of Ill Will: The Story of American Political Cartoons*, New York, 2008.
Doizy, Guillaume & Jean-François Le Petit, *Je suis malade, curieux carnets d'un séjour à l'Hôtel-Dieu par Alfred Le Petit*, Paris, 2007.
Feld, Charles (ed.), *Pilotell. Dessinateur et communard*, Paris, 1969.
Feld, Charles & François Hincker (eds.), *Paris au front d'insurgé, la Commune en images*, Paris, 1970.
Fischer, Roger A., *Them Damned Pictures: Explorations in American Political Cartoon Art*, New York, 1996.
Goldstein, Robert Justin, *Censorship of Political Caricature in Nineteenth-Century France*, Kent, Ohio, 1989.
Grand-Carteret, John, *Les Mœurs et la caricature en France*, Paris, 1888.
Halloran, Fiona Deans, *Thomas Nast: The Father of Modern Political Cartoons*, Chapel Hill, North Carolina, 2013.
Hellmann, Claudia, *Die amerikanischen Präsidentschaftswahlkämpfe von 1864 bis 1895 in den Karikaturen von Thomas Nast*, PhD thesis, Ludwig Maximilian University, Munich, 2006.
Keller, Morton, *The Art and Politics of Thomas Nast*, Oxford, 1968.
Kneiß, Daniela, *Die Republik im Zwielicht: Zur Metaphorik von Licht und Finsternis in der französischen Bildpublizistik 1871–1914*, Munich, 2010.
[Le Petit, Alfred], *Alfred Le Petit, Photographe "maudit"*, Paris, 2005.
Leclercq, Pierre-Robert, *André Gill. Les Dessins de presse et la censure*, Paris, 2015.
Leonard, Thomas C., *The Power of the Press: The Birth of American Political Reporting*, Oxford, 1986.
Mitchell, J.A., "Contemporary American Caricature", *Scribner's Magazine*, vol. 6, 1889, pp. 728–745.
Paine, Albert Bigelow, *Thomas Nast: His Period and His Pictures*, New York, 1904.
Roob, Alexander, "Thomas Nast and Theodor Kaufmann: Higher Forms of Hieroglyph", meltonpriorinstitut.org, feature, November 2012 (accessed 23 May 2018).
Rütter, Raimund (ed.), *Die Karikatur zwischen Republik und Zensur. Bildsatire in Frankreich 1830 bis 1880*, Marburg, 1991.
St. Hill, Thomas Nast, *Thomas Nast: Cartoons and Illustrations*, New York, 1974.
Schleicher, Regina, *Antisemitismus in der Karikatur: Zur Bildpublizistik in der französischen Dritten Republik und im deutschen Kaiserreich (1871–1914)*, Frankfurt, 2007.
Summers, Mark Wahlgren, *The Press Gang: Newspapers and Politics, 1865–1878*, Chapel Hill, North Carolina, 1994.
Tillier, Bertrand, *Le Potager républicain, caricatures d'Alfred Le Petit*, Montreuil, 2003.
Ueding, Gert, *Wilhelm Busch: das 19. Jahrhundert en miniature*, Frankfurt, 2007.
Vallès, Jules, *Jacques Vingtras: L'Enfant – Le Bachelier – L'Insurgé*, Paris, 1950.
Valmy-Baysse, Jean, *André Gill, L'Impertinent* (1927), Paris, 1991.
Vinson John, *Thomas Nast: Political Cartoonist*, Jackson, Mississippi, 2014.
West, Richard Samuel, *Satire on Stone: The Political Cartoons of Joseph Keppler*, Chicago, 1988.

The Golden Age of Illustrated Journalism
Glanzzeit des Bildjournalismus
Splendeur du journalisme illustré

Agnew, Jeremy, *The Creation of the Cowboy Hero: Fiction, Film and Fact*, Jefferson, North Carolina, 2015.
Alkon, Paul K., *Science Fiction before 1900: Imagination Discovers Technology*, New York, 1994.
Allen, Douglas, *Frederic Remington and the Spanish-American War*, New York, 1971.
Braun, Alexander, *Winsor McCay, Comics, Filme, Träume*, Bonn, 2012.
Briessen, Fritz van, *Shanghai-Bildzeitung (1884–98). Eine Illustrierte aus dem China des ausgehenden 19. Jahrhunderts*, Zurich, 1977.
Brown, Joshua, *Beyond the Lines: Pictorial Reporting, Everyday Life, and the Crisis of Gilded Age America*, Oakland, California, 2002.
Burns, Sarah, *Inventing the Modern Artist: Art and Culture in Gilded Age America*, New Haven, 1996.
Campbell, W. Joseph, *Yellow Journalism: Puncturing the Myths, Defining the Legacies*, Santa Barbara, 2001.
Canemaker, John, *Winsor McCay: His Life and Art* (1987), New York, 2005.
Carruthers, Jane, *Melton Prior: War Artist in Southern Africa, 1895 to 1900*, Johannesburg, 1987.
Carter, Albert Charles Robinson, *The Work of War Artists in South Africa* (1900), Kimberley, 1999.
Cornebise, Alfred, *Art from the Trenches: America's Uniformed Artists in World War I*, College Station, Texas, 1991.
Dixmier, Michel & Véronique Willemin, *L'œil de la police: Crimes et châtiments à la Belle Epoque*, Paris, 2007.
Dobson, Sebastian, Anne Nishimura Morse & Frederic Sharf, *A Much Recorded War: The Russo-Japanese War in History and Imagery*, Boston, 2005.
Doß, Kurt, *Der Hamburger Maler und Zeichner C.W. Allers. Erfolg und Tragik eines Künstlers zur Kaiserzeit*, Hamburg, 1981.
Evans, Arthur B., *Vintage Visions: Essays on Early Science Fiction*, Middletown, Connecticut, 2014.
Faulstich, Werner (ed.), *Kulturgeschichte des 20. Jahrhunderts. Das Erste Jahrzehnt*, Paderborn, 2006.
Ferber, Christian, *Berliner Illustrierte Zeitung. Zeitbild, Chronik, Moritat für Jedermann 1892–1945*, Berlin, 1982.
Gallatin, Albert Eugene, *Art and the Great War*, New York, 1919.
Gamboni, Dario, *The Destruction of Art: Iconoclasm and Vandalism since the French Revolution*, London, 1997.
Geffroy, Gustave (ed.), *La Grande Guerre par les artistes, 1914–1915*, Paris, 1915.
Gooch, John (ed.), *The Boer War: Direction, Experience and Image*, London & New York, 2000.
Gretton, Thomas, "European Illustrated Weekly Magazines, *c.* 1850–1900: A Model and a Counter-Model for the Work of José Guadalupe Posada", *Anales del Instituto de Investigaciones Estéticas*, no. 70, 1997, pp. 99–125.
Harrington, Peter, *British Artists and War: The Face of Battle in Paintings and Prints, 1700–1914*, London, 1993.
Harrington, Peter & Frederic A. Sharf, *"A Splendid Little War": The Spanish-American War, 1898: The Artists' Perspective*, London, 2006.
Hassrick, Peter H. (ed.), *Frederic Remington: A Catalogue Raisonné*, Cody, Wyoming, 2005 (2 vols.).
Heinzelmann, Tobias, *Die Balkankrise in der osmanischen Karikatur. Die Satire-Zeitschriften Karagöz, Kalem und Cem 1908–1914*, Istanbul & Stuttgart, 1999.
Hogarth, Paul, *Artists on Horseback*, New York, 1972.
Hülk, Walburga & Gregor Schuhen (eds.), *Haussmann und die Folgen: vom Boulevard zur Boulevardisierung*, Tübingen, 2012.
Jaccaci, August F., "Daniel Urrabieta y Vierge: The Father of Modern Illustration", *The Century Illustrated Monthly Magazine*, June 1893, pp. 186–203.
Jähn, Hannes (ed.), *The Works of Jose Guadalupe Posada*, Frankfurt, 1976.
Johnson, Peter, *Frontline Artists*, London, 1978.
Keegan, John, *The First World War: An Illustrated History*, London, 2002.
Keller, Ulrich, "Blut und Silber. Die Inszenierung der Kuba-Invasion von 1898 in der amerikanischen Bildpresse", *Fotogeschichte*, issue 97, 2005, pp. 40ff.
Keller, Ulrich, "Der Weltkrieg der Bilder. Organisation, Zensur und Ästhetik der Bildreportage 1914–1918", *Fotogeschichte*, issue 130, 2013, pp. 5–50.
Keller, Ulrich, "Verdun, 1916. Die Schlacht der Bildreportagen", *Fotogeschichte*, issue 130, 2013, pp. 51–84.
Kleeblatt, Norman L., *The Dreyfus Affair: Art, Truth, and Justice*, Los Angeles, 1987.
Kobre, Sidney, *The Yellow Press and Gilded Age Journalism*, Tallahassee, 1964.
Koch-Gotha, Fritz, *Koch-Gotha-Album*, Berlin, 1914.
Koch-Gotha, Fritz, *Gezeichnetes Leben*, Berlin, 1957.
Korff, Kurt, "Die Berliner Illustrirte", in: Max Osborn (ed.), *Fünfzig Jahre Ullstein, 1877–1927*, Berlin, 1927, pp. 279–302.
Küster, Bernd (ed.), *Der Erste Weltkrieg und die Kunst. Von der Propaganda zum Widerstand*, Oldenburg, 2008.
Laffin, John (ed.), *The Western Front Illustrated, 1914–18*, London, 1992.
le Ray, Eric, *Marinoni, le fondateur de la presse moderne (1823–1904)*, Paris, 2009.
López, Mercurio, *José Guadalupe Posada. Ilustrador de cuadernos populares*, Mexico City, 2005.
Lorenz, Detlef, "Nimm mich mit – eine illustrierte Zeitschrift der wilhelminischen Ära", in: Wolfgang Brückner, Konrad Vanja, Detlef Lorenz, Alberto Milano & Sigrid Nagy (eds.), *Arbeitskreis Bild Druck Papier. Tagungsband Amsterdam 2007*, Münster, 2008, pp. 155–179.
Luckhardt, Ulrich, *Lyonel Feininger: Die Karikaturen und das zeichnerische Frühwerk*, Munich, 1987.
MacKenzie, John M., *Imperialism and Popular Culture*, Manchester, 1987.
Marschall, Richard, *Daydreams and Nightmares: The Fantastic Visions of Winsor McCay, 1898–1934*, Seattle, 1988.
Marthold, Jules, *Daniel Vierge – Sa vie, son œuvre*, Paris, 1895.
Morton, Marsha, *Max Klinger and Wilhelmine Culture: On the Threshold of German Modernism*, Farnham, 2014.
Paris, Michael, *Warrior Nation: Images of War in British Popular Culture, 1850–2000*, London, 2000.
Pascal, Janet B., *Jacob Riis: Reporter and Reformer*, New York, 2005.
Pennell, Joseph, *The Adventures of an Illustrator*, London, 1925.
Price, Julius M., *On the Path of Adventure*, London, 1919.
Prior, Melton, *Campaigns of a War Correspondent*, London, 1912.
Reed, Walt (ed.), *The Illustrator in America, 1900–1960's*, New York, 1966.
Roeder, Katherine, *Wide Awake in Slumberland: Fantasy, Mass Culture, and Modernism in the Art of Winsor McCay*, Jackson, Mississippi, 2014.
Schneider, William Howard, *An Empire for the Masses: The French Popular Image of Africa, 1870–1900*, Westport, Connecticut, 1982.
Schwartz, Vanessa R., *Spectacular Realities: Early Mass Culture in Fin-de-Siècle Paris*, Berkeley, 1998.
Smith, Francis Hopkinson (ed.), *American Illustrators*, New York, 1893.

Smythe, Ted Curtis, *The Gilded Age Press, 1865–1900*, Santa Barbara, 2003.

Soppelsa, Peter S., *The Fragility of Modernity: Infrastructure and Everyday Life in Paris, 1870–1914*, PhD thesis, University of Michigan, 2009.

Stern, Madeleine B., *Purple Passage: The Life of Mrs. Frank Leslie* (1953), New York, 1971.

Taft, Robert, *Artists and Illustrators of the Old West, 1850–1900*, New York, 1953.

Thomson, Richard, *The Troubled Republic: Visual Culture and Social Debate in France, 1889–1900*, New Haven, 2004.

Thomson, Richard, *Art of the Actual: Naturalism and Style in Early Third Republic France, 1880–1900*, New Haven, 2013.

Timm, Regine, *Fritz Koch-Gotha*, Berlin, 1971.

Tullio, Contino, *La storia per immagini di Achille Beltrame, 1899–1944*, Pinerolo, 2002.

Valentin, Sylvia, *Journalismus in Frankreich im 19. Jahrhundert, die Veränderung der Pressewelt im kritischen Dialog*, graduate thesis, University of Vienna, 2000.

Villiers, Frederic, *Peaceful Personalities and Warriors Bold*, London, 1907.

Villiers, Frederic, *Villiers: His Five Decades of Adventure*, New York & London, 1920 (2 vols.).

Villoro, Juan, Mercurio López, Helia Bonilla, Montserrat Gali & Rafael Barajas, *Posada: A Century of Skeletons*, n. p., 2014.

Walz, Robin, *Pulp Surrealism: Insolent Popular Culture in Early Twentieth-Century Paris*, Berkeley, 2000.

Weisberg, Gabriel P. (ed.), *Illusions of Reality: Naturalismus 1875–1918*, Stuttgart, 2010.

Westwell, Ian, *The Ultimate Illustrated History of World War I*, London, 2009.

Wirth, Irmgard (ed.), *Berliner Pressezeichner der zwanziger Jahre. Ein Kaleidoskop Berliner Lebens*, Berlin, 1977.

Ye, Xiaoqing, *The Dianshizhai Pictorial: Shanghai Urban Life, 1884–1898*, Ann Arbor, 2003.

Yochelson, Bonnie & Daniel Czitrom, *Rediscovering Jacob Riis: Exposure Journalism and Photography in Turn-of-the-Century New York*, Chicago, 2007.

Zentner, Christian, *Illustrierte Geschichte des Ersten Weltkriegs*, Munich, 1980.

The Illustration Revolution
Revolution der Illustration
Révolution de l'illustration

Abélès, Luce & Catherine Charpin, *Arts incohérents, académie du dérisoire*, Paris, 1992.

Antliff, Allan, *Anarchist Modernism: Art, Politics, and the First American Avant-Garde*, Chicago, 2001.

Appelbaum, Stanley, *French Satirical Drawings from "L'Assiette Au Beurre"*, New York, 1978.

Auriol, Georges, *Steinlen et la rue*, Paris, 1930.

Bachollet, Raymond, *Juan Gris, dessinateur de presse: de Madrid à Montmartre, catalogue raisonné 1904–1912*, Paris, 2003.

Baker, Nicholson & Margaret Brentano, *The World on Sunday: Graphic Art in Joseph Pulitzer's Newspaper (1898–1911)*, New York, 2005.

Balzer, Jens & Lambert Wiesing, *Outcault. Die Erfindung des Comic*, Bochum, 2010.

Banta, Martha, *Barbaric Intercourse: Caricature and the Culture of Conduct, 1841–1936*, Chicago, 2002.

Bee, Andreas (ed.), *Alphonse Allais: Album Primo-Avrilesque*, Heidelberg, 1993.

Beffel, John Nicholas (ed.), *Art Young: His Life and Times*, New York, 1939.

Bihl, Luc, *Adolphe Willette, Pierrot de Montmartre*, Précy-sous-Thil, 1991.

Blackbeard, Bill, *R.F. Outcault's the Yellow Kid: A Centennial Celebration of the Kid Who Started the Comics*, Northampton, Massachusetts, 1995.

Bodinier, Jean-Louis, Fabienne Dumont, Serge Fauchereau, Arlette Le More & Agnès Marcetteau-Paul, *Jules Grandjouan, 1875–1968*, Nantes, 1998.

Brullé, Pierre, Marie-Pierre Salé, Markéta Theinhardt & Petr Wittlich, *Vers des temps nouveaux: Kupka, œuvres graphiques, 1894–1912*, Paris, 2002.

Cabanne, Pierre, *Dialogues with Marcel Duchamp* (1967), London, 1971.

Cabanne, Pierre, *Henri de Toulouse-Lautrec: le peintre de la vie moderne / The Reporter of Modern Life*, Paris, 2003.

Cate, Phillip Dennis, *The Graphic Arts and French Society, 1871–1914*, New Brunswick, New Jersey, 1988.

Cate, Phillip Dennis & Mary Shaw (eds.), *The Spirit of Montmartre: Cabarets, Humor, and the Avant-garde, 1875–1905*, New Brunswick, New Jersey, 1996.

Cate, Phillip Dennis & Susan Gill (eds.), *Théophile-Alexandre Steinlen*, Layton, Utah, 1982.

Chalupa, Pavel, *L'Assiette au Beurre par François Kupka*, Javorník, 1998.

Charpin, Catherine, *Les Arts incohérents (1882–1893)*, Paris, 1990.

Crafton, Donald, *Émile Cohl, Caricature, and Film*, Princeton, 1990.

Crane, Walter, *An Artist's Reminiscences*, New York, 1907.

D'Axa, Zo, *De Mazas à Jérusalem* (1895), Paris, 2012.

D'Axa, Zo, *Les Feuilles de Zo d'Axa*, Paris, 1900.

Demm, Eberhard (ed.), *Der Erste Weltkrieg in der internationalen Karikatur*, Hanover, 1988.

Dickerman, Leah, *ROSTA: Bolshevik Placards, 1919–1921; Handmade Political Posters from the Russian Telegraph Agency*, New York, 1994.

Didier, Bénédicte, *Petites revues et esprit bohème à la fin du XIXe siècle, 1878–1889*, Paris, 2009.

Dittmar, Peter, *Steinlen. Théophile Alexandre Steinlen – ein poetischer Realist in der Epoche des Jugendstils*, Zurich, 1984.

Dixmier, Élisabeth & Michel Dixmier, *L'Assiette au Beurre: revue satirique illustrée, 1901–1912*, Paris, 1974.

Dixmier, Michel (ed.), *Jossot caricatures: De la révolte à la fuite en Orient (1866–1951)*, Paris, 2011.

Dixmier, Michel & Louis Bretonnière, *L'Art social à la Belle Époque: Aristide Delannoy, Jules Grandjouan, Maximilien Luce: trois artistes engagés*, Auxerre, 2006.

Dumont, Fabienne, Joël Moris & Marie-Hélène Jouzeau, *Jules Grandjouan créateur de l'affiche politique illustrée en France*, Paris, 2001.

Duwakin, Wiktor, *ROSTA-Fenster. Majakowski als Dichter und bildender Künstler* (1967), Dresden, 1975.

Eastman, Max, *Journalism versus Art*, New York, 1916.

Fitzgerald, Richard, *Art and Politics: Cartoonists of the "Masses" and "Liberator"*, New York, 1973.

Gambone, Robert L., *Life on the Press: The Popular Art and Illustrations of George Benjamin Luks*, Jackson, Mississippi, 2009.

Glasmeier, Michael & Wolfgang Till (eds.), *Gestern oder im 2. Stock. Karl Valentin, Komik und Kunst seit 1948*, Munich, 2009.

Goergen, Annabelle, *L'Exposition internationale du surréalisme, Paris 1938. Die Ausstellung als Werk. Einflüsse aus dem 19. Jahrhundert unter dem Aspekt der Kohärenz*, Munich, 2008.

Goldstein, Robert Justin, *Censorship of Political Caricature in Nineteenth-Century France*, Kent, Ohio, 1989.

Grand-Carteret, John, *L'Affaire Dreyfus et l'image*, Paris, 1898.

Halperin, Joan Ungersma, *Félix Fénéon: Aesthete and Anarchist in Fin-de-Siècle Paris*, New Haven, 1988.

Herszkowicz, Sophie, *Les Arts incohérents*, Paris, 2010.

Hervouët, Philippe, *L'Infréquentable Jules: Jules Grandjouan, 1875–1968*, Nantes, 1999.

Hiekisch-Picard, Sepp, "Die Zeitschriften *Gil Blas illustré*, *Le Rire* und *L'Assiette au Beurre*", in: Gerhard Langemeyer (ed.), 1986, pp. 27–33.

Hopmans, Anita, *The Van Dongen Nobody Knows: Early and Fauvist Drawings, 1895–1920*, Rotterdam, 1996.

Hopmans, Anita, "Au haut de la Butte: Van Dongen's Early Years in Paris", in: Max Hollein & Ingrid Pfeiffer (eds.), *Esprit Montmartre*, Munich, 2014, pp. 255–261.

Houfe, Simon, *Fin de Siècle: The Illustrators of the Nineties*, London, 1992.

Hulten, Pontus, Jennifer Gough-Cooper & Jacques Caumont, *Marcel Duchamp: Work and Life; Ephemerides on and about Marcel Duchamp and Rrose Sélavy, 1887–1968*, Cambridge, Massachusetts, 1993.

Hünig, Wolfgang K., *British and German Cartoons as Weapons in World War I: Invectives and Ideology of Political Cartoons, a Cognitive Linguistics Approach*, Bern, 2002.

King, David & Cathy Porter (eds.), *Blood and Laughter: Caricatures from the 1905 Revolution*, London, 1983.

Kleeblatt, Norman L., *The Dreyfus Affair: Art, Truth, and Justice*, Los Angeles, 1987.

Kneißl, Daniela, *Die Republik im Zwielicht: Zur Metaphorik von Licht und Finsternis in der französischen Bildpublizistik 1871–1914*, Munich, 2010.

Koch, Ursula E. & Markus Behmer (eds.), *Grobe Wahrheiten – Wahre Grobheiten – Feine Striche – Scharfe Stiche. Jugend, Simplicissimus und andere Karikaturen-Journale der Münchner "Belle Époque"*, Munich, 1996.

Koechlin, Noémie, *Jules Grandjouan: dessinateur de presse et illustrateur*, Nantes, 2003.

Krain, Peter, *Willibald Krain. Als Künstler gefeiert – verboten – vergessen*, Hamburg, 2007.

Kunzle, David, *The History of the Comic Strip*, vol. 2: *The Nineteenth Century*, Berkeley, 1990.

Kunzle, David, "The Voices of Silence: Willette, Steinlen, and the Introduction of the Silent Strip in the *Chat Noir*, with a German Coda", in: Robin Varnum & Christina T. Gibbons (eds.), *The Language of Comics: Word and Image*, Jackson, Mississippi, 2001, pp. 3–18.

Langemeyer, Gerhard (ed.), *Bilderwelten II. Satirische Illustrationen im Frankreich der Jahrhundertwende aus der Sammlung von Kritter*, Dortmund, 1986.

Leighten, Patricia, *The Liberation of Painting: Modernism and Anarchism in Avant-Guerre Paris*, Chicago, 2013.

Maresca, Peter (ed.), *Society Is Nix: Gleeful Anarchy at the Dawn of the American Comic Strip, 1895–1915*, New York, 2013.

Mathews, Nancy Mowll, *Moving Pictures: American Art and Early Film, 1880–1910*, Manchester, Vermont, 2005.

O'Neill, Morna, *"Art and Labour's Cause Is One": Walter Crane and Manchester, 1880–1915*, Manchester, 2008.

O'Neill, Morna, *Walter Crane: The Arts and Crafts, Painting, and Politics*, New Haven, 2010.

O'Neill, William L., *Echoes of Revolt: The Masses, 1911–1917*, Chicago, 1989.

Reff, Theodore & Florence Valdes-Forain, *Jean-Louis Forain: The Impressionist Years*, Memphis, Tennessee, 1995.

Robbins, Kevin C., "Roving Anarchist Flâneurs: The Visual Politics of Popular Protest via Parisian Street Art in *L'Assiette au Beurre* (1900–1914)", in: Richard Wrigley (ed.), *The Flâneur Abroad: Historical and International Perspectives*, Newcastle, 2004, pp. 223–255.

Roob, Alexander, "Die ROSTA-Fenster der bolschewistischen Kunstarmee. Graphischer Bildjournalismus und Avantgarde", in: Susanne Altmann & Petra Lewey (eds.), *Re-bellion, Re-ligion, Re-form. Künstler agieren im Umbruch*, Zwickau, 2015, pp. 25–31.

Scholz, Dieter, *Pinsel und Dolch. Anarchistische Ideen in Kunst und Kunsttheorie 1840–1920*, Berlin, 1999.

Shattuck, Roger, *The Banquet Years: The Origins of the Avant-Garde in France, 1885 to World War I*, London, 1968.

Shikes, Ralph, "Five Artists in the Service of Politics in the Pages of *L'Assiette au Beurre*", in: Henry Armand Millon & Linda Nochlin (eds.), *Art and Architecture in the Service of Politics*, Cambridge, Massachusetts, 1978, pp. 162–192.

Slavs and Tatars (eds.), *Molla Nasreddin: The Magazine That Would've, Could've, Should've*, Zurich, 2011.

Tillier, Bertrand, *La Commune de Paris, révolution sans image? – Politique et représentations dans la France républicaine, 1871–1914*, Seyssel, 2004.

Traeger, Jörg, *Bilder vom Elend. Käthe Kollwitz im Simplicissimus*, Munich, 1998.

Viltard, Henri (ed.), *Henri Gustave Jossot: Le Fœtus récalcitrant* (1939), Paris, 2011.

Vogt, Tobias, *Artikel der Kunst. Alltagsobjekt und Wortspiel in den Pariser Bildkünsten des 19. Jahrhunderts*, Paderborn, 2019.

Weisberg, Gabriel P. (ed.), *Montmartre and the Making of Mass Culture*, New Brunswick, New Jersey & London, 2001.

Weiss, Jeffrey, *The Popular Culture of Modern Art: Picasso, Duchamp, and Avant-Gardism*, New Haven, 1994.

Willette, Adolphe, *Feu Pierrot, 1857–19?*, Paris, 1919.

Zurier, Rebecca, *Art for the Masses: A Radical Magazine and Its Graphics, 1911–1917*, Philadelphia, 1988.

Zurier, Rebecca, *Picturing the City: Urban Vision and the Ashcan School*, New York, 2006.

Index of Persons

Index of Periodicals

Photo Credits

Unless stated otherwise, all images in the book are from the Melton Prior Institute in Düsseldorf: http://www.meltonpriorinstitut.org/

The editors wish to thank Jürgen Seidel, of Siegburg, who photographed the works from the Melton Prior Institute for this book. Our thanks also go to the museums, libraries, archives and other institutions mentioned in the captions and in the credits for their kind assistance.

Abbreviations:
The following abbreviations are used:
l. = left, r. = right, t. = top, t.l. = top left, t.r. = top right, b. = bottom, b.l. = bottom left, b.r. = bottom right, m. = middle, m.l. = middle left, m.r. = middle right.

akg-images: pp. 222 t., 260 t.; akg-images / The British Library: p. 83; akg-images / Erich Lessing: p. 119 b.
Artefact / Alamy Stock Foto: p. 315
Artokoloro / Alamy Stock Foto: p. 256 b.l. and b.r.
Photo © Beaux-Arts de Paris, Dist. RMN-Grand Palais / image Beaux-arts de Paris: p. 85 t. and b.
Beinecke Rare Book & Manuscript Library, Yale University: p. 571 t.
© BnF: p. 187
Photo © BnF, Dist. RMN-Grand Palais / image BnF: pp. 96, 311
bpk: p. 241; bpk | DeAgostini / New Picture Library: p. 255
bpk | Kupferstichkabinett, SMB / Jörg P. Anders: p. 415 b.; Dietmar Katz: p. 23; Volker-H. Schneider: p. 90 t. and b.
bpk | The Metropolitan Museum of Art: p. 39
bpk | The Solomon R. Guggenheim Foundation | Art Resource, New York: p. 261 b.r.
bpk | Staatsbibliothek zu Berlin, Abteilung Historische Drucke, p. 20
Bridgeman Images: pp. 251 r., 257 t.l. and t.r.
© Brooklyn Museum of Art / Designated Purchase Fund / Bridgeman Images: p. 87 t.
© British Library Board. All Rights Reserved / Bridgeman Images: pp. 584/585
© The Trustees of the British Museum: pp. 4/5, 30, 35, 44, 46/47, 53 t.
Hs 22474 © Germanisches Nationalmuseum, Nuremberg: pp. 24–25

Getty Museum Collection: p. 261 b.l.
Heritage Images / Fine Art Images / akg-images: p. 296 b.
© Kunsthalle Bremen – ARTOTHEK: p. 38
© Look and Learn / Bridgeman Images: p. 457
Look and Learn / Illustrated Papers Collection / Bridgeman Images: p. 256 t.l. and t.r.
Mondadori Portfolio / Electa / Bridgeman Images: p. 257 m.l. and m.r.
Sovfoto / UIG / Bridgeman Images: p. 497
The Stapleton Collection / Bridgeman Images: pp. 13, 560 b.l., 581
Universitäts- und Landesbibliothek Düsseldorf: pp. 168 t. and b., 169, 170 b., 173
USC Libraries, University of Southern California Los Angeles: p. 560 b.r.
Digital image, The Museum of Modern Art, New York / Scala, Florence: p. 431 b.
The Ohio State University Billy Ireland Cartoon Library & Museum: pp. 526/527, 529
Photo © RMN-Grand Palais / Philippe Bernard: p. 84
Photo © RMN-Grand Palais (musée d'Orsay) / Hervé Lewandowski: p. 68
Courtesy Sammlung Gaby und Wilhelm Schürmann, photo: Eric Tschernow: pp. 586, 587 l. and r., 588 l. and r., 589
Courtesy Slavs and Tatars, Berlin: pp. 564, 565
Staatliche Graphische Sammlung München, Munich: p. 257 b.l. and b.r.
Van Gogh Museum, Amsterdam (Vincent van Gogh Foundation): p. 298

Copyright

© Comité Cocteau, Paris / VG Bild-Kunst, Bonn 2023: p. 581
© Robert Crumb: p. 336 m.
© Olaf Gulbransson / VG Bild-Kunst, Bonn 2023: pp. 10, 560 t.
© Succession Picasso / VG Bild-Kunst, Bonn 2023: p. 531
© Jacques Villon / VG Bild-Kunst, Bonn 2023: pp. 507, 535 b.

© VG Bild-Kunst, Bonn 2023
for the works of Lyonel Feininger: p. 476 t. and b.; Albert Gleizes: p. 583; Jules Grandjouan: pp. 534 b., 558 t. and b.; František Kupka: pp. 466, 544/545, 546 t. and b., 547; Jacques Lehmann: p. 582; Bruno Paul: pp. 535 t., 556.

The Author | Acknowledgements

Alexander Roob has been a church painter, an illustrator for comics and also taught graphics and painting at the Kunsthochschule in Hamburg and the Kunstakademie in Stuttgart. As part of his ongoing drawing project *CS* he has investigated hermetic symbolism and the underlying history of sequential and documentary methods of illustration. In 2005 he founded the Melton Prior Institute in Düsseldorf with Clemens Krümmel, which specialises in the history of pictorial journalism and print culture. His book *Alchemy & Mysticism. The Hermetic Museum* has previously been published by TASCHEN.
Roob's research on the history of illustration concentrates chiefly on the dialectics of the inward and the outward gaze together with the period of the Enlightenment and Counter-Enlightenment, which at present he is examining with reference to the influence of William Hogarth on William Blake.

Alexander Roob war Kirchenmaler, zeichnete Comics und lehrte Grafik und Malerei an der Kunsthochschule Hamburg und der Kunstakademie Stuttgart. Im Rahmen seines fortlaufenden Zeichenprojekts *CS* setzt er sich mit hermetischer Emblematik und den Grundlagen sequentiellen und dokumentarischen Zeichnens auseinander. 2005 gründete er in Düsseldorf gemeinsam mit Clemens Krümmel das Melton Prior Institut, das sich der Geschichte der Reportagezeichnung und der Druckkultur widmet. Bei TASCHEN hat er bereits die Publikation *Alchemie & Mystik. Ein hermetisches Museum* vorgelegt.
Roobs illustrationshistorische Forschung konzentriert sich schwerpunktmäßig auf die Dialektik von Außen- und Innenschau sowie von Aufklärung und Gegenaufklärung, die er zurzeit am Beispiel des Einflusses von William Hogarth auf William Blake untersucht.

Alexander Roob a été peintre d'église, auteur de bandes dessinées, il a enseigné le graphisme et la peinture à l'École supérieure des Beaux-Arts de Hambourg et à l'Académie des Beaux-Arts de Stuttgart. Dans le cadre de son projet graphique actuel *CS*, il analyse l'emblématisme hermétique et les principes fondamentaux de l'illustration séquentielle et documentaire. En 2005 il a fondé en collaboration avec Clemens Krümmel le Melton Prior Institut, spécialisé dans l'histoire du dessin de presse et la culture de l'imprimerie. Chez TASCHEN il a déjà publié l'ouvrage *Alchimie & Mystique. Le Musée Hermétique*. Roob concentre ses recherches dans le domaine de l'illustration historique sur la dialectique de la perception interne et externe ainsi que des Lumières et des Anti-Lumières, qu'il étudie à travers l'exemple de l'influence de William Hogarth sur William Blake.

Author's acknowledgements
My thanks go firstly to Benedikt Taschen, for his enthusiasm about this project right from the start together with his intuition and energy as a publisher, which all made this publication possible in the first place. I would also like to thank Clemens Krümmel for his long-standing support, and Ute Kieseyer for her committed and perceptive management of the project. Of especial importance was the inspiration I gained through Alan Rusbridger and Steve Bell of *The Guardian*, who in 2002 introduced me to the unexpectedly vivid and historically rich culture of press illustration in the context of a *CS* drawing project initiated by Kate Macfarlane (Drawing Room).

Benedikt Taschen, den das Projekt von Anfang an begeistert hat, danke ich für seine Intuition und seine verlegerische Tatkraft, die diese Publikation überhaupt ermöglicht haben. Mein besonderer Dank gilt Clemens Krümmel für seine langjährige Unterstützung sowie Ute Kieseyer für ihr engagiertes und umsichtiges Management. Eine außergewöhnliche Bedeutung kommt der Inspiration durch Alan Rusbridger und Steve Bell von *The Guardian* zu, die mich im Jahr 2002 im Rahmen eines von Kate Macfarlane (Drawing Room) initiierten *CS*-Zeichnungsprojekts in eine ungeahnt lebendige und geschichtsträchtige Kultur der Pressegrafik eingeführt haben.

J'exprime ma vive reconnaissance à Benedikt Taschen, qui a porté dès le début le projet avec enthousiame, pour son intuition et son dynamisme éditorial sans lesquels cette publication n'aurait pas vu le jour. Ma gratitude va particulièrement à Clemens Krümmel pour le soutien qu'il m'accorde depuis de longues années, à Ute Kieseyer pour son engagement et sa grande compétence dans la direction de ce projet. Une importance exceptionnelle revient à l'inspiration que m'ont apportée Alan Rusbridger et Steve Bell du *Guardian* qui, en 2002, dans le cadre d'un projet de dessin *CS* lancé par Kate Macfarlane (Drawing Room), m'ont initié à la culture incroyablement vivante et imprégnée d'histoire du graphisme de presse.

For their various suggestions, encouragement and support I would also like to thank the following:
Weiterer Dank für ihre Anregungen, ihre Motivation und ihr Engagement geht an:
Que soient aussi chaleureusement remerciés pour leurs suggestions, leur motivation et leur engagement:

Esther Acevedo-Valdés, Chris Allen, Andreas Bee, Stephan Berg, Fritz Best, Rolf Bier, Nils Büttner, Luis Camnitzer, Nazire Ergün, Theo de Feyter, Thomas Flor, Maurice Garnier, Elena Gatkina, Michael Glasmeier, Herwig Graef, Ulrike Groos, Rudolf Herz, Ben Katchor, Ulrich Keller, Thomas Ketelsen, Stephan Mörsch, Horst Moser, Françoise Pétry, Richard Reisen, Thomas Rieger, Rudolf Rieß, Helmut Ritter, Lena Roob, Lisa Roob, Thomas Ruppel, Astrit Schmidt-Burkhardt, Bernd Schulz, Jürgen Seidel, Hubert Sowa, Patrick Thomas, Pierre Thomé, Susan Turcot, Tobias Vogt, Ursula Walbröl, Susanne Weiß, Georg Winter, He Youzhi & Xiaopeng Zhou.

Imprint

Cover
(from left to right and from top to bottom)

André Gill & Marchandeau, *Untitled*, 1867 (see p. 320 t.)

Pierre Legrain, *An Enemy Company Has Been Destroyed by Our Deadly Hertzian Waves*, 1916 (see p. 577)

Alfred Le Petit, *Damn…*, 1870 (see p. 327)

Raphael Bordallo Pinheiro, *Disturbance in the Chamber*, 1904 (see p. 554)

Rosta Collective (Mikhail Cheremnykh), *And We Are ready for the Spring*, 1921 (see p. 587 r.)

Eugène Bataille (Sapeck), *Mona Lisa Smoking a Pipe*, 1887 (see p. 504)

André Gill, *Ambush*, 1872 (see p. 343)

André Gill & Marchandeau, *And. Gill, by X…*, 1867 (see p. 316 l.)

Spine
(from top to bottom)

Saïd (Alphonse Lévy), *What Bad Luck!*, undated (see p. 332)

André Gill & Ferdinand Lefman, *The Journalism of the Future*, 1875 (see p. 348 t.)

Gustave-Henri Jossot, *All Is Lost, even Honour…*, 1907 (see p. 553 t.)

Back cover
(from left to right and from top to bottom)

André Gill & Marchandeau, *Authentic Portrait of Rocambole*, 1867 (see p. 318)

Juan Gris, *New Year's Gifts: Thank You, Mister Fifteengrand, and See You Next Year, if the Butter Hasn't Melted by then…*, 1910 (see p. 569 t.)

Carrey, *New York. Accident on the Elevated Railroad*, 1905 (see p. 457)

André Gill & Ferdinand Lefman, *Split Decisions*, 1873 (see p. 345 t.)

Raphael Bordallo Pinheiro, *Mice, Mice and still more Mice!*, 1902 (see p. 555)

André Gill; Yves & Barret, *Hold on Tight, Silly Billy, It's Starting Again!*, 1877 (see p. 358)

Édouard Bernard, *The "Fifteen Thousand"*, 1907 (see p. 493)

André Gill & Marchandeau, *Jules Vallès by Gill*, 1867 (see p. 316 r.)

Winsor McCay, *Confusion*, 1899 (see p. 447)

Endpapers, double spread

Gustave Doré & Soutain, *The History of Holy Russia* (detail), 1854 (see p. 187)

Bernhard Gillam, *Hopelessly Bound to the Stake*, 1883 (see p. 365)

Anonymous, *The Rioters' Railroad to Ruin*, 1877 (see pp. 366/367)

Henri Meyer, *A Crime in Le Kremlin-Bicêtre*, 1897 (see p. 458)

André Gill, *Cham*, 1874 (see p. 348 b.)

Auguste Bouquet & the Becquet Brothers, *Father Saw*, 1832 (see p. 110 t.)

André Gill & Marchandeau, *Authentic Portrait of Rocambole*, 1867 (see p. 318)

Émile Cohl, *Charles Lullier* from *Two Fine Friends*, 1882 (see p. 372)

Paul Iribe, *"I'm here, Captain, You Won't Fall. – Thanks, Mate"*, 1917 (see p. 578 t.)

Paul Klenck (Filozel), *The Crimes of the Executive. Who's Next?*, undated (see p. 334 l.)

Anonymous, *The Redskins and the Phonograph*, 1913 (see p. 481)

Anonymous, *How They Treat Apaches Abroad: "Hard Labour" and the "Cat-o'-Nine-Tails" in England*, 1907 (see p. 459 b.r.)

Endpapers, single spread

James Gillray, *The King of Brobdingnag and Gulliver*, 1803 (see p. 45)

Syd B. Griffin & J. Ottmann, *The Evil Spirits of the Modern Daily Press*, 1888 (see p. 383)

Émile Cohl, *Paul de Cassagnac* from *Two Fine Friends*, 1882 (see p. 373)

Jules Grandjouan, *Down with Monopolies*, 1904 (see p. 558 t.)

Bertall, *Victor Hugo, Ahead of His Time*, 1871 (see p. 339 l.)

Georges Pilotell, *Gather Thistles, Expect Prickles*, undated (see p. 329 b.)

Caran d'Ache, *Mr. Cecil Rhodes – Money is Made from the Blood of Others*, 1900 (see p. 541)

Anonymous, *The Apaches – the Plague of Paris*, 1907 (see p. 459 t.)

Page 1
Gustave-Henri Jossot, *All Is Lost, even Honour…* (detail), 1907 (see p. 553)

Pages 2/3
Auguste Raffet, *The King's Prosecutor* (detail), 1831 (see p. 100)

Pages 4/5
Anonymous, *The Newspapers* (detail), 1814 (see p. 53 t.)

Pages 590/591
Alphonse Allais
Young Recruits Amazed by Their First Sight of Your Azure, O Mediterranean!, 1897
Das Erstaunen junger Rekruten als sie zum ersten Mal Dein Azur erblickten, O Mittelmeer!
Stupeur de jeunes recrues apercevant pour la première fois ton azur, o Méditerranée!
Relief etching
From: Alphonse Allais, *Album primo-avrilesque*, Paris, 1897

Page 604
Daniel Chodowiecki, *Moral Improvement* (detail), 1786 (see p. 23)

EACH AND EVERY TASCHEN BOOK PLANTS A SEED!
TASCHEN is a carbon neutral publisher. Each year, we offset our annual carbon emissions with carbon credits at the Instituto Terra, a reforestation program in Minas Gerais, Brazil, founded by Lélia and Sebastião Salgado. To find out more about this ecological partnership, please check: *www.taschen.com/zerocarbon*
Inspiration: unlimited.
Carbon footprint: zero.

To stay informed about TASCHEN and our upcoming titles, please subscribe to our free magazine at www.taschen.com/magazine, follow us on Instagram and Facebook, or e-mail your questions to contact@taschen.com.

© 2023 TASCHEN GmbH
Hohenzollernring 53, D–50672 Köln
www.taschen.com

Translation: Jane Michael, Munich; Annick Schmidt, Bergisch Gladbach

ISBN 978–3–8365–0786–8
Printed in Italy

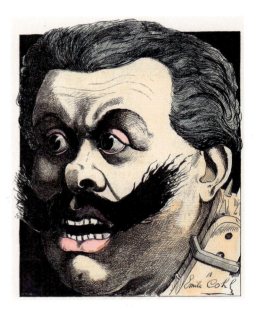

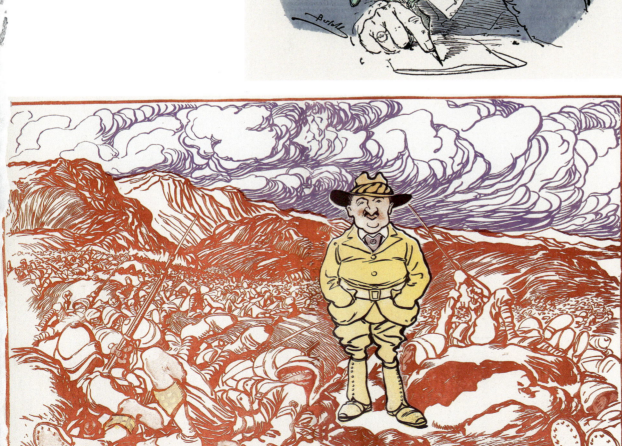

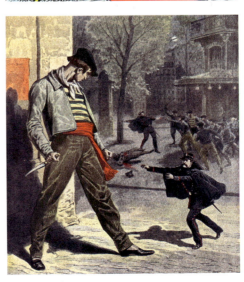

MER NOIRE.

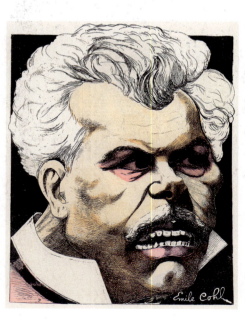